Metuchen, N.J., London, 1982 Studies in Jazz No. 1

Volume II

The Scarecrow Press and the Institute

Benny Carter

A Life in American Music

MORROE BERGER

EDWARD BERGER

JAMES PATRICK

of Jazz Studies, Rutgers University

Copyright © 1982 by Edward Berger
Manufactured in the United States of America

VOLUME II

Chronology	3
Discography	29
Introduction	31
Section One: Carter as Instrumentalist	33
Index of Artists	241
Index of Tune Titles	255
Section Two: Carter as Arranger and Composer	267
Master List of Arrangements and Compositions	268
Index of Artists Who Have Recorded Carter Arrangements and/or Compositions	345
Sound Tracks	378
Chronological Index of Compositions and Arrangements	381
A Basic Selection of Benny Carter's LPs	391
Filmography	393
Bibliography	397
Discographical Addenda	415

CHRONOLOGY

This Chronology supplies details of Benny Carter's professional life: his formation and dissolution of regular big bands from 1928 to 1946, his formation of bands for specific engagements since 1946, the dates and places of all his engagements on which information has been found. Most of these details are not given in the text, but the general index includes the names of persons and venues. This Chronology gives the personnel for all the regular and pickup bands, led by Carter, for which such information has been found; to save space Carter's name is omitted from these lists. Also included are the dates of those issues of Billboard and Down Beat in which their band routes (showing where the bands were or would be playing) listed Carter's bands. The band routes are not always reliable because schedules often changed, but they do provide useful leads.

This Chronology omits Carter's recording dates and the films he wrote for. This information is given in the Discography and the Filmography. Together, these three compendia embrace the facts of Carter's musical activity.

The sources of the Chronology are: (1) published statements in periodicals and books, which are cited if full details are available and if the source is not too obscure, (2) Carter's careful recollections, backed by his files including photographs, programs, newspaper clippings, etc., and stimulated by the authors' myriad questions to him since 1973, (3) the authors' interviews with many people associated with Carter's career, and (4) the authors' own observations and notes since 1970 when they became associated with Carter. These last three types of primary sources are not cited in this Chronology and are to be taken as the sources of those entries not documented and as supplementing those that are documented.

ABBREVIATIONS

Periodicals

AA	Afro-American (Baltimore)
AN	N.Y. Amsterdam News
BB	Billboard
CD	Chicago Defender
DB	Down Beat
IM	International Musician
IST	Inter-State Tattler
LAT	Los Angeles Times
Met	Metronome
MM	Melody Maker
NYA	N.Y. Age
NYT	N.Y. Times
OW	Orchestra World
PC	Pittsburgh Courier
PT	Philadelphia Tribune
Var	Variety

Instruments

as	alto saxophone
b	bass
bj	banjo
cl	clarinet
d	drums
g	guitar
p	piano
t	trumpet
tb	trombone
ts	tenor saxophone
v	vocalist
vn	violin

Venues

Th	Theater
Bm	Ballroom

Others

JATP	Jazz at the Philharmonic
NARAS	National Academy of Recording Arts and Sciences
NEA	National Endowment for the Arts

CHRONOLOGY

1907   Aug. 8. Born, N.Y.

1917   First music lessons, piano, from mother.

1921   Buys first instrument, cornet, which he exchanges soon for C melody saxophone. Takes saxophone lessons from neighborhood teachers.

1922   Sits in with professional musicians in Harlem.

1923   Family moves from San Juan Hill (N.Y.) to Harlem. Probably first professional job, Connor's Inn, Harlem. Summer. Plays at Asbury Park, N.J., with Rex Stewart, Bobby Stark.

1924   Plays in trio or quartet, Harlem, with Willie the Lion Smith. Switches from C melody to alto saxophone. Possibly first recording, not verified, with Charles Matson group. Plays with June Clark band, N.Y. Plays briefly with Sidney Bechet and James P. Johnson, Kentucky Club, N.Y.

1925   Summer. With June Clark band, Saratoga Springs, N.Y.

        Summer. With Billy Paige's Broadway Syncopators, Capitol Palace, Harlem, and in Pittsburgh.

        Summer. With Earl Hines band, Pittsburgh.

        Fall. Joins Wilberforce Collegians based at Wilberforce U., O., dates in Harlem, New England, Baltimore.

1926   Jan. Leaves Wilberforce Collegians, joins Charlie Johnson band, Small's Paradise, Harlem.

        April. Leaves Charlie Johnson, joins Billy Fowler band at Strand Roof Cascades; also Cameo Club, N.Y.

        April. Joins Duke Ellington band for about two weeks as temporary replacement, Ciro's club, N.Y.

        Sept. With Fowler band in Baltimore and Newark, en route to N.Y. --AA Sept. 11, p. 5.

Oct. Joins Fletcher Henderson band briefly as replacement for Don Redman, at Roseland Bm, N.Y., then returns to Fowler band.

Late. Leaves Fowler, rejoins Charlie Johnson band at Small's Paradise (remaining until Feb. 1928). Starts arranging.

1927 Composes first published song, collaborating with Fats Waller on "Nobody Knows."

With Charlie Johnson band all year.

April 28. Perhaps first arrangement recorded, "P.D.Q. Blues," by F. Henderson.

1928 Jan. 28. First confirmed recording as sideman and of a BC arrangement, with Charlie Johnson's Paradise Ten, N.Y.

Feb. Leaves Johnson, rejoins Collegians at Savoy Bm, Harlem.

Spring. Tours with Collegians, to Graystone Garden, Detroit.

Summer. Elected leader of Collegians--first time leading a band.

Aug. 13. Leads Collegians to victory, in battle of bands, over McKinney's Cotton Pickers led by Don Redman, Graystone Garden, Detroit.

Fall. Leads Collegians as Savoy Play Boys, Savoy Bm, Harlem, intermittently to March 1929. Personnel. Shelton Hemphill, Wardell Jones (t), Henry Hicks, Danny Logan (tb), Ted McCord, Bobby Sands, Gabby Rogers (p), Lavert Hutchison (b, tuba), Talcott Reeves (bj), Bill Beason (d). In late 1928: Clarence Powell (t) added, Elmer Williams (reeds) replaces Sands, Joe Turner (p) replaces Rogers.

Nov. 26-Dec. 2. Leads band, Lafayette Th, Harlem. --AN Nov. 28, p. 8.

1929 Starts playing trumpet regularly.

March, early. Band leaves Savoy after intermittent residency since fall 1928. --IST March 22, p. 10.

March 20. Leads band, one-nighter, Shadowland Bm, Philadelphia. -- PT March 14, p. 6.

July 4. Leads band, one-nighter, Pythian Temple, Pittsburgh. -- PC local edn., June 29, p. 7.

Aug. 4. Leads band, boat-ride, Pittsburgh. --PC local edn., Aug. 3, p. 7.

Aug. 5. Leads band, Pythian Temple, Pittsburgh. --Ibid.

Sept. 13. Leads band, with four others, for reopening of Alhambra BM, Harlem. --AN Sept. 4, p. 8.

Oct.-late Dec. Leads band, Arcadia Bm, N.Y., then disbands.
--OW Oct., pp. 4, 15, 17, and Nov., pp. 15, 16, 21.
Personnel. In Oct. Edward Anderson, Wardell Jones, Shelton Hemphill (t), Henry Hicks, Charlie Green (tb), Bob Carroll, Howard Johnson, Ted McCord (reeds), Joe Turner (p), Lavert Hutchison (b, tuba), Talcott Reeves (bj), Bill Beason (d). --OW Oct., p. 7. In Nov. Russell Procope (as) replaces Johnson, John Truehart (bj) replaces Reeves, omit Anderson. --OW Nov., p. 21.

1930   Jan. Joins F. Henderson band, remains to March 1931. W. C. Allen, pp. 254-255.

1931   March. Leaves F. Henderson to join Chick Webb band.

Aug. Leaves Webb band to join McKinney's Cotton Pickers, Detroit, as musical director (not leader), remaining to April 1932.
Personnel. Doc Cheatham, Joe Smith, Rex Stewart (t), Charlie Green, Quentin Jackson (tb), Elmer Williams, Jimmy Dudley (reeds), Todd Rhodes (p), Billy Taylor (b), Dave Wilborn (g, bj), Cuba Austin (d). Changes: see Discography, Sept. 8.

1932   First BC tune played in a feature film: "Hot Toddy" played on screen by Cab Calloway band in The Big Broadcast of 1932.

April. Leaves McKinney's Cotton Pickers.

Summer. Forms new big band: Benny Carter and His Orchestra.

July 10-23. Leads new band in show, "Connie's Inn Ace in the Hole Revue," Central Th, N.Y. --AN July 13, 20, p. 8.

Aug.-Sept. Leads band, four weeks, in revue "Cocktails of 1932" in a Boston Th (name not given). -NYA Oct. 8, p. 6. Personnel. Leonard Davis, Louis Bacon (t), Dicky Wells (tb), Chu Berry, Hilton Jefferson, Wayman Carver (reeds), Rod Rodriguez (p), Ralph Escudero (b), Bernard Addison (g), Sidney Catlett (d). Also: Alfred C. Thomas, James M. Herbert, instruments not given. --IM Oct., p. 3.

Oct. 7. Leads band in benefit for "Scottsboro Boys," Rockland Palace, Harlem. --NYA Oct. 15, p. 7; PC Oct. 15, p. 6.

Oct. 8-14. Leads band, Lafayette Th, Harlem. --NYA Oct. 15, p. 6.

Oct., late. Leads band, a week, Howard Th, Wash., D.C. Personnel. Leonard Davis, Howard Scott, Shad Collins (t), George Washington, Dicky Wells (tb), Howard Johnson, Wayman Carver (reeds), Rod Rodriguez (p), Ernest Hill (b), Bernard Addison (g), Sidney Catlett (d). --IM Dec., p. 7.

1933   Feb. 9-ca. 23. Leads band to open Empire Bm., N.Y. --N.Y. Daily News, Feb. 9, p. 33; --MM March, p. 185, and May 27, p. 3.

Feb. 11-17. Leads band, Lafayette Th, Harlem. --AN Feb. 8, 15, p. 8.

March 8. Leads band in benefit for "Scottsboro Boys," Savoy Bm, Harlem. --AN March 1, p. 8, "Observations."

April 1-7. Leads band, Lafayette Th, Harlem. --AN April 5, p. 8.

May, late. Leads band, Savoy Bm, Harlem, about two weeks. --MM June 24, p. 5.

June, early. Leads band, Empire Bm, N.Y., to early Aug. --W. C. Allen, P. 285.

June, late. Leads band, Howard Th, Wash., D.C. --AA July 1, p. 9. Personnel. Clifton "Pike" Davis, Otis Johnson, John Brown (t), Wilbur de Paris, Fayette Williams (tb), Johnny Russell, Alberto Socarras (Estacio) (reeds), Rod Rodriguez (p), Ernest Hill (b), Lawrence Lucie (g), Walter Conyers (d). --IM July, p. 5. Other sidemen in late 1933: Shad Collins, Bill Coleman, Lincoln Mills (t), Dicky Wells, Charlie Green (tb), Chu Berry, Hilton Jefferson (reeds), Cozy Cole (d). --Lucie in Dance, World of Swing, p. 349; Cole, ibid., p. 186. See Discography, Oct. 16.

July 22-25, July 29-Aug. 1. Leads band, Harlem Opera House, Harlem. --AN July 19, 26, p. 7.

Oct. 6 ca. Leads band at new Harlem Club, Harlem, remaining to late Feb. 1934. --CD Oct. 7, p. 8; AN Oct. 11, p. 7; Ottley, AN Feb. 21, 1934, p. 9; advt., ibid., Feb. 28, 1934, p. 9.

Oct. 23-29. Leads band, Lafayette Th, Harlem. --AN Oct. 25, p. 7.

Dec. 20-26. Leads band, Harlem Opera House, Harlem. --NYA Dec. 23, p. 6; AN advt., Dec. 20, p. 7 and review, Dec. 27, p. 7; Albertson, p. 191. Bessie Smith was advertised for Dec. 23-26 but did not appear.

1934 Jan. 15 ca. Leads band, several days, Louis Sherry's, club, N.Y. --Var Jan. 23, p. 1.

Jan. 26-Feb. 2. Leads band at reopening, with "new" band-show format, Apollo Th, Harlem. --AN Jan. 24, p. 14, and Jan. 31, p. 8. Personnel. Bill Coleman, Bill Dillard, Lincoln Mills (t), Charlie Green, Keg Johnson (tb), Johnny Russell (reeds), Teddy Wilson (p), Lawrence Lucie (g), Cozy Cole (d). --Cole in Dance, World of Swing, p. 186.

Feb., late. Leaves Harlem Club.

Feb. 16. Leads band in benefit for "Scottsboro Boys," Savoy Bm, Harlem. --NYA Feb. 10, p. 6.

Feb.-April. Leads band, Empire Bm, N.Y. --Rosenkrantz, pp. 7, 32-36; NYA May 12, p. 5, Outram.

Chronology 1934

Spring. Arranges for new Benny Goodman band. --Goodman, pp. 133-134, 139.

May, early, to mid-June. Leads band, Empire Bm, N.Y. --BB band routes, May 5-June 16.

June 1. Breaks arm in auto accident en route from N.Y. to Trenton, N.J. This injury exempted him from military service in World War II.

Nov. 16-22. Leads band, Apollo Th, Harlem. --NYA Nov. 24, p. 4.

Nov. 29. Leads band in Thanksgiving Day dance after Wilberforce-W. Va. St. Coll. football game, Arcadia Bm, Detroit. --PC Dec. 1, sec. 2, p. 1.

Dec. 31. Leads band, New Year's Eve dance, Webster Hall, N.Y. --Labor Defender (International Labor Defense), Jan. 1935, advt. p. 23.

Band routes. BB May 5-June 16.

1935 Jan. Gives up regular band formed in 1932.

Feb. Joins Willie Bryant band as trumpeter and arranger, remaining until May. --NYA March 23, p. 4.

May 24. Sails for France to join Willie Lewis band at Chez Florence, club, Paris, returns to U.S. May 2, 1938. --AN June 8, p. 1.

July. Starts playing with Willie Lewis band, Chez Florence, remaining until ca. March 17, 1936.

1936 Jan. 29, 31. Plays concerts with Quintette of the Hot Club of France in Barcelona. --Tendes; Delaunay, Django Reinhardt, p. 83.

March 18. Arrives London to arrange for BBC dance orchestra. --MM March 21, p. 11.

March 27. BBC dance band broadcasts program of BC compositions and arrangements. --MM April 11, p. 5.

July. Leaves London, arrives Holland.

July 26, 28, 29. Holland. Plays at Kurhaus Hotel, Scheveningen. --De Jazzwereld (The Hague) Sept., p. 3.

July 31. Holland. Plays at Hamdorff Hotel, Laren.

Aug. 6. Holland. Plays at Kurhaus Hotel, Scheveningen. --MM Aug. 15, p. 3.

Aug. 19. Arrives Copenhagen, remains three weeks. --Copenhagen daily press, Aug. 20.

Aug. 20, 27. Copenhagen. Concerts with Kai Ewans band, Tivoli park. --Ibid., Aug. 21, 28.

Sept. 9-13. Stockholm. Sept. 9, 11, concerts with the Swedish Orchestra at Royal Djurgarden Circus. --Orkester Journalen, Oct., pp. 7-13.

Sept. 14. Copenhagen. Concert at Concert Palace. --Rosenkrantz, Politiken, Sept. 15.

Sept. 15. Concert on Danish radio with Kai Ewans band. --B. T. (newspaper) Sept. 16.

Sept. 16-Sept. 29. Plays at National Scala accompanied by Richard Johansen band. --Copenhagen daily press, Sept. 17.

Oct. 2. Returns to London, remaining until March 1937.

Oct. 13. Plays radio concert with BBC dance band. --MM Oct. 17, p. 14.

Fall. Arranges for first film, one tune, "Okay for Sound," Gaumont British, released 1937.

1937 Jan. 10. Leads British band, concert, Hippodrome Th, London. -- MM Jan. 16, p. 1; DB, Feb., p. 5.

Feb. Plays with British band daily for one week, Locarno Bm, Streatham, London. --Musical News and Dance Band (London), March, p. 23.

March 16. Leaves London for Holland to negotiate summer engagement, remains two weeks. --MM March 20, p. 1.

April 6. Arrives in Paris, remaining until May 11.

May 11. Arrives London, remains two weeks, to line up musicians for summer engagement in Holland.

May 17. Leads British band in BBC weekly swing series on radio. --Met May, p. 38.

May 27. In Holland, putting together band for summer.

June 4-Sept. 7. Leads international, interracial band, Kurhaus Hotel, Scheveningen. --De Jazzwereld (The Hague), May, p. 4 and Sept., p. 7. Personnel. Sam Dasberg, Cliff Woodridge (t), George Chisholm (tb), Louis Stephenson, Bertie King, Jimmy Williams (reeds), Justo Barretto or Freddy Johnson (p), Len Harrison (b), Ray Webb (g), Robert Mommarché (d). --Photo in McCarthy, Big Band Jazz, p. 314 and Doctor Jazz, Dec. 1971/Jan. 1972, p. 15; Met Sept., pp. 66-67.

Sept. Leaves Holland for France, remains until April 1938.

Oct. 15-ca. April 20, 1938. Leads band at Boeuf sur le Toit, club, Paris. --MM Oct. 30, p. 1, and March 26, 1938, p. 6. Personnel. Louis Stephenson, Bertie King, Jean Luino (reeds), Yorke de Souza or Frank Etheridge (p), Len Harrison (b), Robert Mommarché or Jacques de Bourgarel (d). --MM Oct. 30, p. 1.

Dec. 17. Leads band, concert, Salle de l'Ecole Normale de Musique, Paris. --Jazz Hot (Paris), Dec. 1937-Jan. 1938, p. 13. Personnel. Jacques Raymond (t), Jesus Pia (ts), Michel Warlop (vn), Garland Wilson (p), Len Harrison (b), Tommy Benford (d). --Ibid.

1938 Feb. 19. Leads band from Paris for Italian students' ball, Zurich. --M. Cook, AN March 19, p. 19.

April 20 ca. Closes at Boeuf sur le Toit, there since Oct. 15, 1937.

April 24. Leaves Paris for London to embark for U.S.

April 27. Sails on Normandie from Southampton, arrives N.Y. May 2.

Summer. Forming new big band. Met Nov., p. 64.

Nov. 25-Dec. 1. Leads new band, Howard Th, Wash., D.C. --AA Nov. 26, pp. 10-11.

1939 March 25. Leads band at annual Beaux Arts ball, Yale U.

March 29. Opens with band at Savoy Bm, Harlem, there intermittently for months at a time until Jan. 1941, using "Melancholy Lullaby" as theme song. --AN July 8, pp. 16-17; BB, July 8, p. 13. Personnel. Lincoln Mills, Louis Bacon, Archie Johnson (t), Tyree Glenn, Vic Dickenson, Jimmy Archey (tb), Ernie Powell, Cass McCord, Jimmy Powell, Carl Frye (reeds), Eddie Heywood, Jr. (p), Hayes Alvis (b), Arnold Adams (g), Ted Fields (d). --AN April 15, p. 21. Foregoing personnel refers to 1939 and into 1940, with these changes from time to time: Bobby Woodlen, Joe Thomas (t) replace Bacon and Johnson; Sammy Davis (reeds) in, Frye out; Ulysses Livingston (g) replaces Adams; Henry "Chick" Morrison (d) replaces Ted Fields. --DB Sept., p. 24.

July, early. Leaves Savoy to tour. --AN July 8, pp. 16-17; BB July 8, p. 13.

July 7-13. Starts tour at Apollo Th, Harlem. --Ibid.

July-Aug. Touring. --Ibid.

Oct.-Nov. Back in Savoy, out Dec. to Feb. 1940. --Burley in AN Oct. 21, p. 20.

Dec. 2-8. Leads band, Roseland Bm, Brooklyn, N.Y. --Burley in AN Dec. 2, p. 20.

Dec. 15. Leads band, Apollo Th, Harlem, with others, in benefit show. --AN Dec. 23, p. 13.

Dec. 22-28. Leads band, Howard Th, Wash., D. C. --BB Dec. 23, band routes; AA Dec. 30, p. 14.

Dec. 24. Leads band, Tuxedo Club, Harrisburg, Pa. --AA ibid.

Dec. 31. Leads band, Celoron Park, N. Y., pier bm. --AA ibid., and BB Dec. 30, band routes. Both wrongly give this as Jamestown University, probably because the Chautauqua adult education program is there. See advt. for this engagement, Jamestown Evening Journal, Dec. 30, p. 10.

Band routes. BB April 1-July 8, Sept. 30-Oct. 28, Dec. 9-30. --DB May-Oct. 15, Dec. 15.

1940 Jan. or Feb. Leads band at Savoy Bm, Pittsburgh. --BB April 27, p. 11.

Jan.-Feb. Touring.

Feb. 23. Leads band in Savoy Bm, Harlem, to Feb. 27 or 28, when BC is taken to alimony jail to end of March, while vocalist Roy Felton fronts band. --Burley in AN March 9 and April 6, p. 20.

March. Band tours, fronted by Roy Felton.

April 6. BC leads band, Golden Gate Bm, Harlem. --MM May 4, p. 4.

June. Leads band on midwestern tour, several weeks. --DB June 15, p. 9. Personnel. Russell Smith, Shad Collins, Bill Coleman (t), Milt Robinson, Sandy Williams, Fernando Arbello (tb), Carl Frye, Stafford Simon, Sammy Davis, George Dorsey (reeds), Sonny White (p), Hayes Alvis (b), Ulysses Livingston (g), Keg Purnell (d). --Ibid.

July 26. Leads band, N. Y. World's Fair, Negro Week. --MM Aug. 7, p. 9.

Sept. 19-25. Leads band, Strand Bm, Philadelphia. --BB Sept. 21, band routes.

Oct. 4-10. Leads band to reopen West End Th, Harlem. --AN Sept. 28, advt., p. 21; review, Oct. 12, p. 20. Personnel. Freddie Webster, Bob Williams (t), Madison Vaughan (tb), George Irish, George James (reeds), Everett Barksdale (g) replacing Livingston, Ann Robinson (v). --DB Oct. 15, p. 9. These are new members only, and all are in personnel given for Famous Door in next item.

Nov. 18-Dec. 2. Leads band, Famous Door, 52d St., N. Y. Personnel. Russell Smith, Bob Williams, Freddie Webster (t), Fernando Arbello, Milt Robinson, Madison Vaughan (tb), Chauncey Haughton, Stafford Simon, George James, George Irish (reeds), Sonny White (p), Hayes Alvis (b), Everett Barksdale (g), Keg Purnell (d), Ann Robinson, Roy Felton (v). --George Simon, Met Nov., p. 16.

Chronology 1940

    Dec. Leads band at Savoy, into Jan. 1941.

    Band routes. BB Sept. 21. --DB Jan. 1-Feb. 15.

1941 Jan. 28-March 2. Leads band, Nick's, club, N.Y. --AN Feb. 1, p. 16; BB Feb. 8, p. 11; New Yorker, "Goings On About Town," Feb. 1-March 1. Personnel. Lincoln Mills, Sidney de Paris, Tom Lindsay (t), Vic Dickenson, Jimmy Archey, Joe Britton (tb), Fred Mitchell, Al Gibson, Bill White, Jim Johnson (reeds), Sonny White (p), Charlie Drayton (b), Chris I. Cruickson (d). --DB Feb. 15, p. 4.

    March 15. Leads band, Princeton U. junior prom. --Daily Princetonian, March 15, p. 1.

    March-May. Touring midwest. --DB Feb. 15, p. 4.

    March 30. Plays at reunion of F. Henderson bands, Café Society, N.Y. --W. C. Allen, p. 407.

    June 21. BC Featured with Vaughn Monroe band, CBS broadcast, Frank Dailey's Meadowbrook, club, Cedar Grove, N.J. --PC June 28, p. 21; NYT radio programs, 5 p.m., June 21, p. 30.

    July, early, to Sept. Touring south, with Maxine Sullivan. --BB July 5, p. 14; DB July 15, p. 29. Personnel. Lincoln Mills, Sidney de Paris, Bobby Johnson (t), Jimmy Archey, Joe Britton, Milt Robinson (tb), Howard Johnson, Frank Powell, Al Sears, Al Gibson (reeds), Sonny White (p), Charlie Drayton (b), Willie Lewis (g), Shep Shepherd (d), Roy Felton (v), Maxine Sullivan (featured v). --DB ibid.

    Sept. or Oct. Gives up big band on return from tour, re-forms big band Feb. 1942.

    Sept. BC named in F. Henderson's "dream band." --W. C. Allen, p. 490.

    Oct. Leads small combo, several weeks, Ritz Carlton Hotel, Boston. --Met Oct., p. 11; DB Nov. 1, p. 2. Personnel. "Little" Benny Harris or Rostelle Reese (t), Eddie Barefield (cl), Sonny White (p), Charlie Drayton (b), Willie Lewis (g), Shep Shepherd (d). --Met ibid.; MM Nov. 8, p. 6.

    Oct. 23 ca.-Dec. 10. Leads small combo, Kelly's Stable, club, 52d St., N.Y. --DB Nov. 1, p. 2; BB Dec. 20, p. 11; New Yorker, Oct. 25, p. 4, and Dec. 13, p. 4. Personnel. Rostelle Reese (t), Al Gibson (reeds), Sonny White (p), Charlie Drayton (b), Willie Lewis (g), Eddie Dougherty (d). Changes probably in Nov.: John Collins (g) replaces Lewis, Dizzy Gillespie (t) replaces Reese.

    Nov. 5. Leads sextet (from Kelly's Stable), concert, Museum of Modern Art, N.Y., with Maxine Sullivan, harpsichordist Sylvia Marlowe, dancer Baby Lawrence. --N.Y. Herald Tribune, Nov. 6, p. 17; New Yorker, Nov. 1, p. 4.

Dec. 10-Feb. 4, 1942. Leads small combo, Famous Door, 52d St., N. Y. --BB Dec. 20, p. 11; DB Feb. 15, p. 2. Personnel. Dizzy Gillespie (t), Al Gibson (reeds), Sonny White (p), Charlie Drayton (b), Kenny Clarke (d). --Met Jan. 1942, pp. 11, 17. Change: Gillespie left briefly, probably in late Dec., for another engagement, and may have been replaced by "Tatti" Smith. --OW Jan., p. 4. Jimmy Hamilton (reeds) replaces Gibson. --DB Feb. 1, 1942, p. 3.

Band routes. BB Feb. 22, May 10, July 5, Nov. 8-22, Dec. 6-27. DB Feb. 15, March 15, Aug. 15-Dec. 1.

1942 Joins ASCAP.

Feb. Assembles a new big band.

Feb. 4. Leaves Famous Door; see entry 1941, Dec. 10.

Feb. Begins to arrange for Mark Warnow's Lucky Strike Hit Parade Orchestra. --DB Feb. 15, p. 2.

March 14. Leads band (one-nighter?), Golden Gate Bm, Harlem. --DB April 1, p. 1. Personnel. Lincoln Mills, Courtney Williams, Nelson Bryant (t), Claude Jones, John "Rocks" McConnell, Alton "Slim" Moore (tb), George Dorsey, Frank Powell, Al Gibson, Fred Mitchell (reeds), Jimmy Phipps (p), Charlie Drayton (b), John Collins (g), Specs Powell (d). --DB April 1, p. 1. Changes in early spring: Sidney de Paris (t) replaces Bryant, DB April 15, p. 3; add Dan Minor (tb). --DB May 15, p. 7.

April 10-16. Leads band, Apollo Th, Harlem; start of tour, featuring Billie Holiday, into May. --DB April 15, p. 3. Personnel. As above, entry for March 14. --MM June 6, p. 5.

April 27-May 3. Leads band, Gaiety Th, N. Y. --BB May 9, p. 18; NYT April 28, p. 24.

May 8. Leads band, opening at Strand Th, Toledo, O., with Billie Holiday. --Toledo Times, May 7.

May. Leads band, Strand Th, Syracuse, N. Y., with Billie Holiday. --Syracuse Post-Standard, May 9; DB June 15, p. 20.

June-July. Touring east (without Billie Holiday).

June 7. Leads band, opening at Tic-Toc Club, Boston, one or two weeks. --OW June, p. 24.

June 14. Leads band, Wagenbach's Hofbrau, Lawrence, Mass.

July 3-9. Leads band, Apollo Th, Harlem. --AN July 4, p. 17.

Sept. Leads band on tour westward, arriving Hollywood in Nov.

Sept. 11-17. Leads band, Royal Th, Baltimore. --DB Sept. 1, band routes.

Chronology 1942 15

Oct. Touring midwest.

Oct. 16 to mid-Nov. Leads band, Rainbow Rendezvous, Salt Lake City. --BB Oct. 3, p. 24; OW Nov., advt., inside front cover.

Nov. BC arrives in Hollywood, settles in L.A. area for good.

Nov. 14-20. Leads band, Lincoln Th, L.A. --BB Nov. 14, band routes.

Nov. 20. Leads band, opening at Billy Berg's Swing Club, L.A., to mid-Jan. 1943. --Met Dec., p. 21; DB Dec. 1, p. 13. Personnel. George Treadwell, Hal Mitchell, William "Chiefie" Scott (t), Earl Hardy, J. J. Johnson, John "Shorty" Haughton, Slim Moore (tb), Ted Barnett, Carroll "Stretch" Ridley, Gene Porter, Eddie De Verteuil (reeds), Teddy Brannon (p), Curly Russell (b), Johnny Smith (g), Alvin Burroughs (d), Savannah Churchill (v). --DB Nov. 15, p. 11. Changes by Jan. 1943: Eddie Davis (reeds) in, Barnett out; Hardy (tb) out; Buddy Rich (d) in, Burroughs out. --"The Lamplighter," L.A. Daily News, Jan. 2, 1943, p. 5. Add Hal Schaefer (p), briefly, late 1942.

Band routes. BB Jan. 10-March 28, May 9, June 13-20, Oct. 3-Nov. 14, Dec. 5-26. DB March 15-July 1, Sept. 1, Oct. 1-Nov. 1.

1943 Jan. BC works on his first Hollywood film, Stormy Weather.

Jan., middle. Band closes at Swing Club.

Jan., middle, to mid-Feb. Leads band, Hollywood Club, Hollywood. --DB Feb. 1, p. 6.

March 17-23. Leads band, Orpheum Th, L.A. --DB March 15, band routes.

April. Leads band, Sweet's Bm, Oakland, several days, perhaps two weeks. --BB April 3, 10, 17, band routes; DB April 1, band routes.

April 7 ca., to May, late. Leads band, Hollywood Club. --BB April 24-May 8, band routes; DB April 15-May 15, band routes. Personnel. Gerald Wilson, Snooky Young, Walter Williams, Fred Trainer (t), Shorty Haughton, J. J. Johnson, Slim Moore (tb), Kirt Bradford, Willard Brown, Gene Porter, Eddie Davis (reeds), Teddy Brannon (p), Curly Russell (b), Oscar Bradley (d), Savannah Churchill (v). Met, April, pp. 17, 33. Changes: add Frank Comstock (tb and arranging). Uan Rasey, Teddy Buckner (t) in, Young, Trainer out; Bumps Myers (reeds) replaces Davis. --DB June 15, p. 2. Add Freddie Webster (t). DB Sept. 1, p. 6. Add Art Pepper (reeds) playing April-Sept. April 10, aircheck: see Discography.

May, late, to July, early. Leads band, Casa Mañana, club, Hollywood. --Met July, p. 20; BB May 22-June 5, June 19-July 10, band routes; DB June 1-July 1, band routes.

July, early, to Aug., early. Leads band, Hollywood Casino. --DB Aug. 1, p. 6.

Aug., early, to mid-Sept. Leads band, Terrace Club, Hermosa Beach, California. --DB Aug. 15-Sept. 15, all p. 6.

Sept., last week. Leads band, Orpheum Th, L. A. --Met Nov., p. 26.

Sept., late, to Dec. Touring Pacific states and south, into spring 1944. --DB Sept. 15, p. 6.

Band routes. BB Jan. 2, Jan. 23-Feb. 13, April 3-May 8, May 22-June 5, June 19-Sept. 4, Sept. 18-Nov. 6, Nov. 20. DB Jan. 15-July 1, Aug. 1-Dec. 1.

1944 Jan. to spring. Continues tour (begun Sept. 1943) to east.

Jan. 28-Feb. 3. Leads band, Apollo Th, Harlem. --Met March, p. 32.

Feb. 24-March 1. Leads band, Loew's State Th, N. Y. --BB March 4, p. 28.

March or April. End of tour, band back in California.

May 16-22. Leads band, Orpheum Th, L. A. --L. A. Examiner, May 17, pt. 2, p. 3.

June 1-July, end. Leads band, Swing Club, Hollywood. --Met June, p. 11, and July, p. 13. Personnel. Milton Fletcher, Tom "Sleepy" Grider, Fatso Ford, Edwin Davis (t), Shorty Haughton, Slim Moore, J. J. Johnson (tb), Porter Kilbert, Bumps Myers, Gene Porter, Willard Brown (reeds), Gerald Wiggins (p), Charlie Drayton (b), Jimmy Edwards (g), Max Roach (d). --Met July, p. 14.

July 31-March 1945. Leads band on tour to east and back to west. Band routes in BB July 29, 1944 to Jan. 20, 1945, and DB Sept. 1, 1944 to March 1, 1945. Some specific engagements reviewed in press: Kansas City, DB Dec. 1, 1944, p. 8; N. Y., DB Dec. 15, 1944, p. 3; Newark, Var Jan. 31, 1945, p. 34; Philadelphia, Var Feb. 14, 1945, p. 18; N. Y., BB March 3, 1945, p. 21. Personnel, on tour ca. December 1944-January 1945. Fats Aradando, Harold Bruce, Red Kelly (t), Charles Greenlea, Buster Scott (tb), Harold Clark, Porter Kilbert, Bumps Myers, Leo Parker, Howard Smith (reeds), Garland Finney (p), Tommy Moultrie (b), Stanley Williams (d). Add Jean Starr (t, v), 1944 and early 1945. --Var Jan. 31, 1945 p. 34.

Band routes. BB June 3, July 29, Aug. 12-Sept. 30, Oct. 14, Oct. 28-Nov. 11, Dec. 9-23. DB Jan. 1-March 1, May 15-Oct. 15, Nov. 15-Dec. 15.

1945 Jan.-March. Continues touring--see 1944, July 31.

Chronology 1945

March 22-28. Leads band, Trocadero, club, Hollywood. --DB March 15, April 15, p. 6.

April 20-May 18. Leads band, Casa Mañana, Culver City. --DB May 1, p. 2.

June 26-July 1. Leads band, Orpheum Th, L.A. --BB July 7, pp. 35-36.

July 3-8. Leads band, Plantation, club, L.A. --DB July 1, band routes.

Aug. BC wins court case to retain ownership of house in L.A. despite restrictive covenant. --DB Sept. 1, p. 6.

Aug. 10-Feb. 13, 1946. Leads band on tour to east. --DB band routes, Aug. 1, 1945-Jan. 28, 1946. Some specific engagements reviewed in press: N.Y., AN Sept. 15, p. 9-B, and Dec. 22, p. 25; Detroit, Detroit Free Press, Feb. 6, 1946, p. 10.

Band routes. BB Jan. 6-20. DB Jan. 1-April 1, May 1, June 1, July 1, Aug. 1, Sept. 1-Oct. 1, Nov. 15-Dec. 15.

1946 Jan.-Feb. 13. Continues touring--see 1945, Aug. 10.

March 19-25. Leads band, Orpheum Th, L.A. --BB March 30, p. 46.

March 26-May 21. Leads band, Trianon, Bm, South Gate, L.A. --Var April 17, p. 58 to May 15, p. 57, L.A. residencies.

April 12. Leads some of his band, concert, UCLA, on first anniversary of death of Franklin D. Roosevelt. --DB May 6, p. 16; California Daily Bruin, April 15, 1946, p. 1.

June 3-8. Leads band, Swing Club, Hollywood. --DB June 3, July 1, band routes. Personnel. Fred Trainer, Calvin Strickland, Walter Williams, Ira Pettiford (t), Candy Ross, Johnny Morris, Al Grey, Charley Johnson (tb), Bob Graettinger, Joe Epps, Harold Clark, Bumps Myers, Willard Brown (reeds), Sonny White (p), Tommy Moultrie (b), Jimmy Cannady (g), Percy Brice (d), Lucy Elliott, Ross (v), Graettinger, Cannady (arranging). --BB June 22, p. 22. Changes as of August in Apollo Th, N.Y.: add Martin "Fuzzy" Gower (reeds), omit Graettinger, Epps; add Reunald Jones (t), Trainer out. --Bérard, pp. 14-15.

July 19-Oct. 19. Leads band on tour east, disbands in Boston. Some specific engagements reviewed in press: N.Y., AN Aug. 3, p. 17; Philadelphia, PT advt., Aug. 31, p. 12; Louisville, Var Oct. 2, p. 20.

Oct. 8 ca.-19. Leads band, Rio, club, Boston. --Boston Globe, advts., Oct. 8, p. 16, and Oct. 19, p. 10.

Oct. 19. BC gives up regular big band permanently on finishing engagement at Rio this day. --DB Nov. 18, p. 5; BB Dec. 14, p. 17.

Oct. 23 ca. BC returns home to California without a band.

Band routes. DB Jan. 1-28, March 25, April 8-22, June 3-Aug. 26, Sept. 23-Oct. 7.

1947 Neighbors threaten, on basis of a restricted covenant, to force BC out of his house in Hollywood; threat fades when such discriminatory agreements are ruled unenforceable.

March. Leads big band, for first time since disbanding, El Patio Th, L.A. --DB March 12, p. 19. Personnel (partial). Fred Trainer, Harry Parr Jones (t), Henry Coker (tb), Lucky Thompson (reeds), Eddie Beal (p), Charlie Drayton (b), Irving Ashby (g), Lee Young (d). --Ibid.

July 2. Leads band, Swing Club, Hollywood, several weeks. --DB July 2, p. 10. Personnel. Harry Parr Jones (t), Henry Coker (tb), Lucky Thompson (reeds), Dodo Marmarosa (p), Tommy Moultrie (b), Henry Tucker Green (d). --Ibid., some errors corrected by BC.

July, late. Leads band, Million Dollar Th, L.A., one week. --Var July 30, p. 44. Personnel. Some of sidemen as for July 2. Wardell Gray (reeds) replaces Thompson. --Ibid.

1948 July, late, into Aug. Leads band, Casbah, club., L.A. --DB Aug. 11, 25, p. 8. Personnel. Gerald Wilson (t), Henry Coker (tb), Bumps Myers (reeds), Gerald Wiggins (p), Charlie Drayton or Benny Booker (b), Lee Young (d).

Aug. 10-16. Leads band, Million Dollar Th, L.A. --DB July 28, Aug. 11, band routes. Personnel. Some of sidemen from previous entry: Coker, Myers, Wiggins.

Sept. 23-Oct. 13. Leads band, Cafe Society Uptown, San Francisco. --DB Nov. 3, p. 7. Personnel. Teddy Buckner (t), Henry Coker (tb), Bumps Myers (reeds), Gerald Wiggins (p), Benny Booker (b), Jesse Price (d). --Ibid.

Band routes. DB July 28, Aug. 11.

1949 June. Appendectomy.

1950 April. Leads band, Million Dollar Th, L.A. --DB May 5, p. 15. Personnel. Ernie Royal (t), Britt Woodman (tb), Bumps Myers (reeds), Gerald Wiggins (p), Ulysses Livingston (g), Lee Young (d). --Ibid.

Dec. 9 ca.-Dec. 21. Leads band, Blue Note, club, Chicago. -- Chicago Tribune, advts., Dec. 9, pt. 2, p. 5, and Dec. 20, pt. 3, p. 4; DB Dec. 29, p. 21. Personnel. Rostelle Reese (t), J. J. Johnson (tb), Al Williams (p), Johnny Williams (b), Joe Harris (d).

Chronology 1950

Dec., late. Leads band at High Hat, club, Boston. Personnel. Same as previous entry.

Band routes. DB Dec. 29.

1951 Feb. 3-ca. 28. Leads band, Black Hawk, club, San Francisco. --DB March 9, p. 9, and March 23, p. 13. Personnel. Bumps Myers (reeds), Sheldon Smith (p), Charlie Drayton (b), Al Bartee or Roy Porter (d). --Ibid.

May 12. Leads band, U. of Oregon, Eugene. --DB June 15, p. 8, L.A. sec. Personnel. Maxwell Davis (reeds), Moe Dieffenbach (p), Ulysses Livingston (g), Billy Hadnott (b), Bill Douglas (d). --Ibid.

Aug.-Sept. Leads band, Club Royal, San Diego, two weeks to a month. --DB Nov. 30, p. 8. Personnel. Gerald Wiggins (p), Ulysses Livingston (g), Charlie Drayton (b), George Jenkins (d), Ruth Olay (v).

Sept. 12-Oct. 9. Leads band, Tiffany, club, L.A. --DB Oct. 19, p. 6; PC Oct. 13, p. 17. Personnel. Herbie Harper (tb), Wardell Gray (reeds), Ernie Freeman (p), Harry Babasin (b), George Jenkins (d). --Ibid.

Nov. to Jan. or Feb., 1952. Leads trio, Astor's Lounge, L.A. --DB Nov. 30, p. 1, and Jan. 25, 1952, p. 13. Personnel. Gerald Wiggins (p), George Jenkins (d). --Ibid.

Band routes. DB Oct. 5-19, Nov. 30-Dec. 28.

1952 Jan., late, or Feb. Closes at Astor's Lounge--see previous entry.

April or May to late June. Leads band, Sardi's, club, L.A. --DB June 4, p. 8, and June 18, p. 13. Personnel. Keg Johnson (tb), Bumps Myers or Ben Webster (reeds), Gerald Wiggins or Fred Otis (p), Charlie Drayton (b), George Jenkins (d). --Ibid., June 4.

Sept. 13. BC makes his first appearance with JATP, Carnegie Hall, N.Y. --DB Sept. 24, p. 1.

Band routes. DB Jan. 11.

1953 Spring. Leads band, touring West Coast. --MM Aug. 8, p. 3. Personnel. George Washington (tb), Ernie Powell (reeds), Ernie Freeman (p), George Bledsoe (b), Al Bartee (d). --Ibid.

April 1. Amalgamation of black and white musicians' unions in L.A. BC plays important role since 1950.

Sept. 19. Plays with JATP, Carnegie Hall, N.Y. --AN Sept. 12, p. 23, and NYT Sept. 20, sec. 2, p. 7.

Nov., early. BC makes his first tour abroad with JATP, in Far East. --Var Nov. 11, p. 51.

1954 Feb. 5-March 9. BC tours Europe with JATP.

Oct. Leads quartet, Keyboard Lounge, Beverly Hills, two weeks. --DB Dec. 1, p. 3. Personnel. Sir Charles Thompson (p), Red Callender (b), Bill Douglas (d).

Nov. Leads trio, Melody Room, Hollywood, two weeks. --Ibid.

1955 May 26-Oct. 13. Leads band, opening of interracial hotel, Moulin Rouge, Las Vegas. --DB June 29, p. 38, and Nov. 16, p. 31.

1956 Jan., early. Heart attack, seven weeks in L.A. hospital.

Summer, ca. Elected chairman of Local 47 committee on arrangers. --DB Aug. 8, p. 39.

1957 Elected to Board of Governors and Executive Committee of National Academy of Recording Arts and Sciences, also to Board of L.A. chapter.

1958 Elected to Executive Board of Composers and Lyricists Guild of America. --DB Dec. 25, pp. 12-13.

Starts composing for television, M Squad.

Oct. 5. Plays for first time at a "jazz festival": Monterey Jazz Festival, its first. --DB Nov. 13, p. 50.

1959 Oct. 3. BC conducts Basie band in BC's Kansas City Suite, at first L.A. Jazz Festival. --DB Nov. 12, pp. 18-19.

1960 June 17-18. Plays, leads BC All-Stars, L.A. Jazz Festival. --DB Aug. 4, pp. 14-16.

July 29-Aug. 7. Leads quartet at The Embers, club, Melbourne, Australia; one concert in Sydney. Personnel. Paul Moer (p), Curtis Counce (b), Frankie Capp (d).

Nov., early, to Dec. 7. Tours Europe with JATP. --DB Dec. 8, p. 11; MM Dec. 3, pp. 3, 9.

1961 Nov., late, to Dec. 2. Plays radio show and four days in night club, Cologne, W. Germany; visits London. --MM Dec. 9, p. 13; Jazzer (Kiel), Dec. 1961, p. 1.

1962 April 16-May 12. Conducts big band accompanying Peggy Lee, Basin St. East, club, N.Y. --DB April 26, p. 54; New Yorker, April 14, May 12, p. 8.

July 7-8. Plays and conducts BC Festival Orch. at first Las Vegas

Chronology 1962

Jazz Festival, featuring own composition Las Vegas Suite (never recorded). --DB Aug. 16, p. 19; MM Sept. 29, suppl. p. 10.

Sept. 21-23. BC musical director, Monterey Jazz Festival. Opening night BC conducts Dizzy Gillespie orch. in The New Continent, by Lalo Schifrin. --DB Nov. 8, pp. 13-15.

1963 Fall. Participates in course on recording arts, at UCLA extension division, conducted in cooperation with NARAS. --DB Nov. 21, p. 11.

1966 Nov.-Dec., early. Tours Europe with JATP. --DB Jan. 26, 1967, pp. 27, 40, 45.

1967 March 26-July, early. Tours U.S. and Canada with JATP, opening at Carnegie Hall, N.Y. --DB March 9, p. 15.

1968 Jan. Substitutes on alto sax for Russell Procope (who substitutes for ill Harry Carney) in Ellington band, about three days, Harrah's, club, Reno.

Feb. Leads quintet, Donte's, club, L.A., three weekends. --DB Feb. 8, p. 14, and Feb. 22, p. 24. Personnel. Billy Byers (tb), Jimmy Jones (p), Red Mitchell (b), Joe Harris (d). --Ibid.

July 5-6. First appearance at Newport Jazz Festival, solos with bands led by Gillespie (July 5) and Ellington (July 6). --DB June 27, p. 10, and Sept. 5, p. 18; Christian Science Monitor, July 12, p. 6.

Oct. 19. Featured soloist, and accompanies Carmen McRae, concert, Royce Hall, UCLA. --LAT Oct. 22, sec. 4, p. 15. Personnel. Norman Simmons (p), Chuck Domanico (b), Frank Severino (d). --Ibid.

Oct. 23-Nov., early. BC in London with group from Newport Jazz Festival. --DB Oct. 31, p. 10; LAT Oct. 20, Calendar sec., p. 40.

Nov. Plays in Ronnie Scott Club, London, ten days. --BB Nov. 23, p. 16.

Nov. 9. Plays with Henri Chaix band, "Jazz in der Aula," in Kantonsschule, Baden, Switzerland. --Badener Tagblatt, Nov. 8.

Nov. 10. Plays with Henri Chaix band at Vieilles Pierres, Geneva.

Nov. 11. Plays at C.N.P.-Capitole Th, Bordeaux.

1969 April 5. Conducts and solos with large orchestra and choir his own extended composition (with lyrics) in honor of the late Martin Luther King, Jr., Pauley Pavilion, UCLA. --LAT April 7, pt. 4, p. 16; DB May 29, p. 33.

1970   Jan. 26-30. Plays and conducts seminars, Baldwin Wallace College, Berea, O.

Feb. 2-3. Leads quartet, conducts seminars, Princeton U. --NYT Feb. 5, p. 34. Personnel. Roland Hanna (p), Ron Carter (b), Grady Tate (d). --Ibid.

May 16-17. Plays and participates in seminar at National College Jazz Festival, U. of Ill., Urbana. --DB July 9, p. 13.

1971   May 30. Conducts and plays with Louis Bellson band, big-band "festival," Disneyland. --DB Aug. 19, p. 44.

June 1-24. Touring Denmark, Sweden, France.

Sept. 4-6. Plays at Dick Gibson's jazz party, Colorado Springs.

1972   Feb. 13-14. Plays (Feb. 13) and conducts seminars (Feb. 14), Eisenhower College, Seneca Falls, N.Y. Personnel. Hank Jones (p), George Duvivier (b), Ron Zito (d).

July 2-3. Newport Jazz Festival, N.Y. July 2 leads Swing Masters, Carnegie Hall; July 3 jam session, Radio City Music Hall. --NYT July 3, p. 7, and July 5, p. 31. Personnel. July 2, Swing Masters: see Discography.

July 4. Guest of honor, New Amsterdam Musical Association (est. 1900), Harlem.

Sept. 2-4. Dick Gibson jazz party, Colorado Springs.

Oct. 6-8. Plays concert and named Fellow, Duke Ellington Fellowship Program, Yale U. --DB Dec. 7, pp. 11, 38.

Oct. 24, ca., to Nov. 8 ca. Touring Europe, Norman Granz management. --DB Dec. 7, p. 10.

1973   April 18-19. Leads seminars and concert (April 19), Princeton U. Personnel. Hank Jones (p), Milt Hinton (b), Ron Zito (d). --NYT April 23, p. 41.

May 21-June, early. Touring Denmark, France.

July 18-28. Touring Japan. Personnel. Gildo Mahones (p), Larry Gales (b), Duffy Jackson (d).

Sept. 1-3. Dick Gibson jazz party, Colorado Springs.

Sept. 17. Leads quartet, L.A. County Museum of Art. --LAT Sept. 20, pt. 4, p. 16. Personnel. Gildo Mahones (p), Larry Gales (b), Duffy Jackson (d). --Ibid.

Sept.-Dec. Visiting professor, fall term, Princeton U.: workshops, seminars, concerts on Oct. 22, Dec. 3. Personnel. Oct. 22, McCarter Th. Clark Terry (t), Hank Jones (p), Bucky Pizzarelli

Chronology 1973

(g), Milt Hinton (b), Grady Tate (d). Personnel. Dec. 3, Alexander Hall: see Discography.

Nov. 10. Participates in workshop and concert conducted by Willie Ruff, Yale U.

Dec., mid. Leads local combo, Bourbon St., club, Toronto. --IM Jan. 1974, p. 21.

1974 Jan. 19. Receives "Jazzboree" award; leads quartet, concert, Paramount Th, Oakland. Personnel. Gildo Mahones (p), Larry Gales (b), Paul Humphrey (d). --Philip Elwood, San Francisco Examiner, Jan. 21, p. 27.

June 11. Receives honorary degree, Doctor of Humanities, Princeton U. --NYT June 12, p. 49; DB Nov. 7, p. 10.

Aug. 31-Sept. 2. Dick Gibson jazz party, Colorado Springs.

Nov. 6-7. Leads sextet in concert (Nov. 7), and seminars, Cornell U. Personnel. Jimmy Nottingham (t), Al Grey (tb), Roland Hanna (p), Milt Hinton (b), Alan Dawson (d).

Nov. Conducts band accompanying Maria Muldaur on U.S. tour. --NYT Nov. 20, p. 54, on Nov. 18 concert, Avery Fisher Hall, N.Y. Personnel. Sweets Edison, Snooky Young (t), Frank Rosolino (tb), Plas Johnson, Sahib Shihab, Tony Ortega (reeds), Marty Harris (p), John Collins (g), John B. Williams, Jr. (b), Earl Palmer (d).

Dec. 22. Conducts band accompanying Maria Muldaur, Troubadour, club, L.A. Personnel. Changes from Nov.: J. J. Johnson (tb) replaces Rosolino, Bud Shank (reeds) replaces Ortega, Mundell Lowe (g) replaces Collins.

1975 June 28. Leads band (also accompanies Maria Muldaur), Newport Jazz Festival, Carnegie Hall, N.Y. --NYT June 30, p. 40.

July. Plays at European festivals, Nice and Montreux.

Aug. 25-30. Leads quartet, Playboy Club, L.A. --LAT Aug. 27, pt. 4, p. 11. Personnel. Gildo Mahones (p), Larry Gales (b), Jimmie Smith (d). --Ibid.

Aug. 31-Sept. 2. Dick Gibson jazz party, Colorado Springs.

Sept. 9. Leads quartet, Ratso's, club, Chicago. --Chicago Daily News, Sept. 10, p. 24. Personnel. Jodie Christian (p), David Shipp (b), Jo Jones (d). --Ibid.

Oct. 26-Nov. 22. Touring Europe with Earl Hines. --Dance, World of Earl Hines, pp. 126, 310.

Dec. 16-Jan. 22, 1976. Leads quintet touring Middle East under auspices of U.S. Dept. of State and USIA. --LAT Jan. 31, 1976, p. 1, and Feb. 8, Calendar sec., pp. 73-75. Personnel. Sweets

Edison (t), Gildo Mahones (p), John B. Williams, Jr. (b), Earl Palmer (d), Millicent Browne (v).

1976   Jan. 1-22.   Continues tour of Middle East. See previous entry.

April 14-16.   Plays with student jazz band with Willie Ruff, Duke U. --The Chronicle, student paper, April 21, p. 9.

May 29-June 6.   Tours Europe with show, "A Night in New Orleans."

June 8-July 3.   Leads quartet, Michael's Pub, N.Y., BC's first club date in N.Y. since 1942 on 52d St. --NYT June 11, p. C4. Personnel.   Ray Bryant (p), Milt Hinton (b), Grady Tate (d). --Ibid.

July 5-17.   Plays with local rhythm section, Buena Vista Village Lounge, Disney World, Fla. --Orlando Sentinel-Star, advt., July 11, p. 9-F.

July 27.   Honored in testimonial dinner by Hollywood Press Club. --BB July 31, p. 41.

Aug.   Accepts three-year term on music advisory panel of NEA.

Sept.   Accepts four-year term on advisory council of Princeton U Music department.

Sept. 4-6.   Dick Gibson jazz party, Colorado Springs.

Sept. 7-8.   Leads quartet, Donte's, club, L.A. --LAT advt. Sept. 5, Calendar sec., p. 76.

Sept. 17.   Plays at Monterey Jazz Festival in tributes to F. Henderson and Armstrong. Receives award from American Music Conference. --DB July 15, p. 6.

Oct. 13-15.   Gives interview on career for Jazz Oral History Project conducted by Smithsonian Institution on behalf of NEA.

1977   Jan.   Awarded prize for Pablo record, The King, by Académie du Disque Français.

Feb. 15.   Leads band for dance, Palladium, L.A.

March 11-April 12.   Visiting lecturer, Princeton U.: workshops, seminars, concerts Alexander Hall March 18 (leading quintet) and April 8 (solos with student P.U. Jazz Ensemble). Personnel. March 18. Joe Newman (t), Bucky Pizzarelli (g), Roland Hanna (p), Richard Davis (b), Richard Pratt (d). Personnel. April 8: see Discography.

April 19-29.   Tours Japan with BC All Stars. Personnel. April 29: see Discography.

May 2-7.   Plays at Kool festival, Hawaii.

May 17-June 11.   Leads quartet, Michael's Pub, N.Y. --NYT May

21, p. 11. Personnel. Ray Bryant (p), Richard Davis (b), Ronnie Bedford (d). --Ibid.

June 23-July 2. Tours England. --Jazz Journal International, Aug., pp. 22-23.

July 7-12. Plays at Nice festival, Grande Parade du Jazz.

July 13-14. Plays at Montreux festival. Personnel. See Discography, July 13, 14.

July 15. Plays at Northsea festival, The Hague.

July 16-18. Plays at San Sebastian (Spain), Biarritz and Montauban (France).

Sept. 3-5. Dick Gibson jazz party, Colorado Springs.

1978 Feb. 19. Inducted into Black Film Makers Hall of Fame, Oakland. --Oakland Tribune, Feb. 19, special sec.; San Francisco Examiner, Feb. 20, p. 22.

March 20. Plays with Jon Hendricks at Meadows Playhouse, Las Vegas.

April 13-21. Tours Japan. Personnel. See Discography, April 15.

April 28-May 12. Tours Canada and Europe with "A Night in New Orleans."

May 14. Leads quintet, concert, Jazz Heritage Series of Smithsonian Institution, at National Museum of Natural History, Wash., D.C. --Washington Post, May 15, p. B8. Personnel. Joe Kennedy, Jr. (vn), Ray Bryant (p), Larry Ridley (b), Freddie Waits (d). --Ibid.

May 16-27. Leads quartet, Rick's Café Américain, Chicago. --Chicago Tribune, May 19, sec. 2, p. 5. Personnel. Jodie Christian (p), John Bany (b), Barrett Deems (d). --Ibid.

May 25. Award made to BC by Center for Afro-American Studies, UCLA.

June 18. Leads ensemble at White House tribute to jazz. Personnel. Roy Eldridge, Clark Terry (t), Illinois Jacquet (ts), Teddy Wilson (p), Milt Hinton (b), Jo Jones (d). --Washington Post, June 19, p. B1.

June 23. Plays in concert, Denver, produced by Dick Gibson.

Sept. 2-4. Dick Gibson jazz party, Colorado Springs.

Sept. 10-11. Plays at festival, Sao Paolo, Brazil. --LAT Oct. 8, Calendar sec., pp. 92-94.

Sept. 14-17. Gives master classes and concert, Capital U. Conservatory of Music, Columbus, O.

Sept. 19-23. Leads quartet, Hong Kong Bar, Century Plaza Hotel, L.A. --LAT Sept. 21, pt. 4, p. 26. Personnel. Gildo Mahones (p), Andy Simpson (b), Jimmie Smith (d). --Ibid.

Oct. 20. Plays with youth band, Yale U. School of Music.

Oct. 21. Plays fund-raising concert, Wooster School, Danbury, Conn.

Oct. 26. Leads band, inauguration of new president, California Institute of Technology, Pasadena. Personnel. Conte Candoli, Bobby Bryant (t), Frank Rosolino (tb), Abe Most, Teddy Edwards (reeds), Gildo Mahones (p), John Collins (g), Monte Budwig (b), Jimmie Smith (d).

Oct. 27-29. Conducts seminars, two concerts (Oct. 28) SUNY Buffalo. In each concert BC solos with student band, then leads and plays with Al Tinney Trio. Personnel, both ensembles: see Discography.

1979 June 1-15. Tours Japan. Personnel. See Discography, June 2.

Aug. 30. Plays at Chicago festival. --Chicago Tribune, Aug. 31, sec. 4, p. 6.

Sept. 1-3. Dick Gibson jazz party, Colorado Springs.

Sept.-Dec. Visiting professor, fall term, Princeton U., teaching in regular course and giving two concerts, Alexander Hall: Oct. 12, leads a sextet; Nov. 10, solos with student ensemble. Personnel, Oct. 12. Dizzy Gillespie (t), Joe Kennedy, Jr. (vn), Barry Harris (p), Larry Ridley (b), Yusef Ali (d). Personnel, Nov. 10: see Discography.

1980 Jan. 25-26. Plays in concert, Paramount Th, Denver, produced by Dick Gibson.

April. Album of BC records appears, Giants of Jazz series, published by Time-Life Records.

June 8. Receives Golden Score award from American Society of Music Arrangers in ceremony, Ambassador Hotel, L.A.

June 11-13. Plays at Stockholm Jazz and Blues Festival with several local groups. Personnel: see Discography.

June 20. Leads quartet, "Tonight Show," NBC-TV, L.A. Personnel. Teddy Wilson (p), Ray Brown (b), Shelly Manne (d).

June 21. Leads quintet, Playboy festival, Hollywood Bowl. --LAT June 23, pt. 6, pp. 1-2. Personnel. Sweets Edison (t), Teddy Wilson (p), Ray Brown (b), Shelly Manne (d). --Ibid.

June 26. Plays with New McKinney Cotton Pickers, honoring Don Redman, Detroit Institute of Arts. --Detroit News, June 26, p. 11B.

June 27-28. Leads quartet, One Step Down, club, Wash., D. C. --Washington Star, June 27, sec. C, p. 11. Personnel. Gus Simms (p), Tommy Cecil (b), Bernard Sweetney (d).

July 3. Leads band, Newport festival, Avery Fisher Hall. --NYT July 5, p. 12. Personnel. Jimmy Maxwell, Doc Cheatham (t), Curtis Fuller (tb), Budd Johnson, Cecil Payne (reeds), Joe Kennedy, Jr. (vn), Ray Bryant (p), Major Holley (b), Oliver Jackson (d).

July 9-24. Leads BC All-Stars (personnel--see July 3 above) in European festivals: France, Holland.

Aug. 10-15. Leads combo, Tivoli garden, Slukefter Jazz Club, Copenhagen. Personnel. Kenny Drew (p), Jesper Lundgaard (b), Ed Thigpen (d).

Sept. 3-7. Leads quintet in three concerts in Japan: Tokyo, Osaka, Yokohama. Aurex festival also features groups led by Benny Goodman, Freddie Hubbard, Dizzy Gillespie. Personnel. Sweets Edison (t), Teddy Wilson (p), Milt Hinton (b), Shelly Manne (d), Helen Humes (v).

Oct. 10. Plays at New Haven, Conn., with Yale Jazz Ensemble (undergraduates), Willie Ruff and Dwike Mitchell in two concerts: for elementary school pupils and for the general public.

Oct. 28. Leads big band in celebrating, over several evenings, 40th anniversary of Palladium Bm, L. A.

1981 March 24-25. Member of ad hoc group convened by the Smithsonian Institution Division of Performing Arts, in Washington, D. C., to discuss its jazz program.

April 14-18. Leads quartet, Sweet Basil's, N. Y. --NYT April 17, p. C15. Personnel. Norman Simmons (p), George Duvivier (b), Ronnie Bedford (d).

April 28-May 3. Concerts in Denmark, Sweden.

May 5-8. Leads combo, Tivoli garden, Slukefter Jazz Club, Copenhagen.

May 25-June 13. Leads quartet, Lyte's, Royal York Hotel, Toronto. Personnel. Carol Britto (p), Dave Field (b), Don Vickery (d).

July 1-21. Tours Japan. Personnel. Bill Berry, Pete Candoli (t), George Bohanon (tb), Frank Wess (ts, flute), Jack Nimitz (bar. sax), Kenny Barron (p), Joe Kennedy, Jr. (violin), George Duvivier (b), Frankie Capp (d).

Aug. 22-23. Leads quartet, Ojai Festival, Ojai, California. Personnel. Roger Kellaway (p), Chuck Domanico (b), John Guerin (d).

Aug. 26. Plays at concert, tribute to Lionel Hampton, Hollywood Bowl. Personnel. Includes Harry Edison, Teddy Wilson.

Sept. 5-7. Dick Gibson jazz party, Colorado Springs.

Sept. 26. Leads sextet, concert, UCLA. (Portions later broadcast over National Public Radio's "Jazz Alive.") Personnel. Bill Berry (cornet), George Bohanon (tb), Roger Kellaway (p), Chuck Domanico (b), John Guerin (d).

Nov. 8. Leads quintet, Bach Dancing and Dynamite Society, Half Moon Bay, California. --San Francisco Examiner, Nov. 13, p. E5. Personnel. Tee Carson (p), Eddie Duran (g), Dean Reilly (b), Benny Barth (d).

Nov. 20-21. Plays in concert, Paramount Th, Denver, produced by Dick Gibson. Personnel. Red Rodney (t), Bill Watrous, Al Grey (tb), Plas Johnson, Buddy Tate (ts), Dick Hyman, Jay McShann (p), Slam Stewart (b), Gus Johnson (d).

Nov. 28. Leads quintet, concert, Smithsonian Institution, Washington, D.C. Personnel. Kenny Barron (p), Joe Kennedy, Jr. (violin), George Duvivier (b), Ronnie Bedford (d).

Dec. 1-5. Leads quartet, Sweet Basil's, N.Y. --NYT Dec. 4, p. C15. Personnel. Kenny Barron (p), George Duvivier (b), Ronnie Bedford (d).

Dec. 15-20. Leads quartet, Parisian Room, L.A. Personnel. Gildo Mahones (p), Larry Gales (b), Harold Jones (d).

1982 Jan. 4-23. Leads quartet, Lyte's, Royal York Hotel, Toronto. Personnel. Carol Britto (p), Dave Young (b), Don Vickery (d).

DISCOGRAPHY

Introduction	31
Section One: Carter as Instrumentalist	33
Index of Artists	241
Index of Tune Titles	255
Section Two: Carter as Arranger and Composer	267
Master List of Arrangements and Compositions	268
Index of Artists Who Have Recorded Carter	
Arrangements and/or Compositions	345
Soundtracks	378
Chronological Index of Compositions and	
Arrangements	381
A Basic Selection of Benny Carter's LPs	391
Filmography	393
Bibliography	397
Discographical Addenda	415

INTRODUCTION*

In possessing such a wide range of talents, Carter has done little to "cooperate" with the discographer. It is easy to develop a workable format for the artist who is primarily a player (extracting the data, of course, may be anything but simple). Documenting the contributions of a composer/arranger is more complex. Carter is unique in the depth of his contributions to every domain discographers seek to cover. Moreover, his career encompasses many musical styles, all types of media, and is extraordinary in its longevity and sustained creativity.

Scope. This discography could not be confined to Carter's playing. Therefore a section has been devoted to his arrangements and compositions, with indexes to show who recorded them and a chronology of their creation.

Nor could any stylistic limitations be imposed, such as attempting to isolate the "jazz" component of his work. Aside from the inevitable arbitrariness of such a distinction, the exclusion of the non-jazz elements would severely distort the total picture of Carter's career. The symbiosis between jazz and popular music is well known and jazz musicians--Carter more than most--have always moved between the two realms. In fact, it would be safe to say that since the 1940s he has devoted more time to arranging and composing for television, films, and popular singers than to his activity as a jazz instrumentalist. Carter himself, unlike some purists, does not view this as an invidious distinction.

We include many private recordings because they provide important documentation of periods in Carter's career when he made few commercial studio recordings (particularly late 1960s and 1970s). Such performances, indeed, may yet become more widely available.

Sources. Rust's and Jepsen's general jazz discographies provide the basis for much of the information in this discography. More specialized artist-discographies and bio-discographies also proved helpful, as did two previous surveys of Carter's recordings: Jörgen Grunnet Jepsen's "Benny Carter Diskografi 1949-1959," Orkester Journalen, December 1959, pp. 56-57; January 1960, p. 34; February 1960, pp. 38-39, and a Carter discography in the Japanese Swing Journal, June 1979, pp. 222-227. The late Walter C. Allen's Hendersonia must be singled out not only for the information provided on Carter's recordings with Henderson but as a model for the presentation of arranging and composing data. Many collectors and researchers helped with the more ephemeral material, such as airchecks, transcriptions, and private recordings.

---

*This introduction is abbreviated from Edward Berger's article in the Journal of Jazz Studies. He invites additions to and corrections of this discography. Portions of the notes on the music are adapted from those in The Giants of Jazz: Benny Carter (Time-Life).

Special problems arose in the documentation of Carter's "popular" music because discographical coverage of this field is far less advanced than of jazz. Consequently, chance played a large role in the discovery of his participation as an instrumentalist on some sessions.

The identification of recorded arrangements by Carter was also problematical. The arranger is truly the stepchild of the recording session. Though his reworking of a composition often becomes an act of greater creativity and musical interest than the piece on which it is based, he is too often viewed as a journeyman.

Aural identification of arrangements is difficult but may be a starting point taken in conjunction with the arranger's known associations. Certainly Carter's arrangements have distinctive stylistic features, not the least of which are his innovative reed voicings. But, as other arrangers have attested, many copied his style--often rather successfully--so that after a time the presence of a flowing reed passage no longer guarantees that it is a Carter arrangement. Furthermore, the special demands of a particular bandleader or contractor often required Carter to treat a piece in a style different from his own. This results in the elimination, or at least the dilution, of some of Carter's trademarks, making it more difficult, even for him, to recognize his own work, especially after many years.

Musician as Source. The artist himself may be the single most valuable source in a project of this kind. Carter's cooperation has been complete. He opened his home to the project. His record collection, scores, memorabilia, and business files provided answers to many problems, as well as clues to a number of items which would otherwise have been overlooked. He submitted to hundreds of hours of interviews and listening, which helped immeasurably in identifying solos and arrangements. Carter's respect for scholarship and research methods led him to divulge even such information as his use of pseudonyms.

This was not the first time Carter willingly submitted to discographical grilling. In 1935 in Paris, Charles Delaunay enlisted Carter's help for his pioneering Hot Discography. It was Delaunay, on a visit to the United States in 1980, who revealed the extent of Carter's assistance. Carter himself never mentioned it, perhaps to avoid the appearance of impatience with this new inquisition.

As far as his credibility as a source is concerned, Carter is not one to claim credit for a solo, arrangement or composition unless he is certain that it is his work. Jelly Roll Morton claimed to have invented jazz in 1902. The Carter interviewer considers himself a success if he gets his subject to admit that he played the saxophone.

SECTION ONE: CARTER AS INSTRUMENTALIST

This section is a chronological listing of all known recordings on which Carter plays. Issued and unissued performances of the following types are included: studio recordings, airchecks, private recordings, transcriptions and some television broadcasts. Carter's playing in films is listed here only when such material has appeared on record (e.g., soundtrack albums). Other film work is documented in the filmography.

Each session includes the following data.

1. Session number appears in brackets at the left and is assigned sequentially to each session, beginning with 1. If sets of recordings made on one date have significant changes in personnel they are assigned different session numbers (e.g., the trio portion of a Jazz At The Philharmonic concert).

2. Date of recording is followed by place of recording (city). Following the date a brief description of the type of recording may appear, including a more precise location (e.g., airchecks, Savoy Ballroom). If no additional descriptive information is present, the session is a studio recording. The leader and/or group appears on the next line. For recent Carter-led sessions, the appropriate LP title(s) are given in parentheses.

3. Personnel. Carter always appears first, with abbreviations summarizing his role(s) on the date (i.e., instruments played, arrangements and/or compositions contributed).

4. Tune titles, Carter's solos, and matrix numbers. Each title is followed by an indication (using initials) of vocalists and/or arrangers, etc. pertinent to that title. Next is a notation of Carter's precise participation on that particular piece. The solo description consists of the number of measures followed by an instrument abbreviation. If Carter's solo is continued after a brief interlude (e.g., bridge) by the ensemble or another soloist, Carter's passages are separated by a + symbol. If Carter returns after a longer interval, the + does not appear between the solo statements. Where Carter is not the only soloist on a given instrument, his solo is identified. The abbreviation "acc." following the instrument means that Carter's playing is accompanying a vocalist or another soloist (i.e., obbligato). An "e" is used to indicate titles on which Carter plays in the ensemble but does not solo. The absence of any solo indication means that we have not heard the item. The abbreviations "arr" and "comp" following the solo description identify the piece as a Carter arrangement or composition. With the advent of the LP, the release of longer performances became feasible. After 1952 the number of measures of Carter's solos is no longer indicated; only the instrument is given.

5. Basic record issue information appears directly below the individual tune titles. Issues are preceded by the type of disc (78: 45: LP: or

T: for transcription). Where helpful, the country of origin of a record issue is indicated by an abbreviation in parentheses after the label name. These listings do not attempt to include every issue of every title, but concentrate on the original issue, major reissues, and those issues (usually recent) not covered in the standard comprehensive discographies. An absence of record issues indicates that the recordings exist or are likely to exist on private tapes. Artist and title indexes to Section One refer to session numbers.

      6. Annotations follow many of the sessions; these annotations concentrate on the commercially issued recordings rather than the less widely-circulated material.

      Armed Forces Radio Service Transcriptions. From 1942 to 1952 Benny Carter participated in approximately thirty AFRS productions including Jubilee shows, Downbeat shows, the Basic Library of Popular Music and the V-Disc program.

      Most of the information for the AFRS listings comes from two major sources: 1) Dr. Ranier E. Lotz, who is carrying out extensive research on the AFRS series and provided drafts of his worksheets for the Jubilee programs involving Carter. 2) Jerry Valburn, who supplied tapes of many of the AFRS shows as well as information about the various series.

      Jubilee. Jubilee shows were half-hour transcriptions distributed overseas for broadcast to United States personnel. Many were especially recorded before a live audience, but occasionally material from other sources was included (e.g., portions of the 1947 "Just Jazz" concerts). Most of the shows featuring Carter were recorded in Los Angeles with comedian Ernie "Bubbles" Whitman as m.c. Later shows originated from the McCornack Hospital in Pasadena, with Gene Norman as host. Musicians donated their services. The Jubilee shows were often extensively edited, with some segments reappearing in later programs. Some were repeated in their entirety, although assigned a new program number. Where specific dates are given in the discography, they come from Dr. Lotz, who has examined AFRS books prior to 1946. He points out that these are not actual recording dates, but probably the dates the transcriptions were edited. He surmises that they are reasonably close to the date of recording and in some cases the same. In any case, these dates should be considered as "not later than" rather than exact.

      Basic Library of Popular Music. According to Jerry Valburn, the AFRS was allowed to take material off the air for inclusion in this transcription series, which served as the source for other programs.

      Downbeat shows. These half-hour transcriptions derived from several sources. Those featuring Carter seem to have drawn primarily from the Basic Library, although some regular commercial studio items are present.

      V-Discs. These were 12-inch 78 rpm discs playable on standard phonographs and distributed directly to the military posts. Some performances were recorded especially for V-Discs; others came from commercial recordings and other AFRS productions. Most of the Carter V-Discs contain performances from Jubilee transcriptions.

      Discographical information about these recordings is highly speculative for several reasons. 1) Original documentation for many of these programs no longer exists. 2) A performance from one source was often used for other types of programs (e.g., Jubilee recordings used in Downbeat shows, commercial recordings reissued on V-Disc, etc.). 3) Dubbed applause and announcements may disguise the original source of the material. 4) A performance may reappear in various programs under different titles (e.g., "Jump Tune," "No Title Jump," "Untitled Jump," and possibly "Jay Jay's Jump" for the Carter orchestra recording of "Polishin' Brass"). On the other hand, several different versions of the same tune may be included on different AFRS programs. 5) The approximately 15 LPs containing Carter AFRS material which have appeared to date include some wrong discographical data.

ABBREVIATIONS

Instruments

tp - trumpet	g - guitar
tb - trombone	b - bass
cl - clarinet	d - drums
ss - soprano saxophone	vib - vibraphone
as - alto saxophone	v - vocal
ts - tenor saxophone	ldr - leader
bs - baritone saxophone	dir - director
p - piano	

Carter's role and solos:

instruments - abbreviated as above

e - ensemble (no solo)

acc - Carter plays accompaniment to vocalist or other soloist (obbligato)

arr - arranger

comp - composer

Record issues (countries of origin)

E - England	I - Italy
F - France	J - Japan
G - Germany	Sw - Sweden

Discography: Section One

CARTER AS INSTRUMENTALIST

[1]	January 24, 1928 New York

CHARLIE JOHNSON'S PARADISE ORCHESTRA

Carter (as, cl, arr) Jabbo Smith, Sidney de Paris (tp) Charlie Irvis (tb) Edgar Sampson (as, violin) Ben Whittet (cl, as) Benny Waters (ts, as) Charlie Johnson (p) Bobby Johnson (banjo) Cyrus St. Clair (tuba) George Stafford (d) McNette Moore (v)

YOU AIN'T THE ONE   v-MM   (e) arr   41639-1
78: UNISSUED   LP: VICTOR 430687, PIRATE MPC521,
RCA (F) 741.065

YOU AIN'T THE ONE   v-MM   (e) arr   41639-2
78: VICTOR 21247   LP: MELODEON MLP7327, RCA (F)
741.065

CHARLESTON IS THE BEST DANCE AFTER ALL   (8as) arr   41640-1
78: VICTOR 21491   LP: MELODEON MLP7326, RCA (F)
741.065, RCA (F) PM42406

CHARLESTON IS THE BEST DANCE AFTER ALL   (8as) arr   41640-2
78: UNISSUED   LP: VICTOR "X" LVA3026, VICTOR 430687,
ONLY FOR COLLECTORS OFC10, RCA (F) 741.065

HOT TEMPERED BLUES   (e)   41641-1
78: UNISSUED   LP: VICTOR "X" LVA3026, VICTOR
430687, RCA (F) 741.065

HOT TEMPERED BLUES   (e)   41641-2
78: VICTOR 21247   LP: ONLY FOR COLLECTORS OFC10,
RCA (F) 741.065

* * *

This session is generally considered to be Carter's first, but he recalls making a recording much earlier (probably 1924) with blues singer Clara Smith. Carter, who would have been 17 at the time, remembers that he was contacted by Charles Matson, who played piano on the date. In an attempt to identify the recording more precisely, Carter perused Clara Smith titles of that time, and sessions with unidentified alto saxophone accompaniments were played for him (he was not yet doubling on clarinet). He could not recognize any of these titles or recordings. If indeed he played on one of them it may never have been issued, or perhaps he substituted for a saxophonist whose name remains as the accompanist.

Although Carter's playing on this 1928 date is limited to an eight-bar statement on "Charleston," we get our first extended look at Carter's incipient arranging style. The two Carter arrangements are not, however, his first on record. "PDQ Blues," recorded by Fletcher Henderson on April 28, 1927, is probably by Carter. While obviously drawing on past elements (e.g., the trumpet section breaks à la Armstrong/Oliver), Carter's special treatment of the reeds is evident in both arrangements. "Charleston," in particular, has a full chorus of the section displaying some of the characteristic lines and voicings--although with the prevailing choppier phrasing--which would mark his later work. His brief solo appearance (the eight-bar bridge within Jabbo Smith's solo trumpet chorus) is also unmistakably Carter in tone. He has difficulty in the second measure of his solo in take 2, possibly one reason the first take was chosen for issue.

[2]	Mid November, 1928 New York
	HENDERSON'S HAPPY SIX ORCHESTRA

Carter (as) Rex Stewart (cornet) Charlie Green (tb) Buster Bailey (cl) Fletcher Henderson (p) Charlie Dixon or Clarence Holiday (banjo) Coleman Hawkins (bass sax)

OLD BLACK JOE'S BLUES (2as)   3491-A
78: CAMEO 9033   LP: COLUMBIA CL1683

* * *

This is Carter's first recording with the Henderson group, although he was not to become a regular member of the band until 1930.

[3]	December 12, 1928 New York
	FLETCHER HENDERSON AND HIS ORCHESTRA

Carter (as, v, arr) Rex Stewart, Bobby Stark (tp) Charlie Green (tb) Buster Bailey (cl, as) Coleman Hawkins (ts) Fletcher Henderson (p) Clarence Holiday (banjo) June Cole (tuba) Kaiser Marshall (d)

COME ON, BABY (8+8as) (v) arr   147421-3
78: COLUMBIA 14392-D   LP: COLUMBIA CL1684

EASY MONEY (e) arr   147422-2
78: COLUMBIA 14392-D   LP: COLUMBIA CL1683

* * *

Carter's brief solo contribution to this date is in two parts and shows a growing confidence and forceful attack, with an ambitious break at the end of the first eight measures. He has some intonation problems during the second eight-bar spot.

His first recorded vocal is also his only attempt at scat-singing and makes up in energetic good humor what it lacks in technique.

Walter C. Allen lists Charlie Green with a question mark; Carter, after hearing these recordings, believes the trombonist is Green.

[4]   September 18, 1929 New York
        THE CHOCOLATE DANDIES

Carter (as, cl, v) Rex Stewart, Leonard Davis (tp) J. C. Higginbotham (tb) Don Redman (as, cl, v) Coleman Hawkins (ts) Fats Waller (p) Bobby Johnson (banjo) Cyrus St. Clair (tuba) George Stafford (d)

THAT'S HOW I FEEL TODAY   (16+8as)   402965-C
78: OKEH 8728 LP: PARLOPHONE (E) PMC7038,
SWAGGIE S1249, ODEON (J) EMI OR-8065

SIX OR SEVEN TIMES v-BC, DR (16as) (vocal duet   402966-D
    with DR) (16as trades with DR-v)+(16as trades
    with ensemble)
78: OKEH 8728 LP: FOLKWAYS FP69, FOLKWAYS
FJ2808, PARLOPHONE (E) PMC7038, SWAGGIE S1249,
ODEON (J) EMI OR-8065, TIME-LIFE STL-J10

                        *   *   *

This was the first of Carter's several associations with recording groups named "Chocolate Dandies." He himself was to lead sessions under this now anachronistic designation in 1930, 1933, and as late as 1946. Here, Don Redman is in charge.

The riff which opens and closes "Six Or Seven Times" later became the basis of Count Basie's "One O'Clock Jump." The piece includes a sixteen-bar conversation between Carter and Redman, with Redman's scat-singing replies to Carter's alto statements. (For a discussion of Carter's solo on this piece, see chapter 3.)

[5]   November 5, 1929 New York
        McKINNEY'S COTTON PICKERS

Carter (as) Joe Smith, Leonard Davis, Sidney de Paris (tp) Claude Jones (tb) Don Redman (as, v, arr) Coleman Hawkins, Theodore McCord (cl, ts) Fats Waller (p) Dave Wilborn (banjo) Billy Taylor (tuba) Kaiser Marshall (d) John Nesbitt (arr)

PLAIN DIRT arr-JN (e)   57064-2
78: VICTOR V-38097 LP: RCA (F) 741.088, RCA
(F) 42407, RCA (J) RA-47

GEE, AIN'T I GOOD TO YOU v-DR, arr-DR (16as)   57065-1
78: VICTOR V-38097 LP: RCA LPV520, RCA (E)
RD7561, RCA (F) 741.088, RCA (F) PM42407, RCA
(J) RA-47

[6]   November 6, 1929 New York
        McKINNEY'S COTTON PICKERS

Carter (as, cl) Joe Smith, Leonard Davis, Sidney de Paris (tp) Claude Jones (tb) Don Redman (as, v, arr) Coleman Hawkins, Theodore McCord (cl, ts) Fats Waller (p) Dave Wilborn (banjo) Billy Taylor (tuba) Kaiser Marshall (d)

I'D LOVE IT (32as)   57066-2

78: VICTOR V-38133   LP: RCA LPV520, RCA (E)
RD7561, RCA (F) 741.088, TIME-LIFE STL-J10, RCA
(F) PM42407

THE WAY I FEEL TODAY   v-DR (e)   57067-1
78: VICTOR V-38102   LP: RCA LPV520, RCA (E)
RD7561, RCA (F) 741.109, RCA (F) PM42407, RCA
(J) RA-47

MISS HANNAH   v-DR (16cl)   57068-2
78: VICTOR V-38102   LP: RCA LPV520, RCA (E)
RD7561, RCA (F) 741.109, RCA (F) PM42407, RCA
(J) RA-47

[7]	November 7, 1929 New York
	McKINNEY'S COTTON PICKERS

Carter (as) Joe Smith, Leonard Davis, Sidney de Paris (tp) Claude Jones
(tb) Don Redman (as, v, arr) Coleman Hawkins, Theodore McCord (cl, ts)
Fats Waller (p) Dave Wilborn (banjo) Billy Taylor (tuba) Kaiser Marshall (d)

PEGGY (e)   57139-3
78: VICTOR V-38133   LP: RCA (E) RD7561, RCA
LPV520, RCA (F) 741.109, RCA (F) PM43258

WHEREVER THERE'S A WILL, BABY   v-DR (e)   57140-2
78: VICTOR 22736   LP: RCA (E) RD7561, RCA
LPV501, RCA (F) 741.109, TIME-LIFE STL-J06,
RCA (F) PM43258

WHEREVER THERE'S A WILL, BABY   v-DR (e)   57140-3
78: UNISSUED   LP: RCA (J) RA-5314, RCA (F)
741.109, RCA (F) PM43258

NOTE: RCA (J) RA-47 contains one of the two takes of "Wherever..."

* * *

The personnel for these three sessions [5, 6, 7] is an augmented recording version of the regular McKinney's Cotton Pickers, for which Don Redman was then musical director; Carter would replace him two years later. Carter credits Redman's leadership for the precise execution of the Cotton Pickers and remembers him as "one of the sweetest and most generous men I ever knew." Whenever they recorded together, the self-effacing Redman usually delegated the alto or clarinet solos to Carter.

Carter's alto chorus on "I'd Love It" is his longest recorded solo outing to date and already shows some of the characteristics that have been the cornerstones of his style to the present. There are hints of the long, graceful lines to come, and a clear demonstration of his uncanny ability to conceive a solo as a whole.

Carter's clarinet solo on "Miss Hannah" is his first on record. He recalls taking up the clarinet when he joined Charlie Johnson's band at Small's Paradise: "In fact, that may have been one of the conditions of the job, because in those days everybody doubled."

November 7, 1929 [7]

There have been several attempts in recent years to re-create the unique feel of the McKinney's Cotton Pickers. Carter, himself, who was in charge of one such effort in 1975, comments on the difficulty of the task: "The entire rhythmic conception was different then; it's so hard to find players familiar with that approach to rhythm. It takes four people thinking alike."

[8]   October 3, 1930 New York
      FLETCHER HENDERSON AND HIS ORCHESTRA

Carter (cl, as, v, arr) Russell Smith, Bobby Stark, Rex Stewart (tp) Jimmy Harrison (tb, v) Claude Jones (tb) Harvey Boone (as) Coleman Hawkins (ts) Fletcher Henderson (p) Clarence Holiday (g) John Kirby (b) Walter Johnson (d) John Nesbitt (arr)

CHINATOWN, MY CHINATOWN arr-JN (16cl)   150857-1
78: COLUMBIA 2329-D LP: COLUMBIA CL1684,
TIME-LIFE STL-J10

SOMEBODY LOVES ME v-BC, JH, CJ (e) (v in   150858-3
     vocal trio) arr
78: COLUMBIA 2329-D LP: COLUMBIA CL1684,
SMITHSONIAN P2-13710

* * *

Carter's first recording session as a regular member of the Fletcher Henderson orchestra includes a high-speed clarinet ride through "Chinatown." The almost reckless abandon of this solo is not typical of his clarinet work, and when he heard it almost 50 years later his first response was, "Did I do that?" In later years he preferred to play clarinet on slower "mood" pieces to which he applied a rounded, full, lower register tone, once described by Whitney Balliett as "the ideal sound for the instrument."

(For a discussion of Carter's arrangement of "Somebody Loves Me," see chapter 3.)

[9]   November 3, 1930 New York
      McKINNEY'S COTTON PICKERS

Carter (as) Rex Stewart, Buddy Lee, Langston Curl (tp) Ed Cuffee (tb) Don Redman (cl, as, v) Prince Robinson (cl, ts) Todd Rhodes (p, celeste) Dave Wilborn (banjo, g) Ralph Escudero (tuba) Cuba Austin (d)

TALK TO ME v-DR (8as)   64605-1
78: VICTOR 22640 LP: RCA LPV520, RCA (F)
FPM1-7007, RCA (F) PM43258

TALK TO ME v-DR (8as)   64605-2
78: UNISSUED LP: PIRATE MPC518, RCA (F)
FPM1-7007, RCA (F) PM43258

ROCKY ROAD v-DR (8as)   64606-1
78: VICTOR 22932 LP: RCA LPV520, RCA (E)
RD7561, RCA (F) FPM1-7007, RCA (F) PM43258

[10]	November 4, 1930 New York

McKINNEY'S COTTON PICKERS

Carter (cl, as, arr) Rex Stewart, Buddy Lee, Langston Curl (tp) Ed Cuffee (tb) Don Redman (cl, as) Prince Robinson (cl, ts) Todd Rhodes (p, celeste) Dave Wilborn (banjo, g) Ralph Escudero (tuba) Cuba Austin (d) Bill Coty (v)

LAUGHING AT LIFE   v-Coty (e)   64607-1
78: UNISSUED LP: GAPS 080, RCA (F) FPM1-7007,
RCA (F) PM43258

LAUGHING AT LIFE   v-Coty (e)   64607-2
78: VICTOR 23020   LP: RCA (F) FPM1-7007, RCA
(F) PM43258

NEVER SWAT A FLY   v-Coty (8cl)+(16cl over ensemble)+   64608-1
      (8cl over ensemble) arr
78: VICTOR 23020   LP: RCA (E) RD7561, RCA (F)
FPM1-7007, RCA (F) PM43258

NEVER SWAT A FLY   v-Coty (8cl)+(16cl over ensemble)+   64608-2
      (8cl over ensemble) arr
78: UNISSUED LP: GAPS 080, RCA (F) FPM1-7007,
RCA (F) PM43258

[11]	November 5, 1930 New York

McKINNEY'S COTTON PICKERS

Carter (as) Rex Stewart, Buddy Lee, Langston Curl (tp) Ed Cuffee (tb) Don Redman (cl, as) Prince Robinson (cl, ts) Todd Rhodes (p) Dave Wilborn (banjo, g, v) Ralph Escudero (tuba) Cuba Austin (d) George Bias (v)

I WANT YOUR LOVE   v-DW (4as)   63195-1
78: UNISSUED   LP: RCA(F) FPM1-7007, RCA (F)
PM43258

I WANT YOUR LOVE   v-DW (4as)   63195-2
78: VICTOR 22683   LP: RCA (F) FPM1-7007, RCA
(F) PM43258

HELLO!   v-DW (e)   63196-2
78: VICTOR 23031   LP: RCA (F) FXM1-7059, RCA
(F) PM43258

AFTER ALL, YOU'RE ALL I'M AFTER   v-GB (8as)   64609-2
78: VICTOR 23024   LP: RCA (F) FXM1-7059, RCA
(F) PM43258

I MISS A LITTLE MISS   v-GB (e)   64610-2
78: VICTOR 23024   LP: GAPS 080, RCA (F) FXM1-
7059, RCA (F) PM43258

*   *   *

Exactly one year after his first recordings with McKinney's Cotton Pickers, Carter sat in with the band for three more sessions [9, 10, 11]. He replaced George Thomas who was injured in, and later died as a result of, an auto accident.

November 5, 1930 [11]

The November 4 session includes one of only two McKinney recordings of Carter arrangements ("Never Swat A Fly"). The other took place almost a year later, after Carter had become musical director of the group.

[12]   December 2, 1930   New York
       FLETCHER HENDERSON AND HIS ORCHESTRA

Carter (cl, as, arr) Russell Smith, Bobby Stark, Rex Stewart (tp) Jimmy Harrison, Claude Jones (tb) Harvey Boone (as) Coleman Hawkins (ts) Fletcher Henderson (p) Clarence Holiday (g) John Kirby (tuba) Walter Johnson (d)

KEEP A SONG IN YOUR SOUL   (16as) arr   150997-2
78: COLUMBIA 2352-D   LP: COLUMBIA CL1684,
SMITHSONIAN P2-13710, TIME-LIFE STL-J10

WHAT GOOD AM I WITHOUT YOU   (4cl)+(cl coda)   150998-2
78: COLUMBIA 2352-D   LP: GAPS 090

* * *

(For a discussion of Carter's arranging masterpiece, "Keep A Song In Your Soul," see chapter 3.)

[13]   December 4, 1930   New York
       THE CHOCOLATE DANDIES

Carter (as, v, arr, comp) Rex Stewart (tp) Jimmy Harrison (tb) Coleman Hawkins (ts) Horace Henderson (p) Benny Jackson (g) John Kirby (b)

GOODBYE BLUES   (16as)(v) arr, comp   404566-A
78: COLUMBIA 35679   45: ODEON SOF3553   LP:
PARLOPHONE PMC7038, SWAGGIE S1249, CBS (F)
68227, ODEON (J) EMI OR-8065, ELECTROLA 1C
054-06 312

   NOTE: Rust lists Bobby Stark (tp) for Stewart; Allen's *Hendersonia*
   suggests Stewart. Carter agrees that it is Stewart.

[14]   December 8, 1930   New York
       FLETCHER HENDERSON AND HIS ORCHESTRA

Carter (as, cl) probably regular Henderson personnel

WE'RE FRIENDS AGAIN   E 35668
78: BRUNSWICK, UNISSUED

WHAT GOOD AM I WITHOUT YOU   E 35669
78: BRUNSWICK, UNISSUED

[15]   December 31, 1930   New York
       THE CHOCOLATE DANDIES

Carter (cl, as, arr, comp) Bobby Stark (tp) Jimmy Harrison (tb, v) Coleman Hawkins (ts) Horace Henderson (p) Benny Jackson (g) John Kirby (tuba)

CLOUDY SKIES (8as)+(4as over ensemble) 404596-B
78: COLUMBIA 35679 45: ODEON SOF3553 LP:
PARLOPHONE (E) PMC7038, SWAGGIE S1249, CBS
(F) 68227, ODEON (J) EMI OR-8065, ELECTROLA 1C
054-06 316

GOT ANOTHER SWEETIE NOW v-JH (e) arr 404597-B
78: COLUMBIA 36009 LP: PARLOPHONE (E)
PMC7038, SWAGGIE S1249, CBS (F) 68227, ODEON
(J) EMI OR-8065, ELECTROLA 1C 054-06 313

BUGLE CALL RAG (12as) (16cl) arr 404598-B
78: COLUMBIA 2543-D 45: ODEON SOF3553 LP:
PARLOPHONE (E) PMC7038, FOLKWAYS FP75,
FOLKWAYS FJ2811, SWAGGIE S1249, CBS (F) 68227,
ODEON (J) EMI OR-8065, TIME-LIFE STL-J06,
ELECTROLA 1C 054-06 318

DEE BLUES (12cl)(12cl) comp 404599-B
78: COLUMBIA 2543-D 45: ODEON SOF3553 LP:
PARLOPHONE (E) PMC7038, SWAGGIE S1249, CBS
(F) 68227, ODEON (J) EMI OR-8065, COLUMBIA
CG33557, TIME-LIFE STL-J10, ELECTROLA 1C
054-06 316

* * *

Perhaps the most famous of the Chocolate Dandies dates, this session's personnel is again drawn from the Henderson orchestra. Carter's sketchy arrangements were designed to provide a loose framework for the solos, which are the main focus of the session. One of the sides, "Dee Blues," was completely impromptu; musicians were told that another number was needed and the blues was a natural choice.

There are excellent contributions on all four titles by Jimmy Harrison including the vocal on his own tune "Got Another Sweetie Now." The great trombonist, a close friend of Carter, died seven months later of stomach cancer. Carter's clarinet work is superb on "Bugle Call Rag" where he plays the "Ole Miss" strain, and on "Dee Blues" where he opens and closes the record. The former also contains the first of many examples of Carter's soloing on two instruments in the same piece.

[16]   February 5, 1931 New York
         FLETCHER HENDERSON AND HIS ORCHESTRA

Carter (cl, as, arr) Russell Smith, Rex Stewart, Bobby Stark (tp) Jimmy Harrison (tb, v) Claude Jones (tb) Harvey Boone (as) Coleman Hawkins (ts) Fletcher Henderson (p) Clarence Holiday (g) John Kirby (tuba, b) Walter Johnson (d) Lois Deppe (v) Bill Challis (arr)

I'VE FOUND WHAT I WANTED IN YOU v-LD (e) 151274-2
78: COLUMBIA 2414-D LP: GAPS 090

MY GAL SAL arr-Challis (e) 151275-1
78: COLUMBIA 2586-D LP: COLUMBIA CL1684

MY PRETTY GIRL v-LD (32cl acc) arr 151276-2

February 5, 1931 [16]

78: COLUMBIA 2586-D   LP: JAZZ PANORAMA
LP4, JOKER SM3077

SWEET AND HOT   v-JH (e) arr   151277-2
78: COLUMBIA 2414-D   LP: COLUMBIA CL1684

---

[17]   March 30, 1931   New York
       CHICK WEBB AND HIS ORCHESTRA

Carter (cl, as, arr, comp) Shelton Hemphill, Louis Hunt (tp) Louis Bacon (tp, v) Jimmy Harrison (tb) Hilton Jefferson (cl, as) Elmer Williams (cl, ts) Don Kirkpatrick (p) John Trueheart (banjo, g) Elmer James (b) Chick Webb (d)

HEEBIE JEEBIES   (e) arr   F-36432-
78: VOCALION 1607, BRUNSWICK 6898   LP: DECCA
DL79222, MCA (F) 510.014, MCA 1303

BLUES IN MY HEART   v-LB (e) arr, comp   F-36433-A
78: BRUNSWICK 6156, BRUNSWICK 6898   LP:
JAZUM 46

SOFT AND SWEET   (e) arr   F-36434-
78: VOCALION 1607   LP: DECCA DL79222, MCA
(F) 510.014, MCA 1303

>   NOTE: Title appears on Brunswick 6156 as "I'm Left With The
>   Blues In My Heart."

* * *

This session took place during Carter's brief tenure with Webb. Although he does not solo, Carter makes his presence felt through his arrangements. This recording of "Blues In My Heart" is one of the first of what is Carter's most widely recorded composition (over 50 versions to date). It was ante-dated only by the "King Carter And His Royal Orchestra" version, recorded a week earlier. Although his name appears as leader, Carter did not participate in the King Carter date.

---

[18]   September 8, 1931   Camden, N.J.
       McKINNEY'S COTTON PICKERS

Carter (cl, as, arr) Rex Stewart, Joe Smith, Doc Cheatham (tp) Ed Cuffee (tb) Quentin Jackson (tb, v) Hilton Jefferson (cl, alt) Prince Robinson (ts) Todd Rhodes (p) Dave Wilborn (g) Billy Taylor (b) Cuba Austin (d)

DO YOU BELIEVE IN LOVE AT SIGHT   v-QJ (e) arr   68300-1
78: UNISSUED   LP: RCA 430272, RCA (E) RD7561,
RCA (F) FXM1-7059

DO YOU BELIEVE IN LOVE AT SIGHT   v-QJ (e) arr   68300-2
78: VICTOR 22811   LP: RCA (F) FXM1-7059

WRAP YOUR TROUBLES IN DREAMS   v-QJ (32cl acc)   70495-1
78: VICTOR 22811   LP: GAPS 080, RCA (F)
FXM1-7059

WRAP YOUR TROUBLES IN DREAMS   v-QJ (32cl acc)   70495-2
78: UNISSUED   LP: RCA (F) FXM1-7059

* * *

Carter's first and only recording session as musical director of McKinney's Cotton Pickers features the second of the two Carter arrangements recorded by that group. The bridge of the first chorus is a characteristic Carter reed passage. Carter's own solo work is restricted to some lovely clarinet behind the vocal chorus. Chilton, Davies and Wright question the identity of the vocalist; when the recordings were played for Doc Cheatham, however, he confirmed that the vocals are, indeed, by Jackson.

[19]	ca. June 23, 1932 New York
	BENNY CARTER AND HIS ORCHESTRA

Carter (as) Louis Bacon, Frankie Newton, Unknown (tp) Dicky Wells (tb) Wayman Carver (as, flute) Chu Berry (ts) Unknown (p) Unknown (g) Richard Fullbright (b) Sid Catlett (d) Unknown Female (v)

TELL ALL YOUR DAY DREAMS TO ME   v-unknown (32as)   1765-1
78: CROWN 3321, VARSITY 6004

* * *

The first record made by a regular Carter orchestra is a highly sought-after collector's item, but certainly not on musical grounds. Carter cannot remember making this record and the identity of the vocalist is a mystery to him. It is quite obviously not a Carter arrangement, and although the alto solo chorus is unmistakably his, the style sounds like the Carter of a few years before. This could almost have been a deliberate attempt to fit in with an arrangement and vocal which must have sounded nostalgic even then, and in no way foreshadowed the innovative and influential Carter orchestra recordings of the next year.

Rust lists Teddy Wilson as pianist, but this does not seem possible, given Wilson's activities at the time. He did not join Carter until October 1933. The other personnel are highly speculative.

[20]	October 5, 1932 New York
	KING CARTER AND HIS ORCHESTRA

Carter (as, arr, comp) Louis Bacon, Frankie Newton, Unknown (tp) Dicky Wells, Unknown (tb) Wayman Carver (as, flute) Chu Berry, Unknown (ts) Unknown (p) Unknown (g) Richard Fullbright (b) Sid Catlett (d)

HOT TODDY   arr, comp   73772-
78: VICTOR-UNISSUED

JAZZ COCKTAIL   arr, comp   73773-
78: VICTOR-UNISSUED

BLACK JAZZ   73774-
78: VICTOR-UNISSUED

NOTE: A test pressing of one of these titles is rumored to exist.

March 14, 1933 [21]   47

| [21]   March 14, 1933 New York
         BENNY CARTER AND HIS ORCHESTRA

Carter (cl, as, tp, v, arr, comp) Shad Collins, Leonard Davis, Bill Dillard (tp)
George Washington, Wilbur de Paris (tb) Howard Johnson (as) Chu Berry
(ts) Nicholas Rodriguez (p) Lawrence Lucie (g) Ernest Hill (b) Sid Catlett
(d) Spike Hughes (arr)

SWING IT   (v)(32as) arr   265090-2
78: COLUMBIA CB-628 LP: FAMILY (I) SFR736,
PRESTIGE 7643, REGAL (E) 1108, WORLD RECORDS
(E) SHB42

SYNTHETIC LOVE   (16+8tp)(v)(16cl) arr, comp   265091-3
78: COLUMBIA CB-636 LP: FAMILY (I) SFR736,
PRESTIGE 7643, REGAL (E) 1108, WORLD RECORDS
(E) SHB42

SIX BELLS STAMPEDE   arr-SH (e)   265092-2
78: COLUMBIA CB-628 LP: MUSIC FOR PLEASURE
(E) MFP1085, FAMILY (I) SFR736, PRESTIGE 7643,
REGAL (E) 1038, WORLD RECORDS (E) SHB42

LOVE, YOU'RE NOT THE ONE FOR ME   (v)(4+4+8as)   265093-2
          arr, comp
78: COLUMBIA CB-636 LP: FAMILY (I) SFR736,
PRESTIGE 7643, REGAL (E) 1108, WORLD RECORDS (E)
SHB42

                              *   *   *

     The first real recording dates for the Carter band were set up for British
Columbia by John Hammond, with the purpose of releasing the sides in England. Hammond describes contracting for the Carter sessions (as well as
those by Fletcher Henderson, Benny Goodman, and others) during a trip to
England "in the spring of 1933" (Hammond, p. 105). This first Carter orchestra session, however, seems to have antedated that trip which, according to Hammond, took place after the Spike Hughes dates (April/May 1933)
(Hammond, p. 108). It is possible that these recordings were already "in
the can" and released after the Hammond agreement with British Columbia.

     Three of the four pieces contain Carter vocals; he sounds most na-
tural and convincing on "Swing It."

     "Synthetic Love" opens with Carter's first recorded trumpet solo.
He stays close to the melody, which he delivers in a bright, full tone--even
at low volume--reminiscent of Doc Cheatham. Cheatham had given Carter
encouragement and technical advice in his return to the instrument, which
was his first love and remains his favorite. "Six Bells," composed and
arranged by Spike Hughes, is a preview of the sessions with the Carter band
led by Hughes a month later.

| [22]   April 18, 1933 New York
         SPIKE HUGHES AND HIS NEGRO ORCHESTRA

Carter (cl, as, v) Shad Collins, Leonard Davis, Bill Dillard (tp) Dicky Wells,
Wilbur de Paris, George Washington (tb) Wayman Carver, Howard Johnson

(cl, as) Coleman Hawkins (ts) Nicholas Rodriguez (p) Lawrence Lucie (g)
Ernest Hill (b) Kaiser Marshall, Sid Catlett (d) Spike Hughes (arr, comp)

NOCTURNE (8cl) 13257-A
78: DECCA F-3563 LP: DECCA (E) ACE OF CLUBS
ACL1153, LONDON LL1387, DECCA (SW) LK4173

SOMEONE STOLE GABRIEL'S HORN (v)(8as) 13258-A
78: DECCA F-3563 LP: DECCA (E) ACE OF CLUBS
ACL1153

PASTORALE (16as) 13259-A
78: DECCA F-3606 LP: DECCA (E) ACE OF CLUBS
ACL1153, LONDON LL1387, DECCA (SW) LK4173

BUGLE CALL RAG (16as) 13260-A
78: DECCA F-3606 LP: DECCA (E) ACE OF CLUBS
ACL1153, LONDON LL1387, DECCA (SW) LK4173

   NOTE: Catlett (d) on last two titles.

[23]   May 18, 1933   New York
       SPIKE HUGHES AND HIS NEGRO ORCHESTRA

Carter (cl, as) Henry Allen, Leonard Davis, Bill Dillard (tp) Dicky Wells,
Wilbur de Paris, George Washington (tb) Wayman Carver (cl, as, flute)
Howard Johnson (cl, as) Coleman Hawkins, Chu Berry (ts) Luis Russell (p)
Lawrence Lucie (g) Ernest Hill (b) Sid Catlett (d) Spike Hughes (arr, comp)

ARABESQUE (e) 13352-A
78: DECCA F-3639 LP: DECCA (E) ACE OF CLUBS
ACL1153, LONDON LL1387, DECCA (SW) LK4173

FANFARE (24cl) 13353-A
78: DECCA F-3639 LP: DECCA (E) ACE OF CLUBS
ACL1153, LONDON LL1387, DECCA (SW) LK4173

SWEET SORROW BLUES (e) 13354-A
78: DECCA F-5101 LP: DECCA (E) ACE OF CLUBS
ACL1153, LONDON LL1387, DECCA (SW) LK4173

MUSIC AT MIDNIGHT (12as)(8cl) 13355-A
78: DECCA F-3836 LP: DECCA (E) ACE OF CLUBS
ACL1153, LONDON LL1387, DECCA (SW) LK4173

SWEET SUE, JUST YOU (32as) 13356-A
78: DECCA F-3972 LP: DECCA (E) ACE OF CLUBS
ACL1153, LONDON LL1387, DECCA (SW) LK4173,
TIME-LIFE STL-J06, SMITHSONIAN P15470

   NOTE: Personnel for last title: Carter, Allen, Wells, Carver,
   Hawkins, Berry, Lucie, Rodriguez, Hughes (b), Catlett.

[24]   May 19, 1933   New York
       SPIKE HUGHES AND HIS NEGRO ORCHESTRA

May 19, 1933 [24]

Carter (cl, as, ss) Henry Allen, Howard Scott, Leonard Davis or Bill Dillard (tp) Dicky Wells, Wilbur de Paris, George Washington (tb) Wayman Carver (as, flute) Howard Johnson (cl, as) Coleman Hawkins, Chu Berry (ts) Nicholas Rodriguez (p) Lawrence Lucie (g) Ernest Hill (b) Sid Catlett (d) Spike Hughes (arr, comp)

AIR IN D FLAT (e) 78: DECCA F-5101 LP: DECCA (E) ACE OF CLUBS ACL1153, LONDON LL1387, DECCA (SW) LK4173	13359-A
DONEGAL CRADLE SONG (e) 78: DECCA F-3717 LP: DECCA (E) ACE OF CLUBS ACL1153, LONDON LL1387, DECCA (SW) LK4173, TIME-LIFE STL-J06	13360-A
FIREBIRD (e) [on soprano] 78: DECCA F-3717 LP: DECCA (E) ACE OF CLUBS ACL1153, LONDON LL1387, DECCA (SW) LK4173	13361-A
MUSIC AT SUNRISE (e) 78: DECCA F-3836 LP: DECCA (E) ACE OF CLUBS ACL1153	13362-A
HOW COME YOU DO ME LIKE YOU DO v-HA (e) 78: DECCA F-3972 LP: DECCA (E) ACE OF CLUBS ACL1153, LONDON LL1387, DECCA (SW) LK4173, SMITHSONIAN P15470	13363-A

NOTE: Personnel on last title: Allen (also v), Wells, Carver, Hawkins, Berry, Rodriguez, Lucie, Hughes (b), Catlett.

* * *

Spike Hughes had been impressed by the musicianship of the Carter orchestra at a rehearsal and the band became the nucleus for these three sessions [22, 23, 24] of his music. Soloists like Henry Allen and Coleman Hawkins were added. Carter is not heavily featured as a soloist but as Raymond Horricks observes, "No one else but Carter ... would have been capable of leading a saxophone section on to produce such a unique variety of tonal blends. Throughout all these sessions, the composer and rehearsal leader complemented each other perfectly, so that their names became inseparable" (Liner notes to London LL1387).

The label of the original issue of "Someone Stole Gabriel's Horn" lists Monette Moore as vocalist; Carter filled in when she failed to appear.

[25]	October 10, 1933 New York THE CHOCOLATE DANDIES

Carter (as, tp, arr, comp) Max Kaminsky (tp) Floyd O'Brien (tb) Chu Berry (ts) Teddy Wilson (p) Lawrence Lucie (g) Sid Catlett, Mezz Mezzrow (d) Ernest Hill (b)

BLUE INTERLUDE (32as) arr, comp 78: DECCA 18255 45: IL JAZZ (I) LP: PRESTIGE 7643, PARLOPHONE (E) PMC7038, SWAGGIE S1249	265156-2

I NEVER KNEW (8as)(8as)(8tp[2nd 8-bar solo]) arr   265157-1
78: COLUMBIA 2875-D LP: PRESTIGE 7643,
PARLOPHONE (E) PMC7038, SWAGGIE S1249, TIME-
LIFE STL-J10

ONCE UPON A TIME (32tp)(10tp) arr, comp   265158-1
78: OKEH 41568, DECCA 18255 LP: PRESTIGE
7643, PARLOPHONE (E) PMC7038, SWAGGIE S1249,
FOLKWAYS FP71, FOLKWAYS FJ2809, TIME-LIFE
STL-J10

KRAZY KAPERS (8as)(32as) arr, comp   265159-2
78: OKEH 41568 LP: PRESTIGE 7643, PARLO-
PHONE (E) PMC7038, SWAGGIE S1249, TIME-LIFE
STL-J10

NOTES: I1 Jazz 45rpm disc has no issue number. Carter's solo on "I Never Knew" is reproduced vocally by The Cats And The Fiddle on their June 27, 1939 recording "Gangbusters" (reissued on Bluebird AXM2-5531). An alternate take of "Once Upon A Time" is known to exist.

* * *

This reincarnation of the Chocolate Dandies bore a clearer Carter stamp than the other recordings made under that name. With the exception of Max Kaminsky and Floyd O'Brien, all of the personnel were regular members of Carter's orchestra. Furthermore, three of the four tunes recorded on the date were Carter's own compositions, and his arrangements were far more structured than the loose framework he provided for the 1930 Chocolate Dandies. The producer, John Hammond, was a great admirer of those 1930 recordings and hoped to recapture their spirit.

Perhaps most significant about the session is the presence of Teddy Wilson, who had arrived the day before from Chicago to join the Carter orchestra. His playing here shows why Carter was so eager to have him. He already displays--fully formed--many of the components of his style: the dancing right-hand lines, with bouncing tremolos and sparkling runs, complemented by a lightly striding left. More importantly, he shares with Carter the rare ability to create an improvised solo with a logical sense of direction, without losing the spark of spontaneity.

In spite of the obvious maturity of his playing, Wilson cites the two major influences in the further development of his style after his arrival in New York as his study of classical music, and "...being around Benny Carter. He played that flowing saxophone every night and that came out in my playing." (Interview with Phil Schaap, March 5, 1980.) Keg Johnson, whom Carter had recruited along with Wilson in Chicago, joined the trombone section.

Carter, who had given listeners a taste of his trumpet with a cautious solo on his March 14 date, now felt confident enough to feature himself extensively on the instrument. The result, "Once Upon A Time," is one of the great Carter trumpet solos; indeed it is one of the greatest trumpet solos in jazz history. The ending shows an Armstrong influence, with soaring half-valve effects and a pronounced vibrato. The tune, written for this session, is a typical Carter composition: an attractive and deceptively simple melody with interesting chord changes. It is also typical of Carter

October 10, 1933 [25] 51

in another sense: he never recorded or played it again. It thus joins a long line of Carter melodies which, because they were never plugged, did not attain the popularity they deserved.

On "Krazy Kapers," the supposed replacement of Sid Catlett, who probably had another engagement, by the ubiquitous Mezz Mezzrow is disputed by John Hammond who states, "Mezzrow tried to play drums, but I asked him to leave the studio." (The Giants of Jazz: Benny Carter, p. 36.)

[26]	October 16, 1933 New York
	BENNY CARTER AND HIS ORCHESTRA

Carter (cl, as, arr, comp) Eddie Mallory, Bill Dillard, Dick Clark (tp) J. C. Higginbotham, Fred Robinson, Keg Johnson (tb) Wayman Carver (as, flute) Glyn Paque (as) Johnny Russell (ts) Teddy Wilson (p) Lawrence Lucie (g) Ernest Hill (b) Sid Catlett (d)

DEVIL'S HOLIDAY (8as) arr, comp 265160-1
78: COLUMBIA 2898-D LP: MUSIC FOR PLEASURE
(E) MFP1085, PRESTIGE 7643, FAMILY (I) SFR736,
REGAL (E) 1038, WORLD RECORDS (E) SHB42

LONESOME NIGHTS (e) arr, comp 265161-1
78: OKEH 41567 LP: MUSIC FOR PLEASURE
(E) MFP1085, PRESTIGE 7643, FAMILY (I) SFR736,
REGAL (E) 1038, WORLD RECORDS (E) SHB42

SYMPHONY IN RIFFS (e) arr, comp 265162-2
78: COLUMBIA 2898-D LP: PARLOPHONE (E)
PMC1222, PRESTIGE 7643, FAMILY (I) SFR736,
REGAL (E) 1108, WORLD RECORDS (E) SHB42

BLUE LOU (4+4as) arr 265163-2
78: OKEH 41567 LP: MUSIC FOR PLEASURE
(E) MFP1085, PRESTIGE 7643, FAMILY (I) SFR736,
REGAL (E) 1038, WORLD RECORDS (E) SHB42,
TIME-LIFE STL-J20

* * *

These are the only recordings of the 1932-33 Carter band at its peak. Unlike the March 14 session, there are no distracting vocals and, of course, the band personnel includes the great Teddy Wilson. Also, the saxophone section has been expanded from three to four. Carter takes full advantage of the addition by providing several innovative four-part saxophone choruses. Carter's solo contributions on the four pieces total only 16 measures, yet because of his writing, this session must be counted among his most significant.

The impact of these influential arrangements, "Symphony In Riffs" and "Lonesome Nights," can be gauged by the large number and variety of bands which recorded them precisely as Carter wrote them. Over a 25-year period "Symphony In Riffs" was recorded by Tommy Dorsey, Gene Krupa, Glenn Miller, Artie Shaw and Glen Gray (by some of these more than once). "Lonesome Nights" (later called "Take My Word") was made by Benny Goodman, Charlie Barnet, Bunny Berigan, Artie Shaw and Cab Calloway. "Lonesome Nights" also inspired two similar pieces, "Puddin' Head Serenade," recorded by Andy Kirk (March 31, 1936 and April 10, 1936) and "I'm Alone With You," recorded by Jimmie Lunceford (December 14, 1939). No doubt other bands had these Carter compositions in their books, but never recorded them. Even the lesser known title "Devil's Holiday" was recorded in its original arrangement by the bands of Charlie Barnet, Bunny Berigan and Charlie Spivak.

The session also affords a good opportunity to assess the importance of Carter as lead alto player. A comparison of the intricate saxophone choruses in "Lonesome Nights" as played by the bands named above with the original version demonstrates the difference Carter's presence in the section makes in the tonal blending and precision of execution.

The final number of the session "Blue Lou" is the first recording of the Edgar Sampson classic.

The musicians who played in this band all recall it with reverence. Trumpeter Bill Coleman, who was asked to join soon after his return from Europe with Lucky Millinder, missed playing on these recordings because he was spending a few days in New Jersey and could not be reached. He joined soon afterward and remarks, "The salary was not great, but the other musicians, like myself, admired and loved Benny to the point where they would have worked with him for the pleasure of playing his arrangements, if a job actually could not pay. We all hated to see this band of Benny's break up and I considered and still do consider it the best band I ever played with." (Coleman, interview, Jazz Oral History Project, 1978.) Ernest Hill, the bass player for these recordings, told Johnny Simmen, "It was a new pleasure every night to go on that bandstand and play Benny's music." (Liner notes to Prestige 7643.)

(For an analysis of "Lonesome Nights," see chapter 3.)

---

[27]   November 6, 1933   New York
       MEZZ MEZZROW AND HIS ORCHESTRA

Carter (as, tp, v, arr, comp) Max Kaminsky, Freddy Goodman, Ben Gusick (tp) Floyd O'Brien (tb, arr) Mezz Mezzrow (cl, as, arr) Johnny Russell (ts) Teddy Wilson (p) Clayton Duerr (g) Pops Foster (b) Jack Maisel (d)

FREE LOVE (e) arr, comp   14272-A
78: BRUNSWICK 7551   LP: FAMILY (I) SFR736

DISSONANCE arr-MM (e)   14273-A
78: BRUNSWICK 7551   LP: FAMILY (I) SFR736,
COLUMBIA KG31564, TAX (SW) M-8031

SWINGIN' WITH MEZZ arr-MM, FO (18tp)(4tp)   14274-A
78: BRUNSWICK 6778   LP: FAMILY (I) SFR736,
TAX (SW) M-8031

LOVE, YOU'RE NOT THE ONE FOR ME (v) arr, comp   14275-A
78: BRUNSWICK 6778   LP: FAMILY (I) SFR736,
TAX (SW) M-8031

* * *

November 6, 1933 [27] 53

In 1933 Mezz Mezzrow tried to form an interracial band, not just for recording (which was already fairly common), but for public performance. Although this project failed, Mezzrow did succeed in leading two mixed recording sessions--this one and one on May 7, 1934.

Although Carter acknowledges that the fact that Mezz always "took care of all the boys' needs" may have taken him further in musical circles than his talent warranted, he respected Mezzrow as a musician with a sincere and spirited, if not highly polished, style.

Carter's solo work is limited to the trumpet on "Swingin' With Mezz," a solo which drew praise from Louis Armstrong, himself. In Really the Blues (p. 269), Mezzrow quotes a letter he received from Louis Armstrong in which Armstrong writes about the recordings made on this date:

> Say Gate ... how wonderful your records are. Everybody enjoys them very much. All of them are perfect. My favorite one is Love your not the one for me and the one where your trumpet player hits that F right square in the face Yea man. By the way who is that fellow? Who ever he is hes mess (Mezz) I aint no playin Hes perfect....

Mezzrow claims these remarks were made about "Dissonance"; however, it is undoubtedly Carter's solo on "Swingin' With Mezz" to which Armstrong was referring.

---

[28] March 23, 1934 New York
       CHARLIE BARNET AND HIS ORCHESTRA

Carter (tp, as) includes Charlie Barnet (ts, v) Helen Heath, Jackie Martin (v) Toots Camarata (tp) Red Norvo (vib)

| BUTTERFINGERS v-HH | 14985- |
| 78: UNISSUED | |

| INFATUATION v-HH (e) | 14986- |
| 78: BANNER 33015 LP: AJAX LP104 | |

| I LOST ANOTHER SWEETHEART v-JM (e) | 14987-1 |
| 78: BANNER 33033 LP: AJAX LP104 | |

| EMALINE v-CB (e) | 14888-1 |
| 78: BANNER 33033 LP: AJAX LP104 | |

NOTE: Personnel is uncertain.

---

[29] March 29, 1934 New York
       CHARLIE BARNET AND HIS ORCHESTRA

Carter (tp, as) includes Charlie Barnet (ts, v) Helen Heath, Jackie Martin (v) Toots Camarata (tp) Red Norvo (vib)

| BUTTERFINGERS v-HH (e) | 14985- |
| 78: BANNER 33015 LP: AJAX LP104 | |

| BABY, TAKE A BOW v-JM (e) | 15020- |
| 78: BANNER 33029 LP: AJAX LP104 | |

THIS IS OUR LAST NIGHT TOGETHER v-JM (e)   15021-
78: BANNER 33029   LP: AJAX LP104

---

[30]   May 7, 1934 New York
         MEZZ MEZZROW AND HIS ORCHESTRA

Carter (as) Max Kaminsky, Reunald Jones, Chelsea Quealey (tp) Floyd O'Brien (tb, arr) Mezz Mezzrow (cl, as, arr) Bud Freeman (ts) Willie 'The Lion' Smith (p) John Kirby (b) Chick Webb (d) Alex Hill (arr)

OLD FASHIONED LOVE   arr-AH (e)   82392-1
78: VICTOR 25202   LP: VICTOR (F) 130.219, RCA
(F) 741.046, RCA (F) PM42406

APOLOGIES   arr-MM (24as)   82393-1
78: VICTOR 25019   LP: RCA (F) 130.219, RCA
(F) 741.046, TIME-LIFE STL-J10, RCA (F) PM42406

SENDIN' THE VIPERS   arr-MM (16as)   82394-1
78: VICTOR 25019   LP: RCA (F) 130.219, RCA
(F) 741.046, RCA (F) PM42406

35TH AND CALUMET   arr-FO (24as)   82395-1
78: VICTOR 25202   LP: RCA (F) 130.219, RCA
(F) 741.046, RCA (F) PM42406

                    *   *   *

The second of the two Mezzrow sessions is the only known collaboration on record between Carter and Willie "The Lion" Smith and Carter and Bud Freeman. "The Lion" had helped Carter many years earlier to adjust from the C-melody to the alto saxophone.

   The personnel was noteworthy as Mezzrow points out (p. 269) with a number of leaders and future leaders present: Smith, Carter, Freeman, Kirby and Webb.

   Carter's growling entrance on "Apologies" is unlike anything he had played before on record. Perhaps it was an early subconscious attempt to shed the "urbane" label that was already becoming a cliché in describing his playing. His reaction 45 years later was, "Is that me?" The piece, which is derived from "Dippermouth Blues," ends abruptly with Webb's drum solo chorus ending four bars short of the expected twelve. The record had already well exceeded the normal three-minute average for 78's.

---

[31]   September 25, 1934 New York
         FLETCHER HENDERSON AND HIS ORCHESTRA

Carter (as) Russell Smith, Irving Randolph, Henry Allen (tp) Keg Johnson, Claude Jones (tb) Buster Bailey (cl) Hilton Jefferson, Russell Procope (as) Ben Webster (ts) Fletcher Henderson, Horace Henderson (p, arr) Lawrence Lucie (g) Elmer James (b) Walter Johnson (d) Russ Morgan (arr)

WILD PARTY   arr-RM, p-HH (e)   38723-A
78: DECCA 342   LP: DECCA DL9228, DECCA (E)
ACE OF HEARTS AH61, WORLD RECORDS SHB42,
MCA (F) 510.060, MCA 1318

September 25, 1934 [31]

RUG CUTTER'S SWING arr-HH, p-FH (e) 38724-A
78: DECCA 342, LP: DECCA DL9228, DECCA (E)
ACE OF HEARTS AH61, WORLD RECORDS SHB42,
MCA (F) 510.060, MCA 1318

HOTTER THAN 'ELL arr-HH, p-FH (e) 38725-A
78: DECCA 555 LP: DECCA DL9228, DECCA
(E) ACE OF HEARTS AH61, WORLD RECORDS
SHB42, MCA (F) 510.060, MCA 1318

LIZA p-FH and HH (32as[1st solo; 2nd alto solo--8 bars-- 38728-A
is Procope])
78: DECCA 555 LP: DECCA DL9228, DECCA (E)
ACE OF HEARTS AH61, WORLD RECORDS SHB42,
MCA (F) 510.060, MCA 1318

* * *

Carter was reunited with his old employer, Fletcher Henderson, for this date. It also brought him together with two alto players, Hilton Jefferson and Russell Procope, whose styles in some ways closely resembled his own. This similarity is particularly striking in Jefferson's solo on "Wild Party."

[32] October 19, 1934 New York
ALEX HILL AND HIS HOLLYWOOD SEPIANS

Carter (tp, arr) Joe Thomas (tp) Claude Jones (tb) Albert Nicholas (cl) George James (as) Gene Sedric (ts) Garnet Clark (p) Eddie Gibbs (g) Billy Taylor (b) Harry Dial (d) Alex Hill (v, arr)

SONG OF THE PLOW v-AH, arr-AH (e) 16141-1
78: VOCALION 2848, BRUNSWICK 02078 LP:
JAZZ DOCUMENT 7999

LET'S HAVE A JUBILEE v-AH (16tp) arr 16142-1
78: VOCALION 2848, VOCALION S-70 LP:
JAZZ DOCUMENT 7999

* * *

For many years, discographers disagreed about Carter's presence on this and an earlier (September 10) Alex Hill session. Carter seems to have played only on the later date. He confirmed the muted trumpet which opens "Let's Have A Jubilee" as his. He also identified the arrangement of this Alex Hill composition as his. Irving Mills commissioned him to make this arrangement, which was first recorded on October 4, 1934 by the Mills Blue Rhythm Band.

[33] December 13, 1934 New York
BENNY CARTER AND HIS ORCHESTRA

Carter (cl, as, arr, comp) Russell Smith, Otis Johnson, Irving Randolph (tp) Benny Morton, Keg Johnson (tb) Ben Smith, Russell Procope (as) Ben Webster (ts) Teddy Wilson (p) Clarence Holiday (g) Elmer James (b) Walter Johnson (d) Charles Holland (v)

SHOOT THE WORKS   (e) arr, comp   16412-1
78: VOCALION 2898   LP: TAX (SW) M-8031

DREAM LULLABY   (16cl with ensemble) (8cl with   16413-1
    ensemble) arr, comp
78: VOCALION 2898   LP: TAX (SW) M-8031,
TIME-LIFE STL-J21

EVERYBODY SHUFFLE   (4+4as)(16as) arr, comp   16414-1
78: VOCALION 2870   LP: TAX (SW) M-8031

SYNTHETIC LOVE   v-CH (e) arr, comp   16415-1
78: VOCALION 2870

*   *   *

These are the last recordings of the band Carter had formed in 1932. With engagements slacking off and no prospects for steady work for his men, within a few weeks of this session Carter reluctantly disbanded. The legend of this band has grown steadily; many of its illustrious alumni have called it the finest unit in which they ever played. By this session, Carter was already putting together personnels on a job-to-job basis, drawing from the Fletcher Henderson band to fill some slots.

For this occasion, Carter supplied three new originals; the final number was his "Synthetic Love," previously recorded at the March 14, 1933, date. This time, Carter modestly relegated the vocal to Charles Holland.

The most important solo voices are those of Ben Webster on tenor, Benny Morton on trombone and Irving Randolph on trumpet. The two up-tempo arrangements, "Shoot The Works" and "Everybody Shuffle," were obviously not attempts at the type of innovative ensemble writing of a "Lonesome Nights." Rather they feature brief sax-section passages and well-balanced brass and reed riffs, which serve to complement the excellent solos.

"Dream Lullaby" is the first of several similar wistful, melancholy compositions by Carter, who seemed attracted to dreams and lullabies--e.g., "Melancholy Lullaby," "Lullaby To A Dream," "Lullaby In Blue." It particularly foreshadowed "Just A Mood," one recording of which also featured Carter's clarinet (late April 1936).

[34]	December 28, 1934 New York
	BUSTER BAILEY & HIS SEVEN CHOCOLATE DANDIES

Carter (as) Henry Allen (tp) J. C. Higginbotham (tb) Buster Bailey (cl) Charlie Beal (p) Danny Barker (g) Elmer James (b) Walter Johnson (d) Fletcher Henderson (arr)

CALL OF THE DELTA   (8as)   16445-1
78: VOCALION 2887   LP: RARITIES 17

CALL OF THE DELTA   (8as)   16445-2
78: COLUMBIA 35677   LP: MERITT 13/14

SHANGHAI SHUFFLE   (8as)(16as)   16446-1
78: VOCALION 2887   LP: RARITIES 17

January 2, 1935 [35]   57

[35]   January 2, 1935 New York
         BOB HOWARD AND HIS ORCHESTRA

Carter (tp, as) Buster Bailey (cl) Teddy Wilson (p) Clarence Holiday (g)
Elmer James (b) Cozy Cole (d) Bob Howard (v)

IT'S UNBELIEVABLE   v-BH (16+8tp)   39217-A
78: BRUNSWICK 02097   LP: RARITIES 48

IT'S UNBELIEVABLE   v-BH (16+8tp)   39217-B
78: DECCA 347   LP: RARITIES 48

WHISPER SWEET   v-BH (4tp)(16tp)   39218-A
78: BRUNSWICK RL-221   LP: RARITIES 48

WHISPER SWEET   v-BH (4tp)(16tp)   39218-B
78: DECCA 347   LP: RARITIES 48

THROWIN' STONES AT THE SUN   v-BH (e)   39219-A
78: DECCA 343, BRUNSWICK RL-221   LP:
RARITIES 48

YOU FIT INTO THE PICTURE   v-BH (16+8as)(16tp)   39220-A
78: DECCA 343, BRUNSWICK 02111   LP:
RARITIES 48

[36]   February 25, 1935 New York
         BOB HOWARD AND HIS ORCHESTRA

Carter (tp) Ben Webster (ts) Teddy Wilson (p) Clarence Holiday (g) Elmer
James (b) Cozy Cole (d) Bob Howard (v)

THE GHOST OF DINAH   v-BH (e)   39387-A
78: DECCA 400   LP: RARITIES 48

PARDON MY LOVE   v-BH (2tp)(16tp)   39388-A
78: DECCA 400   LP: RARITIES 48

PARDON MY LOVE   v-BH (2tp)(16tp)   39388-B
78: UNISSUED   LP: RARITIES 61

[37]   March 4, 1935 New York
         BOB HOWARD AND HIS ORCHESTRA

Carter (tp, as) Rex Stewart (cornet) Barney Bigard (cl) Teddy Wilson (p)
Clarence Holiday (g) Elmer James (b) Cozy Cole (d) Bob Howard (v)

STAY OUT OF LOVE   v-BH (e)   39390-A
78: DECCA 439   LP: RARITIES 48

I'LL NEVER CHANGE   v-BH (8tp)   39391-A
78: DECCA 439   LP: RARITIES 48

WHERE WERE YOU ON THE NIGHT OF JUNE   39392-A
        THE THIRD   v-BH (e)
78: DECCA 407   LP: CORAL CJE100, RARITIES 48

(LOOK'S LIKE I'M) BREAKIN' THE ICE   v-BH (16+8as)   39393-A
78: DECCA 407   LP: RARITIES 48

>   NOTE: Coral CJE100 contains only excerpt (Wilson's solo) of
>   "Where were you..."

[38]	May 7, 1935 New York
	BOB HOWARD AND HIS ORCHESTRA

Carter (tp) Russell Procope (cl, as) Teddy Wilson (p) Clarence Holiday (g) Billy Taylor (b) Cozy Cole (d) Bob Howard (v)

CORINNE CORINNA   v-BH and impromptu v by   39518-A
    musicians (24tp)
78: DECCA 484   LP: RARITIES 48

EV'RY DAY   v-BH (4tp)(16+8tp)   39519-A
78: DECCA 460   LP: RARITIES 48

A PORTER'S LOVE SONG TO A CHAMBERMAID   39520-A
    v-BH (32tp with ensemble)
78: DECCA 460   LP: RARITIES 48

I CAN'T DANCE (I GOT ANTS IN MY PANTS)   39521-A
    v-BH (8tp)(16+8tp)
78: DECCA 484   LP: RARITIES 48

[39]	May 8, 1935 New York
	WILLIE BRYANT AND HIS ORCHESTRA

Carter (tp) Robert Cheek, Richard Clark (tp) Edgar Battle (tp, valve tb, arr) John "Shorty" Haughton, Robert Horton, Eddie Durham (tb) Glyn Paque (cl, as) Stanley Payne (as) Ben Webster, Johnny Russell (ts) Teddy Wilson (p) Arnold Adams (g) Louis Thompson (b) Cozy Cole (d) Willie Bryant (v) Alex Hill (arr)

RIGAMAROLE   (e)   89817-1
78: VICTOR 25038   LP: RCA (F) FXM1-7084,
BLUEBIRD AXM2-5502, RCA (J) RA-56

LONG ABOUT MIDNIGHT   v-WB, arr-AH (e)   89818-1
78: VICTOR 25045   LP: RCA (F) FXM1-7084,
BLUEBIRD AXM2-5502, RCA (J) RA-56

THE SHEIK (OF ARABY) (32tp)   89819-2
78: VICTOR 25038   LP: RCA (F) FXM1-7084,
BLUEBIRD AXM2-5502, RCA (J) RA-56, TIME-
LIFE STL-J20

JERRY THE JUNKER   v-WB (e)   89820-1
78: VICTOR 25045   LP: RCA (F) FXM1-7084,
BLUEBIRD AXM2-5502, RCA (J) RA-56

* * *

[34-39] While Carter's own orchestra was breaking up, he took part in the date under the leadership of his former Henderson colleague Buster Bailey.

May 8, 1935 [39]

The first of four sessions featuring singer/comedian Bob Howard followed five days later; the other Howard recordings came after Carter had followed several of his former sidemen into Willie Bryant's orchestra in February 1935.

On the Bob Howard recordings, and with Willie Bryant, Carter played trumpet almost exclusively. "I jumped at the chance to play trumpet in somebody's section; it was a lot of fun for me."

Teddy Wilson, who preceded Carter in the Bryant band, recalls that the band "improved a great deal because after awhile Benny Carter joined as the musical director and Willie's band really began to sound like something after Benny took over." (Interview with Phil Schaap, March 5, 1980.) Carter, who was not formally named "musical director," did arrange for the band and was heavily featured as a soloist. Unfortunately, at his one recording session with Bryant, none of his arrangements were recorded, and he solos on only one title.

[40] January 17, 1936 Paris
WILLIE LEWIS AND HIS ORCHESTRA

Carter (tp, as, arr, comp) Alex Renard (tp) Bobby Martin (tp, v) Billy Burns (tb) George Johnson (as) Willie Lewis (as, v) Joe Hayman, Coco Kiehn (ts) Herman Chittison (p) John Mitchell (g) June Cole (b) Ted Fields (d)

I'VE GOT A FEELING YOU'RE FOOLING v-WL   CPT-2450
    (8as) arr
78: PATHE PA-803   LP: PATHE CO54-11416,
ON THE LOOSE 5

STAY OUT OF LOVE   v-WL (32tp acc) arr   CPT-2451-1
78: PATHE PA-816   LP: PATHE CO54-11416,
ON THE LOOSE 5

RHYTHM IS OUR BUSINESS   v-BM (4tp break +   CPT-2452-1
    32tp) arr
78: PATHE PA-803   LP: PATHE CO54-11416,
ON THE LOOSE 5

JUST A MOOD   (16as) arr, comp   CPT-2453-1
78: PATHE PA-816   LP: PATHE CO54-11416,
ON THE LOOSE 5

ALL OF ME   (32+coda tp) arr   CPT-2454-1
78: PATHE PA-817   LP: PATHE CO54-11416,
ON THE LOOSE 5

STAR DUST   (24tp+coda [last chorus; muted tp in   CPT-2455-1
    1st chorus is probably Martin]) arr
78: PATHE PA-817   LP: PATHE CO54-11416,
ON THE LOOSE 5, TIME-LIFE STL-J10

* * *

Carter's first recording date in Europe finds him still featured primarily on trumpet and includes some of his finest work of the period on that instrument. The Willie Lewis orchestra, for which Carter had left the United

States in May of 1935, was, as Carter puts it, "almost a society band." French writer Charles Delaunay, who met Carter at that time, was less charitable. "It was simply not a good band," he recalls. He describes its home base, the posh Chez Florence, as rather hostile to the small coterie of jazz fans anxious to see Carter. "It was very difficult to get in if the maître d' didn't know you. You practically had to be the Duke of Windsor!"

The music recorded at this session was, indeed, atypical of the Lewis' Chez Florence repertoire, and Carter doubts that most of these arrangements were ever played in the club.

Carter's writing for reeds is his most ambitious since the October 16, 1933, "Lonesome Nights"/"Symphony In Riffs" date. "Stay Out Of Love" and "Rhythm Is Our Business" both have short saxophone ensemble passages but the real reed showcases are "All Of Me" and "Stardust." The former opens with a dazzling chorus by the sax section; Carter was to incorporate this chorus for an expanded section in a 1940 recording of the same tune.

Judging by the saccharine opening of "Stardust," one might suspect the arrangement was geared to the Chez Florence clientele, but another fine reed chorus intervenes. Carter's writing is full of brief asides and double-time passages, while still preserving the melody. The brass play the first eight bars of the last chorus to allow Carter, who had been leading the saxes, to switch to trumpet for his solo.

Carter's trumpet work here ranks among his best on record. In the brisk "Rhythm Is Our Business" he is at his most Armstrong-like. Despite an occasional fluff on "All Of Me," he shows more of the high note trumpet facility that attracted Armstrong himself to Carter's playing on the Mezzrow date two years earlier. He ends the piece with a spectacular series of ascending arpeggios, culminating in an effortless climb to high E-flat (F concert).

His solo on "Stardust" is even more impressive. Here he takes subtle liberties with the time, in places anticipating the melody and elsewhere falling daringly behind, only to catch up with a flurry of 16th notes. The full tone is, again, reminiscent of Armstrong's, as is the use of glissandi.

Carter's composition, "Just A Mood," was used as the Lewis orchestra's theme for broadcast to England. The recording here features Carter on alto; he made another version several months later in England on clarinet.

---

[41]   April 15, 1936   London
         BENNY CARTER AND HIS ORCHESTRA

Carter (tp, as, ts, cl, v, arr, comp) Max Goldberg, Tommy McQuater, Duncan Whyte (tp) Ted Heath, Bill Mulraney (tb) Andy McDevitt (cl, as) E. O. Pogson (as) Buddy Featherstonhaugh (ts) Pat Dodd (p) George Elliot (g) Al Burke (b) Ronnie Gubertini (d)

SWINGIN' AT MAIDA VALE   (16cl)(16+8as) arr, comp   S-103-2
78: VOCALION S-4 LP: DECCA (E) ACE OF
CLUBS ACL1167, EVEREST FS225, TIME-LIFE STL-J10

SWINGIN' AT MAIDA VALE   (16cl)(16+8as) arr, comp   S-103-3
78: UNISSUED-TEST EXISTS

April 15, 1936 [41]

NIGHTFALL (8cl)(32ts) arr, comp   S-104-2
78: VOCALION S-4   LP: DECCA (E) ACE OF
CLUBS ACL1167, EVEREST FS225

BIG BEN BLUES (v)(12as)+(12as alternating with   S-105-2
    ensemble) arr, comp
78: VOCALION S-7   LP: DECCA (E) ACE OF
CLUBS ACL1176, ON THE LOOSE 1

THESE FOOLISH THINGS (4as intro)(16tp)(8cl)   S-106-1
    (8as)(2as) arr
78: VOCALION S-5   LP: ON THE LOOSE 1,
INTERCORD (G) 158001

THESE FOOLISH THINGS (4as intro)(16tp)(8cl)   S-106-3
    (8as)(2as) arr
78: UNISSUED-TEST EXISTS

*   *   *

After nine months in France, Carter accepted Henry Hall's invitation to become arranger for the BBC dance orchestra. Five of Carter's arrangements for it were recorded commercially (see Arrangement section) and, within the constraints imposed by the musical format and instrumentation, they represent skillful marriages of jazz and dance music. But Carter's major impact on the British jazz scene came from a series of records made for Vocalion, which signed him within 24 hours of his arrival there.

    Within the month Carter led the first of these sessions, giving notice of his intent to produce first-rate swing music using only British musicians. The players were Britain's finest. Carter found them to be excellent readers, but as soloists they lacked real individuality. So many were Scots that the press dubbed them "Benny Carter and His Highland Swing."

    Carter frequently soloed on two and sometimes three instruments in the same piece, which elicited accusations of grandstanding from some writers, notably John Hammond. The English press, and certainly the musicians themselves, had nothing but praise for these records, and felt it only natural that Carter should be so prominent. Moreover, there were plenty of opportunities for solo work by the sidemen.

    For his first British session Carter prepared four new arrangements, three of which were his own compositions.

    "Swingin' At Maida Vale" refers to the section of London where the BBC studios were located and where Carter lived. The British soloists include the future bandleader Ted Heath on trombone, trumpeter Duncan Whyte, and a very Hawkins-like Buddy Featherstonhaugh.

    "Nightfall," a lovely melancholy melody which Carter states on clarinet, also features his first recorded solo on tenor. Carter has no trouble adjusting to the unfamiliar horn which he borrowed from Featherstonhaugh.

    "Big Ben Blues" includes a humorous vocal parody of blues lyrics by Carter. "These Foolish Things" finds him switching deftly from alto to trumpet to clarinet and back to alto. The third take of "These Foolish Things" is slower than the issued version; there is a minor fluff in the trumpet solo which may have contributed to the choice of take 1.

[42]	Late April, 1936 London

BENNY CARTER AND HIS ORCHESTRA

Carter (tp, as, cl, arr, comp) Tommy McQuater, Duncan Whyte (tp) Andy McDevitt (cl) Buddy Featherstonhaugh (ts) Pat Dodd (p) George Elliot (g) Al Burke (b) Ronnie Gubertini (d)

WHEN DAY IS DONE   arr   S-107-1
78: UNISSUED

WHEN DAY IS DONE   (32tp)(32as)(tp coda) arr   S-107-2
78: VOCALION S-11   LP: DECCA (E) ACE OF
CLUBS ACL1167

WHEN DAY IS DONE   (32tp)(32as)(tp coda) arr   S-107-3
78: UNISSUED   LP: ON THE LOOSE 5

I'VE GOT TWO LIPS   (32cl with ensemble)(32as) arr   S-108-3
78: VOCALION S-9   LP: DECCA (F) ACE OF
CLUBS ACL1167, EVEREST FS225

I'VE GOT TWO LIPS   (32cl with ensemble)(32as) arr   S-108-2
78: UNISSUED   LP: ON THE LOOSE 1

JUST A MOOD   (4cl)(16cl)(4cl) arr, comp   S-109
78: UNISSUED-TEST EXISTS

JUST A MOOD   (4cl)(16cl)(4cl) arr, comp   S-109-2
78: VOCALION S-11   LP: DECCA (F) ACE OF
CLUBS ACL1167, EVEREST FS225

SWINGIN' THE BLUES   (24as)(24tp [2nd solo; 1st   S-110-1
     is McQuater]) arr, comp
78: VOCALION S-5   LP: ON THE LOOSE 1

* * *

The information on take 1 of "When Day Is Done" comes from an article by Carter entitled "My Nine Lives," which appeared in the May-June issue of Swing Music (page 71). Carter writes: "You may also be interested to know that we made two masters on "When Day Is Done" in one of which I played a piano chorus. Whether that one will be selected for release hasn't yet been decided."

[43]	Mid June, 1936 London

BENNY CARTER AND HIS ORCHESTRA

Carter (tp, cl, as, ts, p, arr, comp) Max Goldberg, Tommy McQuater (tp) Leslie Thompson (tp, tb) Lew Davis, Ted Heath (tb) Freddy Gardner, Andy McDevitt (cl, as) Buddy Featherstonhaugh (ts) Billy Munn (p) Albert Harris (g) Wally Morris (b) George Elrick (d) Elisabeth Welch (v)

SCANDAL IN A FLAT   (8ts) arr, comp   S-115-2
78: VOCALION S-14   LP: DECCA (E) ACE OF
CLUBS ACL1176, ON THE LOOSE 2

ACCENT ON SWING   (4as)+(8as with ensemble)   S-116-1
     arr, comp

Mid June, 1936 [43]

78: VOCALION S-14 LP: DECCA (E) ACE OF
CLUBS ACL1167, EVEREST FS225

YOU UNDERSTAND (16p)(20) arr, comp   S-117-2
78: VOCALION S-27 LP: DECCA (E) ACE OF
CLUBS ACL1176, EVEREST FS221, ON THE LOOSE 2

GIN AND JIVE (32as) (8cl[2nd solo]) arr, comp   S-118
78: UNISSUED-TEST EXISTS

IF ONLY I COULD READ YOUR MIND (32ts)   S-119-1
    (8cl) arr, comp
78: VOCALION S-27 LP: DECCA (E) ACE OF
CLUBS ACL1167, EVEREST FS225

I GOTTA GO v-EW (20tp)(10as) arr, comp   S-120-1
78: UNISSUED-TEST EXISTS

I GOTTA GO v-EW (20ts)(10as) arr, comp   S-120-2
78: VOCALION S-16 LP: ON THE LOOSE 2

NOTE: "You Understand" was included by mistake on Everest FS221, which is an Ellington reissue. The Carter recording appears in place of a track labelled "I'm Crazy 'Bout My Baby." The Carter piece immediately precedes Ellington's on the Decca anthology ACL1176, which apparently was the source of the Everest issue.

* * *

The full orchestra returns for these recordings which feature Carter on no less than five instruments.

The trumpet soloist on "Accent On Swing" is Tommy McQuater, who was one of the few original solo voices among the British musicians. His brash exuberance, though occasionally bordering on the uncontrollable, lent excitement to a number of these British sides. Carter, himself, in a letter to a friend in January 1937, singles out McQuater. "There are quite a few good players over here but not yet on a par with our boys. There is one though I think is very good and that is Tommy McQuater, the trumpet player. His style is quite individual to a degree and he has a terrific attack at times."

"Accent On Swing" also contains Carter's first writing featuring the British saxophone section, a 16-bar passage in the last chorus.

"You Understand," one of Carter's favorites of his British recordings, includes his first piano work on record.

The unissued uptempo Carter original, "Gin And Jive," has Carter on alto and briefly on clarinet in the final chorus; the earlier clarinet work is by McDevitt. It may have been withheld because of a number of reed squeaks in Featherstonhaugh's opening tenor solo. It was rerecorded at the January 11-16, 1937, session and that version was issued. This arrangement became a staple of the Carter 1939 band's book at the Savoy as "Savoy Stampede," under which title it was recorded on June 29 (along with another piece premiered in England, "Scandal In A Flat").

[44]	June 20, 1936 London
	BENNY CARTER AND HIS SWING QUARTET

Carter (tp, as, ts, comp) Gene Rodgers (p) Bernard Addison (g) Wally Morris (b) George Elrick (d) Elisabeth Welch (v)

WHEN LIGHTS ARE LOW   v-EW (32as)(16tp acc) comp   S-121-1
78: VOCALION S-16   LP: DECCA (E) ACE OF
CLUBS ACL1167, EVEREST FS225

WALTZING THE BLUES   (24ts)(24as)(24tp) comp   S-122-1
78: VOCALION S-19   LP: DECCA (E) ACE OF
CLUBS ACL1167, EVEREST FS225, TIME-LIFE STL-J10

WALTZING THE BLUES   (24ts)(24as)(24tp) comp   S-122-2
78: UNISSUED-TEST EXISTS

TIGER RAG   (96ts)(16tp)   S-123-1
78: VOCALION S-19   LP: ON THE LOOSE 2

* * *

For his first small-group recordings in Europe Carter took advantage of the presence of two visiting Americans--pianist Gene Rodgers, who was part of the touring "Radcliffe and Rodgers" act, and Bernard Addison, the guitarist from the early 1930s Carter orchestra who was then accompanying the Mills Brothers.

The two Carter originals on this date became classics but in quite different ways. This is the first recording of "When Lights Are Low." This piece, composed by Carter (with lyrics by Spencer Williams), has endured for some forty-five years as a favorite of jazzmen from Lionel Hampton to Miles Davis and Eric Dolphy.

"Waltzing The Blues," on the other hand, has been one of the most controversial recordings in the history of jazz. It is the first recorded attempt at playing the blues in 3/4 or waltz time and foreshadowed other efforts which expanded the notion of "acceptable" jazz time signatures by such artists as Max Roach, Sonny Rollins, Dave Brubeck and Don Ellis. Coincidentally, a tune with the same title, composed by Clarence Gaskill, had been recorded in 1923 by the Victor Arden-Phil Ohman orchestra (Victor 19017), but this was a straight waltz and had nothing to do with the blues or jazz. Carter's recording was prompted by Leonard Feather who, as early as 1933, had proposed a jazz record in 3/4 time (Vocalion announcement no. 8, mid-September 1936). Carter, after experimenting with the idea on piano, decided it was worth a try. The result was a tune based on a 24-bar blues chorus rather than the more conventional twelve. Carter takes one chorus each on tenor, alto, and trumpet, separated by piano and guitar solo choruses. The unissued test of take 2 follows the same pattern. Carter's solos are quite different here, with no obvious flaws to account for its rejection in favor of take 1.

The British music press heralded the recording with headlines such as "REVOLUTION IN JAZZ!!," "Benny Carter's Hot Waltz Record," and "What's It All About?" The <u>Melody Maker</u> ran a forum of reviews and debates on the merits of the experiment (September 12, 1936). The jury of critics, who wrote under pseudonyms, was anything but unanimous. "Rophone," hot records critic for the <u>Melody Maker</u>: "Benny has started some-

thing which others were either too scared or too unobservant to start."
"Pick-Up," the commercial records critic for the Melody Maker: "This is all very exciting, but if it is to be seriously regarded as a dance record, hot or cold, it fails lamentably." "Swing-High," reviewer of hot records in Rhythm: "I have never been more completely at a loss for words than when I first heard the record. It just didn't seem possible that after 25 years of jazz records somebody could have produced one so completely and radically different." Leonard Hibbs in Swing Music: "No jazz swing, no waltz swing (by Viennese standards) but a record of the utmost interest because of Benny Carter's three perfect solos."

The severest indictment came from "Mike" (the noted writer and composer Spike Hughes and a great Carter admirer): "Waltzing The Blues is an idea that has as much prospect of posterity as a mule. And it isn't even as useful ... what the hell's the matter with the blues anyway that 4-in-a-bar is no longer enough?" Hughes also thought "Waltzing The Blues" was a misnomer, suggesting that "blue-ing the waltz" was "nearer the mark." (Melody Maker, October 3, 1936, p. 5.)

Not to be outdone, John Hammond called it "affected, 'clever' in the most odious sense of the word" and defended the blues as "simple folk music, far too pure for defilement at the hands of sophisticates." (Rhythm, November 1936, p. 13.)

Carter himself characteristically disclaims any attempt to "revolutionize jazz" and was quite surprised by the controversy. Although he still feels today that "three is almost a more natural swing feeling than four," Carter never continued the 3/4 experiment; it was almost 30 years before he recorded another piece in waltz time.

In the face of the strong reactions on all sides to "Waltzing The Blues," the commercial recordings critic for Rhythm, "Swing-Low," injected a welcome note of sanity into the debate: "As to whether the record proves anything or not I really do not care, as it has got me under its spell to such an extent that I only wish to be left alone to enjoy it."

"Tiger Rag" is Carter's most extensive tenor feature on record. He plays three effortless, rollicking choruses and then caps the performance with a brief appearance on trumpet.

[45]	August 2, 1936 Hilversum, Holland Airchecks
	BENNY CARTER WITH AVRO ORCHESTRA

Carter (cl, as, comp) Unknown (tp, b, d) Klaas Van Beeck (p)

NIGHTFALL   (8cl)(32as) comp

SOPHISTICATED LADY   (32+16as)

    NOTE: Piano and bass accompaniment only on second title.

[46]	August 26, 1936 Copenhagen
	BENNY CARTER WITH KAI EWANS' ORCHESTRA

Carter (tp, as, cl, arr, comp) Axel Skouby, Olaf Carlsson, Kurt Pederson (tp) Peter Rasmussen, Palmer Traulsen (tb) Kai Ewans (as) Aage Voss (cl, as)

Knut Knutsson, Anker Skjoldborg (ts) Christian Jensen (p) Ulrik Neumann (g) Kelof Nielsen (b) Eric Kragh (d) Leo Mathiesen (arr)

BLUE INTERLUDE (32as)(16tp)(8cl)(8as with   OCS-435-2
   ensemble + coda) arr, comp
78: HMV X-4699   LP: ON THE LOOSE 2

BUGLE CALL RAG arr-LM (4tp break)(4tp break+   OCS-436-2
   8tp+4tp break+8tp)(32as)
78: HMV X-4698   LP: ON THE LOOSE 2

[47]	August 29, 1936 Copenhagen
	BENNY CARTER WITH KAI EWANS' ORCHESTRA

Carter (tp, as, cl, v, arr, comp) Axel Skouby, Olaf Carlsson, Kurt Pederson (tp) Peter Rasmussen, Palmer Traulsen (tb) Kai Ewans (as, v) Aage Voss (cl, as) Knut Knutsson, Henry Hagemann-Larsen (ts) Christian Jensen (p) Ulrik Neumann (g) Kelof Nielsen (b) Eric Kragh (d) Leo Mathiesen (arr)

MEMPHIS BLUES v-KE, arr-LM (12tp)(12cl)   OCS-450-2
78: HMV X-4698   LP: ON THE LOOSE 2

WHEN LIGHTS ARE LOW (v)(32as)(8tp) arr, comp   OCS-451-2
78: HMV X-4699   LP: ON THE LOOSE 2

               * * *

Carter's visit to Holland was arranged by Danish bandleader/musician/entrepreneur Kai Ewans. His activities in Copenhagen included two concerts as well as two recording sessions [46, 47] with Evans's orchestra.

    "Blue Interlude" is a new arrangement of the composition Carter first recorded with the Chocolate Dandies in 1933.

    On this second recording of "When Lights Are Low," Carter himself does the vocal. His alto chorus here departs far more from the melody than that on the British recording made two months earlier. Soon after this recording Kai Ewans adopted "When Lights Are Low" as the theme song of his orchestra. It became so closely associated with the popular bandleader that as late as 1978, after he had retired to the United States, people still whistled the tune to him whenever he was spotted in Copenhagen.

[48]	September 12, 1936 Stockholm
	BENNY CARTER MED SONORA SWING BAND

Carter (as, tp, arr) Thore Ehrling (tp) Uno Gorling (tb) Charles Redland (cl) Zilas Gorling (ts) Stig Holm (p) Olle Sahlin (g) Thore Jederby (b) Sture Aberg (d)

SOME OF THESE DAYS (32as)(56tp)+(8tp with   1879-A
   ensemble)[1st tp solo - muted - is by
   Ehrling] arr
78: SONORA 3188   LP: SONORA SOLP106, ON
THE LOOSE 2

SOME OF THESE DAYS (32as)(48tp)+(8tp with   1879-B

September 12, 1936 [48]

ensemble) [1st tp solo - muted - is by
Ehrling] arr
78: UNISSUED LP: SONORA SOLP106, ON THE
LOOSE 2

---

[49]　Same Session
　　　BENNY CARTER MED ALL STAR ORCHESTRA

Carter (cl, as, tp, arr) Gosta Petersson, Thore Ehrling, Rune Ander (tp) Uno Gorling, George Vernon (tb) Tony Mason, Olle Thalen (as) Zilas Gorling (ts) Evert Haden (p) Olle Sahlin (g) Thore Jederby (b) Gosta Heden (d)

GLOAMING　arr　　　　　　　　　　　　　　　　　　　　　　1880-A
78: UNISSUED

GLOAMING　(16+8tp [2nd chorus; 1st chorus　　　　　　　1880-B
　　bridge by Ehrling])(4+4cl)　arr
78: SONORA 3188　LP: SONORA SOLP106, ON
THE LOOSE 2

　　　　　　　　　　　　　*　*　*

Carter's brief stay in Sweden included two concerts and this recording session [48, 49] with Swedish musicians. Because of the large number of local musicians who wanted to play with him, the two tunes were recorded with somewhat different personnels.

"Some Of These Days," made with a nine-piece group, is capped by some spectacular Carter trumpet, still very much in the Armstrong mold. On both takes Carter begins the last chorus with an interpolation of "Dark Eyes," one of the very few instances of his use of "quotes" (a device he generally dislikes). On the A take (issued), Carter solos on trumpet for the entire final chorus; on the B take the bridge of that chorus is taken by Sahlin on guitar.

The attractive "Gloaming," recorded by the larger ensemble, was composed by the trumpet player Thore Ehrling. The Nordiska Music Publishing Company had commissioned Carter to do an arrangement of a piece by a Swedish composer. The company sent Carter one work by each of the four leading writers of dance music and Carter selected "Gloaming." The trumpet on the bridge of the first chorus is the composer's; the rest of the trumpet work and the clarinet solo are by Carter.

In general the rhythm sections on Carter's Scandinavian recordings seem to be a little less rigid than those with which he recorded in Britain. According to the Swedish press, however, the fans in Stockholm may have been somewhat less sophisticated, applauding in the wrong places at Carter's concerts. When asked about this report Carter responded, "Wherever they applauded I was glad to accept it."

---

[50]　October 13, 1936　London
　　　ELISABETH WELCH

Carter (tp, cl, as) Gene Rodgers (p) Ivor Mairants (g) Wally Morris (b) Elisabeth Welch (v)

POOR BUTTERFLY v-EW (32as acc)(32as)(16as acc)   S-124-1
78: VOCALION 526   LP: ON THE LOOSE 2

DROP IN NEXT TIME YOU'RE PASSING v-EW   S-125-1
    (32as)(32as acc)(16tp acc)
78: VOCALION 515   LP: ON THE LOOSE 2,
TAX (SW) M-8031

THE MAN I LOVE v-EW (28cl acc)(16tp)   S-126-2
78: VOCALION 515   LP: ON THE LOOSE 2,
TAX (SW) M-8031

THAT'S HOW THE FIRST SONG WAS BORN v-EW   S-127-1
    (8tp)(32tp acc)(8tp)(10tp acc)
78: VOCALION 526   LP: ON THE LOOSE 2

[51]   October 19, 1936 London
        BENNY CARTER AND HIS SWING QUINTET

Carter (cl, as) Tommy McQuater (tp) Gerry Moore (p) Albert Harris (g)
Wally Morris (b) Al Craig (d)

THERE'LL BE SOME CHANGES MADE (8cl)   S-130-1
78: UNISSUED-TEST EXISTS

THERE'LL BE SOME CHANGES MADE (18cl)   S-130-2
78: VOCALION S-46   LP: DECCA (E) ACE OF
CLUBS ACL1167, DECCA (E) ACE OF CLUBS ACL1105

JINGLE BELLS (16cl)(32as)(8cl)   S-131-1
78: VOCALION S-39   LP: ON THE LOOSE 3,
TIME-LIFE STL-J10

JINGLE BELLS (16cl)(32as)(8cl)   S-131-2
78: UNISSUED   LP: ON THE LOOSE 3

ROYAL GARDEN BLUES (12cl)(24as)   S-132-1
78: VOCALION S-46   LP: DECCA (E) ACE OF
CLUBS ACL1167, EVEREST FS225

CARRY ME BACK TO OLD VIRGINNY (8as)(32as)   S-133-1
78: VOCALION S-39   LP: ON THE LOOSE 3

* * *

Soon after his return to England, Carter participated in two small-group sessions [50, 51]. For the first, he was part of a drumless quartet providing the accompaniment for the vocals of Elisabeth Welch, who has recently had a comeback in New York. For jazz fans, the most interesting moments are provided by Carter's alto on the first two titles, as well as Gene Rodgers's piano.

The quintet date features some excellent Red Allen-style solos by McQuater. Guitarist Albert Harris, who later became a noted teacher and composer in Hollywood, contributes some polished solos.

The first take of "Jingle Bells" is slightly faster than the originally issued second take. The question has been raised whether both trumpet solo

October 19, 1936 [51]

choruses are by the same trumpeter. In both takes the first chorus is open and the second muted. In take 2 there is practically no pause between the two choruses, necessitating a rather deft application of the straight mute by McQuater.

[52]	Between January 11 and 16, 1937 London
	BENNY CARTER AND HIS ORCHESTRA

Carter (tp, as, v, arr, comp) Leslie Thompson, Tommy McQuater, possibly Max Goldberg (tp) Lew Davis, Bill Mulraney (tb) Freddy Gardner, Andy McDevitt (cl, as) George Evans, Buddy Featherstonhaugh (ts) Eddie Macauley (p) Albert Harris (g) Wally Morris (b) Al Craig (d)

GIN AND JIVE (32as)(8as) arr, comp   S-140-1
78: UNISSUED-TEST EXISTS

GIN AND JIVE (32as)(8as) arr, comp   S-140-2
78: VOCALION S-57, VOCALION S-58, LP:
DECCA (E) ACE OF CLUBS ACL1167, EVEREST
FS225

NAGASAKI (v)(32as) arr   S-141-1
78: VOCALION S-69 LP: ON THE LOOSE 3

NAGASAKI (v)(32as) arr   S-141-2
78: UNISSUED-TEST EXISTS

THERE'S A SMALL HOTEL (16tp)(v) arr   S-142-1
78: VOCALION S-58 LP: ON THE LOOSE 3

THERE'S A SMALL HOTEL (16tp) arr   S-142-2
78: VOCALION S-57 LP: ON THE LOOSE 3

I'M IN THE MOOD FOR SWING (16tp) arr, comp   S-143-1
78: UNISSUED-TEST EXISTS

I'M IN THE MOOD FOR SWING (16tp) arr, comp   S-143-2
78: VOCALION S-69 LP: ON THE LOOSE 3

    NOTE: "Gin And Jive" later recorded by Carter under title "Savoy Stampede."

[53]	Same Session
	INFORMAL POST-SESSION

Carter (p, comp) possibly Max Goldberg (tp) Freddy Gardner (as, v) Al Craig (d)

RAMBLING IN C v-FG? (16p) comp   S-144
78: UNISSUED-TEXT EXISTS LP: ON THE
LOOSE 5

STARS AND YOU (18p) comp   S-145
78: UNISSUED-TEST EXISTS

* * *

[52, 53] Immediately following his successful Hippodrome concert, Carter returned to the studio with the English big band for his last recordings in London. Another try at "Gin And Jive," which had been rejected at the mid-June 1936 session, yielded an acceptable take.

Carter demonstrates his vocal dexterity on the tongue-twisting lyrics of "Nagasaki." The arrangement is similar, but not identical, to one Carter had done two years earlier for Charlie Barnet (recorded January 21, 1935).

Both takes of "Small Hotel" were issued simultaneously, an unusual procedure explained by Leonard Feather who produced the session. After the first take, which included both a trumpet solo and a vocal chorus by Carter, Feather suggested that the recording might be improved if Carter substituted an alto solo for the vocal. On the second take Carter did eliminate the vocal, but assigned the saxophone solo to Freddy Gardner. This was Carter's expression of pique at the disparagement of his singing. "It was a way of putting me down," Feather recalls. "To cover all sides we issued both takes." A Vocalion Swing Records press leaflet issued in mid-February 1937 (No. 16) describes the recordings at some length, but deliberately fails to note that the alto solo on the instrumental version is not by Carter. For years, it was thought to be his by many listeners. Vocalion concluded its pitch by advising the music lover, "If you prefer to have the vocal version of 'Small Hotel' all you have to do is ask for record S. 58 instead of S. 57," to which Carter asked many years later, "I wonder what they did with all those surplus copies of S. 58?"

Carter recorded both "Gin And Jive" and "I'm In The Mood For Swing" again after his return to the United States. In a similar arrangement, the latter was recorded by an illustrious Lionel Hampton group at Carter's first session back in New York.

The final two items were recorded informally after the session ended [53]. These demos of two Carter compositions, neither of which was recorded again, were discovered on a test pressing in Carter's own collection. He identified the piano work as his own, and the alto as that of Freddy Gardner, whom he also believes sings the scat vocal in "Rambling in C." There is a brief passage of muted trumpet in the first title, and the muted trumpet opens the second. It does not sound like McQuater and Carter suggested that it might be Max Goldberg.

[54]	March 24, 1937 Laren, Holland
	BENNY CARTER AND THE RAMBLERS

Carter (tp, as, ts, cl, arr) George Van Helvoirt, Jack Bulterman (tp) Marcel Thielemans (tb) Wim Poppink, Andre Van Der Ouderaa (cl, as) Sal Doof (ts) Freddy Johnson (p) Jack Pet (b) Kees Kranenburg (d) Theo Uden Masman (dir)

BLACK BOTTOM   (8as)(16+8tp)(32cl)(8as)(cl coda)   AM 368-1
78: DECCA F-42121, VOCALION S-94 LP:
DECCA (F) 154.062, ON THE LOOSE 3

RAMBLER'S RHYTHM   (24as)(32tp)(8as)   AM 369-2
78: DECCA F-44076, DECCA F-42110, VOCALION
S-94, LP: DECCA (F) 154.062, ON THE LOOSE 3

NEW STREET SWING   (32as)(4+4+8cl)+(8cl with   AM 370-1
    ensemble)

March 24, 1937 [54]

78: DECCA F-42165, DECCA F-42110, VOCALION
S-81, LP: DECCA (F) 154.062, ON THE LOOSE 3

I'LL NEVER GIVE IN   (16+8tp)(12ts) arr   AM 371-2
78: DECCA F-42121, DECCA F-42110, VOCALION
S-81, LP: DECCA (F) 154.062, ON THE LOOSE 3

* * *

During a brief, exploratory visit to Holland to conclude an agreement for his summer's engagement in Scheveningen, Carter recorded with this Dutch radio band. He was also reunited with his boyhood friend Freddy Johnson.

The session was held in a makeshift studio at the Hamdorff Hotel in Laren, where Carter had played one night the previous summer.

The first three tunes were from the Rambler's book and were completed in the morning. According to trumpeter Jack Bulterman (reported by Evert Kaleveld in the liner notes to On The Loose 3), Carter's arrangement of Freddy Johnson's "I'll Never Give In" was not ready. Carter seems to have spent the lunch hour in the studio "writing the arrangement, by hand, for all instruments. But at the convened time, one hour later, everyone had his part ready waiting for him."

The Ramblers provide excellent backing for perhaps the most impressive showcase to date for Carter's talents as a multi-instrumentalist. He takes all the solos here, except for an occasional spot for Johnson's piano. Playing four instruments, and switching as many as four times in a single piece with only a few measures between solos, Carter might be accused of gimmickry were it not for the technical mastery, coherence, and beauty of each of these solo statements.

[55]   April 28, 1937   Paris
        COLEMAN HAWKINS AND HIS ALL STAR JAM BAND

Carter (as, tp, arr) André Ekyan (as) Alix Combelle (cl, ts) Coleman Hawkins (ts) Stephane Grappelly (p) Django Reinhardt (g) Eugene D'Hellemmes (b) Tommy Benford (d)

HONEYSUCKLE ROSE   (8as) arr   OLA 1742-1
78: SWING 1, HMV B-8754   45: HMV 7EG8393,
HMV (F) 7EMF26, LP: PATHE FELP174,
ODEON CLP1890, PATHE CHTX240-551,
PRESTIGE 7633, PATHE (F) C054-16004, TIME-
LIFE STL-J06, WORLD RECORDS SM643

CRAZY RHYTHM   (32as[2nd solo]) arr   OLA 1743-1
78: SWING 1, HMV B-8754   45: HMV 7EG8393,
HMV (F) 7EMF26, LP: PATHE FELP174,
ODEON CLP1890, PATHE CHTX240-551,
PRESTIGE 7633, PATHE (F) C054-16004, TIME-LIFE
STL-J06, WORLD RECORDS SM643

OUT OF NOWHERE   (32tp)   OLA 1744-1
78: HMV K-8511, HMV B-8812   45: HMV
7EG8393 LP: PATHE FELP174, ODEON CLP1890,
PATHE CHTX240-551, PRESTIGE 7633, PATHE
(F) C054-16004, WORLD RECORDS SM643

SWEET GEORGIA BROWN   (32tp[theme])(32tp)   OLA 1745-1
   (64tp with ensemble)
78: HMV K-8511, HMV B-8812 45: HMV 7EG8393,
LP: PATHE FELP174, ODEON CLP1890, PATHE
CHTX240-551, PRESTIGE 7633, PATHE (F)
C054-16004, TIME-LIFE STL-J06, WORLD
RECORDS SM643

* * *

Carter's first recorded meeting in Europe with Coleman Hawkins turned out to be a landmark session. The idea for the sax quartet was Charles Delaunay's who, along with Hugues Panassié, launched their new Swing label with this date. Delaunay recalls that Carter, who was supposed to furnish four arrangements, arrived with none and sketched out the ensemble passages of "Honeysuckle Rose" and "Crazy Rhythm" on the spot. The final title was in the nature of an informal jam. Part of Delaunay's plan was to pair Carter and Hawkins with their French counterparts André Ekyan and Alix Combelle.

"Honeysuckle Rose" is basically all Hawkins, set off by Django's tasteful fills and some lovely sax ensemble passages, with Carter's incomparable lead alto quite prominent. Carter also solos on the bridge in the last chorus.

The Frenchmen rise to the occasion in "Crazy Rhythm," Ekyan and Combelle turning in, according to Delaunay, among their best performances ever. As Dan Morgenstern notes (liner notes to Prestige 7633), Carter pays Combelle the supreme compliment of incorporating a figure from the latter's bridge into his own. (For an analysis of Carter's solo, see chapter 3.) Hawkins's solo is one of his greatest on record; after one sensational chorus, apparently all he was allotted, Django is heard urging him to continue, which he does without breaking stride. It is difficult to believe Combelle's contention that Carter "advised" Hawkins how this tune should be played (Delaunay, Django Reinhardt, p. 85).

For the last pieces Carter switches to trumpet. On "Out Of Nowhere" he sets the stage for yet another Hawkins milestone, this time in his rhapsodic ballad vein.

[56]   August 17, 1937   The Hague
          BENNY CARTER AND HIS ORCHESTRA

Carter (tp, as, cl, arr, comp) Sam Dasberg, Cliff Woodridge, Rolf Goldstein (tp) George Chisholm, Harry Van Oven (tb) Louis Stephenson (as) Bertie King, Jimmy Williams (ts) Freddy Johnson (p) Ray Webb (g) Len Harrison (b) Robert Montmarche (d)

SKIP IT   (12as) arr, comp   AM 393-3
78: DECCA F-42136, VOCALION S-126 LP:
DECCA (F) 154.062, ON THE LOOSE 4, TAX
(SW) M-8031, TIME-LIFE STL-J10

LAZY AFTERNOON   (16tp)(34as) arr, comp   AM 394-2
78: DECCA F-42130, DECCA F-42165,

August 17, 1937 [56]

VOCALION S-118, LP: DECCA (F) 154.062,
ON THE LOOSE 4, TAX (SW) M-8031

I AIN'T GOT NOBODY (8cl)(16as) arr   AM 395-1
78: DECCA F-42125, VOCALION S-110, LP:
ON THE LOOSE 4

I AIN'T GOT NOBODY (8cl)(16as) arr   AM 395-2
78: BRUNSWICK 03311 LP: DECCA (F)
154.062, ON THE LOOSE 4, TAX (SW) M-8031

BLUES IN MY HEART (34as) arr, comp   AM 396-1
78: DECCA F-42128, VOCALION S-104 LP:
DECCA (F) 154.062, ON THE LOOSE 4, TAX
(SW) M-8031

* * *

Carter played in the summers of 1936 and 1937 in the Dutch seaside resort of Scheveningen. For the second engagement he assembled an international, interracial band with members from six countries. With some changes, this was the group which recorded for Dutch Decca.

Since his arrival in Europe, Carter had hardly exercised his talent for fashioning dazzling saxophone choruses. Having played several months with his international band, Carter apparently felt he could now offer them an arranging challenge. "Skip It" is a tour de force for the reeds. It is a good example of Carter's skill at creating the most intricate reed passages without ever sounding as if he were simply engaging in musical exercises.

Carter's lovely ballad, "Lazy Afternoon," is another of his compositions which deserve to become more popular. It obviously made an impression on one of the reed men in this band, Bertie King, who, almost 20 years later, made the only other recording of it. The two versions of "I Ain't Got Nobody" are quite similar. Rust lists Brunswick 03311(-2) as "never issued" but Harold Flakser has shown us a copy.

The arrangement of "Blues In My Heart" is a novel, almost "symphonic" treatment, which only hints at the melody.

[57]	August 18, 1937 The Hague
	BENNY CARTER AND HIS ORCHESTRA

Carter (tp, as, cl) George Chisholm (tb) Coleman Hawkins (ts) Jimmy Williams (cl, ts) Freddy Johnson (p) Ray Webb (g) Len Harrison (b) Robert Montmarche (d)

SOMEBODY LOVES ME (32tp)(8tp) arr   AM 397-1
78: DECCA F-42128, VOCALION S-104 LP:
DECCA (F) 154.062, ON THE LOOSE 4, TAX
(SW) M-8031

MIGHTY LIKE THE BLUES (16tp)(12cl) arr   AM 398-3
78: DECCA F-42125, VOCALION S-110, BRUNS-
WICK 03311, LP: DECCA (F) 154.062, NEW
WORLD RECORDS NW174, ON THE LOOSE 4,
TAX (SW) M-8031

PARDON ME, PRETTY BABY (32tp)(32as)　　　　AM 399-1
(32tp[4-bar trades with Hawkins]) arr
78: DECCA F-42130, VOCALION S-126 LP:
DECCA (F) 154.062, ON THE LOOSE 4, TAX
(SW) M-8031, TIME-LIFE STL-J10

MY BUDDY (16as)(32tp) arr　　　　　　　　AM 400-1
78: DECCA F-42136, VOCALION S-118 LP:
DECCA (F) 154.062, ON THE LOOSE 4, TIME-
LIFE STL-J10

                                        * * *

For this session the orchestra pared down to an octet, making four sides with guest Coleman Hawkins. The performances have a loose feeling. Carter supplied an occasional arranged passage for cohesion, but the date was meant to display the solo talents of the principals.

    Leonard Feather, visiting Holland, produced this and the previous session for English Vocalion. Looking back, he recalls that there was an "undeclared sense of rivalry" between Carter and Hawkins. Hawkins felt it more, he adds, and was "not too eager" to record as a sideman. Charles Delaunay, who produced the earlier Paris encounter between the saxophonists, and also saw them in Holland, remembers that Hawkins loved the competition of a jam session, but Carter took part only on rare occasions. "I always had the feeling that he preferred writing to playing," says Delaunay. Carter denies there was competition between him and Hawkins. "We may have felt stimulated by each other's company, especially in Europe, but only to make the best music we could, and not in a combative sense." Furthermore, on this session, Carter played mostly trumpet, blunting direct comparison.

    In its own way, this relaxed date was as successful as the Paris session four months earlier. It never became as well known, perhaps because the records were never as widely distributed, nor the reissues as extensive.

[58]	March 7, 1938 Paris
	BENNY CARTER AND HIS ORCHESTRA

Carter (tp, as, arr, comp) Fletcher Allen (as) Bertie King (ts, cl) Alix Combelle (ts) Yorke De Souza (p) Django Reinhardt (g) Len Harrison (b) Robert Montmarche (d)

I'M COMING VIRGINIA (23as) arr　　　　　OSW 4-1
78: SWING 20 LP: ODEON CLP1907, PATHE
(F) C 054-16007, PRESTIGE 7633, TIME-LIFE
STL-J10, WORLD RECORDS SM645

FAREWELL BLUES (32as[2nd solo; 1st is Allen]) arr　　OSW 5-1
78: SWING 36 LP: PATHE CHTX240-551, ODEON
CLP1907, PATHE (F) C 054-16007, PRESTIGE 7633,
WORLD RECORDS SM645

BLUE LIGHT BLUES (12tp with ensemble)(24tp with　　OSW 6-1
    ensemble) comp
78: SWING 20 LP: ODEON CLP1907, PATHE

March 7, 1938 [58]

(F) C 054-16008, PRESTIGE 7633, WORLD
RECORDS SM646

NOTE: "Blue Light Blues" as "Playin' The Blues" on Swing 20.

* * *

Carter's final European recordings were again for the Delaunay-Panassié Swing label and featured the same instrumentation as the famous April 1937 date which inaugurated the label. Two of the musicians from that session, Combelle and Reinhardt, were present along with a couple from Carter's Scheveningen band.

"I'm Coming Virginia" takes full advantage of the reed section from the start with a ravishing ensemble chorus, which embellishes but never obscures the melody. The last chorus is an even more daring reed show. After modulating from F to E-flat, the sax quartet, spurred on by Django's fills, cascades through Carter's masterful reworking of the theme.

The other two tunes are less elaborate, concentrating on the solos.

---

[59]   July 21, 1938 New York
        LIONEL HAMPTON AND HIS ORCHESTRA

Carter (cl, as, arr, comp) Harry James (tp) Dave Matthews (as) Herschel Evans, Babe Russin (ts) Billy Kyle (p) John Kirby (b) Jo Jones (d) Lionel Hampton (vib, v)

I'M IN THE MOOD FOR SWING (32as) arr, comp   024065-1
78: VICTOR 26011 LP: CAMDEN CAL402,
RCA (F) 730.641, BLUEBIRD AXM6-5536, TIME-
LIFE STL-J10, RCA (F) PM42406

SHOE SHINER'S DRAG (12as)(12cl) arr   024066-1
78: VICTOR 26011 LP: CAMDEN CAL402, RCA
(F) 730.641, BLUEBIRD AXM6-5536, TIME-LIFE
STL-J10

ANY TIME AT ALL v-LH (e) arr   024067-1
78: VICTOR 26039 LP: CAMDEN CAL517, RCA
(F) 741.077, BLUEBIRD AXM6-5536

MUSKRAT RAMBLE (16cl) arr   024068-1
78: VICTOR 26017 LP: CAMDEN CAL402, RCA
(F) 730.641, BLUEBIRD AXM6-5536

* * *

By 1938 Carter felt that he needed a change musically. Although satisfied with many of his recordings of the preceding two years, he realized that he had reached the limit of the talents available abroad.

His desire to hear his music performed by top American jazzmen was soon gratified. Within two months of his return to the United States, he took part in one of Lionel Hampton's all-star dates for Victor and the first tune recorded was Carter's composition "I'm In The Mood For Swing," which he had recorded in England using a similar arrangement. The contrast between the two recordings, particularly in the rhythm sections, is startling. Carter's own solo is a marvel; he makes excellent use of space, allowing each idea to be absorbed. During the transition from the bridge to the final eight bars of his solo, Carter lays out almost two full measures, creating a sense of anticipation. His ornate reentry draws a faintly audible exclamation from someone in the studio.

In "Shoe Shiner's Drag," which Hampton suggested he arrange, Carter incorporates elements of Jelly Roll Morton's classic recording, without re-creating it. Morton's blues figure opens and closes the piece which features solos by Carter on alto, James, and Evans. Carter reappears, playing the clarinet chorus allotted to Omer Simeon on Morton's recording, followed by Hampton's vibes and a brief spot by Russin. The bass line carried by the tuba on the Morton recording is played here by the horns behind Carter's clarinet and Hampton's vibraphone solo.

In Hampton's vocal feature, "Anytime At All," Carter has written some lovely reed figures for the opening chorus.

"Muskrat Ramble" resembles "Shoe Shiner's Drag" in many ways: a New Orleans standard given a modern treatment.

---

[60]   July 29, 1938   New York
        TEDDY WILSON AND HIS ORCHESTRA

Carter (as) Jonah Jones (tp) Ben Webster (ts) Teddy Wilson (p) John Kirby (b) Cozy Cole (d) Nan Wynn (v)

NOW IT CAN BE TOLD   v-NW (32as)   23305-1
78: BRUNSWICK 8199   LP: TAX (SW) M-8032

LAUGH AND CALL IT LOVE   v-NW (4as)(8as)   23306-2
78: BRUNSWICK 8207   LP: TAX (SW) M-8032

ON THE BUMPY ROAD TO LOVE   v-NW (32as)   23307-1
78: BRUNSWICK 8207   LP: TAX (SW) M-8032,
TIME-LIFE STL-J10

A-TISKET, A-TASKET   v-NW (32as)   23308-1
78: BRUNSWICK 8199   LP: TAX (SW) M-8032

                         *   *   *

The first of Carter's several appearances on Teddy Wilson's all-star dates for Brunswick yielded several excellent, and often overlooked, alto solos, particularly those on the last two titles. British critic Benny Green once wrote that Carter's perfectly paced, flowing effort on the unlikely title "Bumpy Road" managed to convince him that the "forgotten jingle ... was the ideal jazz vehicle." (Liner notes to Pablo 2310-732.)

---

[61]   October 31, 1938   New York
        TEDDY WILSON AND HIS ORCHESTRA

Carter (as, arr) Harry James (tp) Benny Morton (tb) Edgar Sampson (as) Lester Young, Herschel Evans (ts) Teddy Wilson (p) Al Casey (g) Walter Page (b) Jo Jones (d) Billie Holiday (v)

October 31, 1938 [61]

EVERYBODY'S LAUGHING v-BH (e)   23642-1
78: BRUNSWICK 8259   LP: SONY (J) SOPH67,
COLUMBIA JG34840

HERE IT IS TOMORROW AGAIN v-BH (e) arr   23643-1
78: BRUNSWICK 8259   LP: SONY (J) SOPH67,
COLUMBIA JG34840

[62]	November 9, 1938 New York
	TEDDY WILSON AND HIS ORCHESTRA

Carter (as, arr) Harry James (tp) Benny Morton (tb) Edgar Sampson (as)
Lester Young, Herschel Evans (ts) Teddy Wilson (p) Al Casey (g) Walter
Page (b) Jo Jones (d) Billie Holiday (v)

SAY IT WITH A KISS v-BH (e) arr   23687-1
78: BRUNSWICK 8270   LP: COLUMBIA CL2427,
COLUMBIA KG32127, SONY (J) SOPH67, COLUMBIA
JG34840

APRIL IN MY HEART v-BH (20as) arr   23688-1
78: BRUNSWICK 8265   LP: RARETONE (I)
RTR24011 SONY (J) SOPH67

APRIL IN MY HEART v-BH arr   23688-2
78: UNISSUED-TEST EXISTS

I'LL NEVER FAIL YOU v-BH (e) arr   23689-1
78: BRUNSWICK 8265   LP: RARETONE (I)
RTR24011, SONY (J) SOPH67

THEY SAY v-BH (12as) arr   23690-1
78: BRUNSWICK 8270   LP: TIME-LIFE STL-
J10, SONY (J) SOPH67, TWO FLAT DISC 5006

THEY SAY v-BH (12as) arr   23690-2
78: UNISSUED   LP: COLUMBIA CL2427,
COLUMBIA KG32127, SONY (J) SOPH67

* * *

These two sessions [61, 62] were Carter's first recordings with Billie
Holiday, whom he had known for four or five years. While most of the
Wilson-Holiday sessions were impromptu affairs, for these Wilson asked
Carter to provide arrangements.

For the personnel Wilson drew heavily on the Count Basie band,
which Billie had left in February of that year. Carter's arrangements are
good examples of his ability to provide a vocalist with tasteful accompaniment which is unobtrusive without being bland. The reed figures which
cushion the vocal in "They Say" are unmistakably Carter's, but do not detract from the lyric. Singers to the present day are aware of Carter's
knack. In a 1976 Down Beat blindfold test Sarah Vaughan listened to a
Carter arrangement for pop singer Maria Muldaur. She was unable to
identify the vocalist, but instantly spotted the arrangement as Carter's.

Carter remembers that recording with Billie Holiday was never
"just another gig," but rather a special musical occasion marked by the

empathy that existed between the players and the vocalist who truly appreciated and understood their work.

[63]	November 22, 1938 New York
	BLUE LU BARKER ACC. BY DANNY BARKER'S FLY CATS

Carter (tp) Buster Bailey (cl) Sam Price (p) Danny Barker (g) Wellman Braud (b) Blue Lu Barker (v)

I FEEL LIKE LYING IN ANOTHER WOMAN'S   64767-
HUSBAND'S ARMS v-BLB
78: UNISSUED

GIVE ME SOME MONEY v-BLB   64768-
78: UNISSUED

I GOT WAYS LIKE THE DEVIL v-BLB (12tp acc)   64769-
    (12tp)+(24tp acc)
78: DECCA 7560 LP: JAZZ ARCHIVES JA47

THAT MADE HIM MAD v-BLB (4tp intro)+(16tp   64770-A
    acc)
78: DECCA 7538 LP: JAZZ ARCHIVES JA47

*   *   *

Rust lists Carter as the trumpeter on a previous Blue Lu Barker date (6-11-38) but it is definitely not Carter; it is probably Red Allen. This confusion with Red Allen is also apparent on the Jazz Archives LP; although it is entitled Red Allen and the Blues Singers vol. 2 it contains these two Blue Lu Barker items on which Carter is the trumpeter.

[64]	January 20, 1939 New York
	NAT GONELLA WITH JOHN KIRBY'S ORCHESTRA

Carter (as) Nat Gonella (tp, v) Buster Bailey (cl) Billy Kyle (p) Brick Fleagle (g) John Kirby (b) Jack Maisel (d)

YOU MUST HAVE BEEN A BEAUTIFUL BABY   64909-A
    v-NG (20as)
78: PARLOPHONE F-1353 LP: HISTORIA (G)
H639, WORLD RECORDS (E) SH369

JUST A KID NAMED JOE v-NG (as intro)(8as)   64910-A
78: PARLOPHONE F-1376 LP: HISTORIA (G)
H639, WORLD RECORDS (E) SH369

JEEPERS CREEPERS v-NG (16as)   64911-A
78: PARLOPHONE F-1376 LP: HISTORIA (G)
H639, WORLD RECORDS (E) SH369

I MUST SEE ANNIE TONIGHT v-NG (4+4as   64912-A
    [horns trade])(4+8as[horns trade])
78: PARLOPHONE F-1353 LP: HISTORIA (G)
H639, WORLD RECORDS (E) SH369

*   *   *

January 20, 1939 [64]

The British trumpeter and vocalist led this session of top American jazzmen while on a visit to New York. Carter's solo on the first title is quite "modern." He discards the melody entirely and, using a restrained attack, plays long lines incorporating a dazzling series of runs halfway into his chorus.

[65]	January 30, 1939 New York
	TEDDY WILSON AND HIS ORCHESTRA

Carter (as, cl) Roy Eldridge (tp) Ernie Powell (ts) Teddy Wilson (p) Danny Barker (g) Milt Hinton (b) Cozy Cole (d) Billie Holiday (v)

WHAT SHALL I SAY v-BH (4as intro)(32cl acc) 24044-1
78: BRUNSWICK 8314 LP: SONY (J) SOPH68,
TWO FLAT DISC 5007

IT'S EASY TO BLAME THE WEATHER v-BH 24045-1
 (16cl)(8as)(2as break)
78: BRUNSWICK 8314 LP: SONY (J) SOPH68,
TWO FLAT DISC 5007

IT'S EASY TO BLAME THE WEATHER v-BH 24045-2
78: UNISSUED-TEST EXISTS

MORE THAN YOU KNOW v-BH (16as) 24046-1
78: BRUNSWICK 8319 LP: RARETONE (I)
RTR24011, SONY (J) SOPH68

MORE THAN YOU KNOW v-BH (16as) 24046-2
78: UNISSUED LP: COLUMBIA CL2428,
COLUMBIA KG32127, SMITHSONIAN P13708

SUGAR v-BH (16+8as) 24047-1
78: BRUNSWICK 8319 LP: FOLKWAYS FJ2804,
FOLKWAYS FP59, COLUMBIA CL2428, COLUMBIA KG32127, SONY (J) SOPH67

* * *

Although Carter does not arrange, he plays a greater role as a soloist here than on the previous dates with Billie Holiday. The first two titles have some lovely Carter clarinet accompaniment, with his alto contributing melodic solos to "More Than You Know" and "Sugar."

[66]	April 17, 1939 New York Airchecks, Savoy Ballroom
	BENNY CARTER AND HIS ORCHESTRA

Carter (as, tp, arr, comp) Collective Personnel for Savoy Ballroom Airchecks: Lincoln Mills, Louis Bacon, Joe Thomas, Archie Johnson, Bobby Woodlen (tp) Tyree Glenn (tb, vib) Vic Dickenson, Jimmy Archey (tb) Jimmy Powell, Carl Frye (as) Ernie Powell, Castor McCord (ts) Sammy Davis, Eddie Heywood (p) Ulysses Livingston, Arnold Adams (g) Hayes Alvis (b) Henry Morrison, Ted Fields, Keg Purnell (d)

MELANCHOLY LULLABY (16as)+(8as with ensemble)+
 (8as) arr, comp

I'M COMING VIRGINIA (24as) arr

GIN AND JIVE (32as) arr, comp

MORE THAN YOU KNOW (32tp)(8tp) arr

HONEYSUCKLE ROSE (incomplete) (32as[interrupted by signoff]) arr

>   NOTE: The personnel given above is a general one for the period of the band's residencies at the Savoy in 1939. It covers the airchecks recorded on April 22, April 29, May 6, May 8, May 13, May 20, May 27, June 10, June 12, June 17, July 24, October 9, October 14, October 23 and October 28. The personnel is not repeated for each session; only pertinent vocalist and arranger credits are noted.

* * *

A few months after his return from Europe, Carter put together an orchestra of top musicians. He fondly remembers them as "terrific guys, fine musicians and great friends--I loved every one of them. There was no drinking, no drugs and no trouble."

The band spent long periods during 1939 and 1940 in residence at the Savoy Ballroom in Harlem. These airchecks from that legendary venue are the earliest recorded examples of the orchestra, antedating its first commercial sides by two months.

Carter wrote "Melancholy Lullaby" specifically as a theme song, and used it to open many of his appearances and broadcasts into the mid-forties. Leonard Feather has called the melody "the loveliest of all the big band themes." It was also admired by some of the top bandleaders; Glenn Miller, Jimmy Dorsey, Gene Krupa and Artie Shaw all recorded or played it over the air.

The opening and closing sax ensemble passages of "I'm Coming Virginia" are based on the arrangement recorded by Carter in Paris on March 7, 1938.

"Gin And Jive" also derives from his European period; this arrangement was first recorded in London in June 1936.

Carter's commercial recording of "More Than You Know" (November 1, 1939) was to become one of his most celebrated trumpet solos. In this earlier version, some of the ideas which went into that classic are already apparent.

---

[67] April 20, 1939 New York
      LEONARD FEATHER'S ALL STAR JAM BAND

Carter (tp, as) Bobby Hackett (cornet, g) Pete Brown (as, tp) Joe Marsala (cl) Billy Kyle (p) Hayes Alvis (b) Cozy Cole (d)

TWELVE BAR STAMPEDE (12tp)(24as)   65437-A
78: DECCA 18111 LP: BRUNSWICK (G) 87527,
MCA (F) 510.071, TIME-LIFE STL-J10, MCA 1324

April 20, 1939 [67]

FEATHER BED LAMENT (12tp)   65438-A
78: DECCA 18111 LP: BRUNSWICK (G) 87527,
MCA (F) 510.071, MCA 1324

MEN OF HARLEM (16tp)(16as)   65439-A
78: DECCA 18118 LP: BRUNSWICK (G) 87527,
MCA (F) 510.071, TIME-LIFE STL-J10, MCA 1324

OCEAN MOTION (32tp)   65440-A
78: DECCA 18118 LP: BRUNSWICK (G) 87527,
MCA (F) 510.071, STASH ST104, MCA 1324

    NOTE: On MCA (F) 510.071 and MCA 1324 LPs titles for "Men
    Of Harlem" and "Ocean Motion" are reversed.

* * *

    Leonard Feather, who had played an important role in Carter's British
recordings, was by now settled in the United States. This date was his
idea, and he wrote the tunes as well.

    The personnel is a discographer's nightmare because of the multi-
instrumental talents of these versatile artists. Carter plays trumpet and
alto which is, of course, not unusual for him. Bobby Hackett plays his
lyrical cornet, but he also plays guitar, which was his original instrument.
Pete Brown, a truly original alto stylist, is heard here on trumpet as well.

    This was Carter's only session with Brown, Marsala and Hackett.
On this date Brown set down some of his greatest playing on record. His
infectious bounce on alto seems to have rubbed off on Carter, especially in
"Twelve Bar Stampede." The tune ends with Carter, Hackett and Brown
riffing on brass.

    In "Men Of Harlem," a jaunty melody which Feather based on the
traditional Welsh air "Men Of Harlech," Carter and Brown both solo on alto
and trumpet. Carter's alto statement is almost perfectly symmetrical in
structure, with its deliberately placed highest note (high F, concert A-flat)
occurring exactly midway. In a rare appearance on trumpet, Brown conveys
the same irrepressible jump feeling that he does on alto.

    The solo sequence for this session is as follows: "Twelve Bar
Stampede"--Carter (tp), Brown (as), Kyle (p), Marsala (cl), Carter (as),
Hackett (cornet), Marsala (cl); "Feather Bed Lament"--Brown (as), Kyle
(p), Marsala (cl), Carter (tp), Marsala (cl); "Men Of Harlem"--Brown (as),
Carter (tp), Marsala (cl), Kyle (p), Carter (as), Brown (tp); "Ocean Mo-
tion"--Kyle (p), Marsala (cl), Brown (as), Carter (tp).

[68]   April 22, 1939 New York Airchecks, Savoy Ballroom
         BENNY CARTER AND HIS ORCHESTRA

Carter (as, tp, cl, arr, comp) Louis Bacon (v) for Collective Personnel for the
Period See 4/17/39.

MELANCHOLY LULLABY (16as)+(8as with ensemble)+
         (8as) arr, comp

TEA FOR TWO (16as) (4as with ensemble) arr

SCANDAL IN A FLAT   (16as) arr, comp

I AIN'T GOT NOBODY   (16as) arr

I'M IN THE MOOD FOR SWING   (32as)(16tp) arr, comp

BETWEEN THE DEVIL AND THE DEEP BLUE SEA
    v-LB (8tp) arr

HONEYSUCKLE ROSE   (32as)(32tp)(8cl arr

STAR DUST   (32tp)(20tp+coda) arr

MELANCHOLY LULLABY (incomplete)   (16as)+(8as
    with ensemble)+(8as) arr, comp

* * *

For his repertoire, Carter continues to mix material he had recorded in Europe with newer scores. Except for adaptations from earlier arrangements, like "Stardust," the distinctive saxophone ensemble passages which marked Carter's past work are strangely absent during this period. Carter offers two explanations for this apparent change in his arranging style. First, he was forced to put together a book for his new band rather quickly and could not afford the time required to write and rehearse complex saxophone choruses. Second, he felt at the time that his band might have wider popular appeal without them. Such figures began to reappear more consistently after 1940.

[69]	April 25, 1939 New York
	JERRY KRUGER AND HER ORCHESTRA

Carter (tp, arr) Ernie Powell (ts) Eddie Heywood (p) Hayes Alvis (b) Henry Morrison (d) Jerry Kruger (v)

RAIN, RAIN, GO AWAY   v-JK (8tp) arr   WM-1021-A
78: VOCALION 4927   LP: CBS (F) 65384

SUMMERTIME   v-JK (16tp) arr   WM-1022-A
78: VOCALION 4927   LP: CBS (F) 65384,
NOSTALGIA BOOK CLUB 1005

* * *

Rust lists Buck Clayton (tp) and Lester Young (ts) but George Simon (writing at the time under the pseudonym Gordon Wright, Metronome, August 1939, p. 24) reports Carter and Ernie Powell (of Carter's band) on those instruments. Carter confirms this contemporary review, adding that the arrangements were likely his and that the drummer was probably Henry Morrison, also in his band then.

[70]	April 29, 1939 New York Airchecks, Savoy Ballroom
	BENNY CARTER AND HIS ORCHESTRA

Carter (tp, cl, as) for Collective Personnel for the Period See 4/17/39 Mercedes Carter (v) Andy Gibson (arr)

April 29, 1939 [70]

WHEN IRISH EYES ARE SMILING arr-AG (32tp)

WE'VE COME A LONG WAY TOGETHER v-MC (8cl)

BLUE SKIES (32as)(8as with ensemble)

[71] May 6, 1939 New York Airchecks, Savoy Ballroom
BENNY CARTER AND HIS ORCHESTRA

Carter (as, cl, arr, comp) for Collective Personnel for the Period See 4/17/39 Mercedes Carter (v)

MELANCHOLY LULLABY (16as)+(8as with ensemble)+
  (8as) arr, comp

I'M COMING VIRGINIA v-MC (24as) arr

HAVE MERCY v-MC (2as break)(18+9as)

SUGARFOOT STOMP (incomplete) (24cl)(12as[interrupted by signoff])

SOLID MAMA (e)

[72] May 8, 1939 New York Airchecks, Savoy Ballroom
BENNY CARTER AND HIS ORCHESTRA

Carter (as) for Collective Personnel for the Period See 4/17/39 Mercedes Carter (v) Phil Lang (arr)

HAVE MERCY v-MC (2as break)(18+9as)

PLYMOUTH ROCK arr-PL (e)

[73] May 13, 1939 New York Airchecks, Savoy Ballroom
BENNY CARTER AND HIS ORCHESTRA

Carter (as, tp, arr, comp) for Collective Personnel for the Period See 4/17/39 Mercedes Carter (v)

THE LADY'S IN LOVE WITH YOU v-MC (4as)(16as)

A HOME IN THE CLOUDS v-MC (16tp)(8tp)(8tp)
  arr, comp

I CRIED FOR YOU v-MC (16tp)(8tp) arr

PATTY CAKE v-MC (e) arr

* * *

This is one of two airchecks by Carter of "A Home in The Clouds," the tune that was first recorded by Benny Goodman (February 9, 1939, with a vocal by Martha Tilton). The composer credits for this tune are somewhat vague, with Carter's name mysteriously omitted from many issues.

[74]   May 20, 1939   New York   Airchecks, Savoy Ballroom
BENNY CARTER AND HIS ORCHESTRA

Carter (as, cl, arr, comp) for Collective Personnel for the Period See 4/17/39 Mercedes Carter (v)

LIEBESTRAUM (e)
LP: TAX (SW) M-8004, HOT 'N SWEET (F)
HOL6426

MY HEART HAS WINGS   v-MC (16as) arr
LP: TAX (SW) M-8004, HOT 'N SWEET (F)
HOL6426

LADY BE GOOD (32as) arr
LP: TAX (SW) M-8004, HOT 'N SWEET (F)
HOL6426

BIG WIG IN THE WIGWAM   v-MC (4+16+8cl)
LP: TAX (SW) M-8004, HOT 'N SWEET (F)
HOL6426

MELANCHOLY LULLABY (incomplete) (16as)+
     (8as with ensemble)+(8as [interrupted by signoff])
LP: TAX (SW) M-8004, HOT 'N SWEET (F)
HOL6426

[75]   May 27, 1939   New York   Airchecks, Savoy Ballroom
BENNY CARTER AND HIS ORCHESTRA

Carter (as, arr) for Collective Personnel for the Period See 4/17/39 Mercedes Carter (v)

HOW STRANGE   v-MC (16as) arr

TEA FOR TWO   v-MC (2as)(16as)(4as) arr

[76]   June 10, 1939   New York   Airchecks, Savoy Ballroom
BENNY CARTER AND HIS ORCHESTRA

Carter (as, tp, arr) for Collective Personnel for the Period See 4/17/39

BLUE EVENING   (32as)+(32as[Carter covers when vocalist - probably Mercedes Carter - misses cue]) arr

BYE BYE BLUES   (12+12tp)

[77]   June 12, 1939   New York   Aircheck, Savoy Ballroom
BENNY CARTER AND HIS ORCHESTRA

Carter (as) for Collective Personnel for the Period See 4/17/39

CLEMENTINE   (24as)

[78]	June 17, 1939 New York Aircheck, Savoy Ballroom
	BENNY CARTER AND HIS ORCHESTRA

Carter (tp) for Collective Personnel for the Period See 4/17/39

STRANGE ENCHANTMENT (16+8tp)

[79]	June 29, 1939 New York
	BENNY CARTER AND HIS ORCHESTRA

Carter (as, arr, comp) Joe Thomas, Lincoln Mills, Bobby Woodlen (tp) Jimmy Archey, Vic Dickenson (tb) Tyree Glenn (tb, vib) Jimmy Powell, Carl Frye (as) Ernie Powell, Castor McCord (ts) Eddie Heywood (p) Ulysses Livingston (g) Hayes Alvis (b) Henry Morrison (d) Phil Lang (arr)

PLYMOUTH ROCK   arr-PL (12as)   WM-1046-A
78: VOCALION 4984   LP: TAX (SW) M-8004

SAVOY STAMPEDE   (32as) arr, comp   WM-1047-A
78: VOCALION 5112   LP: EPIC LG3127, TAX
(SW) M-8004

MELANCHOLY LULLABY   (16as)+(8as with ensemble)   WM-1048-A
     (8as) arr, comp
78: VOCALION 4984   LP: TAX (SW) M-8004,
TIME-LIFE STL-J10

SCANDAL IN A FLAT   (4+16as) arr, comp   WM-1049-A
78: VOCALION 5112   LP: TAX (SW) M-8004

                              *   *   *

For his new band's first commercial recording session, Carter chose four tunes from his Savoy repertoire and for which there also exist earlier airchecks.

"Savoy Stampede" is the new title for "Gin And Jive," which he recorded in England. "Scandal In A Flat" also premiered in England, but the arrangement differs from the 1936 version, as well as from that used on the three Savoy airchecks.

The Carter band theme, "Melancholy Lullaby," features Carter playing the melody straight (as befits a "signature") as well as Eddie Heywood and Tyree Glenn.

[80]	July 24, 1939 New York Airchecks, Savoy Ballroom
	BENNY CARTER AND HIS ORCHESTRA

Carter (as, tp, cl, arr, comp) for Collective Personnel for the Period See 4/17/39 Dell St. John (v) Phil Lang (arr)

MELANCHOLY LULLABY (incomplete)   (16as)+(8as
     with ensemble)+(8as[interrupted by signoff])
     arr, comp

PLYMOUTH ROCK   arr-PL (12as)

A HOME IN THE CLOUDS v-DSJ (16tp)(8tp)(8tp)
    arr, comp

LADY BE GOOD (16as with ensemble)+(8as)+(8as
    with ensemble) arr

SCANDAL IN A FLAT (16as) arr, comp

I'M IN THE MOOD FOR SWING (32as)(16tp)
    arr, comp

BLUE EVENING v-DSJ (32as) arr

HONEYSUCKLE ROSE (32as)(8cl) arr

BYE BYE BLUES (32tp with ensemble)

MELANCHOLY LULLABY (incomplete) (8as)+(8as
    with ensemble)+(8as[interrupted by signoff])
    arr, comp

---

[81] August 15, 1939 New York
    ETHEL WATERS ACCOM. BY EDDIE MALLORY & HIS
    ORCHESTRA

Carter (as) Eddie Mallory (tp) Tyree Glenn (tb, vib) Castor McCord (cl, ts) Reginald Beane (p) Danny Barker (g) Milt Hinton (b) Ethel Waters (v)

BREAD AND GRAVY v-EW (e)   041552
78: BLUEBIRD B-10415 LP: RCA (F) 741.067

DOWN IN MY SOUL v-EW (e)   041553
78: BLUEBIRD B-11284 LP: RCA (F) 741.067

GEORGIA ON MY MIND v-EW (e)   041554
78: BLUEBIRD B-11028 LP: RCA (F) 741.067

STOP MYSELF FROM WORRYIN' OVER YOU v-EW (e)   041555
78: BLUEBIRD B-11284 LP: RCA (F) 741.067

OLD MAN HARLEM v-EW (e)   041556
78: BLUEBIRD B-11028 LP: RCA (F) 741.067

PUSH OUT v-EW with chorus by the band (28as)   041557
78: BLUEBIRD B-10415 LP: RCA (F) 741.067,
RCA (F) PM42406

---

[82] August 31, 1939 New York
    BENNY CARTER AND HIS ORCHESTRA

Carter (as, cl, arr, comp) Joe Thomas, Lincoln Mills, Eddie Mullens (tp) Jimmy Archey, Vic Dickenson, Tyree Glenn (tb) Jimmy Powell, Carl Frye (as) Ernie Powell, Castor McCord (ts) Eddie Heywood (p) Ulysses Livingston (g) Hayes Alvis (b) Henry Morrison (d) Dell St. John (v)

WHEN LIGHTS ARE LOW v-DSJ (16as with   WM-1069-A

August 31, 1939 [82]

    ensemble)+(8as) arr, comp
78: UNISSUED LP: COLUMBIA CL2162

THE FABLE OF A FOOL (32as)(4as) arr, comp   WM-1070-A
78: VOCALION 5294 LP: TAX (SW) M-8031

RIFF ROMP (16+8as)(8cl) arr, comp   WM-1071-A
78: VOCALION 5294 LP: TAX (SW) M-8031,
TIME-LIFE STL-J10

                  * * *

Carter's second Vocalion session yielded his first U.S. recording of his "When Lights Are Low" for which he provided a lively new arrangement. Oddly enough, judging from the recorded evidence, Carter never played this melody over the air from the Savoy, although there are many airchecks of far less worthy tunes. "I knew lots of song pluggers, of course, and they came to the Savoy regularly. I would play tunes to help a friend and try for a hit, but I should also have done more of what other leaders did, promote my own tunes." "When Lights Are Low" was not helped by this version, however, which was not issued on 78.

"Fable Of A Fool" was mistakenly listed on the original label as "The Favor Of A Fool" and appears that way on subsequent issues and in reference sources.

The final Carter original of the date is an uptempo flag waver "Riff Romp," which effectively juxtaposes brass and reed figures, and includes a trombone choir on the bridge of the third chorus. Another interesting feature of Carter's writing for brass is the difficult but perfectly executed ascending run by the trumpets which caps this performance.

[83]	September 11, 1939 New York
	LIONEL HAMPTON AND HIS ORCHESTRA

Carter (as, arr, comp) Dizzy Gillespie (tp) Coleman Hawkins, Ben Webster, Chu Berry (ts) Clyde Hart (p) Charlie Christian (g) Milt Hinton (b) Cozy Cole (d) Lionel Hampton (vib, v)

WHEN LIGHTS ARE LOW (8as) arr, comp   041406-1
78: VICTOR 26371 LP: RCA (F) 731.048,
SMITHSONIAN COLLECTION OF CLASSIC JAZZ,
BLUEBIRD AXM6-5536, RCA (F) PM42417

WHEN LIGHTS ARE LOW (8as) arr, comp   041406-2
78: UNISSUED LP: BLUEBIRD AXM6-5536,
RCA (F) PM42406, RCA (F) PM42417

ONE SWEET LETTER FROM YOU v-LH (e) arr   041407-1
78: VICTOR 26393 LP: RCA CAMDEN CAL517,
RCA (F) 731.048, BLUEBIRD AXM6-5536, RCA
(F) PM42417

HOT MALLETS (8as)   041408-1
78: VICTOR 26371 LP: RCA LPM2318, RCA
CAMDEN CAL517, RCA (F) 731.048, BLUEBIRD
AXM6-5536, RCA (F) PM42417

EARLY SESSION HOP (8as) arr   041409-1
78: VICTOR 26393   LP: RCA LPV501, RCA
(F) 731.048, BLUEBIRD AXM6-5536, RCA (F)
PM42417, TIME-LIFE STL-J21

> NOTE: On RCA LPM2318 track listed as "When Lights Are Low" is actually "Hot Mallets."

* * *

"When Lights Are Low" finally received its due with this all-star recording, Carter's first with Dizzy Gillespie, and a rare summit meeting of the three leading tenor voices of the day.

The tenor soloist on "When Lights Are Low" is Hawkins. He launches his solo on take 1 with a 4-bar break, whereas take 2 has a brief ensemble introduction. Hampton is even more imaginative on the second take, which was probably rejected because of some audible fluffs by Gillespie in the final ensemble. In his autobiography, Gillespie recalls the date, for which he believes he got the call because the "name" trumpet players were all on the road. "Milt Hinton and Cozy Cole probably told Hamp there's a new trumpet player in Cab's band ... they brought me down to this record date, and talk about giants, man, this was superroyalty ... man, I was so scared ... all them kings were in there, and I was just a young dude." (Gillespie, p. 102.)

The rhythmic accompaniment of "When Lights Are Low" is singled out by André Hodeir as "the apex of the ascending curve that symbolizes the evolution of swing." (Jazz: Its Evolution And Essence, New York, 1961, pp. 215-17.)

(For an analysis and transcription of Carter's solo on "When Lights Are Low" see chapter 3.)

Gillespie, apparently recovered from his bout of nerves, opens "Hot Mallets," with a solo which he, and several other musicians on the date, believe was a departure for him and a harbinger of things to come. Hampton describes it as "the first time I heard be-bop played on a trumpet." (Gillespie, To Be Or Not To Bop, p. 105.) Carter's fluid alto solo occurs on the bridge of Gillespie's chorus.

[84]   September 22, 1939 New York
         ETHEL WATERS ACC. BY EDDIE MALLORY AND HIS
         ORCHESTRA

Carter (as) Eddie Mallory (tp) Garvin Bushell (cl) Reginald Beane (p) Charles Turner (b) Ethel Waters (v)

BABY, WHAT ELSE CAN I DO   v-EW (e)   042717
78: BLUEBIRD B-10517   LP: RCA (F) 741.067

I JUST GOT A LETTER   v-EW (16as)   042718
78: BLUEBIRD B-10517   LP: RCA (F) 741.067,
RCA (F) 42406

[85]   October 9, 1939 New York Airchecks, Savoy Ballroom
         BENNY CARTER AND HIS ORCHESTRA

October 9, 1939 [85]

Carter (as, tp, arr, comp) for Collective Personnel for the Period See 4/17/39 Dell St. John (v)

MELANCHOLY LULLABY   (16as)+(8as with ensemble)+
(8as) arr, comp

SAVOY STAMPEDE   (32as)(16tp [last chorus]) arr, comp

SCANDAL IN A FLAT   (4+16as) arr, comp

RUSSIAN LULLABY   (16as)

THERE'S ONLY ONE IN LOVE   v-DSJ (incomplete) (e)

BYE BYE BLUES (incomplete)   (32tp with ensemble)

[86]   October 14, 1939 New York Airchecks, Savoy Ballroom
BENNY CARTER AND HIS ORCHESTRA

Carter (as, tp, arr, comp) for Collective Personnel for the Period See 4/17/39 Dell St. John (v) Fred Norman (arr) Phil Lang (arr)

MELANCHOLY LULLABY   (16as)+(8as with ensemble)+
(8as) arr, comp

CHINA BOY   probably arr-FN (32as)

IT'S FUNNY TO EVERYONE BUT ME   v-DSJ (16as)

PLYMOUTH ROCK   arr-PL (12as)

I'LL SEE YOU IN MY DREAMS   (32tp)

WHAT'S NEW   v-DSJ (e) arr

STRANGE ENCHANTMENT   (16+8tp)

LAST NIGHT   v-DSJ (e)

RIFF ROMP   (32as) arr, comp

MELANCHOLY LULLABY (incomplete)   (16as)+(8as
with ensemble)+(8as [interrupted by signoff])
arr, comp

[87]   October 23, 1939 New York Airchecks, Savoy Ballroom
BENNY CARTER AND HIS ORCHESTRA

Carter (as, arr) for Collective Personnel for the Period See 4/17/39 Dell St. John (v) Fred Norman (arr)

BLUE ORCHIDS   (32as)(8as with ensemble) arr

CHINA BOY probably arr: FN (32as)

WHAT'S NEW   v-DSJ (e) arr

[88]	October 28, 1939 New York Airchecks, Savoy Ballroom
	BENNY CARTER AND HIS ORCHESTRA

Carter (as, arr) for Collective Personnel for the Period See 4/17/39 Dell
St. John, Roy Felton (v)

LILACS IN THE RAIN   v-DSJ (16as) arr

VAGABOND DREAMS   v-RF (20as) arr

[89]	November 1, 1939 New York
	BENNY CARTER AND HIS ORCHESTRA

Carter (tp, as, arr, comp) Irving Randolph, Lincoln Mills, Joe Thomas, Eddie
Mullens (tp) Jimmy Archey, Vic Dickenson (tb) Tyree Glenn (tb, vib) Jimmy
Powell, Carl Frye (as) Ernie Powell, Sammy Davis (ts) Eddie Heywood (p)
Ulysses Livingston (g) Hayes Alvis (b) Keg Purnell (d) Roy Felton (v)

SHUFFLEBUG SHUFFLE   (16as) arr, comp   WM-1109-
78: VOCALION 5508   LP: TAX (SW) M-8004

VAGABOND DREAMS   v-RF (20as) arr   WM-1110-1
78: VOCALION 5224   LP: TAX (SW) M-8004

LOVE'S GOT ME DOWN AGAIN   v-RF (8as) arr   WM-1111-1
78: VOCALION 5224   LP: TAX (SW) M-8004,
NOSTALGIA BOOK CLUB 1005

MORE THAN YOU KNOW   v-RF (32tp)(8tp+coda) arr   WM-1112-1
78: VOCALION 5508   LP: TAX (SW) M-8004,
TIME-LIFE STL-J10

* * *

"More Than You Know" is one of Carter's most impressive trumpet features, and is a milestone in his stylistic development on that instrument. He hinted at this treatment in an earlier aircheck version (April 17, 1939). "More Than You Know" can be viewed as exemplifying the second of three stages in his trumpet playing. The earliest, best demonstrated by "Once Upon A Time" (October 10, 1933), was a more direct approach, very much in the Armstrong mold. In "More Than You Know" the phrasing is more ornate, containing intricate filigrees and multinoted runs. He treats the chord changes differently as well, assimilating them with subtle arpeggio figures rather than attacking them head on.

The solo is in two parts, separated by Roy Felton's vocal. The first chorus again shows Carter's ability to achieve a full tone even at low volume, a skill he credits to the early technical advice of Doc Cheatham. His range has become even more commanding than two or three years before, as shown by the climb to high F to end the piece.

His tone retains its characteristic delicate vibrato; this tone would change over the next five years before the recording of the third of the Carter trumpet display pieces, "I Surrender Dear" (May 21, 1944).

[90]	December 14, 1939 New York
	VARSITY SEVEN

December 14, 1939 [90]

Carter (tp, as) Danny Polo (cl) Coleman Hawkins (ts) Joe Sullivan (p) Ulysses Livingston (g, v) Artie Bernstein (b) George Wettling (d) Jeanne Burns (v)

IT'S TIGHT LIKE THAT   v-JB (24tp with ensemble)   US-1158-1
78: VARSITY 8147   LP: STORYVILLE SLP703,
PHOENIX LP3

EASY RIDER   v-JB, UL (8tp with ensemble)   US-1159-1
78: VARSITY 8147   LP: STORYVILLE SLP703,
PHOENIX LP3

SCRATCH MY BACK   (24as)   US-1160-1
78: VARSITY 8135   LP: STORYVILLE SLP703,
PHOENIX LP3, TIME-LIFE STL-J06

SAVE IT, PRETTY MAMA   v-JB (16tp)(4tp with   US-1161-1
  ensemble)+(4tp with ensemble)
78: VARIETY 8135   LP: STORYVILLE SLP703,
PHOENIX LP3

---

[91]   December 21, 1939   New York
        LIONEL HAMPTON AND HIS ORCHESTRA

Carter (tp) Edmond Hall (cl) Coleman Hawkins (ts) Joe Sullivan (p) Freddie Green (g) Artie Bernstein (b) Zutty Singleton (d) Lionel Hampton (vib)

DINAH   (32tp)   046024-1
78: VICTOR 26557   LP: RCA LPM2318, RCA
(F) 731.048, BLUEBIRD AXM6-5536, RCA (F)
PM42417, TIME-LIFE STL-J06

DINAH   (32tp)   046024-2
78: UNISSUED   LP: RCA LPV501, RCA (F)
741.077, BLUEBIRD AXM6-5536, RCA (F) PM42417

MY BUDDY   (e)   046025-1
78: VICTOR 22608   LP: RCA (F) 731.048,
BLUEBIRD AXM6-5536, RCA (F) PM42417

SINGIN' THE BLUES   (8tp with ensemble)   046026-1
78: VICTOR 26557   LP: RCA (F) 741.049,
BLUEBIRD AXM6-5536, RCA (F) PM42417

---

[92]   January 3, 1940   New York
        COLEMAN HAWKINS' ALL STAR OCTET

Carter (tp) J. C. Higginbotham (tb) Danny Polo (cl) Coleman Hawkins (ts) Gene Rodgers (p) Lawrence Lucie (g) Johnny Williams (b) Walter Johnson (d)

WHEN DAY IS DONE   (16tp)(8tp with ensemble)   046156-1
78: BLUEBIRD B-10693   LP: RCA (F) 730.625,
TIME-LIFE STL-J06

THE SHEIK OF ARABY   (32tp)(8tp with ensemble)   046157-1

78: BLUEBIRD B-10770 LP: RCA LPV501,
RCA (F) 730.625, QUINTESSENCE JAZZ SERIES
QJ25131, TIME-LIFE STL-J06

MY BLUE HEAVEN   (32tp)(8tp with ensemble)   046158-1
78: BLUEBIRD B-10770   LP: RCA LPM1393,
RCA (F) 730.625

BOUNCING WITH BEAN   (32tp)(16tp with ensemble)   046159-1
78: BLUEBIRD B-10693   LP: RCA (F) 730.625,
TIME-LIFE STL-J06

---

[93]   January 15, 1940   New York
        VARSITY SEVEN

Carter (tp, comp) Danny Polo (cl) Coleman Hawkins (ts) Joe Sullivan (p)
Ulysses Livingston (g) Artie Shapiro (b) George Wettling (d) Joe Turner (v)

HOW LONG, HOW LONG BLUES v-JT (8tp)   US-1284-1
    (8tp with ensemble)
78: VARSITY 8173   LP: STORYVILLE SLP703,
PHOENIX LP3

SHAKE IT AND BREAK IT v-JT (16tp)(16tp with   US-1285-1
    ensemble)
78: VARSITY 8179   LP: STORYVILLE SLP703,
PHOENIX LP3

A PRETTY GIRL IS LIKE A MELODY   (16tp with   US-1286-1
    ensemble)(16tp)+(16tp with ensemble)
78: VARSITY 8179   LP: STORYVILLE SLP703,
PHOENIX LP3

POM POM   (16tp) comp   US-1287-1
78: VARSITY 8173   LP: STORYVILLE SLP703,
PHOENIX LP3

---

[94]   January 30, 1940   New York
        BENNY CARTER AND HIS ORCHESTRA

Carter (tp, as, arr, comp) Russell Smith, Lincoln Mills, Joe Thomas (tp)
Jimmy Archey, Vic Dickenson, Gene Simon (tb) Jimmy Powell, Carl Frye
(as) Stanley Payne, Coleman Hawkins (ts) Eddie Heywood (p) Ulysses Livingston (g) Hayes Alvis (b) Keg Purnell (d) Roy Felton (v)

SLEEP   (24as) arr   M-1126-1
78: VOCALION 5399   LP: COLUMBIA KG32945,
CBS (E) 88134, TAX (SW) M-8004, TIME-LIFE
STL-J10

AMONG MY SOUVENIRS v-RF (32as)(17tp) arr   M-1127-1
78: VOCALION 5458   LP: TAX (SW) M-8004

FISH FRY   (32tp) arr, comp   M-1128-1
78: VOCALION 5458   LP: TAX (SW) M-8004,
TIME-LIFE STL-J10

January 30, 1940 [94]

SLOW FREIGHT (8tp)(16+8tp)(8tp)[tp on bridge M-1129-1
    of 3rd chorus is Joe Thomas] arr
78: VOCALION 5399 LP: TAX (SW) M-8004,
TIME-LIFE STL-J10

    NOTE: Alternate takes are known to exist of these titles.

                    *   *   *

The Carter band was given a boost on its next Vocalion date by the presence of Coleman Hawkins.

   The first tune, "Sleep," is the highlight of the session. Carter takes Fred Waring's theme song, originally a waltz, and turns it into an uptempo swinger. The arrangement is distinguished by Carter's imaginative use of complementary riffs to introduce and back each soloist. After Hawkins's driving solo, muted brass back Heywood, swelling reeds, Thomas, and a new brass figure appears behind Carter's own solo. The last chorus includes a brief trombone choir passage and some exciting drumming by Keg Purnell, who added some punch to the Carter rhythm section. Carter remembers arranging "Sleep" specifically for this session. Because of the blistering tempo, he remarks, "Had we been able to play it every night for a week or so before, it would have felt more comfortable, not just for the soloist but for those playing parts."

   Carter's original "Fish Fry" remained in his band's book for the next six years. On this first recording, Hawkins contributes a rough-edged solo. Carter's full chorus of muted trumpet contains two fluffs, one just before the bridge and one on it. These imperfections do not seem to faze him as he delivers a solo which is both heated and relaxed.

   One in a long tradition of railroad songs in jazz, "Slow Freight" was originally composed and arranged by Buck Ram, but Down Beat reported that "since most of the swing records followed Carter's interpretation he was delegated to revise the stock." (September 1, 1940, p. 18) One of Carter's added touches was the electric guitar simulating a train whistle. Carter plays the soulful muted trumpet which opens and closes the piece as well as the muted solos before and after Hawkins's bridge on the second chorus. The open trumpet solo on the bridge of the third chorus is by Joe Thomas.

[95]   February 2, 1940   New York
        THE QUINTONES

Carter (as) The Quintones (v) Joe Thomas (tp) Coleman Hawkins (ts) Eddie Heywood (p) Hayes Alvis (b) Keg Purnell (d) Buck Ram (dir)

HONEY BUNNY BOO v-Q (e)   WM-1130-A
78: VOCALION 5596

THE FIVE LITTLE QUINTS v-Q (e)   WM-1131-A
78: VOCALION 5409

HARMONY IN HARLEM v-Q (e)   WM-1132-A
78: VOCALION 5596

MIDNIGHT JAMBOREE v-Q (e)   WM-1133-A
78: VOCALION 5409

NOTE: This personnel is listed by Rust as probable; the presence of Hawkins has been questioned, and the lack of any alto solos makes confirmation of Carter's participation impossible.

---

[96]   February 7, 1940   New York
METRONOME ALL-STAR BAND

Carter (as) Charlie Spivak, Harry James, Ziggy Elman (tp) Jack Teagarden, Jack Jenney (tb) Benny Goodman (cl) Toots Mondello (as) Eddie Miller, Charlie Barnet (ts) Jess Stacy (p) Charlie Christian (g) Bob Haggart (b) Gene Krupa (d) Fletcher Henderson (arr)

KING PORTER STOMP (e)	26489-A

78: COLUMBIA 35389   LP: COLUMBIA CL2528, HARMONY HL7044, QUEEN-DISC Q009, SONY (J) SONP50419

KING PORTER STOMP (e)	26489-B

LP: PHONTASTIC NOST7610

---

[97]   Same Session
METRONOME ALL-STAR NINE

Carter (as) Harry James (tp) Jack Teagarden (tb) Benny Goodman (cl) Eddie Miller (ts) Jess Stacy (p) Charlie Christian (g) Bob Haggart (b) Gene Krupa (d)

ALL STAR STRUT (12as)	26490-A

78: COLUMBIA 35389   LP: COLUMBIA CL2528, HARMONY HL7044, COLUMBIA G30779, QUEEN-DISC Q009, SONY (J) SONP50419

ALL STAR STRUT	26490-B

78: UNISSUED   LP: SONY (J) SONP50419

---

[98]   February 14, 1940   New York
FREDDIE RICH AND HIS ORCHESTRA

Carter (as, arr) Nat Natoli, Red Solomon, Roy Eldridge (tp) Larry Altpeter (tb) Sid Stoneburn, Sid Perlmutter (cl, as) Babe Russin, Frank Chase, Stafford Simon (ts) Clyde Hart (p) Ken Binford (g) Hayes Alvis (b) Johnny Williams (d) Rosemary Calvin (v)

TILL WE MEET AGAIN (8as) arr	26514-A

78: VOCALION 5507

A HOUSE WITH A LITTLE RED BARN v-RC	26515-A

(e) arr
78: VOCALION 5420

I'M FOREVER BLOWING BUBBLES (32as) arr	26516-

78: VOCALION 5507

HOW HIGH THE MOON v-RC (8as)	26517-

78: VOCALION 5420

[99]	May 5, 1940 New York Airchecks, NBC's 'Chamber Music Society of Lower Basin St.' CARTER WITH THE CHAMBER MUSIC SOCIETY OF LOWER BASIN ST.

Carter (as, tp) Henry Levine (tp) Jack Epstein (tb) Alfie Evans (cl) Rudolph Adler (ts) Tony Colucci (g) Henry Patent (b) Nat Levine (d) Franklyn Marks (arr)

HONEYSUCKLE ROSE (2as break+32+32+18
      with ensemble)
LP: JOKER (I) SM3115, SAGA (E) 6927, KINGS OF JAZZ (I) KLJ20027, HOT 'N SWEET (F) HOL6426

STAR DUST (4tp intro+32+32+coda)
LP: JOKER (I) SM3115, SAGA (E) 6927, HOT 'N SWEET (F) HOL6426

    NOTE: Personnel from Hot 'N Sweet LP; Carter recalled arranger.

[100]	May 20, 1940 New York BENNY CARTER AND HIS ORCHESTRA

Carter (as, cl, arr, comp) Bill Coleman, Shad Collins, Russell Smith (tp) Sandy Williams, Milton Robinson (tb) Carl Frye, George Dorsey (as) Stafford Simon, Sammy Davis (ts) Sonny White (p) Ulysses Livingston (g) Hayes Alvis (b) Keg Purnell (d)

NIGHT HOP (16as with ensemble)+(8as)   67781-A
      arr, comp
78: DECCA 3294 LP: DECCA DL79242, MCA 1323

POM POM (8cl)(8cl) arr, comp   67782-A
78: DECCA 3262 LP: DECCA DL79242, MCA (F) 510.178-180, MCA 1323

O.K. FOR BABY (16as) arr, comp   67783-A
78: DECCA 3294 LP: BRUNSWICK (F) 87.505, DECCA DL79242, MCA (F) 510.178-180, TIME-LIFE STL-J10, MCA 1323

SERENADE TO A SARONG (8+8as) arr, comp   67784-A
78: DECCA 3262 LP: DECCA DL79242, MCA 1323

                              * * *

The Carter orchestra's first sides for Decca are among the best recorded representations of the band of the period. Several important personnel changes have taken place. Shad Collins and Bill Coleman, both of whom had played in Carter's 1933 orchestra, are in the trumpet section and Sammy Davis has replaced Ernie Powell as principal tenor soloist. Perhaps most significant is the addition on piano of Sonny White, formerly Billie Holiday's accompanist. White was to remain with Carter, with a few interruptions, until 1946.

    Leonard Feather reported in the Melody Maker (June 1940) that "Carter went into the studio not knowing what numbers he was going to do, which resulted in the usual clambake with the supervisor. Finally they picked out four Carter originals which all came out very well."

In spite of the apparent informality of the session, this latest edition of the Carter orchestra sounds even tighter and better drilled than the Savoy band of the previous year.

"Night Hop" and "O.K. For Baby" are relaxed swingers. The latter is notable for the excellent balance between the reeds and the brass, and the dynamic shadings in the sections.

"Pom Pom" is a big-band version of the Carter tune previously recorded by smaller ensembles including the Varsity Seven and Joe Sullivan's Cafe Society Orchestra. Carter's very personal clarinet tone is well captured.

"Serenade To A Sarong" is an impressionistic mood piece with an "Oriental" flavor, with brief contributions by Carter's alto and Sandy Williams's growling trombone.

This session is yet another example of Carter's reluctance to promote his own music. He never again recorded, or possibly even played, these four excellent pieces. "O.K. For Baby" did, however, become part of the Jimmie Lunceford band's book in an arrangement by Lonnie Wilfong and was also recorded by Les Brown among others. "Pom Pom" was revived six years later by Eddie Heywood, who recorded it with a small group.

This was guitarist Ulysses Livingston's last session as a regular member of the Carter orchestra. Livingston combined music with a career as a quality control engineer for Hughes Aircraft, which included work on the NASA "Survivor" program. He remains close friends with Carter and remembers the thrill of playing Carter's music: "His arrangements were enlightening; a revelation. He was the first to include flatted fifths, augmented ninths and other features that became popular later. We used to eagerly put in extra rehearsal time to get things to sound the way he wanted." Livingston also recalls the circumstances of his leaving the band: "No one ever wanted to leave Benny. In 1940, during a period when the band wasn't working too regularly, I got an offer from the Gale agency to join Ella Fitzgerald. When Benny found out about it he said, 'Ulysses, it's a great opportunity--you've got to take it.' I said, 'No way, I'm not leaving.' So Benny told me, 'In that case, you're fired!' So I had to go, but that was the only way I would have left Benny Carter."

[101]	May 25, 1940 New York
	THE CHOCOLATE DANDIES

Carter (as, p) Roy Eldridge (tp) Coleman Hawkins (ts) Bernard Addison (g) John Kirby (b) Sid Catlett (d)

SMACK (64as)(8as)   R2995
78: COMMODORE 533 LP: MAINSTREAM
56037, ATLANTIC SD2-306, COMMODORE
XFL14936, LONDON 6.24056, TIME-LIFE
STL-J10

SMACK (64as)(8as)   R2995-4

May 25, 1940 [101]

78: UNISSUED LP: ATLANTIC SD2-306,
COMMODORE XFL14936, LONDON 6.24056

I SURRENDER DEAR (4p intro+piano acc) R2996
78: COMMODORE 1506 LP: MAINSTREAM
56037, ATLANTIC SD2-306, COMMODORE
XFL14936, LONDON 6.24056

I SURRENDER DEAR (4p intro+piano acc) R2996-
78: UNISSUED LP: ATLANTIC SD2-306,
COMMODORE XFL14936, LONDON 6.24056

I CAN'T BELIEVE THAT YOU'RE IN LOVE WITH R2997
ME (64as)
78: COMMODORE 1506 LP: MAINSTREAM 56037,
MAINSTREAM 56017, ATLANTIC SD2-306, COM-
MODORE XFL14936, LONDON 6.24056, SMITH-
SONIAN COLLECTION OF CLASSIC JAZZ

I CAN'T BELIEVE THAT YOU'RE IN LOVE WITH R2997-1
ME (32as)
78: UNISSUED LP: COMMODORE XFL14936,
LONDON 6.24056

NOTES: Second version of "I Surrender Dear" is a composite of
alternate takes (possibly 1 and 2). Smithsonian LP contains only
excerpt of R2997.

* * *

Carter's only appearance on the Commodore label was another Leonard
Feather production. Milt Gabler, the founder of the label, recalls that
"you never saw him [Carter] on 52nd Street blowing, sitting in. He was
always too busy with his big bands or writing and arranging." (Giants of
Jazz, p. 47.)

Feather's intent was to bring together some of the illustrious Fletcher Henderson alumni and, since Henderson himself was unable to be present,
it was decided to go without a piano.

These were Carter's first small-group recordings with Roy Eldridge, who has always maintained that his own style derived as much from
the influence of saxophonists Carter and Hawkins in particular, as from
trumpeters.

The first tune was dedicated to Fletcher Henderson whose nickname
was "Smack." It is unusual for that time--an improvised performance from
the beginning, based on chord changes sketched out by Feather. Carter's
opening two choruses follow the same general pattern in both takes. His
playing is more rhythmic than usual, as he builds excitement by hitting the
beat head on. There is a pronounced difference, however, between the 8-
bar bridges played by Carter after Hawkins's solo chorus in the two takes.
In the first version, Carter's return is a dramatic departure from the hot
choruses preceding it. He plays a descending melodic figure with a detached coolness, which foreshadows later styles. In the alternate take,
Carter's first two measures hint at a similar approach but he then takes a
different direction.

"I Surrender Dear" is a ballad feature for Hawkins and Eldridge, with Carter providing a piano introduction and accompaniment.

In his remarkable solo on "I Can't Believe" (issued take) Carter elaborates upon the prescient ideas suggested in "Smack." Beginning with the last eight measures of his first solo chorus, Carter seems to discard the chord changes, melody line, and even the AABA 32-bar song structure itself. He plays a 16-bar melodic statement which begins with a descending figure similar to that present on his bridge in "Smack" (issued version) and carries it over into his second chorus. In the 9th measure of that chorus he introduces yet another repeated descending figure which carries through the transition to the bridge. Here he adds to the startling effect by deliberately falling behind the beat. He recovers in the middle of the bridge and finishes the chorus in more conventional fashion.

The recently discovered alternate take of "I Can't Believe" is completely different, with the tempo almost half that of the issued version.

---

[102]   June 1940   New York
         BUSTER BAILEY AND HIS SEXTET

Carter (as) Charlie Shavers (tp) Buster Bailey (cl) Billy Kyle (p) John Kirby (b) Zutty Singleton (d) Judy Ellington (v)

SEEMS LIKE A MONTH OF SUNDAYS v-JE (e)	US-1841-1

78: VARSITY 8358   LP: RARITIES 17, STORYVILLE SLP701, SAVOY SJL2246

FABLE OF A ROSE v-JE (4as)(4as)	US-1842-1

78: VARSITY 8358   LP: RARITIES 17, STORYVILLE SLP701, SAVOY SJL2246

PINETOP'S BOOGIE WOOGIE (12+12as)	US-1843-1

78: VARSITY 8365   LP: RARITIES 17, STORYVILLE SLP701, SMITHSONIAN P2-14584, STORYVILLE (G) 6.28474, SAVOY SJL2246

ECCENTRIC RAG (16as)	US-1844-1

78: VARSITY 8365   LP: RARITIES 17, STORYVILLE SLP701, SMITHSONIAN P2-14584, SAVOY SJL2246

* * *

This personnel is essentially the John Kirby sextet with Carter and Singleton substituting for Russell Procope and O'Neil Spencer. Although the arrangements are less structured than the sextet's usual recordings, the session naturally has a Kirby-like feel.

---

[103]   October 15, 1940   New York
         BILLIE HOLIDAY ACC. BY BENNY CARTER AND
         HIS ALL STAR ORCHESTRA

Carter (as, cl, arr) Bill Coleman (tp) Benny Morton (tb) Georgie Auld (ts) Sonny White (p) Ulysses Livingston (g) Wilson Myers (b) Yank Porter (d) Billie Holiday (v)

ST. LOUIS BLUES v-BH (12cl acc)(12cl) arr   28874-1
78: OKEH 6064, COLUMBIA 30229 LP: SONY
(J) SOPH69

ST. LOUIS BLUES v-BH (12cl acc)(12cl) arr   28874-2
78: OKEH 6064   LP: COLUMBIA CL2428,
COLUMBIA KG32127, COLUMBIA CG30782,
SONY (J) SOPH69

LOVELESS LOVE v-BH (e) arr   28875-1
78: OKEH 6064, COLUMBIA 30229 LP: SONY
(J) SOPH69

LOVELESS LOVE (e) arr   28875-2
78: UNISSUED   LP: COLUMBIA CG30782

NOTE: Both takes of "St. Louis Blues" appear on various copies
of Okeh 6064. One take of each title on Two Flat Disc 5007.

[104]	October 15, 1940 New York
	BENNY CARTER AND HIS ALL STAR ORCHESTRA

Carter (cl) Bill Coleman (tp) Benny Morton (tb) Georgie Auld (ts) Sonny
White (p) Ulysses Livingston (g) Wilson Myers (b) Yank Porter (d) Joe
Turner (v)

JOE TURNER BLUES v-JT (12cl acc)   28876-1
78: OKEH 6001

JOE TURNER BLUES v-JT (12cl acc)   28876-2
78: UNISSUED LP: MERITT 10

BEALE STREET BLUES v-JT (e)   28877-1
78: OKEH 6001

BEALE STREET BLUES v-JT (e)   28877-2
78: UNISSUED LP: MERITT 10

                        *   *   *

[103, 104] Carter's role here was to provide accompaniment for two great
jazz vocalists, Billie Holiday and Joe Turner. His playing is confined to
the tasteful clarinet obbligatos and one solo clarinet chorus on "St. Louis
Blues."

[105]	October 23, 1940 New York
	BENNY CARTER AND HIS ORCHESTRA

Carter (as, arr) Russell Smith, Jonah Jones, Bobby Williams (tp) Milton
Robinson, Madison Vaughan (tb) Chauncey Haughton (as) George James (as,
bs) George Irish, Stafford Simon (ts) Sonny White (p) Everett Barksdale (g)
Hayes Alvis (p) Keg Purnell (d) Roy Felton, The Mills Brothers (v)

BY THE WATERMELON VINE, LINDY LOU v-RF, MB   68284-A
       (16as) arr
78: DECCA 3545 LP: MCA CORAL 62100

THE LAST KISS YOU GAVE ME v-RF (8as) arr   68285-A
78: DECCA 3588

BOOGIE WOOGIE SUGAR BLUES (18as)(4+2as) arr   68286-A
78: DECCA 3588

I'VE BEEN IN LOVE BEFORE v-RF (16as) arr   68287-A
78: DECCA 3545

* * *

This session, his second for Decca, ended in a dispute which led Carter to break with that label. At his first Decca session (May 20, 1940) Carter had enjoyed a free rein in choice of material: four excellent big-band sides resulted. But by this date, some five months later, the company had formed definite ideas about how the band was to sound and what it should play. Vocals were given high priority, with three of the four tunes featuring Roy Felton. The Mills Brothers were brought in for one sentimental ballad dating back to 1914. The final straw, however, was the single instrumental number, a boogie-woogie interpretation of Clyde McCoy's "Sugar Blues," complete with laughing saxophone and trumpet. "Someone at the studio had the idea that this would make the band more commercially successful," Carter recalls. "I went along at first, but the results were just not what I wanted my orchestra to sound like." Carter failed in an attempt to prevent the record's release. Less than a month later he signed with Bluebird.

[106]   November 13, 1940 New York
        UNA MAE CARLISLE AND HER JAM BAND

Carter (tp) Everett Barksdale (g) Slam Stewart (b) Zutty Singleton (d) Una Mae Carlisle (p, v)

WALKIN' BY THE RIVER v-UMC (4tp intro)(32tp)   057641-1
78: BLUEBIRD B-11033 LP: RCA (F) FXM1-7124,
RCA (F) PM42406

[107]   November 19, 1940 New York
        BENNY CARTER AND HIS ORCHESTRA

Carter (cl, as, arr, comp) Russell Smith, Sidney De Paris, Bobby Williams (tp) Milton Robinson, Madison Vaughan, Benny Morton (tb) Chauncey Haughton (as) George James (as, bs) George Irish, Stafford Simon (ts) Sonny White (p) Everett Barksdale (g) Hayes Alvis (b) Keg Purnell (d) Roy Felton (v)

ALL OF ME (14cl) arr   057656-1
78: BLUEBIRD B-10962 LP: RCA (F) 430.686,
RCA (F) 741.073, RCA (J) RA-57, TIME-LIFE
STL-J10, RCA (F) PM42406, RCA (F) PM43259

THE VERY THOUGHT OF YOU v-RF (16as) arr   057657-1
78: BLUEBIRD B-10962 LP: RCA (F) 430.686,
RCA (F) 741.073, RCA (F) PM42406

COCKTAILS FOR TWO (32as)(10as) arr   057658-1
78: BLUEBIRD B-10998 45: HMV (F) 7EMF26

November 19, 1940 [107]   101

LP: RCA (F) 430.686, RCA (F) 741.073, RCA
(J) RA-57, RCA (F) PM42406

TAKIN' MY TIME (32as) arr, comp   057659-1
78: BLUEBIRD B-10998 LP: RCA (F) 430.686,
RCA (F) 741.073, RCA (F) PM42406

                              *   *   *

This was the first of four sessions by Carter for RCA's Bluebird label
over a one-year period. Aside from the personnel changes, the date is
significant because of a shift to the two-alto, two-tenor, one-baritone reed
section which was rapidly becoming the big band standard. The first tune,
"All Of Me," takes full advantage of the added depth of the baritone with a
typically supple sax section chorus, an expanded version of the one Carter
had recorded four years earlier with the Willie Lewis band in Paris.
Carter's burnished, rounded clarinet tone is almost in the New Orleans
tradition.

     The standards, "The Very Thought Of You" and "Cocktails For Two,"
both have Carter alto solos which elegantly paraphrase the melodies.

[108]	January 16, 1941 New York
	METRONOME ALL STAR BAND

Carter (as) Harry James, Ziggy Elman, Cootie Williams (tp) Tommy Dorsey, J. C. Higginbotham (tp) Benny Goodman (cl) Toots Mondello (as) Coleman Hawkins, Tex Beneke (ts) Count Basie (p) Charlie Christian (g) Artie
Bernstein (b) Buddy Rich (d)

BUGLE CALL RAG (e)   060331-1
78: VICTOR 27314 LP: RCA (F) 731.089,
RCA (F) PM42046

ONE O'CLOCK JUMP (12as)   060332-1
78: VICTOR 27314 LP: RCA (F) 731.089,
RCA (F) PM42046

[109]	January 21, 1941 New York
	BENNY CARTER AND HIS ORCHESTRA

Carter (as, arr, comp) Russell Smith, Sidney De Paris, Jonah Jones (tp)
Vic Dickenson, Jimmy Archey, Joe Britton (tb) George Dorsey, Bill White
(as) George Irish, Fred Mitchell (ts) Sonny White (p) Herb Thomas (g) Ted
Sturgis (b) J. C. Heard (d) Roy Felton (v)

CUDDLE UP, HUDDLE UP (16as) arr, comp   060351-1
78: BLUEBIRD B-11197 LP: RCA (F) 430.686,
RCA (F) 741.073, RCA (F) PM42406

EV'RY GOODBYE AIN'T GONE arr, comp   060352-1
78: UNISSUED

BABALU (intro+16as) arr   060353-1
78: BLUEBIRD B-11090 LP: RCA (F) 430.686,
RCA (F) 741.073, RCA (F) PM42406, RCA (J) RA-57

THERE I'VE SAID IT AGAIN v-RF (8as) arr   060354-1
78: BLUEBIRD B-11090 LP: RCA (F) 430.686,
RCA (F) 741.073, RCA (F) PM42406

* * *

"Cuddle Up" is reminiscent of "O.K. For Baby" (May 20, 1940) with all sections beautifully integrated. The arrangement features declamatory brass, a rich 16-measure reed passage, and a brief trombone choir.

[109A]   March 22, 1941 Cedar Grove, N.J. Airchecks, CBS
                Broadcast "Matinee at the Meadowbrook"
          BENNY CARTER WITH THE GENE KRUPA ORCHESTRA

Includes Carter (as, arr) Gene Krupa (d)

THERE'LL BE SOME CHANGES MADE   (36+20as)

ROCKIN' CHAIR   (intro+32+28+coda tp) arr

[110]   April 1, 1941 New York
         BENNY CARTER AND HIS ORCHESTRA

Carter (tp, as, arr, comp) Doc Cheatham, Lincoln Mills, Sidney De Paris (tp) Vic Dickenson, Jimmy Archey, Joe Britton (tb) Ernie Purce, Eddie Barefield (as) Fred Williams, Ernie Powell (ts) Sonny White (p) Herb Thomas (g) Charles Drayton (b) Al Taylor (d) Maxine Sullivan (v)

MIDNIGHT   v-MS (16as) arr   063700-1
78: BLUEBIRD B-11288 LP: RCA (F) 430.686,
RCA (F) 741.073, RCA (F) PM42406

MY FAVORITE BLUES   (24tp) arr, comp   063701-1
78: BLUEBIRD B-11288 LP: RCA LEJ-2, RCA
(F) 430.686, RCA (F) 741.073, RCA (F) PM42406,
RCA (J) RA-57

LULLABY TO A DREAM   (32tp)(2tp) arr, comp   063702-2
78: UNISSUED LP: RCA (F) 741.073, RCA (F)
PM42406, RCA (J) RA-57

WHAT A DIFFERENCE A DAY MADE   v-MS (e) arr   063703-1
78: BLUEBIRD B-11197 LP: RCA (F) 430.686,
RCA (F) 741.073, RCA (F) PM42406

* * *

For his third Bluebird date, Carter drew on the talents of Maxine Sullivan (who was soon to tour with the orchestra). Some veterans of Carter's various orchestras have returned, including trumpeters Doc Cheatham and Lincoln Mills, and tenorman Ernie Powell.

Carter plays trumpet for the two originals. The medium-fast "My Favorite Blues" opens with Carter's muted solo followed by Vic Dickenson. A brief reed passage leads into Sonny White's piano and Ernie Powell's tenor spot.

April 1, 1941 [110]

Carter plays his lovely piece "Lullaby To A Dream" on open horn, with Eddie Barefield taking the lead alto part.

[111]   June 26, 1941   New York
           ARTIE SHAW AND HIS ORCHESTRA

Carter (as) Henry Allen (tp) J. C. Higginbotham (tb) Artie Shaw (cl, arr) Sonny White (p) Jimmy Shirley (g) Billy Taylor (b) Shep Shepherd (d) Laura Newell (harp) 12 violins, violas and violincellos, Lena Horne (v)

CONFESSIN' (16+8as [trades with Higginbotham])   066146-1
78: UNISSUED LP: CAMDEN CAL584, RCA
VPM6062, RCA (F) FXM1-7336, BLUEBIRD
AXM2-5576

LOVE ME A LITTLE LITTLE v-LH (8+8as)   066147-1
78: VICTOR 27509 LP: RCA LPM1570, RCA
(F) FXM1-7336, BLUEBIRD AXM2-5576

BEYOND THE BLUE HORIZON   066148-1
78: UNISSUED LP: BLUEBIRD AXM2-5576

DON'T TAKE YOUR LOVE FROM ME v-LH (e)   066149-1
78: VICTOR 27509 LP: RCA VPM6039, RCA
(F) FXM1-7336, RCA (J) RA-5445/6, BLUEBIRD
AXM2-5576

                          *   *   *

Carter's only appearance on record with Artie Shaw came at a time when Shaw was experimenting with strings. Here he added some top jazz solo talents.

In the liner notes to French RCA FXM1-7336, Jean-Pierre Daubresse attributes the arrangements from this session to Carter. Mr. Shaw, however, has verified that he, Shaw, was actually the arranger (letter dated 5/31/77).

[112]   October 16, 1941   New York
           BENNY CARTER AND HIS ORCHESTRA

Carter (as, arr, comp) Nathaniel Williams, Emmett Berry, Rostelle Reese (tp) Jimmy Archey, Benny Morton, John McConnell (tb) Ernie Purce, George James (as) Ernie Powell, Al Gibson (ts) Sonny White (p) Willie Lewis (g) Charles Drayton (b) Shep Shepherd (d)

SUNDAY (8+32as) arr   066792-1
78: BLUEBIRD B-11341 45: HMV (F) 7EMF26
LP: RCA (F) 430.686, RCA (F) 741.073, RCA
(J) RA-57, RCA (F) PM42406, TIME-LIFE STL-
J10, RCA (F) PM43259

ILL WIND (20as)(14as) arr   066793-2
78: UNISSUED LP: RCA (J) RA-5335, RCA (F)
741.073, RCA (J) RA-57, RCA (F) PM42406, TIME-
LIFE STL-J10

BACK BAY BOOGIE (24as) arr, comp   066794-1
78: BLUEBIRD B-11341 LP: RCA (F) 430.686,
RCA (F) 741.073, RCA (J) RA-57, RCA (F)
PM42406, TIME-LIFE STL-J10

TREE OF HOPE (2as break)(8as) arr, comp   066795-1
78: UNISSUED LP: RCA (F) 741.073, RCA
(F) PM42406

* * *

Carter's last Bluebird date was strictly instrumental. "Sunday" has an excellent Carter alto solo, in which he cleverly alternates melody with playing on the changes.

His alto really sings the melody of "Ill Wind," allowing each note to ripen before moving on. The arrangement uses an interesting sequence of ensemble voicings. A rich reed passage leads to an unexpected and effective moment of silence, before a more forceful swinging bridge is carried by the brass.

"Back Bay Boogie" is based on a riff Carter used to play with his sextet at the Ritz Carlton Hotel in Boston--hence the title. The arrangement is a showstopper and Carter used it often in situations calling for the frantic uptempos that came into vogue during World War II. The boogie motif is supplied by pianist White. In subsequent air checks and transcriptions of this piece Carter adhered closely to the pattern of his forceful solo here.

[113]   December 31, 1941 New York
         METRONOME ALL STAR BAND

Carter (as) Harry James, Cootie Williams, Roy Eldridge (tp) J. C. Higginbotham, Lou McGarity (tb) Benny Goodman (cl) Toots Mondello (as) Vido Musso, Tex Beneke (ts) Count Basie (p) Freddie Green (g) Doc Goldberg (b) Gene Krupa (d)

ROYAL FLUSH (8as [2nd solo])   32079-1
78: COLUMBIA 36499 LP: SONY (J)
SONP50419

ROYAL FLUSH (8as [2nd solo])   32079-2
78: UNISSUED LP: COLUMBIA CL2528, HARMONY HL7044, QUEEN-DISC Q009, SONY (J)
SONP50419

DEAR OLD SOUTHLAND (16as)   32080-1
78: UNISSUED LP: HARMONY HL7044,
QUEEN-DISC Q009, SONY (J) SONP50419

[114]   January 16, 1942 New York
         METRONOME ALL STAR LEADERS

Carter (as) Cootie Williams (tp) J. C. Higginbotham (tb) Benny Goodman (cl) Charlie Barnet (ts) Count Basie (p) Alvino Rey (g) John Kirby (b) Gene Krupa (d)

January 16, 1942 [114]   105

I GOT RHYTHM (16+8as)   32261-1
78: COLUMBIA C-601 LP: COLUMBIA
CL2528, HARMONY HL7044, QUEEN-DISC
Q009, SONY (J) SONP50419

I GOT RHYTHM (16+8as)   32261-2
78: COLUMBIA 36499 LP: SONY (J) SONP50419

I GOT RHYTHM (16+8as)   32261-3
78: UNISSUED LP: SONY (J) SONP50419,
TAX (SW) M-8039

[115]	February 9, 1942 New York
	MARK WARNOW AND HIS ORCHESTRA

Carter (cl, as, arr) Russ Case, Ivor Lloyd, Nat Natoli (tp) Cliff Heather, Larry Altpeter (tb) Sid Trucker, Ezell Watson, Bernie Ladd, Reggie Merrill, Babe Russin (reeds) Arnold Fidus, Bernard Ocke, Max Pilzer, Jules Sherter, Max Silverman, Waldo Mayo, M. Polikoff, Leo Kahn (violin) Bernie Lazaroff (p) Ben Mortell (g) R. Berman (harp) Sam Shoobe (b) John Williams (d) The Hit Paraders, Joan Edwards, Barry Wood (v)

THESE FOOLISH THINGS v-BW arr   071783-1
78: VICTOR 27867

TI-PI-TIN v-HP, JE, BW (e)   071784-1
78: VICTOR 27865

ALL THE THINGS YOU ARE v-JE   071785-1
78: VICTOR 27866

THE MUSIC GOES ROUND AND ROUND v-HP   071786-1
     (e) arr
78: VICTOR 27868

                                            *   *   *

Carter's tenure as arranger for Mark Warnow's Hit Parade network broadcasts included this one commercial recording session. The string arrangements were Carter's first since his work for Henry Hall in England. As Carter recalls, the Hit Parade scores had to be turned out on short notice: "You didn't know until a few days before the broadcast what the hit of the week would be." He adds, "In every arrangement the introduction would have to start with part of the melody of the song, so that it would be immediately recognizable."

[116]	December 18, 1942 Los Angeles AFRS Jubilee #4
	BENNY CARTER AND HIS ORCHESTRA

Carter (as, arr) George Treadwell, Hal Mitchell, Chiefie Scott (tp) Earl Hardy, J. J. Johnson, John "Shorty" Haughton, Alton Moore (tb) Ted Barnett, Stretch Ridley, Gene Porter, Eddie De Verteuil (reeds) Ted Brannon (p) Johnny Smith (g) Curly Russell (b) Alvin Burroughs (d) Savannah Churchill (v)

STOMPIN' AT THE SAVOY

ALL I NEED IS YOU   v-SC

I CAN'T GET STARTED   arr

OL' MAN RIVER   (32as) arr

>NOTE: Tentative listing of personnel based on Carter's opening at the Swing Club in Los Angeles, November 1942 (Down Beat, November 15, 1942, p. 11).

[117]   Probably Late 1942   Los Angeles   AFRS Basic Library of Popular Music P-8
BENNY CARTER AND HIS ORCHESTRA

Carter (as, arr) Carter Band Personnel Probably Similar to 12-18-42 Jubilee #4 Listing, Savannah Churchill (v)

WHY DON'T YOU DO RIGHT   v-SC

ILL WIND   v-SC   arr?

>NOTE: This may be Carter's arrangement of "Ill Wind" as first recorded October 16, 1941.

[117A]   January 1, 1943 (New Year's Eve)   Hollywood   Aircheck
BENNY CARTER AND HIS ORCHESTRA

Includes Carter (as)

ONE O'CLOCK JUMP   (24as)

[118]   January 23, 1943   Los Angeles
FATS WALLER AND HIS RHYTHM

Carter (tp, comp) Alton Moore (tb) Gene Porter (cl, ts) Irving Ashby (g) Fats Waller (p, v) Slam Stewart (b) Zutty Singleton (d) Ada Brown (v)

MOPPIN' AND BOPPIN'   (16+8tp)(16+8tp with   D6-V6-6215
    ensemble) comp
78:   20TH CENTURY FOX TCF202, VICTOR 40-
4003   LP: HMV C3737, SOUNTRAK STK103, RCA
(J) RA-80, RCA (F) PM42361

AIN'T MISBEHAVIN'   v-FW   (12tp)+(8tp acc)   D6-V6-6216
78:   20TH CENTURY FOX TCF203, VICTOR 40-
4003, LP: HMV C3737, CAMDEN CAL473,
SOUNTRAK STK103, RCA (J) RA-80, RCA (F)
PM42361, TIME-LIFE STL-J15

THAT AIN'T RIGHT   v-FW, AB (8tp with ensemble)   VP 471
    (8tp acc)(12tp acc)
78:   20TH CENTURY FOX TCF201   LP: SWAGGIE
S1227, ALAMAC QSR2438, JAZZ ANTHOLOGY
JA5104, RCA (J) RA-80

>NOTE: "That Ain't Right" appears as "It Ain't Right" on Swaggie LP.

January 23, 1943 [118]

* * *

These recordings, which were among Waller's last, are from the soundtrack of the film Stormy Weather. Carter's only other recordings with Waller were the 1929 Chocolate Dandies and McKinney's sessions.

Carter recalls their composition "Moppin' And Boppin'": "Fats had part of the tune, I think the beginning, and he asked me to finish it with him." This was not their first collaboration; in 1927 a tune called "Nobody Knows How Much I Love You" was registered with the U.S. copyright office. Carter and Waller were the composers, Bud Allen the lyricist. Andy Razaf recorded it January 17, 1928, under the pseudonym Johnny Thompson, with Fats supplying piano accompaniment.

[119]　　January-February 1943　Los Angeles
　　　　SOUNDTRACK OF FILM STORMY WEATHER

Carter (as, arr) Large Orchestra With Strings and Vocal Chorus, Lena Horne, Bill 'Bojangles' Robinson (v) David Raksin (arr)

STORMY WEATHER　v-LH (e) arr
LP:　SOUNTRAK STK103

STORMY WEATHER　vocal chorus (5as)(5as) arr
　　　[last 29 measures]
LP:　SOUNTRAK STK103

I CAN'T GIVE YOU ANYTHING BUT LOVE
　　　v-LH, BR, chorus (e) arr [instrumental
　　　section only]
LP:　SOUNTRAK STK103

AIN'T THAT SOMETHIN'　v-BR (e) arr
LP:　SOUNTRAK STK103

GOOD FOR NOTHIN' JOE　v-LH (e) arr
LP:　SOUNTRAK STK103

[120]　　January-February 1943　Los Angeles
　　　　BENNY CARTER WITH CAB CALLOWAY AND HIS ORCHESTRA

Carter (as) Shad Collins, Jonah Jones, Russell Smith, Lammar Wright (tp) Tyree Glenn, Quentin Jackson, Keg Johnson (tb) Andy Brown (cl, as) Hilton Jefferson (as) Al Gibson, Illinois Jacquet (ts) Greely Walton (bs) Benny Payne (p) Danny Barker (g) Milt Hinton (b) J. C. Heard (d) Cab Calloway (leader)

BODY AND SOUL　(32as [1st solo])
78:　20TH CENTURY FOX TCF207/TCF211
LP:　SPOTLITE SPJ148

* * *

This performance was originally issued in two parts on a limited Twentieth Century-Fox 12-inch pressing. It took place on the sound stage during the

filming of the picture Stormy Weather but was not intended for use in the
film. Personnel is from the Spotlite LP. The soloists are, in order:
Jacquet (ts), Carter (as), Jefferson (as).

---
[121]   March 24, 1943   Los Angeles   Radio Show, "Blueberry Hill"
         BENNY CARTER AND HIS ORCHESTRA

Carter (tp, as, arr, comp) Gerald Wilson, Snooky Young, Walter Williams,
Fred Trainer (tp) John "Shorty" Haughton, J. J. Johnson, Alton Moore
(tb) Kirt Bradford, Willard Brown, Gene Porter, Eddie Davis (reeds) Ted
Brannon (p) Curly Russell (b) Oscar Bradley (d) The Charioteers (v)

FISH FRY   (32tp) arr, comp
LP: IAJRC 17

I CAN'T GET STARTED   (32as) arr

JOSHUA FIT DE BATTLE OF JERICHO   v-C (e)

AIN'T THAT SOMETHIN' (incomplete) (e)

>   NOTE: "Fish Fry" announced as "Blueberry Hill Fish Fry," and
>   listed on IAJRC LP as "Blueberry Hill Jamboree."

* * *

This show was the pilot for what was to be the civilian version of the Jubilee series. It was aired over the CBS network.

The source for the tentative personnel is a Leonard Feather report
on a Benny Carter engagement in April-May 1943 at the Hollywood Club
(Metronome, April 1943, pp. 17, 33).

---
[122]   March-April 1943   Los Angeles   Soundtrack of Film
                      The Gang's All Here
         ALICE FAYE WITH BENNY GOODMAN AND HIS ORCHESTRA

Carter (as, arr) Benny Goodman (cl) Lee Castaldo, Ray Linn, Bobby Guyer
(tp) Miff Mole, Charlie Castaldo (tb) Hymie Schertzer, Leonard Kaye (as)
Jon Walton, Bob Taylor (ts) Joe Rushton (bs) Jess Stacy (p) Bart Roth (g)
Gus Van Camp (b) Louis Bellson (d) strings, Alice Faye (v)

NO LOVE, NO NOTHIN'   v-AF (14as) arr
LP: CLASSIC INTERNATIONAL FILMUSICALS
3003

---
[123]   April 10, 1943   Los Angeles   Airchecks, Hollywood Club
         BENNY CARTER AND HIS ORCHESTRA

Carter (as, tp, v, arr, comp) Gerald Wilson, Snooky Young, Walter Williams,
Fred Trainer (tp) Alton Moore, John "Shorty" Haughton (tb) J. J. Johnson
(tb, arr) Kirt Bradford, Willard Brown, Gene Porter, Eddie Davis (reeds)
Ted Brannon (p) Curly Russell (b) Oscar Bradley (d) Savannah Churchill (v)

MELANCHOLY LULLABY (incomplete)   (4+4as)
        arr, comp

April 10, 1943 [123]

I'VE HEARD THAT SONG BEFORE v-SC (6tp)

BLUE SKIES v-SC with "Benny Carter Quartet"
(Carter and three others) (4+4+4as)(v)

WITHOUT A SONG probably arr-JJJ (e)

ONE O'CLOCK JUMP probably arr-JJJ (20as)

ILL WIND (10+10+14as) arr

BACK BAY BOOGIE (incomplete) (24as) arr, comp

> NOTE: Personnel from Leonard Feather report in Metronome (April 1943, pp. 17, 33). Eddie Davis not same as Eddie "Lockjaw" Davis.

[124]   May or Later 1943   Los Angeles   AFRS Basic Library
of Popular Music P-33
BENNY CARTER AND HIS ORCHESTRA

Carter (as, tp, arr, comp) Carter Band Personnel Probably Similar to 10-25-43 Capitol Recording Session, Savannah Churchill (v) Frank Comstock (arr)

SLEEP (24as) arr
LP: ALAMAC QSR2449

I USED TO LOVE YOU v-SC, arr-FC (16+8as)
LP: ALAMAC QSR2449

ILL WIND (20as)(14as) arr
LP: PALM CLUB 12, ALAMAC QSR2449, SWING TREASURY ST109, HOT 'N SWEET (F) HOL6426

FISH FRY (32tp) arr, comp
LP: PALM CLUB 12, ALAMAC QSR2449, HOT 'N SWEET (F) HOL6426

> NOTE: The tenor saxophone soloist is probably Bumps Myers, who joined Carter in May 1943.

[125]   October 25, 1943 San Francisco
BENNY CARTER AND HIS ORCHESTRA

Carter (as, arr, comp) Claude Dunson, Vernon 'Jake' Porter, Teddy Buckner, Freddie Webster (tp) Alton Moore, J. J. Johnson, John "Shorty" Haughton (tb) Porter Kilbert (as) Willard Brown (as, bs) Gene Porter, Bumps Myers (ts) Ted Brannon (p) Ulysses Livingston (g) Curly Russell (b) Oscar Bradley (d) Savannah Churchill (v) Frank Comstock (arr)

POINCIANA   arr-FC (16as with ensemble)
(8as)(as coda)
78: CAPITOL 144 T: VA TRANSCRIPTION
HERE'S TO VETERANS 335, LP: CAPITOL
(E) LC6649, HITS H1002, CAPITOL (G) 1 C
056-85610 M

JUST A BABY'S PRAYER AT TWILIGHT 94
v-SC, arr-FC (e)
78: CAPITOL 165   LP: CAPITOL (G) 1 C
056-85610 M

HURRY HURRY v-SC, arr-FC (8as) comp 95
78: CAPITOL 144   45: IL JAZZ (I)

LOVE FOR SALE (16as) arr 96
78: CAPITOL 100   LP: CAPITOL M11057,
CAPITOL (G) 1 C 056-85610 M

  NOTE: Il Jazz 45 rpm has no issue number; Capitol M11057 also issued under number 5C 052-80850.

* * *

  In 1942 Ella Mae Morse and Freddie Slack helped to put Capitol Records on firm ground with a huge hit "Cow Cow Boogie," which Carter had composed with Don Raye and Gene DePaul. A year later Carter himself made his first recordings for the label.

  The personnel is entirely different from Carter's East Coast orchestra, although his old friend, guitarist Ulysses Livingston, has returned.

  Some of the influential modernists, such as J. J. Johnson and Freddie Webster, are beginning to make their presence felt. One of the most important additions was tenor saxophonist Bumps Myers, who was to become a mainstay of the orchestra over the next three years. Myers was a consistent and exciting soloist as well as one of Carter's closest friends.

  Carter was now busy enough to hire Frank Comstock to help arrange for the orchestra. Comstock deeply admired Carter and brought so sympathetic an understanding of Carter's style to his work that his arrangements were often credited to Carter. Carter did not attempt to dictate to his arranger. "I left it up to him. He knew the band and he used to sit in with us occasionally." Although Carter hired Comstock because of the increasing demands on his time by film assignments, he had a secondary motive. "I was also hoping someone would come up with a hit for the band --a big seller. My thinking wasn't too bad because the arrangements he [Comstock] made really were bigger sellers than anything I had done."

[126] 1943 Los Angeles   Soundtrack of Film Thousands Cheer
    LENA HORNE WITH BENNY CARTER AND HIS ORCHESTRA

Carter (as, arr) Lena Horne (v)

HONEYSUCKLE ROSE v-LH (e) arr
LP: MCA2-11002, HOLLYWOOD SOUNDSTAGE SS409

[127] 1943 Los Angeles   AFRS Basic Library of Popular Music P-34
    BENNY CARTER AND HIS ORCHESTRA

Carter (as, arr) Carter Band Personnel May Be Similar to 10-25-43 Capitol Session, Savannah Churchill (v) Frank Comstock (arr)

1943 [127]

SWANEE RIVER   arr-FC (16+8as)
LP: PALM CLUB 12, ALAMAC QSR2449, HOT
'N SWEET (F) HOL6426

ALL OF ME   (14as) arr
LP: PALM CLUB 12, ALAMAC QSR2449, HOT
'N SWEET (F) HOL6426

HONEYSUCKLE ROSE possibly arr: FC (32as)
LP: PALM CLUB 12, ALAMAC QSR2449

MIDNIGHT   v-SC (16as) arr
LP: ALAMAC QSR2449

[128]   1943 Los Angeles AFRS Basic Library of Popular Music P-40
         BENNY CARTER AND HIS ORCHESTRA

Carter (as) Carter Band Personnel May Be Similar to 12-25-43 Capitol Session, Savannah Churchill (v) Frank Comstock (arr)

PRELUDE TO A KISS   arr-FC (16as)
LP: ALAMAC QSR2449

I HEARD YOU CRIED LAST NIGHT   v-SC (8+12as)
LP: ALAMAC QSR2449

ON THE ALAMO   arr-FC (16as)(32as)
LP: ALAMAC QSR2449

[129]   1943 Los Angeles AFRS Basic Library of Popular Music P-86
         BENNY CARTER AND HIS ORCHESTRA

Carter (as) Rex Stewart (cornet) Remainder of Carter Band Personnel May Be Similar to 12-25-43 Capitol Session

BOY MEETS HORN   (e)
T: AFRS DOWNBEAT #218   LP: BLACK JACK
LP3010, SPOTLITE SPJ147

* * *

This is a feature for Rex Stewart who, according to John Chilton, gigged with Carter in July 1943. The Downbeat show includes a brief interview with Carter (added later) in which he discusses his career and the formation of his band. He mentions touring the country, "winding up at the present time at the Orpheum Theater here in Los Angeles." Carter first played at the Orpheum March 17-23, 1943, and returned for the last week in September.

[130]   May 21, 1944   Los Angeles
         BENNY CARTER AND HIS ORCHESTRA

Carter (as, tp, arr) John Carroll, Karl George, Edwin Davis, Milton Fletcher (tp) Alton Moore, J. J. Johnson, John "Shorty" Haughton, Bart Varsalona (tb) Porter Kilbert (as) Willard Brown (as, bs) Gene Porter, Bumps Myers (ts) Gerald Wiggins (p) W. J. Edwards (g) Charles Drayton (b) Max Roach (d) Dick Gray (v)

I CAN'T ESCAPE FROM YOU   (6as) arr   254
78:   CAPITOL 40048   LP: CAPITOL (E)
LC6649, CAPITOL M11057, CAPITOL (G)
1 C 056-85610 M

I'M LOST   v-DG (8as) arr   255
78:   CAPITOL 165

I CAN'T GET STARTED   (32as)(4as) arr   256
78:   CAPITOL 48015   LP: CAPITOL (E)
LC6649, CAPITOL M11057, CAPITOL (G)
1 C 056-85610 M

I SURRENDER DEAR   (32tp)(40tp)(tp coda) arr   257
78:   CAPITOL 200   LP: CAPITOL H235,
CAPITOL M11057, CAPITOL (G) 1 C 056-
85610 M, TIME-LIFE STL-J10

NOTE: Capitol M11057 also issued under number 5C 052-80850.

* * *

"I Can't Escape From You" is one of the great Carter sax section features, with a full chorus allotted to the reeds. Although comparable to "Lonesome Nights" or "Skip It" in concept, this arrangement has harmonic and rhythmic innovations which give it a modern flavor.

This is Carter's first commercial recording of "I Can't Get Started," which he has consistently chosen as a ballad feature at concerts down to the 1980s. In later versions it evolved into something of a set piece--a dazzling technical display with a spectacular coda. Here the melody is more explicit, although the last eight measures of Carter's solo foreshadow the later virtuoso approach.

"I Surrender Dear" marks the final step in the evolution of Carter's trumpet style from the Armstrong influence of his early work to the more ornamented approach suggested by "More Than You Know." The tone has become drier and Carter makes greater use of tonguing. The piece is in two parts. After Carter's decorative exposition of the melody at moderate tempo in the first chorus, the pace doubles. Carter's trumpet soars over the ensemble and climaxes in a break. His crisply-played ascending two-note figures come to a slightly premature end, before the ensemble returns. A fat-toned trumpet coda and flight to high E-flat end the record. In subsequent performances he usually re-created the sensational solo he had improvised at this session. "That was what you tried to do when a record achieved some degree of success," he explains. "If you varied it too much, people would come up to you and say, 'Oh, but that's not the way you played it on the record!'"

These are the first commercial recordings of Max Roach with the Carter orchestra. Carter recalls that Roach brought excitement to the band, but occasionally the men had trouble picking up after one of his drum solos. "We were on the edge of our seats," Carter recalls. "You never knew where 'one' was!"

June 12, 1944 [131]

[131]	June 12, 1944 Los Angeles AFRS Jubilee #83
	BENNY CARTER AND HIS ORCHESTRA

Carter (as, tp, arr) Milton Fletcher, Sleepy Grider, Fatso Ford, Edwin Davis (tp) John "Shorty" Haughton, Alton Moore, J. J. Johnson (tb) Porter Kilbert, Bumps Myers, Gene Porter, Willard Brown (reeds) Gerald Wiggins (p) Jimmy Edwards (g) Charles Drayton (b) Max Roach (d) Savannah Churchill (v)

JAY JAY'S JUMP

THEN YOU'VE NEVER BEEN BLUE   v-SC

I SURRENDER DEAR   arr

OL' MAN RIVER   arr

> NOTES: Tentative listing of personnel from Carter engagement at the Swing Club, Los Angeles, June 1944 reported by Barry Ulanov (Metronome, July 1944, p. 14). "Jay Jay's Jump" may be the same as "Polishin' Brass," arranged and composed by J. J. Johnson. "I Surrender Dear" probably features Carter on tp. From this show on Ernie "Bubbles" Whitman serves as m. c. for the Jubilee series.

[132]	July 11, 1944 Los Angeles AFRS Jubilee #87
	BENNY CARTER AND HIS ORCHESTRA

Carter (as, tp, arr) Carter Band Personnel Probably Similar to 6-12-44 Jubilee #83, Savannah Churchill (v) Frank Comstock (arr)

SWEET GEORGIA BROWN   (32tp)(16as) arr

I LOST MY SUGAR IN SALT LAKE CITY   v-SC
     (4as intro)

STAR DUST   (32tp)(28tp+coda) arr

ROSE ROOM   arr-FC (16as)
LP: JAZZ SOCIETY AA502, JAZZ ANTHOLOGY
JA5123, KAYDEE KD2, SWEET 'N HOT (F) HOL6426

[133]	September 11, 1944? New York Recorded for V-Disc--Unissued
	BENNY CARTER AND HIS ORCHESTRA

Carter (as, tp, arr) Bumps Myers (ts) Probably Regular Band Personnel

AMONG MY SOUVENIRS   (32as)(16tp) arr   32633

* * *

The date given above is listed on the sleeve of the acetate and is probably only approximate. Band routes show the Carter orchestra on tour at this time, but probably not in New York. There is a brief tenor solo at the end which is quite likely Bumps Myers.

[134]	Possibly January or November 1944　New York　Aircheck, Apollo Theater
	BENNY CARTER AND HIS ORCHESTRA

Carter (as, arr, comp) Probably Regular Carter Band Personnel for the Period

BACK BAY BOOGIE   arr, comp

[135]	1944　Los Angeles　AFRS Basic Library of Popular Music P-238
	BENNY CARTER AND HIS ORCHESTRA

Carter (as, arr) Carter Band Personnel May Be Similar to 6-12-44 Jubilee #83, Savannah Churchill (v)

TWO AGAIN   v-SC (16as) arr
T:　AFRS DOWNBEAT #218

I NEVER MENTION YOUR NAME   v-SC (e) arr
T:　AFRS DOWNBEAT #218

I LOST MY SUGAR IN SALT LAKE CITY
　　　v-SC (4as intro)
T:　AFRS DOWNBEAT #215

    NOTE: On dubbed narrative to Downbeat #218 Carter notes that he used "Two Again" as a theme song for some time.

[136]	February 26, 1945　New York
	TIMMIE ROGERS AND HIS ORCHESTRA

Carter (as) William Johnson, Talib Dawud, Felix Barboza, Loyal Walker (tp) Alton Moore, John "Shorty" Haughton, George Washington, J. J. Johnson (tb) Porter Kilbert, Jewell Grant (as) Harold Clark, Don Byas (ts) Willard Brown (bs) Rufus Webster (p) Herman Mitchell (g) Charles Drayton (b) Max Roach (d) Timmie Rogers (v)

DADDY-O   v-TR (e)　　　　　　　　　　　　　　　　W1256
78:　REGIS 7001

GOOD DEAL   v-TR (e)　　　　　　　　　　　　　　　W1258
78:　REGIS 7001

CAPACITY
78:　UNISSUED

IF YOU CAN'T SMILE AND SAY YES DON'T
　　　CRY AND SAY NO
78:　UNISSUED

[137]	February 27, 1945　New York
	SAVANNAH CHURCHILL AND HER ALL STAR ORCHESTRA

Carter (as, tp, arr) William Johnson, Talib Dawud, Felix Barboza, Loyal Walker (tp) Alton Moore, John "Shorty" Haughton, George Washington, J. J.

February 27, 1945 [137]

Johnson (tb) Porter Kilbert, Jewell Grant, Harold Clark, Willard Brown, Don Byas (reeds) Rufus Webster (p) Herman Mitchell (g) Charles Drayton (b) Max Roach (d) Savannah Churchill (v)

ALL ALONE v-SC (e) arr W1261
78: MANOR 1004 LP: BLUE STAR (F) 116

DADDY DADDY v-SC (12tp acc) arr W1262
78: MANOR 1004 LP: BLUE STAR (F) 116

NOTE: Label of Manor 1004 states "trombone solo by Jay Jay" ("Daddy Daddy") and "tenor solo Don Byas" ("All Alone").

[138] March 19, 1945 Los Angeles AFRS Jubilee #125
BENNY CARTER AND HIS ORCHESTRA

Carter (as, tp, arr) Irving Lewis, Fred Trainer, Gerald Wilson, Emmett Berry, Paul Cohen (tp) J. J. Johnson, George Washington, Louis Taylor (tb) Porter Kilbert, Jewell Grant (as) Bumps Myers, Harold Clark (ts) John Taylor (bs) Rufus Webster (p) Herman Mitchell (g) Charles Drayton (b) Max Roach (d) Timmie Rogers (v)

SWEET GEORGIA BROWN (32tp)(16as) arr
LP: PALM CLUB 12, JAZZ SOCIETY AA502,
JAZZ ANTHOLOGY JA5123, GOLDEN ERA
LP15058, SWEET 'N HOT (F) HOL6426, JOYCE
LP5007

DADDY-O v-TR (e)
LP: JOYCE LP5007

JUST YOU, JUST ME (8as)(16tp)(8tp) arr
LP: PALM CLUB 12

ADDITIONAL ISSUES: All on Jubilee #219; "Sweet Georgia Brown" on AFRS Downbeat.

* * *

This tentative personnel is based on Carter's recording session for Capitol on April 9, 1945. The presence of Bumps Myers and J. J. Johnson is confirmed by Carter's announcement of the soloists following "Sweet Georgia Brown" on the AFRS Downbeat show. This announcement is not present on the Jubilee show.

[139] March 26, 1945 Los Angeles AFRS Jubilee #126
BENNY CARTER AND HIS ORCHESTRA

Carter (as, tp, v, arr, comp) Carter Band Personnel Probably Similar to 3-19-45 (Jubilee #125) Barney Bigard (cl) Timmie Rogers, Betty Roche (v) Arthur Treacher, Nat King Cole (spoken v)

JUBILEE JUMP (8tp [2nd solo])
LP: EXTREME RARITIES 1007, JAZZ SOCIETY
AA502, JAZZ ANTHOLOGY JA5123, KAYDEE KD2,
HOT 'N SWEET (F) HOL6426, JOYCE LP5007

TROUBLE, TROUBLE v-BR (e)
LP: JOYCE LP5007

COMEDY SKETCH v-AT, NKC (spoken v)
LP: JOYCE LP5007

GOOD DEAL v-TR (e)
LP: JOYCE LP5007

TEA FOR TWO (e)
LP: SUNBEAM SB214, BLACK JACK LP3003,
JOYCE LP5007, SPOTLITE SPJ147

BACK BAY BOOGIE (4as break)+(24as) arr, comp
LP: SUNBEAM SB214, JOYCE LP5007

> NOTE: "Tea For Two" is a feature for Bigard.
>
> ADDITIONAL ISSUES: "Jubilee Jump" on Jubilee #131 and #207; "Tea For Two" on Jubilee #207 and #292; "Trouble..." and "Back Bay Boogie" on Jubilee #207.

---

[140]   March 30, 1945   Los Angeles
        CAPITOL INTERNATIONAL JAZZMEN

Carter (as, comp) Bill Coleman (tp) Buster Bailey (cl) Coleman Hawkins (ts) Nat King Cole (p) Oscar Moore (g) John Kirby (b) Max Roach (d) Kay Starr (v)

YOU CAN DEPEND ON ME (16as)   599
78: CAPITOL 283 45: IL JAZZ (I) LP:
CAPITOL M11031, CAPITOL (G) 1 C 056-
85610 M

IF I COULD BE WITH YOU v-KS (18as)   600
78: CAPITOL 10031 LP: CAPITOL (E)
LC6520, CAPITOL M11031

STORMY WEATHER v-KS (8as)   601
78: CAPITOL 283 LP: CAPITOL (G) 1 C
056-85610 M

RIFFAMAROLE (24as) comp   602
78: CAPITOL 10031 45: IL JAZZ (I) LP:
TULIP TLP105, CAPITOL M11031

> NOTE: Il Jazz 45 rpm has no issue number; Capitol M11031 also issued under number 5C 052-80806.

* * *

Capitol took advantage of the presence in Los Angeles of this dream personnel. The group derived its name from the long periods of time Carter, Hawkins and Coleman had spent in Europe.

Considering the magnitude of talent, the results are less than spectacular. Hawkins is the dominant soloist on the two instrumentals. Carter

March 30, 1945 [140] 117

sounds as if he is distracted in the middle of his solo on "You Can Depend On Me, " and falls into a predictable pattern on his boppish blues original "Riffamarole. " Cole's piano is superb throughout.

Bill Coleman has fond memories of this date, once calling it "one of the greatest thrills of my life, " because it was his first chance to record with both Hawkins and Carter.

Nat Cole was also glad to participate because, as producer Dave Dexter recounts in his autobiography, the pianist was "being castigated by the Eastern critics ... for deserting jazz to become a pop singer. " (Dexter, Playback, p. 98.)

[141]	Early 1945? Los Angeles AFRS Jubilee?
	BENNY CARTER AND HIS ORCHESTRA

Carter (as, tp, arr) Carter Band Personnel Unknown but Probably Includes J. J. Johnson (tb) Bumps Myers (ts) Frank Comstock (arr)

SOMEBODY LOVES ME   (8as) arr
T: AFRS DOWNBEAT # ?

MOONGLOW   arr-FC (16+8as)
T: AFRS DOWNBEAT # ?

ROSE ROOM   arr-FC (16as)
T: AFRS DOWNBEAT # 215

STAR DUST   (32tp)(28tp+coda) arr
T: AFRS DOWNBEAT # 97, AFRS DOWNBEAT # 215 ?
LP: SPOTLITE SPJ147

AFTER YOU'VE GONE   arr-FC (38as)
T: AFRS DOWNBEAT # ?

* * *

Although all of these recordings were included on AFRS Downbeat shows, their original source is not known. They may have been made for the Jubilee series and probably were not all done at the same time.

Carter has identified the trombone soloist on "Stardust" as J. J. Johnson, who probably left the band in early April 1945.

Although "Moonglow" is announced as a Carter arrangement, it is by Frank Comstock.

[142]	April 2, 1945 Los Angeles AFRS Jubilee #127
	BENNY CARTER AND HIS ORCHESTRA

Carter (as, tp) Carter Band Personnel Probably Similar to 3-19-45 (Jubilee #125) Timmie Rogers (v) Frank Comstock (arr)

ROSITA   arr-FC (32tp)(16as)
LP: JAZZ SOCIETY AA502, JAZZ ANTHOLOGY
JA5123, KAYDEE KD2

IF YOU CAN'T SMILE AND SAY YES DON'T
   CRY AND SAY NO   v-TR (e)

> NOTE: "Rosita" announced and listed on Jazz Society and Jazz Anthology LPs as "Slick Mix."

---

[143]   April 9, 1945   Los Angeles
BENNY CARTER AND HIS ORCHESTRA

Carter (as, arr, comp) Irving Lewis, Fred Trainer, Gerald Wilson, Emmett Berry, Paul Cohen (tp) Henry Coker, Alton Moore, George Washington, Louis Taylor (tb) Jewell Grant, Porter Kilbert (as) Bumps Myers, Harold Clark (ts) John Taylor (bs) Rufus Webster (p) Herman Mitchell (g) Charles Drayton (b) Max Roach (d) Larry Stewart (v)

JUNE COMES AROUND   v-LS   610
78: UNISSUED

MALIBU   (16+8as)(8as)   arr, comp   611
78: CAPITOL 200   T: HERE'S TO VETERANS 26

> NOTE: Veterans transcription contains only excerpt of "Malibu."

* * *

"Malibu" is one of Carter's most haunting melodies and his arrangement highlights its stark simplicity. An errie background of swelling reeds and muted brass back Carter's alto, which carries the theme. The only other soloist is Henry Coker, who plays the eight-bar trombone bridge.

Quincy Jones cites this record as one which made him want to become an arranger. "I dug his record of 'Malibu' when I was in high school and he's been my idol ever since."

---

[144]   April 16, 1945   Los Angeles   AFRS Jubilee #129
BENNY CARTER AND HIS ORCHESTRA

Carter (as, arr) Carter Band Personnel Probably Similar to 4-9-45 Recording Date for Capitol, Barney Bigard (cl) Judy Carroll (v)

UNIDENTIFIED TITLE   (e)

EELIBUJ BLUES   (e)
LP: SPOTLITE SPJ147

PLAY ME THE BLUES   v-JC (e)

OL' MAN RIVER   (16as)   arr
LP: SWING TREASURY 109

> NOTES: Carter believes that the first title may have been an original by one of the band members. "Eelibuj" features Bigard.
>
> ADDITIONAL ISSUES: All on Jubilee #220.

April 30, 1945 [145]   119

[145]	April 30, 1945 Los Angeles AFRS Jubilee #131
	BENNY CARTER AND HIS ORCHESTRA

Carter (as, arr) Carter Band Personnel Probably Similar to 4-9-45 Recording Date for Capitol, Judy Carroll (v)

SOMEBODY LOVES ME   (8as) arr
LP: JAZZ SOCIETY AA502, JAZZ ANTHOLOGY
JA5123, PROBABLY MUSIDISC CCV2521

DARLING   v-JC (e)

SLEEP   (24as) arr
LP: JAZZ SOCIETY AA502, JAZZ ANTHOLOGY
JA5123, SWEET 'N HOT (F) HOL 6426

> ADDITIONAL ISSUES: "Somebody..." and "Sleep" on Jubilee #246; Jubilee #131 also includes version of "Jubilee Jump" from #126 (March 26, 1945).

[146]	May 8, 1945 Los Angeles AFRS Jubilee #132
	BENNY CARTER AND HIS ORCHESTRA

Carter (tp, as, arr, comp) Carter Band Personnel Probably Similar to 4-9-45 Recording Date for Capitol Except from Here on Percy Brice (d) Replaces Max Roach, Helen Humes (v)

FISH FRY   (32tp) arr, comp
LP: SUNBEAM SB214

UNLUCKY WOMAN   v-HH (e)
LP: SUNBEAM SB214

FIESTA IN BRASS   (e)

> NOTE: "Unlucky Woman" listed on Sunbeam LP as "Blues"; although the m.c. announces that Humes is backed on this title by Carter, Carter does not believe that the trumpet accompaniment is his.
>
> ADDITIONAL ISSUES: "Unlucky Woman" on Jubilee #136 and #222.

[147]	June 4, 1945 Los Angeles AFRS Jubilee #136
	BENNY CARTER AND HIS ORCHESTRA

Carter (as, tp, arr) Carter Band Personnel Probably Similar to 5-8-45 (Jubilee #132), Helen Humes (v) Frank Comstock (arr)

SUNDAY   (8as)(32as) arr
LP: JAZZ SOCIETY AA502, JAZZ ANTHOLOGY
JA5123

HABANERA   arr-FC (16as)
LP: JAZZ SOCIETY AA502, JAZZ ANTHOLOGY
JA5123

I CRIED FOR YOU   v-HH (tp acc)

EARLY BOYD (8as)
LP: JAZZ SOCIETY AA502, JAZZ ANTHOLOGY
JA5123, EXTREME RARITIES 1007

    ADDITIONAL ISSUES: All on Jubilee #222.

| [148] | September 24, 1945   Los Angeles   AFRS Jubilee #149 |

Carter (as) Unidentified Orchestra with Strings, Dick Haymes (v)

I'M GONNA LOVE THAT GAL   v-DH

IT MIGHT AS WELL BE SPRING   v-DH

    NOTE: Carter's presence not confirmed.

    ADDITIONAL ISSUES: Both titles on Jubilee #223.

| [149] | November 16-22, 1945   Chicago   Live Recording or Aircheck, Regal Theater |
| BENNY CARTER AND HIS ORCHESTRA |

Carter (as, tp, v, arr, comp) Probably Regular Band Personnel for the Period

THE HONEYDRIPPER   (v)(8tp)

MALIBU   (16+8as)(8as) arr, comp

| [150] | December 12, 1945   New York |
| BENNY CARTER AND HIS ORCHESTRA |

Carter (as, tp, arr, comp) Louis Gray, Wallace Jones, Lewis Botton, Idrees Sulieman (tp) Alton Moore, Charley Johnson, Al Grey, Johnny Morris (tb) Joe Epps, Porter Kilbert (as) Willard Brown (as, bs) Bumps Myers, Harold Clark (ts) Rufus Webster (p) James Cannady (g) Thomas Moultrie (b) Percy Brice (d) Frank Comstock (arr)

CUTTIN' TIME   (32as) arr, comp   838
78: UNISSUED   LP: CAPITOL M11057,
CAPITOL (G) 1 C 056-85610 M

BUNBELINA   arr, comp   839
78: UNISSUED

PRELUDE TO A KISS   arr-FC (16as)   847
78: CAPITOL 40048   LP: PICKWICK
SPC3281, PICKWICK PTP2072, CAPITOL
M11057, CAPITOL (G) 1 C 056-85610 M

JUST YOU, JUST ME   (6as)(16tp)(8tp) arr   848
78: UNISSUED   LP: CAPITOL M11057,
CAPITOL (G) 1 C 056-85610 M

    NOTE: Capitol M11057 also issued under number 5C 052-80850.

December 12, 1945 [150]   121

                                    *   *   *

There is some confusion over the first title from this session. The Capitol files show this tune as "Forever Blue" and the Capitol Jazz Classics
LP lists that title. Carter, however, remembers writing "Forever Blue"
and does not believe that this is it. Furthermore, the title does not seem
to correspond to this uptempo non-blues swinger. This same composition
and arrangement was performed on an AFRS Jubilee show where it is announced as "Cuttin' Time." In any case, this arrangement and "Just You,
Just Me" show a marked be-bop influence, particularly in the brass writing.
The trumpet and tenor soloists on "Cuttin' Time" are Idrees Sulieman (who
was Leonard Graham at the time) and Bumps Myers. On "Just You, Just
Me" Carter has some reed trouble which may have prevented the record's
release. Although the notes to the Capitol Jazz Classics LP state that
Sulieman is the trumpet soloist on "Just You, Just Me," it is certainly
Carter, with Myers again featured on tenor.

[151]	January 5, 1946 New York
	BENNY CARTER AND HIS ORCHESTRA

Carter (as, v, arr, comp) Probably Louis Gray, Wallace Jones, Lewis Botton,
Idrees Sulieman (tp) Charley Johnson, Al Grey, Johnny Morris (tb) Joe
Epps, Porter Kilbert (as) Willard Brown (as, bs) Bumps Myers, Harold
Clark (ts) Rufus Webster (p) James Cannady (g) Thomas Moultrie (b) Percy
Brice (d) Bixy Harris (v) Gil Fuller (arr)

JUMP CALL   (32as) arr, comp   166
78: DELUXE 1008   LP: AUDIOLAB 1505,
EMBER CJS802, JAZZ SELECTION 602

PATIENCE AND FORTITUDE   v-BH, arr-GF   167
       (16as)(v)
78: DELUXE 1008

[152]	January 7, 1946 New York
	BENNY CARTER AND HIS ORCHESTRA

Carter (as, tp) Emmett Berry, Shorty Rogers, Joe Newman (tp) Neal Hefti
(tp, arr) Trummy Young, Alton Moore, Sandy Williams, Dicky Wells (tb)
Russell Procope (as) Willard Brown (as, bs) Tony Scott (cl, as) Flip Phillips,
Don Byas (ts) Sonny White (p) Al Casey (g) John Simmons (b) J. C. Heard
(d) James Cannady (arr)

DIGA DIGA DOO   arr-JC (32as)   168
78: DELUXE 1028   LP: AUDIOLAB 1505,
EMBER CJS802, JAZZ SELECTION 606

WHO'S SORRY NOW   arr-NH (32tp)   169
78: DELUXE 1009   LP: AUDIOLAB 1505,
EMBER CJS802, JAZZ SELECTION 606

SOME OF THESE DAYS   arr-NH (8as with ensemble)+   170
       (8as)
78: DELUXE 1012   LP: AUDIOLAB 1505,
EMBER CJS802

[153]	January 8, 1946 New York

BENNY CARTER AND HIS ORCHESTRA

Carter (as, arr, comp) Emmett Berry, Shorty Rogers, Joe Newman, Neal Hefti (tp) Al Grey, Trummy Young, Alton Moore, Sandy Williams (tb) Russell Procope (as) Willard Brown (as, bs) Tony Scott (cl, as) Dexter Gordon, Don Byas (ts) Sonny White (p) Freddie Green (g) John Simmons (b) J. C. Heard (d) Maxine Sullivan (v) Frank Comstock (arr)

I'M THE CARING KIND   v-MS (8as) arr, comp   171
78: DELUXE 1012   LP: AUDIOLAB 1549,
AUDIOLAB 1505, EMBER CJS802

LOOKING FOR A BOY   v-MS (e) arr   172
78: DELUXE 1009   LP: AUDIOLAB 1505,
EMBER CJS802

ROSE ROOM   arr-FC (16as)   173
78: DELUXE 1028   45: DELUXE DEP282   LP:
AUDIOLAB 1505, EMBER CJS802

NOTE: Although Audiolab 1549 is a Billy Eckstine release, it mistakenly contains "I'm The Caring Kind."

* * *

The first of these three Deluxe sessions [151-153] was done with the regular Carter orchestra, but for the second and third dates an all-star group of New York musicians was brought in. Carter cites two reasons for this curious shift in personnel: "The producers wanted some big names on the date. Also, they went to Gil Fuller, Neal Hefti, and Budd Johnson for arrangements. Not all of the players in my band could just walk into the studio and read, and these arrangements were all new to us."

Gil Fuller, one of the pioneer bebop arrangers, provided the chart for "Patience And Fortitude." With appropriately boppish ensemble accents spurring him on, Carter here, more than in any other solo to date, shows that he was absorbing some of the rhythmic and harmonic features of the new style without abandoning his own. "I certainly paid attention to what the younger musicians in my band and others were playing and tried to understand it. But I made no attempt to incorporate anything in particular into my own playing. I'm sure what I heard must have affected me, but the change was purely subconscious."

Carter's vocal exchanges with Bixie Harris are among his more successful attempts at singing on record.

The first arrangement played on the all-star date was far removed from the boppish flavor of "Patience And Fortitude." "Diga Diga Doo" is definitely a product of the 1930s with solos by Dicky Wells, Flip Phillips, Joe Newman, Carter, Sonny White, and J. C. Heard.

Carter opens "Who's Sorry Now" on trumpet, and his rather nostalgic reading of the melody is somewhat incongruent with Neal Hefti's arrangement. The two tenor spots are by Phillips, and Al Casey solos on electric guitar.

Soloists on "Some Of These Days" are Trummy Young, Sonny White, Carter, probably Emmett Berry, and Don Byas.

January 8, 1946 [153]

Maxine Sullivan interprets Carter's attractive composition "I'm The Caring Kind" as well as "Looking For A Boy." The latter features some excellent Carter sax ensemble writing in the first chorus. The six-man section, which includes no less than Don Byas and Dexter Gordon, blends together well. The tenor solo is by Gordon.

"Rose Room" is one of those Frank Comstock scores which capture the essence of Carter's reed section so faithfully. Even the original 78 label credits Carter as arranger of this piece which features solos by Emmett Berry, Carter, John Simmons, Don Byas and Trummy Young.

[154]   March 31, 1946   Los Angeles   Airchecks from Club
                         'The Streets of Paris'
        BENNY CARTER

Carter (as) Miles Davis, Howard McGhee (tp) Al Grey, Possibly Britt Woodman (tb) Bumps Myers, Unknown (ts) Sonny White (p) James Cannady (g) Thomas Moultrie (b) Percy Brice (d)

JUST YOU, JUST ME   (32as with ensemble)(32as)

DON'T BLAME ME   (20as)(32as)

SWEET GEORGIA BROWN   (64as)

                    *   *   *

The personnel for this informal session is confusing. It seems to change after the first title, for which the soloists are announced. Following "Just You, Just Me" there is a presentation of the Esquire Gold alto sax award to Carter and for the final two tunes, other soloists seem to sit in. Tentative identifications of these were offered by Carter. "Just You, Just Me": all soloists named by announcer--Carter (as), Myers (ts), Davis (tp), Cannady (g), Carter (as) fades into Grey (tb), White (p). "Don't Blame Me": Carter (as) fades into ? (tb), White (p), ? (ts), Davis (tp) fades into Carter (as), Cannady (g). The tb soloist is probably not Grey; Carter has suggested Woodman. The ts solo is not by Myers. "Sweet Georgia Brown": tp over ensemble (may be Davis), Carter (as), Grey (tb), Myers (ts), Moultry (b) fades into Cannady (g), McGhee (tp); announcer interrupts after third chorus.

During his brief tenure with Carter, Miles Davis made no commercial recordings with the band but seems to have been present on several of the airchecks and AFRS programs. Carter remembers him as "very quiet," getting along well with the others in the band. He adds, "When Miles joined me it was quite clear that he was already thinking along different lines. But he was a good reader and certainly had no trouble with the book."

[155]   April 7, 1946
        ARNOLD ROSS QUARTET

Carter (as) Arnold Ross (p) Allan Reuss (g) Artie Bernstein (b) Nick Fatool (d)

THE MOON IS LOW   (32as)(32as)   HL145-1
78:   UNISSUED-TEST EXISTS

THE MOON IS LOW (32as)(16as)　　　　　　　　HL145-2
78: UNISSUED LP: EMARCY MG26029,
TRIP TLP5543

STAIRWAY TO THE STARS (16as)(16as)　　　　HL146
78: KEYNOTE 648 LP: EMARCY MG26029,
TRIP TLP5543

BYE BYE BLUES (32as[theme])+(32as)(32as)　　HL147
78: KEYNOTE 648 LP: EMARCY MG26029,
TRIP TLP5543

I DON'T KNOW WHY (16as[theme])(8as)
78: UNISSUED LP: EMARCY MG26029,
TRIP TLP5543

* * *

Although Arnold Ross was the nominal leader, Carter's alto is the major focus of this excellent session. The instrumentation is significant because these are Carter's first recordings with only a rhythm section since the Swing Quartet date ten years earlier in England. His playing in this setting was to change little throughout the 1950s and 1960s, when he recorded often this way.

[156]　　April 30, 1946 Southgate, California Airchecks
　　　　　　　　　　　　Trianon Ballroom
　　　　　　BENNY CARTER AND HIS ORCHESTRA

Carter (as, tp, arr, comp) Probably 4 of These 5: Miles Davis, Fred Trainer, Calvin Strickland, Walter Williams, Ira Pettiford (tp) Candy Ross (tb, v) Johnny Morris, Al Grey, Charley Johnson (tb) Bob Graettinger, Joe Epps, Harold Clark, Bumps Myers, Willard Brown (reeds) Sonny White (p) James Cannady (g) Thomas Moultrie (b) Percy Brice (d) Lucy Elliott (v) J. J. Johnson, Neal Hefti (arr)

I'M GONNA MAKE BELIEVE I'VE GOT
　　　　MYSELF A SWEETHEART v-CR (8as)

I COVER THE WATERFRONT (4tp intro)+(32tp)
　　　arr

I'M THE CARING KIND v-LE (8as) arr, comp

POLISHIN' BRASS (incomplete) arr-JJJ (e)

WHO'S SORRY NOW arr-NH

　　　　NOTE: "Polishin' Brass" announced as "Comin' On At The Trianon."

* * *

This probable personnel is based on a review of the band at a June 5 show at the Swing Club in Los Angeles (Billboard, June 22, 1946, p. 22) and photos in Carter's collection. Miles Davis was not listed in the review but is known to have been with the band from January to May 1946.

May 5, 1946 [157]   125

[157]	May 5, 1946 Southgate, California Airchecks, Trianon Ballroom
	BENNY CARTER AND HIS ORCHESTRA

Carter (as, tp, arr, comp) probably 4 of these 5: Miles Davis, Fred Trainer, Calvin Strickland, Walter Williams, Ira Pettiford (tp) Candy Ross (tb, v) Johnny Morris, Al Grey, Charley Johnson (tb) Bob Graettinger, Joe Epps, Harold Clark, Bumps Myers, Willard Brown (reeds) Sonny White (p) James Cannady (g) Thomas Moultrie (b) Percy Brice (d) Lucy Elliott (v) J. J. Johnson (arr)

MY GUY'S COME BACK   v-LE (16tp)

DREAM CASTLE   (16+4as)(4as) arr, comp

BACK BAY BOOGIE (incomplete) (24as[interrupted]) arr, comp

NIGHT AND DAY   v-LE (4as intro)(16as)(8tp) arr

IF I CAN'T HAVE YOU   v-CR (e) arr, comp

POLISHIN' BRASS   arr-JJJ (e)

WHERE OR WHEN (incomplete) (12as[interrupted by signoff]) arr

    NOTES: "Polishin' Brass" announced as "Comin' On At The Trianon." See note on personnel from preceding session.

[158]	April-May 1946 Los Angeles AFRS Jubilee #184
	BENNY CARTER AND HIS ORCHESTRA

Carter (as, tp, arr, comp) probably 4 of these 5: Miles Davis, Fred Trainer, Calvin Strickland, Walter Williams, Ira Pettiford (tp) Candy Ross, Johnny Morris, Al Grey, Charley Johnson (tb) Bob Graettinger, Joe Epps, Harold Clark, Bumps Myers, Willard Brown (reeds) Sonny White (p) James Cannady (g) Thomas Moultrie (b) Percy Brice (d) Kay Starr (v) Neal Hefti (arr)

WHO'S SORRY NOW   arr-NH (32as)
LP: QUEEN-DISC Q009

SHE'S FUNNY THAT WAY   v-KS (tp acc)

ON THE SUNNY SIDE OF THE STREET   v-KS
    (tp acc)

I CAN'T GET STARTED   (32as)(4as) arr
LP: JAZZ SOCIETY AA502, JAZZ ANTHOLOGY JA5123

JUMP CALL   (32as) arr, comp
78: V-DISC 701   LP: JAZZ SOCIETY AA502, JAZZ ANTHOLOGY JA5123, SPOTLITE SPJ147

    NOTES: "She's Funny..." announced and sung as "He's..." "Jump

Call" as "Melodrama In A V-Disc Record Room" on V-Disc 701.
See note on personnel from 4-30-46 session.

ADDITIONAL ISSUES: "Jump Call" on Jubilee #186.

* * *

Carter believes the trumpet soloist on "Jump Call" is Miles Davis. Although the style is rather different from that of Davis's recordings of the period with Charlie Parker, it has often been pointed out that the Parker recordings may not be representative. Carter recalls that Davis was far more technically proficient at that time than he is usually given credit for. Furthermore, he states that Davis did solo often with the band, and could easily have been featured here and on "Just You, Just Me" from the next session.

[159]	April-May 1946 Los Angeles AFRS Jubilee #186
	BENNY CARTER AND HIS ORCHESTRA

Carter (as, arr) See Personnel and Notes for Previous Jubilee Session, Lucy Elliott (v)

JUST YOU, JUST ME (8as)(8as) arr
LP: SPOTLITE SPJ147

LOVER MAN v-LE

  NOTE: This Jubilee show also includes the version of "Jump Call" from Jubilee #184.

[160]	Same Show

Carter (as) Charlie Parker, Willie Smith (as) Nat King Cole (p) Oscar Moore (g) Johnny Miller (b) Buddy Rich (d)

BODY AND SOUL (56as)
LP: SOUNDS 1206

CHEROKEE (e)
LP: SOUNDS 1206

* * *

[159, 160] Only one of two instances of Parker and Carter together on record, this session is disappointing in that the medley format precluded any interaction between the soloists, although they come together briefly on "Cherokee." "Body And Soul" is Carter's feature in a two-part medley; the first part was Smith's solo on "Tea For Two."

   The Spotlight LP credits Miles Davis with the trumpet solo on "Just You, Just Me." Carter agrees. The solo sounds somewhat more characteristic of the style Davis displayed on other recordings of the period.

[161]	May-June 1946 Los Angeles AFRS Jubilee #191
	BENNY CARTER AND HIS ORCHESTRA

May-June 1946 [161]

Carter (as, tp, arr, comp) Fred Trainer, Calvin Strickland, Walter Williams, Ira Pettiford (tp) Candy Ross, Johnny Morris, Al Grey, Charley Johnson (tb) Bob Graettinger, Joe Epps, Harold Clark, Bumps Myers, Willard Brown (reeds) Sonny White (p) James Cannady (g) Thomas Moultrie (b) Percy Brice (d) Lucy Elliott, Herb Jeffries (v) Calvin Jackson, J. J. Johnson (arr)

MR. COED   arr-CJ (e)
LP: PALM CLUB 12, QUEEN-DISC Q009

I'M THE CARING KIND   v-LE (8as) arr, comp

FRIM FRAM SAUCE   v-LE (16tp with ensemble)

SHE'S FUNNY THAT WAY   v-HJ (e)

POLISHIN' BRASS   arr-JJJ (e)
LP: PALM CLUB 12, EXTREME RARITIES 1007, SPOTLITE SPJ147

NOTES: Personnel from Carter engagement at Swing Club, Los Angeles, June 5, 1946 (Billboard, June 22, 1946, p. 22) and photos in Carter collection. "Polishin' Brass" on Palm Club as "Jump Tune," on Extreme Rarities as "No Title Jump," and on Spotlite as "untitled original."

[162]   Ca. July 1946   Los Angeles   AFRS Jubilee #193
BENNY CARTER AND HIS ORCHESTRA

Carter (as, cl, tp, arr, comp) Carter Band Personnel Probably Similar to May-June 1946 Jubilee #191 Listing, The Delta Rhythm Boys (v) James Cannady, Frank Comstock (arr)

CUTTIN' TIME   (32as) arr, comp
LP: EXTREME RARITIES 1007

ON THE SUNNY SIDE OF THE STREET   v-DRB (e)

STAR DUST   arr-JC (e)

PRELUDE TO A KISS   arr-FC (16as)
78: V-DISC 823   LP: QUEEN-DISC Q009

I COVER THE WATERFRONT   (4tp intro)+(32tp) arr
LP: EXTREME RARITIES 1007

HELLO, GOODBYE, FORGET IT   v-DRB (e)

BACK BAY BOOGIE   (24as)(48cl) arr, comp
78: V-DISC 678   LP: QUEEN-DISC Q009

NOTES: Presence of Bumps Myers, Candy Ross and Sonny White confirmed by announcement of soloists on "I Cover The Waterfront." "Stardust" is a feature for James Cannady on pedal steel guitar. The introduction to this performance is included on Spotlite SPJ147, but the version which follows on that LP is from an AFRS Downbeat show.

[163]	Ca. July 1946 Los Angeles AFRS Jubilee #203
	BENNY CARTER AND HIS ORCHESTRA

Carter (as, tp, v, arr, comp) Carter Band Personnel Probably Similar to May-June 1946 Jubilee #191 Listing, Lucy Elliott (v) Gil Fuller, J. J. Johnson (arr)

LOVE FOR SALE   (4as)(32as) arr
LP: JAZZ ANTHOLOGY JA5123, JAZZ SOCIETY AA502

I GOT IT BAD AND THAT AIN'T GOOD   v-LE (16as)
LP: QUEEN-DISC Q009

PATIENCE AND FORTITUDE   v-LE, BC arr-GF (v)(16as)
LP: QUEEN-DISC Q009

WITHOUT A SONG probably arr: JJJ (e)
LP: JAZZ SOCIETY AA502, JAZZ ANTHOLOGY JA5123

OOFDAH (24tp [1st solo; 2nd is Walter Williams])
        arr, comp
LP: JAZZ SOCIETY AA502, JAZZ ANTHOLOGY JA5123

    ADDITIONAL ISSUES: "Love For Sale," "Without A Song" and "Oofdah" on Jubilee #297; "I Got It Bad" on Jubilee #295.

[164]	Ca. July 1946 Los Angeles AFRS Jubilee #205
	BENNY CARTER AND HIS ORCHESTRA

Carter (as, tp, arr, comp) Carter Band Personnel Probably Similar to May-June 1946 Jubilee #191, Vivian Garry (v)

I SURRENDER DEAR   (32tp)(40tp+coda) arr
LP: QUEEN-DISC Q009

I'M IN THE MOOD FOR LOVE   v-VG (as acc)

MALIBU (16as)(8as)(8as) arr, comp

WHAT IS THIS THING CALLED LOVE   (16+8as)

    NOTE: Presence of Sonny White, Thomas Moultry and Percy Brice confirmed by announcement by Vivian Garry before "I'm In The Mood For Love." Candy Ross and Harold Clark announced as soloists by m.c. on "What Is This Thing Called Love."

    ADDITIONAL ISSUES: Jubilee #292 contains all except "What Is This Thing...." In its place "Tea For Two" (featuring Barney Bigard) is repeated from Jubilee #126.

[165]	August 23, 1946 New York
	BENNY CARTER AND HIS CHOCOLATE DANDIES

August 23, 1946 [165]

Carter (as, cl, arr, comp) Buck Clayton (tp) Al Grey (tb) Ben Webster (ts) Sonny White (p) John Simmons (b) Sid Catlett (d, v)

SWEET GEORGIA BROWN (32cl) 78: SWING 258 LP: PRESTIGE 7604, PATHE C054-16026, RCA (F) 75.594	D6VB 2694
OUT OF MY WAY v-SC (e) arr 78: SWING 226 LP: PRESTIGE 7604, PATHE C054-16026, RCA (F) 75.594	D6VB 2695
WHAT'LL IT BE (8as)(32as) comp 78: SWING 226 LP: PRESTIGE 7604, PATHE C054-16026, RCA (F) 75.594	D6VB 2696
CADILLAC SLIM (32as [trades with Webster]) +(32as) 78: SWING 258 LP: PRESTIGE 7604, PATHE C054-16026, RCA (F) 75.594, TIME-LIFE STL-J10	D6VB 2697

* * *

The last of Carter's Chocolate Dandies sessions took place while Carter was in New York leading his band at the Apollo Theater. Charles Delaunay and Hugues Panassié were anxious to revive their Swing label, and Delaunay traveled to the United States to arrange for several sessions in a variety of styles.

Panassié was a great admirer of Mezz Mezzrow, and insisted that he be hired to supervise the sessions, one of which featured some of the leading exponents of bebop. When Delaunay questioned Mezzrow's participation in a session centered around a music for which he had little sympathy, Mezzrow quickly countered with an authentic-sounding legality: Delaunay could not supervise these dates because he was a Frenchman.

The sides have an informal air; the only writing seems to be the introduction and background to Catlett's vocal feature "Out Of My Way." Al Grey's solos on "Out Of My Way" and "Cadillac Slim" are probably his first on record. Grey, who had joined Carter's orchestra a few months earlier, recalls the importance of his stay with Carter: "...the biggest thing about him from my point of view was that he taught me how to phrase." (Dance, The World of Count Basie, p. 205.)

Carter's clarinet chorus on "Sweet Georgia Brown" is his last recording on that instrument. "I was more concerned with devoting time to the trumpet which I preferred to the clarinet and even to the alto," he recalls. Whitney Balliett writes, "One of the persistent sorrows of jazz is Carter's abandonment of the clarinet...," adding that his recordings "suggest that Carter might easily have been the jazz clarinetist." (Balliett, Such Sweet Thunder, p. 20.)

The highlight of the session is "Cadillac Slim," an "I Got Rhythm" variant credited to Catlett. The melody is very similar to Billy Strayhorn's "Raincheck," recorded by the Ellington band in 1941. Ben Webster may have been the link since he was prominent in the Ellington recording as well. Webster's solo generates an electricity reminiscent of his famous solo on "Cottontail," and is followed by an inspired series of 4-bar exchanges with Carter. Carter flies through the first 16 measures of his chorus. As on several other recordings, when he reaches the bridge, he adopts a cooler, more detached approach, before resuming the rapid pace. Pianist White shares the next chorus with Grey, who makes the most of his eight bars. Clayton's piercing, yet warm sound and relaxed phrasing are complemented by Catlett's accompaniment. Throughout the session his rim shots, fills and bass drum explosions, perfectly timed, constantly spur the soloists.

---
[166]   August 1946   New York
BENNY CARTER AND HIS ORCHESTRA

Carter (as, arr, comp) Paul Cohen, Ira Pettiford, Walter Williams (tp) Al Grey, Candy Ross (tb) Bumps Myers (ts) Willard Brown (as, bs) Sonny White (p) James Cannady (g) Thomas Moultrie (b) Percy Brice (d) Lucy Elliott (v)

RE-BOP BOOGIE   (24as) arr, comp   236
78: DELUXE 1044   45: DELUXE DEP282   LP:
PARLOPHONE GEP8568

TWELVE O'CLOCK JUMP   (32as) arr, comp   237
78: DELUXE 1041   LP: PARLOPHONE GEP8566,
AUDIOLAB 1505, EMBER CJS802

YOUR CONSCIENCE TELLS YOU SO   v-LE (8as) arr, comp   238
78: DELUXE 1041   45: DELUXE DEP282   LP:
PARLOPHONE GEP8568

MEXICAN HAT DANCE   (4as)   239
78: DELUXE 1044   45: DELUXE DEP282   LP:
PARLOPHONE GEP8568, AUDIOLAB 1505, EMBER CJS802

> NOTE: Ember CJS802 and Audiolab 1505 lists "Re-bop Boogie" but track is actually "Twelve O'Clock Jump" which appears twice.

* * *

Carter's final Deluxe date was made with his regular orchestra. The strange hybrid, "Re-bop Boogie," and "Twelve O'Clock Jump" again show the rhythmic influence of the new music on Carter's writing, particularly for the brass. The last tune was arranged by Budd Johnson.

---
[167]   1946   Los Angeles
ERNIE ANDREWS WITH THE CALVIN JACKSON ORCHESTRA

Carter (as) Manny Klein (tp) Calvin Jackson (p) Dave Barbour (g) Red Callender (b) Jackie Mills (d) Ernie Andrews, The Air Crew (v)

BABY I'M GONE   (8as)
78: G & G 1028, EXCLUSIVE 55X

---
[168]   Ca. 1946   Los Angeles   AFRS Jubilee #207
BENNY CARTER AND HIS ORCHESTRA

Carter (as) For General Personnel for This Period See May-June 1946 Jubilee #191 Listing, Jimmy Durante (v)

Ca. 1946 [168]

WHO WILL BE WITH YOU WHEN I'M FAR AWAY v-JD (e)

CHICAGO (incomplete) (32as)

NOTE: Rest of show repeats Jubilee #126.

---

[169]   March 1947   Pasadena, California   AFRS Jubilee #230,
              from McCornack Hospital
        BENNY CARTER AND THE ALL STARS FROM BLACK &
        WHITE RECORDS

Carter (as) Gerald Wilson (tp) Murray McEachern (tb) Barney Bigard (cl)
Phil Moore (p) Al Hendrickson (g) Red Callender (b) Hal West (d)

STOMPIN' AT THE SAVOY (88as)
LP: QUEEN-DISC Q009

* * *

The m.c. for this session is Lena Horne and the announcer is Gene Norman; hereafter Norman serves as m.c. The date is established when Lena Horne says that "Carter is leading a band at the El Patio Theater in a review called Sumpin's Jumpin'."

---

[170]   Probably Early 1947   Pasadena, California   AFRS Jubilee #246,
              Possibly from McCornack Hospital
        BENNY CARTER AND HIS ORCHESTRA

Carter (as, arr, comp) Unknown Personnel Probably Including Henry Coker (tb) Dexter Gordon (ts) Sonny White (p) Dave Barbour (g) Peggy Lee (v) The Pied Pipers (v) Frank Comstock (arr)

JUMP CALL (32as) arr, comp
LP: EXTREME RARITIES 1007, SPOTLITE SPJ147

SUGAR v-PL (e)

MY GAL SAL v-PP (e)
LP: SPOTLITE SPJ147

PRELUDE TO A KISS arr-FC (16as)

NOTES: "Jump Call" listed on Extreme Rarities LP as "Bugle Call Rag." This show concludes with a repeat of "Somebody Loves Me" from Jubilee #131.

* * *

Because Carter no longer maintained a big band after October 1946, it is impossible to establish a consistent personnel for this session and others from this period. Carter certainly used some of the musicians who had been with him for the past several years, but he also drew on other available talent to put together groups for varying periods of time. This may explain the likely presence of Dexter Gordon on this date. Although Carter cannot recall Gordon playing with him at this time, several sources maintain that the solo on "Jump Call" and the brief tenor passage on "My Gal

Sal" are by Gordon, who was then on the West Coast. These recordings were played for Bob Porter and Michael Cuscuna, two Dexter Gordon specialists, who concur that it is he.

---

[171]   April 22, 1947 Los Angeles
LUCKY THOMPSON AND HIS LUCKY SEVEN

Carter (as, arr, comp) Neal Hefti (tp) Lucky Thompson (ts) Bob Lawson (bs) Dodo Marmarosa (p) Barney Kessel (g) Red Callender (b) Lee Young (d)

JUST ONE MORE CHANCE   (e)   D7VB510-
78: VICTOR 20-2504   LP: RCA LPV544, RCA (F) 741.106

FROM DIXIELAND TO BEBOP   (e)   D7VB511'J'
78: UNISSUED-TEST EXISTS

FROM DIXIELAND TO BEBOP   (e)   D7VB511'K'
78: UNISSUED-TEST EXISTS

FROM DIXIELAND TO BEBOP   (e)   D7VB511-
78: VICTOR 20-3142   LP: RCA LPV544, RCA (F) 741.106

BOULEVARD BOUNCE   (32+16as) arr, comp   D7VB512'B'
78: UNISSUED-TEST EXISTS

BOULEVARD BOUNCE   (32+16as) arr, comp   D7VB512'D'
78: UNISSUED-TEST EXISTS

BOULEVARD BOUNCE   (32+16as) arr, comp   D7VB512'H'
78: UNISSUED   LP: RCA LPV544, RCA (F) 741.106

BOPPIN' THE BLUES   (24as)   D7VB513-
78: VICTOR 20-2504, VICTOR 20-3142 LP: RCA LPV3046, RCA LPV519, RCA (F) 741.106

* * *

Carter does not solo on "Just One More Chance," an extended ballad feature for Thompson, nor on the humorous three-minute capsule history of jazz, "From Dixieland To Be-bop."

Carter's own "Boulevard Bounce," however, is a feature for him and is particularly interesting because of the existence of three complete takes, none of which, oddly enough, was issued on 78.

He has no trouble negotiating the bebop head on the last title, and his brief solo is in the spirit of the piece.

(For an analysis of Carter's solo on the "H" take of "Boulevard Bounce" see chapter 3.)

---

[172]   April 29, 1947 Pasadena, California Concert, Civic Auditorium
GENE NORMAN'S 'JUST JAZZ'

April 29, 1947 [172]

Carter (as) Howard McGhee (tp) Vic Dickenson (tb) Wardell Gray (ts) Erroll Garner (p) Irving Ashby (g) Red Callender (b) Jackie Mills (d)

ONE O'CLOCK JUMP MM 914
78: MODERN 20-641 T: AFRS JUBILEE 262
LP: MODERN LP1207, CROWN CLP5004, VOGUE
CMDGN766, CROWN CST293, CROWN CST420,
UNITED SUPERIOR US7722

TWO O'CLOCK JUMP MM 915
78: MODERN 20-641 LP: MODERN LP1207,
CROWN CLP5004, VOGUE CMDGN766, CROWN
CST293, CROWN CST420, UNITED SUPERIOR US7722

THREE O'CLOCK JUMP (84as) MM 916
78: MODERN 20-642 LP: MODERN LP1207, CROWN
CLP5004, VOGUE CMDGN766, CROWN CST293,
CROWN CST420, UNITED SUPERIOR US7722

FOUR O'CLOCK JUMP MM 917
78: MODERN 20-642 LP: MODERN LP1207,
CROWN CLP5004, VOGUE CMDGN766, CROWN
CST420, UNITED SUPERIOR US7722

[173]   Same Concert

Carter (as) Chuck Peterson (tp) Vic Dickenson (tb) Charlie Barnet (ts) Dodo Marmarosa (p) Irving Ashby (g) Red Callender (b) Jackie Mills (d)

PERDIDO (part one) MM 1000
78: MODERN 20-660 T: AFRS JUBILEE 261
LP: CROWN CP5008, VOGUE (E) E2296, JAZZ
SELECTION 633, SWING HOUSE SWH10

PERDIDO (part two) (96as) MM 1001
78: MODERN 20-660 T: AFRS JUBILEE 261
LP: CROWN CP5008, VOGUE (E) E2296, JAZZ
SELECTION 633, SWING HOUSE SWH10

NOTE: Jepsen lists mx MM 1002 "Just You, Just Me" as by this same group, but it is by Erroll Garner with rhythm section only.

* * *

[172, 173] In a jam atmosphere which foreshadowed his appearances with Jazz at the Philharmonic, Carter turns in two genuinely exciting solos. His playing has none of the forced frenzy of some of his JATP work; his solos here are shorter and perhaps the novelty of the concept had yet to wear off.

The first four titles comprise one continuous performance which was divided for release on 78.

"Perdido" was also one performance, divided into two parts when originally issued. The 78 version is also edited: Vic Dickenson's solo, which opens the tune, has been eliminated and Barnet's solo has been cut from five choruses to three. This edited version may be on some of the LP's, except the Swing House, which contains the complete performance.

[174]	May 29, 1947 Los Angeles
	THE HOLLYWOOD HUCKSTERS

Carter (as) Charlie Shavers (tp) Benny Goodman (cl, v) Dave Cavanaugh (ts, arr) Joe Koch (bs) Red Norvo (vib, xylophone) Jimmy Rowles (p) Irving Ashby (g) Red Callender (b) Lee Young (d) Stan Kenton (v)

I APOLOGIZE (4as) 2006
78: CAPITOL 48013 45: CAPITOL 7-1230 LP: CAPITOL EAP 2-441, CAPITOL T441, CAPITOL (J) EMI CR8811

THEM THERE EYES (16as) 2007
78: CAPITOL 40022 LP: CAPITOL EBF 322, CAPITOL H322, CAPITOL (E) LC6563, CAPITOL (J) EMI CR8811

HAPPY BLUES v-BG, SK (12as) 2008
78: CAPITOL 40022 45: CAPITOL 7-1230 LP: BANDSTAND 7106, CAPITOL (J) EMI CR8811

* * *

Dave Dexter brought this unusual personnel together. When asked why he did not participate in the vocal repartee between Goodman and Kenton on "Happy Blues," Carter replied, "Because it was just a put-on; they would have asked me to sing only if it were serious!"

[175]	May 31, 1947 Los Angeles Aircheck, Bocage Hotel?
	BENNY CARTER AND THE KING COLE TRIO

Carter (as) Nat King Cole (p) Oscar Moore (g) Johnny Miller (b)

COCKTAILS FOR TWO (32+24as)

[176]	Early June 1947 Pasadena, California Gene Norman's 'Just Jazz,'
	Civic Auditorium
	BENNY CARTER AND THE ALL STARS

Carter (as) Chuck Peterson (tp) Vic Dickenson (tb) Charlie Barnet (ts) Dodo Marmarosa (p) Irving Ashby (g) Red Callender (b) Jackie Mills (d)

HOW HIGH THE MOON (64as)
T: AFRS JUBILEE 262 LP: SWING TREASURY ST109

[177]	June 16, 1947 Los Angeles
	JULIA LEE AND HER BOY FRIENDS

Carter (as) Bobby Sherwood (tp) Vic Dickenson (tb) Dave Cavanaugh (ts) Red Norvo (xylophone) Julia Lee (p, v) Jack Marshall (g) Red Callender (b) Sam 'Baby' Lovett (d) Joe Alexander (v)

MAMA DON'T ALLOW IT v-JL (16as) 2061
78: CAPITOL 1589 45: CAPITOL F1589 LP: CAPITOL (E) LC6563, CAPITOL (J) EMI CR8811, CHARLY CRB1039

June 16, 1947 [177] 135

DOUBTFUL BLUES v-JL (e) 2062
78: CAPITOL 40056

AIN'T IT A CRIME v-JL (e) 2063
78: CAPITOL 838 LP: CAPITOL (E) LC6563

KNOCK ME A KISS v-JL, JA (e) 2064
78: UNISSUED LP: CHARLY CRB1039

[178] June 18, 1947 Los Angeles
JULIA LEE AND HER BOY FRIENDS

Carter (as) Red Nichols (cornet) Vic Dickenson (tb) Dave Cavanaugh (ts) Red Norvo (xylophone) Julia Lee (p, v) Jack Marshall (g) Red Callender (b) Sam 'Baby' Lovett (d)

COLD HEARTED DADDY v-JL (e) 2065
78: CAPITOL 15300 LP: CAPITOL (E) CL13323

MY SIN v-JL (16as) 2066
78: CAPITOL 40056 LP: CAPITOL T1057

WHEN YOU'RE SMILING v-JL (16as) 2067
78: CAPITOL 40082 LP: CAPITOL T1057, CAPITOL
(G) 1 C 056-85610 M

I WAS WRONG v-JL (8as) 2068
78: CAPITOL 40028 LP: CAPITOL T1057, CAPITOL
T2038, TULIP TLP103, CAPITOL (G) 1 C 056-85610 M

[179] Ca. July 1947 Pasadena, California AFRS Jubilee #248,
Probably from McCornack Hospital
BENNY CARTER AND HIS ORCHESTRA

Carter (as, arr, comp) Unknown Personnel Probably Including Henry Coker (tb) Lucky Thompson (ts) Sonny White (p) The Pied Pipers (v)

FISH FRY (16as) arr, comp

LINDA v-PP (e)

SAME OLD DREAM v-PP (e)

JUST YOU, JUST ME (incomplete) (8as) arr
LP: SPOTLITE SPJ147

* * *

The trombone and tenor solos on "Just You, Just Me" sound like Coker and Thompson, who were working with Carter on and off during this time.

    This show also includes a version of Carter's composition "Lonely Woman" sung by Peggy Lee, accompanied by piano and guitar.

[180] September 22, 1947 Los Angeles
JOE ALEXANDER WITH DAVE CAVANAUGH'S MUSIC

Carter (as, comp) Ernie Royal (tp) Clint Neagley (tb) Dave Cavanaugh, Babe
Russin (ts) Joe Koch (bs) Juan Panalle (p) Jack Marshall (g) Harry Babasin
(b) Lee Young (d) Joe Alexander (v)

FOR YOU v-JA	2263
78: CAPITOL 40055	

WHEN I CLOSE MY EYES v-JA	2264
78: CAPITOL 40055	

I'M A THREE TIME LOSER v-JA comp	2265
78: CAPITOL 40079	

SO LONG DARLING v-JA (12as)	2266
78: CAPITOL 15274	

[181]   October 14, 1947   Los Angeles
         TEN CATS AND A MOUSE

Carter (ts) Dave Barbour (tp) Billy May, Bobby Sherwood (tb) Paul Weston
(cl) Eddie Miller (as) Dave Cavanaugh (bs) Red Norvo (p) Hal Derwin (g)
Frank Devol (b) Peggy Lee (d)

JA-DA (16ts [trades with tb])	2343
78: CAPITOL 15015	

THREE O'CLOCK JUMP (12ts)	2344
78: CAPITOL 15015	

*   *   *

In this Capitol novelty the musicians switch instruments. Carter on tenor
was nothing new, of course.

[182]   Same Date
         RED NORVO'S NINE

Carter (as, arr, comp) Bobby Sherwood (cornet) Dave Cavanaugh, Eddie
Miller (ts) Arnold Ross (p) Dave Barbour (g) Billy Hadnott (b) Jesse Price
(d) Red Norvo (vib)

HOLLYRIDGE DRIVE (16as) arr, comp	2345
78: CAPITOL 15083 45: CAPITOL 6F-1225, LP: CAPITOL (J) EMI CR8811, CAPITOL (G) 1 C 056-85609 M	

UNDER A BLANKET OF BLUE (8as)	2346
78: CAPITOL 15083 45: CAPITOL 6F-1225, LP: CAPITOL H322, CAPITOL T795, CAPITOL (E) CL13405, CAPITOL (E) LC6563, CAPITOL (J) EMI CR8811, CAPITOL (G) 1 C 056-85609 M	

*   *   *

Carter's lovely composition and small-group arrangement "Hollyridge Drive"
was named for the Beverly Hills street on which he lived.

October 20, 1947 [183]

[183]	October 20, 1947 Los Angeles

KAY STARR WITH DAVE CAVANAUGH'S MUSIC

Carter (as) Uan Rasey, Joe Triscari, George Seaburg, Irv Stumph (tp) Hoyt Bohannon, Lloyd Ulyate, Lou McGarity, Ed Kusby (tb) Clint Neagley (as) John Hamilton, Jack Crowlet, Dave Cavanaugh (ts) Joe Koch (bs) Arnold Ross (p) George Van Eps (g) Billy Hadnott (b) Lee Young (d) Dan Lube (viola)

MANY HAPPY RETURNS v-KS (e)   2348
78: CAPITOL 15137

YOU'VE GOTTA SEE MAMA EV'RY NIGHT OR YOU   2349
CAN'T SEE MAMA AT ALL v-KS (e)
78: CAPITOL 497 LP: CAPITOL T211, CAPITOL
T1468, CAPITOL (E) CL13047

WAS THAT THE HUMAN THING TO DO v-KS (e)   2350
78: CAPITOL 40066

THEN I'LL BE TIRED v-KS (e)   2351
78: CAPITOL 40066

NOTE: Last title by smaller group (no brass, possibly fewer reeds).

[184]	November 11, 1947 Los Angeles

JULIA LEE AND HER BOY FRIENDS

Carter (as, tb, comp) Geechie Smith (tp) Dave Cavanaugh (ts) Julia Lee (p, v) Jack Marshall (g) Red Callender (b) Sam 'Baby' Lovett (d)

PAGAN LOVE SONG v-JL (e [on tb])   2441
78: CAPITOL 1149

ALL I EVER DO IS WORRY v-JL (8tb)   2442
78: CAPITOL 15106

TAKE IT OR LEAVE IT v-JL (4+4as) comp   2443
78: CAPITOL 57-70006 LP: CHARLY CRB1039

THAT'S WHAT I LIKE v-JL (e)   2444
78: CAPITOL 15060 LP: CAPITOL (G)
1 C 056-85610 M, CHARLY CRB1039

KING SIZE PAPA v-JL (4+4as) comp   2445
78: CAPITOL 40082 LP: CAPITOL T2038, CAPITOL
(E) CL13055, CAPITOL (E) LC6535, CHARLY CRB1039

BLUES FOR SOMEONE v-JL (e)   2446
78: CAPITOL 57-70051

I'M FOREVER BLOWING BUBBLES v-JL (32as)   2447
78: CAPITOL 1149

BREEZE, BLOW MY BABY BACK TO ME (e)   2448
78: CAPITOL 1589 45: CAPITOL F1589

[185]	November 13, 1947 Los Angeles
	JULIA LEE AND HER BOY FRIENDS

Carter (as, tb, comp) Vic Dickenson (tb) Dave Cavanaugh (ts) Julia Lee (p, v) Jack Marshall (g) Billy Hadnott (b) Sam 'Baby' Lovett (d)

I DIDN'T LIKE IT THE FIRST TIME   v-JL (16as) comp   2458
78: CAPITOL 15367   LP: CAPITOL (E) LC6535, CHARLY CRB1039

CRAZY WORLD   v-JL (12as [trades with Dickenson -   2460
   Carter starts])
78: CAPITOL 15060   LP: CAPITOL T2038

TELL ME DADDY   v-JL (12as)   2461
78: CAPITOL 15144   LP: CAPITOL (E) LO6535

CHRISTMAS SPIRITS   v-JL (e)   2462
78: CAPITOL 15203

* * *

These two sessions [184, 185] comprise Carter's total recorded output on trombone. "I had been playing trombone occasionally and had written some things for my band where I played in the trombone section. Dave Dexter suggested that I play it on these dates." Carter can be heard riffing with the ensemble on trombone in "Pagan Love Song," and he takes an 8-bar solo on "All I Ever Do Is Worry."

    Vic Dickenson joined the group for the second session, and he and Carter play a trombone-duet chorus on "Crazy World," with Carter leading and Dickenson providing the more intricate fills. Carter achieves a full sound on the instrument, especially on "All I Ever Do Is Worry." He himself notes that he became more proficient on the horn after this date but never again recorded on it. Trombonist Al Grey, who played in the Carter orchestra, recalls Carter's initial efforts: "One day he decided to pick up the trombone. Though I was only a newcomer, I thought I sounded pretty good. So he played, and I was soon saying to myself, 'Well, well, you'd better take note here!'" (Dance, The World of Count Basie, p. 205.)

    These sessions also marked the first use by Carter of the pseudonym "Johnny Gomez" under which he co-composed "King Size Papa" and "I Didn't Like It The First Time" (subtitled "The Spinach Song"). Apparently Carter preferred not to have his name attached to these tunes, whose double-entendre lyrics were somewhat risqué for that time.

[186]	November 25, 1947 Los Angeles
	FREDDIE SLACK AND HIS ORCHESTRA

Carter (as, arr, comp) Chuck Peterson, Jim Salco, Jack Trainer, Gerald Wilson (tp) Hoyt Bohannon, Tommy Pederson (tb) Jewell Grant (as) Bumps Myers, Vido Musso (ts) Chuck Gentry (bs) Freddie Slack (p) Ulysses Livingston (g) Harry Babasin (b) Henry Green (d)

BOOGIE MINOR   (e) arr, comp   2596
78: CAPITOL 10134   LP: CAPITOL (E) H83,
CAPITOL (E) LC6529

November 25, 1947 [186]

ST. LOUIS BLUES (e) arr 2597
78: UNISSUED LP: CAPITOL H323, BIG BAND
ARCHIVES 1202

CHOPSTICK BOOGIE (e) arr 2598
78: CAPITOL 10132 LP: CAPITOL (E) H83,
CAPITOL (E) LC6529, BIG BAND ARCHIVES 1202

* * *

These three Carter arrangements are centered around the boogie-woogie piano stylings of the leader. Of particular interest are the excellent brass and reed figures in "St. Louis Blues."

[187] 1947 Los Angeles
ANITA O'DAY WITH RALPH BURNS AND HIS ORCHESTRA & BENNY CARTER AND HIS ORCHESTRA

Carter (as, arr, comp) 12 Piece Orchestra Including Ray Linn (tp) Ray Sims (tb) Ralph Burns (p, arr) Don Lamond (d) Anita O'Day (v)

HOW HIGH THE MOON v-AO (e) SRC 657
78: SIGNATURE 15185 LP: SIGNATURE LSP8,
CORAL CRL56073, BOB THIELE MUSIC BBM1-0595,
RCA (J) PG-86

I AIN'T GETTIN' ANY YOUNGER v-AO (e) arr, comp SRC 658
78: SIGNATURE 15217 LP: SIGNATURE LSP8,
CORAL CRL56073, BOB THIELE MUSIC BBM1-0595,
RCA (J) PG-86

MALAGUENA v-AO (e) SRC 659
78: SIGNATURE 15181 LP: SIGNATURE LSP8,
CORAL CRL56073, BOB THIELE MUSIC BBM1-0595,
RCA (J) PG-86

KEY LARGO v-AO (e) arr, comp SRC 660
78: SIGNATURE 15185 LP: CORAL CRL56073,
BOB THIELE MUSIC BBM1-0595, RCA (J) PG-86

NOTE: First three titles--Ralph Burns And His Orchestra; last title--Benny Carter And His Orchestra.

* * *

Two Carter compositions were premiered at this session. The boppish blues "I Ain't Gettin' Any Younger" was later recorded by Woody Herman. The alto solo on this version is not by Carter.

The Latin-flavored "Key Largo" was recorded by a variety of artists, including Sarah Vaughan. Carter believes he may have written the bridge with co-composer Karl Suessdorf providing the "A" section. Carter's arrangement for O'Day has some lush reed background figures with Carter prominent on lead alto.

[188] 1947 Los Angeles
LEE RICHARDSON ACC. BY BENNY CARTER'S ALL STARS

Carter (as) Lee Richardson (v) Others Unknown

IT'S TOO SOON TO KNOW 801
78: DELUXE 3196, DELUXE 3197

AM I ASKING FOR TOO MUCH 802
78: DELUXE 3195

WHEN I THINK OF YOU 803
78: DELUXE 3196

A FOOL FOR YOU 804
78: DELUXE 3197

[189] Late 1947 or Early 1948 Pasadena, California AFRS Jubilee
#276, from McCornack Hospital
BENNY CARTER AND HIS ORCHESTRA

Carter (as, arr, comp) Mary Lou Williams (p) Unknown Carter Band Personnel Probably Including Henry Coker (tb) Bumps Myers (ts)

LOVER (32as)

HOLLYRIDGE DRIVE (16as) arr, comp

ROLL 'EM (e)
LP: SPOTLITE SPJ147

CONGOROO (32as) arr, comp

  NOTES: Mary Lou Williams plays only on "Roll 'Em." "Hollyridge Drive" is by a small group from the orchestra.

[190] January 1948 Los Angeles
BENNY CARTER AND HIS ORCHESTRA

Carter (as, arr) Lew Obergh (tp) Henry Coker (tb) Bumps Myers (ts) Cyril Haynes (p) Jack Marshall (g) Dallas Bartley (b) Henry Green (d) Bob Decker, Emma Lou Welch, The Enchanters (v)

BABY, YOU'RE MINE FOR KEEPS v-ELW (8as) arr
78: REINA 101

YOU'LL NEVER BREAK MY HEART AGAIN v-ELW, E
(8as) arr
78: REINA 101

AN OLD LOVE STORY v-ELW, E (8as) arr
78: REINA 102

CHILPANCINGO v-BD, E (12as) arr
78: REINA 102

REINA v-BD, E (4as intro)(16as) arr
78: REINA 103

January 1948 [190]

LET US DRINK A TOAST TOGETHER   arr
78: REINA 103

* * *

This session was similar in concept, but on a smaller scale, to the work Carter was to do for amateur songwriter Bob Friedman some 25 years later. Here Harry Atwood hired Carter to provide an appropriate showcase for his compositions and issued the sides on his own label.

These recordings are of little jazz interest except for good alto and guitar solos on "Chilpancingo."

[191]   March 30, 1948 Pasadena, California AFRS Jubilee #284, from
                        McCornack Hospital
         BENNY CARTER AND HIS ORCHESTRA

Carter (as, arr, comp) Unknown Personnel

CONGOROO   arr, comp

ORIGINAL JELLY ROLL BLUES

BOP BOUNCE   arr, comp

* * *

The date is from an AFRS script for this show, which was a jazz retrospective, tracing the history of the music. Along with the Carter band were Peggy Lee, Pete Daley's Chicagoans and the Deep River Boys. Also included were recordings by Jelly Roll Morton of "King Porter Stomp" and "Winin' Boy Blues."

The script originally listed "Sleep" which was crossed out in favor of "Little Bo Bop Has Lost Her Beep." Rainer E. Lotz lists the title as "Bop Bounce." It is not known whether these are the same composition.

On the script "Congoroo" is crossed out and the title "Bamboula" is substituted. These are probably the same composition.

[192]   December 14, 1948 Los Angeles
         CLARENCE CLUMP WITH ORCHESTRA [Clump is pseudonym for
             Carter]

Carter (v, comp) Possibly Henry Coker (tb) Unknown (as) Possibly Dave Cavanaugh (ts) Unknown (p, g, b, d) Clarence Clump (v)

HAPPY GO LUCKY YOU AND BROKEN HEARTED ME   (v)   3800-2D-5
78: CAPITOL 15363

I DON'T WANT IT NO MORE   (v) comp   3801-3D-4
78: CAPITOL 15363

* * *

After many years Carter revealed his identity as the mysterious Clarence Clump on these humorous sides put together by Carter and Dave Dexter. Although bearing a standard Capitol label and issue-number, the disc must have had a limited pressing and appears in very few Capitol catalogs.

Carter sings the first title with mock seriousness, using a British accent. A tenor saxophone is audible: Carter suggests Dave Cavanaugh.

Carter sings the double-entendre lyrics to "I Don't Want It No More" with no special accent. There are brief alto (not Carter), tenor and trombone (Carter suggests Henry Coker) solos and an impromptu vocal group. Capitol files show the session as non-union and no personnel records were kept.

Carter used a double pseudonym on this last title; not only did he sing it under the name "Clarence Clump," but again he used "Johnny Gomez" to mask his role as co-composer.

---
[193]   May 1949   Los Angeles
         BENNY CARTER AND HIS ALL STARS

Carter (as, comp) Possibly Chuck Peterson (tp) Vic Dickenson (tb) Ben Webster (ts) Dodo Marmarosa (p) John Simmons or Charles Drayton (b) Jackie Mills (d)

COTTONTAIL   (e)   MM1767
78: MODERN 858   LP: RIVERBOAT (F) 900.267

TIME OUT FOR THE BLUES   (e)   MM1768
78: MODERN 858   LP: CROWN CLP5009, RIVERBOAT
(F) 900.267, TIME-LIFE STL-J21

SURF BOARD   (e) comp   MM1813
78: MODERN 865   LP: IAJRC 15, RIVERBOAT (F) 900.267

YOU ARE TOO BEAUTIFUL   (e)   MM1814
78: MODERN 865   LP: CROWN CLP5009, RIVERBOAT
(F) 900.267

                        *   *   *

This date has several puzzling aspects. First, Carter remembers it as a Ben Webster session. This possibility is given credence by the fact that Webster is the featured soloist on all sides, with Carter himself not soloing at all. The records may have been issued under Carter's name in error, someone mistaking "Benny" for "Ben."

Dubbed applause is audible on the original issues of "Time Out For The Blues" and "Cottontail," a re-creation by Webster of his famous 1940 solo.

---
[194]   July 8, 1949   Los Angeles
         KITTY WHITE ACC. BY DAVE CAVANAUGH'S ORCH.

Carter (as, comp) Parr Jones, Vernon Smith, Mickey Mangano (tp) George Washington (tb) Marvin Johnson (as) Dave Cavanaugh, Maxwell Davis (ts)

July 8, 1949 [194]

Chuck Waller (bs) Charlie Davis (p) Billy Hadnott (b) Jackie Mills (d) Kitty White (v)

I'M PLAYING WITH FIRE v-KW (e)	4654
78: CAPITOL 57-70061 LP: CAPITOL (E) CL13549	
A MAN IS GOOD v-KW	4655
78: CAPITOL 57-70032	
OO-WEE v-KW (e)	4656
78: CAPITOL 57-70061	
IT PAYS TO ADVERTISE comp	4657
78: CAPITOL 57-70032 LP: CAPITOL (E) CL13549	

[195]   September 22, 1949 Los Angeles
JOE ROBINSON WITH BENNY CARTER'S ORCHESTRA

Carter (as, arr, comp) Teddy Buckner (tp) Bumps Myers (ts) Chuck Waller (bs) Gerald Wiggins (p) Gene Phillips (g) Charles Drayton (b) Jackie Mills (d) Joe Robinson (v)

ROLL WITH THE BOOGIE v-JR (e) arr, comp	D9VB747-1
78: VICTOR 22-0054 45: VICTOR 50-0038	
IF I CAN'T HAVE YOU v-JR (e) arr, comp	D9VB748-1
78: VICTOR 22-0054 45: VICTOR 50-0038	
SUSPICIOUS OF MY WOMAN v-JR (e) arr, comp	D9VB749-1
78: VICTOR 22-0067 45: 50-0052	
SUSPICIOUS OF MY WOMAN v-JR (e) arr, comp	D9VB749-2
78: UNISSUED	
DON'T SCREAM, DON'T SHOUT v-JR (e) arr	D9VB750-1
78: VICTOR 22-0067 45: 50-0052	
DON'T SCREAM, DON'T SHOUT arr	D9VB750-2
78: UNISSUED	

* * *

Carter used his "Johnny Gomez" pseudonym for his compositions "Roll With The Boogie" and "Suspicious Of My Woman." He wrote the ballad "If I Can't Have You" under his own name, assuming the role of lyricist as well.

All titles except "Suspicious ..." have good solos by Bumps Myers.

[196]   1949 Los Angeles
DEBBIE ANDREWS

Carter (as) Debbie Andrews (v) Others Unknown

I LOST YOU v-DA
78:   MERCURY 8282

I AIN'T GOT NOBODY   v-DA
78: MERCURY 8282

[197]   October 21, 1950   Los Angeles
           AL HIBBLER WITH THE ELLINGTONIANS

Carter (as) Mercer Ellington (mellophone, arr) Harry Carney (bs) Billy Strayhorn (p, arr) Dave Barbour (g) Wendell Marshall (b) Charlie Smith (d) Al Hibbler (v)

STORMY WEATHER   v-AH arr-BS (e)   M4019
78: MERCER 1956   LP: MERCER LP1004, BRUNSWICK
BL54036

CHERRY   v-AH arr-ME (e)   M4020
78: MERCER 1956   LP: MERCER LP1004, BRUNSWICK
BL54036

STAR DUST   v-AH (e)   M4021
78: MERCER 1965   LP: MERCER LP1004, BRUNSWICK
BL54036

HONEYSUCKLE ROSE   v-AH (e)   M4022
78: MERCER 1965   LP: MERCER LP1004, BRUNSWICK
BL54036, JAZZ SELECTION JS652

[198]   November 6, 1950   New York
           THE THREE FLAMES WITH ORCH. UNDER THE DIRECTION OF
           BENNY CARTER

Carter (as) The Three Flames: Tiger Haynes (g) Roy Testamark (p, v) Bill Pollard (b, v) Unknown vib. and d.

SKY FULL OF SUNSHINE   v-TF (as, arr)   44616
78: COLUMBIA 39078

SUCCOTASH BABY   v-TF (4as intro)(12as acc)(8as acc)   44618
78: COLUMBIA 39078

STICK AROUND   v-TF   ZSP5445
78 AND/OR 45: COLUMBIA 39259

GO WAY GAL   v-TF   ZSP5447
78 AND/OR 45: COLUMBIA 39259

           NOTE: Last two titles may be from same session; Carter's presence not confirmed.

[199]   December 27, 1951   Los Angeles
           BEN WEBSTER SEXTET

Carter (as, comp) Maynard Ferguson (tp) Ben Webster (ts) Gerald Wiggins (p) John Kirby (b) George Jenkins (d)

RANDALL'S ISLAND   (e) comp   4720

December 27, 1951 [199]   145

78: MERCURY 8265 LP: EMARCY MG36050, EMARCY
MG26006, MERCURY (F) MEP 14076, TRIP TLP5555

OLD FOLKS (e)   4721
78: MERCURY 8298 LP: EMARCY MG26006, MERCURY
(F) MEP14076

KING'S RIFF (24as) comp   4722
78: MERCURY 8298 LP: EMARCY MG36050, EMARCY
MG26006, MERCURY (F) MEP14076, TRIP TLP5555

                          *   *   *

Carter provided two blues--the boppish "Randall's Island" and the basic "King's Riff"--for this session showcasing the talents of his good friend Ben Webster.

The date was one of the last for John Kirby, who was in poor health and whom Carter had assisted after Kirby's move to the West Coast.

---
[200]   April 23, 1952   Los Angeles   AFRS Jubilee #366
          BENNY CARTER QUINTET

Carter (as, tp?, comp) Unknown TP and Rhythm Section

LADY BE GOOD

CRUISIN' comp

---
[201]   June or July 1952   Los Angeles
          JAM SESSION (NORMAN GRANZ)

Carter (as, comp) Charlie Shavers (tp) Johnny Hodges, Charlie Parker (as) Flip Phillips, Ben Webster (ts) Oscar Peterson (p) Barney Kessel (g) Ray Brown (b) J. C. Heard (d)

JAM BLUES (84as [1st as solo])   802-2
LP: CLEF MGC4001, CLEF MGC601, VERVE MGV8002,
VERVE MGV8049, VERVE VE-2-2508, VERVE (F) 2683-043,
VERVE (J) MV2530, BOOK OF THE MONTH CLUB BOMC10-5604

WHAT IS THIS THING CALLED LOVE (96as [2nd as solo])   803-3
         (horns trade 4 bars at end for 3 choruses, Carter 1st)
LP: CLEF MGC4002, CLEF MGC602, VERVE MGV8002,
VERVE MGV8050, VERVE V8486, VERVE VE-2-2508,
VERVE (E) 2683-043

ISN'T IT ROMANTIC (32as)   804-4
LP: CLEF MGC4001, CLEF MGC601, VERVE MGV8002,
VERVE MGV8049, VERVE VE-2-2508, VERVE (E) 2683-043,
VERVE (J) MV2530, BOOK OF THE MONTH CLUB BOMC10-5604

FUNKY BLUES (24as [3rd as solo])   805-2
LP: CLEF MGC4002, CLEF MGC602, VERVE MGV8002,
VERVE MGV8050, VERVE V8486, VERVE VE-2-2508,
VERVE (E) 2683-043

NOTE: "Isn't It Romantic" is Carter's feature in ballad medley.

* * *

In one of his most intriguing jam session productions, Norman Granz brought together Carter, Parker and Hodges for the only recordings including all three of the shapers of the jazz alto saxophone. As is Granz's stated preference, the date was a loose affair, with the blues a common meeting ground much of the time.

The air of competition which pervades many such gatherings and which one might expect, given the extraordinary personnel, did not materialize, at least as far as Carter was concerned. "I don't recall any sense of rivalry at the date. I wouldn't say we felt 'pitted' against each other; more like 'combined.'" He then added with a smile, "It all went very smoothly--how else could it go with three so-called giants?"

In many spots Carter's playing seems stylistically closer to Parker's than it does to that of his own contemporary, Hodges. This is particularly evident in the standard "What Is This Thing Called Love." Hodges, who solos first among the altoists, uses the melody as a base, paraphrasing, reshaping and changing its emphasis, whereas Carter and Parker go directly to the changes. Indications of Carter's assimilation of new developments are evident, including an increased use of tonguing, and some boppish rhythmic figures. Carter notes the difference in approach between himself and Hodges: "What Johnny had was so uniquely his that he felt no need to change. I'm sure my own style was not so set."

As for any direct effect Parker may have had on him, he adds, "I never took any of the published Parker solos and practiced them endlessly as many of the younger saxophonists have done. But I have looked at them, and I've always tried to keep listening."

Carter has continued his efforts to keep abreast of musical developments. His record collection includes items by Sun Ra and Muhal Richard Abrams among others, and during the 1980 Newport Jazz Festival he made a special point of attending a concert by the World Saxophone Quartet.

[202]   July 26, 1952 Los Angeles
         BENNY CARTER AND HIS ORCHESTRA

Carter (as, arr, comp) Ernie Royal (tp) Milt Bernhart (tb) Ben Webster (ts) Bob Lawson (bs) Gerald Wiggins (p) Ulysses Livingston (g) Curtis Counce (b) George Jenkins (d)

LULLABY IN BLUE   (32+2as) arr, comp   E2VB6903-1
78: VICTOR 20-5389   45: RCA 47-5389   LP: RCA
(F) PM42406

MAMA LOU   arr, comp   E2VB6904-1
78: UNISSUED

ROCKIN' ALONG   (32as) arr, comp   E2VB6905-1
78: UNISSUED T: HERE'S TO VETERANS 335   LP:
HITS H1002

CRUISIN'   (36as) arr, comp   E2VB6906-1

July 26, 1952 [202]

```
78:  VICTOR 20-5389 T:  HERE'S TO VETERANS 335
45:  RCA 47-5389, LP:  RCA (F) PM42406
```

NOTES: "Rockin' Along" on Hits LP as "Rock Alone." RCA LP lists -2 for matrices 6903 and 6906.

* * *

Until the recent two-record French RCA Benny Carter issue, Carter's 1952 RCA dates were not readily available. The sides vary from highly commercial production numbers, replete with choruses, strings and echo, to some forays into near-R&B.

The personnel comes from the RCA files in New York. The French RCA LP lists New York as the place of recording and suggests a different personnel with a full big-band instrumentation (a personnel actually present on the October 2, 1952, session). Carter, however, remembers the location as Los Angeles, and aural evidence confirms the personnel and instrumentation shown above.

"Lullaby In Blue" is an attractive mood piece stated by Carter's alto with little embellishment and a lot of echo.

"Rockin' Along" is a riff tune which, although originally unissued, somehow made its way onto LP via a Veteran's Administration transcription. The sound quality is poor, and the alto break with which Carter opens his solo is marred by a very conspicuous reed squeak.

"Cruisin'," another uptempo riff tune, this time based on the blues, is more successful.

[203]   August 18, 1952   Los Angeles
        BENNY CARTER AND HIS ORCHESTRA

Carter (as, arr) Rubin Zarchy, Ray Linn, Manny Klein (tp) Bill Schaefer, Pullman Pederson (tb) Phil Shuken, Jess Carneol, Ted Nash, Sal Franzella (reeds) Paul Smith (p) Al Hendrickson (g) Phil Stephenson (b) Milt Holland (d) Harry Bluestone, Mischa Russell, Nick Pisani, Felix Slatkin, Erno Neufeld, Ben Gill (violins) Eleanor Slatkin (cello) Paul Robyn, William Hymanson (viola) Gail Laughton (harp) Ray Linn, Burton Dole, Maxwell Smith, Gil Mershon, Sue Allen, Delores Dahl, Gloria Wood, Dorothy McArty (v)

```
WISH YOU WERE HERE  vocal group arr            E2VB6957-1
78:  UNISSUED

WANNA GO HOME  vocal group (8as) arr           E2VB7304-1
78:  VICTOR 20-5005  45:  RCA 47-5005  LP:
RCA (F) PM42406

GEORGIA ON MY MIND  (32as)(4as+ coda) arr      E2VB7305
78:  UNISSUED   LP:  RCA (F) PM42406

YOU BELONG TO ME  (32as) arr                   E2VB7306-1
78:  VICTOR 20-5005  45:  RCA 47-5005  LP:
RCA (F) PM42406
```

* * *

This is one of Carter's most "commercial" dates. His alto echoes through an ethereal background of strings and voices.

Once again the French RCA LP gives New York as the location and September 1952 as the date. Carter recalls Los Angeles, and the RCA files list the personnel and date as above.

"Georgia On My Mind" was not issued until 1980 when it was included on the French RCA two-record set. The liner notes list October 2, 1952 as the recording date but RCA files and the general sound of the piece indicate this session as its source.

[204]	September 13, 1952 New York Concert, Carnegie Hall
	JAZZ AT THE PHILHARMONIC

Carter (as) Roy Eldridge, Charlie Shavers (tp) Lester Young, Flip Phillips (ts) Hank Jones, Oscar Peterson (p) Barney Kessel (g) Ray Brown (p) Buddy Rich (d)

JAM SESSION BLUES (108as)
LP: CLEF MG VOL. 15, VERVE MG VOL. 8, VERVE (J) MV9073/75

COCKTAILS FOR TWO (32as)
LP: CLEF MG VOL. 15, VERVE MG VOL. 8

PERDIDO (e)
LP: CLEF MG VOL. 15, VERVE MG VOL. 8, VERVE (E) 2615-040, VERVE (E) 2332-060

COTTONTAIL (32as)
LP: CLEF MG VOL. 15, VERVE MG VOL. 8, VERVE MGV 8368

THE TRUMPET BATTLE (128as)
LP: CLEF MG VOL. 15, VERVE MG VOL. 8, VERVE (J) MV9073/75

NOTE: "Cocktails..." is Carter's feature in ballad medley; Jones plays piano on medley, Peterson elsewhere.

*   *   *

Carter has always been ambivalent about the often combative atmosphere of Norman Granz's extravaganzas. The idea of several horns, without arrangements, playing endless crowd-pleasing solo choruses in an artificial recreation of a jam session is basically antithetical to his musical philosophy. "I found playing these long solos somewhat unpleasant. I've always felt that after I've said what I had to say there's no point in milking the audience for applause. Sometimes after I'd finish a solo, Norman would be waiting in the wings and would say, 'You were just getting started, Benny!'"

Consequently, on some JATP recordings Carter sounds bored and detached. On others he actually seems to be subtly mocking the JATP concept by going overboard in achieving the required frenzy. Such is the impression given by his solo on "Jam Session Blues."

September 13, 1952 [204]

    Carter seems more at home in the ballad medley portion of the JATP format, and his "Cocktails For Two" here is a typically virtuoso performance.

    Jepsen gives the date of this recording as October 11, 1952, but may be confusing it with an October 11 concert--also at Carnegie--featuring Nat King Cole, the Stan Kenton Orchestra, Sarah Vaughan and others (see New York Times, October 11, 1952, p. 17 and New Yorker, October 4, 1952, p. 12 and October 11, 1952, p. 12). Down Beat and New Yorker for September and October 1952 show the JATP concert as September 13. Also, a review in the New York Times, September 15, p. 15, mentions the identical personnel as on this recording.

[205]   September 1952   New York
        BENNY CARTER WITH THE OSCAR PETERSON TRIO AND
        BUDDY RICH (ALONE TOGETHER)

Carter (as) Oscar Peterson (p) Barney Kessel (g) Ray Brown (b) Buddy Rich (d) Horns and String Section-Joe Glover (arr, cond)

ISN'T IT ROMANTIC arr-JG (32+16as+ coda)	871-7
78: CLEF 89026 LP: NORGRAN MGN1058, VERVE MGV8148	
SOME OTHER SPRING arr-JG (intro+ 32+16as)	872-4
45: NORGRAN EPN45 LP: NORGRAN MGN1058, VERVE MGV8148	
THESE THINGS YOU LEFT ME arr-JG (34as)(10as+ coda)	873-1
45: NORGRAN EPN45 LP: NORGRAN MGN1058, VERVE MGV8148	

[205A]   September 1952   New York
        BENNY CARTER WITH THE OSCAR PETERSON TRIO AND
        BUDDY RICH (ALONE TOGETHER)

Carter (as) Oscar Peterson (p) Barney Kessel (g) Ray Brown (b) Buddy Rich (d)

GONE WITH THE WIND (64as)+(16as trades with piano) (32as+ coda)	874-5
78: NORGRAN 111 LP: NORGRAN MGN1058, VERVE MGV8148, VERVE (E) 2683-043	
I GOT IT BAD AND THAT AIN'T GOOD (48as)	875-2
45: CLEF EPC187 LP: NORGRAN MGN1058, VERVE MGV8148, VERVE (E) 2683-043	
LONG AGO AND FAR AWAY (64as)(36as)	876-9
45: CLEF EPC187 LP: NORGRAN MGN1058, VERVE MGV8148, VERVE (E) 2683-043	
I'VE GOT THE WORLD ON A STRING (48as)	877-3
78: NORGRAN 111 LP: NORGRAN MGN1058, VERVE MGV8148, VERVE (E) 2683-043	

[205B] September 1952 New York
BENNY CARTER WITH THE OSCAR PETERSON TRIO AND
BUDDY RICH (ALONE TOGETHER)

Carter (as, arr, comp) Oscar Peterson (p) Barney Kessel (g) Ray Brown (b) Buddy Rich (d) Horns and String Section-Joe Glover (arr, cond)

ROUND MIDNIGHT (32+16as+ coda) arr 878-5
45: NORGRAN EPN45 LP: NORGRAN MGN1058, VERVE
MGV8148, VSP 38

ALONE TOGETHER arr-JG (72+16as) 879-3
45: NORGRAN EPN46 LP: NORGRAN MGN1058, VERVE
MGV8148

BEWITCHED, BOTHERED AND BEWILDERED (48as+coda) arr 880-4
78: NORGRAN 120 45: BLUE STAR (F) GM8512 LP:
NORGRAN MGN1058, VERVE MGV8148

COCKTAILS FOR TWO (32+12as+coda) arr 881-6
78: NORGRAN 120 45: BLUE STAR (F) GM8512 LP:
NORGRAN MGN1058, VERVE MGV8148

KEY LARGO (64as)(12as) arr, comp 882-7
78: CLEF 89026 LP: NORGRAN MGN1058, VERVE MGV8148

[206] Probably September 1952 New York
BENNY CARTER QUINTET (COSMOPOLITE)

Carter (as) Oscar Peterson (p) Barney Kessel (g) Ray Brown (b) J. C. Heard (d)

STREET SCENE (48as) 938
78: CLEF 89044 LP: NORGRAN MGN1070, VERVE
MGV8160, VERVE (J) MV2635

IMAGINATION (36as)(12as+ coda) 939-2
78: CLEF 89065 LP: NORGRAN MGN1070, VERVE
MGV8160, VERVE (J) MV2635

PICK YOURSELF UP (64as)(36as) 940
78: CLEF 89044 LP: NORGRAN MGN1070, VERVE
MGV8160, VERVE (J) MV2635

I GET A KICK OUT OF YOU (52as) 941-3
78: CLEF 89065 LP: NORGRAN MGN1070, VERVE
MGV8160, VERVE (J) MV2635

[207] October 2, 1952 New York
BENNY CARTER AND HIS ORCHESTRA

Carter (as, arr, comp) Doc Cheatham, Taft Jordan, Dick Vance (tp) Tyree Glenn, Claude Jones, Frank Rehak (tb) Eddie Barefield (as) Art Drelinger, Lucky Thompson (ts) Willard Brown (bs) Billy Taylor (p) Rene Hall (g) Joe Benjamin (b) Chris Colombus (d)

LOVE IS CYNTHIA (28as)+(10as with ensemble) arr   E2VB7382-1
78: VICTOR 20-5133   45: VICTOR 47-5133, HMV 7M189,
LP: RCA (F) PM42406

SUNDAY AFTERNOON (32as)(16as) arr, comp   E2VB7383-1
78: VICTOR 20-5133   45: 47-5133, LP: RCA (F)
PM42406

* * *

On "Love Is Cynthia," an Alfred Newman melody from the film The Snows Of Kiliminjaro, Carter re-creates the melodic solo he played on the film's soundtrack.

---

[208]   Same Date
      SAVANNAH CHURCHILL

Carter (as) as above add Savannah Churchill (v) and vocal group

WALKIN' BY THE RIVER   v-SC (as acc)   E2VB7384-1
78: VICTOR 20-5031

IF I DIDN'T LOVE YOU SO   v-SC (as acc)   E2VB7385-1
78: VICTOR 20-5031

---

[209]   August 3, 1953   Los Angeles
      JAM SESSION (NORMAN GRANZ)

Carter (as) Harry Edison (tp) Willie Smith (as) Stan Getz, Wardell Gray (ts) Buddy DeFranco (cl) Count Basie (organ, p) Arnold Ross (p) Freddie Green (g) John Simmons (b) Buddy Rich (d)

APPLE JAM (as [1st solo])   1259-6
LP: CLEF MGC4003, VERVE MGV8051, VSP 31,
VERVE (E) 2304-421

LADY BE GOOD (as [1st solo])   1260-2
LP: CLEF MGC4004, VERVE MGV8052, VERVE (J)
MV2518, BOOK OF THE MONTH CLUB BOMC20-5605

BLUES FOR THE COUNT (as [1st solo])   1261-2
LP: CLEF MGC4004, VERVE MGV8052, BOOK OF THE
MONTH CLUB BOMC20-5605

I HADN'T ANYONE TILL YOU (as)   1262-4
LP: CLEF MGC4003, VERVE MGV8051, VERVE (E)
2304-421

>NOTES: Last title is Carter's feature in ballad medley; Ross is pianist. Beginning with this session, the number of measures of Carter's solos is no longer given.

* * *

Although similar to the JATP in format, this studio session manages to avoid some of the crowd-pleasing excesses of Granz's live productions.

Consequently Carter is able to turn in some thoughtful solos without fear of being accused of malingering. Particularly interesting is his playing on "Blues For The Count," which benefits from Basie's excellent organ accompaniment.

This is Carter's first recording with Harry "Sweets" Edison; the two became very close and collaborated many times over the next three decades.

[210]   September 10, 1953   Los Angeles
          BUDDY RICH AND HIS ALL STARS

Carter (as, arr, comp) Harry Edison (tp) Milt Bernhart (tb) Georgie Auld (ts) Bob Lawson (bs) Jimmy Rowles (p) John Simmons (b) Buddy Rich (d)

LET'S FALL IN LOVE   (as) arr   1266
78: CLEF 89094   LP: NORGRAN EPN37, VERVE (E)
2683-035

ME AND MY JAGUAR   (e) arr, comp   1267
78: CLEF 89094   LP: NORGRAN EPN37, VERVE (E)
2683-035

JUST BLUES   (as)   1268
LP: NORGRAN EPN37, VERVE (E) 2683-035

[211]   Early September 1953   Los Angeles
          LOUIS BELLSON ORCHESTRA

Carter (as) Harry Edison, Maynard Ferguson, Conrad Gozzo, Ray Linn (tp) Hoyt Bohannon, Herb Harper, Tommy Pederson (tb) Willie Smith (as) Wardell Gray, Bumps Myers (ts) Bob Lawson (bs) Jimmy Rowles (p) Barney Kessel (g) John Simmons (b) Louis Bellson (d)

CAXTON HALL SWING   (e)   1250
78: CLEF 89093   LP: NORGRAN MGN14, NORGRAN
MGN1046, VERVE MGV8137

FOR EUROPEANS ONLY   (e)   1251
78: NORGRAN 108   LP: NORGRAN MGN14, NORGRAN
MGN1046, VERVE MGV8137

PHALANGES   (e)   1252
78: CLEF 89093   LP: NORGRAN MGN14, NORGRAN
MGN1046, VERVE MGV8137

SKIN DEEP   (e)   1253
78: UNISSUED   45: NORGRAN EPN104   LP: NORGRAN
MGN14, NORGRAN MGN1046, VERVE MGV8137

[212]   September 19, 1953   New York   Concert, Carnegie Hall
          JAZZ AT THE PHILHARMONIC

Carter (as) Charlie Shavers, Roy Eldridge (tp) Bill Harris (tb) Willie Smith (as) Lester Young, Ben Webster, Flip Phillips (ts) Oscar Peterson (p) Herb Ellis (g) Ray Brown (b) J. C. Heard, Gene Krupa (d)

September 19, 1953 [212]

COOL BLUES (as)
LP: CLEF MG VOL. 16, VERVE MG VOL. 9, BARCLAY GLP6918

FLAMINGO (as)
LP: CLEF MG VOL. 16, VERVE MG VOL. 9, BARCLAY GLP6918

ONE O'CLOCK JUMP (as)
LP: CLEF MG VOL. 16, VERVE MG VOL. 9, BARCLAY GLP6920

FLYING HOME (e)
LP: CLEF MG VOL. 16, VERVE MG VOL. 9, BARCLAY GLP6920

> NOTES: "Flamingo" is Carter's feature in ballad medley. Young does not play on "Cool Blues." Krupa is the drummer on "Flying Home"; Heard on other titles.

[213] Same Concert
       GENE KRUPA TRIO

Carter (as) Oscar Peterson (p) Gene Krupa (d)

INDIANA (as)
LP: CLEF MG VOL. 16, VERVE MG VOL. 9

SOMEBODY LOVES ME (as)
LP: CLEF MG VOL. 16, VERVE MG VOL. 9

LAURA (as)
LP: CLEF MG VOL. 16, VERVE MG VOL. 9, VERVE (J)
MV9073/75

STOMPIN' AT THE SAVOY (as)
LP: CLEF MG VOL. 16, VERVE MG VOL. 9, VERVE (J)
MV9073/75

* * *

[212, 213] Carter's 17 12-bar choruses on "Cool Blues" constitute one of his longest solos on record. His wild performance is the epitome of the JATP spirit, and the crowd responds appropriately. Carter's effort seems to have adversely affected his tone, which is harsher than usual for the rest of the concert.

On this JATP tour Carter was featured in a new context, as a member (with Oscar Peterson) of the Gene Krupa trio. This setting seems more to his liking, although Krupa's bass drum is overbearing at times.

Jepsen lists this date as September 23, but contemporary reports indicate September 19 (New York Amsterdam News advertisement, September 12, 1953, p. 23, and article in New York Times, September 20, 1953, section 2, p. 7).

[214] Late September 1953   Location Unknown
       JAZZ AT THE PHILHARMONIC

Carter (as) Roy Eldridge, Charlie Shavers (tp) Bill Harris (tb) Willie Smith (as) Lester Young, Ben Webster, Flip Phillips (ts) Oscar Peterson (p) Herb Ellis (g) Ray Brown (b) Gene Krupa (d)

CONCERT BLUES (as)
LP: CLEF MG VOL. 16

* * *

This item was added as a "bonus" ten-inch LP to Clef MG volume 16 and is not from the same concert as the rest of that volume.

[215] Between November 4 and 9, 1953 Tokyo Concert, Nichigeki Theater
JAZZ AT THE PHILHARMONIC

Carter (as) Roy Eldridge, Charlie Shavers (tp) Willie Smith (as) Flip Phillips, Ben Webster (ts) Oscar Peterson (p) Herb Ellis (g) Ray Brown (b) J. C. Heard (d)

JAM SESSION BLUES (as)
LP: VERVE (J) MV9061, VERVE 2660-112, PABLO LIVE 2620-104, VERVE (J) MV9076/78

J. C. HEARD DRUM SOLO (e)
LP: VERVE (J) MV9061, VERVE 2660-112, PABLO LIVE 2620-104, VERVE (J) MV9076/78

COTTONTAIL (e)
LP: VERVE (J) MV9061, VERVE 2660-112, PABLO LIVE 2620-104, VERVE (J) MV9076/78

FLAMINGO (as)
LP: VERVE (J) MV9061, VERVE 2660-112, PABLO LIVE 2620-104, VERVE (J) MV9076/78

NOTE: "Flamingo" is Carter's feature in ballad medley. "Jam Session Blues" appears as "Tokyo Blues" and "J. C. Heard Drum Solo" as "Up" on Pablo Live set.

[216] Same Concert
GENE KRUPA TRIO

Carter (as) Oscar Peterson (p) Gene Krupa (d)

COCKTAILS FOR TWO (as)
LP: VERVE (J) MV9061, VERVE 2660-112, PABLO LIVE 2620-104, VERVE (J) MV9076/78

INDIANA (as)
LP: VERVE (J) MV9061, VERVE 2660-112, PABLO LIVE 2620-104, VERVE (J) MV9076/78

DON'T BE THAT WAY (as)
LP: VERVE (J) MV9061, VERVE 2660-112, PABLO LIVE 2620-104, VERVE (J) MV9076/78

November 4-9, 1953 [216]   155

STOMPIN' AT THE SAVOY   (as)
LP: VERVE (J) MV9061, VERVE 2660-112, PABLO LIVE
2620-104, VERVE (J) MV9076/78

[217]	Same Concert

Carter (as) Roy Eldridge, Charlie Shavers (tp) Willie Smith (as) Flip Phillips, Ben Webster (ts) Oscar Peterson (p) Herb Ellis (g) Ray Brown (b) Ella Fitzgerald (v)

PERDIDO   (e)
LP: VERVE (J) MV9063, VERVE 2660-112, PABLO LIVE
2620-104, VERVE (J) MV9076/78

[218]	Between November 4 and 9, 1953 Tokyo Concert, Nichigeki Theater
	JAZZ AT THE PHILHARMONIC

Carter (as) Roy Eldridge, Charlie Shavers (tp) Willie Smith (as) Flip Phillips, Ben Webster (ts) Oscar Peterson (p) Herb Ellis (g) J. C. Heard (d)

COTTONTAIL   (e)
UNISSUED

FLAMINGO   (as)
UNISSUED

J. C. HEARD DRUM SOLO   (e)
UNISSUED

   NOTE: "Flamingo" is Carter's feature in ballad medley.

[219]	Between November 4 and 9, 1953 Tokyo Concert, Nichigeki Theater
	JAZZ AT THE PHILHARMONIC

Carter (as) Roy Eldridge, Charlie Shavers (tp) Willie Smith (as) Flip Phillips, Ben Webster (ts) Oscar Peterson (p) Herb Ellis (g) J. C. Heard (d)

FLAMINGO   (as)
UNISSUED

J. C. HEARD DRUM SOLO   (e)
UNISSUED

   NOTE: "Flamingo" is Carter's feature in ballad medley.

                         *   *   *

[215-219] The date given for the concert on the Pablo Live issue, November 18, 1953, is certainly incorrect. Carter's passport shows him leaving Japan November 15 for Honolulu. A Variety report from Tokyo (November 11, 1953, p. 51) describes the opening on November 4 of a six-day engagement at the Nichigeki Theater. The commercially issued recording and the two unissued portions of concerts listed after it are probably from this

period, although their correct order is not known. Variety also reports a projected two days of dates in Osaka and Nagoya, probably November 10-12, and a November 13-14 engagement for servicemen at the U.S. Ernie Pyle Theater. This schedule would coincide with the November 15 departure from Japan shown in Carter's passport.

The Japanese Verve issues contain an informal "After Hours Session" on which Carter does not seem to play.

His playing with the trio and on his ballad feature is far superior to the Carnegie Hall September JATP recordings. The interaction among Krupa, Peterson and Carter is more balanced, and his tone is back to normal.

[220]   December 8, 1953   Los Angeles
           BEN WEBSTER AND HIS ORCHESTRA

Carter (as) Harry Edison (tp) Ben Webster (ts) Oscar Peterson (p) Herb Ellis (g) Ray Brown (b) Alvin Stoller (d)

THAT'S ALL   1362-2
UNISSUED

THAT'S ALL   (e)   1362-5
78: NORGRAN 103   LP: NORGRAN MGN1001, VERVE
MGV8020, VERVE (E) 2683-049, VERVE (J) MV2554,
VERVE UMV2081

PENNIES FROM HEAVEN   (e)   1363-2
78: NORGRAN 115   LP: NORGRAN MGN1001, VERVE
MGV8020, METRO 2356-075, VERVE (J) MV2554, VERVE
UMV2081, TIME-LIFE STL-J21

JIVE AT SIX   (as)   1365-2
78: NORGRAN 103   LP: NORGRAN MGN1001, VERVE
MGV8020, METRO 2356-075, VERVE (J) MV2554, VERVE
UMV2081

JIVE AT SIX   1365-5
UNISSUED

DON'T GET AROUND MUCH ANYMORE   (e)   1366-3
78: UNISSUED   45: NORGRAN EPN15   LP: NORGRAN
MGN1001, VERVE MGV8020, VERVE (E) 2683-049, VERVE
(J) MV2554, VERVE UMV2081

[221]   December 31, 1953   Los Angeles
           BENNY CARTER AND HIS ORCHESTRA (COSMOPOLITE)

Carter (as, arr, comp) Gerald Wiggins (p) Red Callender (b) Bill Douglas (d) Horn and String Sections

I'LL BE AROUND   (as) arr   1482-5
45: NORGRAN EPN18   LP: NORGRAN MGN1070,
VERVE MGV8160, VERVE (J) MV2635

December 31, 1953 [221]

BEAUTIFUL LOVE (as) arr   1483
45: NORGRAN EPN18   LP: NORGRAN MGN1070, VERVE
MGV8160, VERVE (J) MV2635

BLUE STAR (as) arr, comp   1484-2
45: NORGRAN EPN18   LP: NORGRAN MGN1070, VERVE
MGV8160, VERVE (J) MV2635

FLAMINGO (as) arr   1485-4
78: CLEF 89109   45: NORGRAN EPN18   LP: NORGRAN
MGN1070, VERVE MGV8160, VERVE (J) MV2635

    NOTE: Two takes (-1, -5) were made of "Beautiful Love."

[221A]   January 4, 1954 Los Angeles
        BENNY CARTER AND HIS ORCHESTRA (COSMOPOLITE)

Carter (as, arr, comp) Gerald Wiggins (p) Red Callender (b) Bill Douglas (d)
Horn and String Sections

WITH A SONG IN MY HEART (as) arr   1490
45: NORGRAN EPN17   LP: NORGRAN MGN1070, VERVE
MGV8160, VERVE (J) MV2635

CAN'T WE BE FRIENDS (as) arr   1491-3
78: CLEF 89109   45: NORGRAN EPN18   LP: NORGRAN
MGN1070, VERVE MGV8160, VERVE (J) MV2635

SYMPHONY (as) arr   1492
45: NORGRAN EPN17   LP: NORGRAN MGN1070, VERVE
MGV8160, VERVE (J) MV2635

I'M SORRY (as) arr, comp   1493-3
45: NORGRAN EPN17   LP: NORGRAN MGN1070, VERVE
MGV8160, VERVE (J) MV2635

    NOTE: Two takes (-2, -7) were made of "With A Song" and three
of "Symphony" (-5, -6, -8). "I'm Sorry" appears on LP as "Sorry."

                          *   *   *

[221]-[221A] Among his most successful recordings with strings, these dates
epitomize the facet of Carter's playing which critics like to call "urbane."
Coming at a time when listeners had become accustomed to a less "legiti-
mate" alto sound, they also show why some critics labeled his tone "saccharine."

    Carter's arrangements here are skillfully crafted; he never has to
compete with the strings, as some jazz soloists have had to do in similar
settings.

    Two lovely original ballads, "Blue Star" and "I'm Sorry" are intro-
duced here, and Carter lavishes his fullest and purest tone on them.

    Uptempo delights include "Symphony" and "With A Song in My Heart."

[221B]	June 23, 1954 Los Angeles
	BENNY CARTER (PLAYS PRETTY/MOONGLOW)

Carter (as) Don Abney (p) George Duvivier (b) Louis Bellson (d)

MOONGLOW (as) 1780-1
45: NORGRAN EPN87 LP: NORGRAN MGN1015, VERVE MGV2025

MY ONE AND ONLY LOVE (as) 1781-2
45: NORGRAN EPN87 LP: NORGRAN MGN1015, VERVE MGV2025

OUR LOVE IS HERE TO STAY (as) 1782-3
45: NORGRAN EPN87 LP: NORGRAN MGN1015, VERVE MGV2025

THIS CAN'T BE LOVE (as) 1783-5
45: NORGRAN EPN88 LP: NORGRAN MGN1044, VERVE MGV8135

TENDERLY (as) 1784-3
45: NORGRAN EPN87 LP: NORGRAN MGN1015, VERVE MGV2025

UNFORGETTABLE (as) 1785-2
45: NORGRAN EPN88 LP: NORGRAN MGN1015, VERVE MGV2025

RUBY (as) 1786-5
45: NORGRAN EPN88 LP: NORGRAN MGN1015, VERVE MGV2025

MOON SONG (as) 1787
45: NORGRAN EPN88 LP: NORGRAN MGN1015, VERVE MGV2025

NOTE: Two takes (-3, -4) were made of "Moon Song."

[222]	June 25, 1954 Los Angeles
	ART TATUM-BENNY CARTER-LOUIS BELLSON

Carter (as, comp) Art Tatum (p) Louis Bellson (d)

MY BLUE HEAVEN (as) 1788-1
45: CLEF EPC320 LP: CLEF MGC643, VERVE MGV8013, METRO 2682-024, PABLO 2310-733, PABLO 2625-706

BLUES IN B FLAT (as) 1789-2
45: CLEF EPC319 LP: CLEF MGC643, VERVE MGV8013, METRO 2682-024, PABLO 2310-732, PABLO 2625-706, TIME-LIFE STL-J10

BLUES IN C (as) 1790-1
LP: VERVE MGV8227, METRO 2682-024, PABLO 2310-732, PABLO 2625-706

June 25, 1954 [222]

A FOGGY DAY (as) LP: VERVE MGV8227, METRO 2682-024, PABLO 2310-732, PABLO 2625-706	1791-2
BLUES IN MY HEART (as) comp 45: CLEF EPC318 LP: CLEF MGC643, VERVE MGV8013, METRO 2682-024, PABLO 2310-733, PABLO 2625-706	1792-1
STREET OF DREAMS (as) 45: CLEF EPC320 LP: CLEF MGC643, VERVE MGV8013, METRO 2682-024, PABLO 2310-732, PABLO 2625-706	1793-2
IDAHO (as) 45: CLEF EPC320 LP: CLEF MGC643, VERVE MGV8013, METRO 2682-024, PABLO 2310-733, PABLO 2625-706	1794-2
YOU'RE MINE, YOU (as) LP: VERVE MGV8227, METRO 2682-024, PABLO 2310-733, PABLO 2625-706	1795-1
UNDECIDED (as) LP: VERVE MGV8227, METRO 2682-024, PABLO 2310-732, PABLO 2625-706	1796-2
UNDER A BLANKET OF BLUE (as) LP: VERVE MGV8227, METRO 2682-024, PABLO 2310-732, PABLO 2625-706	1797-2
MAKIN' WHOOPEE (as) UNISSUED	1798-1
MAKIN' WHOOPEE (as) LP: VERVE MGV8227, METRO 2682-024, PABLO 2310-733, PABLO 2625-706	1798-2
OLD FASHIONED LOVE (as) 45: CLEF EPC318 LP: CLEF MGC643, VERVE MGV8013, METRO 2682-024, PABLO 2310-733, PABLO 2625-706	1799-1
'S WONDERFUL (as) 45: CLEF EPC319 LP: CLEF MGC643, VERVE MGV8013, METRO 2682-024, PABLO 2310-732, PABLO 2625-706	1800-2
HANDS ACROSS THE TABLE (as) 45: CLEF EPC319 LP: CLEF MGC643, VERVE MGV8013, METRO 2682-024, PABLO 2310-733, PABLO 2625-706	1801-1

* * *

Carter and Tatum were brought together in the studio for the first and only time by Norman Granz. This marathon session (14 tunes in one day) points up the many similarities between their styles. Both have flawless technique and are most at home with the more sophisticated standards, which they reshape with elegant multinoted embellishments. But both men have another, more earthy side, and perhaps most surprising are their superb collaborations on the blues, especially the "Blues in B Flat."

If Tatum was ever criticized it was for his alleged inability to subordinate his great solo gifts to a secondary accompanying role. Carter, however, found his backing solid and imaginative. Nor did the absence of a bass bother Carter, who recalls, "With Art Tatum, no bass was needed. It would only get in the way." He adds that the only inhibiting factor in playing with the pianist was "the feeling of awe he generated, and the question of whether you could keep up with what he was doing."

[223]	August 2, 1954 Los Angeles
	MEL TORME

Carter (as, arr) large orchestra, George Cates (dir) Matty Matlock (cl) Mel Torme (v)

TUTTI FRUTTI v-MT (as) arr   L7770
LP: CORAL CRL57044, VOCALION VL73905

IT DON'T MEAN A THING IF IT AIN'T GOT THAT SWING   L7771
    v-MT (e) arr
LP: CORAL CRL57044, VOCALION VL73905

ROSE O'DAY v-MT (e)   L7772
LP: CORAL CRL57044, VOCALION VL73905

HOLD TIGHT v-MT (e)   L7773
LP: CORAL CRL57044, VOCALION VL73905

I'SE A MUGGIN' v-MT (e)   L7774
LP: CORAL CRL57044

[224]	August 3, 1954 Los Angeles
	MEL TORME

Carter (as) large orchestra, George Cates, Sonny Burke (dir) Conrad Gozzo (tp) Georgie Auld (ts) Al Pellegrini (p) Mel Torme (v) Billy May (arr)

ALL OF YOU v-MT arr-BM (e)   L7775
LP: CORAL CRL57044

SPELLBOUND v-MT (e)   L7776
LP: CORAL CRL57044

CEMENT MIXER v-MT (e)   L7777
LP: CORAL CRL57044

FLAT FOOT FLOOGIE v-MT (e)   L7778
LP: CORAL CRL57044

THE HUT-SUT SONG v-MT (e)   L7779
LP: CORAL CRL57044

    NOTE: Burke (dir) on "Cement Mixer" and "Flat Foot"; Cates on others.

[225]	September 14, 1954 New York
	NEW JAZZ SOUNDS

September 14, 1954 [225]

Carter (as) Dizzy Gillespie (tp) Bill Harris (tb) Oscar Peterson (p) Herb Ellis (g) Ray Brown (b) Buddy Rich (d)

LAURA (as) LP: NORGRAN MGN1015, VERVE MGV2025	1955-1
THAT OLD BLACK MAGIC (as) LP: NORGRAN MGN1044, VERVE MGV8135, VERVE (J) MV2549	1956-2
ANGEL EYES (as) LP: NORGRAN MGN1044, VERVE MGV8135, VERVE (J) MV2549	1957-3
THE SONG IS YOU (as) LP: NORGRAN MGN1044, VERVE MGV8135, VERVE (J) MV2549	1958-8
MARRIAGE BLUES (as) LP: NORGRAN MGN1044, VERVE MGV8135, VERVE (J) MV2549	1959-1
JUST ONE OF THOSE THINGS (as) LP: NORGRAN MGN1044, VERVE MGV8135, VERVE (J) MV2549	1960-1

NOTE: Gillespie plays on last two titles only.

* * *

Carter's first recorded collaboration with Dizzy Gillespie since the famous "Hot Mallets" session of 1939 with Lionel Hampton was not planned. Gillespie dropped by the studio during this session and, as the liner notes (Verve MGV8135) report, asked to sit in. Although the two titles with Gillespie are the highlights, the date as a whole is also consistently inspired, with Harris's gruff trombone contrasting well with Carter's smooth alto.

[225A] September 20, 1954 New York Studio Session for Norgran--
                                        Unissued
            BENNY CARTER TRIO

Carter (as) Teddy Wilson (p) Jo Jones (d)

LITTLE GIRL BLUE	1988-5
JUNE IN JANUARY	1989-4
JEEPERS CREEPERS	1990-2
ROSETTA	1991-2
BIRTH OF THE BLUES	1992-1
WHEN YOUR LOVER HAS GONE	1993-3
THE MOON IS LOW	1994-1
THIS LOVE OF MINE	1995-3

[225B]   November 12, 1954   Los Angeles
         BENNY CARTER

Carter (as) Oscar Peterson (p) Herb Ellis (g) Ray Brown (b) Bobby White (d)

DON'T YOU THINK   2042-1
UNISSUED

WILL YOU STILL BE MINE   2043-2
UNISSUED

A FOGGY DAY (as)   2044-1
LP: NORGRAN MGN1035, VERVE MGV8126, COLUMBIA
(E) 33CX10072, VERVE (J) KL5021

WE'LL BE TOGETHER AGAIN   2045-2
UNISSUED

YOU TOOK ADVANTAGE OF ME (as)   2046-1
LP: NORGRAN MGN1035, VERVE MGV8126, COLUMBIA
(E) 33CX10072, VERVE (J) KL5021

POINCIANA (as)   2047-2
LP: NORGRAN MGN1035, VERVE MGV8126, COLUMBIA
(E) 33CX10072, VERVE (J) KL5021

PRISONER OF LOVE (as)   2048-1
LP: NORGRAN MGN1035, VERVE MGV8126, COLUMBIA
(E) 33CX10072, VERVE (J) KL5021

FRENESI (as)   2049-2
LP: NORGRAN MGN1044, VERVE MGV2025, VERVE
MGV8135, COLUMBIA (E) 33CX10049

[226]   December 23, 1954   Los Angeles
         BIG DAVE (CAVANAUGH) AND HIS ORCHESTRA

Carter (as) Dave Cavanaugh, Plas Johnson, Ted Romersa, Mort Friedman (reeds) Don Robertson (p) Jack Marshall (g) Mike Rubin (b) Roy Harte (d) The Hard Tops, (i.e.) Buck Stapleton, Allan Copeland, Harold Dickenson, Tom Kenny, Charles Schrouder (v)

ROCK AND ROLL PARTY   v-HT   13339
45?: CAPITOL 3028

YOUR KIND OF LOVE   v-HT   13340
45?: CAPITOL 3028

[227]   1954   Los Angeles
         PEGGY LEE WITH ORCH. CONDUCTED BY JOSEPH LILLEY

Carter (as, arr) Peggy Lee (v) Large Orchestra with Strings

LOVE, YOU DIDN'T DO RIGHT BY ME   v-PL (as) arr   L7706
78: DECCA 29250

1954 [227]

SISTERS v-PL (e)   L7707
78: DECCA 29250

---

[228] Ca. 1954 Los Angeles
    PEGGY LEE

Carter (as) Unknown Rhythm Section, Peggy Lee (v)

BOUQUET OF BLUES (as)
45: DECCA 9-29373

---

[229] January 7, 1955 Los Angeles
    LORD BUCKLEY & THE ROYAL COURT ORCH. UNDER THE
    DIRECTION OF HIS GRACE, SIR HARRY M. G.

Carter (as) Maury Harris (tp) Milt Bernhart (tb) Ted Nash (ts?) Edwin Cole (p) Red Callender (b) Lou Singer (d) Harry Geller (dir) Lord Buckley (v)

FRIENDS, ROMANS, COUNTRYMEN v-LB (as acc)   F2PB-0402
LP: RCA LPM3246, RCA LPV580

HIAWATHA v-LB (e)   F2PB-0403
LP: RCA LPM3246

BOSTON TEA PARTY v-LB (e)   F2PB-0404
LP: RCA LPM3246

BAA BAA BLACK SHEEP v-LB (e)   F2PB-0405
UNISSUED?

  NOTE: On the first title musical accompaniment is present throughout only on RCA LPV580; apparently, the music track was omitted on the original issue, except for brief passages at the beginning and end of this piece.

---

[230] March 23, 1955 Los Angeles
    ROY ELDRIDGE-BENNY CARTER QUINTET (URBANE JAZZ)

Carter (as, comp) Roy Eldridge (tp) Bruce MacDonald (p) John Simmons (b) Alvin Stoller (d)

I STILL LOVE HIM SO (as) comp   2296-1
LP: VERVE MGV8202, ARS G413

THE MOON IS LOW (as)   2297-1
LP: VERVE MGV8202, ARS G413

THE MOON IS LOW (as)   2297-3
78: CLEF 89143

CLOSE YOUR EYES (as)   2298-4
78: CLEF 89143 LP: VERVE MGV8202, ARS G413

I MISSED MY HAT (as)   2299-2
LP: VERVE MGV8202, ARS G413

POLITE BLUES (as)   2300-1
LP: VERVE MGV8202, ARS G413

I REMEMBER YOU (as)   2301-2
LP: VERVE MGV8202, ARS G413

   NOTE: "I Remember You" is Carter's feature in ballad medley.

                            * * *

Carter and Eldridge are both in top form and each seems inspired by the other. "I Still Love Him So" is a Carter ballad which is a favorite of Eldridge's. The trumpeter first recorded it in Paris in 1951 and redid it in 1976 for Pablo.

   The LP version of "The Moon Is Low" is more than twice as long as the 78 and is far superior, with space for both Carter and Eldridge to stretch out as well as two full choruses of 8-bar trades between the two horns. Both versions have the same riff in the out-chorus, but on the 78 Eldridge has some problems executing it.

[231]   - reassigned

[232]   May 4, 1955   New York
EARL BOSTIC

Carter (as) Elmon Wright, John Coles (tp) Earl Bostic (as) Benny Golson (ts) Frank Flynn (vib) Stash O'Laughlin (p) Ulysses Livingston (g) George Tucker (b) Granville Hogan (d) String Section

DREAM (e)   K9626
45: KING 4815 LP: KING LP515, PARLOPHONE (E)
R4061, POLYDOR 623229

BEYOND THE BLUE HORIZON (e)   K9627
45: KING 4829 LP: KING LP515, PARLOPHONE (E)
R4208, POLYDOR 623229

EAST OF THE SUN (e)   K9628
45: KING 4815 LP: KING LP515, PARLOPHONE (E)
R4061, POLYDOR 623229

FOR ALL WE KNOW (e)   K9629
45: KING 4829 LP: KING LP558, PARLOPHONE (E) R4208

[233]   August 23, 1955   Los Angeles
BILLIE HOLIDAY AND HER ORCHESTRA

Carter (as) Harry Edison (tp) Jimmy Rowles (p) Barney Kessel (g) John Simmons (b) Larry Bunker (d) Billie Holiday (v)

I DON'T WANT TO CRY ANYMORE   v-BH (as acc)   2438-2
45: CLEF EPC368 LP: VERVE MGV8026, VERVE (J)
MV2595, VERVE (E) 2304-114, VERVE VE-2-2515

August 23, 1955 [233]

PRELUDE TO A KISS v-BH (as) 2439-2
LP: CLEF MGC713, VERVE MGV8096, VERVE (J)
MV2596, VERVE (E) 2304-114, VERVE VE-2-2515

GHOST OF A CHANCE v-BH (as acc) 2440-1
45: CLEF EPC369 LP: VERVE MGV8026, VERVE (J)
MV2595, VERVE (E) 2304-114, VERVE VE-2-2515

WHEN YOUR LOVER HAS GONE v-BH (e) 2441-3
LP: CLEF MGC713, VERVE MGV8096, VERVE (J)
MV2596, VERVE (E) 2304-114, VERVE VE-2-2515

PLEASE DON'T TALK ABOUT ME WHEN I'M GONE 2443-2
v-BH (as)
LP: CLEF MGC713, VERVE MGV8096, VERVE (J)
MV2596, VERVE 2-V6S-8816, VERVE (E) 2304-114,
VERVE VE-2-2515

IT HAD TO BE YOU v-BH (as acc) 2444-1
45: CLEF EPC368 LP: VERVE MGV8026, VERVE (J)
MV2595, VERVE (E) 2304-114, VERVE VE-2-2515

NICE WORK IF YOU CAN GET IT v-BH (as acc) 2445-5
LP: CLEF MGC713, VERVE MGV8096, VERVE (J)
MV2596, VERVE (E) 2304-114, VERVE VE-2-2515

[233A]   August 25, 1955 Los Angeles
         BILLIE HOLIDAY AND HER ORCHESTRA

Carter (as) Harry Edison (tp) Jimmy Rowles (p) Barney Kessel (g) John Simmons (b) Larry Bunker (d) Billie Holiday (v)

COME RAIN OR COME SHINE v-BH (as acc) 2446-3
LP: CLEF MGC669, VERVE MGV8026, VERVE (J)
MV2595, VERVE (E) 2304-114, VERVE VE-2-2515

WHAT'S NEW v-BH (as) 2448-3
LP: CLEF MGC669, VERVE MGV8096, VERVE (J)
MV2596, VERVE 2-V6S-8816, VERVE (E) 2304-115,
VERVE VE-2-2529

A FINE ROMANCE v-BH (as acc) 2449-8
45: CLEF EPC368 LP: VERVE MGV8026, VERVE (J)
MV2595, VERVE (E) 2304-115, VERVE VE-2-2529

I GET A KICK OUT OF YOU v-BH (as) 2451-3
45: CLEF EPC369 LP: VERVE MGV8026, VERVE (J)
MV2595, VERVE (E) 2304-115, VERVE VE-2-2529

ISN'T IT A LOVELY DAY v-BH (as) 2453-3
LP: CLEF MGC669, VERVE MGV8026, VERVE (J)
MV2595, VERVE (E) 2304-115, VERVE VE-2-2529

---

[234]   December 2, 1955 Los Angeles
         SESSION AT MIDNIGHT

Carter (as, tp) Shorty Sherock, Harry Edison (tp) Murray McEachern (tb, as) Gus Bivona (cl) Willie Smith (as) Plas Johnson, Babe Russin (ts) Jimmy Rowles (p) Al Hendrickson (g) Mike Rubin (b) Irv Cottler (d)

MOTEN SWING (as [2nd solo])
LP: CAPITOL T707, CAPITOL (DENMARK) 6E-052-81006

MAKING THE SCENE (tp [2nd solo])
LP: CAPITOL T707, CAPITOL (DENMARK) 6E-052-81006

SWEET GEORGIA BROWN (as)
LP: CAPITOL T707, CAPITOL (DENMARK) 6E-052-81006

BLUE LOU (tp [Edison, Carter, Sherock trade fours in that order]) (as [McEachern, Carter, Smith trade fours in that order])
LP: CAPITOL T707, CAPITOL (DENMARK) 6E-052-81006

STOMPIN' AT THE SAVOY (as [1st solo])
LP: CAPITOL T707, CAPITOL (DENMARK) 6E-052-81006

SESSION AT MIDNIGHT (as [2nd solo])
LP: CAPITOL T707, CAPITOL (DENMARK) 6E-052-81006

[235] - reassigned

[236] 1955 Los Angeles
ALFRED NEWMAN AND HIS ORCHESTRA

Carter (as, arr) Large Orchestra with Strings, Alfred Newman (conductor)

TO AVA (as) arr
LP: DECCA DL8123

* * *

This is another recording of the theme written by Alfred Newman which Carter played in the film The Snows of Kiliminjaro. It is known variously as "To Ava" (after Ava Gardner who starred), "Blue Mountain," and "Love Is Cynthia."

[237] February 25, 1957 Los Angeles
QUINCY JONES' ALL STARS

Carter (as) Herb Geller, Charlie Mariano, Art Pepper (as) Lou Levy (p) Red Mitchell (b) Shelly Manne (d) Quincy Jones (dir) Jimmy Giuffre, Lennie Niehaus (arr, comp)

BE MY GUEST arr&comp-LN (as [4th 16b solo, 4th in trades])
LP: ABC PARAMOUNT ABC186, HMV CLP1157, ABC (J) YW8511

DANCIN' PANTS arr&comp-JG (as [2nd solo])
LP: ABC PARAMOUNT ABC186, HMV CLP1157, ABC (J) YW8511

February 25, 1957 [237]

KING'S ROAD BLUES   arr&comp-LN (as [1st solo])
LP: ABC PARAMOUNT ABC186, HMV CLP1157, ABC
(J) YW8511

* * *

Quincy Jones directed this date which brings Carter together with three of
the younger West Coast alto men. The catchy originals by Niehaus and
Giuffre provide an excellent basis for a comparison of the alto styles.

[238]   Ca. February 1957   Los Angeles
        STARS FOR DEFENSE DIXIELAND JAMBOREE

Carter (as) Charlie Teagarden, Red Nichols, Dick Cathcart, Conrad Gozzo,
Frank Beach, John Best (tp) Jack Teagarden (tb, v) Moe Schneider, King
Jackson, Murray McEachern, Warren Smith, Bill Schaefer (tb) Chuck Gentry, Wayne Songer, Matty Matlock, Eddie Miller, Babe Russin (reeds) Stan
Wrightsman, Al Pellegrini (p) Al Hendrickson, Nappy Lamare (g) Morty Corb
(b) Phil Stevens (tuba) Jack Sperling, Nick Fatool (d)

SOUTH RAMPART STREET PARADE   (e)
T: STARS FOR DEFENSE   LP: BLACK JACK LP3009,
FANFARE LP-2-102

BASIN STREET BLUES   v-JT (e)
T: STARS FOR DEFENSE   LP: FANFARE LP-2-102

MILENBERG JOYS   (as)
T: STARS FOR DEFENSE   LP: BLACK JACK LP3009,
FANFARE LP-2-102

   NOTE: The Fanfare LP contains two versions of "South Rampart
   Street Parade," designated no. 1 and no. 2. The liner notes list
   no. 2 from this session and no. 1 as from a 1949 session but aural
   evidence indicates the reverse.

[239]   June 3, 1957   Los Angeles   TV Show Soundtrack
        BOBBY TROUP'S STARS OF JAZZ

Carter (as) Pete Jolly (p) Unknown (g, b, d)

THIS CAN'T BE LOVE   (as)
LP: CALLIOPE CAL320

LAURA   (as)
LP: CALLIOPE CAL320

TAKE THE A TRAIN   (as)
LP: CALLIOPE CAL320

[240]   June 11, 1957   Los Angeles
        BENNY CARTER (JAZZ GIANT)

Carter (as, arr) Frank Rosolino (tb) Ben Webster (ts) Andre Previn (p) Barney
Kessel (g) Leroy Vinnegar (b) Shelly Manne (d)

OLD FASHIONED LOVE (as) arr
LP: CONTEMPORARY C3555/S7028

BLUE LOU (as) arr
LP: CONTEMPORARY C3555/S7028

*   *   *

This is the first of four sessions comprising Carter's Jazz Giant, one of his finest LPs of the 1950s. The album was to have been completed on August 6, but Carter became ill at the last moment. (The session, which was continued without him, resulted in the Barney Kessel album Let's Cook, Contemporary S7603.)

Carter's arrangements consist primarily of opening and closing riffs which allow maximum space for the string of superb solos.

[241]	July 22, 1957 Los Angeles
	BENNY CARTER (JAZZ GIANT)

Carter (as, tp, arr, comp) Frank Rosolino (tb) Ben Webster (ts) Jimmy Rowles (p) Barney Kessel (g) Leroy Vinnegar (b) Shelly Manne (d)

A WALKIN' THING (as) arr, comp
LP: CONTEMPORARY C3555/S7028

I'M COMING VIRGINIA (tp) arr
LP: CONTEMPORARY C3555/S7028

*   *   *

The second Jazz Giant session opens with the first recording of a catchy Carter original, "A Walkin' Thing."

"I'm Coming Virginia" is Carter's first trumpet feature on record in over ten years. After 1946 he found that the increasing demands of arranging and composing for films precluded his devoting sufficient time to the instrument. Lester Koenig of Contemporary Records was a great admirer of Carter's trumpet, however, and Carter recalls, "He was always after me to record on trumpet and I finally acquiesced." His solo, while containing none of the bravura of an "I Surrender Dear," shows excellent control and the typically bright singing tone, delicate vibrato, and varied dynamics which have always distinguished Carter's trumpet work.

[242]	October 7, 1957 Los Angeles
	BENNY CARTER (JAZZ GIANT)

Carter (as, tp, arr, comp) Frank Rosolino (tb) Ben Webster (ts) Andre Previn (p) Barney Kessel (g) Leroy Vinnegar (b) Shelly Manne (d)

HOW CAN YOU LOSE (tp)(as) arr, comp
LP: CONTEMPORARY C3555/S7028

[243]	December 6 and 12, 1957 Los Angeles
	HENRI RENE & HIS ORCHESTRA--BENNY CARTER, SOLO SAXOPHONE

December 6 and 12, 1957 [243]

Carter (as) John Towner Williams (p) Al Hendrickson (g) Joe Mondragon (b) Lou Singer or Irv Cottler (d) 12 violins, 4 violas, Henri Rene (dir)

FRANKIE (as)
LP: RCA LPM1583

TAB (as)
LP: RCA LPM1583

PAT (as)
LP: RCA LPM1583

DINO (as)
LP: RCA LPM1583

JOHNNY (as)
LP: RCA LPM1583

>NOTE: Despite the label designations, Carter solos only on the titles listed above.

* * *

There is little of jazz interest in this "easy listening" date. Carter's role as featured soloist is to play the themes and occasional obbligatos behind the strings. Henri Rene's music is supposed to depict some of the singing idols of women of the day and was issued under the dated title "Music For The Weaker Sex."

[243A]   1957   Los Angeles
SOUNDTRACK OF FILM THE SUN ALSO RISES

Carter (C-melody sax) with P/B/D

I LOVE YOU   (C-melody sax)
LP: KAPP KDL7001

SWINGIN' DOWN THE LANE   (C-melody sax)
LP: KAPP KDL7001

YOU DO SOMETHING TO ME   (C-melody sax)
LP: KAPP KDL7001

THE CARTER CHARLESTON   (C-melody sax)
LP: KAPP KDL7001

>NOTE: First three tunes played in medley; accordion added on last.

[244]   April 21, 1958   Los Angeles
BENNY CARTER (JAZZ GIANT)

Carter (as) Andre Previn (p) Barney Kessel (g) Leroy Vinnegar (b) Shelly Manne (d)

AIN'T SHE SWEET (as)
LP: CONTEMPORARY C3555/S7028

BLUES MY NAUGHTY SWEETIE GAVE TO ME   (as)
LP: CONTEMPORARY C3555/S7028

* * *

To finish the Jazz Giant album, Carter recorded two selections with just the rhythm section. His alto solos are perhaps the strongest on the album.

[245]   September 1958   Los Angeles
        FRANK DEVOL AND HIS ORCHESTRA

Carter (as) Large Orchestra, Frank Devol (dir) Albert Harris (comp)

CIRCE (as)
LP: COLUMBIA CL1287

MORPHEUS (as)
LP: COLUMBIA CL1287

* * *

Carter is featured soloist on these pieces written by Albert Harris. Harris, guitarist on several of Carter's 1936-1937 British recordings, moved to Hollywood, where he has become a composer of note.

[246]   September or Early October 1958
        SOUNDTRACK OF FILM THE FIVE PENNIES

Carter (as, arr) Collective Personnel: Red Nichols (tp, cornet) Louis Armstrong (tp, v) Bobby Goodrich, Clyde Hurley, Dick Cathcart (tp) Warren Smith, Pete Beilman, Elmer Schneider (tb) Heinie Beau (cl) Wayne Songer (as) Eddie Miller (ts) Joe Rushton (bs) Stan Wrightsman, Gene Plummer (p) George Van Eps, Allan Reuss (g) Morty Corb (b) Jack Sperling, Nick Fatool, Shelly Manne (d) Danny Kaye (v)

AFTER YOU'VE GONE   (as acc)
LP: DOT DLP9500

BILL BAILEY, WON'T YOU PLEASE COME HOME   v-LA, DK
     (e) arr
LP: DOT DLP9500

BATTLE HYMN OF THE REPUBLIC   v-LA (e)
LP: DOT DLP9500, DOT DLP25878

JUST THE BLUES   (e) arr
LP: DOT DLP9500, DOT DLP25878

* * *

Carter does not solo on his only recordings with Louis Armstrong. He arranged and conducted (but did not play) on a session for him in 1955.

Carter may play in the ensemble on other selections on the soundtrack album, but is clearly audible on the four listed above.

September or Early October 1958 [246]

In addition to the two arrangements listed, Carter arranged the following tunes in the film which do not appear on the soundtrack album: "Washington And Lee Swing," "Runnin' Wild," "Tiger Rag" and "Sleepy Time."

[247]   October 24, 1958   Los Angeles
         BOBBY TROUP AND HIS STARS OF JAZZ

Carter (as) Collective Personnel: Buddy Childers, Conte Candoli, Pete Candoli, Ollie Mitchell, Al Porcino, Ray Triscari, Stu Williamson (tp) Shorty Rogers (tp, arr) Milt Bernhart, Harry Betts, Bob Enevoldsen, John Halliburton, Dick Nash, Frank Rosolino, Kenny Shroyer (tb) Paul Horn, Bud Shank (fl, as) Bob Cooper, Plas Johnson, Richie Kamuca (ts) Bill Holman (ts, bs) Chuck Gentry (bs) Jimmy Rowles (p, arr) Red Norvo (vib) Barney Kessel (g) Monty Budwig, Joe Mondragon (b) Mel Lewis, Shelly Manne (d) Bobby Troup (v)

PLEASE BE KIND   v-BT (as)
LP: RCA LPM1959

AS LONG AS I LIVE   v-BT (e)
LP: RCA LPM1959

IS YOU IS OR IS YOU AIN'T MY BABY   v-BT (e)
LP: RCA LPM1959

PERDIDO   v-BT
UNISSUED

NOTE: Personnel listed is for three sessions; Carter plays on this one only.

[248]   November 2, 1958   Los Angeles
         BENNY CARTER QUARTET WITH EARL HINES (SWINGIN' THE TWENTIES)

Carter (as, tp) Earl Hines (p) Leroy Vinnegar (b) Shelly Manne (d)

MARY LOU   (as)
LP: CONTEMPORARY M3561/S7561, VOGUE (E) LAC12225, CONTEMPORARY (F) CHTX240.630

IF I COULD BE WITH YOU   (tp)
LP: CONTEMPORARY M3561/S7561, VOGUE (E) LAC12225, CONTEMPORARY (F) CHTX240.630

IN A LITTLE SPANISH TOWN   (as)
LP: CONTEMPORARY M3561/S7561, VOGUE (E) LAC12225, CONTEMPORARY (F) CHTX240.630

JUST IMAGINE   (as)
LP: CONTEMPORARY M3561/S7561, VOGUE (E) LAC12225, CONTEMPORARY (F) CHTX240.630

SWEET LORRAINE   (as)
LP: CONTEMPORARY M3561/S7561, VOGUE (E) LAC12225, CONTEMPORARY (F) CHTX240.630

A MONDAY DATE (as)
LP: CONTEMPORARY M3561/S7561, VOGUE (E) LAC12225,
CONTEMPORARY (F) CHTX240.630

SOMEONE TO WATCH OVER ME (tp)
LP: CONTEMPORARY M3561/S7561, VOGUE (E) LAC12225,
CONTEMPORARY (F) CHTX240.630

ALL ALONE (tp)
LP: CONTEMPORARY M3561/S7561, VOGUE (E) LAC12225,
CONTEMPORARY (F) CHTX240.630

WHO'S SORRY NOW (as)
LP: CONTEMPORARY M3561/S7561, VOGUE (E) LAC12225,
CONTEMPORARY (F) CHTX240.630

THOU SWELL (as)
LP: CONTEMPORARY M3561/S7561, VOGUE (E) LAC12225,
CONTEMPORARY (F) CHTX240.630

LAUGH, CLOWN, LAUGH (as)
LP: CONTEMPORARY M3561/S7561, VOGUE (E) LAC12225,
CONTEMPORARY (F) CHTX240.630

MY BLUE HEAVEN (as)
LP: CONTEMPORARY M3561/S7561, VOGUE (E) LAC12225,
CONTEMPORARY (F) CHTX240.630

* * *

Carter's first recording with Hines is a generally successful date, featuring updated versions of 1920s standards. Lester Koenig again persuaded Carter to play trumpet, which he does effectively on three tunes.

[249]	1958 Los Angeles
	DON EVANS WITH ORCH. UNDER THE DIRECTION OF BENNY CARTER

Carter (as, arr, comp) Unknown Rhythm Section, Don Evans (v)

HOW LONG IS A MOMENT v-DE (as) arr, comp
45: DOME 100-2

NOTE: Dome is Carter's own label.

[250]	1958 Los Angeles
	THE SMART SET

Carter (as) Includes Dick Cathcart (tp) Ted Nash (as, flute) Bob Enevoldsen (ts) Red Norvo (vib) The Smart Set (v) Jimmy Joyce (arr)

THE LONESOME ROAD v-SS (e)
LP: WARNER BROS. W1258

CARELESS v-SS (e)
LP: WARNER BROS. W1258

1958 [250]

IT'S ALL RIGHT WITH ME   v-SS (e)
LP: WARNER BROS. W1258

I HEAR MUSIC   v-SS (e)
LP: WARNER BROS. W1258

FIVE FOOT TWO, EYES OF BLUE   v-SS (e)
LP: WARNER BROS. W1258

---

[251]   1958   Los Angeles
KITTY WHITE

Carter (as) Jimmy Rowles (p) Bill Pitman (g) Larry Bunker (vib) Red Callender (b) Alvin Stoller (d) Carlos Vidal (bongos, conga) Kitty White (v)

PLEASE BE PATIENT   v-KW (as)
LP: ROULETTE R52020

FOREVER YOUNG   v-KW (as)
LP: ROULETTE R52020

SO HELP ME   v-KW (as)
LP: ROULETTE R52020

IT WAS SO BEAUTIFUL   v-KW (as)
LP: ROULETTE R52020

---

[252]   Ca. 1958   Los Angeles
KITTY WHITE WITH BENNY CARTER AND HIS ORCHESTRA

Carter (as, arr) Gale Robinson (French horn) Unknown (tb, p, g, b, d) Kitty White (v)

THE OLD MAN AND THE SEA   v-KW (as acc) arr
45:   GNP 141X

I AM YOUR DREAM   v-KW (as) arr
45:   GNP 141X

---

[253]   Late 1958 or Early 1959   Los Angeles
BENNY CARTER AND HIS ORCHESTRA (ASPECTS/JAZZ CALENDER)

Carter (as, arr, comp) Conrad Gozzo, Shorty Sherock, Pete Candoli, Uan Rasey (tp) Tommy Pederson, George Roberts, Herb Harper (tb) Buddy Collette, Bill Green, Justin Gordon, Chuck Gentry (reeds) Arnold Ross (p) Bobby Gibbons (g) Joe Comfort (b) Shelly Manne (d) Larry Bunker (vib, bongos)

JUNE IN JANUARY   (as) arr
LP: UNITED ARTISTS UAL4017/UAS5017, UNITED ARTISTS UAL4080/UAS5080, UNITED ARTISTS (J) GXF3039

FEBRUARY FIESTA   (as) arr
LP: UNITED ARTISTS UAL4017/UAS5017, UNITED ARTISTS UAL4080/UAS5080, UNITED ARTISTS (J) GXF3039

I'LL REMEMBER APRIL (as) arr
LP: UNITED ARTISTS UAL4017/UAS5017, UNITED ARTISTS
UAL4080/UAS5080, UNITED ARTISTS (J) GXF3039

SEPTEMBER SONG (as) arr
LP: UNITED ARTISTS UAL4017/UAS5017, UNITED ARTISTS
UAL4080/UAS5080, UNITED ARTISTS (J) GXF3039

ONE MORNING IN MAY (as)
LP: UNITED ARTISTS UAL4017/UAS5017, UNITED ARTISTS
UAL4080/UAS5080, UNITED ARTISTS (J) GXF3039

AUGUST MOON (as) comp
LP: UNITED ARTISTS UAL4017/UAS5017, UNITED ARTISTS
UAL4080/UAS5080, UNITED ARTISTS (J) GXF3039

    NOTE: Carter with p, g, b, d, vib on last two titles. See comments for next session.

[254]   Late 1958 or Early 1959 Los Angeles
BENNY CARTER AND HIS ORCHESTRA (ASPECTS/JAZZ CALENDER)

Carter (as, arr, comp) Al Porcino, Stu Williamson, Ray Triscari, Joe Gordon (tp) Frank Rosolino, Tommy Pederson, Russ Brown (tb) Buddy Collette, Bill Green, Jewell Grant, Plas Johnson (reeds) Gerald Wiggins (p) Barney Kessel (g) Joe Comfort (b) Shelly Manne (d)

MARCH WIND (as) arr, comp
LP: UNITED ARTISTS UAL4017/UAS5017, UNITED ARTISTS
UAL4080/UAS5080, UNITED ARTISTS (J) GXF3039

JUNE IS BUSTIN' OUT ALL OVER (as) arr
LP: UNITED ARTISTS UAL4017/UAS5017, UNITED ARTISTS
UAL4080/UAS5080, UNITED ARTISTS (J) GXF3039

SLEIGH RIDE IN JULY (as) arr
LP: UNITED ARTISTS UAL4017/UAS5017, UNITED ARTISTS
UAL4080/UAS5080, UNITED ARTISTS GXF3039

SOMETHING FOR OCTOBER (as) arr, comp
LP: UNITED ARTISTS UAL4017/UAS5017, UNITED ARTISTS
UAL4080/UAS5080, UNITED ARTISTS GXF3039

SWINGIN' IN NOVEMBER (as) arr, comp
LP: UNITED ARTISTS UAL4017/UAS5017, UNITED ARTISTS
UAL4080/UAS5080, UNITED ARTISTS (J) GXF3039

ROSES IN DECEMBER (as) arr
LP: UNITED ARTISTS UAL4017/UAS5017, UNITED ARTISTS
UAL4080/UAS5080, UNITED ARTISTS (J) GXF3039

* * *

[253, 254] Jazz Calendar is a good representation of Carter's big-band writing during the period when he was recording almost exclusively with smaller groups. He also supplied original compositions for those months without appropriate tunes.

Late 1958 or Early 1959 [254]

Dates for Carter's three United Artists LPs range from 1959 to 1962 in various sources. Carter believes they were all recorded in a one-year period, ca. 1958. Hal Schaefer, who was with United Artists at the time, concurs. Schaefer conceived the theme for the Aspects/Jazz Calendar session (originally entitling it A Year of Joy--12 Swinging Months) and the Can Can album (as well as playing piano on the latter). He joined United Artists in April 1958 and was not involved in Carter's last album for the label, Sax à la Carter.

[255]   Late 1958 or 1959   New York
        BENNY CARTER--HAL SCHAEFER (CAN CAN)

Carter (as) Hal Schaefer (p) John Drew (p) Gus Johnson (d) Teddy Charles (vib)

ANYTHING GOES (as)
LP: UNITED ARTISTS UAL3055/UAS6055, UNITED ARTISTS UAL4073/UAS5073

ALL THROUGH THE NIGHT (as)
LP: UNITED ARTISTS UAL3055/UAS6055, UNITED ARTISTS UAL4073/UAS5073

WALTZ DOWN THE AISLE (as)
LP: UNITED ARTISTS UAL3055/UAS6055, UNITED ARTISTS UAL4073/UAS5073

BUDDIE BEWARE (as)
LP: UNITED ARTISTS UAL3055/UAS6055, UNITED ARTISTS UAL4073/UAS5073

YOU'RE THE TOP (as)
LP: UNITED ARTISTS UAL3055/UAS6055, UNITED ARTISTS UAL4073/UAS5073

[256]   Late 1958 or 1959   New York
        BENNY CARTER--HAL SCHAEFER (CAN CAN)

Carter (as) Hal Schaefer (p) Joe Benjamin (b) Gus Johnson (d) Ted Sommer (percussion)

I LOVE PARIS (as)
LP: UNITED ARTISTS UAL3055/UAS6055, UNITED ARTISTS UAL4073/UAS5073

C'EST MAGNIFIQUE (as)
LP: UNITED ARTISTS UAL3055/UAS6055, UNITED ARTISTS UAL4073/UAS5073

IT'S ALL RIGHT WITH ME (as)
LP: UNITED ARTISTS UAL3055/UAS6055, UNITED ARTISTS UAL4073/UAS5073

ALLEZ-VOUS EN (as)
LP: UNITED ARTISTS UAL3055/UAS6055, UNITED ARTISTS UAL4073/UAS5073

I AM IN LOVE (as)
LP: UNITED ARTISTS UAL3055/UAS6055, UNITED
ARTISTS UAL4073/UAS5073

* * *

[255, 256] Although there has been some dispute over the place of recording, both Carter and Hal Schaefer recall that this date and the final one for United Artists (session [267]) were made in New York.

[257]   January 5, 1959   Los Angeles
          HELEN HUMES

Carter (tp) Frank Rosolino (tb) Teddy Edwards (ts) Andre Previn (p) Leroy Vinnegar (b) Shelly Manne (d) Helen Humes (v)

BILL BAILEY, WON'T YOU PLEASE COME HOME   v-HH (tp)
45: CONTEMPORARY 366   LP: CONTEMPORARY M3571/S7571,
VOGUE (E) LAC12245

WHEN THE SAINTS GO MARCHING IN   v-HH (tp)
45: CONTEMPORARY 366   LP: CONTEMPORARY M3571/S7571,
VOGUE (E) LAC12245

AIN'T MISBEHAVIN'   v-HH (tp acc)
CONTEMPORARY M3571/S7571, VOGUE (E) LAC12245

BILL   v-HH (e)
45: CONTEMPORARY M3571/S7571, VOGUE (E) LAC12245

[258]   January 9 and 12, 1959   Los Angeles
          BARBARA DANE

Carter (tp) Herb Harper or John Halliburton (tb) Plas Johnson (ts) Earl Hines (p) Leroy Vinnegar (b) Shelly Manne (d) Barbara Dane (v)

LIVIN' WITH THE BLUES   v-BD (tp acc)
LP: DOT DLP3177, DOT SDLP25177, DOT DLP25878

HOW LONG, HOW LONG BLUES   v-BD (tp acc)
LP: DOT DLP3177, DOT SDLP25177

IF I COULD BE WITH YOU   v-BD (tp)
LP: DOT DLP3177, DOT SDLP25177

IN THE EVENIN'   v-BD (tp acc)
LP: DOT DLP3177, DOT SDLP25177

BYE BYE BLACKBIRD   v-BD (tp)
LP: DOT DLP3177, DOT SDLP25177

A HUNDRED YEARS FROM TODAY   v-BD (tp acc)
LP: DOT DLP3177, DOT SDLP25177

MECCA FLAT BLUES   v-BD (tp acc)
LP: DOT DLP3177, DOT SDLP25177

January 9 and 12, 1959 [258]

WHY DON'T YOU DO RIGHT   v-BD (e)
LP: DOT DLP3177, DOT SDLP25177

PORGY   v-BD (tp acc)
LP: DOT DLP3177, DOT SDLP25177

SINCE I FELL FOR YOU   v-BD (tp acc)
LP: DOT DLP3177, DOT SDLP25177

* * *

[257, 258] In a supporting role, Carter turns in some of his best trumpet work of the period on these sessions featuring vocalists Helen Humes and Barbara Dane.

[259]   January 26, 1959   Los Angeles
        EARL BOSTIC

Carter (as) Earl Bostic (as) Bill Green, Plas Johnson (ts) Buddy Collette (reeds) Sir Charles Thompson (p) Rene Hall (g) Herb Gordy (b) Earl Palmer (d) Elmer Schmidt (vib)

THAT OLD BLACK MAGIC   (e)   K10231
45:   KING 5454, KING EP452   LP: KING LP640,
KING LP786, PARLOPHONE (E) PMC1119

WHILE WE'RE YOUNG   (e)   K10232
45:   KING EP454   LP: KING LP640, PARLOPHONE
(E) PMC1119

MOONLIGHT IN VERMONT   (e)   K10233
45:   KING EP452   LP: KING LP640, PARLOPHONE
(E) PMC1119

FULL MOON AND EMPTY ARMS   (e)   K10234
45:   KING 5454, KING EP453   LP: KING LP640,
PARLOPHONE (E) PMC1119

I THINK OF YOU   (e)   K10235
45:   KING EP453   LP: KING LP640, PARLOPHONE
(E) PMC1119

AUTUMN SERENADE   (e)   K10236
45:   KING EP454   LP: KING LP640, PARLOPHONE
(E) PMC1119

[260]   January 27, 1959   Los Angeles
        HELEN HUMES

Carter (tp) Frank Rosolino (tb) Teddy Edwards (ts) Andre Previn (p) Leroy Vinnegar (b) Mel Lewis (d) Helen Humes (v)

'TAIN'T NOBODY'S BIZNESS IF I DO   v-HH (tp)
45:   CONTEMPORARY 368   LP: CONTEMPORARY
M3571/S7571, VOGUE (E) LAC12245

AMONG MY SOUVENIRS v-HH (e)
CONTEMPORARY M3571/S7571, VOGUE (E) LAC12245

I GOT IT BAD AND THAT AIN'T GOOD v-HH (tp acc)
CONTEMPORARY M3571/S7571, VOGUE (E) LAC12245

A GOOD MAN IS HARD TO FIND v-HH (e)
CONTEMPORARY M3571/S7571, VOGUE (E) LAC12245

[261]   February 10, 1959 Los Angeles
        HELEN HUMES

Carter (tp) Frank Rosolino (tb) Teddy Edwards (ts) Andre Previn (p) Leroy Vinnegar (b) Shelly Manne (d) Helen Humes (v)

TROUBLE IN MIND v-HH (tp acc)
45: CONTEMPORARY 368 LP: CONTEMPORARY M3571/S7571, VOGUE (E) LAC12245

YOU CAN DEPEND ON ME v-HH (tp)
CONTEMPORARY M3571/S7571, VOGUE (E) LAC12245

STAR DUST v-HH (tp)
CONTEMPORARY M3571/S7571, VOGUE (E) LAC12245

WHEN I GROW TOO OLD TO DREAM v-HH (tp)
CONTEMPORARY M3571/S7571, VOGUE (E) LAC12245

[262]   March 1959 Los Angeles
        THE MUSIC FROM M SQUAD

Carter (as, ss, arr, comp) Collective Personnel: Pete Candoli, Frank Beach, Don Fagerquist, Maury Harris (tp) Frank Rosolino, Pete Carpenter, Joe Howard, George Roberts (tb) John Towner Williams (p, arr, comp) Red Mitchell, Joe Mondragon (b) Alvin Stoller (d) Stanley Wilson (cond)

M SQUAD THEME (as)
LP: RCA LPM/LSP2062

THE CHASE (as)
LP: RCA LPM/LSP2062

THE SEARCH (e) arr, comp
LP: RCA LPM/LSP2062

PHANTOM RAIDERS (as) arr, comp
LP: RCA LPM/LSP2062

LONELY BEAT (ss)
LP: RCA LPM/LSP2062

THE JUKE BOX (as) arr, comp
LP: RCA LPM/LSP2062

THE MUGGER (as) arr, comp
LP: RCA LPM/LSP2062

March 1959 [262]

THE DISCOVERY (as)
LP: RCA LPM/LSP2062

THE LATE SPOT (as)
LP: RCA LPM/LSP2062

THE CHA-CHA CLUB (as)
LP: RCA LPM/LSP2062

A LADY SINGS THE BLUES (as) arr
LP: RCA LPM/LSP2062

THE END (as)
LP: RCA LPM/LSP2062

* * *

This album features music performed on the soundtrack of the TV series, for which Carter composed, arranged and played. Of particular interest is Carter's only recorded solo on soprano saxophone in "Lonely Beat."

[263]   July 28, 1959   Los Angeles
        SOUNDTRACK OF FILM ON THE BEACH

Carter (as) Large Orchestra

ON THE BEACH-SOUNDTRACK ALBUM
LP: ROULETTE R25098

   NOTE: Carter plays in the orchestra but does not solo on this album.

[264]   Probably November-December 1959   Los Angeles
        SAM COOKE

Carter (as) Vocal Group and Orchestra Including: Pete Candoli, Conte Candoli (tp) Conrad Gozzo, Milt Bernhart (tb) Jewell Grant (as) Jackie Kelso, Plas Johnson (ts) Ernie Freeman (p) Red Callender (b) Earl Palmer (d) Sam Cooke (v) Rene Hall (arr)

LOVER MAN   v-SC (as acc)
LP: KEEN A2004, UP FRONT UPF160, RCA APL1-0899, TRIP TLX9517, RCA (E) HY1030

'TAIN'T NOBODY'S BIZNESS IF I DO   v-SC (as acc)
LP: KEEN A2004, UP FRONT UPF160, RCA APL1-0899, TRIP TLX9517, TRIP TOP 16-2, RCA (E) HY1030

SOLITUDE   v-SC (as acc)
LP: KEEN A2004, UP FRONT UPF160, RCA APL1-0899, TRIP TLP8030, RCA (E) HY1030

LOVER, COME BACK TO ME   v-SC (as acc)
LP: KEEN A2004, UP FRONT UPF160, RCA APL1-0899, TRIP TLP8030, TRIP TOP 16-2, RCA (E) HY1030

COMES LOVE   v-SC (as acc)
LP: KEEN A2004, TRIP TLP8030

GOOD MORNING HEARTACHE   v-SC (e)
LP: KEEN A2004, UP FRONT UPF160, RCA APL1-0899,
TRIP TLX9517, TRIP TOP 16-2, RCA (E) HY1030

LET'S CALL THE WHOLE THING OFF   v-SC (e)
LP: KEEN A2004, UP FRONT UPF160, RCA APL1-0899,
TRIP TLX9517, SPRINGBOARD SPX6003, RCA (E) HY1030

GOD BLESS THE CHILD   v-SC (e)
LP: KEEN A2004, UP FRONT UPF160, TRIP TLP8030,
TRIP TOP 16-2

CRAZY IN LOVE WITH YOU   v-SC (e)
LP: KEEN A2004, UP FRONT UPF160, RCA APL1-0899,
TRIP TLP8030, RCA (E) HY1030

THEY CAN'T TAKE THAT WAY FROM ME   v-SC (e)
LP: KEEN A2004, RCA APL1-0899, TRIP TLP8030, RCA
(E) HY1030

I GOT A RIGHT TO SING THE BLUES   v-SC (e)
LP: KEEN A2004, RCA APL1-0899, TRIP TLP8030, TRIP
TOP 16-2, RCA (E) HY1030

SHE'S FUNNY THAT WAY   v-SC (e)
LP: KEEN A2004, TRIP TLP8030

   NOTES: Strings, vocal group present on "Good Morning Heartache," "God Bless The Child," "Crazy In Love With You" and "She's Funny That Way." "Lover Man" as "Lover Girl" on Up Front and Trip; "Crazy In Love" as "Crazy She Calls Me" on RCA.

*   *   *

Rene Hall put together this album as a tribute to Billie Holiday, who died several months earlier.   Carter wrote the liner notes for the original issue, Keen A2004.

[265]   1959 Los Angeles   Soundtrack from Film The Gene Krupa Story
         GENE KRUPA

Carter (as) Pete Candoli, Conrad Gozzo, Ray Triscari, Joe Triscari (tp) Ed Kusby, Murray McEachern, Tommy Pederson, George Roberts (tb) Heinie Beau (as, cl) Jerry Casper, Dave Harris (ts) Dave Pell (bs) Jimmy Rowles (p) Barney Kessel (g) Morty Corb (b) Gene Krupa, Shelly Manne (d) Jerry Williams, John Williams (percussion) Ruby Lane, Anita O'Day (v) Leith Stevens (arr)

MAIN TITLE   (e)
LP: VERVE MGV15010, HMV CLP1352, HMV CSD1296

SPIRITUAL JAZZ   (e)
LP: VERVE MGV15010, HMV CLP1352, HMV CSD1296

CHEROKEE . (as)
LP: VERVE MGV15010, HMV CLP1352, HMV CSD1296

INDIANA MONTAGE (e)
LP: VERVE MGV15010, HMV CLP1352, HMV CSD1296

OAHU DANCE/CHEROKEE (FINALE) (e)
LP: VERVE MGV15010, HMV CLP1352, HMV CSD1296

I LOVE MY BABY v-RL (e)
LP: VERVE MGV15010, HMV CLP1352, HMV CSD1296

MEMORIES OF YOU v-AO (e)
LP: VERVE MGV15010, HMV CLP1352, HMV CSD1296

[266]   Same Session

Carter (as) Red Nichols (c) Moe Schneider (tb) Heinie Beau (cl) Eddie Miller (ts) Jess Stacy (p) Barney Kessel (g) Morty Corb (b) Gene Krupa (d)

ROYAL GARDEN BLUES (e)
LP: VERVE MGV15010, HMV CLP1352, HMV CSD1296

INDIANA JAM SESSION (as)
LP: VERVE MGV15010, HMV CLP1352, HMV CSD1296

WAY DOWN YONDER IN NEW ORLEANS (e)
LP: VERVE MGV15010, HMV CLP1352, HMV CSD1296

[267]   Probably 1959
BENNY CARTER QUARTET (SAX ALA CARTER)

Carter (as, ts) Jimmy Rowles (p) Leroy Vinnegar (b) Mel Lewis (d)

FAR AWAY PLACES (as)
LP: UNITED ARTISTS UAL4094/UAS5094

AND THE ANGELS SING (as)
LP: UNITED ARTISTS UAL4094/UAS5094

EVERYTHING I HAVE IS YOURS (as)
LP: UNITED ARTISTS UAL4094/UAS5094

I UNDERSTAND (as)
LP: UNITED ARTISTS UAL4094/UAS5094

ALL OR NOTHING AT ALL (as)
LP: UNITED ARTISTS UAL4094/UAS5094

I'LL NEVER SMILE AGAIN (as)
LP: UNITED ARTISTS UAL4094/UAS5094

IF I LOVED YOU (as)
LP: UNITED ARTISTS UAL4094/UAS5094

I SHOULD CARE (as)
LP: UNITED ARTISTS UAL4094/UAS5094

FOR ALL WE KNOW (as)
LP: UNITED ARTISTS UAL4094/UAS5094

GHOST OF A CHANCE   (as)
LP: UNITED ARTISTS   UAL4094/UAS5094

THE ONE I LOVE   (as)
LP: UNITED ARTISTS   UAL4094/UAS5094

MOON OF MANAKOORA   (as) (ts [Carter dubbed tenor part])
LP: UNITED ARTISTS   UAL4094/UAS5094

---

[268]   March 1, 1960   Los Angeles
        NAT KING COLE

Carter (as) Large Orchestra with Strings and Vocal Group, Nat King Cole (v) Nelson Riddle (arr, cond)

WILD IS LOVE   v-NKC (e)
LP: CAPITOL (S) WAK1392

HUNDREDS AND THOUSANDS OF GIRLS   v-NKC (as [2 bars])
LP: CAPITOL (S) WAK1392

TELL HER IN THE MORNING   v-NKC (e)
LP: CAPITOL (S) WAK1392

PICK UP   v-NKC (e)
LP: CAPITOL (S) WAK1392

BEGGAR FOR THE BLUES   v-NKC (e)
LP: CAPITOL (S) WAK1392

STAY WITH IT   v-NKC (e)
LP: CAPITOL (S) WAK1392

WILD IS LOVE FINALE   v-NKC (e)
LP: CAPITOL (S) WAK1392

---

[269]   November 21, 1960   Stockholm   Concert, Konserthuset
        JAZZ AT THE PHILHARMONIC

Carter (as, comp) Dizzy Gillespie (tp) J. J. Johnson (tb) Cannonball Adderley (as) Lalo Schifrin (p) Art Davis (b) Chuck Lampkin (d)

BERNIE'S TUNE   (as [1st solo])
LP: VERVE MGV8539, VERVE (E) VLP9045, BARCLAY GLP3638, VERVE 2V6S-8823

SWEDISH JAM   (as [2nd solo]) comp
LP: VERVE MGV8539, VERVE (E) VLP9045, BARCLAY GLP3638, VERVE 2V6S-8823

---

[270]   Same Session

Carter (as, comp) Roy Eldridge (tp) Coleman Hawkins, Don Byas (ts) Lalo Schifrin (p) Art Davis (b) Jo Jones (d)

November 21, 1960 [269]

INDIANA (as)
LP: VERVE V6-8541, VERVE (E) VLP9047, BARCLAY GLP3640

TAKE THE A TRAIN (as)
LP: VERVE V6-8541, VERVE (E) VLP9047, BARCLAY GLP3640

THE NEARNESS OF YOU (as)
LP: VERVE V6-8541, VERVE (E) VLP9047, BARCLAY GLP3640

A JAZZ PORTRAIT OF BRIGITTE BARDOT (as) comp
LP: VERVE V6-8541, VERVE (E) VLP9047, BARCLAY GLP3640

> NOTE: "The Nearness Of You" is Carter's feature in the ballad medley.

* * *

[269, 270] This version of JATP features Carter with two different generations of stars. Obviously inspired, he turns in his best recorded JATP work. Some stylistic adjustment in his playing with the different groups is evident. With the modernists his tone is slightly more strident. Also, his lines are less symmetrical; each phrase seems stimulated by the one preceding, rather than fitting into a larger scheme as on "Indiana" or "Take The A Train."

This is Carter's only recording with Cannonball Adderley, who named him, along with Charlie Parker, as his major influence.

Jepsen gives November 22 as the concert date, but Carter's passport shows he left Sweden on November 21. Also, the reproduction of a poster on the cover of Verve V8541 shows the date as November 21.

[271]	Probably Same Date and Location
	JAZZ AT THE PHILHARMONIC

Carter (as) Lalo Schifrin (p) Art Davis (b) Jo Jones (d)

THE NEARNESS OF YOU (as)
LP: UNISSUED

> NOTE: This piece is part of a ballad medley probably recorded at a different concert performance of JATP on the same day as the issued items.

[272]	1960 Los Angeles
	ELLA FITZGERALD-HAROLD ARLEN SONGBOOK

Carter (as) Large Orchestra, Ella Fitzgerald (v) Billy May (arr, dir)

BLUES IN THE NIGHT   v-EF (as)
LP: VERVE MGV4057, VERVE V6-4046, VERVE SELECT DOUBLE (E) 2683-064

LET'S FALL IN LOVE   v-EF (as)
LP: VERVE MGV4057, VERVE V6-4046, VERVE SELECT DOUBLE (E) 2683-064

THIS TIME THE DREAM'S ON ME   v-EF (as)
LP: VERVE MGV4057, VERVE V6-4046, VERVE SELECT
DOUBLE (E) 2683-064

>NOTE: Carter plays in the ensemble on other tunes from this session.

[273]   April 14-15, 1961   Los Angeles
PEGGY LEE ACC. BY QUINCY JONES' ORCHESTRA

Carter (as, arr) Frank Beach, Bob Fowler, Conrad Gozzo, Manny Klein, Al Porcino, Jack Sheldon (tp) Vernon Friley, Lewis McGreery, Frank Rosolino (tb) Bob Knight (bass tb) Bill Green (as) Plas Johnson, Bill Perkins (ts) Jack Nimitz (bs) Lou Levy, Jimmy Rowles (p) Dennis Budimir (g) Max Bennett (b) Stan Levey (d) Chano Pozo (conga, bongos) Peggy Lee (v) Quincy Jones (arr)

BOSTON BEANS   v-PL (e)
LP: CAPITOL (S) T1671

KANSAS CITY BLUES   v-PL (e)
LP: CAPITOL (S) T1671

BASIN STREET BLUES   v-PL (e)
LP: CAPITOL (S) T1671

GOING TO CHICAGO BLUES   v-PL (e)
LP: CAPITOL (S) T1671

NEW YORK CITY BLUES   v-PL (e)
LP: CAPITOL (S) T1671

LOS ANGELES BLUES   v-PL (e)
LP: CAPITOL (S) T1671

SAN FRANCISCO BLUES   v-PL (e) arr
LP: CAPITOL (S) T1671

I LOST MY SUGAR IN SALT LAKE CITY   v-PL (e)
LP: CAPITOL (S) T1671

ST. LOUIS BLUES   v-PL (e)
LP: CAPITOL (S) T1671

FISHERMAN'S WHARF   v-PL (e)
LP: CAPITOL (S) T1671

THE GRAIN BELT BLUES   v-PL (e)
LP: CAPITOL (S) T1671

THE TRAIN BLUES   v-PL (e)
LP: CAPITOL (S) T1671

ORANGE BLUES   v-PL (e)
LP: CAPITOL (S) T1671

[274]   June 6, 1961   Los Angeles
           ALFRED NEWMAN

Carter (as, arr) Horns / 24 Violins / Rhythm Section, Alfred Newman (cond, comp)

LAURA (as) arr
LP: CAPITOL ST1652, ANGEL S36066

THE BAD AND THE BEAUTIFUL (as) arr
LP: CAPITOL ST1652, ANGEL S36066

[275]   October 30-31, 1961   New York
           COUNT BASIE AND HIS ORCHESTRA

Carter (as, arr, comp) Sonny Cohn, Al Aarons, Thad Jones, Snooky Young (tp) Henry Coker, Quentin Jackson, Benny Powell (tb) Frank Wess (as) Frank Foster, Budd Johnson (ts) Charlie Fowlkes (bs) Count Basie (p) Sam Herman (g) Ed Jones (b) Sonny Payne (d)

THE BASIE TWIST (e) arr, comp   16356
45: ROULETTE 4403   LP: ROULETTE R25176

THE TROT (e) arr, comp   16357
45: ROULETTE 4403   LP: ROULETTE R52086,
COLUMBIA (E) 33SX1496, ROULETTE RE118, VOGUE 500021

THE LEGEND (e) arr, comp
LP: ROULETTE R52086, COLUMBIA (E) 33SX1496,
ROULETTE RE118, VOGUE 500021

GOIN' ON (e) arr, comp
LP: ROULETTE R52086, COLUMBIA (E) 33SX1496,
ROULETTE RE118, VOGUE 500021

[276]   November 1-2, 1961   New York
           COUNT BASIE AND HIS ORCHESTRA

Carter (as, arr, comp) Sonny Cohn, Al Aarons, Thad Jones, Snooky Young (tp) Henry Coker, Quentin Jackson, Benny Powell (tb) Frank Wess (as) Frank Foster, Budd Johnson (ts) Charlie Fowlkes (bs) Count Basie (p) Sam Herman (g) Ed Jones (b) Sonny Payne (d) Dizzy Gillespie (cowbell)

EASY MONEY (e) arr, comp
LP: ROULETTE R52086, COLUMBIA (E) 33SX1496,
ROULETTE RE118, VOGUE 500021

WHO'S BLUE (e) arr, comp
LP: ROULETTE R52086, COLUMBIA (E) 33SX1496,
ROULETTE (E) 2683-013, ROULETTE RE118, VOGUE 500021

AMOROSO (e) arr, comp
LP: ROULETTE R52086, COLUMBIA (E) 33SX1496,
ROULETTE RE118, VOGUE 500021

THE SWIZZLE (e) arr, comp
LP: ROULETTE R52086, COLUMBIA (E) 33SX1496,
ROULETTE RE118, VOGUE 500021

TURNABOUT (e) arr, comp
LP: ROULETTE R52086, COLUMBIA (E) 33SX1496,
ROULETTE (E) 2683-013, ROULETTE RE118, VOGUE 500021

   NOTE: Gillespie plays cowbell on "Amoroso" only.

*   *   *

[275, 276] This collaboration with Basie--The Legend--is less celebrated than Carter's Kansas City Suite of the previous year (on which Carter did not play). The Legend is just as successful musically, however. While the arrangements are unmistakably Carter's, he has obviously tailored them to the Basie style, with more riffs than usual and plenty of space for the leader's piano fills. The Basie band also proves itself amenable to some of the arranger's trademarks, the reed section capturing the distinctive Carter sound on "Easy Money" and "Turnabout."

   Carter plays on the album only because Basie asked him to fill in for Marshall Royal at the last minute. He agreed, provided that he not be called upon to solo and that Frank Wess play lead alto.

[277]   November 13, 1961 New York
         BENNY CARTER AND HIS ORCHESTRA (FURTHER DEFINITIONS)

Carter (as, arr) Phil Woods (as) Coleman Hawkins, Charlie Rouse (ts) Dick Katz (p) John Collins (g) Jimmy Garrison (b) Jo Jones (d)

HONEYSUCKLE ROSE (as) arr
LP: IMPULSE A(S)#12, HMV (E) CLP1624/CSD1480, IMPULSE (J) YP8519, WORLD RECORD CLUB (E) T864, KING (J) SH3002

THE MIDNIGHT SUN WILL NEVER SET (as) arr
LP: IMPULSE A(S)#12, HMV (E) CLP1624/CSD1480, IMPULSE AS9258, IMPULSE (J) YP8519, WORLD RECORD CLUB (E) T864, KING (J) SH3002

CHERRY (as) arr
LP: IMPULSE A(S)#12, HMV (E) CLP1624/CSD1480, IMPULSE (J) YP8519, WORLD RECORD CLUB (E) T864, KING (J) SH3002

CRAZY RHYTHM (as) arr
LP: IMPULSE A(S)#12, HMV (E) CLP1624/CSD1480, IMPULSE (J) YP8519, WORLD RECORD CLUB (E) T864, KING (J) SH3002

[278]   November 15, 1961 New York
         BENNY CARTER AND HIS ORCHESTRA (FURTHER DEFINITIONS)

Carter (as, arr, comp) Phil Woods (as) Coleman Hawkins, Charlie Rouse (ts) Dick Katz (p) John Collins (g) Jimmy Garrison (b) Jo Jones (d)

November 15, 1961 [278]

DOOZY (as) arr, comp
LP: IMPULSE A(S)#12, HMV (E) CLP1624/CSD1480, IMPULSE (J) YP8519, WORLD RECORD CLUB (E) T864, KING (J) SH3002

BLUE STAR (as) arr, comp
LP: IMPULSE A(S)#12, HMV (E) CLP1624/CSD1480, IMPULSE (J) YP8519, WORLD RECORD CLUB (E) T864, KING (J) SH3002

COTTONTAIL (as) arr
LP: IMPULSE A(S)#12, HMV (E) CLP1624/CSD1480, IMPULSE ASH9272-3, IMPULSE (J) YP851, WORLD RECORD CLUB (E) T864, KING (J) SH3002

BODY AND SOUL (as) arr
LP: IMPULSE A(S)#12, HMV (E) CLP1624/CSD1480, IMPULSE ASH9253-3, IMPULSE (J) YP8519, WORLD RECORD CLUB (E) T864, KING (J) SH3002

* * *

[277, 278] Further Definitions is considered by many not only Carter's finest overall album, but one of the greatest jazz records of the last 30 years. Intended as a "retrospective" of the epic 1937 Hawkins Paris date, the session pairs Carter and Hawkins with two leading voices of a later generation of reed players. The instrumentation is the same as on the earlier date.

Carter and Hawkins are superb throughout, but perhaps their most outstanding contributions come on the ballads, "Blue Star" and "The Midnight Sun" and Hawkins's work on "Body And Soul."

There are arranging delights in every piece, with a perfect balance between solo and ensemble passages. The sax quartet blends perfectly and the sound of Carter's lead alto has never been captured more clearly.

Two of the pieces have a particularly "retrospective" flavor: on "Cottontail" Carter has included the original Ellington saxophone chorus, and "Body And Soul" opens with a sax ensemble reading of the first eight measures of Hawkins's classic 1939 solo.

[279]   1961   New York
   PEARL BAILEY WITH LOUIS BELLSON AND HIS ORCHESTRA

Carter (as, arr) Louis Bellson (d, arr) Pearl Bailey (v)

TIRED v-PB (e) arr
LP: ROULETTE R25144

THAT'S GOOD ENOUGH FOR ME v-PB (e)
LP: ROULETTE R25144

IT TAKES TWO TO TANGO v-PB (e)
LP: ROULETTE R25144

ROW ROW ROW ROW v-PB (e) arr
LP: ROULETTE R25144

MA, HE'S MAKIN' EYES AT ME   v-PB (e)
LP: ROULETTE R25144

TOOT TOOT TOOTSIE   v-PB (e) arr
LP: ROULETTE R25144, ROULETTE RE101

ST. LOUIS BLUES   v-PB (e)
LP: ROULETTE R25144

LEGALIZE MY NAME   v-PB (e)
LP: ROULETTE R25144

FIFTEEN YEARS   v-PB (e)
LP: ROULETTE R25144

AC-CENT-UATE THE POSITIVE   v-PB (e)
LP: ROULETTE R25144

CHERRY'S AT TOP OF THE TREE   v-PB (e)
LP: ROULETTE R25144

OLD, TIRED AND TORN   v-PB (e)
LP: ROULETTE R25144

---

[280]   1961   Los Angeles
         SOUNDTRACK OF FILM THE FLOWER DRUM SONG

FLOWER DRUM SONG-SOUNDTRACK ALBUM
LP: DECCA DL79098, MCA 2069

>   NOTE: Carter played in the orchestra and assisted in the orchestration of parts of this production.

---

[281]   1961   Los Angeles
         DAVE PELL--TRIBUTE TO JOHN KIRBY

Carter (as) Ray Linn (tp) Dave Pell (cl) John Towner Williams (p, arr, comp) Lyle Ritz (b) Frankie Capp (d) Harry Betts (arr) Marty Paich (arr, comp) Med Flory (arr)

ROSE ROOM (original Kirby sextet arr)   (as [re-creation of Procope solo])
LP: CAPITOL (S) T1687

ROYAL GARDEN BLUES (original arr adapted by HB)   (as)
LP: CAPITOL (S) T1687

ANITRA'S DANCE (original arr transcribed by MP)   (as)
LP: CAPITOL (S) T1687

IT FEELS SO GOOD (original arr transcribed by MF)   (as)
LP: CAPITOL (S) T1687

TOOTSIE ROLL   arr&comp-MP (as)
LP: CAPITOL (S) T1687

1961 [281]

DOUBLE WALK arr&comp-JTW (as)
LP: CAPITOL (S) T1687

UNDECIDED arr-JTW (as)
LP: CAPITOL (S) T1687

BLUE SKIES (original arr adapted by HB) (as)
LP: CAPITOL (S) T1687

COQUETTE (original arr transcribed by MF) (as)
LP: CAPITOL (S) T1687

OPUS 5 (original arr adapted by HB) (as)
LP: CAPITOL (S) T1687

20TH CENTURY CLOSET arr-JTW (as)
LP: CAPITOL (S) T1687

THEN I'LL BE HAPPY (as)
LP: CAPITOL (S) T1687

* * *

Dave Pell organized this session as a tribute to Carter's close friend John Kirby. The repertoire includes several of the Kirby sextet's arrangements, as well as some originals by Marty Paich and John Williams played in the Kirby style. The group is quite successful in capturing the flavor of the Kirby band. On "Rose Room," Carter plays Russell Procope's original solo note-for-note, coming close to Procope's distinctive timbre and vibrato. This is the only instance of Carter attempting such a re-creation on record.

[282] April 10, 1962   Los Angeles
       BBB & CO

Carter (as, tp, comp) Shorty Sherock (tp) Barney Bigard (cl) Ben Webster (ts) Jimmy Rowles (p) Dave Barbour (g) Leroy Vinnegar (b) Mel Lewis (d)

OPENING BLUES (as)
LP: SWINGVILLE/STATUS 2032, PRESTIGE (F) FELP15002, PRESTIGE (J) SMJ7572, PRESTIGE MPP2513

LULA (as) comp
LP: SWINGVILLE/STATUS 2032, PRESTIGE (F) FELP15002, PRESTIGE (J) SMJ7572, PRESTIGE MPP2513

WHEN LIGHTS ARE LOW (tp [8-bar sequence in 1st chorus: Carter, Sherock, Carter]) (as) comp
LP: SWINGVILLE/STATUS 2032, PRESTIGE (F) FELP15002, PRESTIGE (J) SMJ7572, PRESTIGE MPP2513

YOU CAN'T TELL THE DIFFERENCE WHEN THE SUN GOES DOWN BLUES (as)
LP: SWINGVILLE/STATUS 2032, PRESTIGE (F) FELP15002, PRESTIGE (J) SMJ7572, PRESTIGE MPP2513

* * *

This date does not live up to the potential of its personnel. The repertoire lacks a focus, with most of the session taken up by the two extended blues.

[283]   May 1963   Paris
STANLEY WILSON ORCH. WITH BENNY CARTER, GUEST SOLOIST

Carter (as, arr, comp) Maurice Van Der (p) Pierre Culloz (g) Pierre Michelot (b) Lionel Galli (violin) Christian Garros (d) Strings / Horns / Vocal Choir Directed by Christiene Legrand, Stanley Wilson (arr)

UNDER PARIS SKIES vocal group   (as) arr
LP: CHARTER CLS105

IF YOU LOVE ME, REALLY LOVE ME   (as)
LP: CHARTER CLS105

COMME CI, COMME CA vocal group   (as)
LP: CHARTER CLS105

DOMINO   (as) arr
LP: CHARTER CLS105

CHERCHEZ LA FEMME   arr-SW (as) comp
LP: CHARTER CLS105

MY PLACE vocal group   (as)
LP: CHARTER CLS105

IF YOU GO   (as) arr
LP: CHARTER CLS105

DANCE WITH ME vocal group   (as) arr
LP: CHARTER CLS105

I WISH YOU LOVE   (as)
LP: CHARTER CLS105

[284]   May 1963   Paris Studio recording-Unissued
STANLEY WILSON ORCH. WITH BENNY CARTER, GUEST SOLOIST

Carter (as, arr) Maurice Van Der (p) Pierre Culloz (g) Pierre Michelot (b) Christian Garros (d) Orchestra Including 20 Strings, Stanley Wilson, John Towner Williams (arr)

THE VERY THOUGHT OF YOU   arr-SW (as)

HE NEEDS ME   arr-JTW (as)

NEVER MORE   arr-SW (as)

WHAT KIND OF FOOL AM I   (as) arr

ROOM WITH A VIEW   arr-JTW (as)

THE BRITISH GRENADIERS   arr-JTW (e)

POOR LITTLE RICH GIRL (as) arr

SHOW ME THE WAY TO GO HOME (as) arr

THESE FOOLISH THINGS arr-SW (as)

SERENADE TO A WEALTHY WIDOW arr-SW (as)

GREENSLEEVES arr-JTW (e)

ROSES OF PICARDY (as) arr

[285] May 1963 Paris
BENNY CARTER (BENNY CARTER IN PARIS/AUTUMN LEAVES)

Carter (as, arr, comp) Maurice Van Der (p) Pierre Michelot (b) Christian Garros (d) Christiene Legrand, Alice Herald, Jeanette Beaucamont (vocal group)

AROUND THE WORLD IN 80 DAYS vocal group (as) arr
LP: 20TH CENTURY FOX TFM3134, MOVIETONE 71020/S72020

I'LL CLOSE MY EYES (as)
LP: 20TH CENTURY FOX TFM3134, MOVIETONE 71020/S72020

CUANDO CALIENTE EL SOL vocal group (as) arr
LP: 20TH CENTURY FOX TFM3134, MOVIETONE 71020/S72020

SMILE (as)
LP: 20TH CENTURY FOX TFM3134, MOVIETONE 71020/S72020

BLACK KNIGHT vocal group (as) arr
LP: 20TH CENTURY FOX TFM3134

AUTUMN LEAVES (as)
LP: 20TH CENTURY FOX TFM3134, MOVIETONE 71020/S72020

CHEROKEE vocal group (as) arr
LP: 20TH CENTURY FOX TFM3134, MOVIETONE 71020/S72020

WALTZ GAY (as) comp
LP: 20TH CENTURY FOX TFM3134, MOVIETONE 71020/S72020

VOUS QUI PASSEZ SANS ME VOIR vocal group (as) arr
LP: 20TH CENTURY FOX TFM3134, MOVIETONE 71020/S72020

BAGATELLE (as) comp
LP: 20TH CENTURY FOX TFM3134, MOVIETONE 71020/S72020

THE GYPSY   vocal group   (as) arr
LP: 20TH CENTURY FOX TFM3134, MOVIETONE
71020/S72020

BLUES FOR BENNY   (as)
LP: 20TH CENTURY FOX TFM3134

* * *

[283, 284, 285]   Carter traveled to Paris in order to record three albums. Two were to be part of a series conceived by Stanley Wilson called "The World Of Sights And Sounds" for Panel Productions, founded by Carter and Wilson.   Two albums in the series were recorded, but only the first, Stop One: Paris was released.   (The second was to be Stop Two: London.)

The sessions featured arrangements of songs of the country named. Of greater jazz interest was the Paris session with rhythm section alone, although some may find the presence of a vocal group on half the tracks distracting.

[286]	May 1963 Paris
	KPM MUSIC LIBRARY

Carter (as, arr, comp) 19 Piece Orchestra Including: Maurice Van Der (p) Pierre Culloz (g) Pierre Michelot (b) Christian Garros (d)

LONELY AFFAIR - A   (as) arr, comp
78:   KPM (E) 155

LONELY AFFAIR - B   arr, comp
78:   KPM (E) 155

LONELY AFFAIR - C   arr, comp
78:   KPM (E) 155

LONELY AFFAIR - D   arr, comp
78:   KPM (E) 155

BE COOL - A   (as) arr, comp
78:   KPM (E) 156

BE COOL - B   arr, comp
78:   KPM (E) 156

BE COOL - C   arr, comp
78:   KPM (E) 156

DISCOVERY   arr, comp
78:   KPM (E) 156

HEELS UP   arr, comp
78:   KPM (E) 156

JAZZ WALTZ - A   (as) arr, comp
78:   KPM (E) 157

JAZZ WALTZ - B   arr, comp
78:   KPM (E) 157

JAZZ WALTZ - C   arr, comp
78:   KPM (E) 157

METROPOLE   arr, comp
78:   KPM (E) 157

GOTTA GO HOME   arr, comp
78:   KPM (E) 157

BLUE YONDER - A   arr, comp
78:   KPM (E) 158

BLUE YONDER - B   arr, comp
78:   KPM (E) 158

SHOW BREAK - 1   arr, comp
78:   KPM (E) 158

SHOW BREAK - 2   arr, comp
78:   KPM (E) 158

IMMINENT   arr, comp
78:   KPM (E) 158

CATFISH ROW   arr, comp
78:   KPM (E) 158

CATFISH ROW - LINK 1   arr, comp
78:   KPM (E) 158

CATFISH ROW - LINK 2   arr, comp
78:   KPM (E) 158

ONE WAY OUT   arr, comp
78:   KPM (E) 158

VINHO VERDE   (as) arr, comp
78:   KPM (E) 159

* * *

These recordings were made for the Keith Prowse Music Recorded Library Catalog (London) which furnishes music for films and TV productions. Several versions of some pieces were recorded to provide a variety of tempos and moods. Also, a number of very short transitional passages and endings were included.

Carter probably does not play except where noted as a soloist but, for completeness, all titles have been listed.

[287]	August 1964 Los Angeles
	BENNY CARTER

Carter (as, arr, comp) Skeets Herfurt, Bill Green (as) Harry Klee, Jack Dumont, Paul Horn (as) Plas Johnson, Babe Russin, Carrington Visor (ts) Bill Hood, Chuck Gentry (bs) Gerald Wiggins (p) John Collins (g) Joe Comfort (b) Alvin Stoller (d) Lalo Schifrin (arr)

TICKLE TOE (as) arr
LP: VEE-JAY VJLP2501

ALTO EGO (as) arr, comp
UNISSUED

WATERMELON MAN arr-LS (as)
UNISSUED

SHANGRI-LA (as) arr
UNISSUED

RIGHT HERE WITH YOU (as) arr
UNISSUED

MEMORIES OF YOU (as) arr
UNISSUED

FAIRY TALES (as) arr
UNISSUED

THE GREAT LIE (as) arr
UNISSUED

GIRL FROM IPANEMA (as) arr
UNISSUED

I WANNA BE AROUND (as) arr
UNISSUED

DON'T GET AROUND MUCH ANYMORE (as) arr
UNISSUED

ON GREEN DOLPHIN STREET (as) arr
UNISSUED

* * *

This ambitious project featuring Carter leading ten reeds was produced by Lee Young for Vee Jay Records. The only item ever released appeared on an anthology compiled by Leonard Feather (Encyclopedia Of Jazz, Jazz Of The 60's, Vol. 1--Giants Of The Saxophones).

[287A] Ca. 1964 Studio Recording--Unissued
BENNY CARTER

Carter (as, ss, comp) Ten Piece Band Including Rex Stewart, Teddy Buckner (tp) Ben Webster (ts) Rozelle Gayle (p)

DUKE STEPS OUT

HOW COME YOU DO ME LIKE YOU DO

QUEER NOTIONS

BLUES IN MY HEART comp

[288]　　March 30-April 1, 1965　Los Angeles
　　　　PEARL BAILEY

Carter (as, arr, comp) Large Orchestra Including Harry Edison (tp) Pearl Bailey (v) Louis Bellson (arr)

PLEASURES AND PALACES　v-PB (e) arr
LP:　ROULETTE (S)R25300

TAKE BACK YOUR MINK　v-PB (e) arr
LP:　ROULETTE (S)R25300

WHAT IS A MAN　v-PB (e) arr
LP:　ROULETTE (S)R25300

I SHOULDA QUIT WHEN I WAS AHEAD　v-PB (e) arr
LP:　ROULETTE (S)R25300

WHO'S TIRED　v-PB (e) arr
LP:　ROULETTE (S)R25300

PUSHING FORTY　v-PB arr-LB (e)
LP:　ROULETTE (S)R25300

THE GENTLEMAN IS A DOPE　v-PB arr-LB (e)
LP:　ROULETTE (S)R25300

A MAN IS A NECESSARY EVIL　v-PB (e) arr
LP:　ROULETTE (S)R25300

LOOK AT THAT FACE　v-PB (e) arr
LP:　ROULETTE (S)R25300

BIG NOBODY　v-PB (e) arr
LP:　ROULETTE (S)R25300

YOU'D BETTER THINK IT OVER　v-PB (e) arr, comp
LP:　ROULETTE (S)R25300

HEY THERE　v-PB (e) arr
LP:　ROULETTE (S)R25300

[289]　　March 2, 1966　Los Angeles
　　　　BENNY CARTER (ADDITIONS TO FURTHER DEFINITIONS)

Carter (as, arr, comp) Bud Shank (as) Buddy Collette, Teddy Edwards (ts) Bill Hood (bs) Don Abney (p) Barney Kessel (g) Ray Brown (b) Alvin Stoller (d)

IF DREAMS COME TRUE　(as) arr
LP:　IMPULSE A(S)9116, HMV (E) CLP/CSD3576,
IMPULSE (J) YP8520

FANTASTIC, THAT'S YOU　(as) arr
LP:　IMPULSE A(S)9116, HMV (E) CLP/CSD3576,
IMPULSE (J) YP8520

COME ON BACK   (as) arr, comp
LP: IMPULSE A(S)9116, HMV (E) CLP/CSD3576,
IMPULSE (J) YP8520

PROHIBIDO   (as) arr, comp
LP: IMPULSE A(S)9116, HMV (E) CLP/CSD3576,
IMPULSE (J) YP8520

[290]	March 4, 1966 Los Angeles
	BENNY CARTER (ADDITIONS TO FURTHER DEFINITIONS)

Carter (as, arr, comp) Bud Shank (as) Bill Perkins, Teddy Edwards (ts) Bill Hood (bs) Don Abney (p) Mundell Lowe (g) Al McKibbon (b) Alvin Stoller (d)

DOOZY   (as) arr, comp
LP: IMPULSE A(S)9116, HMV (E) CLP/CSD3576,
IMPULSE (J) YP8520

WE WERE IN LOVE   (as) arr, comp
LP: IMPULSE A(S)9116, HMV (E) CLP/CSD3576,
IMPULSE (J) YP8520

TITMOUSE   (as) arr, comp
LP: IMPULSE A(S)9116, HMV (E) CLP/CSD3576,
IMPULSE (J) YP8520

ROCK BOTTOM   (as) arr, comp
LP: IMPULSE A(S)9116, HMV (E) CLP/CSD3576,
IMPULSE (J) YP8520

*   *   *

[289, 290]   This album does not equal Further Definitions (1961) but affords many pleasant moments. Aside from some excellent new material, Carter updates the 1961 "Doozy." Here it is taken at a faster tempo and a middle ensemble-section consisting of three 12-bar choruses and an 8-bar bridge has been added.

[291]	Between June 28 and July 1, 1967
	CONCERT TOUR, JAZZ AT THE PHILHARMONIC

Carter (as) Clark Terry (tp) Zoot Sims, Paul Gonsalves (ts) Oscar Peterson (p) Sam Jones (b) Bobby Durham (d)

NOW'S THE TIME   (as)
LP: PABLO (E) 2335-721, PABLO 2625-704

WEE DOT   (as)
LP: PABLO (E) 2335-721, PABLO 2625-704

I CAN'T GET STARTED   (as)
LP: PABLO (E) 2335-721, PABLO 2625-704, TIME-LIFE
STL-J10

   NOTE: Carter with rhythm section only on last title.

Between June 28 and July 1, 1967 [292]

| [292] | Same Tour |

Carter (as) Johnny Hodges (as) Coleman Hawkins (ts) Oscar Peterson (p)
Sam Jones (b) Louis Hayes (d)

C-JAM BLUES (as)
LP: PABLO (F) 2335-722, PABLO 2625-704

| [293] | Same Tour |
| | BENNY CARTER WITH THE DUKE ELLINGTON ORCH. |

Carter (as) Cat Anderson, Mercer Ellington, Herb Jones, Cootie Williams (tp) Buster Cooper, Chuck Connors, Lawrence Brown (tb) Russell Procope, Johnny Hodges (as) Jimmy Hamilton, Paul Gonsalves (ts) Harry Carney (bs) Duke Ellington (p) John Lamb (b) Rufus Jones (d)

SATIN DOLL (as)
LP: PABLO (E) 2335-723, PABLO 2625-704

PRELUDE TO A KISS (as)
LP: PABLO (E) 2335-723, PABLO 2625-704

* * *

[291, 292, 293] This material, issued as the "World's Greatest Jazz Concert," was recorded on a tour produced by Norman Granz. It was billed as a JATP event, and it is not known at which concert or concerts the issued recordings were made. Performances were given in various cities in the United States and Canada.

As usual, Carter is more at home with the ballad portion, playing one of his best versions of "I Can't Get Started." Carter has chosen to explore many lovely ballads over the years but always returns to Vernon Duke's standard. Oscar Peterson's daring uptempo introduction works perfectly. Carter embellishes the melody without obscuring it; he departs from it temporarily to create a complementary inlay of perfectly executed runs and arpeggios, returning just in time to keep the melodic thread intact. Despite the many times he has played this piece, Carter once again provides a stunning coda, moving one of the players to exclaim, "Play it, Benny!"

During the preceding jam numbers, "Now's The Time" and "Wee Dot," Carter has some reed trouble. He plays with atypical abandon on the way-up "Wee Dot." Yielding to his stated preference, he takes a brief three choruses, unheard of at a JATP concert. His restraint catches the other musicians off guard; they continue to riff in anticipation of the other half of his solo.

"C-Jam Blues" marks the last time Carter and Coleman Hawkins recorded together. The tenor saxophonist's health was failing and his playing sounds weak and disjointed. Carter recalls touring with him: "We had a lot of nice conversation and a lot of laughs together. But it was very difficult to get him to eat; he was drinking more than he was eating. After the concert in Toronto, he had dinner brought up to the hotel room, and on the next day the food was there, practically untouched."

Carter's masterful collaboration with Johnny Hodges on "Prelude To A Kiss" is historic. It is their only recording together, with the exception of the 1952 Norman Granz studio-date. Hodges, on his home ground, is the more aggressive voice, but the piece provides valuable insights into the contrasting tonal and melodic approaches of the two architects of the swing alto style. (Alto solo sequence: Hodges (8b), Carter (8b), Hodges (8b), Carter (8b), Hodges (8b), Carter (4b), Hodges [ending].)

[294]   May 28, 1968   Los Angeles
ELLA FITZGERALD WITH BENNY CARTER'S MAGNIFICENT SEVEN

Carter (as, arr) Harry Edison (tp) Georgie Auld (ts) Jimmy Jones (p) John Collins (g) Bob West (b) Panama Francis (d) Ella Fitzgerald (v)

NO REGRETS   v-EF
LP: CAPITOL ST2960, CAPITOL SL6751

I'VE GOT A FEELING YOU'RE FOOLING   v-EF
LP: CAPITOL ST2960, CAPITOL SL6751

DON'T BLAME ME
LP: CAPITOL ST2960, CAPITOL SL6751

DEEP PURPLE   v-EF
LP: CAPITOL ST2960, CAPITOL SL6751

RAIN   v-EF
LP: CAPITOL ST2960, CAPITOL SL6751

YOU'RE A SWEETHEART   v-EF (e)
LP: CAPITOL ST2960, CAPITOL SL6751

ON GREEN DOLPHIN STREET   v-EF
LP: CAPITOL ST2960

HOW AM I TO KNOW   v-EF
LP: CAPITOL ST2960

JUST FRIENDS
LP: CAPITOL ST2960

I CRIED FOR YOU   v-EF
LP: CAPITOL ST2960

SEEMS LIKE OLD TIMES   v-EF (e)
LP: CAPITOL ST2960

YOU STEPPED OUT OF A DREAM   v-EF
LP: CAPITOL ST2960

[295]   May 29, 1968   Los Angeles
ELLA FITZGERALD WITH BENNY CARTER'S MAGNIFICENT SEVEN

Carter (as, arr) Harry Edison (tp) Georgie Auld (ts) Jimmy Jones (p) John Collins (g) Bob West (b) Louis Bellson (d) Ella Fitzgerald (v)

May 29, 1968 [295]

IF I GIVE MY HEART TO YOU v-EF
LP: CAPITOL ST2960

ONCE IN A WHILE v-EF
LP: CAPITOL ST2960

EBB TIDE (as)
LP: CAPITOL ST2960

THE LAMP IS LOW v-EF
LP: CAPITOL ST2960

WHERE ARE YOU v-EF
LP: CAPITOL ST2960

THINKING OF YOU v-EF (as acc)
LP: CAPITOL ST2960

MY MOTHER'S EYES v-EF
LP: CAPITOL ST2960

TRY A LITTLE TENDERNESS v-EF
LP: CAPITOL ST2960

I GOT IT BAD AND THAT AIN'T GOOD (as)
LP: CAPITOL ST2960

EVERYTHING I HAVE IS YOURS v-EF
LP: CAPITOL ST2960

I NEVER KNEW I COULD LOVE ANYBODY LIKE I'M LOVING YOU v-EF
LP: CAPITOL ST2960

GOODNIGHT, MY LOVE v-EF
LP: CAPITOL ST2960

[296]   June 3, 1968   Los Angeles
ELLA FITZGERALD WITH BENNY CARTER'S MAGNIFICENT SEVEN

Carter (as, arr) Harry Edison (tp) Georgie Auld (ts) Jimmy Jones (p) John Collins (g) Bob West (b) Louis Bellson (d) Ella Fitzgerald (v)

CANDY v-EF
LP: CAPITOL ST2960, CAPITOL SL6751

ALL I DO IS DREAM OF YOU v-EF
LP: CAPITOL ST2960, CAPITOL SL6751

SPRING IS HERE
LP: CAPITOL ST2960, CAPITOL SL6751

720 IN THE BOOKS v-EF
LP: CAPITOL ST2960, CAPITOL SL6751

IT HAPPENED IN MONTEREY v-EF
LP: CAPITOL ST2960, CAPITOL SL6751

WHAT CAN I SAY AFTER I'M SORRY   v-EF (e)
LP: CAPITOL ST2960, CAPITOL SL6751

FOUR OR FIVE TIMES   v-EF (e)
LP: CAPITOL ST2960

MAYBE   v-EF
LP: CAPITOL ST2960

TAKING A CHANCE ON LOVE
LP: CAPITOL ST2960

ELMER'S TUNE   v-EF
LP: CAPITOL ST2960

AT SUNDOWN   v-EF
LP: CAPITOL ST2960

IT'S A WONDERFUL WORLD   v-EF (e)
LP: CAPITOL ST2960

* * *

[294, 295, 296] This album, 30 By Ella, presents a large number of standards in medley form. Two medleys were recorded at each of the three sessions; the first six and last six tunes listed each comprise a medley. Although Carter plays only where indicated, the complete contents of each medley has been noted. Carter also worked out the transitions between the pieces. Each medley included one instrumental featuring one of the band members.

[297]   November 9, 1968   Baden, Switzerland   Broadcast of Concert,
                Jazz in der Aula
          BENNY CARTER WITH HENRI CHAIX AND HIS ORCHESTRA

Carter (as, arr, comp) Jo Gagliardi (tp) Andre Faist (tb) Roger Zufferey (as) Michel Pilet (ts) Marc Erbetta (bs) Henri Chaix (p) Alain Du Bois (b) Romano Cavicchiolo (d)

SWINGIN' IN NOVEMBER   (as) arr, comp

BLUE LOU   (as)

EASY MONEY   (as) arr, comp

ROSE ROOM   (as)

SWINGIN' THE BLUES   (as)

I CAN'T GET STARTED   (as)

TITMOUSE   (as) arr, comp

MARCH WIND   (as) arr, comp

PERDIDO   (as)

November 9, 1968 [297]

BODY AND SOUL (as)

C-JAM BLUES (as)

'S WONDERFUL (as)

UNDECIDED (as)

---
[298]   1968 Los Angeles
         NANCY WILSON

Carter (as, arr) Large Orchestra with Strings, Nancy Wilson (v) Jimmy Jones (arr)

I'M YOUR SPECIAL FOOL   v-NW (e)
LP: CAPITOL ST148

PRISONER OF MY EYES   v-NW (e) arr
LP: CAPITOL ST148

PLAYER PLAY ON   v-NW (e)
LP: CAPITOL ST148

ONLY LOVE   v-NW (e)
LP: CAPITOL ST148

LOOKING BACK   v-NW (e)
LP: CAPITOL ST148

IF WE ONLY HAVE LOVE   v-NW (e)
LP: CAPITOL ST148

IN A LONG WHITE ROOM   v-NW (e)
LP: CAPITOL ST148

YOU'D BETTER GO   v-NW (e)
LP: CAPITOL ST148

QUIET SOUL   v-NW (e)
LP: CAPITOL ST148

WHAT DO YOU SEE IN HER   v-NW (e)
LP: CAPITOL ST148

WE COULD LEARN TOGETHER   v-NW (e)
LP: CAPITOL ST148

NOTE: Strings on "Only Love" and "If We Only Have Love."

---
[299]   1968 Los Angeles
         NANCY WILSON

Carter (as) John Audino, Bobby Bryant, Pete Candoli, Harry Edison, Clyde Reesinger (tp) Chuck Cooper, Ed Kusby, Lew McCreary, Dick Nash, Tommy Pederson, Kenny Shroyer (tb) Chuck Gentry, Justin Gordon, Bill Green, Arthur Herbert, Plas Johnson (reeds) Jimmy Jones (p, arr) Donn Trenner (p)

Bob Bain, Mundell Lowe (g) Buster Williams, Carol Kaye (b) Shelly Manne (d) Larry Bunker, Gene Estes, Victor Feldman (percussion) Nancy Wilson (v)

OUT OF THIS WORLD   v-NW (e)
LP: CAPITOL ST2970

THIS BITTER EARTH   v-NW (e)
LP: CAPITOL ST2970

BY MYSELF   v-NW (e)
LP: CAPITOL ST2970

WHEN THE SUN COMES OUT   v-NW (as acc)
LP: CAPITOL ST2970

ALONE WITH MY THOUGHTS OF YOU   v-NW (e)
LP: CAPITOL ST2970

IT ONLY TAKES A MOMENT   v-NW (e)
LP: CAPITOL ST2970

PEACE OF MIND   v-NW (e)
LP: CAPITOL ST2970

ON THE OTHER SIDE OF THE TRACKS   v-NW (e)
LP: CAPITOL ST2970

BELOW, ABOVE   v-NW (e)
LP: CAPITOL ST2970

THE RULES OF THE ROAD   v-NW (e)
LP: CAPITOL ST2970

BLACK IS BEAUTIFUL   v-NW (e)
LP: CAPITOL ST2970

[300]   September 4-6, 1971   Colorado Springs   Recorded Live for
BASF-Unissued
COLORADO JAZZ PARTY

Carter (as) Clark Terry (tp) Carl Fontana (tb) Victor Feldman (p) Lyn Christie (b) Alan Dawson (d)

TERRY CLOTH

WHEN I FALL IN LOVE

THE SHADOW OF YOUR SMILE

MY FOOLISH HEART

A TIME FOR LOVE

RIFFTIDE

[301]	As Above

Carter (as) Dick Hyman (p) Larry Ridley (b) Duffy Jackson (d)

ALL THE THINGS YOU ARE

WHAT'S NEW

STOMPIN' AT THE SAVOY

[302]	As Above

Carter (as) Joe Newman (tp) Vic Dickenson (tb) James Moody, Bob Wilber (reeds) Dick Hyman (p) Larry Ridley (b) Alan Dawson (d)

IN A LITTLE SPANISH TOWN

BODY AND SOUL

IT'S THE TALK OF THE TOWN

LAURA

YOU'VE CHANGED

TANGERINE

LESTER LEAPS IN

[303]	As Above

Carter (as) Teddy Wilson (p) Milt Hinton (b) Cliff Leeman (d)

ROSETTA

I CAN'T GET STARTED

'S WONDERFUL

MAKIN' WHOOPEE

* * *

[300-303] Although portions of the Jazz Party were released on BASF 25099, Carter refused to allow any of his own work to be issued: "I wasn't told about the recording until I arrived, and I simply didn't want to be represented that way on record."

[304]	July 2, 1972 New York Broadcast, Newport Jazz Festival Concert, Carnegie Hall
	BENNY CARTER AND THE SWINGMASTERS

Carter (as, arr, comp) Harry Edison, Joe Thomas, Taft Jordan, Carl Warwick, Jimmy Nottingham (tp) Tyree Glenn, Benny Morton, Dicky Wells, Quentin Jackson (tb) Earle Warren, Howard Johnson (as) Buddy Tate, Budd

Johnson (ts) Haywood Henry (bs, cl) Teddy Wilson (p) Bernard Addison (g)
Milt Hinton (b) Jo Jones (d)

HONEYSUCKLE ROSE   (as) arr

DOOZY   (as) arr, comp

BLUES FOR BEGINNERS   (e) arr, comp

THE JUKE BOX   (as) arr, comp

I CAN'T GET STARTED   (as) arr

SLEEP   (as) arr

YOU ARE   (as) arr, comp

* * *

This emotional reunion of many of the swing era's seminal figures, including former Carter band members Joe Thomas, Tyree Glenn, Dicky Wells and Teddy Wilson, was a high point of the first Newport Jazz Festival in New York.

[305]   July 3, 1972   New York   Newport Jazz Festival Concert, Radio City Music Hall
MIDNIGHT JAM SESSION

Carter (as) Bobby Hackett (tp) Vic Dickenson (tb) Bud Freeman (ts) Red Norvo (vib) Teddy Wilson (p) Jim Hall (g) Larry Ridley (b) Bobby Rosengarden, Gene Krupa (d)

IN A MELLOTONE   (as)

BLUES   (as)

HONEYSUCKLE ROSE   (as)

NOTES: This session was probably recorded, but was not included on the commercially issued LPs of the Festival. Krupa plays on last tune only.

[306]   October 7, 1972   New Haven, Conn.
CONCERT, YALE UNIVERSITY

Carter (as) Harry Edison (tp) Duke Ellington (p) Ray Brown (b) Jo Jones (d) Joe Williams (v)

TAKE THE A TRAIN   (as)

SATIN DOLL   (as)

ROCKS IN MY BED   v-JW (as)

JUST SQUEEZE ME   v-JW (as)

October 7, 1972 [306]

EVERYDAY I HAVE THE BLUES   v-JW (as)

    NOTE: This concert was to benefit the Duke Ellington Fellowship Program--"Conservatory Without Walls." Tapes may exist.

[307]   November 7, 1972   Malmo, Sweden   Concert Recording
        JAZZ AT THE PHILHARMONIC

Carter (as) Roy Eldridge (tp) Al Grey (tb) Eddie "Lockjaw" Davis (ts) Oscar Peterson (p) Niels Pedersen (b) Louis Bellson (d)

JIM DOGS BLUES (as)
LP: UNIQUE JAZZ (I) 002

THE NEARNESS OF YOU (as)
LP: UNIQUE JAZZ (I) 002

UNDECIDED (as)
LP: UNIQUE JAZZ (I) 002

    NOTES: Date and location of this bootleg JATP issue from contemporary reports in Orkester Journalen. Carter with rhythm only on "Nearness Of You."

[308]   April 19, 1973   Princeton, New Jersey   Concert, Princeton
        University
        BENNY CARTER AND HIS ALL STARS

Carter (as) Hank Jones (p) Milt Hinton (b) Ron Zito (d)

NIGHT IN TUNISIA (as)

UNDECIDED (as)

ROBBINS NEST (as)

THE SHADOW OF YOUR SMILE (as)

HONEYSUCKLE ROSE (as)

IN A MELLOTONE (as)

A DAY IN THE LIFE OF A FOOL (MANHA DE CARNIVAL) (as)

ALL THE THINGS YOU ARE (as)

ONE GOOD BLUES (as)

SWEET GEORGIA BROWN (as)

HOW HIGH THE MOON (as)

[309]   October 22, 1973   Princeton, New Jersey   Concert, Princeton
        University
        BENNY CARTER AND HIS ALL STARS

Carter (as, comp) Clark Terry (tp, flugelhorn, v) Hank Jones (p) Bucky Pizzarelli (g) Milt Hinton (b) Grady Tate (d, v)

UNDECIDED   (as)

THE SHADOW OF YOUR SMILE   (as)

SATIN DOLL   (as)

WHEN LIGHTS ARE LOW   (as) comp

BLUES

BLUE MONK   (e)

MY GAL   v-CT (as)

BLUE MONK   (e)

TAKE THE A TRAIN   (as)

PERDIDO   (as)

BLUE STAR   (as) comp

DOOZY   (as) comp

IN A MELLOTONE   (as)

SWEET GEORGIA BROWN   (as)

    NOTE: "Blues"/"Blue Monk"/"My Gal"/"Blue Monk" played in medley.

[310]   November 10, 1973   New Haven, Conn.   Yale University
BENNY CARTER AND HIS ORCHESTRA

Carter (as, arr, comp) Earle Warren (as) Billy Mitchell, Charlie Rouse (ts) Cecil Payne (bs) Dwike Mitchell (p) Willie Ruff (b) Grady Tate (d)

DOOZY   (as) arr, comp

PROHIBIDO   (as) arr, comp

I CAN'T GET STARTED   (as)

ROCK BOTTOM   (as) arr, comp

IF DREAMS COME TRUE   (as) arr

    NOTE: Carter with rhythm only on "I Can't Get Started."

[311]   December 3, 1973   Princeton, New Jersey   Concert, Princeton University
BENNY CARTER AND HIS ORCHESTRA

December 3, 1973 [311]

Carter (as, arr, comp) Jon Faddis, Joe Newman, Victor Paz, Ernie Royal (tp) Eddie Bert, Dickie Harris, Quentin Jackson, Jimmy Knepper (tb) George Dorsey (as) Jerry Dodgion (as, flute) Budd Johnson, Billy Mitchell (ts) George Barrow (bs) Roland Hanna (p) Wally Richardson (g) Major Holley (b) Mousie Alexander (d) Ray Barretto (conga) Hale Smith (v)

DOOZY (as) arr, comp

WHEN LIGHTS ARE LOW (as) arr, comp

YOU ARE (e) arr, comp

SOUVENIR (as) arr, comp

HONEYSUCKLE ROSE (as) arr

BLUES FOR BEGINNERS v-HS (as) arr, comp

COALITION (as) arr, comp

I CAN'T GET STARTED (as) arr

COTTONTAIL (e) arr

A KISS FROM YOU (e) arr, comp

A WALKIN' THING (as) arr, comp

SLEEP (as) arr

THE NEARNESS OF YOU (as)

THE JUKE BOX (as) arr, comp

NOTES: "Souvenir" announced as "That's How It Goes"; title changed later. "A Kiss From You" formerly entitled "Lydia." "The Nearness Of You" is Carter's feature in ballad medley.

[312]   November 7, 1974 Ithaca, New York   Concert, Cornell University
          BENNY CARTER AND HIS ALL STARS

Carter (as) Jimmy Nottingham (tp, flugelhorn) Al Grey (tb) Roland Hanna (p) Milt Hinton (b) Alan Dawson (d)

IN A MELLOTONE (as)

ON GREEN DOLPHIN STREET (as)

MISTY (as)

UNDECIDED (as)

PERDIDO (as)

STOMPIN' AT THE SAVOY (as)

BROADWAY (as)

I CAN'T GET STARTED (as)

COTTONTAIL (as)

[313]   December 22, 1974   Los Angeles Broadcast of Concert,
                               The Troubadour
          MARIA MULDAUR

Carter (as, arr, comp) Snooky Young, Harry Edison (tp) J. J. Johnson (tb) Bud Shank (as, cl, flute) Plas Johnson (ts) Sahib Shihab (bs) Marty Harris (p, electric p) Mundell Lowe (g) John B. Williams (b) Earl Palmer (d) Maria Muldaur (v)

SQUEEZE ME   v-MM (e) arr

ANY OLD TIME   v-MM (e) arr

GEE, AIN'T I GOOD TO YOU   v-MM (e) arr

SWEETHEART   v-MM (e) arr

DOOZY   (e) arr, comp

IT DON'T MEAN A THING IF IT AIN'T GOT THAT SWING
      v-MM (e)

LOVER MAN   v-MM (as) arr

WALKIN' ONE AND ONLY   v-MM (e) arr

DON'T YOU MAKE ME HIGH   v-MM (e) arr

I'M A WOMAN   v-MM (e) arr

IT AIN'T THE MEAT IT'S THE MOTION   v-MM (e) arr

[314]   July 16, 1975   Montreux, Switzerland   Montreux Jazz Festival
                               Concert
          JAZZ AT THE PHILHARMONIC

Carter (as) Roy Eldridge (tp) Clark Terry (tp, flugelhorn) Zoot Sims (ts) Tommy Flanagan (p) Joe Pass (g) Keter Betts (b) Bobby Durham (d)

FOR YOU   (as)
LP: PABLO 2310-748

AUTUMN LEAVES   (as)
LP: PABLO 2310-748

IF I HAD YOU   (as)
LP: PABLO 2310-748

I NEVER KNEW   (as)
LP: PABLO 2310-748

July 16, 1975 [314]

SUNDAY (as)
LP: PABLO 2625-707

* * *

Those listening to Carter at live performances in the early 1970s noticed a change in his style. His tone acquired a new edge, his attack became more forceful. The clearest evidence of change on record is Carter's remarkable solo on "Autumn Leaves." At several points Carter descends into the lower register for a decidedly non-"urbane" honk. He also plays behind the beat, exploring the chord changes with almost mockingly deliberate arpeggios. Once again, Carter seems to have assimilated those features of more recent styles necessary to keep his own sound current.

[314A]　July 17, 1975　Nice, France
　　　　　INTERNATIONAL JAZZ FESTIVAL - LA GRANDE PARADE DU
　　　　　JAZZ

Carter (as) Bobby Hackett (tp) Vic Dickenson (tb) Barney Bigard (cl) Joe Venuti (violin) Teddy Wilson, Earl Hines (p) Red Norvo (vib) George Duvivier (b) Bobby Rosengarden (d)

FOR YOU (as)

MONDAY DATE (as)

ROSETTA (as)

　　　NOTE: Wilson plays on first title, Hines on second. Both play on
　　　"Rosetta," with Hines soloing first.

[314B]　July 18, 1975　Nice, France
　　　　　INTERNATIONAL JAZZ FESTIVAL - LA GRANDE PARADE DU
　　　　　JAZZ

Carter (as) Bobby Hackett (tp) Teddy Wilson (p) Larry Ridley (b) David Lee (d)

BODY AND SOUL (as)

WHAT IS THIS THING CALLED LOVE (as)

[314C]　July 21, 1975　Nice, France
　　　　　INTERNATIONAL JAZZ FESTIVAL - LA GRANDE PARADE DU
　　　　　JAZZ

Carter (as) Bob Wilber (ss) Earle Warren (as) Teddy Wilson (p) Major Holley (b) Panama Francis (d)

THE JEEP IS JUMPIN' (as)

I GOT IT BAD AND THAT AIN'T GOOD (as)

PERDIDO (as)

NOTE: Carter with rhythm section only on "I Got It Bad"; "Perdido" fades during Carter's solo.

[314D] Same Date
INTERNATIONAL JAZZ FESTIVAL - LA GRANDE PARADE DU JAZZ

Carter (as) Harry Edison, Clark Terry (tp) Zoot Sims (ts) Teddy Wilson (p) Major Holley (b) Ray Mosca (d)

LADY BE GOOD   (as)

[315]   September 9, 1975   Chicago   Club Date, Ratso's
BENNY CARTER

Carter (as) Jody Christian (p) Dave Shipp (b) Jo Jones (d)

IN A MELLOTONE   (as)

ALL THE THINGS YOU ARE   (as)

MISTY   (as)

THREE LITTLE WORDS   (as)

AUTUMN LEAVES   (as)

AS TIME GOES BY   (as)

BYE BYE BLACKBIRD   (as)

I FOUND A NEW BABY   (as)

[316]   September 10, 1975   Chicago   TV Show Soundstage, WTTW-TV Studios
A TRIBUTE TO JOHN HAMMOND

Carter (as) Benny Morton (tb) Teddy Wilson (p) George Benson (g) Milt Hinton (b) Jo Jones (d) Red Norvo (vib) Helen Humes (v)

RIFF INTERLUDE   (as)

JOHN'S IDEA   (as)

SONG OF THE WANDERER   v-HH (as)

[317]   December 18, 1975   Istanbul, Turkey   Concert, Park Hotel-U.S. State Dept. Tour
BENNY CARTER QUINTET

Carter (as) Harry Edison (tp) Gildo Mahones (p) John B. Williams (b) Earl Palmer (d)

IN A MELLOTONE   (as)

December 18, 1975 [317]   211

UNDECIDED (as)

MISTY (as)

HONEYSUCKLE ROSE (as)

STOMPIN' AT THE SAVOY (as)

TAKE THE A TRAIN (as)

>   NOTE: All titles except "Honeysuckle Rose" and "Stompin' At The Savoy" aired over Turkish TV and radio.

[318]   December 21, 1975 Ankara, Turkey Concert, Turkish-American Assoc. -U. S. State Dept. Tour
        BENNY CARTER QUINTET

Carter (as) Harry Edison (tp) Gildo Mahones (p) John B. Williams (b) Earl Palmer (d)

IN A MELLOTONE (as)

UNDECIDED (as)

MISTY (as)

HONEYSUCKLE ROSE (as)

STOMPIN' AT THE SAVOY (as)

PERDIDO (as)

[319]   Same Concert

Carter (as,p) Harry Edison (tp) Tuna Otenel (as,p) Selcuk Sun (b) Erol Pekcan (d)

JUMPIN' WITH SYMPHONY SID (as)

>   NOTE: For this piece Carter and Edison were joined by some Turkish musicians. Carter plays piano accompaniment while Otenel solos on alto.

[320]   December 22, 1975 Ankara, Turkey Broadcast, Turkish Radio/ Television-U. S. State Dept. Tour
        BENNY CARTER QUINTET

Carter (as) Harry Edison (tp) Gildo Mahones (p) John B. Williams (b) Earl Palmer (d)

BLUES (e)

UNDECIDED (as)

IN A MELLOTONE (as)

I CAN'T GET STARTED   (as)

PERDIDO (incomplete)   (e)

[321]   December 22, 1975 Ankara, Turkey Concert, Turkish-American
                            Assoc. -U. S. State Dept. Tour
           BENNY CARTER QUINTET

Carter (as) Harry Edison (tp) Gildo Mahones (p) John B. Williams (b) Earl Palmer (d) Millicent Browne (v)

IN A MELLOTONE   (as)

UNDECIDED   (as)

HONEYSUCKLE ROSE   (as)

STOMPIN' AT THE SAVOY   (as)

MISTY   (as)

PERDIDO   (as)

EVERYDAY I HAVE THE BLUES   v-MB (as)

[322]   December 24, 1975 Tehran, Iran Concert, City Theater-U. S.
                            State Dept. Tour
           BENNY CARTER QUINTET

Carter (as) Harry Edison (tp) Gildo Mahones (p) John B. Williams (b) Earl Palmer (d)

IN A MELLOTONE   (as)

UNDECIDED   (as)

HONEYSUCKLE ROSE   (as)

MISTY   (as)

PERDIDO   (as)

JINGLE BELLS   (as)

[323]   December 25, 1975 Tehran, Iran Concert, City Theater-U. S.
                            State Dept. Tour
           BENNY CARTER QUINTET

Carter (as) Harry Edison (tp) Gildo Mahones (p) John B. Williams (p) Earl Palmer (d)

IN A MELLOTONE   (as)

UNDECIDED   (as)

December 25, 1975 [323]

HONEYSUCKLE ROSE (as)

SUPERSWEET (as)

I CAN'T BELIEVE THAT YOU'RE IN LOVE WITH ME (as)

MISTY (as)

PERDIDO (as)

[324] December 30, 1975 Islamabad, Pakistan Concert, Liaquat Memorial Hall-U. S. State Dept. Tour
BENNY CARTER QUINTET

Carter (as) Harry Edison (tp) Gildo Mahones (p) John B. Williams (b) Earl Palmer (d) Millicent Browne (v)

IN A MELLOTONE (as)

UNDECIDED (as)

MISTY (as)

HONEYSUCKLE ROSE (as)

SUPERSWEET (as)

EVERYDAY I HAVE THE BLUES v-MB (as)

PERDIDO (e)

[325] December 31, 1975 Lahore, Pakistan Concert, Foreman Christian College-U. S. State Dept. Tour
BENNY CARTER QUINTET

Carter (as) Harry Edison (tp) Gildo Mahones (p) John B. Williams (b) Earl Palmer (d) Millicent Browne (v)

SUPERSWEET (as)

EVERYDAY I HAVE THE BLUES v-MB (as)

TAKE THE A TRAIN (as)

> NOTE: Due to a power failure, only part of this concert was recorded.

[326] January 1, 1976 Karachi, Pakistan Concert, American Center-U. S. State Dept. Tour
BENNY CARTER QUINTET

Carter (as) Harry Edison (tp) Gildo Mahones (p) John B. Williams (b) Earl Palmer (d) Millicent Browne (v)

IN A MELLOTONE (as)

UNDECIDED (as)

MISTY (as)

PERDIDO (as)

SUPERSWEET (as)

EVERYDAY I HAVE THE BLUES   v-MB (as)

TAKE THE A TRAIN (as)

    NOTE: This concert was filmed for Karachi television.

[327]   January 2, 1976   Karachi, Pakistan Concert, Pakistan-American Cultural Center-U. S. State Dept. Tour
BENNY CARTER QUINTET

Carter (as) Harry Edison (tp) Gildo Mahones (p) John B. Williams (b) Earl Palmer (d) Millicent Browne (v)

IN A MELLOTONE (as)

UNDECIDED (as)

I CAN'T GET STARTED (as)

PERDIDO (as)

SUPERSWEET (as)

EVERYDAY I HAVE THE BLUES   v-MB (as)

TAKE THE A TRAIN (as)

    NOTE: This concert was filmed for Karachi television.

[328]   January 3, 1976   Karachi, Pakistan Broadcast, Karachi TV-U. S. State Dept. Tour
BENNY CARTER QUINTET

Carter (as, comp) Harry Edison (tp) Gildo Mahones (p) John B. Williams (b) Earl Palmer (d) Millicent Browne (v)

UNDECIDED (as)

IN A MELLOTONE (as)

BLUE STAR (as) comp

SUPERSWEET (as)

ONLY TRUST YOUR HEART (as) comp

WHEN LIGHTS ARE LOW   v-MB (as) comp

January 3, 1976 [328]

ALL THAT JAZZ   v-MB (as) comp

PERDIDO   (as)

[329]   January 5, 1976 Kuwait Concert/Seminar, Aldar Gallery-U.S. State Dept. Tour
BENNY CARTER QUINTET

Carter (as) Harry Edison (tp) Gildo Mahones (p) John B. Williams (b) Earl Palmer (d) Millicent Browne (v)

UNDECIDED   (as)

HONEYSUCKLE ROSE   (as)

EVERYDAY I HAVE THE BLUES   v-MB (as)

WHEN THE SAINTS GO MARCHING IN   (as)

MISTY   (as)

SUPERSWEET   (e)

JUMPIN' AT THE WOODSIDE   (as)

IN A MELLOTONE   (as)

PERDIDO   (as)

NOTE: Williams became ill after the first number and no bass is present thereafter.

[330]   January 6, 1976 Kuwait Concert, Kuwait Hilton-U.S. State Dept. Tour
BENNY CARTER QUINTET

Carter (as) Harry Edison (tp) Gildo Mahones (p) John B. Williams (b) Earl Palmer (d) Millicent Browne (v)

IN A MELLOTONE   (as)

UNDECIDED   (as)

MISTY   (as)

PERDIDO   (as)

SUPERSWEET   (as)

EVERYDAY I HAVE THE BLUES   v-MB (as)

TAKE THE A TRAIN   (as)

[331]   January 11, 1976 Damascus, Syria Concert, Al Hamra Theatre-U.S. State Dept. Tour
BENNY CARTER QUINTET

Carter (as) Harry Edison (tp) Gildo Mahones (p) John B. Williams (b) Earl Palmer (d) Millicent Browne (v)

IN A MELLOTONE   (as)

UNDECIDED   (as)

MISTY   (as)

PERDIDO   (as)

SUPERSWEET   (as)

EVERYDAY I HAVE THE BLUES   v-MB (as)

TAKE THE A TRAIN   (as)

  NOTE: Concert filmed for television.

[332] January 13, 1976 Irbid, Jordan Concert, Irbid Trade School-U.S. State Dept. Tour
  BENNY CARTER QUINTET

Carter (as) Harry Edison (tp) Gildo Mahones (p) John B. Williams (b) Earl Palmer (d) Millicent Browne (v)

UNDECIDED   (as)

MISTY   (as)

PERDIDO   (as)

SUPERSWEET   (as)

EVERYDAY I HAVE THE BLUES   v-MB (as)

TAKE THE A TRAIN   (as)

[333] January 14, 1976 Amman, Jordan Concert, Greek Orthodox Club-U.S. State Dept. Tour
  BENNY CARTER QUINTET

Carter (as) Harry Edison (tp) Gildo Mahones (p) John B. Williams (b) Earl Palmer (d) Millicent Browne (v)

IN A MELLOTONE   (as)

MISTY   (as)

PERDIDO   (as)

SUPERSWEET   (as)

EVERYDAY I HAVE THE BLUES   v-MB (as)

TAKE THE A TRAIN   (as)

January 14, 1976 [334]

[334]	January 14, 1976 Amman, Jordan Concert, University of Jordan-U. S. State Dept. Tour
	BENNY CARTER QUINTET

Carter (as) Harry Edison (tp) Gildo Mahones (p) John B. Williams (b) Earl Palmer (d) Millicent Browne (v)

IN A MELLOTONE (as)

MISTY (as)

PERDIDO (as)

SUPERSWEET (as)

EVERYDAY I HAVE THE BLUES v-MB (as)

[335]	January 16, 1976 Cairo, Egypt Concert, American University of Cairo-U. S. State Dept. Tour
	BENNY CARTER QUINTET

Carter (as) Harry Edison (tp) Gildo Mahones (p) John B. Williams (b) Earl Palmer (d) Millicent Browne (v)

UNDECIDED (as)

IN A MELLOTONE (as)

MISTY (as)

PERDIDO (as)

SUPERSWEET (as)

EVERYDAY I HAVE THE BLUES v-MB (as)

[336]	Same Concert

Carter (as) Harry Edison (tp) Said Salama (ts) Gildo Mahones (p) John B. Williams (b) Bib Hanein (timbales) Salah Ragab (d)

CARAVAN (as)

> NOTE: For this piece Carter was joined by members of the Cairo University jazz band.

[337]	January 19, 1976 Alexandria, Egypt Concert, Sayed Darwish Theatre-U. S. State Dept. Tour
	BENNY CARTER QUINTET

Carter (as) Harry Edison (tp) Gildo Mahones (p) John B. Williams (b) Earl Palmer (d) Millicent Browne (v)

IN A MELLOTONE (as)

UNDECIDED (as)

MISTY (as)

PERDIDO (as)

SUPERSWEET (as)

EVERYDAY I HAVE THE BLUES v-MB (as acc)

I CAN'T BELIEVE THAT YOU'RE IN LOVE WITH ME (as)

[338]   February 11, 1976 Los Angeles
          BENNY CARTER (THE KING)

Carter (as, comp) Milt Jackson (vib) Tommy Flanagan (p) Joe Pass (g) John B. Williams (b) Jake Hanna (d)

A WALKIN' THING   (as) comp
PABLO 2310-768

MY KIND OF TROUBLE IS YOU   (as) comp
PABLO 2310-768

EASY MONEY   (as) comp
PABLO 2310-768

BLUE STAR   (as) comp
PABLO 2310-768

I STILL LOVE HIM SO   (as) comp
PABLO 2310-768

GREEN WINE   (as) comp
PABLO 2310-768

MALIBU   (as) comp
PABLO 2310-768

BLUES IN D FLAT   (as) comp
PABLO 2310-768

ALL THAT JAZZ   comp
UNISSUED

* * *

The King, in a sense, was Carter's "comeback" date; it had been ten years since his last album as a leader. This session is valuable if only because it documents a number of fine Carter compositions, some of which had previously existed only in obscure versions ("Green Wine," and "My Kind Of Trouble Is You"). Also included were new interpretations of earlier classics ("Malibu," "Blue Star").

[339]   April 27, 1976 Los Angeles
          CARTER, GILLESPIE, INC.

April 27, 1976 [339]

Carter (as, comp) Dizzy Gillespie (tp, comp) Tommy Flanagan (p) Joe Pass (g) Al McKibbon (b) Mickey Roker (d, v)

SWEET AND LOVELY   (as)
PABLO 2310-781

BROADWAY   (as)
PABLO 2310-781

THE COURTSHIP   (as) comp
PABLO 2310-781

CONSTANTINOPLE   (as)
PABLO 2310-781

NOBODY KNOWS THE TROUBLE I'VE SEEN   v-MR
PABLO 2310-781

NIGHT IN TUNISIA   (as)
PABLO 2310-781

* * *

This session is an intriguing and highly enjoyable reunion. Although Gillespie takes the initiative (he set the tempos and suggested most of the music), Carter sounds much more at ease than on his own date two months earlier.

Most of the tracks are impromptu with the solo routines and endings in some cases evolving on the spot.

Carter supplied a new composition, "The Courtship," an insinuating 38-bar melody.

(For an analysis of Carter's solo on "A Night In Tunisia" see chapter 3.)

[340]   May 6, 1976   Los Angeles
        BASIE JAM #2 AND #3

Carter (as, comp) Clark Terry (tp) Al Grey (tb) Eddie "Lockjaw" Davis (ts) Count Basie (p) Joe Pass (g) John Heard (b) Louis Bellson (d)

MAMA DON'T WEAR NO DRAWERS   (as) comp
LP: PABLO 2310-786

DOGGIN' AROUND   (as)
LP: PABLO 2310-786

KANSAS CITY LINE   (as) comp
LP: PABLO 2310-786

JJJJUMP   (as) comp
LP: PABLO 2310-786

BYE BYE BLUES   (as)
LP: PABLO 2310-840

MOTEN SWING   (as)
LP: PABLO 2310-840

I SURRENDER DEAR   (as)
LP: PABLO 2310-840

SONG OF THE ISLANDS   (as)
LP: PABLO 2310-840

* * *

Carter's exuberant playing is one of the highlights of this informal gathering. He credits Count Basie's ideal backing with spurring on the soloists: "He stays out of the way and feeds you perfectly. His choice of chords, spacing, and, above all, taste set him apart."

[341]   June 19, 1976 New York Club Date, Michael's Pub
        BENNY CARTER QUARTET

Carter (as, tp, comp) Ray Bryant (p) Milt Hinton (b) Grady Tate (d)

THREE LITTLE WORDS   (as)

EASY MONEY   (as) comp

MISTY   (as)

IN A MELLOTONE   (as)(tp)

ALL THE THINGS YOU ARE   (as)

LAURA (as)

BLUES (tp)

IT DON'T MEAN A THING IF IT AIN'T GOT THAT SWING   (as)

MEMORIES OF YOU   (as)

OVER THE RAINBOW   (tp)

EASY MONEY   (as) comp

WHAT ARE YOU DOING THE REST OF YOUR LIFE   (as)

THESE FOOLISH THINGS   (features Hinton)

DON'T BLAME ME   (tp)

TAKE THE A TRAIN   (as)

MEAN TO ME   (as)

    NOTE: "Memories Of You"/"Over The Rainbow" and "What Are You Doing"/"These Foolish Things"/"Don't Blame Me" are medleys.

[342]   June 24, 1976 New York Club Date, Michael's Pub
        BENNY CARTER QUARTET

June 24, 1976 [342]

Carter (as, tp, comp) Ray Bryant (p) Milt Hinton (b) Grady Tate (d)

THREE LITTLE WORDS (as)

ROBBINS NEST (as)(tp)

I CAN'T GET STARTED (as)

EASY MONEY (as)(tp) comp

BLUE LOU (as)

WAVE (as)

POOR BUTTERFLY (tp)(as)

ON GREEN DOLPHIN STREET (as)

I COVER THE WATERFRONT (tp)

MOONGLOW (tp)(as)

ALL THE THINGS YOU ARE (as)(tp)

BUT NOT FOR ME (tp)

SWEET GEORGIA BROWN (tp)

BLUES IN MY HEART (tp) comp

[343] July 3, 1976 New York Club Date, Michael's Pub
BENNY CARTER QUARTET

Carter (as, tp, comp) Ray Bryant (p) Milt Hinton (b) Grady Tate (d, v)

EASY MONEY (as) comp

ALL THE THINGS YOU ARE (as)

WAVE (as)

BLUES IN MY HEART (tp)(as) comp

UNDECIDED (incomplete) (as)

HERE'S THAT RAINY DAY (as)

DON'T BLAME ME (tp)

I'LL NEVER BE THE SAME (features Bryant)

THESE FOOLISH THINGS (features Hinton)

BODY AND SOUL v-GT (tp)

> NOTE: "Don't Blame Me"/"I'll Never Be The Same"/"These Foolish Things" played in medley.

[344]   September 17, 1976 Monterey, California Airchecks?, Monterey
                            Jazz Festival Concert
        BENNY CARTER - TRIBUTE TO FLETCHER HENDERSON

Carter (as) Gene Coe, Blue Mitchell, Cat Anderson, Bill Berry (tp) Britt Woodman, Benny Powell, Jimmy Cleveland, Tricky Lofton (tb) Russell Procope (cl) Marshall Royal, Unknown (as) Richie Kamuca, Don Menza (ts) Jack Nimitz (bs) Dave Frishberg (p) Mundell Lowe (g) Monty Budwig (b) Frankie Capp (d)

WRAPPIN' IT UP

BIG JOHN SPECIAL

CHRISTOPHER COLUMBUS

KING PORTER STOMP

>   NOTE: These tunes were scored by Mundell Lowe based on the
>   original Fletcher/Horace Henderson arrangements.

[345]   Same Concert
        TRIBUTE TO LOUIS ARMSTRONG

Carter (tp) Harry Edison, Doc Cheatham, Dizzy Gillespie, Clark Terry, Jon Faddis (tp) Dave Frishberg (p) Mundell Lowe (g) Monty Budwig (b) Frankie Capp (d)

CONFESSIN' (tp)

STRUTTIN' WITH SOME BARBECUE (e)

[346]   November 30, 1976 New York Studio Recording for Pablo--Unissued
        BENNY CARTER

Carter (as, tp, comp) Ray Bryant (p) Milt Hinton (b) Grady Tate (d)

A TEA VISTA (as) comp

JOHNNY (as) comp

STROLL (as) comp

BODY AND SOUL (tp)

MISTY (as)

[347]   Same Date Studio recording for Pablo--Unissued
        BENNY CARTER

Carter (as, tp, arr, comp) Harry Edison (tp) Eddie "Lockjaw" Davis (ts) Ray Bryant (p) Milt Hinton (b) Grady Tate (d)

SUMMER NIGHT (as) arr, comp

November 30, 1976 [347]

THREE LITTLE WORDS (as)

BLUES (tp)

    NOTE: "Summer Night" also known as "Wonderland."

[348]   March 18, 1977   Princeton, N.J.   Concert, Princeton University
BENNY CARTER SEXTET

Carter (as, comp) Joe Newman (tp) Roland Hanna (p) Bucky Pizzarelli (g) Richard Pratt (d)

UNDECIDED (as)

EASY MONEY (as) comp

HERE'S THAT RAINY DAY (as)

SOUTH SIDE SAMBA (as) comp

GREEN WINE (as) comp

YESTERDAYS (as)

SATIN DOLL (as)

ST. THOMAS (as)

BLUE STAR (as) comp

ON GREEN DOLPHIN STREET (as)

THE COURTSHIP (as) comp

PERDIDO (as)

IN A MELLOTONE (as)

[349]   April 8, 1977   Princeton, N.J.   Concert, Princeton University
BENNY CARTER WITH THE PRINCETON UNIVERSITY JAZZ
ENSEMBLES

Carter (as, arr, comp) Ernie Rivera, Randy Rydell, Steve Silliman, Bill Ash, Bill McHenry (tp) Bob Gibbons, Myles Connors, Barry Welch, Dave Preston (tb) Brian Ewart, Mike Zelner, Gary Monheit, Rob Kaminsky, Rick Sonnenfeld (reeds) John Novaria (p) Steve Wexler (g) Todd Beany (b) John Pittenger (d)

SOUVENIR (as) arr, comp

COTTONTAIL (as) arr

    NOTE: "Souvenir" previously entitled "That's How It Goes."

[350]   Same Concert

Carter (as, arr, comp) John Dolan, Tom Orlofsky, Ben Ballard, Doug Abbott, Bob McKillip (tp) Ben Monderer, Tony Maoicco, Jim Huffman, Ken Marantz (tb) Art Fogartie, Leslie Ritts, Tim McNally, Jon Healy, Steve Mathews (reeds) Jeff Presslaff (p) Joe Defrisco (b) Jon Stroup (d) Frank Foster (arr, comp)

WHEN LIGHTS ARE LOW (as) arr, comp

I CAN'T GET STARTED (as) comp

DOOZY (as) arr, comp

WHO, ME? arr&comp-FF (as)

[351]   April 29, 1977 Tokyo Concert, Koseinenkin Kaikan Hall
          BENNY CARTER ALL STARS

Carter (as, tp, arr, comp) Cat Anderson (tp) Joe Newman (tp, v) Britt Woodman (tb) Budd Johnson (ts, ss) Cecil Payne (bs, flute) Nat Pierce (p, arr) Mundell Lowe (g) George Duvivier (b) Harold Jones (d)

SQUATTY ROO (as) arr
LP: PABLO LIVE 2308-216, PABLO LIVE (J) MTF1815,
PABLO 2310-853

THEM THERE EYES (as) arr
LP: PABLO LIVE 2308-216, PABLO LIVE (J) MTF1815

IN A SENTIMENTAL MOOD (e) arr
UNISSUED

SOUTH SIDE SAMBA (as) arr, comp
UNISSUED

NUAGES (e) arr
UNISSUED

WHEN IT'S SLEEPY TIME DOWN SOUTH (e) arr
LP: PABLO LIVE 2308-216, PABLO LIVE (J) MTF1815,
MAXELL JAZZ II SAMPLER

CONFESSIN' (tp) arr
LP: PABLO LIVE 2308-216, PABLO LIVE (J) MTF1815,
MAXELL JAZZ II SAMPLER

WHEN YOU'RE SMILING v-JN (e) arr
LP: PABLO LIVE 2308-216, PABLO LIVE (J) MTF1815,
MAXELL JAZZ II SAMPLER

CHINATOWN, MY CHINATOWN (e) arr
UNISSUED

THINGS AIN'T WHAT THEY USED TO BE (as) arr
UNISSUED

ALL MY LOVE (e) arr
UNISSUED

April 29, 1977 [351]

GIRL TALK   arr-NP (e)
UNISSUED

SOUVENIR   (as) arr, comp
UNISSUED

JITTERBUG WALTZ   (as) arr
UNISSUED

GOD BLESS THE CHILD   (as) arr
UNISSUED

IT DON'T MEAN A THING IF IT AIN'T GOT THAT SWING   (as) arr
LP: PABLO LIVE 2308-216, PABLO LIVE (J) MTF1815, PABLO 2310-853

COTTONTAIL   (e) arr
UNISSUED

   NOTES: "Sleepy Time"/"Confessin'"/"When You're Smiling" played as medley in tribute to Louis Armstrong. "Souvenir" previously known as "That's How It Goes."

* * *

  Carter's triumphant tour of Japan resulted in this live recording, which includes his first trumpet playing on a commercial release since 1962. Carter remarks, "I was being very careful, like treading on eggs!" In spite of the layoff, on "Confessin'" he achieves a lovely tone without straining. "That's what Cuban Bennett used to do and what Doc Cheatham does. I think it's the way the instrument should be played."

  Carter put together an interesting book for this small "big band." At the request of the Japanese he included several pieces in tribute to some of the departed jazz creators. Of particular interest is "Chinatown," which features a transcription played by the three trumpets (Carter, Newman and Anderson) of Louis Armstrong's famous November 3, 1931 solo.

[352] July 13, 1977 Montreux, Switzerland Montreux Jazz Festival
            Concert
     BENNY CARTER FOUR (BENNY CARTER FOUR, MONTREUX '77)

Carter (as, tp)   Ray Bryant (p)   Niels Pedersen (b)   Jimmie Smith (d)

THREE LITTLE WORDS   (as)
LP: PABLO LIVE 2308-204, TIME LIFE STL-J10, PABLO 2310-853

IN A MELLOTONE   (as)(tp)
LP: PABLO LIVE 2308-204, PABLO 2310-853

WAVE   (as)
LP: PABLO LIVE 2308-204, PABLO 2310-853

UNDECIDED   (as)
LP: PABLO LIVE 2308-204

BODY AND SOUL (tp)(as)
LP: PABLO LIVE 2308-204

ON GREEN DOLPHIN STREET (as)
LP: PABLO LIVE 2308-204

HERE'S THAT RAINY DAY (as)
LP: PABLO LIVE 2308-204

* * *

Carter has always amazed his followers with his ability to maintain his command of the alto even after long layoffs. Such is his mastery that he does not usually practice regularly; he prepares only for a specific engagement. In the mid-1970s, as he returned to a more active playing schedule, undertaking several extended club dates and concert tours, his playing became awesome.

Norman Granz caught Carter at just such a peak at the 1977 Montreux Jazz Festival and the result is the Carter album of the 1970s. With him is Ray Bryant, with whom Carter first played at a New York club in 1976. The two achieved instant rapport, and Carter has since called on Bryant whenever possible for concerts, recordings and tours.

Every track is superb. On two tunes Carter plays trumpet as well, muted on "Mellotone" and open on "Body And Soul." Despite some fluffs on the latter, it is a striking statement which prompted contemporary trumpet star Freddie Hubbard to exclaim in a Downbeat blindfold test, "What!! Are you kiddin'? Benny Carter! Oh, man, he should play more trumpet. That is unbelievable!!" (April 20, 1978, p. 35.)

One witness reported that in the usually noisy musicians' lounge at Montreux, there was complete silence, as those who had played or were waiting to go on watched Carter's set on the TV monitor. When he returned after the performance he received a standing ovation from his peers. As Gary Giddins wrote in his review of this record, "excepting pianists and Joe Venuti, I don't think any septuagenarian jazzman has ever played with such unimpeded authority." (Village Voice, February 6, 1978, p. 56.)

[353]   July 14, 1977   Montreux, Switzerland   Montreux Jazz Festival
                          Concert
         COUNT BASIE JAM

Carter (as) Roy Eldridge (tp, v) Vic Dickenson, Al Grey (tb) Zoot Sims (ts) Count Basie (p) Ray Brown (b) Jimmie Smith (d)

ROOKIE BLUES (as)
LP: PABLO LIVE 2308-209

SHE'S FUNNY THAT WAY (e)
LP: PABLO LIVE 2308-209

THESE FOOLISH THINGS (as)
LP: PABLO LIVE 2308-209

KIDNEY STEW v-RE (e)
LP: PABLO LIVE 2308-209

July 14, 1977 [353]

I GOT IT BAD AND THAT AIN'T GOOD (e)
LP: PABLO LIVE 2308-209

JUMPIN' AT THE WOODSIDE (e)
LP: PABLO LIVE 2308-209

FREEPORT JUMP (as)
LP: PABLO LIVE 2620-105

[354]   April 15, 1978 Tokyo Concert, Nakano Sun Plaza Hotel
        BENNY CARTER ALL STAR ORCHESTRA

Carter (as, tp, arr, comp) Al Aarons, Ernie Royal (tp) Joe Newman (tp, v) Britt Woodman (tb) Budd Johnson (ts, arr) Buddy Collette (ts, cl, flute) Cecil Payne (bs, flute) Nat Pierce (p, arr) Mundell Lowe (g) George Duvivier (b, arr, comp) Gus Johnson (d)

SWEET GEORGIA BROWN   arr-NP (as)

THEM THERE EYES   (as) arr

LOVER MAN   arr-NP (as)

DOOZY (e) arr, comp

EKE'S BLUES   arr&comp-GD (as)

IT DON'T MEAN A THING IF IT AIN'T GOT THAT SWING   (as) arr

THINGS AIN'T WHAT THEY USED TO BE   (as) arr

WHEN IT'S SLEEPY TIME DOWN SOUTH   (e) arr

CONFESSIN'   (tp) arr

WHEN YOU'RE SMILING   v-JN (e) arr

BROADWAY (incomplete)   arr-NP (e)

BODY AND SOUL   (tp)

GIRL TALK   arr-NP (e)

ROSETTA   arr-BJ (as)

COTTONTAIL   (e) arr

    NOTE: "Sleepy Time"/"Confessin'"/"When You're Smiling" played as medly in tribute to Louis Armstrong; "Body And Soul"/"Girl Talk" part of medley.

[355]   Ca. April 19, 1978 Tokyo Concert, Nakano Sun Plaza Hotel
        BENNY CARTER ALL STAR ORCHESTRA

Carter (as, tp, arr) Joe Newman (tp, v) Al Aarons, Ernie Royal (tp) Britt Woodman (tb) Budd Johnson (ts, arr) Buddy Collette (ts, cl, flute) Cecil Payne (bs, flute) Nat Pierce (p, arr) Mundell Lowe (g) George Duvivier (b, arr, comp) Gus Johnson (d)

SWEET GEORGIA BROWN   arr-NP (as)

THEM THERE EYES   (as) arr

EKE'S BLUES   arr&comp-GD (as)

IT DON'T MEAN A THING IF IT AIN'T GOT THAT SWING   (as) arr

THINGS AIN'T WHAT THEY USED TO BE   (as) arr

WHEN IT'S SLEEPY TIME DOWN SOUTH   (e) arr

CONFESSIN'   (tp) arr

WHEN YOU'RE SMILING   v-JN (e) arr

BROADWAY   arr-NP (as)

DON'T BLAME ME   (tp)

I CAN'T GET STARTED   (as)

GIRL TALK   arr-NP (e)

ROSETTA   arr-BJ (as)

COTTONTAIL   (e) arr

    NOTE: "Sleepy Time"/"Confessin'"/"When You're Smiling" played as medley in tribute of Louis Armstrong; "Don't Blame Me"/"I Can't Get Started"/"Girl Talk" part of medley.

[356]   May 14, 1978 Washington, D.C.   Concert, Smithsonian Institution
                            Jazz Heritage Series
      BENNY CARTER

Carter (as, comp) Joe Kennedy (violin) Ray Bryant (p) Larry Ridley (b) Freddie Waits (d)

ON GREEN DOLPHIN STREET   (as)

EASY MONEY   (as) comp

MISTY   (as)

WAVE   (as)

PERDIDO   (as)

IN A MELLOTONE   (as)

ALL THE THINGS YOU ARE   (as)

COTTONTAIL   (as)

[357]   June 18, 1978   Washington, D. C.   NPR Broadcast of White House Concert
TRIBUTE TO THE 25TH ANNIVERSARY OF THE NEWPORT JAZZ FESTIVAL

Carter (as) Roy Eldridge, Clark Terry (tp) Illinois Jacquet (ts) Teddy Wilson (p) Milt Hinton (b) Jo Jones (d)

IN A MELLOTONE   (as)

LADY BE GOOD   (as)

[358]   October 28, 1978   Buffalo, N. Y.   Concert (1st), State University of N. Y.
BENNY CARTER WITH THE UNIV. OF BUFFALO JAZZ ENSEMBLE, SAM FALZONE, DIR.

Carter (as, arr, comp) Tony Gorruso, Norm Friedman, Ken Koleff, Mitch Robinson (tp) Craig Brown, Wallace Kotarski, Bruce Caldwell (tb) Sam Falzone, David Markiewicz, Steve Rosenthal, Mike Stalteri, Phil Lamacchia, Jonathan Schnepps, Michael Colquhoun, Robert Sowyrda (reeds) Randolph Noel, Kevin Doyle (p) Tony Logan, Rick Harris (g) Hans Halt (b) Charles Fadale (d)

WHEN LIGHTS ARE LOW   (as) arr, comp

LYDIA   (e) arr, comp

I CAN'T GET STARTED   (as) arr

HONEYSUCKLE ROSE   (as) arr

[359]   Same Concert
BENNY CARTER WITH THE AL TINNEY TRIO

Carter (as) Al Tinney (p) Lou Hackney (b) Jerry McClam (d)

IN A MELLOTONE   (as)

WHAT'S NEW   (as)

ON GREEN DOLPHIN STREET   (as)

TWELVE BAR BLUES   (as)

UNDECIDED   (as)

TAKE THE A TRAIN   (as)

[360]   Same Date--2nd Concert
BENNY CARTER WITH THE UNIV. OF BUFFALO JAZZ ENSEMBLE, PHIL SIMS, DIR.

Carter (as, arr, comp) Mike Reade, Mitch Robinson, Chris Conlon, Jerry Saratini (tp) Phil Sims, Craig Brown, Walter Koslowski, Wallace Kotarski,

James Ford, Denis Bourden (tb) Chuck Briem, Gary White, Jeff Hackworth, Carl Kesselman, Daven Skrzynski (reeds) David Billowus, Leslie Glassman (p) Rick Harris (g) Manuel Guevara (b) Bob Chaplin (d)

WHEN LIGHTS ARE LOW   (as) arr, comp

A WALKIN' THING   (as) arr, comp

BLUES FOR BEGINNERS   (as) arr, comp

I CAN'T GET STARTED   (as) arr

HONEYSUCKLE ROSE   (as) arr

[361]   Same Concert
         BENNY CARTER WITH THE AL TINNEY TRIO

Carter (as) Al Tinney (p) Lou Hackney (b) Jerry McClam (d)

IN A MELLOTONE   (as)

ON GREEN DOLPHIN STREET   (as)

LOVER MAN   (as)

PERDIDO   (as)

BODY AND SOUL   (as)

CHEROKEE   (as)

ALL THE THINGS YOU ARE   (as)

[362]   March 14, 1979
         OSCAR PETERSON

Carter (as) Clark Terry (tp) Zoot Sims (ts) Oscar Peterson (p) Milt Jackson (vib) John Heard (b) Grady Tate (d)

THEME FOR CELINE   (as)
PABLO TODAY   2312-103

THE HAPPY HOUR   (as)
PABLO TODAY   2312-103

PARTY TIME U.S.A.   (as)
PABLO TODAY   2312-103

ELLIOT   (as)
PABLO TODAY   2312-103

THEME FOR SUSANNAH   (as)
PABLO TODAY   2312-103

NOTE: The music for this album, The Silent Partner, is based on Oscar Peterson's score for the film of the same name.

[363] June 2, 1979   Tokyo   Concert, Kosei Nenkin Hall
BENNY CARTER JAZZ ALL STAR ORCHESTRA

Carter (as, arr, comp) Cat Anderson, Joe Newman (tp) Jimmy Cleveland (tb)
Budd Johnson (ts, arr) Cecil Payne (bs, flute) Joe Kennedy (violin) Ray Bryant
(p) George Duvivier (b) Harold Jones (d)

SHAVERS' TUNE   arr-BJ (as)
PADDLE WHEEL (J) GP3199

SOUTH SIDE SAMBA   (as) arr, comp
PADDLE WHEEL (J) GP3199

I CAN'T GET STARTED   (as)
PADDLE WHEEL (J) GP3199

    NOTE: "I Can't Get Started" is Carter's feature in ballad medley.

[364] October 12, 1979   Princeton, N.J.   Concert, Princeton University
BENNY CARTER SEXTET

Carter (as) Dizzy Gillespie (tp) Joe Kennedy (violin) Barry Harris (p) Larry
Ridley (b) Yusef Ali (d) Stanley Jordan (g)

AIN'T MISBEHAVIN'   (as)

STRAIGHT, NO CHASER   (as)

GEE, AIN'T I GOOD TO YOU   (as)

BROADWAY   (as)

PERDIDO   (as)

ON GREEN DOLPHIN STREET   (as)

ALL THE THINGS YOU ARE   (as)

CARAVAN   (as)

BLUES   (as)

    NOTE: Jordan plays on "All The Things You Are" and "Blues" only.

[365] November 10, 1979   Princeton, N.J.   Concert, Princeton University
BENNY CARTER WITH THE PRINCETON UNIVERSITY JAZZ
ENSEMBLE

Carter (as, comp) Tony Branker (tp, arr) Bill Ash, John Dolan, John Hill,
Burns Stanfield (tp) Matt Geymann, Doug Green, Ben Monderer, Jon Reingold (tb) Mike Connor, Tom Falin, Amy Leenhouts, Tim McNally, Steve
Ratner (reeds) Emery Snyder (p) Steve Wexler (b, arr) Jeff Penny (d) James
Capolupo (dir)

FEASANT PHEATHERS   arr-SW (as) comp

THE COURTSHIP   arr-SW (as) comp

ORNITHOLOGY   arr-TB (as)

---

[366]   Same Concert
        BENNY CARTER WITH THE PRINCETON UNIVERSITY JAZZ
        SEXTET

Carter (as) Tony Branker, John Dolan (tp) Ben Monderer (tb) Emery Snyder (p) Steve Wexler (b) Jeff Penny (d)

NIGHT IN TUNISIA   (as)

MISTY (Carter with rhythm)   (as)

WHAT IS THIS THING CALLED LOVE   (as)

---

[367]   June 11, 1980   Stockholm   TV Broadcast, Stockholm Jazz and
        Blues Festival
        BENNY CARTER WITH ARNE DOMNERUS & HIS ORCH.

Carter (as) Jan Allan (tp) Arne Domnerus (as) Claes Rosendahl (ts) Bengt Hallberg (p) Rune Gustafsson (g) Georg Riedel (b) Egil Johansen (d)

EASY MONEY   (as) comp

MISTY   (as)

HONEYSUCKLE ROSE   (as)

JEEP'S BLUES   (as)

        NOTE: Carter with rhythm on first title.

---

[368]   June 12, 1980   Stockholm   TV Broadcast, Stockholm Jazz and
        Blues Festival
        BENNY CARTER WITH KUSTBANDET

Carter (as) 12-Piece Swedish Band

UNKNOWN TITLES

---

[369]   June 13, 1980   Stockholm   TV Broadcast, Stockholm Jazz and
        Blues Festival
        BENNY CARTER QUARTET

Carter (as) Tommy Flanagan (p) Red Mitchell (b) Rune Carlsson (d)

THREE LITTLE WORDS   (as)

SOMETIMES I'M HAPPY   (as)

HERE'S THAT RAINY DAY   (as)

June 13, 1980 [369]

ON THE SUNNY SIDE OF THE STREET   (as)

BLUES   (as)

PERDIDO   (as)

* * *

At this concert Carter literally performed a musical miracle. The festival was held outdoors and, although the musicians were under cover, the audience was being drenched by a rainstorm. After playing "Here's That Rainy Day," Carter picked up the tempo, segued into "Sunny Side Of The Street," and during his solo the rain stopped. A Swedish newspaper ran a photo of Carter with the caption, "The Man Who Stopped The Rain!"

---

[370]   June 20, 1980   Los Angeles Television Broadcast, The Tonight Show
PLAYBOY JAZZ FESTIVAL GROUP

Carter (as) Teddy Wilson (p) Ray Brown (b) Shelly Manne (d)

BLUE LOU   (as)

I CAN'T BELIEVE THAT YOU'RE IN LOVE WITH ME   (as)

> NOTE: This group, with the addition of Harry "Sweets" Edison, performed the next day at the Playboy Jazz Festival in the Hollywood Bowl.

[370A]   June 26, 1980   Detroit National Public Radio Broadcast of Concert, Detroit Institute of Arts
TRIBUTE TO DON REDMAN

Carter (as) Doc Cheatham (tp, v) Dave Wilborn (v) with Rhythm Section

GEE, AIN'T I GOOD TO YOU   v-DC (as acc)

HONEYSUCKLE ROSE   (as)

MISTY   (as)

I WANT A LITTLE GIRL   v-DW, DC (as)

[370B]   Same Concert
NEW McKINNEY'S COTTON PICKERS

Carter (as, arr) Doc Cheatham (tp) Dave Wilborn, Orrin Foslien (v) with the New McKinney's Cotton Pickers

CHERRY   v-DW (e)

NEVER SWAT A FLY   v-OF (e) arr

MISS HANNAH   v-DW (e)

PLAIN DIRT   (e)

HELLO v-DW (e)

    NOTE: Carter plays lead alto on these titles. "Never Swat" is a McKinney's arrangement which Carter believes is his own, although it is usually credited to Redman.

[370C]   Same Concert
           RE-CREATION OF DON REDMAN ORCHESTRA

Includes Carter (as) Doc Cheatham (tp) Orchestra Conducted by Dave Hutson, Dave Wilborn (v)

HOW'M I DOIN' v-DW (as)

DOWN, DOWN, DOWN (e)

HOW DO YOU CALL A MAN A TWO TIMIN' MAN... V-DW (e)

I GOTCHA (e)

REDMAN BLUES (as)

---
[371]   August 17, 1980   Copenhagen   Studio Recording for Sonet
        BENNY CARTER

Carter (as) Kenny Drew (p) Jesper Lundgaard (b) Ed Thigpen (d)

UNKNOWN TITLES

---
[372]   September 3, 1980   Tokyo   Aurex Jazz Festival
        GENTLEMEN OF SWING

Carter (as) Harry Edison (tp) Teddy Wilson (p) Milt Hinton (b) Shelly Manne (d)

HONEYSUCKLE ROSE (as)
LP: EAST WORLD (J) EWJ80188

MISTY (as)
LP: EAST WORLD (J) EWJ80188

SOMETIMES I'M HAPPY (as)
LP: EAST WORLD (J) EWJ80188

[372A]   September 7, 1980 Yokohama, Japan Aurex Jazz Festival
        GENTLEMEN OF SWING

Carter (as) Harry Edison (tp) Teddy Wilson (p) Milt Hinton (b) Shelly Manne (d)

IN A MELLOTONE (as)
LP: EAST WORLD (J) EWJ80188

IDAHO (as)
LP: EAST WORLD (J) EWJ80188

September 7, 1980 [372A]   235

HONEYSUCKLE ROSE (as)
UNISSUED

[372B]   September 1980
          KEI ISHIGURO

Carter (as) Norrio Maeda (p) Yasur Arakawa (b) Takeshi Inomata (d) Kei
Ishiguro (v)

MISTY NIGHT   v-KI (as)
LP: VICTOR (J) SJX30032

MY DEAR OLD LOVE   v-KI (as)
LP: VICTOR (J) SXJ30032

[373]   February 4-5, 1981   Los Angeles
         TERESA BREWER

Carter (as) Oscar Brashear (flugelhorn) Mike Lang (p) Chuck Domanico (b)
Shelly Manne (d) Teresa Brewer (v)

SOPHISTICATED LADY   (feature for Carter) (as)
LP: COLUMBIA FC37363

SOLITUDE   v-TB (as)
LP: COLUMBIA FC37363

COME SUNDAY   v-TB (as)
LP: COLUMBIA FC37363

DUKE'S PLACE   v-TB (as)
LP: COLUMBIA FC37363

IT DON'T MEAN A THING IF IT AIN'T GOT THAT SWING   v-TB (as)
LP: COLUMBIA FC37363

DON'T GET AROUND MUCH ANYMORE   v-TB (as)
LP: COLUMBIA FC37363

I'M BEGINNING TO SEE THE LIGHT   v-TB (as)
LP: COLUMBIA FC37363

[374]   April 18, 1981   New York   Club Date, Sweet Basil
         BENNY CARTER QUARTET

Carter (as, v, comp) Norman Simmons (p) George Duvivier (b) Ronnie Bedford
(d)

IN A MELLOTONE (as)

BLUE STAR (as) comp

UNDECIDED (as)

ALL THE THINGS YOU ARE (as)

EASY MONEY (as) comp

WHAT IS THIS THING CALLED LOVE (as)

MISTY (as)

SOUTH SIDE SAMBA (as) comp

SOUVENIR (as) comp

ALL THAT JAZZ (as)(v) comp

[375]   July 1981 Japan (13 Concerts--see note below)
         BENNY CARTER ALL STARS

Carter (as, tp, arr, comp) Bill Berry (cornet) Pete Candoli (tp, v) George Bohanon (tb) Frank Wess (ts, flute) Jack Nimitz (bs) Kenny Barron (p) Joe Kennedy (violin) George Duvivier (b, arr) Frankie Capp (d)

THINGS AIN'T WHAT THEY USED TO BE (as) arr

MOOD INDIGO (as) arr

I'M BEGINNING TO SEE THE LIGHT (as) arr

THE COURTSHIP (as) arr, comp

WHEN IT'S SLEEPY TIME DOWN SOUTH (e) arr

CONFESSIN' (tp) arr

WHEN YOU'RE SMILING v-PC (e) arr

CHINATOWN (e) arr

EKE'S BLUES GD-comp & arr (tp)(as)

AIN'T MISBEHAVIN' (tp)

MISTY (as)

SOUTH SIDE SAMBA (as) arr, comp

COTTONTAIL (e) arr

NOTE: Carter gave 13 concerts during a three week tour of Japan; all performances exist on tape. The usual program consisted of the tunes listed here, although some variations occurred from concert to concert. Schedule: July 3-Yokohama, July 4-Tokyo (two concerts), July 7-Kushiro, July 9-Tokushima, July 10-Tsuruoka, July 11-Tokyo, July 12-Toyama, July 14-Osaka, July 15-Shimonoseki, July 16-Shizuoka, July 17-Tokyo, July 20-Mito.

"Sleepy Time," "Confessin'," "When You're Smiling" played as medley in tribute to Louis Armstrong.

"Chinatown" includes a transcription, played by the three trumpets, of Louis Armstrong's 11/3/31 solo.

"Ain't Misbehavin'" and "Misty" are Carter features in a medley.

[376]   July 17, 1981 Tokyo Television Show
NANCY WILSON WITH BENNY CARTER, GUEST SOLOIST

Carter (as) Nancy Wilson (v) with Large Studio Orchestra

I'M BEGINNING TO SEE THE LIGHT   v-NW (as)

BUT BEAUTIFUL   v-NW (as acc)

[377]   July 18, 1981 Tokyo
BENNY CARTER WITH THE KAZUO YASHIRO TRIO
(STREET OF DREAMS)

Carter (as, comp) Kazuo Yashiro (p) Kohji Tohyama (b) Ikuo Shiozaki (g)

AFTER YOU'VE GONE (as)
LP: LOB (J) LDC-1030

EASY LIVING (as)
LP: LOB (J) LDC-1030

WHEN LIGHTS ARE LOW (as) comp
LP: LOB (J) LDC-1030

MARI (as)
LP: LOB (J) LDC-1030

LIKE SOMEONE IN LOVE (as)
LP: LOB (J) LDC-1030

STREET OF DREAMS (as)
LP: LOB (J) LDC-1030

ROSETTA (as)
LP: LOB (J) LDC-1030

CHIYO (as)
LP: LOB (J) LDC-1030

[378]   September 26, 1981 Los Angeles National Public Radio Broadcast
of Concert, UCLA
BENNY CARTER SEXTET

Carter (as, comp) Bill Berry (cornet) George Bohanon (tb) Roger Kellaway (p) Chuck Domanico (b) John Guerin (d)

WHEN LIGHTS ARE LOW (as) comp

BLUE STAR (as) comp

SOUTH SIDE SAMBA (as) comp

[379]	November 28, 1981	Washington, D. C.	Concert, Smithsonian Institution
	BENNY CARTER		

Carter (as, comp) Joe Kennedy (violin) Kenny Barron (p) George Duvivier (b) Ronnie Bedford (d)

EASY MONEY   (as) comp

ON GREEN DOLPHIN STREET   (as)

BLUE STAR   (as) comp

LIKE SOMEONE IN LOVE   (as)

SOUTH SIDE SAMBA   (as) comp

HONEYSUCKLE ROSE   (as)

MISTY   (as)

TAKE THE A TRAIN   (as)

COTTONTAIL   (as)

AUTUMN LEAVES   (as)

   NOTE: Concert videotaped for Public Television.

[380]	December 4, 1981 New York Club Date, Sweet Basil
	BENNY CARTER QUARTET

Carter (as, comp) Kenny Barron (p) George Duvivier (b) Ronnie Bedford (d)

ON GREEN DOLPHIN STREET   (as)

EASY MONEY   (as) comp

LOVER MAN   (as)

IN A MELLOTONE   (as)

TAKE THE A TRAIN   (as)

BROADWAY   (as)

BLUE STAR   (as) comp

PERDIDO   (as)

ALL OF ME   (as)

THERE IS NO GREATER LOVE   (as)

MEAN TO ME   (as)

ALL THE THINGS YOU ARE   (as)

December 4, 1981 [380]

MOOD INDIGO (as)

HONEYSUCKLE ROSE (as)

[381]   December 5, 1981 New York Club Date, Sweet Basil
         BENNY CARTER QUARTET

Carter (as, comp) Kenny Barron (p) George Duvivier (b) Ronnie Bedford (d)

EASY MONEY (as) comp

UNDECIDED (as)

LOVER MAN (as)

ON GREEN DOLPHIN STREET (as)

IN A MELLOTONE (as)

HONEYSUCKLE ROSE (as)

TAKE THE A TRAIN (as)

MALIBU (as) comp

ON GREEN DOLPHIN STREET (as)

MISTY (as)

ALL OF ME (as)

SOUTH SIDE SAMBA (as) comp

BLUE STAR (as) comp

ALL THE THINGS YOU ARE (as)

THE COURTSHIP (as) comp

MEAN TO ME (as)

PERDIDO (as)

BLUES (as)

INDEX OF ARTISTS

Note: Numbers refer to Session Numbers, not page numbers.

Aarons, Al 275, 276, 354, 355
Abbott, Doug 350
Aberg, Sture 48
Abney, Don 221B, 289, 290
Adams, Arnold 39, 66
Adderley, Cannonball 269
Addison, Bernard 44, 101, 304
Adler, Rudolph 99
Air Crew, The 167
Alexander, Joe 177, 180
Alexander, Mousie 311
Ali, Yusef 364
Allan, Jan 367
Allen, Fletcher 58
Allen, Henry 23, 24, 31, 34, 111
Allen, Sue 203
Altpeter, Larry 98, 115
Alvis, Hayes 66, 67, 69, 79, 82, 89, 94, 95, 98, 100, 105, 107
Ander, Rune 49
Anderson, Cat 293, 344, 351, 363
Andrews, Debbie 196
Andrews, Ernie 167
Arakawa, Yasur 372B
Archey, Jimmy 66, 79, 82, 89, 94, 109, 110, 112
Armstrong, Louis 246
Ash, Bill 349, 365
Ashey, Irving 118, 172, 173, 174, 176
Audino, John 299
Auld, Georgie 103, 104, 210, 224, 294, 295, 296
Austin, Cuba 9, 10, 11, 18

Babasin, Harry 180, 186
Bacon, Louis 17, 19, 20, 66, 68
Bailey, Buster 2, 3, 31, 34, 35, 63, 64, 102, 140
Bailey, Pearl 279, 288
Bain, Bob 299

Ballard, Ben 350
Barbour, Dave 167, 170, 181, 182, 197, 282
Barboza, Felix 136, 137
Barefield, Eddie 110, 207
Barker, Blue Lu 63
Barker, Danny 34, 63, 65, 81, 120
Barksdale, Everett 105, 106, 107
Barnet, Charlie 28, 29, 96, 114, 173, 176
Barnett, Ted 116
Barretto, Ray 311
Barron, Kenny 375, 379, 380, 381
Barrow, George 311
Bartley, Dallas 190
Basie, Count 108, 113, 114, 209, 275, 276, 340, 353
Battle, Edgar 39
Beach, Frank 238, 262, 273
Beal, Charlie 34
Beane, Reginald 81, 84
Beany, Todd 349
Beau, Heinie 246, 265, 266
Beaucamont, Jeanette 285
Bedford, Ronnie 374, 379, 380, 381
Beilman, Pete 246
Bellson, Louis 122, 211, 221B, 222, 279, 288, 295, 296, 307, 340
Beneke, Tex 108, 113
Benford, Tommy 55
Benjamin, Joe 207, 256
Bennett, Max 273
Benson, George 316
Berman, R. 115
Bernhart, Milt 202, 210, 229, 247, 264
Bernstein, Artie 90, 91, 108, 155
Berry, Bill 344, 375, 378
Berry, Chu 19, 20, 21, 23, 24, 25, 83

241

Berry, Emmett 112, 138, 143, 152, 153
Bert, Eddie 311
Best, John 238
Betts, Harry 247, 281
Betts, Keter 314
Bias, George 11
Bigard, Barney 37, 139, 144, 169, 282, 314A
Billowus, David 360
Binford, Ken 98
Bivona, Gus 234
Bluestone, Harry 203
Bohannon, Hoyt 183, 186, 211
Bohanon, George 375, 378
Boone, Harvey 8, 12, 16
Bostic, Earl 232, 259
Botton, Lewis 150, 151
Bourden, Denis 360
Bradford, Kirt 121, 123
Bradley, Oscar 121, 123, 125
Branker, Tony 365, 366
Brannon, Ted 116, 121, 123, 125
Brashear, Oscar 373
Braud, Wellman 63
Brewer, Teresa 373
Brice, Percy 146, 150, 151, 154, 156, 157, 158, 161, 166
Briem, Chuck 360
Britton, Joe 109, 110
Brown, Ada 118
Brown, Andy 120
Brown, Craig 358, 360
Brown, Lawrence 293
Brown, Pete 67
Brown, Ray 201, 204, 205, 205A-B, 206, 212, 214, 215, 217, 220, 225, 225B, 289, 306, 353, 370
Brown, Russ 254
Brown, Willard 121, 123, 125, 130, 131, 136, 137, 150, 151, 152, 153, 156, 157, 158, 161, 166, 207
Browne, Millicent 321, 324, 325, 326, 327, 328, 329, 330, 331, 332, 333, 334, 335, 337
Bryant, Bobby 299
Bryant, Ray 341, 342, 343, 346, 347, 352, 356, 363
Bryant, Willie 39
Buckley, Lord 229
Buckner, Teddy 125, 195, 287A
Budimir, Dennis 273
Budwig, Monty 247, 344, 345
Bulterman, Jack 54
Bunker, Larry 233, 233A, 251, 253, 299

Burke, Al 41, 42
Burke, Sonny 224
Burns, Billy 40
Burns, Jeanne 90
Burns, Ralph 187
Burroughs, Alvin 116
Bushell, Garvin 84
Byas, Don 136, 137, 152, 153, 270

Caldwell, Bruce 358
Callender, Red 167, 169, 171, 172, 173, 174, 176, 177, 178, 184, 221, 229, 251, 264
Calloway, Cab 120
Calvin, Rosemary 98
Camarata, Toots 28, 29
Candoli, Conte 247, 264
Candoli, Pete 247, 253, 262, 264, 265, 299, 375
Cannady, James 150, 151, 152, 154, 156, 157, 158, 161, 162, 166
Capolupo, James 365
Capp, Frankie 281, 344, 345, 375
Carlisle, Una Mae 106
Carlsson, Olaf 46, 47
Carlsson, Rune 369
Carneol, Jess 203
Carney, Harry 197, 293
Carpenter, Pete 262
Carroll, John 130
Carroll, Judy 144, 145
Carter, Mercedes 70, 71, 72, 73, 74, 75
Carver, Wayman 19, 20, 22, 23, 24, 26
Case, Russ 115
Casey, Al 61, 62, 152
Casper, Jerry 265
Castaldo, Charlie 122
Castaldo, Lee 122
Cates, George 223, 224
Cathcart, Dick 238, 246, 250
Catlett, Sid 19, 20, 21, 22, 23, 24, 25, 26, 101, 165
Cavanaugh, Dave 174, 177, 178, 180, 181, 182, 183, 184, 185, 192, 194, 226
Cavicchiolo, Romano 297
Chaix, Henri 297
Challis, Bill 16
Chaplin, Bob 360
Charioteers, The 121
Charles, Teddy 255
Chase, Frank 98
Cheatham, Doc 18, 110, 207, 345, 370A-C

Index of Artists

Cheek, Robert 39
Childers, Buddy 247
Chisholm, George 56, 57
Chittison, Herman 40
Christian, Charlie 83, 96, 97, 108
Christian, Jody 315
Christie, Lyn 300
Churchill, Savannah 116, 117, 123, 124, 125, 127, 128, 131, 132, 135, 137, 208
Clark, Dick 26
Clark, Garnet 32
Clark, Harold 136, 137, 138, 143, 150, 151, 156, 157, 158, 161
Clark, Richard 39
Clayton, Buck 165
Cleveland, Jimmy 344, 363
Clump, Clarence 192
Coe, Gene 344
Cohen, Paul 138, 143, 166
Cohn, Sonny 275, 276
Coker, Henry 143, 170, 179, 189, 190, 192, 275, 276
Cole, Cozy 35, 36, 37, 38, 39, 60, 65, 67, 83
Cole, Edwin 229
Cole, June 3, 40
Cole, Nat King 139, 140, 160, 175, 268
Coleman, Bill 100, 103, 104, 140
Coles, John 232
Collette, Buddy 253, 254, 259, 289, 354, 355
Collins, John 277, 278, 287, 294, 295, 296
Collins, Shad 21, 22, 100, 120
Colombus, Chris 207
Colquhoun, Michael 358
Colucci, Tony 99
Combelle, Alix 55, 58
Comfort, Joe 253, 254, 287
Comstock, Frank 124, 125, 127, 128, 132, 141, 142, 147, 150, 153, 162, 170
Conlon, Chris 360
Connor, Mike 365
Connors, Chuck 293
Connors, Myles 349
Cooke, Sam 264
Cooper, Bob 247
Cooper, Buster 293
Cooper, Chuck 299
Copeland, Allan 226
Corb, Morty 238, 246, 265, 266
Cottler, Irv 234, 243

Coty, Bill 10
Counce, Curtis 202
Craig, Al 51, 52, 53
Crowlet, Jack 183
Cuffee, Ed 9, 10, 11, 18
Culloz, Pierre 283, 284, 286
Curl, Langston 9, 10, 11

D'Hellemmes, Eugene 55
Dahl, Delores 203
Dane, Barbara 258
Dasberg, Sam 56
Davis, Art 269, 270, 271
Davis, Charlie 194
Davis, Eddie 121, 123
Davis, Eddie "Lockjaw" 307, 340, 347
Davis, Edwin 130, 131
Davis, Leonard 4, 5, 6, 7, 21, 22, 23, 24
Davis, Lew 43, 52
Davis, Maxwell 194
Davis, Miles 154, 156, 157, 158
Davis, Sammy 66, 89, 100
Dawson, Alan 300, 302, 312
Dawud, Talib 136, 137
De Paris, Sidney 1, 5, 6, 7, 107, 109, 110
De Paris, Wilbur 21, 22, 23, 24
De Souza, Yorke 58
De Verteuil, Eddie 116
Decker, Bob 190
DeFranco, Buddy 209
Defrisco, Joe 350
Delta Rhythm Boys, The 162
Deppe, Lois 16
Derwin, Hal 181
Devol, Frank 181, 245
Dial, Harry 32
Dickenson, Harold 226
Dickenson, Vic 66, 79, 82, 89, 94, 109, 110, 172, 173, 176, 177, 178, 185, 193, 302, 305, 314A, 353
Dillard, Bill 21, 22, 23, 24, 26
Dixon, Charlie 2
Dodd, Pat 41, 42
Dodgion, Jerry 311
Dolan, John 350, 365, 366
Dole, Burton 203
Domanico, Chuck 373, 378
Domnerus, Arne 367
Doof, Sal 54
Dorsey, George 100, 109, 311
Dorsey, Tommy 108
Douglas, Bill 221

Doyle, Kevin 358
Drayton, Charles 110, 112, 130, 131, 136, 137, 138, 143, 193, 195
Drelinger, Art 207
Drew, John 255
Drew, Kenny 371
Du Bois, Alain 297
Duerr, Clayton 27
Dumont, Jack 287
Dunson, Claude 125
Durante, Jimmy 168
Durham, Bobby 291, 314
Durham, Eddie 39
Duvivier, George 221B, 314A, 351, 354, 355, 363, 374, 375, 379, 380, 381

Edison, Harry 209, 210, 211, 220, 233, 233A, 234, 288, 294, 295, 296, 299, 304, 306, 313, 314D, 317, 318, 319, 320, 321, 322, 323, 324, 325, 326, 327, 328, 329, 330, 331, 332, 333, 334, 335, 336, 337, 345, 347, 372, 372A
Edwards, Jimmy 131
Edwards, Joan 115
Edwards, Teddy 257, 260, 261, 289, 290
Edwards, W. J. 130
Ehrling, Thore 48, 49
Ekyan, Andre 55
Eldridge, Roy 65, 98, 101, 113, 204, 212, 214, 215, 217, 218, 219, 230, 270, 307, 314, 353, 357
Ellington, Duke 293, 306
Ellington, Judy 102
Ellington, Mercer 197, 293
Elliot, George 41, 42
Elliott, Lucy 156, 157, 159, 161, 163, 166
Ellis, Herb 212, 214, 215, 217, 218, 219, 220, 225, 225B
Elman, Ziggy 96, 108
Elrick, George 43, 44
Enchanters, The 190
Enevoldsen, Bob 247, 250
Epps, Joe 150, 151, 156, 157, 158, 161
Epstein, Jack 99
Erbetta, Marc 297
Escudero, Ralph 9, 10, 11
Estes, Gene 299
Evans, Alfie 99
Evans, Don 249

Evans, George 52
Evans, Herschel 59, 61, 62
Ewans, Kai 46, 47
Ewart, Brian 349

Fadale, Charles 358
Faddis, Jon 311, 345
Fagerquist, Don 262
Faist, Andre 297
Falin, Tom 365
Falzone, Sam 358
Fatool, Nick 155, 238, 246
Faye, Alice 122
Featherstonhaugh, Buddy 41, 42, 43, 52
Feldman, Victor 299, 300
Felton, Roy 88, 89, 94, 105, 107, 109
Ferguson, Maynard 199, 211
Fidus, Arnold 115
Fields, Ted 40, 66
Fitzgerald, Ella 217, 272, 294, 295, 296
Flanagan, Tommy 314, 338, 339, 369
Fleagle, Brick 64
Fletcher, Milton 130, 131
Flory, Med 281
Flynn, Frank 232
Fogartie, Art 350
Fontana, Carl 300
Ford, Fatso 131
Ford, James 360
Foslien, Orrin 370B
Foster, Frank 275, 276, 350
Foster, Pops 27
Fowler, Bob 273
Fowlkes, Charlie 275, 276
Francis, Panama 294, 314C
Franzella, Sal 203
Freeman, Bud 30, 305
Freeman, Ernie 264
Friedman, Mort 226
Friedman, Norm 358
Friley, Vernon 273
Frishberg, Dave 344, 345
Frye, Carl 66, 79, 82, 89, 94, 100
Fullbright, Richard 19, 20
Fuller, Gil 151, 163

Gagliardi, Jo 297
Galli, Lionel 283
Gardner, Freddy 43, 52, 53
Garner, Erroll 172
Garrison, Jimmy 277, 278

Index of Artists

Garros, Christian 283, 284, 285, 286
Garry, Vivian 164
Gayle, Rozelle 287A
Geller, Harry 229
Geller, Herb 237
Gentry, Chuck 186, 238, 247, 253, 287, 299
George, Karl 130
Getz, Stan 209
Geymann, Matt 365
Gibbons, Bob 349
Gibbons, Bobby 253
Gibbs, Eddie 32
Gibson, Al 112, 120
Gibson, Andy 70
Gill, Ben 203
Gillespie, Dizzy 83, 225, 269, 276, 339, 345, 364
Giuffre, Jimmy 237
Glassman, Leslie 360
Glenn, Tyree 66, 79, 81, 82, 89, 120, 207, 304
Glover, Joe 205, 205B
Goldberg, Doc 113
Goldberg, Max 41, 43, 52, 53
Goldstein, Rolf 56
Golson, Benny 232
Gonella, Nat 64
Gonsalves, Paul 291, 293
Goodman, Benny 96, 97, 108, 113, 114, 122, 174
Goodman, Freddy 27
Goodrich, Bobby 246
Gordon, Dexter 153, 170
Gordon, Joe 254
Gordon, Justin 253, 299
Gordy, Herb 259
Gorling, Uno 48, 49
Gorling, Zilas 48, 49
Gorruso, Tony 358
Gozzo, Conrad 211, 224, 238, 253, 264, 265, 273
Graettinger, Bob 156, 157, 158, 161
Grant, Jewell 136, 137, 138, 143, 186, 254, 264
Grappelly, Stephane 55
Gray, Dick 130
Gray, Louis 150, 151
Gray, Wardell 172, 209, 211
Green, Bill 253, 254, 259, 273, 287, 299
Green, Charlie 2, 3
Green, Doug 365
Green, Freddie 91, 113, 153, 209
Green, Henry 186, 190

Grey, Al 150, 151, 153, 154, 156, 157, 158, 161, 165, 166, 307, 312, 340, 353
Grider, Sleepy 131
Gubertini, Ronnie 41, 42
Guerin, John 378
Guevara, Manuel 360
Gusick, Ben 27
Gustafsson, Rune 367
Guyer, Bobby 122

Hackett, Bobby 67, 305, 314A-B
Hackney, Lou 359, 361
Hackworth, Jeff 360
Haden, Evert 49
Hadnott, Billy 182, 183, 185, 194
Hagemann-Larsen, Henry 47
Haggart, Bob 96, 97
Hall, Edmond 91
Hall, Jim 305
Hall, Rene 207, 259, 264
Hallberg, Bengt 367
Halliburton, John 247, 258
Halt, Hans 358
Hamilton, Jimmy 293
Hamilton, John 183
Hampton, Lionel 59, 83, 91
Hanein, Bib 336
Hanna, Jake 338
Hanna, Roland 311, 312, 348
Hard Tops, The 226
Hardy, Earl 116
Harper, Herb 211, 253, 258
Harris, Albert 43, 51, 52, 245
Harris, Barry 364
Harris, Bill 212, 214, 225
Harris, Bixy 151
Harris, Dave 265
Harris, Dickie 311
Harris, Marty 313
Harris, Maury 229, 262
Harris, Rick 358, 360
Harrison, Jimmy 8, 12, 13, 15, 16, 17
Harrison, Len 56, 57, 58
Hart, Clyde 83, 98
Harte, Roy 226
Haughton, Chauncey 105, 107
Haughton, John "Shorty" 39, 116, 121, 123, 125, 130, 131, 136, 137
Hawkins, Coleman 2, 3, 4, 5, 6, 7, 8, 12, 13, 15, 16, 22, 23, 24, 55, 57, 83, 90, 91, 92, 93, 94, 95, 101, 108, 140, 270, 277, 278, 292
Hayes, Louis 292

Hayman, Joe 40
Haymes, Dick 148
Haynes, Cyril 190
Haynes, Tiger 198
Healy, Jon 350
Heard, J. C. 109, 120, 152, 153, 201, 206, 212, 215, 218, 219
Heard, John 340, 362
Heath, Helen 28, 29
Heath, Ted 41, 43
Heather, Cliff 115
Heden, Gosta 49
Hefti, Neal 152, 153, 156, 158, 171
Hemphill, Shelton 17
Henderson, Fletcher 2, 3, 8, 12, 16, 31, 34, 96
Henderson, Horace 13, 15, 31
Hendrickson, Al 169, 203, 234, 238, 243
Henry, Haywood 304
Herald, Alice 285
Herbert, Arthur 299
Herfurt, Skeets 287
Herman, Sam 275, 276
Heywood, Eddie 66, 69, 79, 82, 89, 94, 95
Hibbler, Al 197
Higginbotham, J. C. 4, 26, 34, 92, 108, 111, 113, 114
Hill, Alex 30, 32, 39
Hill, Ernest 21, 22, 23, 24, 25, 26
Hill, John 365
Hines, Earl 248, 258, 314A
Hinton, Milt 65, 81, 83, 120, 303, 304, 308, 309, 312, 316, 341, 342, 343, 346, 347, 357, 372, 372A
Hit Paraders, The 115
Hodges, Johnny 201, 292, 293
Hogan, Granville 232
Holiday, Billie 61, 62, 65, 103, 233, 233A
Holiday, Clarence 2, 3, 8, 12, 16, 33, 35, 36, 37, 38
Holland, Charles 33
Holland, Milt 203
Holley, Major 311, 314C-D
Holm, Stig 48
Holman, Bill 247
Hood, Bill 287, 289, 290
Horn, Paul 247, 287
Horne, Lena 111, 119, 126
Horton, Robert 39
Howard, Bob 35, 36, 37, 38
Howard, Joe 262
Huffman, Jim 350

Hughes, Spike 21, 22, 23, 24
Humes, Helen 146, 147, 257, 260, 261, 316
Hunt, Louis 17
Hurley, Clyde 246
Hutson, Dave 370C
Hyman, Dick 301, 302
Hymanson, William 203

Inomata, Takeshi 372B
Irish, George 105, 107, 109
Irvis, Charlie 1
Ishiguro, Kei 372B

Jackson, Benny 13, 15
Jackson, Calvin 161, 167
Jackson, Duffy 301
Jackson, King 238
Jackson, Milt 338, 362
Jackson, Quentin 18, 120, 275, 276, 304, 311
Jacquet, Illinois 120, 357
James, Elmer 17, 31, 33, 34, 35, 36, 37
James, George 32, 105, 107, 112
James, Harry 59, 61, 62, 96, 97, 108, 113
Jederby, Thore 48, 49
Jefferson, Hilton 17, 18, 31, 120
Jeffries, Herb 161
Jenkins, George 199, 202
Jenney, Jack 96
Jensen, Christian 46, 47
Johansen, Egil 367
Johnson, Archie 66
Johnson, Bobby 1, 4
Johnson, Budd 275, 276, 304, 311, 351, 354, 355, 363
Johnson, Charley 150, 151, 156, 157, 158, 161
Johnson, Charlie 1
Johnson, Freddy 54, 56, 57
Johnson, George 40
Johnson, Gus 255, 256, 354, 355
Johnson, Howard 21, 22, 23, 24, 304
Johnson, J. J. 116, 121, 123, 125, 130, 131, 136, 137, 138, 141, 156, 157, 161, 163, 269, 313
Johnson, Keg 26, 31, 33, 120
Johnson, Marvin 194
Johnson, Otis 33
Johnson, Plas 226, 234, 247, 254, 258, 259, 264, 273, 287, 299, 313
Johnson, Walter 8, 12, 16, 31, 33,

Index of Artists

34, 92
Johnson, William 136, 137
Jolly, Pete 239
Jones, Claude 5, 6, 7, 8, 12, 16, 31, 32, 207
Jones, Ed 275, 276
Jones, Hank 204, 308, 309
Jones, Harold 351, 363
Jones, Herb 293
Jones, Jimmy 294, 295, 296, 298, 299
Jones, Jo 59, 61, 62, 225A, 270, 271, 277, 278, 304, 306, 315, 316, 357
Jones, Jonah 60, 105, 109, 120
Jones, Parr 194
Jones, Quincy 237, 273
Jones, Reunald 30
Jones, Rufus 293
Jones, Sam 291, 292
Jones, Thad 275, 276
Jones, Wallace 150, 151
Jordan, Stanley 364
Jordan, Taft 207, 304
Joyce, Jimmy 250

Kahn, Leo 115
Kaminsky, Max 25, 27, 30
Kaminsky, Rob 349
Kamuca, Richie 247, 344
Katz, Dick 277, 278
Kaye, Carol 299
Kaye, Danny 246
Kaye, Leonard 122
Kellaway, Roger 378
Kelso, Jackie 264
Kennedy, Joe 356, 363, 364, 375, 379
Kenny, Tom 226
Kenton, Stan 174
Kessel, Barney 171, 201, 204, 205, 205A-B, 206, 211, 233, 233A, 240, 241, 242, 244, 247, 254, 265, 266, 289
Kesselman, Carl 360
Kiehn, Coco 40
Kilbert, Porter 125, 130, 131, 136, 137, 138, 143, 150, 151
King, Bertie 56, 58
Kirby, John 8, 12, 13, 15, 16, 30, 59, 60, 64, 101, 102, 114, 140, 199
Kirkpatrick, Don 17
Klee, Harry 287
Klein, Manny 167, 203, 273
Knepper, Jimmy 311
Knight, Bob 273

Knutsson, Knut 46, 47
Koch, Joe 174, 180, 183
Koleff, Ken 358
Koslowski, Walter 360
Kotarski, Wallace 358, 360
Kragh, Eric 46, 47
Kranenburg, Kees 54
Kruger, Jerry 69
Krupa, Gene 96, 97, 109A, 113, 114, 212, 213, 214, 216, 265, 266, 305
Kusby, Ed 183, 265, 299
Kyle, Billy 59, 64, 67, 102

Ladd, Bernie 115
Lamacchia, Phil 358
Lamare, Nappy 238
Lamb, John 293
Lamond, Don 187
Lampkin, Chuck 269
Lane, Ruby 265
Lang, Mike 373
Lang, Phil 72, 79, 80, 86
Laughton, Gail 203
Lawson, Bob 171, 202, 210, 211
Lazaroff, Bernie 115
Lee, Buddy 9, 10, 11
Lee, David 314B
Lee, Julia 177, 178, 184, 185
Lee, Peggy 170, 181, 227, 228, 273
Leeman, Cliff 303
Leenhouts, Amy 365
Legrand, Christiene 283, 285
Levey, Stan 273
Levine, Henry 99
Levine, Nat 99
Levy, Lou 237, 273
Lewis, Irving 138, 143
Lewis, Mel 247, 260, 267, 282
Lewis, Willie (guitar) 112
Lewis, Willie (alto sax, leader) 40
Linn, Ray 122, 187, 203, 211, 281
Livingston, Ulysses 66, 79, 82, 89, 90, 93, 94, 100, 103, 104, 125, 186, 202, 232
Lloyd, Ivor 115
Lofton, Tricky 344
Logan, Tony 358
Lovett, Sam "Baby" 177, 178, 184, 185
Lowe, Mundell 290, 299, 313, 344, 345, 351, 354, 355
Lube, Dan 183
Lucie, Lawrence 21, 22, 23, 24, 25, 26, 31, 92

Lundgaard, Jesper 371

Macauley, Eddie 52
MacDonald, Bruce 230
Maeda, Norrio 372B
Mahones, Gildo 317, 318, 320, 321, 322, 323, 324, 325, 326, 327, 328, 329, 330, 331, 332, 333, 334, 335, 336, 337
Mairants, Ivor 50
Maisel, Jack 27, 64
Mallory, Eddie 26, 81, 84
Mangano, Mickey 194
Manne, Shelly 237, 240, 241, 242, 244, 246, 247, 248, 253, 254, 257, 258, 261, 265, 299, 370, 372, 372A, 373
Maoicco, Tony 350
Marantz, Ken 350
Mariano, Charlie 237
Markiewicz, David 358
Marks, Franklyn 99
Marmarosa, Dodo 171, 173, 176, 193
Marsala, Joe 67
Marshall, Jack 177, 178, 180, 184, 185, 190, 226
Marshall, Kaiser 3, 5, 6, 7, 22
Marshall, Wendell 197
Martin, Bobby 40
Martin, Jackie 28, 29
Masman, Theo Uden 54
Mason, Tony 49
Mathews, Steve 350
Mathiesen, Leo 46, 47
Matlock, Matty 223, 238
Matthews, Dave 59
May, Billy 181, 224, 272
Mayo, Waldo 115
McArty, Dorothy 203
McClam, Jerry 359, 361
McConnell, John 112
McCord, Castor 66, 79, 81, 82
McCord, Theodore 5, 6, 7
McCreary, Lew 299
McDevitt, Andy 41, 42, 43, 52
McEachern, Murray 169, 234, 238, 265
McGarity, Lou 113, 183
McGhee, Howard 154, 172
McGreery, Lewis 273
McHenry, Bill 349
McKibbon, Al 290, 339
McKillip, Bob 350
McNally, Tim 350, 365
McQuater, Tommy 41, 42, 43, 51, 52

Menza, Don 344
Merrill, Reggie 115
Mershon, Gil 203
Mezzrow, Mezz 25, 27, 30
Michelot, Pierre 283, 284, 285, 286
Miller, Eddie 96, 97, 181, 182, 238, 246, 266
Miller, Johnny 160, 175
Mills, Jackie 167, 172, 173, 176, 193, 194, 195
Mills, Lincoln 66, 79, 82, 89, 94, 110
Mills Brothers, The 105
Mitchell, Billy 310, 311
Mitchell, Blue 344
Mitchell, Dwike 310
Mitchell, Fred 109
Mitchell, Hal 116
Mitchell, Herman 136, 137, 138, 143
Mitchell, John 40
Mitchell, Ollie 247
Mitchell, Red 237, 262, 369
Mole, Miff 122
Mondello, Toots 96, 108, 113
Monderer, Ben 350, 365, 366
Mondragon, Joe 243, 247, 262
Monheit, Gary 349
Montmarche, Robert 56, 57, 58
Moody, James 302
Moore, Alton 116, 118, 121, 123, 125, 130, 131, 136, 137, 143, 150, 152, 153
Moore, Gerry 51
Moore, Monette 1
Moore, Oscar 140, 160, 175
Moore, Phil 169
Morgan, Russ 31
Morris, Johnny 150, 151, 156, 157, 158, 161
Morris, Wally 43, 44, 50, 51, 52
Morrison, Henry 66, 69, 79, 82
Mortell, Ben 115
Morton, Benny 33, 61, 62, 103, 104, 107, 112, 304, 316
Mosca, Ray 314D
Moultrie, Thomas 150, 151, 154, 156, 157, 158, 161, 166
Muldaur, Maria 313
Mullens, Eddie 82, 89
Mulraney, Bill 41, 52
Munn, Billy 43
Musso, Vido 113, 186
Myers, Bumps 125, 130, 131, 133, 138, 141, 143, 150, 151, 154, 156, 157, 158, 161, 166, 186, 189, 190, 195, 211
Myers, Wilson 103, 104

Index of Artists

Nash, Dick 247, 299
Nash, Ted 203, 229, 250
Natoli, Nat 98, 115
Neagley, Clint 180, 183
Nesbitt, John 5, 8
Neufeld, Erno 203
Neumann, Ulrik 46, 47
Newell, Laura 111
Newman, Alfred 236, 274
Newman, Joe 152, 153, 302, 311, 348, 351, 354, 355, 363
Newton, Frankie 19, 20
Nicholas, Albert 32
Nichols, Red 178, 238, 246, 266
Niehaus, Lennie 237
Nielsen, Kelof 46, 47
Nimitz, Jack 273, 344, 375
Noel, Randolph 358
Norman, Fred 86, 87
Norvo, Red 28, 29, 174, 177, 178, 181, 182, 247, 250, 305, 314A, 316
Nottingham, Jimmy 304, 312
Novaria, John 349

O'Brien, Floyd 25, 27, 30
O'Day, Anita 187, 265
O'Laughlin, Stash 232
Obergh, Lew 190
Ocke, Bernard 115
Orlofsky, Tom 350
Otenel, Tuna 319

Page, Walter 61, 62
Paich, Marty 281
Palmer, Earl 259, 264, 313, 317, 318, 320, 321, 322, 323, 324, 325, 326, 327, 328, 329, 330, 331, 332, 333, 334, 335, 337
Panalle, Juan 180
Paque, Glyn 26, 39
Parker, Charlie 160, 201
Pass, Joe 314, 338, 339, 340
Patent, Henry 99
Payne, Benny 120
Payne, Cecil 310, 351, 354, 355, 363
Payne, Sonny 275, 276
Payne, Stanley 39, 94
Paz, Victor 311
Pedersen, Niels 307, 352
Pederson, Kurt 46, 47
Pederson, Pullman 203
Pederson, Tommy 186, 211, 253, 254, 265, 299

Pekcan, Erol 319
Pell, Dave 265, 281
Pellegrini, Al 224, 238
Penny, Jeff 365, 366
Pepper, Art 237
Perkins, Bill 273, 290
Perlmutter, Sid 98
Pet, Jack 54
Peterson, Chuck 173, 176, 186, 193
Peterson, Oscar 201, 204, 205, 205A-B, 206, 212, 213, 214, 215, 216, 217, 218, 219, 220, 225, 225B, 291, 292, 307, 362
Petersson, Gosta 49
Pettiford, Ira 156, 157, 158, 161, 166
Phillips, Flip 152, 201, 204, 212, 214, 215, 217, 218, 219
Phillips, Gene 195
Pied Pipers, The 170, 179
Pierce, Nat 351, 354, 355
Pilet, Michel 297
Pilzer, Max 115
Pisani, Nick 203
Pitman, Bill 251
Pittenger, John 349
Pizzarelli, Bucky 309, 348
Plummer, Gene 246
Pogson, E. O. 41
Polikoff, M. 115
Pollard, Bill 198
Polo, Danny 90, 92, 93
Poppink, Wim 54
Porcino, Al 247, 254, 273
Porter, Gene 116, 118, 121, 123, 125, 130, 131
Porter, Vernon "Jake" 125
Porter, Yank 103, 104
Powell, Benny 275, 276, 344
Powell, Ernie 65, 66, 69, 79, 82, 89, 110, 112
Powell, Jimmy 66, 79, 82, 89, 94
Pozo, Chano 273
Pratt, Richard 348
Presslaff, Jeff 350
Preston, Dave 349
Previn, Andre 240, 242, 244, 257, 260, 261
Price, Jesse 182
Price, Sam 63
Procope, Russell 31, 33, 38, 152, 153, 293, 344
Purce, Ernie 110, 112
Purnell, Keg 66, 89, 94, 95, 100, 105, 107

Quealey, Chelsea 30
Quintones, The 95

Ragab, Salah 336
Raksin, David 119
Ram, Buck 95
Randolph, Irving 31, 33, 89
Rasey, Uan 183, 253
Rasmussen, Peter 46, 47
Ratner, Steve 365
Reade, Mike 360
Redland, Charles 48
Redman, Don 4, 5, 6, 7, 9, 10, 11
Reese, Rostelle 112
Reesinger, Clyde 299
Rehak, Frank 207
Reingold, Jon 365
Reinhardt, Django 55, 58
Renard, Alex 40
Rene, Henri 243
Reuss, Allan 155, 246
Rey, Alvino 114
Rhodes, Todd 9, 10, 11, 18
Rich, Buddy 108, 160, 204, 205, 205A-B, 209, 210, 225
Richardson, Lee 188
Richardson, Wally 311
Riddle, Nelson 268
Ridley, Larry 301, 302, 305, 314B, 356, 364
Ridley, Stretch 116
Riedel, Georg 367
Ritts, Leslie 350
Ritz, Lyle 281
Rivera, Ernie 349
Roach, Max 130, 131, 136, 137, 138, 140, 143, 146
Roberts, George 253, 262, 265
Robertson, Don 226
Robinson, Bill "Bojangles" 119
Robinson, Fred 26
Robinson, Gale 252
Robinson, Joe 195
Robinson, Milton 100, 105, 107
Robinson, Mitch 358, 360
Robinson, Prince 9, 10, 11, 18
Robyn, Paul 203
Roche, Betty 139
Rodgers, Gene 44, 50, 92
Rodriguez, Nicholas 21, 22, 24
Rogers, Shorty 152, 153, 247
Rogers, Timmie 136, 138, 139, 142
Roker, Mickey 339
Romersa, Ted 226
Rosendahl, Claes 367

Rosengarden, Bobby 305, 314A
Rosenthal, Steve 358
Rosolino, Frank 240, 241, 242, 247, 254, 257, 260, 261, 262, 273
Ross, Arnold 155, 182, 183, 209, 253
Ross, Candy 156, 157, 158, 161, 166
Roth, Bart 122
Rouse, Charlie 277, 278, 310
Rowles, Jimmy 174, 210, 211, 233, 233A, 234, 241, 247, 251, 265, 267, 273, 282
Royal, Ernie 180, 202, 311, 354, 355
Royal, Marshall 344
Rubin, Mike 226, 234
Ruff, Willie 310
Rushton, Joe 122, 246
Russell, Curly 116, 121, 123, 125
Russell, Johnny 26, 27, 39
Russell, Luis 23
Russell, Mischa 203
Russin, Babe 59, 98, 115, 180, 234, 238, 287
Rydell, Randy 349

Sabatini, Jerry 360
Sahlin, Olle 48, 49
Salama, Said 336
Salco, Jim 186
Sampson, Edgar 1, 61, 62
Schaefer, Bill 203, 238
Schaefer, Hal 255, 256
Schertzer, Hymie 122
Schifrin, Lalo 269, 270, 271, 287
Schmidt, Elmer 259
Schneider, Elmer 246
Schneider, Moe 238, 266
Schnepps, Jonathan 358
Schrouder, Charles 226
Scott, Chiefie 116
Scott, Howard 24
Scott, Tony 152, 153
Seaburg, George 183
Sedric, Gene 32
Shank, Bud 247, 289, 290, 313
Shapiro, Artie 93
Shavers, Charlie 102, 174, 201, 204, 212, 214, 215, 217, 218, 219
Shaw, Artie 111
Sheldon, Jack 273
Shepherd, Shep 111, 112
Sherock, Shorty 234, 253, 282
Sherter, Jules 115

Index of Artists

Sherwood, Bobby 177, 181, 182
Shihab, Sahib 313
Shiozaki, Ikuo 377
Shipp, Dave 315
Shirley, Jimmy 111
Shoobe, Sam 115
Shroyer, Kenny 247, 299
Shuken, Phil 203
Silliman, Steve 349
Silverman, Max 115
Simmons, John 152, 153, 165, 193, 209, 210, 211, 230, 233, 233A
Simmons, Norman 374
Simon, Gene 94
Simon, Stafford 98, 100, 105, 107
Sims, Phil 360
Sims, Ray 187
Sims, Zoot 291, 314, 314D, 353, 362
Singer, Lou 229, 243
Singleton, Zutty 91, 102, 106, 118
Skjoldborg, Anker 46
Skouby, Axel 46, 47
Skrzynski, Daven 360
Slack, Freddie 186
Slatkin, Eleanor 203
Slatkin, Felix 203
Smart Set, The 250
Smith, Ben 33
Smith, Charlie 197
Smith, Geechie 184
Smith, Hale 311
Smith, Jabbo 1
Smith, Jimmie 352, 353
Smith, Joe 5, 6, 7, 18
Smith, Johnny 116
Smith, Maxwell 203
Smith, Paul 203
Smith, Russell 8, 12, 16, 31, 33, 94, 100, 105, 107, 109, 120
Smith, Vernon 194
Smith, Warren 238, 246
Smith, Willie 160, 209, 211, 212, 214, 215, 217, 218, 219, 234
Smith, Willie "The Lion" 30
Snyder, Emery 365, 366
Solomon, Red 98
Sommer, Ted 256
Songer, Wayne 238, 246
Sonnenfeld, Rick 349
Sowyrda, Robert 358
Sperling, Jack 238, 246
Spivak, Charlie 96

St. Clair, Cyrus 1, 4
St. John, Dell 80, 82, 85, 86, 87, 88
Stacy, Jess 96, 97, 122, 266
Stafford, George 1, 4
Stalteri, Mike 358
Stanfield, Burns 365
Stapleton, Buck 226
Stark, Bobby 3, 8, 12, 15, 16
Starr, Kay 140, 158
Stephenson, Louis 56
Stephenson, Phil 203
Stevens, Leith 265
Stevens, Phil 238
Stewart, Larry 143
Stewart, Rex 2, 3, 4, 8, 9, 10, 11, 12, 13, 16, 18, 37, 129, 287A
Stewart, Slam 106, 118
Stoller, Alvin 220, 230, 251, 262, 287, 289, 290
Stoneburn, Sid 98
Strayhorn, Billy 197
Strickland, Calvin 156, 157, 158, 161
Stroup, Jon 350
Stumph, Irv 183
Sturgis, Ted 109
Sulieman, Idrees 150, 151
Sullivan, Joe 90, 91, 93
Sullivan, Maxine 110, 153
Sun, Selcuk 319

Tate, Buddy 304
Tate, Grady 309, 310, 341, 342, 343, 346, 347, 362
Tatum, Art 222
Taylor, Al 110
Taylor, Billy (tuba, bass) 5, 6, 7, 18, 32, 38, 111
Taylor, Billy (piano) 207
Taylor, Bob 122
Taylor, John 138, 143
Taylor, Louis 138, 143
Teagarden, Charlie 238
Teagarden, Jack 96, 97, 238
Terry, Clark 291, 300, 309, 314, 314D, 340, 345, 357, 362
Testamark, Roy 198
Thalen, Olle 49
Thielemans, Marcel 54
Thigpen, Ed 371
Thomas, Herb 109, 110
Thomas, Joe 32, 66, 79, 82, 89, 94, 95, 304
Thompson, Leslie 43, 52
Thompson, Louis 39

Thompson, Lucky 171, 179, 207
Thompson, Sir Charles 259
Three Flames, The 198
Tinney, Al 359, 361
Tohyama, Kohji 377
Torme, Mel 223, 224
Trainer, Fred 121, 123, 138, 143, 156, 157, 158, 161
Trainer, Jack 186
Traulsen, Palmer 46, 47
Treacher, Arthur 139
Treadwell, George 116
Trenner, Donn 299
Triscari, Joe 183, 265
Triscari, Ray 247, 254, 265
Troup, Bobby 247
Trucker, Sid 115
Trueheart, John 17
Tucker, George 232
Turner, Charles 84
Turner, Joe 93, 104

Ulyate, Lloyd 183

Van Beeck, Klaas 45
Van Camp, Gus 122
Van Der, Maurice 283, 284, 285, 286
Van Der Ouderaa, Andre 54
Van Eps, George 183, 246
Van Helvoirt, George 54
Van Oven, Harry 56
Vance, Dick 207
Varsalona, Bart 130
Vaughan, Madison 105, 107
Venuti, Joe 314A
Vernon, George 49
Vidal, Carlos 251
Vinnegar, Leroy 240, 241, 242, 244, 248, 257, 258, 260, 261, 267, 282
Visor, Carrington 287
Voss, Aage 46, 47

Waits, Freddie 356
Walker, Loyal 136, 137
Waller, Chuck 194, 195
Waller, Fats 4, 5, 6, 7, 118
Walton, Greely 120
Walton, Jon 122
Warren, Earle 304, 310, 314C
Warwick, Carl 304
Washington, George 21, 22, 23, 24, 136, 137, 138, 143, 194
Waters, Benny 1

Waters, Ethel 81, 84
Watson, Ezell 115
Webb, Chick 17, 30
Webb, Ray 56, 57
Webster, Ben 31, 33, 36, 39, 60, 83, 165, 193, 199, 201, 202, 212, 214, 215, 217, 218, 219, 220, 240, 241, 242, 282, 287A
Webster, Freddie 125
Webster, Rufus 136, 137, 138, 143, 150, 151
Welch, Barry 349
Welch, Elisabeth 43, 44, 50
Welch, Emma Lou 190
Wells, Dicky 19, 20, 22, 23, 24, 152, 304
Wess, Frank 275, 276, 375
West, Bob 294, 295, 296
West, Hal 169
Weston, Paul 181
Wettling, George 90, 93
Wexler, Steve 349, 365, 366
White, Bill 109
White, Bobby 225B
White, Gary 360
White, Kitty 194, 251, 252
White, Sonny 100, 103, 104, 105, 107, 109, 110, 111, 112, 152, 153, 154, 156, 157, 158, 161, 165, 166, 170, 179
Whittet, Ben 1
Whyte, Duncan 41, 42
Wiggins, Gerald 130, 131, 195, 199, 202, 221, 254, 287
Wilber, Bob 302, 314C
Wilborn, Dave 5, 6, 7, 9, 10, 11, 18, 370A-C
Williams, Bobby 105, 107
Williams, Buster 299
Williams, Cootie 108, 113, 114, 293
Williams, Elmer 17
Williams, Fred 110
Williams, Jerry 265
Williams, Jimmy 56, 57
Williams, Joe 306
Williams, John 115, 265
Williams, John B. 313, 317, 318, 320, 321, 322, 323, 324, 325, 326, 327, 328, 329, 330, 331, 332, 333, 334, 335, 336, 337, 338
Williams, John Towner 243, 262, 281, 284
Williams, Johnny 92, 98
Williams, Mary Lou 189
Williams, Nathaniel 112
Williams, Sandy 100, 152, 153

Index of Artists

Williams, Walter 121, 123, 156, 157, 158, 161, 166
Williamson, Stu 247, 254
Wilson, Gerald 121, 123, 138, 143, 169, 186
Wilson, Nancy 298, 299, 376
Wilson, Stanley 262, 283, 284
Wilson, Teddy 25, 26, 27, 33, 35, 36, 37, 38, 39, 60, 61, 62, 65, 225A, 303, 304, 305, 314A-D, 316, 357, 370, 372, 372A
Wood, Barry 115
Wood, Gloria 203
Woodlen, Bobby 66, 79
Woodman, Britt 154, 344, 351, 354, 355
Woodridge, Cliff 56
Woods, Phil 277, 278
Wright, Elmon 232
Wright, Lammar 120
Wrightsman, Stan 238, 246
Wynn, Nan 60

Yashiro, Kazuo 377
Young, Lee 171, 174, 180, 183
Young, Lester 61, 62, 204, 212, 214
Young, Snooky 121, 123, 275, 276, 313
Young, Trummy 152, 153

Zarchy, Rubin 203
Zelner, Mike 349
Zito, Ron 308
Zufferey, Roger 297

INDEX OF TUNE TITLES

Note: Numbers refer to Session Numbers, not page numbers.

A Tea Vista 346
A-Tisket, A-Tasket 60
Ac-cent-uate the Positive 279
Accent on Swing 43
After All, You're All I'm After 11
After You've Gone 141, 246, 377
Ain't It a Crime 177
Ain't Misbehavin' 118, 257, 364, 375
Ain't She Sweet 244
Ain't That Somethin' 119, 121
Air in D Flat 24
All Alone 137, 248
All I Do Is Dream of You 296
All I Ever Do Is Worry 184
All I Need Is You 116
All My Love 351
All of Me 40, 107, 127, 380, 381
All of You 224
All or Nothing at All 267
All Star Strut 97
All that Jazz 328, 338, 374
All the Things You Are 115, 301, 308, 315, 341, 342, 343, 356, 361, 364, 374, 380, 381
All Through the Night 255
Allez-Vous En 256
Alone Together 205B
Alone with My Thoughts of You 299
Alto Ego 287
Am I Asking for Too Much 188
Among My Souvenirs 94, 133, 260
Amoroso 276
And the Angels Sing 267
Angel Eyes 225
Anitra's Dance 281
Any Old Time 313
Any Time at All 59
Anything Goes 255
Apologies 30
Apple Jam 209

April in My Heart 62
Arabesque 23
Around the World in 80 Days 285
As Long as I Live 247
As Time Goes By 315
At Sundown 296
August Moon 253
Autumn Leaves 285, 314, 315, 379
Autumn Serenade 259

Baa Baa Black Sheep 229
Babalu 109
Baby I'm Gone 167
Baby, Take a Bow 29
Baby, What Else Can I Do 84
Baby, You're Mine for Keeps 190
Back Bay Boogie 112, 123, 134, 139, 157, 162
Bad and the Beautiful (The) 274
Bagatelle 285
Basie Twist (The) 275
Basin Street Blues 238, 273
Battle Hymn of the Republic 246
Be Cool - A 286
Be Cool - B 286
Be Cool - C 286
Be My Guest 237
Beale Street Blues 104
Beautiful Love 221
Beggar for the Blues 268
Below, Above 299
Bernie's Tune 269
Between the Devil and the Deep Blue Sea 68
Bewitched, Bothered and Bewildered 205B
Beyond the Blue Horizon 111, 232
Big Ben Blues 41
Big John Special 344
Big Nobody 288
Big Wig in the Wigwam 74
Bill 257
Bill Bailey, Won't You Please Come

Home 246, 257
Birth of the Blues 225A
Black Bottom 54
Black Is Beautiful 299
Black Jazz 20
Black Knight 285
Blue Evening 76, 80
Blue Interlude 25, 46
Blue Light Blues 58
Blue Lou 26, 234, 240, 297, 342, 370
Blue Monk 309
Blue Orchids 87
Blue Skies 70, 123, 281
Blue Star 221, 278, 309, 328, 338, 348, 374, 378, 379, 380, 381
Blue Yonder - A 286
Blue Yonder - B 286
Blues 305, 309, 320, 341, 347, 364, 369, 381
Blues for Beginners 304, 311, 360
Blues for Benny 285
Blues for Someone 184
Blues for the Count 209
Blues in B Flat 222
Blues in C 222
Blues in D Flat 338
Blues in My Heart 17, 56, 222, 287A, 342, 343
Blues in the Night 272
Blues My Naughty Sweetie Gave to Me 244
Body and Soul 120, 160, 278, 297, 302, 314B, 343, 346, 352, 354, 361
Boogie Minor 186
Boogie Woogie Sugar Blues 105
Bookie Blues 353
Bop Bounce 191
Boppin' the Blues 171
Boston Beans 273
Boston Tea Party 229
Boulevard Bounce 171
Bouncing with Bean 92
Bouquet of Blues 228
Boy Meets Horn 129
Bread and Gravy 81
(Look's Like I'm) Breakin' the Ice 37
Breeze, Blow My Baby Back to Me 184
British Grenadiers (The) 284
Broadway 312, 339, 354, 355, 364, 380
Buddie Beware 255
Bugle Call Rag 15, 22, 46, 108

Bunbelina 150
But Beautiful 376
But Not for Me 342
Butterfingers 28, 29
By Myself 299
By the Watermelon Vine, Lindy Lou 105
Bye Bye Blackbird 258, 315
Bye Bye Blues 76, 80, 85, 155, 340

C-Jam Blues (see also Duke's Place) 292, 297
C'est Magnifique 256
Cadillac Slim 165
Call of the Delta 34
Can't We Be Friends 221
Candy 296
Capacity 136
Caravan 336, 364
Careless 250
Carry Me Back to Old Virginny 51
Carter Charleston (The) 243A
Catfish Row 286
Catfish Row - Link 1 286
Catfish Row - Link 2 286
Caxton Hall Swing 211
Cement Mixer 224
Cha-Cha Club (The) 262
Charleston Is the Best Dance After All 1
Chase (The) 262
Cherchez la Femme 283
Cherokee 160, 265, 285, 361
Cherry 197, 277, 370B
Cherry's at Top of the Tree 279
Chicago 168
Chilpancingo 190
China Boy 86, 87
Chinatown, My Chinatown 8, 351, 375
Chiyo 377
Chopstick Boogie 186
Christmas Spirits 185
Christopher Columbus 344
Circe 245
Clementine 77
Close Your Eyes 230
Cloudy Skies 15
Coalition 311
Cocktails for Two 107, 175, 204, 205B, 216
Cold Hearted Daddy 178
Come on Back 289
Come on, Baby 3
Come Rain or Come Shine 233A
Come Sunday 373

Index of Tune Titles

Comedy Sketch 139
Comes Love 264
Comme Ci, Comme Ca 283
Concert Blues 214
Confessin' 111, 345, 351, 354, 355, 375
Congoroo 189, 191
Constantinople 339
Cool Blues 212
Coquette 281
Corinne Corinna 38
Cottontail 193, 204, 215, 218, 278, 311, 312, 349, 351, 354, 355, 356, 375, 379
Courtship (The) 339, 348, 365, 375, 381
Crazy in Love with You 264
Crazy Rhythm 55, 277
Crazy World 185
Cruisin' 200, 202
Cuando Caliente el Sol 285
Cuddle Up, Huddle Up 109
Cuttin' Time 150, 162

Daddy Daddy 137
Daddy-O 136, 138
Dance with Me 283
Dancin' Pants 237
Darling 145
Day in the Life of a Fool (Manha de Carnival) (A) 308
Dear Old Southland 113
Dee Blues 15
Deep Purple 294
Devil's Holiday 26
Diga Diga Doo 152
Dinah 91
Dino 243
Discovery 286
Discovery (The) 262
Dissonance 27
Do You Believe in Love at Sight 18
Doggin' Around 340
Domino 283
Don't Be that Way 216
Don't Blame Me 154, 294, 341, 343, 355
Don't Get Around Much Anymore 220, 287, 373
Don't Scream, Don't Shout 195
Don't Take Your Love from Me 111
Don't You Make Me High 313
Don't You Think 225B
Donegal Cradle Song 24
Doozy 278, 290, 304, 309, 310, 311, 313, 350, 354

Double Walk 281
Doubtful Blues 177
Down, Down, Down 370C
Down in My Soul 81
Dream 232
Dream Castle 157
Dream Lullaby 33
Drop in Next Time You're Passing 50
Duke Steps Out 287A
Duke's Place (see also C-Jam Blues) 373

Early Boyd 147
Early Session Hop 83
East of the Sun 232
Easy Living 377
Easy Money (Comp: C. Austin) 3
Easy Money (Comp: B. Carter) 276, 297, 338, 341, 342, 343, 348, 356, 367, 374, 379, 380, 381
Easy Rider 90
Ebb Tide 295
Eccentric Rag 102
Eelibuj Blues 144
EKE's Blues 354, 355, 375
Elliot 362
Elmer's Tune 296 ·
Emaline 28
End (The) 262
Ev'ry Day 38
Ev'ry Goodbye Ain't Gone 109
Everybody Shuffle 33
Everybody's Laughing 61
Everyday I Have the Blues 306, 321, 324, 325, 326, 327, 329, 330, 331, 332, 333, 334, 335, 337
Everything I Have Is Yours 267, 295

Fable of a Fool (The) 82
Fable of a Rose 102
Fairy Tales 287
Fanfare 23
Fantastic, That's You 289
Far Away Places 267
Farewell Blues 58
Feasant Pheathers 365
Feather Bed Lament 67
February Fiesta 253
Fiesta in Brass 146
Fifteen Years 279
Fine Romance (A) 233A
Firebird 24
Fish Fry 94, 121, 124, 146, 179

Fisherman's Wharf 273
Five Foot Two, Eyes of Blue 250
Five Little Quints (The) 95
Flamingo 212, 215, 218, 219, 221
Flat Foot Floogie 224
Flower Drum Song-Soundtrack Album 280
Flying Home 212
Foggy Day (A) 222, 225B
Fool for You (A) 188
For All We Know 232, 267
For Europeans Only 211
For You 180, 314, 314A
Forever Young 251
Four O'clock Jump 172
Four or Five Times 296
Frankie 243
Free Love 27
Freeport Jump 353
Frenesi 225B
Friends, Romans, Countrymen 229
Frim Fram Sauce 161
From Dixieland to Bebop 171
Full Moon and Empty Arms 259
Funky Blues 201

Gee, Ain't I Good to You 5, 313, 364, 370A
Gentleman Is a Dope (The) 288
Georgia on My Mind 81, 203
Ghost of a Chance 233, 267
Ghost of Dinah (The) 36
Gin and Jive 43, 52, 66
Girl from Ipanema 287
Girl Talk 351, 354, 355
Give Me Some Money 63
Gloaming 49
Go Way Gal 198
God Bless the Child 264, 351
Goin' On 275
Going to Chicago Blues 273
Gone with the Wind 205A
Good Deal 136, 139
Good for Nothin' Joe 119
Good Man Is Hard to Find (A) 260
Good Morning Heartache 264
Goodbye Blues 13
Goodnight, My Love 295
Got Another Sweetie Now 15
Gotta Go Home 286
Grain Belt Blues (The) 273
Great Lie (The) 287
Green Wine 338, 348
Greensleeves 284
Gypsy (The) 285

Habanera 147
Hands Across the Table 222
Happy Blues 174
Happy Go Lucky You and Broken Hearted Me 192
Happy Hour (The) 362
Harmony in Harlem 95
Have Mercy 71, 72
He Needs Me 284
Heebie Jeebies 17
Heels Up 286
Hello! 11, 370B
Hello, Goodbye, Forget It 162
Here It Is Tomorrow Again 61
Here's that Rainy Day 343, 348, 352, 369
Hey There 288
Hiawatha 229
Hold Tight 223
Hollyridge Drive 182, 189
Home in the Clouds (A) 73, 80
Honey Bunny Boo 95
Honeydripper (The) 149
Honeysuckle Rose 55, 66, 68, 80, 99, 126, 127, 197, 277, 304, 305, 308, 311, 317, 318, 321, 322, 323, 324, 329, 358, 360, 367, 370A, 372, 372A, 379, 380, 381
Hot Mallets 83
Hot Tempered Blues 1
Hot Toddy 20
Hotter than 'Ell 31
House with a Little Red Barn (A) 98
How Am I to Know 294
How Can You Lose 242
How Come You Do Me Like You Do 24, 287A
How Do You Call a Man a Two-timin' Man 370C
How High the Moon 98, 176, 187, 308
How Long Is a Moment 249
How Long, How Long Blues 93, 258
How Strange 75
How'm I Doin' 370C
Hundred Years from Today (A) 258
Hundreds and Thousands of Girls 268
Hurry Hurry 125
Hut-Sut Song (The) 224

I Ain't Gettin' Any Younger 187
I Ain't Got Nobody 56, 68, 196
I Am in Love 256

Index of Tune Titles

I Am Your Dream 252
I Apologize 174
I Can't Believe that You're in Love with Me 101, 323, 337, 370
I Can't Dance (I Got Ants in My Pants) 38
I Can't Escape from You 130
I Can't Get Started 116, 121, 130, 158, 291, 297, 303, 304, 310, 311, 312, 320, 327, 342, 350, 355, 358, 360, 363
I Can't Give You Anything but Love 119
I Cover the Waterfront 156, 162, 342
I Cried for You 73, 147, 294
I Didn't Like It the First Time 185
I Don't Know Why 155
I Don't Want It No More 192
I Don't Want to Cry Anymore 233
I Feel Like Lying in Another Woman's Husband's Arms 63
I Found a New Baby 315
I Get a Kick Out of You 206, 233A
I Got a Right to Sing the Blues 264
I Got It Bad and that Ain't Good 163, 205A, 260, 295, 314C, 353
I Got Rhythm 114
I Got Ways Like the Devil 63
I Gotcha 370C
I Gotta Go 43
I Hadn't Anyone Till You 209
I Hear Music 250
I Heard You Cried Last Night 128
I Just Got a Letter 84
I Let a Song Go Out of My Heart 373
I Lost Another Sweetheart 28
I Lost My Sugar in Salt Lake City 132, 135, 273
I Lost You 196
I Love My Baby 265
I Love Paris 256
I Love You 243A
I Miss a Little Miss 11
I Missed My Hat 230
I Must See Annie Tonight 64
I Never Knew 25, 314
I Never Knew I Could Love Anybody Like I'm Loving You 295
I Never Mention Your Name 135
I Remember You 230
I Should Care 267

I Shoulda Quit When I Was Ahead 288
I Still Love Him So 230, 338
I Surrender Dear 101, 130, 131, 164, 340
I Think of You 259
I Understand 267
I Used to Love You 124
I Wanna Be Around 287
I Want a Little Girl 370A
I Want Your Love 11
I Was Wrong 178
I Wish You Love 283
I'd Love It 6
I'll Be Around 221
I'll Close My Eyes 285
I'll Never Be the Same 343
I'll Never Change 37
I'll Never Fail You 62
I'll Never Give In 54
I'll Never Smile Again 267
I'll Remember April 253
I'll See You in My Dreams 86
I'm a Three Time Loser 180
I'm a Woman 313
I'm Beginning to See the Light 373, 375, 376
I'm Coming Virginia 58, 66, 71, 241
I'm Forever Blowing Bubbles 98, 184
I'm Gonna Love that Gal 148
I'm Gonna Make Believe I've Got Myself a Sweetheart 156
I'm in the Mood for Love 164
I'm in the Mood for Swing 52, 59, 68, 80
I'm Lost 130
I'm Playing with Fire 194
I'm Sorry 221
I'm the Caring Kind 153, 156, 161
I'm Your Special Fool 298
I'se a Muggin' 223
I've Been in Love Before 105
I've Found What I Wanted in You 16
I've Got a Feeling You're Fooling 40, 294
I've Got the World on a String 205A
I've Got Two Lips 42
I've Heard that Song Before 123
Idaho 222, 372A
If Dreams Come True 289, 310
If I Can't Have You 157, 195
If I Could Be with You 140, 248, 258
If I Didn't Love You So 208

If I Give My Heart to You   295
If I Had You   314
If I Loved You   267
If Only I Could Read Your Mind   43
If We Only Have Love   298
If You Can't Smile and Say Yes Don't Cry and Say No   136, 142
If You Go   283
If You Love Me, Really Love Me   283
Ill Wind   112, 117, 123, 124
Imagination   206
Imminent   286
In a Little Spanish Town   248, 302
In a Long White Room   298
In a Mellotone   305, 308, 309, 312, 315, 317, 318, 320, 321, 322, 323, 324, 326, 327, 328, 329, 330, 331, 333, 334, 335, 337, 341, 348, 352, 356, 357, 359, 361, 372A, 374, 380, 381
In a Sentimental Mood   351
In the Evenin'   258
Indiana   213, 216, 270
Indiana Jam Session   266
Indiana Montage   265
Infatuation   28
Is You Is or Is You Ain't My Baby   247
Isn't It a Lovely Day   233A
Isn't It Romantic   201, 205
It Ain't the Meat It's the Motion   313
It Don't Mean a Thing If It Ain't Got that Swing   223, 313, 341, 351, 354, 355, 373
It Feels So Good   281
It Had to Be You   233
It Happened in Monterey   296
It Might as Well Be Spring   148
It Only Takes a Moment   299
It Pays to Advertise   194
It Takes Two to Tango   279
It Was So Beautiful   251
It's a Wonderful World   296
It's All Right with Me   250, 256
It's Easy to Blame the Weather   65
It's Funny to Everyone but Me   86
It's the Talk of the Town   302
It's Tight like That   90
It's Too Soon to Know   188
It's Unbelievable   35

J. C. Heard Drum Solo   215, 218, 219
Ja-Da   181
Jam Blues   201
Jam Session Blues   204, 215
Jay Jay's Jump   131
Jazz Cocktail   20
Jazz Portrait of Brigitte Bardot (A)   270
Jazz Waltz - A   286
Jazz Waltz - B   286
Jazz Waltz - C   286
Jeep Is Jumpin' (The)   314C
Jeep's Blues   367
Jeepers Creepers   64, 225A
Jerry the Junker   39
Jim Dogs Blues   307
Jingle Bells   51, 322
Jitterbug Waltz   351
Jive at Six   220
JJJJump   340
Joe Turner Blues   104
John's Idea   316
Johnny (Comp: H. Rene)   243
Johnny (Comp: B. Carter)   346
Joshua Fit de Battle of Jericho   121
Jubilee Jump   139
Juke Box (The)   262, 304, 311
Jump Call   151, 158, 170
Jumpin' at the Woodside   329, 353
Jumpin' with Symphony Sid   319
June Comes Around   143
June in January   225A, 253
June Is Bustin' Out All Over   254
Just a Baby's Prayer at Twilight   125
Just a Kid Named Joe   64
Just a Mood   40, 42
Just Blues   210
Just Friends   294
Just Imagine   248
Just One More Chance   171
Just One of Those Things   225
Just Squeeze Me   306
Just the Blues   246
Just You, Just Me   138, 150, 154, 159, 179

Kansas City Blues   273
Kansas City Line   340
Keep a Song in Your Soul   12
Key Largo   187, 205B
Kidney Stew   353
King Porter Stomp   96, 344
King Size Papa   184
King's Riff   199
King's Road Blues   237

Index of Tune Titles

Kiss from You (A) 311
Knock Me a Kiss 177
Krazy Kapers 25

Lady Be Good 74, 80, 200, 209, 314D, 357
Lady Sings the Blues (A) 262
Lady's in Love with You (The) 73
Lamp Is Low (The) 295
Last Kiss You Gave Me (The) 105
Last Night 86
Late Spot (The) 262
Laugh and Call It Love 60
Laugh, Clown, Laugh 248
Laughing at Life 10
Laura 213, 225, 239, 274, 302, 341
Lazy Afternoon 56
Legalize My Name 279
Legend (The) 275
Lester Leaps In 302
Let Us Drink a Toast Together 190
Let's Call the Whole Thing Off 264
Let's Fall in Love 210, 272
Let's Have a Jubilee 32
Liebestraum 74
Like Someone in Love 377, 379
Lilacs in the Rain 88
Linda 179
Little Girl Blue 225A
Livin' with the Blues 258
Liza 31
Lonely Affair - A 286
Lonely Affair - B 286
Lonely Affair - C 286
Lonely Affair - D 286
Lonely Beat 262
Lonesome Nights 26
Lonesome Road (The) 250
Long About Midnight 39
Long Ago and Far Away 205A
Look at that Face 288
Looking Back 298
Looking for a Boy 153
Los Angeles Blues 273
Love for Sale 125, 163
Love Is Cynthia 207
Love Me a Little Little 111
Love, You Didn't Do Right by Me 227
Love, You're Not the One for Me 21, 27
Love's Got Me Down Again 89
Loveless Love 103

Lover 189
Lover Man 159, 264, 313, 354, 361, 380, 381
Lover, Come Back to Me 264
Lula 282
Lullaby in Blue 202
Lullaby to a Dream 110
Lydia 358

M Squad Theme 262
Ma, He's Makin' Eyes at Me 279
Main Title 265
Makin' Whoopee 222, 303
Making the Scene 234
Malaguena 187
Malibu 143, 149, 164, 338, 381
Mama Don't Allow It 177
Mama Don't Wear No Drawers 340
Mama Lou 202
Man I Love (The) 50
Man Is a Necessary Evil (A) 288
Man Is Good (A) 194
Many Happy Returns 183
March Wind 254, 297
Mari 377
Marriage Blues 225
Mary Lou 248
Maybe 296
Me and My Jaguar 210
Mean to Me 341, 380, 381
Mecca Flat Blues 258
Melancholy Lullaby 66, 68, 71, 74, 79, 80, 85, 86, 123
Memories of You 265, 287, 341
Memphis Blues 47
Men of Harlem 67
Metropole 286
Mexican Hat Dance 166
Midnight 110, 127
Midnight Jamboree 95
Midnight Sun Will Never Set (The) 277
Mighty Like the Blues 57
Milenberg Joys 238
Miss Hannah 6, 370B
Misty 312, 315, 317, 318, 321, 322, 323, 324, 326, 329, 330, 331, 332, 333, 334, 335, 337, 341, 346, 356, 366, 367, 370A, 372, 379, 381
Misty Night 372B
Monday Date 248, 314A, 374, 375
Mood Indigo 375, 380
Moon Is Low (The) 155, 225A, 230
Moon of Manakoora 267
Moon Song 221B
Moonglow 141, 221B, 342

Moonlight in Vermont   259
Moppin' and Boppin'   118
More Than You Know   65, 66, 89
Morpheus   245
Moten Swing   234, 340
Mr. Coed   161
Mugger (The)   262
Music at Midnight   23
Music at Sunrise   24
Music Goes Round and Round (The)   115
Muskrat Ramble   59
My Blue Heaven   92, 222, 248
My Buddy   57, 91
My Dear Old Love   372B
My Favorite Blues   110
My Foolish Heart   300
My Gal   309
My Gal Sal   16, 170
My Guy's Come Back   157
My Heart Has Wings   74
My Kind of Trouble Is You   338
My Mother's Eyes   295
My One and Only Love   221B
My Place   283
My Pretty Girl   16
My Sin   178

Nagasaki   52
Nearness of You (The)   270, 271, 307, 311
Never More   284
Never Swat a Fly   10, 370B
New Street Swing   54
New York City Blues   273
Nice Work If You Can Get It   233
Night and Day   157
Night Hop   100
Night in Tunisia   308, 339, 366
Nightfall   41, 45
No Love, No Nothin'   122
No Regrets   294
Nobody Knows the Trouble I've Seen   339
Nocturne   22
Now It Can Be Told   60
Now's the Time   291
Nuages   351

O. K. for Baby   100
Oahu Dance/Cherokee (Finale)   265
Ocean Motion   67
Ol' Man River   116, 131, 144
Old Black Joe's Blues   2
Old Fashioned Love   30, 222, 240

Old Folks   199
Old Love Story (An)   190
Old Man and the Sea (The)   252
Old Man Harlem   81
Old, Tired and Torn   279
On Green Dolphin Street   287, 294, 312, 342, 348, 352, 356, 359, 361, 364, 379, 380, 381
On the Alamo   128
On the Beach-Soundtrack Album   263
On the Bumpy Road to Love   60
On the Other Side of the Tracks   299
On the Sunny Side of the Street   158, 162, 369
Once in a While   295
Once Upon a Time   25
One Good Blues   308
One I Love (The)   267
One Morning in May   253
One O'clock Jump   108, 117A, 123, 172, 212
One Sweet Letter from You   83
One Way Out   286
Only Love   298
Only Trust Your Heart   328
Oo-wee   194
Oofdah   163
Opening Blues   282
Opus 5   281
Orange Blues   273
Original Jelly Roll Blues   191
Ornithology   365
Our Love Is Here to Stay   221B
Out of My Way   165
Out of Nowhere   55
Out of This World   299
Over the Rainbow   341

Pagan Love Song   184
Pardon Me, Pretty Baby   57
Pardon My Love   36
Party Time U.S.A.   362
Pastorale   22
Pat   243
Patience and Fortitude   151, 163
Patty Cake   73
Peace of Mind   299
Peggy   7
Pennies from Heaven   220
Perdido   173, 204, 217, 247, 297, 309, 312, 314C, 318, 320, 321, 322, 323, 324, 326, 327, 328, 329, 330, 331, 332, 333, 334, 335, 337, 348, 356, 361, 364, 369, 380, 381

Index of Tune Titles 263

Phalanges 211
Phantom Raiders 262
Pick Up 268
Pick Yourself Up 206
Pinetop's Boogie Woogie 102
Plain Dirt 5, 370B
Play Me the Blues 144
Player Play On 298
Please Be Kind 247
Please Be Patient 251
Please Don't Talk About Me When I'm Gone 233
Pleasures and Palaces 288
Plymouth Rock 72, 79, 80, 86
Poinciana 125, 225B
Polishin' Brass 156, 157, 161
Polite Blues 230
Pom Pom 93, 100
Poor Butterfly 50, 342
Poor Little Rich Girl 284
Porgy 258
Porter's Love Song to a Chambermaid (A) 38
Prelude to a Kiss 128, 150, 162, 170, 233, 293
Pretty Girl Is Like a Melody (A) 93
Prisoner of Love 225B
Prisoner of My Eyes 298
Prohibido 289, 310
Push Out 81
Pushing Forty 288

Queer Notions 287A
Quiet Soul 298

Rain 294
Rain, Rain, Go Away 69
Rambler's Rhythm 54
Rambling in C 53
Randall's Island 199
Re-Bop Boogie 166
Redman Blues 370C
Reina 190
Rhythm Is Our Business 40
Riff Interlude 316
Riff Romp 82, 86
Riffamarole 140
Rifftide 300
Rigamarole 39
Right Here with You 287
Robbins Nest 308, 342
Rock and Roll Party 226
Rock Bottom 290, 310
Rockin' Along 202
Rockin' Chair 109A

Rocks in My Bed 306
Rocky Road 9
Roll 'Em 189
Roll with the Boogie 195
Room with a View 284
Rose O'Day 223
Rose Room 132, 141, 153, 281, 297
Roses in December 254
Roses of Picardy 284
Rosetta 225A, 303, 314A, 354, 355, 377
Rosita 142
Round Midnight 205B
Row Row Row Row 279
Royal Flush 113
Royal Garden Blues 51, 266, 281
Ruby 221B
Rug Cutter's Swing 31
Rules of the Road (The) 299
Russian Lullaby 85

'S Wonderful 222, 297, 303
Same Old Dream 179
San Francisco Blues 273
Satin Doll 293, 306, 309, 348
Save It, Pretty Mama 90
Savoy Stampede 79, 85
Say It with a Kiss 62
Scandal in A Flat 43, 68, 79, 80, 85
Scratch My Back 90
Search (The) 262
Seems Like a Month of Sundays 102
Seems Like Old Times 294
Sendin' the Vipers 30
September Song 253
Serenade to a Sarong 100
Serenade to a Wealthy Widow 284
Session at Midnight 234
720 in the Books 296
Shadow of Your Smile (The) 300, 308, 309
Shake It and Break It 93
Shanghai Shuffle 34
Shangri-La 287
Shavers' Tune 363
She's Funny that Way 158, 161, 264, 353
Sheik of Araby (The) 39, 92
Shoe Shiner's Drag 59
Shoot the Works 33
Show Break - 1 286
Show Break - 2 286
Show Me the Way to Go Home 284
Shufflebug Shuffle 89
Since I Fell for You 258

Singin' the Blues 91
Sisters 227
Six Bells Stampede 21
Six or Seven Times 4
Skin Deep 211
Skip It 56
Sky Full of Sunshine 198
Sleep 94, 124, 145, 304, 311
Sleigh Ride in July 254
Slow Freight 94
Smack 101
Smile 285
So Help Me 251
So Long Darling 180
Soft and Sweet 17
Solid Mama 71
Solitude 264, 373
Some of These Days 48, 152
Some Other Spring 205
Somebody Loves Me 8, 57, 141, 145, 213
Someone Stole Gabriel's Horn 22
Someone to Watch over Me 248
Something for October 254
Sometimes I'm Happy 369, 372
Song Is You (The) 225
Song of the Islands 340
Song of the Plow 32
Song of the Wanderer 316
Sophisticated Lady 45, 373
South Rampart Street Parade 238
South Side Samba 348, 351, 363, 374, 375, 378, 379, 381
Souvenir 311, 349, 351, 374
Spellbound 224
Spiritual Jazz 265
Spring Is Here 296
Squatty Roo 351
Squeeze Me 313
St. Louis Blues 103, 186, 273, 279
St. Thomas 348
Stairway to the Stars 155
Star Dust 40, 68, 99, 132, 141, 162, 197, 261
Stars and You 53
Stay Out of Love 37, 40
Stay with It 268
Stick Around 198
Stompin' at the Savoy 116, 169, 213, 216, 234, 301, 312, 317, 318, 321
Stop Myself from Worryin' over You 81
Stormy Weather 119, 140, 197
Straight, No Chaser 364
Strange Enchantment 78, 86
Street of Dreams 222, 377

Street Scene 206
Stroll 346
Struttin' with Some Barbecue 345
Succotash Baby 198
Sugar 65, 170
Sugarfoot Stomp 71
Summer Night 347
Summertime 69
Sunday 112, 147, 314
Sunday Afternoon 207
Supersweet 323, 324, 325, 326, 327, 328, 329, 330, 331, 332, 333, 334, 335, 337
Surf Board 193
Suspicious of My Woman 195
Swanee River 127
Swedish Jam 269
Sweet and Hot 16
Sweet and Lovely 339
Sweet Georgia Brown 55, 132, 138, 154, 165, 234, 308, 309, 342, 354, 355
Sweet Lorraine 248
Sweet Sorrow Blues 23
Sweet Sue, Just You 23
Sweetheart 313
Swing It 21
Swingin' at Maida Vale 41
Swingin' Down the Lane 243A
Swingin' in November 254, 297
Swingin' the Blues 42, 297
Swingin' with Mezz 27
Swizzle (The) 276
Symphony 221
Symphony in Riffs 26
Synthetic Love 21, 33

Tab 243
'Tain't Nobody's Bizness If I Do 260, 264
Take Back Your Mink 288
Take It or Leave It 184
Take the A Train 239, 270, 306, 309, 317, 325, 326, 327, 330, 331, 332, 333, 341, 359, 379, 380, 381
Takin' My Time 107
Taking a Chance on Love 296
Talk to Me 9
Tangerine 302
Tea for Two 68, 75, 139
Tell All Your Day Dreams to Me 19
Tell Her in the Morning 268
Tell Me Daddy 185
Tenderly 221B
Terry Cloth 300

Index of Tune Titles

That Ain't Right 118
That Made Him Mad 63
That Old Black Magic 225, 259
That's All 220
That's Good Enough for Me 279
That's How I Feel Today 4
That's How the First Song Was Born 50
That's What I Like 184
Them There Eyes 174, 351, 354, 355
Theme for Celine 362
Theme for Susannah 362
Then I'll Be Happy 281
Then I'll Be Tired 183
Then You've Never Been Blue 131
There Is No Greater Love 380
There I've Said It Again 109
There'll Be Some Changes Made 51, 109A
There's a Small Hotel 52
There's Only One in Love 85
These Foolish Things 41, 115, 284, 341, 343, 353
These Things You Left Me 205
They Can't Take That Way from Me 264
They Say 62
Things Ain't What They Used to Be 351, 354, 355, 375
Thinking of You 295
35th and Calumet 30
This Bitter Earth 299
This Can't Be Love 221B, 239
This Is Our Last Night Together 29
This Love of Mine 225A
This Time the Dream's on Me 272
Thou Swell 248
Three Little Words 315, 341, 342, 347, 352, 369
Three O'clock Jump 172, 181
Throwin' Stones at the Sun 35
Ti-Pi-Tin 115
Tickle Toe 287
Tiger Rag 44
Till We Meet Again 98
Time for Love (A) 300
Time Out for the Blues 193
Tired 279
Titmouse 290, 297
To Ava 236
Toot Toot Tootsie 279
Tootsie Roll 281
Train Blues (The) 273
Tree of Hope 112
Trot (The) 275

Trouble in Mind 261
Trouble, Trouble 139
Trumpet Battle (The) 204
Try a Little Tenderness 295
Turnabout 276
Tutti Frutti 223
Twelve Bar Blues 359
Twelve Bar Stampede 67
Twelve O'clock Jump 166
20th Century Closet 281
Two Again 135
Two O'clock Jump 172

Undecided 222, 281, 297, 307, 308, 309, 312, 317, 318, 320, 321, 322, 323, 324, 326, 327, 328, 329, 330, 331, 332, 335, 337, 343, 348, 352, 359, 374, 381
Under a Blanket of Blue 182, 222
Under Paris Skies 283
Unforgettable 221B
Unidentified Title 144
Unlucky Woman 146

Vagabond Dreams 88, 89
Very Thought of You (The) 107, 284
Vinho Verde 286
Vous Qui Passez Sans Me Voir 285

Walkin' by the River 106, 208
Walkin' One and Only 313
Walkin' Thing (A) 241, 311, 338, 360
Waltz Down the Aisle 255
Waltz Gay 285
Waltzing the Blues 44
Wanna Go Home 203
Was that the Human Thing to Do 183
Watermelon Man 287
Wave 342, 343, 352, 356
Way Down Yonder in New Orleans 266
Way I Feel Today (The) 6
We Could Learn Together 298
We Were in Love 290
We'll Be Together Again 225B
We're Friends Again 14
We've Come a Long Way Together 70
Wee Dot 291
What a Difference a Day Made 110

What Are You Doing the Rest of Your Life   341
What Can I Say After I'm Sorry   296
What Do You See in Her   298
What Good Am I Without You   12, 14
What Is a Man   288
What Is This Thing Called Love   164, 201, 314B, 366, 374
What Kind of Fool Am I   284
What Shall I Say   65
What'll It Be   165
What's New   86, 87, 233A, 301, 359
When Day Is Done   42, 92
When I Close My Eyes   180
When I Fall in Love   300
When I Grow Too Old to Dream   261
When I Think of You   188
When Irish Eyes Are Smiling   70
When It's Sleepy Time Down South   351, 354, 355, 375
When Lights Are Low   44, 47, 82, 83, 282, 309, 311, 328, 350, 358, 360, 377, 378
When the Saints Go Marching In   257, 329
When the Sun Comes Out   299
When You're Smiling   178, 351, 354, 355, 375
When Your Lover Has Gone   225A, 233
Where Are You   295
Where or When   157
Where Were You on the Night of June the Third   37
Wherever There's a Will, Baby   7
While We're Young   259
Whisper Sweet   35
Who Will Be with You When I'm Far Away   168
Who, Me?   350

Who's Blue   276
Who's Sorry Now   152, 156, 158, 248
Who's Tired   288
Why Don't You Do Right   117, 258
Wild Is Love   268
Wild Is Love Finale   268
Wild Party   31
Will You Still Be Mine   225B
Wish You Were Here   203
With a Song in My Heart   221
Without a Song   123, 163
Wrap Your Troubles in Dreams   18
Wrappin' It Up   344

Yesterdays   348
You Ain't the One   1
You Are   304, 311
You Are Too Beautiful   193
You Belong to Me   203
You Can Depend on Me   140, 261
You Can't Tell the Difference When the Sun Goes Down Blues   282
You Do Something to Me   243A
You Fit into the Picture   35
You Must Have Been a Beautiful Baby   64
You Stepped Out of a Dream   294
You Took Advantage of Me   225B
You Understand   43
You'd Better Go   298
You'd Better Think It Over   288
You'll Never Break My Heart Again   190
You're a Sweetheart   294
You're Mine, You   222
You're the Top   255
You've Changed   302
You've Gotta See Mamma Ev'ry Night   183
Your Conscience Tells You So   166
Your Kind of Love   226

Discography: Section Two

CARTER AS ARRANGER AND COMPOSER

This section presents Benny Carter's recorded work as an arranger and composer. It is divided into three parts: 1) master list of arrangements and compositions, 2) index of artists, 3) chronological index.

1. Master list of arrangements and compositions. This is an alphabetical listing by title of all known recorded Carter arrangements and compositions. Arrangements and compositions are merged into a single list. Each title is followed by the composer credits (Benny Carter is abbreviated as "BC"). Unless otherwise noted, Carter is presumed to have composed the music to a piece, not its lyric. For Carter compositions with lyrics, the lyricist is specified; for non-Carter compositions no distinction between lyricist and composer is made.

Date provided for each recording include 1) date, 2) leader and/or group (if Carter is the leader "BC" appears), 3) vocalist (if any)--if the leader is the vocalist a "v" appears after the name; other vocalists appear in parentheses, 4) instrumentation (an approximate listing which is given only for the first recording of Carter arrangements), 5) record issues--these are not comprehensive; usually only the most recent LP is shown. An asterisk following the date of recording indicates that Carter played on the session, and the reader may refer to Section One of the discography for record issue information (which is not repeated here).

Each Carter arrangement of a piece is listed under that title in chronological order by the date of its first recording, which is underscored. Subsequent recordings of the same arrangement appear chronologically (without underscoring) under the first recording of that arrangement. Within each title, new arrangements are separated by one space; multiple recordings of the same arrangement have no spaces between them.

All recordings listed under titles which Carter did not compose are, of course, his arrangements. Under titles which Carter did compose, however, all recordings of that piece are listed, including many which he did not arrange. Such recordings (i. e. "head" arrangements of Carter's compositions, or Carter's compositions arranged by others) are set off by one space and marked with a •.

2. Index of artists. This is an alphabetical listing of artists or groups who have recorded Carter arrangements or compositions. The titles recorded appear in chronological order under each leader's name. "See" and "see also" references are provided from all vocalists, co-leaders and some prominent accompanists or groups, to the leader under whose name the recording was issued. Following the tune title an "a" and/or "c" identifies the recording as a Carter arrangement or composition (or both). Multiple recordings by the same artist of a Carter arrangement or composition are indicated by listing the additional recording dates directly under the title. No record issues are given, as this information appears in the master list. Film soundtrack recordings are listed by title in a separate section following the artist index. Only recordings of Carter film arrangements and compositions which have been issued on disc are included here (see filmography for more comprehensive film lists).

Carter himself does not appear in this index; the number of recordings of his arrangements and compositions by his own groups would make such a list unwieldy. Moreover, by perusing Section One of the discography the reader can readily locate the Carter arrangements and compositions recorded on Carter-led dates. Similarly, arrangements and compositions recorded by vocalists on Carter-led sessions are not enumerated; rather, the vocalist's name appears in the index with a list of recording dates at which he or she performed a Carter arrangement or composition (e. g., Maxine Sullivan--see BC 4/1/44). The reader is thus referred to the appropriate session(s) in Section One.

3. Chronological index. This is a year-by-year listing of Carter arrangements and compositions (indicated by "a" and/or "c"). The year under which a given title appears is the year of the first recording of that arrangement or composition. Readers should note that this is only an approximate indication of the period to which a work belongs; the actual date of creation may, of course, be much earlier. In the few instances where the creation of an arrangement or composition is known to greatly antedate its first recording, this is noted. Similarly, for an arrangement by Carter of an earlier composition, the original year of composition is noted.

MASTER LIST OF ARRANGEMENTS AND COMPOSITIONS

A TEA VISTA (BC)
- 11/30/76*   BC

ACCENT ON SWING (BC)
mid 6/36   BC   3tp/2tb/3as/1ts/p/g/b/d

AFTER YOU'VE GONE (T. Layton/H. Creamer)
9/61   Jonah Jones with Glen Gray & the Casa Loma Orch.   6tp/4tb/2as/2ts/1bs/p/g/b/d   Capitol T1713

1962   Sarah Vaughan (v)   4tp/4tb/5reeds/p/g/b/d/vib/v
Roulette R(S)52092, Roulette (E) 2682-043

AGAIN (D. Cochran/L. Newman)
8/30/74   Yujiro Ishihara (v)   2tp/1tb/1as/2ts/1bs/p/g/b/d/
14violins/4violas/4celli/v   Continental (J) CO1
NOTE: Instrumental tracks recorded 8/30/74, Los Angeles; vocal added later in Japan.

AIN'T I (BC)
11/65   film soundtrack: A Man Called Adam   1tp/1tb/
1ts/p/b/d   Reprise 6180

AIN'T MISBEHAVIN' (Waller/Brooks/Razaf)
2/15-16/79   Ella Fitzgerald with Count Basie's Orch.   4tp/
4tb/5reeds/p/g/b/d/v   Pablo Today 2312-132

AIN'T THAT SOMETHING?
Jan.-Feb. 1943*   film soundtrack: Stormy Weather (Bill Robinson-v)   large orch/v

ALL ALONE (I. Berlin)
2/27/45*   Savannah Churchill (v) & Her All Star Orch.
4tp/4tb/5reeds/p/g/b/d/v

ALL ALONE AND LONESOME (BC/lyrics: Paul Herrick)
1953   Ernie Andrews (v) with Benny Carter's Orch.
large orch/v   78: Trend 2502

ALL MY LOVE (P. Durand)
4/29/77*   BC   2tp/1tb/3reeds/p/g/b/d

ALL OF ME (G. Marks/S. Simons)
1/17/36*   Willie Lewis & His Orch.   2tp/1tb/2as/2ts/p/g/b/d

Discography: Arranger/Composer

11/19/40*   BC 3tp/3tb/2as/2ts/1bs/p/g/b/d   NOTE: The
                     saxophone chorus in this arrangement is based on
                     the one recorded by Willie Lewis.
1943*   (AFRS Basic Library P-34) BC

ALL THAT I CAN DO IS THINK OF YOU (Bob Friedman)
11/71-3/72   Carmen McRae (v) large orch/v Temponic
                     TB29562

ALL THAT JAZZ (BC/lyrics: Al Stillman)
11/65   film soundtrack: A Man Called Adam 1tp/1tb/
                     1ts/p/b/d Reprise 6180

• 11/65   film soundtrack: A Man Called Adam (Mel
                     Torme-v) Reprise 6180

• 11/65   film soundtrack: A Man Called Adam (Mel
                     Torme-v) Reprise 6180

• 1/3/76*   BC (Millicent Browne-v)

• 4/18/81*   BC (BC-v)

ALL THE TIME (Bob Friedman)
11/71-3/72   Carmen McRae (v) large orch/v Temponic
                     TB29562

ALL TORE DOWN (D. Wyatt)
1968   Don Wyatt (v) large orch with strings/v NOTE:
                     Recorded for Dome Records--unissued.

ALTO EGO (BC)
8/64*   BC 2ss/4as/3ts/2bs/p/g/b/d

ALWAYS ON MY MIND (Green/Newell)
1/63   Sarah Vaughan (v) 4fr. horns/p/g/b/d/tuba/v
                     Roulette R(S)52104

ALWAYS ON SUNDAY (Bob Friedman)
11/71-3/72   Joe Williams (v) large orch with strings/chorus/
                     v Temponic TB29561

AMONG MY SOUVENIRS (H. Nicholls/E. Leslie)
1/30/40*   BC (Roy Felton-v) 3tp/3tb/3as/2ts/p/g/b/d/v
9/11/44?*   BC

AMOROSO (BC)
11/1-2/61*   Count Basie & His Orch. 4tp/3tb/2as/2ts/1bs/p/
                     g/b/d

1/22-24/62   Louis Bellson Orch. 5tp/3tb/1fr. horn/1tuba/2as/
                     2ts/1bs/p/g/b/d/vib Roulette R52087, Roulette
                     (E) 2934-020

ANY OLD TIME (J. Rodgers)
12/22/74*   Maria Muldaur (v) 2tp/1tb/1as/1ts/1bs/p/g/b/d/v

ANY TIME AT ALL (Van Heusen/J. Dorsey)
7/21/38*   Lionel Hampton (v) & His Orch. 1tp/2as/2ts/p/
                     b/d/vib/v

APOLLO JUMPS (BC)
9/61   Jonah Jones with Glen Gray & the Casa Loma
                        Orch. 6tp/4tb/2as/2ts/1bs/p/g/b/d Capitol
                        T1713

APRIL IN MY HEART (H. Carmichael/H. Melnardi)
11/9/38*   Teddy Wilson & His Orch. (Billie Holiday-v)
                        1tp/1tb/2as/2ts/p/g/b/d/v

AROUND THE WORLD IN EIGHTY DAYS (V. Young)
5/63*   BC 1as/p/b/d/vocal group

AS TIME GOES BY (H. Hupfeld)
8/30/74   Yujiro Ishihara (v) 2tp/1tb/1as/2ts/1bs/p/g/b/d/v
                        Continental (J) C01 NOTE: Instrumental tracks
                        recorded 8/30/74, Los Angeles; vocal added later
                        in Japan.

ASK (BC/lyrics: H. C. Mahr)
ca. 1958   Lois Peters (v) with the Ravenscroft Singers &
                        Orch. 5brass/4woodwinds/rhythm section/strings/
                        v 45: Decca 9-30269 [copyrighted as ASK, BE-
                        LIEVING THAT YOU WILL RECEIVE]

ASK, BELIEVING THAT YOU WILL RECEIVE see ASK

AUGUST MOON (BC)
• late 1958 or   BC
early 1959*

AUTUMN LEAVES (J. Kosma)
10/57   "Mucho Calor" (features Art Pepper) 1tp/1as/
                        1ts/p/b/d/bongo/conga Andex A3002

BABALU (Margarita Lecuona)
1/21/41*   BC 3tp/3tb/3as/2ts/p/g/b/d

BABY, DON'T YOU QUIT NOW (J. Mercer/J. Rowles)
1968   Pearl Bailey (v) with the Louis Bellson Orch.
                        4tp/4tb/5reeds/p/g/b/d/v Project 3 PR5022SD,
                        Project 3 PR4003SD

BABY WON'T YOU PLEASE COME HOME (Warfield/Williams)
early 1950's   Ruby Lane (v) large orch with strings/v 45:
                        Colpix CP139

BABY, YOU'RE MINE FOR KEEPS (H. Atwood/L. Herscher)
1/48*   BC (Emma Lou Welch-v) 1tp/1tb/1as/1ts/p/g/
                        b/d/v

BACK BAY BOOGIE (BC)
10/16/41*   BC 3tp/3tb/3as/2ts/p/g/b/d
4/10/43*   BC
possibly Jan. or   BC
Nov. 1944*
3/26/45*   (AFRS Jubilee #126) BC
5/5/46*   BC
ca. 6/46*   (AFRS Jubilee #193) BC

Discography: Arranger/Composer   271

BACK HOME AGAIN IN INDIANA   see   INDIANA

BACK IN YOUR OWN BACKYARD (A. Jolson/B. Rose/D. Dreyer)
  ca. 1951   Patti Page (v) with Herb Geller Orch. large orch/v 78: Mercury 5463

THE BAD AND THE BEAUTIFUL (D. Raksin)
  1961*   Alfred Newman large orch with horns/strings

BAGATELLE (BC)
  • 5/63*   BC

BAMBOULA   see   CONGOROO

THE BASIE TWIST (BC)
  10/30-31/61*   Count Basie & His Orch. 4tp/3tb/2as/2ts/1bs/p/g/b/d

BAUBLES, BANGLES AND BEADS (R. Wright/G. Forrest)
  9/61   Jonah Jones with Glen Gray & the Casa Loma Orch. 6tp/4tb/2as/2ts/1bs/p/g/b/d Capitol T1713, Capitol (G) 1C 054-81710

BE ANYTHING (I. Gordon)
  2/60   Dakota Staton (v) large orch with strings/v Capitol T1427

BE-BOP BOOGIE   see   RE-BOP BOOGIE

BE COOL (BC)
  5/63*   KPM Music Library 4tp/4tb/2fr. horns/5reeds/p/g/b/d

  5/63*   KPM Music Library 4tp/4tb/2fr. horns/5reeds/p/g/b/d

  5/63*   KPM Music Library 4tp/4tb/2fr. horns/flutes/p/g/b/d

            NOTE: See notes for this session in chronological section of discography.

A BEAUTIFUL FRIENDSHIP (S. Styne/D. Kahn)
  2/19/64   Billy Eckstine (v) 1tp/1tb/2reeds/p/g/b/d/v/vocal group Mercury SR60916, Mercury MG20916

BEAUTIFUL LOVE (Young/Van Alstyne/Gillespie/King)
  12/31/53*   BC horns/strings/p/b/d

BETWEEN 18th AND 19th ON CHESTNUT STREET (W. Osborne/D. Rodgers)
  1955   Freddie Slack 1tp/1tb/1ts/1bs/p/g/b/d Emarcy MG36094, Wing MGW60003

BETWEEN THE DEVIL AND THE DEEP BLUE SEA (H. Arlen/T. Koehler)
  4/27/55   Ella Fitzgerald (v) with Benny Carter Orch. 3tp/1tb/2as/2ts/p/g/b/d/v Decca DL8155, MCA Coral CB20024, MCA Coral (G) 0082.050-2

BEWITCHED, BOTHERED AND BEWILDERED (Rodgers/Hart)
9/52* BC with the Oscar Peterson Trio & Buddy Rich
horns/strings/p/g/b/d

BIG BEN BLUES (BC--words & music)
4/15/36* BC (v) 3tp/2tb/3as/2ts/p/g/b/d/v

BIG NOBODY (Wellington/Chaudet)
Mar. 30-Apr. 1 Pearl Bailey (v) 4tp/4tb/5reeds/p/g/b/d/v
1965*

BILL BAILEY, WON'T YOU PLEASE COME HOME (H. Cannon)
Sept.-Oct. 1958* film soundtrack: The Five Pennies (Louis Armstrong, Danny Kaye-v) probably 1tp/1tb/1cl/1as/
1ts/p/g/b/d/v

BLACK BUTTERFLY (Duke Ellington)
8/14/79 Zoot Sims 4tp/4tb/2as/2ts/1bs/p/g/b/d Pablo
Today 2312-120 NOTE: This arrangement was
written for Sarah Vaughan, but at session Sims
substituted as featured soloist.

BLACK NIGHT (J. Williams)
5/63* BC 1as/p/b/d/vocal group

BLAZIN' (Sanders)
5/16/29 Fletcher Henderson & His Orch. 3tp/2tb/3reeds/
p/banjo/tuba/d Columbia CL1684, Smithsonian
P2-13710

BLITZEN (L. Feather)
1/22-24/62 Louis Bellson Orch. 5tp/3tb/1fr. horn/1tuba/2as/
2ts/1bs/p/g/b/d/vib Roulette R52087, Roulette
(E) 2934-020

BLUE EVENING (G. Jenkins/J. Bishop)
6/10/39* BC 3tp/3tb/2as/2ts/p/g/b/d
7/24/39* BC (Dell St. John-v)

BLUE FIVE JIVE (BC)
9/6-11/60 Count Basie & His Orch. 4tp/3tb/2as/2ts/1bs/p/
g/b/d Roulette (S)R52056, Roulette RE124 NOTE:
See note on recording date under Kansas City Suite;
one of ten pieces comprising the Suite.

BLUE INTERLUDE (BC/lyrics: M. Kurtz/I. Mills)
10/10/33* The Chocolate Dandies 1tp/1tb/1as/1ts/p/g/b/d

• 12/19/34 Chuck Richards (v) 78: Vocalion 2877

8/8/36 Benny Goodman & His Orch. (Martha Tilton-v)
3tp/2tb/2as/2ts/p/g/b/d/v Bluebird AXM2-5566

8/26/36* BC with Kai Ewans' Orch. 3tp/2tb/3as/2ts/p/g/b/d

• 10/27/38 Cab Calloway (v) & His Orch. Two Flat Disc
5008

• 12/2/38 Artie Shaw & His Orch. arr: Jerry Gray (aircheck) Hindsight 139

Discography: Arranger/Composer

● 9/20/56   Bertie King Jazz Group   Nixa (E) NJT506

NOTE: Melody Maker (May 30, 1936) reports that Carter was commissioned by Henry Hall to arrange this tune. It may have been broadcast by Hall and the B.B.C. Dance Orchestra and may be the same as the arrangement recorded on 8/26/36*. The Whiteman Archive at Williams College has a non-Carter arrangement of this title from the Whiteman book. There are no known recordings.

BLUE LIGHT BLUES (BC)
● 3/7/38*   BC [also entitled PLAYIN' THE BLUES]

BLUE LOU (E. Sampson)
10/16/33*   BC 3tp/3tb/3as/1ts/p/g/b/d

6/11/57*   BC 1as/1tb/1ts/p/g/b/d

BLUE MOON (Rodgers/Hart)
1/15/35   Benny Goodman & His Orch.   3tp/2tb/2as/2ts/p/g/b/d/v Sunbeam SB140

BLUE MOUNTAIN (A. Newman)
10/2/52*   BC 3tp/3tb/2as/2ts/1bs/p/g/b/d (as Love Is Cynthia)

1955*   Alfred Newman & His Orch. (as To Ava)

NOTE: This piece was composed by Newman for the film The Snows of Kiliminjaro (1952). Carter also solos on the soundtrack. [also entitled LOVE IS CYNTHIA and TO AVA]

BLUE ORCHIDS (H. Carmichael)
10/23/39*   BC 3tp/3tb/2as/2ts/p/g/b/d

BLUE PRELUDE (J. Bishop/G. Jenkins)

11/56   Billy Daniels (v) accompanied by Benny Carter's Orch. 4tp/4tb/2as/2ts/1bs/p/g/b/d/v Verve MGV2072

THE BLUE ROOM (Rodgers/Hart)
ca. 12/40   Jean Omer & His Swing Orch. 3tp/2tb/4reeds/p/g/b/d 78: Decca (Belgium) 9010

BLUE SKIES (I. Berlin)
11/56   Billy Daniels (v) accompanied by Benny Carter's Orch. 4tp/4tb/2as/2ts/1bs/p/g/b/d/v Verve MGV2072

BLUE STAR (BC)
12/31/53*   BC horns/strings/p/b/d
11/15/61*   BC 2as/2ts/p/g/b/d
● 10/22/73*   BC
● 1/3/76*   BC

- 2/11/76*   BC
- 3/18/77*   BC
- 4/18/81*   BC
- June-July 1981   Eddie Johnson Nessa n-22
- 9/26/81*   BC
- 11/28/81*   BC
- 12/4/81*   BC
- 12/5/81*   BC

BLUE TRAIN   (BC)
1965   Pat Dorn Orch.   4tp/4tb/2as/2ts/1bs/p/g/b/d
                    45: Capitol test pressing (may have been issued commercially)

BLUE YONDER   (BC)
5/63*   KPM Music Library   4tp/4tb/2fr. horns/5reeds/p/
                    g/b/d/xylophone

5/63*   KPM Music Library   4tp/4tb/2fr. horns/5reeds/p/
                    g/b/d

                    NOTE: See notes for this session in chronological section of discography.

BLUEBERRY HILL FISH FRY   see   FISH FRY

BLUEBERRY HILL JAMBOREE   see   FISH FRY

BLUEBIRDS IN THE MOONLIGHT   (R. Rainger/L. Robin)
10/9/39   Glenn Miller & His Orch. (Marion Hutton-v) 4tp/
                    4tb/5reeds/p/g/b/d/v   RCA (E) LFM1-7512, RCA AXM2-5534
11/17/39   Glenn Miller & His Orch. (Marion Hutton-v) (broadcast)
11/25/39   Glenn Miller & His Orch. (Marion Hutton-v) (aircheck)   RCA Victor LPT6701

BLUES FOR BEGINNERS   (BC)
7/2/72*   BC   5tp/4tb/3as/2ts/1bs/p/g/b/d
12/3/73*   BC   (Hale Smith-scat v)
10/28/78*   BC

BLUES FOR THE WEEPERS   (L. Magid/M. Rich)
1965   Lou Rawls (v)   2tp/4tb/2reeds/p/g/b/d/v   Capitol T2273

BLUES IN D FLAT   (BC)
- 2/11/76*   BC

BLUES IN MY HEART   (BC/lyrics: I. Mills/M. Parish)
3/23/31   King Carter & His Royal Orch. (Dick Rogers [pseudonym for Dick Robertson]-v)   3tp/2tb/3reeds/p/banjo/b/d/v   78: Columbia 2439-D

                    NOTE: May be same arrangement as 3/30/31* Chick Webb.

3/30/31*   Chick Webb & His Orch. (Louis Bacon-v)   3tp/1tb/2as/1ts/p/g/b/d/v

Discography: Arranger/Composer

- 5/6/31   Cab Calloway & His Orch.   78: Banner 32221
- 9/15/31   Mildred Bailey (v) with the Casa Loma Orch. arr: Gene Gifford   78: Brunswick 6190
- 9/16/31   Bert Lown & His Hotel Biltmore Orch. (Elmer Feldkamp-v) The Old Masters TOM18
- 9/23/31   Washboard Rhythm Kings (Eddie Miles-v)   78: Victor 23301
- ca. 9/31   Eubie Blake & His Orch. (Dick Robertson-v)   78: Crown 3197
- 10/5/31   Greta Keller (v)   78: Decca (F) F-2592
- 10/16/31   Fletcher Henderson & His Orch. (Les Reis-v) Jazz Panorama LP4
- 1931-1934   Ethel Waters (v) with the Herman Chittison Trio   78: Victor 20-2459
- ca. 1931   Lee Sims   78: Brunswick 6212
- 2/10/32   Spike Hughes & His Orch. (Joey Shields-v) arr: Spike Hughes   78: Parlophone R-1175
- 2/12/32   Ray Noble & His Orch. (Al Bowlly-v) arr: Ray Noble   Monmouth-Evergreen MES7021, World Records SM624
- 2/23/32   Guy Lombardo & His Royal Canadians (Carmen Lombardo-v) arr: Carmen Lombardo?   78: Brunswick 20104   NOTE: Medley: "Between the Devil and the Deep Blue Sea introducing Blues in My Heart."
- ca. 1932   Jack Payne & His Orch.   78: Imperial (E) 2665

3/27/36   Henry Hall & the B.B.C. Dance Orch.   large orch. (B.B.C. broadcast, no known airchecks)

8/17/37*   BC   3tp/3tb/2as/2ts/p/g/b/d

- 7/3/40   Glenn Miller & His Orch. (broadcast)
9/10/40   Glenn Miller & His Orch. (broadcast)
- 1941-1942   Bob Chester & His Orch. (Betty Bradley-v) (aircheck) Big Band International LP2708
- 1943-1944   Glenn Miller & the Army Air Force Band   RCA VPM6080
- 1944-1946   Joe Sullivan   Folkways FA2851
- 2/14/45   Buddy Featherstonhaugh & the Radio Rhythm Club Sextet   78: HMV (E) B9406

• 10/20/45	Lem Davis Sextet Polydor (E) 2460 137 Select NOTE: On the Polydor LP the positions of "Blues in My Heart" and "It Was Meant to Be" are reversed.
• 1/24/46	All Hall's Quintet 78: Wax 101 LP: Crystal 12503
• 1946	Roy Milton & His Solid Senders 78: Roy Milton 111, LP: Riverboat (F) 900.264
• 4/6/50	Chris Powell (v) & His Blue Flames 78: Columbia 30216
• 10/6-9/50	Sidney Bechet avec Claude Luter et son Orch. Scepter SM537, Up Front 186
• ca. 1950	Pee Wee Crayton (v?) Crown CLP5171
• 1951	Johnny Moore (Billy Valentine?-v) 78: Hollywood 425
• ca. 1951	Eddie "Lockjaw" Davis Quartet Roost LP2227
• 1/14/53	Sticks McGhee (v) & His Buddies 78: King 4628
• 12/28/53	Art Tatum Clef MGC612, Pablo 2625-703
• 6/25/54*	Art Tatum - BC
• 4/6/55	Bertie King Jazz Group Jazz Today (E) JTL5
• 4/9/56	Sammy Price Club Francais du Disque 72
• 5/24/56	Bill Coleman (v?) Columbia (F) ESDF1119
• 1956-1957	Sam Taylor 45: MGM 12325, MGM E3553
• 7/25/57	Lee Wiley (v) arr: Bill Finegan RCA LPM1566
• 8/57	George Shearing Quintet with Dakota Staton (v) Capitol T1003
• 1958	Mae Barnes (v) Vanguard VSD2016
• 1958	Ann Richards (v) arr: Warren Baker Capitol T1087
• ca. 1958	Bobby Hackett arr: Stan Applebaum Capitol T1172
• 2/27/59	Arnott Cobb Prestige LP7184
• 1959	Helen Merrill (v) arr: Jimmy Jones Metrojazz E1010, Metrojazz (J) MM2086
• ca. 1959	John Buzon Trio Liberty LRP3108

Discography: Arranger/Composer

- 1960   Plas Johnson arr: Gerald Wilson or Rene Hall Capitol (S)T1503
- 1962   Jonah Jones Capitol T1405
- 1962   Mark Murphy (v) Riverside RM441, Riverside (J) SMJ6091
- 1964   Harry Edison with Benny Carter's Orch. arr: Dick Hazard Vee Jay VJS3065
- ca. 1964*   BC
- 10/20/69   Count Basie & His Orch. arr: Chico O'Farrill BASF MPS MC25111
- 3/1-2/71   Joe Williams (v) & George Shearing Sheba ST102
- 4/22/72   Miss Rhapsody [Viola Wells] (v) Matchbox SDM227, Savoy SJL2233
- 2/9/74   Earle Warren & the Anglo-American All Stars RCA (E) LFL1-5066
- 11/74   Ellis Larkins Halcyon HAL113
- 2/24/75   Sonny Criss Muse 5068
- 5/2/75   Doc Cheatham Black and Blue (F) 33.090, Classic Jazz CJ113
- 5/29/76   Joe Turner (pianist) Classic Jazz CJ138
- 5/30/76   Milt Buckner/Arnett Cobb/Panama Francis Black and Blue (F) 333.093
- 6/24/76*   BC
- 7/21/77   Ellis Larkins Classic Jazz CJ145
- 1/22/79   Jazz Gala '79, Cannes, France (Joe Williams-v) arr: Jimmy Jones Personal Choice PC51001
- 4/14/80   Milt Jackson Pablo Today D2312-124

    NOTE: The Whiteman Archive at Williams College has a non-Carter arrangement of this title from the Whiteman book. There are no known recordings.

BOBBY (Bob Friedman)
<u>11/71-3/72</u>   Carmen McRae (v) large orch/v Temponic TB29562

BODY AND SOUL (J. Green/R. Sour/E. Heyman/F. Eyton)
<u>2/60</u>   Dakota Staton (v) large orch with strings/v Capitol T1427

<u>11/15/61*</u>   BC 2as/2ts/p/g/b/d

BODYGUARD (B. Blalock)
   early 1950's   Bruce Blalock (Ketty Lester?-v) small group/v
                              45: Coral 9-61884

BOOGIE MINOR (BC)
   11/25/47*   Freddie Slack & His Orch.   4tp/2tb/2as/2ts/1bs/
                              p/g/b/d

BOOGIE WOOGIE SUGAR BLUES (C. Williams/L. Fletcher)
   10/23/40*   BC 3tp/2tb/2as/2ts/p/g/b/d

BOP BOUNCE (BC)
   3/30/48*   (AFRS Jubilee #284) BC large orch NOTE:
                              May have been announced under title "Little Bo
                              Bop Has Lost Her Beep." See note for 3/30/48*
                              session.

BOULEVARD BOUNCE (BC)
   4/22/47*   Lucky Thompson & His Lucky Seven 1tp/1as/1ts/
                              1bs/p/g/b/d

BOY MEETS HORN (I. Mills/D. Ellington/R. Stewart)
   9/61   Jonah Jones with Glen Gray & the Casa Loma
                              Orch. 6tp/4tb/2as/2ts/1bs/p/g/b/d   Capitol
                              T1713

BRAZILIAN TWIST (BC)
   1965   Pat Dorn Orch. 4tp/4tb/2as/2ts/1bs/p/g/b/d
                              45: Capitol test pressing (may have been issued
                              commercially)

BUGLE CALL RAG (Pettis/Meyers/Schoebel)
   12/31/30*   The Chocolate Dandies 1tp/1tb/1as/1ts/p/g/tuba

   1955   Horace Heidt & His Musical Knights 3tp/3tb/
                              4reeds/p/g/b/d 45: Magnolia MS1069

BUNBELINA (BC)
   12/12/45*   BC 4tp/4tb/3as/2ts/1bs/p/g/b/d

BUSTED (H. Howard)
   7/16/63   Ray Charles (v), The Raelets (v. group) 4tp/4tb/
                              2as/2ts/1bs/p/g/b/d/v/vocal group 45: ABC
                              Paramount 590X, LP: ABC Paramount 465
                              NOTE: This record won a Grammy Award for
                              Charles. Carter received a certificate from the
                              National Academy of Recording Arts and Sciences
                              in recognition of his nomination for "best back-
                              ground arrangement" of 1963.

BUT NOW I KNOW (E. Townsend)
   1957   Ernie Andrews (v) with Benny Carter's Orch.
                              large orch/v GNP 28, GNP-Crescendo 10008

BY THE WATERMELON VINE, LINDY LOU (T. S. Allen)
   10/23/40*   BC (Roy Felton, The Mills Brothers-v) 3tp/2tb/
                              5 reeds/p/g/b/d/v/vocal group

Discography: Arranger/Composer

BYE BYE BABY (L. Handman/W. Hirsch)
10/24/36   Henry Hall & the B. B. C. Dance Orch. (George Elrick-v) large orch/v 78: Columbia (E) FB1400

THE CALL OF THE FAR AWAY HILLS (M. David/V. Young)
8/30/74   Yujiro Ishihara (v) 2tp/1tb/1as/2ts/1bs/p/g/b/d/14violins/4celli/v Continental (J) C01 NOTE: Instrumental tracks recorded 8/30/74, Los Angeles; vocal added later in Japan.

CALLING ALL BARS (L. Feather)
5/18/40   Cab Calloway & His Orch. 3tp/3tb/3as/2ts/p/g/b/d CBS (F) 62950, Jazz Archives JA8

CAN'T BUY ME LOVE (J. Lennon/P. McCartney)
ca. 1966   Keely Smith (v) large orch/v Reprise RS6142

CAN'T WE BE FRIENDS (K. Swift/P. James)
1/4/54*   BC horns/strings/p/b/d

CARE (Bob Friedman)
11/71-3/72   Joe Williams (v) large orch/strings/vocal chorus/v Temponic TB29561

CATFISH ROW (BC)
5/63*   KPM Music Library 4tp/4tb/2fr. horns/5reeds/p/g/b/d NOTE: Two brief thematic transition passages for this piece were recorded at the same session. Both were arranged and composed by Carter. See notes for this session in chronological section of discography.

CHAIN GANG (S. Cooke)
1/3-4/68   Jackie Wilson (v) with the Count Basie Orch. 4tp/4tb/2as/2ts/1bs/p/g/b/d/v Brunswick BL54134

CHAMPAGNE WALTZ (B. Oakland/C. Conrad/M. Drake)
1960-1961   Stanley Wilson Orch. 28violins/4violas/9celli/3b/2harps Time S2041

CHARLESTON IS THE BEST DANCE AFTER ALL (C. Johnson/A. Porter)
1/24/28*   Charlie Johnson's Paradise Orch. 2tp/1tb/3as/cl/1ts/p/banjo/tuba/d

CHARMAINE (E. Rapee/L. Pollack)
1965   Lou Rawls (v) large orch with strings/vocal group/v Capitol T2401

CHERCHEZ LA FEMME (BC)
• 5/63*   Stanley Wilson Orch. arr: Stanley Wilson horns/strings/rhythm section

CHEROKEE (R. Noble)
5/63*   BC 1as/p/b/d/vocal group

CHERRY (D. Redman/R. Gilbert)
11/13/61*   BC 2as/2ts/p/g/b/d

CHICKFEED   (BC)
   5/7/36   Henry Hall & the B. B. C. Dance Orch.   large
   ———   orch   (B. B. C. broadcast, no known airchecks)

CHILPANCINGO   (H. Atwood/L. Herscher)
   1/48*   BC (Bob Decker, The Enchanters-v)   1tp/1tb/1as/
   ———   1ts/p/g/b/d/v/vocal group

CHINATOWN, MY CHINATOWN   (J. Schwartz/W. Jerome)
   4/29/77*   BC   3tp/1tb/2reeds/p/g/b/d
   July 1981*   BC

NOTE: This arrangement includes a transcription, played by three trumpets, of Louis Armstrong's solo from his 11/3/31 recording of "Chinatown."

CHOPSTICK BOOGIE
   11/25/47*   Freddie Slack & His Orch.   4tp/2tb/2as/2ts/1bs/
   ———   p/g/b/d

CHRISTMAS IN NEW ORLEANS   (D. Sherman/J. Van Winkle)
   9/8/55   Louis Armstrong (v) with Benny Carter's Orch.
   ———   3tp/2tb/1cl/2as/2ts/p/b/d/v   78:   Decca 29710,
                        45:   Cid (F) UM95. 504

CHRISTMAS NIGHT IN HARLEM   (R. Scott/M. Parish)
   9/8/55   Louis Armstrong (v) with Benny Carter's Orch.
   ———   3tp/2tb/1cl/2as/2ts/p/b/d/v   78:   Decca 29710,
                        45:   Cid (F) UM95. 504

CIRIBIRIBIN   (Italian; U. S. version by R. Thaler/A. Pestalozza)
   9/61   Jonah Jones with Glen Gray & the Casa Loma
   ———   Orch.   6tp/4tb/2as/2ts/1bs/p/g/b/d   Capitol
                        T1713

CLAUDIA   (BC/lyrics: A. Stillman)
   11/65   film soundtrack: A Man Called Adam   4tp/4tb/
   ———   4reeds/p/g/b/d   Reprise 6180

• 11/65   film soundtrack: A Man Called Adam   1tb/p/b/d
   ———   Reprise 6180

CLOSE YOUR EYES   (B. Petkere)
   2/60   Dakota Staton (v)   large orch with strings/v
   ———   Capitol T1427

COALITION   (BC)
   12/3/73*   BC   3tp/4tb/3as/2ts/1bs/p/g/b/d/conga
   ———

COCKTAILS FOR TWO   (Johnson/Coslow)
   11/19/40*   BC   3tp/3tb/2as/2ts/1bs/p/g/b/d
   ———

   2/2/42   Mark Warnow & His Orch. (Barry Wood-v)   3tp/
   ———   2tb/4reeds/8violins/1harp/p/g/b/d/v   78:   Victor
                        27868

   9/52*   BC with the Oscar Peterson Trio with Buddy Rich
   ———   horns/strings/p/g/b/d

Discography: Arranger/Composer

COLD COLD HEART (H. Williams)
  1965   Lou Rawls (v) large orch with strings/vocal
                    group/v Capitol T2401

COME ON BABY (A. Gottler/S. Clare/M. Pinkard)
  12/12/28*   Fletcher Henderson & His Orch. (BC-v) 2tp/1tb/
                    3reeds/p/banjo/tuba/d/v

COME ON BACK   (BC)
  3/2/66*   BC   2as/2ts/1bs/p/g/b/d

COMES LOVE (S. Stept/C. Tobias/L. Brown)
  11/56   Billy Daniels (v) accompanied by Benny Carter's
                    Orch. 4tp/4tb/2as/2ts/1bs/p/g/b/d/v   Verve
                    MGV2072

CON ALMA (D. Gillespie/Russell)
  ca. 1970   Benard Ito (v) large orch 45: Mercury 72686

CONFESSIN'   (D. Dougherty/E. Reynolds/A. Neiburg)
  4/29/77*   BC   3tp/1tb/2reeds/p/g/b/d
  4/15/78*   BC
  4/19?/78*   BC
  July 1981*   BC

CONGOROO (BC/Lucille Ostrow) also recorded as BAMBOULA
  late 1947 or early   (AFRS Jubilee #276) BC large orch
  1948*
  3/30/48*   (AFRS Jubilee #284) BC NOTE: May have been
                    announced as "Bamboula."

CONGRATULATIONS TO SOMEONE (A. Frisch/R. Alfred)
  2/60   Dakota Staton (v) large orch with strings/v
                    Capitol T1427

COTTONTAIL   (D. Ellington)
  11/15/61*   BC   2as/2ts/p/g/b/d

  12/3/73*   BC   4tp/4tb/3as/2ts/1bs/p/g/b/d
  4/8/77*   BC with the Princeton University Jazz Ensemble

  4/29/77*   BC   2tp/1tb/3reeds/p/g/b/d
  4/15/78*   BC
  4/19?/78*   BC
  July 1981*   BC

THE COURTSHIP   (BC)
  • 4/27/76*   BC, Gillespie, Inc.

  • 3/18/77*   BC

  • 11/10/79*   BC with the Princeton University Jazz Ensemble
                    arr: Steve Wexler

  July 1981*   BC   2tp/1tb/3reeds/1violin/p/b/d

  • 12/5/81*   BC

281

COW COW BOOGIE (BC/D. Raye/G. DePaul)
- 5/21/42 Freddie Slack & His Orch. (Ella Mae Morse-v) Capitol T1802, AJAZ 281
- 10/19/42 Benny Goodman & His Orch. (Peggy Lee-v) (aircheck) Jazz Society AA510
- 11/13/42 Gene Krupa & His Orch. (Anita O'Day-v) (aircheck) Fanfare LP10-110
- 7/27/43 R. A. F. Dance Orch. [The Squadronaires] (Sid Colin-v) 78: Decca F8364
- 11/3/43 Ella Fitzgerald (v) with The Ink Spots (v) Decca DL4129, MCA-2-4016, MCA Coral (G) 0082 050-2
- 3/46 Dave Bowman & His Orch. 78: Signature 28126
- 11/15/46 Chico Cristobal & His Boogie Woogie Boys 78: Blue Star (F) 6
- ca. 1948 Ella Mae Morse (v) 78: Capitol 15188
- 1955 Ray McKinley's Dixie Six (Ray McKinley-v) Grand Award 33-333
- 1955 Freddie Slack & His Orch. (Thelma Gracen-v) arr: Freddie Slack Emarcy MG36094, Wing MGW60003
- ca. 1956 Dick Hyman MGM E3536
- 4/15/58 Art Simmons Wing MGW12150, Wing SEW12505
- 1/8/61 Sir Charles Thompson Columbia CL1663, Columbia CS8463
- 1962 David Swift, with Rene Hall's Orch. arr: Rene Hall Warner Brothers B1441
- 1975 Ray Stevens (v) arr: Ray Stevens Barnaby 4009
- 1976 Charlie Byrd, Barney Kessel, Herb Ellis Concord CJ23
- ca. 1976 Blind John Davis Alligator 4709
- date unknown piano roll played by J. Lawrence Cook Q. R. S. Word Roll 7739

CRACK UP (Coleman/Leigh)
11/65 film soundtrack: A Man Called Adam 1tp/1tb/p/b/d Reprise 6180

CRAZY RHYTHM (Meyer/Kahn/Caesar)
4/28/37* Coleman Hawkins & His All Star Jam Band 2as/2ts/p/g/b/d

Discography: Arranger/Composer

11/13/61*   BC   2as/2ts/p/g/b/d

CRUISIN' (BC)
• 4/23/52*   (AFRS Jubilee #366) BC

7/26/52*   BC   1tp/1tb/3reeds/p/g/b/d

CUANDO CALIENTE EL SOL (C. and M. Rigual)
5/63*   BC   1as/p/b/d/vocal group

CUDDLE UP, HUDDLE UP (BC)
1/21/41*   BC   3tp/3tb/3as/2ts/p/g/b/d

CUTTIN' TIME (BC)
12/12/45*   BC   4tp/4tb/2as/2ts/1bs/p/g/b/d   NOTE: Appears on Capitol LP under title "Forever Blues."
ca. 7/46*   (AFRS Jubilee #193) BC

DADDY DADDY (S. Churchill/I. Berman)
2/27/45*   Savannah Churchill & Her All Star Orch.   4tp/4tb/5reeds/p/g/b/d/v

DANCE WITH ME (Rome/Hornez/Lopez)
5/63*   Stanley Wilson Orch.   horns/strings/vocal group/rhythm section

DAY DREAM (B. Strayhorn)
8/13/79   Sarah Vaughan (v)   1flute/1ts/9violins/3viola/2celli/p/g/b/d/v   NOTE: Recorded for Pablo--unissued.

DEBBIE'S DEBUT
date unknown   Annie Malone (v)   ?/v   45: Kady 45102

DEDICATED TO YOU (S. Chaplin/S. Cahn/H. Zaret)
2/60   Dakota Staton (v)   large orch with strings/v   Capitol T1427

DEE BLUES (BC)
• 12/31/30*   The Chocolate Dandies

DEVIL'S HOLIDAY (BC)   also appears as ON A HOLIDAY
10/16/33*   BC   3tp/3tb/3as/1ts/p/g/b/d
1/21/35   Charlie Barnet & His Orch.   RCA Bluebird AXM2-5526   NOTE: Recorded as "On a Holiday."
4/8/38   Bunny Berigan (probably aircheck)   Jazz Archives JA11
6/2/38   Charlie Barnet & His Orch.   (aircheck)
6/27/38   Bunny Berigan (Thesaurus transcription 563)   IAJRC 5, Collector's Classics CC15, Forsgate Products SAP7500

1/7/47   Charlie Spivak & His Orch.   (AFRS One Night Stand #1259)
1/12/47   Charlie Spivak & His Orch.   (AFRS One Night Stand #1273)

2/12/47 Charlie Spivak & His Orch. (AFRS One Night Stand #1252) Swing Era LP1017

NOTE: The arrangements for Charlie Spivak are probably the same as the five listed above them. The Whiteman Archive at Williams College has an arrangement of this title from the Whiteman book. Carter does not recognize it as his own arrangement. There are no known recordings.

DIRTY HANDS, DIRTY FACE (J. Monaco/E. Leslie)
NOTE: <u>Melody Maker</u> (May 30, 1936) reports that Carter was commissioned by Henry Hall to arrange this tune. It may have been broadcast by Hall and the B.B.C. Dance Orchestra. There are no known airchecks.

DISCOVERY (BC)
<u>5/63</u>* KPM Music Library 4tp/4tb/2fr. horns/5reeds/p/g/b/d NOTE: See notes for this session in chronological section of discography.

DO I NEED YOU (D. Wyatt)
<u>1968</u> Don Wyatt (v) large orch with strings/v NOTE: Unissued

DO YOU BELIEVE IN LOVE AT SIGHT (G. Kahn/T. Fiorito)
<u>9/8/31</u>* McKinney's Cotton Pickers (Quentin Jackson-v) 3tp/2tb/3reeds/p/g/b/d/v

DOMINO (Raye/Plante/Ferrari)
<u>5/63</u>* Stanley Wilson Orch. horns/strings/vocal group/rhythm section

DON'T BURN THE CANDLE AT BOTH ENDS (BC/lyrics: I. Gordon)
• <u>12/8/47</u> Louis Jordan & His Tympany Five (Martha Davis-v) 78: Decca 24483

DON'T COME TOO SOON (BC under pseudonym "Johnny Gomez"/lyrics: I. Gordon)
• <u>4/49</u> Julia Lee (v) & Her Boy Friends 45: Capitol 1111

DON'T EXPLAIN
<u>6/60</u> Dakota Staton (v) large orch with strings/v Capitol T1597

DON'T GET AROUND MUCH ANYMORE (D. Ellington/B. Russell)
<u>8/64</u>* BC 2ss/4as/3ts/2bs/p/g/b/d

DON'T LEAD ME ON (J. Greene/J. Anz)
<u>1953</u> Ernie Andrews (v) with Benny Carter's Orch. large orch/v 78: Trend 68, LP: GNP 28
NOTE: Although the discographies list two versions of this title by Ernie Andrews, one from 1953 (Trend 68) and one from 1957 (GNP 28), both discs contain the same performance, probably recorded in 1953.

Discography: Arranger/Composer 285

DON'T LEAVE ME NOW (Westray/Freed)
6/60 Dakota Staton (v) large orch/v Capitol T1490

DON'T SCREAM, DON'T SHOUT (Gabriel Jones)
9/22/49* Joe Robinson (v) with Benny Carter's Orch.
1tp/1as/1ts/1bs/p/g/b/d/v

DON'T WORRY 'BOUT ME (R. Bloom/T. Koehler)
2/15-16/79 Ella Fitzgerald (v) with Count Basie's Orch.
4tp/4tb/5reeds/p/g/b/d/v Pablo Today 2312-132

DON'T YOU FEEL MY LEG see DON'T YOU MAKE ME HIGH

DON'T YOU MAKE ME HIGH (D. Barker/K. Harris)
12/22/74* Maria Muldaur (v) 2tp/1tb/1as/1ts/1bs/p/g/b/d/v

DOOZY (BC)
11/15/61* BC 2as/2ts/p/g/b/d

1/22-24/62 Louis Bellson Orch. 5tp/3tb/1fr. horn/1tuba/2as/
2ts/1bs/p/g/b/d/vib Roulette R52087, Roulette
(E) 2934-020

3/4/66* BC 2as/2ts/1bs/p/g/b/d
11/10/73* BC

7/2/72* BC 5tp/4tb/3as/2ts/1bs/p/g/b/d

• 10/22/73* BC

12/3/73* BC 4tp/4tb/3as/2ts/1bs/p/g/b/d
4/8/77* BC with the Princeton University Jazz Ensemble

12/22/74* Maria Muldaur 2tp/1tb/2as/1ts/1bs/p/g/b/d
NOTE: This is instrumental feature for band.
4/15/78* BC

DREAM CASTLE (BC)
5/5/46* BC large orch

DREAM LULLABY (BC)
12/13/34* BC 3tp/2tb/1cl/2as/1ts/p/g/b/d

DU BIST DIE LIEBE (Olias/Schwabach/Neiburg)
1965 Lou Rawls (v) large orch/strings/vocal group/v
Capitol T2401

EARLY SESSION HOP (Teddy Wilson/B. Harding)
9/11/39* Lionel Hampton & His Orch. 1tp/1as/3ts/p/g/b/
d/vib

EASY MONEY (C. Austin)
12/12/28* Fletcher Henderson & His Orch. 2tp/1tb/2as/c1/
1ts/p/banjo/tuba/d

EASY MONEY (BC)
11/1-2/61* Count Basie & His Orch. 4tp/3tb/2as/2ts/1bs/p/
g/b/d

```
         8/10/62              Count Basie & His Orch.  NOTE: Recorded live
                              in Stockholm--unissued.
        11/9/68*              BC with Henri Chaix & His Orch.  NOTE: Sim-
                              ilar arrangement but performed by 1tp/1tb/2as/
                              1ts/1bs/p/b/d

       • 2/11/76*             BC

       • 6/19/76*             (two versions) BC

       • 6/24/76*             BC

       • 3/18/77*             BC

       • 4/18/81*             BC

       • 11/28/81*            BC

       • 12/4/81*             BC

       • 12/5/81*             BC
```

ECHOES OF HARLEM   (D. Ellington)
   9/61   Jonah Jones with Glen Gray & the Casa Loma
                       Orch. 6tp/4tb/2as/2ts/1bs/p/g/b/d Capitol T1713

EVEN WHEN YOU CRY   (Q. Jones/M. Bergman/A. Bergman)
   1/3-4/68   Jackie Wilson (v) with the Count Basie Orch.
                       4tp/4tb/2as/2ts/1bs/p/g/b/d/v Brunswick
                       BL54134

EVERYBODY SHUFFLE   (BC)
   10/13/33   Joe Venuti & His Orch. 3tp/2tb/4reeds/p/g/b/d
                       RCA (F) FPM1-7016
   12/13/34*   BC

EVERYBODY'S SOMEBODY'S FOOL   (Hampton/Adams/Adams)
   6/60   Dakota Staton (v) large orch/v Capitol T1490

EV'RY GOODBYE AIN'T GONE   (BC)
   1/21/41*   BC 3tp/3tb/3as/2ts/p/g/b/d

THE FABLE OF A FOOL   (BC)
   8/31/39*   BC 3tp/3tb/3as/2ts/p/g/b/d NOTE: On most
                       issues as "Favor of a Fool."

FAIRY TALES   (G. Shearing)
   8/64*   BC 2ss/4as/3ts/2bs/p/g/b/d

FALLING IN LOVE WITH LOVE   (Rodgers/Hart)
   1962   Sarah Vaughan (v) 4tp/4tb/5reeds/p/g/b/d/vib/v
                       Roulette R(S)52092, Roulette (E) 2682-043

FANTASTIC, THAT'S YOU   (G. Cates/G. Douglas)
   3/2/66*   BC 2as/2ts/1bs/p/g/b/d

FAREWELL BLUES   (Mares/Rappolo/Schoebel)
   3/7/38*   BC 2as/2ts/p/g/b/d

Discography: Arranger/Composer

THE FAVOR OF A FOOL   see   FABLE OF A FOOL

FEASANT PHEATHERS   (BC)
- 11/10/79*   BC with the Princeton University Jazz Ensemble

FEBRUARY FIESTA   (H. Schaefer)
late 1958 or early   BC 4tp/3tb/5reeds/p/g/b/d
1959*

FEUDIN' AND FIGHTIN'   (Dubin/Lane/Lane)
1964   Ray Charles (v) & the Raelets 5tp/3tb/2as/2ts/
                       1bs/p/g/b/d/v ABC Paramount 495

FIRST THINGS FIRST
6/60   Dakota Staton (v) large orch with strings/v 45:
                       Capitol 4465

FISH FRY   (BC)
1/30/40*   BC 3tp/3tb/2as/2ts/p/g/b/d
3/24/43*   BC
May or later 1943*   (AFRS Basic Library P-33) BC
5/8/45*   (AFRS Jubilee #132) BC
ca. 7/47*   (AFRS Jubilee #248) BC

FLAMINGO   (T. Grouya/E. Anderson)
12/31/53*   BC horns/strings/p/b/d

FLOWER DRUM SONG [film title]   (Rodgers/Hammerstein)
                       NOTE: Carter played in the orchestra and as-
                       sisted in the orchestration of parts of this 1961
                       production. The soundtrack is on Decca DL79098
                       (later labelled MCA2069).

A FOGGY DAY   (G. and I. Gershwin)
1/22-24/62   Louis Bellson Orch. 5tp/3tb/1fr. horn/1tuba/2as/
                       2ts/1bs/p/g/b/d/vib Roulette R25167

THE FOLKS WHO LIVE ON THE HILL   (J. Kern/O. Hammerstein II)
6/60   Dakota Staton (v) large orch with strings/v
                       Capitol T1597

FOR SALE - ONE BROKEN HEART   (Hoffman/Saronne)
early 1950's   Ruby Lane (v) large orch with strings 45: Col-
                       pix CP139

FOR YOUR PRECIOUS LOVE   (A. Brooks/R. Brooks/J. Butler)
1/3-4/68   Jackie Wilson (v) with the Count Basie Orch.
                       4tp/4tb/2as/2ts/1bs/p/g/b/d/v 45: Brunswick
                       BR55365, LP: Brunswick BL54134

FOREVER BLUE   (BC)
                       NOTE: This piece by Carter may have been re-
                       corded by his orchestra in 1945 but was never re-
                       leased. A recording for Capitol done on 12/12/45*
                       by Benny Carter was labelled "Forever Blues"
                       but is actually his composition "Cuttin' Time."

FREE LOVE   (BC/E. Sampson)
11/6/33*   Mezz Mezzrow & His Orch.   3tp/1tb/2as/1ts/p/
                    g/b/d

FRIENDLESS   (BC/lyrics: P. Vandervoort)
1/63   Sarah Vaughan (v) with orchestra directed by
                    Benny Carter   4tb/20strings/p/g/b/d/v   Roulette
                    R(S)52104

FRIENDLY ISLANDS   (BC--words & music)
• 1959   Ethel Azama (v)   arr: Paul Conrad   Liberty
                    LRP3104

FUNKY BROADWAY   (A. Christian)
1/3-4/68   Jackie Wilson (v) with the Count Basie Orch.
                    4tp/4tb/2as/2ts/1bs/p/g/b/d/v   Brunswick
                    BL54134

THE GANG'S ALL HERE [film title]
                    NOTE: For Carter's work on this film see the
                    individual title "No Love, No Nothin.'"

A GARDEN IN THE RAIN   (C. Gibbons/J. Dyrenforth)
1962   Sarah Vaughan (v)   4tp/4tb/5reeds/p/g/b/d/vib/v
                    Roulette R(S)52092, Roulette (E) 2682-043

GEE, AIN'T I GOOD TO YOU   (D. Redman/A. Razaf)
1965   Lou Rawls (v)   2tp/4tb/2reeds/p/g/b/d/v   Capitol
                    T2273

12/22/74*   Maria Muldaur (v)   2tp/1tb/1as/1ts/1bs/p/g/b/d/v

GEORGIA ON MY MIND   (H. Carmichael)
8/18/52*   BC   3tp/3tb/2as/2ts/1bs/p/g/b/d

GIN AND JIVE   (BC)   also entitled SAVOY STAMPEDE
mid 6/36*   BC   2tp/2tb/2as/2ts/p/g/b/d
1/11-16/37*   BC
4/17/39*   BC
6/29/39*   BC   (as Savoy Stampede)
10/9/39*   BC   (as Savoy Stampede)

THE GIRL FROM IPANEMA   (Jobim/de Moraes/Gimbel)
8/64*   BC   2ss/4as/3ts/2bs/p/g/b/d

1964   Harry Edison with Benny Carter's Orch.   1tp/4tb/
                    14strings/1harp/p/g/b/d   Vee-Jay VJS3065

THE GIRL UPSTAIRS   (A. Newman)
1955   Alfred Newman & His Orch.   large orch with
                    strings   Decca DL8123

GLOAMING   (T. Ehrling)
9/12/36*   BC   3tp/2tb/3as/1ts/p/g/b/d

GO NOW   (BC)
11/65   film soundtrack: A Man Called Adam   1tp/1tb/p/
                    b/d   Reprise 6180

Discography: Arranger/Composer

GOD BLESS THE CHILD (A. Herzog, Jr./B. Holiday)
4/29/77*   BC 2tp/1tb/3reeds/p/g/b/d

GOD BLESS YOU (Bob Friedman)
11/71-3/72   Joe Williams (v) large orch with strings/v
                        Temponic TB29561

GOIN' ON (BC)
10/30-31/61*   Count Basie & His Orch. 4tp/3tb/2as/2ts/1bs/p/
                        g/b/d

GONNA BUILD A MOUNTAIN (L. Bricusse/A. Newley)
1965   Pat Dorn Orch. 4tp/4tb/2as/2ts/1bs/p/g/b/d
                        45: Capitol test pressing (may have been issued
                        commercially)

GOOD FOR NOTHIN' JOE (R. Bloom)
Jan.-Feb. 1943*   film soundtrack: Stormy Weather (Lena Horne-v)
                        large orch with strings/v

GOODBYE BLUES (BC)
12/4/30*   The Chocolate Dandies (BC-v) 1tp/1tb/1as/1ts/p/
                        g/b/v

GOT ANOTHER SWEETIE NOW (J. Harrison)
12/31/30*   The Chocolate Dandies (Jimmy Harrison-v) 1tp/
                        1tb/1as/1ts/p/g/tuba/v

GOT THAT FEELING (Bob Friedman)
11/71-3/72   Joe Williams (v) large orch/v Temponic
                        TB29561

GOTTA GO HOME (BC)
5/63*   KPM Music Library 4tp/4tb/2fr. horns/5reeds/p/
                        g/b/d NOTE: See notes for this session in
                        chronological section of discography.

GREAT DAY (V. Youmans/B. Rose/E. Eliscu)
1962   Sarah Vaughan (v) 4tp/4tb/5reeds/p/g/b/d/vib/v
                        Roulette R(S)52092, Roulette (E) 2682-043

THE GREAT LIE (Lester Young)
8/64*   BC 2ss/4as/3ts/2bs/p/g/b/d

GREEN DOLPHIN STREET see ON GREEN DOLPHIN STREET

GREEN WINE (BC/lyrics: L. Feather) see also VINHO VERDE
• 2/11/76*   BC

• 3/18/77*   BC

GUIDING LIGHT (BC/lyrics: Romola Robinson) [copyrighted as MY GUID-
ING LIGHT]
• 1960   Dihann Carroll (v) arr: Al Cohn 45: United
                        Artists UA142X

GUMSHOE (BC)
1/22-24/62   Louis Bellson Orch. 5tp/3tb/1fr. horn/1tuba/2as/

                            2ts/1bs/p/g/b/d/vib Roulette R52087, Roulette
                            (E) 2934-020

THE GUNS OF NAVARONE [film soundtrack]
                            NOTE: For Carter's work on this film see the
                            individual title "Yassu."

THE GYPSY   (B. Reid)
    5/63*   BC 1as/p/b/d/vocal group

THE GYPSY IN MY SOUL (M. Jaffe/C. Boland)
    ca. 1959   Dean Jones (v) ?/v MGM K12462

HALLELUJAH (V. Youmans/L. Robin/C. Grey)
    11/56   Billy Daniels (v) accompanied by Benny Carter's
                            Orch. 4tp/4tb/2as/2ts/1bs/p/g/b/d/v Verve
                            MGV2072

HAPPY AS THE DAY IS LONG (H. Arlen/T. Koehler)
    9/11/34   Fletcher Henderson & His Orch. 3tp/2tb/1cl/2as/
                            1ts/p/g/b/d Decca DL9228, MCA 1318, Time-
                            Life STL-J10
    7/29/71   Time-Life series The Swing Era (Billy May-lead-
                            er) Time-Life STL340 NOTE: In the Time-Life
                            series significant swing era performances are
                            "recreated" including imitations of the solos
                            present on the original recordings.

THE HAPPY ONES (Bob Friedman)
    11/71-3/72   Carmen McRae (v) large orch/v Temponic
                            TB29562

A HARD DAY'S NIGHT (J. Lennon/P. McCartney)
    ca. 1966   Keely Smith (v) large orch with strings/v Re-
                            prise RS6142

HARLEM ON PARADE (BC/lyrics: Redd Evans)
  • 1/23/42   Gene Krupa & His Orch. (Anita O'Day-v) 78:
                            Okeh 6607, LP: Ajax 167

A HEART MUST LEARN TO CRY (D. Tiomkin/P. F. Webster)
    ca. 1966   Irma Curry (v) large orch/v 45: Vee-Jay 669

HEEBIE JEEBIES (B. Atkins)
    3/30/31*   Chick Webb & His Orch. 3tp/1tb/2as/cl/1ts/p/
                            g/b/d
    6/26/31   Mills Blue Rhythm Band (Chick Bullock-v) RCA
                            (F) 741.045

HEELS UP (BC)
    5/63*   KPM Music Library 4tp/4tb/2fr. horns/5reeds/p/
                            g/b/d/xylophone NOTE: See notes for this ses-
                            sion in chronological section of discography.

HELLS BELLS (A. Kassel)
    date unknown   Annie Malone (v) ?/v 45: Kady 45102

Discography: Arranger/Composer

HERE IT IS TOMORROW AGAIN
    10/31/38*   Teddy Wilson & His Orch. (Billie Holiday-v)
                            1tp/1tb/2as/2ts/p/g/b/d/v

HERE'S THAT RAINY DAY (J. Van Heusen/J. Burke)
    1971   Pearl Bailey (v) 4tp/4tb/5reeds/p/g/b/d/strings/v
                            RCA LSP4529

HE'S GOT TWO LEFT HANDS see TWO LEFT HANDS

HEY LAWDY MAMA (Easton)
    6/60   Dakota Staton (v) 1tp/1reed/p/g/b/d/v Capitol
                            T1597

HEY THERE (Adler/Ross)
    Mar. 30-Apr. 1   Pearl Bailey (v) 4tp/4tb/5reeds/p/g/b/d/v
    1965*

HIGH SOCIETY LIMBO (BC)
    1965   Pat Dorn Orch. 4tp/4tb/2as/2ts/1bs/p/g/b/d 45:
                            Capitol test pressing (may have been issued com-
                            mercially)

HOBNOBBIN' (BC)
    4/8/77   Princeton University Jazz Ensemble 5tp/4tb/
                            5reeds/p/g/b/d (private tape--concert) NOTE:
                            This Carter composition was published in the
                            Repertory Stage Band Series.

HOLD ME TIGHT, I'M FALLING
    ca. 5/36   Henry Hall & the B. B. C. Dance Orch. large
                            orch (B. B. C. broadcast, no known airchecks)

HOLLYRIDGE DRIVE (BC)
    10/14/47*   Red Norvo's Nine 1cornet/1as/2ts/p/g/b/d
    late 1947 or early   (AFRS Jubilee #276) BC
    1948*

A HOME IN THE CLOUDS (BC/B. Goodman/B. Henderson/K. Parker)
    ● 2/9/39   Benny Goodman & His Orch. (Martha Tilton-v)
                            Jazum 19

    ● 5/1/39   Dick Todd (v), The Three Reasons (v. group)
                            Victor AXM2-5509

    5/13/39*   BC (Mercedes Carter-v) 3tp/3tb/2as/2ts/p/g/b/
                            d/v
    7/24/39*   BC (Dell St. John-v)

    ● 5/17/39   Ray Herbeck & His Music with Romance (Betty
                            Bronson, Kirby Brooks-v) 78: Vocalion 4876

    ● 5/22/39   Shep Fields & His Rippling Rhythm (Hal Derwin-v)
                            78: Bluebird B-10291

    ● 5/26/39   Jimmy Dorsey & His Orch. (Helen O'Connell-v)
                            78: Decca 2522

• 3/69   Bobby Henderson   Chiaroscuro 122

• 3/69   Bobby Henderson   Halcyon (also labelled Chiaroscuro) 102

HONEYSUCKLE ROSE   (T. Waller/A. Razaf)
4/28/37*   Coleman Hawkins & His All Star Jam Band   2as/2ts/p/g/b/d

4/17/39*   BC   3tp/3tb/2as/2ts/p/g/b/d
4/22/39*   BC
7/24/39*   BC

1943*   Lena Horne (v) with Benny Carter's Orch.   large orch/v

11/13/61*   BC   2as/2ts/p/g/b/d

1962   Sarah Vaughan (v)   4tp/4tb/5reeds/p/g/b/d/vib/v
                           Roulette R(S)52092, Roulette (E) 2582-043

7/2/72*   BC   5tp/4tb/3as/2ts/1bs/p/g/b/d
12/3/73*   BC
10/28/78*   BC with the University of Buffalo Jazz Ensemble directed by Sam Falzone
10/28/78*   BC with the University of Buffalo Jazz Ensemble directed by Phil Sims

2/15-16/79   Ella Fitzgerald (v) with Count Basie's Orch.   4tp/4tb/5reeds/p/g/b/d/v   Pablo Today 2312-132

HONGI TONGI HOKI POKI   (BC/lyrics: A. and C. Hanson)
• 1950   Gordon MacRae (v) with the Les Baxter Chorus & Paul Weston & His Orch.   arr: Paul Weston
                           78: Capitol 1021

HOT LIPS   (H. Busse/H. Lange/L. Davis)
9/61   Jonah Jones with Glen Gray & the Casa Loma Orch.   6tp/4tb/2as/2ts/1bs/p/g/b/d   Capitol T1713

HOT TODDY   (BC)
6/9/32   Cab Calloway & His Orch.   3tp/2tb/2ts/p/g/b/d (unissued)
9/21/32   Cab Calloway & His Orch.   Collector's Classics 20
10/5/32*   BC
1932   Cab Calloway (v) & His Orch. in film: The Big Broadcast of 1932
                           NOTE: These are all probably the same arrangement.

A HOUSE IS NOT A HOME   (B. Bacharach/H. David)
1971   Pearl Bailey (v)   4tp/4tb/5reeds/p/g/b/d/strings/v
                           RCA LSP4529

A HOUSE WITH A LITTLE RED BARN   (M. Lewis/N. Hamilton)
2/14/40*   Freddie Rich & His Orch. (Rosemary Calvin-v)
                           3tp/1tb/3as/3ts/p/g/b/d/v

Discography: Arranger/Composer

HOW AM I TO KNOW? (J. King/D. Parker)
11/56 Billy Daniels (v) accompanied by Benny Carter's Orch. 1tp/4reeds/p/g/b/d/strings/v Verve MGV2072

HOW CAN YOU LOSE? (BC)
10/7/57* BC 1tp/1tb/1as/1ts/p/g/b/d

● 10/24-25/60 Art Pepper Quintet Contemporary M3602, Contemporary S7602

HOW DEEP IS THE OCEAN (I. Berlin)
ca. 1958 Lois Peters (v) 5brass/4reeds/rhythm section/strings/v 45: Decca 9-30269

HOW HIGH THE MOON (M. Lewis/N. Hamilton)
2/14/40* Freddie Rich & His Orch. (Rosemary Calvin-v) 3tp/1tb/3as/3ts/p/g/b/d/v

HOW LONG IS A MOMENT (BC/lyrics: P. Zeller)
1958* Don Evans (v) with Orch. under direction of Benny Carter 1as/p/g/b/d/v

HOW STRANGE (H. Stothart/E. Brent/G. Kahn)
5/27/39* BC (Mercedes Carter-v) 3tp/3tb/2as/2ts/p/g/b/d/v

A HUNDRED YEARS FROM TODAY (V. Young/N. Washington)
1957 Martha Davis (v) 4tp/4tb/2as/2ts/1bs/p/g/b/d/v
  NOTE: Recorded for ABC Paramount--unissued.

HURRY HURRY (BC/lyrics: R. Larkin [pseudonym for Dave Dexter])
● 10/25/43* BC (Savannah Churchill-v) arr: Frank Comstock

● 4/6/44 Christine Chatham & Her Orch. (Mabel Smith [Big Maybelle]-v) 78: Decca 8660

● 5/26/44 Lucky Millinder & His Orch. (Wynonie Harris-v) MCA (F) 510.065, MCA 1319

● 1953-1955 Pee Wee Crayton (v) 78: Imperial 5297

● 1958 Ruth Olay (v) arr: Jerry Fielding Mercury MG20390

I AIN'T GETTIN' ANY YOUNGER (BC/lyrics: A. Hanson) also entitled
I AIN'T GONNA WAIT TOO LONG
1947* Anita O'Day (v) 12 piece orch/v

● 12/30/48 Woody Herman (v) & His Orch. arr: Shorty Rogers Capitol (E) CL13060 (as I Ain't Gonna Wait Too Long)

● 1949 Martha Davis (v) Decca 48174

I AIN'T GONNA WAIT TOO LONG see I AIN'T GETTIN' ANY YOUNGER

I AIN'T GOT NOBODY (Spencer Williams)
    8/17/37*   BC   3tp/2tb/2as/2ts/p/g/b/d
    4/22/39*   BC

    1949   Debbie Andrews (v) ?/v 78: Mercury 8282
                       NOTE: Melody Maker (May 30, 1936) reports
                       that Carter was commissioned by Henry Hall to
                       arrange this tune. It may have been broadcast
                       by Hall and the B. B. C. Dance Orchestra and may
                       be the same as the arrangement recorded on 8/17/
                       37*. There are no known airchecks.

I AM YOUR DREAM (Tiomkin/Webster)
    ca. 1958*   Kitty White (v) with Benny Carter & His Orch.
                       1tb/1fr. horn/1as/p/g/b/d/v

I BELIEVE IN YOU (F. Loesser)
    8/61   Peggy Lee (v) 4tp/4tb/5reeds/p/g/b/d/v Capitol
                       T1772

    1962   Sarah Vaughan (v) 4tp/4tb/5reeds/p/g/b/d/vib/v
                       45: Roulette 4516, LP: Roulette R(S)52092,
                       Roulette (E) 2682-043

I CAN'T ESCAPE FROM YOU (L. Robin/R. Whiting)
    5/21/44*   BC   4tp/3tb/2as/2ts/1bs/p/g/b/d

I CAN'T GET STARTED (V. Duke/I. Gershwin)
    12/18/42*   (AFRS Jubilee #4) BC 4tp/3tb/2as/2ts/p/g/b/d
                       NOTE: Probably same arrangement as two below.
    5/21/44*   BC
    Apr.-May 1946*   (AFRS Jubilee #184) BC

    3/24/43*   BC large orch

    2/60   Dakota Staton (v) large orch with strings/v
                       Capitol T1427

    9/61   Jonah Jones with Glen Gray & the Casa Loma
                       Orch. 6tp/4tb/2as/2ts/1bs/p/g/b/d Capitol T1713

    7/2/72*   BC 5tp/4tb/3as/2ts/1bs/p/g/b/d
    12/3/73*   BC
    4/8/77*   BC with the Princeton University Jazz Ensemble
    10/28/78*   BC with the University of Buffalo Jazz Ensemble
                       directed by Sam Falzone
    10/28/78*   BC with the University of Buffalo Jazz Ensemble
                       directed by Phil Sims
                       NOTE: Ending differs slightly on University of
                       Buffalo recordings.

I CAN'T GIVE YOU ANYTHING BUT LOVE (J. McHugh/D. Fields)
    Jan.-Feb. 1943*   film soundtrack: Stormy Weather (Lena Horne,
                       Bill Robinson-v) large orch with strings/v/vocal
                       group

    1962   Sarah Vaughan (v) 4tp/4tb/5reeds/p/g/b/d/vib/v
                       Roulette R(S)52092, Roulette (E) 2682-043

Discography: Arranger/Composer

I COVER THE WATERFRONT   (G. Green/E. Heyman)
4/30/46*   BC   large orch
ca. July 1946*   (AFRS Jubilee #193) BC

I CRIED FOR YOU   (G. Arnheim/A. Lyman/A. Freed)
5/13/39*   BC (Mercedes Carter-v) 3tp/3tb/2as/2ts/p/g/b/d/v

I DIDN'T LIKE IT THE FIRST TIME   (BC under pseudonym "Johnny Gomez"/lyrics: I. Gordon)
• 11/13/47*   Julia Lee (v) & Her Boy Friends   arr: Dave Cavanaugh 1tb/1as/1ts/p/g/b/d/v

I DIDN'T SAY YES (I DIDN'T SAY NO)   (O. Harbach/J. Kern)
1956   Abbey Lincoln (v) large orch/v 45: Liberty F55035

I DON'T KNOW WHAT KIND OF BLUES I'VE GOT   (D. Ellington)
1964   Harry Edison with Benny Carter's Orch. 1tp/4tb/14strings/1harp/p/g/b/d Vee-Jay VJS3065

I DON'T WANT IT NO MORE   (BC under pseudonym "Johnny Gomez"/lyrics: B. Strother, B. Ide)
• 12/14/48*   Clarence Clump (v) with Orch. NOTE: Clarence Clump is a pseudonym for Benny Carter.

I GOT IT BAD   (D. Ellington/P. F. Webster)
8/14/79   Zoot Sims 4tp/4tb/2as/2ts/1bs/p/g/b/d Pablo Today 2312-120 NOTE: This arrangement was written for Sarah Vaughan, but at session Sims substituted as featured soloist.

I GOT RHYTHM   (G. and I. Gershwin)
3/27/36   Henry Hall & the B.B.C. Dance Orch. large orch (B.B.C. broadcast, no known airchecks)

I GOTTA GO   (BC/lyrics: Spencer Williams)
mid 6/36*   BC (Elisabeth Welch-v) 3tp/2tb/4reeds/p/g/b/d/v

I HAVEN'T GOT ANYTHING BETTER TO DO   (P. Vance/L. Pockriss)
1968   Carmen McRae (v) large orch with strings/v Atlantic SD8165

I LET A SONG GO OUT OF MY HEART   (D. Ellington/Mills/Nemo)
8/14/79   Zoot Sims 4tp/4tb/2as/2ts/1bs/p/g/b/d Pablo Today 2312-120 NOTE: This arrangement was written for Sarah Vaughan, but at session Sims substituted as featured soloist.

I LIKE A SHUFFLE BEAT   (P. Vandervoort)
1954   Jimmie Maddin (v) & His Orch. small orch/v 78: Skyway 104

I LONG FOR YOU   (K. E. Beam)
date unknown   Arthur Lee Simpkins (v) p/vib/g/b/d/v/vocal group 45: Miranda 4-56-14

I LOST YOU
1949   Debbie Andrews (v) ?/v 78: Mercury 8282

I LOVE YOU FOR THAT (Fischer/Carey)
   ca. 1951   Frankie Laine (v) & Patti Page (v) with Harry Geller Orch.   large orch/v   78: Mercury 5442

I NEVER KNEW (Fiorito/Kahn)
   10/10/33*   The Chocolate Dandies   2tp/1tb/1as/1ts/p/g/b/d

   5/7/36   Henry Hall & the B. B. C. Dance Orch.   large orch   (B. B. C. broadcast, no known airchecks)

I NEVER LOVED A MAN   see   I NEVER LOVED A WOMAN

I NEVER LOVED A WOMAN   (R. Shannon) [original title: I NEVER LOVED A MAN]
   1/3-4/68   Jackie Wilson (v) with Count Basie's Orch.   4tp/4tb/2as/2ts/1bs/p/g/b/d/v   Brunswick BL54134

I NEVER MENTION YOUR NAME
   1944*   (AFRS Basic Library P-238)   BC (Savannah Churchill-v)   large orch/v

I NEVER MET A STRANGER (D. Redman)
   1971   Pearl Bailey (v)   4tp/4tb/5reeds/p/g/b/d/strings/v   RCA LSP4529

I RESOLVE (Sourwine/Cunningham/Whitcup)
   date unknown   Arthur Lee Simpkins (v)   p/vib/g/b/d/v/vocal group   45: Miranda 4-56-13

I SAID NO (J. Styne/F. Loesser)
   9/29/70   Mrs. Miller (v)   2tp/2tb/2as/1ts/1bs/p/g/b/d/v   45: Mrs. Miller Records (no issue number)

I SHOULDA QUIT WHEN I WAS AHEAD (Livingston/Evans)
   Mar. 30-Apr. 1 1965*   Pearl Bailey (v)   4tp/4tb/5reeds/p/g/b/d/v

I STILL LOVE HIM SO   (BC) [also recorded under title I'D LOVE HIM SO]
   • 3/28/51   Roy Eldridge Quintet   Inner City IC7012 (as I'd Love Him So)

   • 3/23/55*   Roy Eldridge - Benny Carter Sextet

   • 1/16/76   Roy Eldridge   Pablo 2310-766

   • 2/11/76*   BC

I STOLE DE WEDDING BELL   (BC/lyrics: P. Vandervoort)
   1954   Jimmie Maddin (v) & His Orch.   small orch/v   78: Skyway 104

I SURRENDER DEAR (H. Barris/G. Clifford)
   5/21/44*   BC   4tp/3tb/2as/2ts/p/g/b/d
   6/12/44*   (AFRS Jubilee #83?)   BC
   ca. July 1946*   (AFRS Jubilee #205)   BC
   2/17/72   Time-Life series The Swing Era (Billy May-leader)   Time-Life STL353   NOTE: This is a recreation of Carter's 5/21/44* performance including

Discography: Arranger/Composer   297

                              imitations of the solos. Carter's trumpet solo
                              is played by Joe Graves.

I WANNA BE AROUND (J. Mercer)
   8/64*   BC 2ss/4as/3ts/2bs/p/g/b/d

I WANT TO HOLD YOUR HAND (Lennon/McCartney)
   ca. 1966   Keely Smith (v) large orch with strings/v Reprise RS6142

I WAS MADE TO LOVE HER (H. Cosby/L. Hardaway/S. Wonder/S. Moy)
   1/3-4/68   Jackie Wilson (v) with Count Basie's Orch. 4tp/4tb/2as/2ts/1bs/p/g/b/d/v Brunswick BL54134

I WON'T WORRY
   6/60   Dakota Staton (v) large orch with strings/v Capitol T1597

I'D LOVE HIM SO   see I STILL LOVE HIM SO

I'D RATHER BE A ROOSTER (BC/lyrics: P. Vance)
• ca. 1949   Scat Man Crothers (v) 78: London 17008

IF DREAMS COME TRUE (E. Sampson/B. Goodman)
   3/2/66*   BC 2as/2ts/1bs/p/g/b/d
   11/10/73*   BC

IF I CAN'T HAVE YOU (BC--words & music)
   5/5/46*   BC (Candy Ross-v) large orch/v

   9/22/49*   Joe Robinson with Benny Carter's Orch. 1tp/1as/1ts/1bs/p/g/b/d/v

IF I HAD MY LIVE TO LIVE OVER (Tobias/Jaffe/Vincent)
   1965   Lou Rawls (v) 2tp/4tb/2reeds/p/g/b/d/v Capitol T2273

IF I HAD YOU (I. Berlin)
   1/63   Sarah Vaughan (v) 4fr. horns/p/g/b/d/1tuba/v Roulette R(S)52104

IF I LOVE AGAIN (B. Oakland/J. P. Murray)
   6/60   Dakota Staton (v) large orch/v Capitol T1490

IF IT'S THE LAST THING I DO (S. Cahn/S. Chaplin)
   1965   Lou Rawls (v) 2tp/4tb/2reeds/p/g/b/d/v Capitol T2273

IF ONLY I COULD READ YOUR MIND (BC/L. Feather)
   mid 6/36*   BC 3tp/2tb/2as/2ts/p/g/b/d

IF YOU GO (Parsons/Emer)
   5/63*   Stanley Wilson Orch. horns/strings/rhythm section

I'LL BE AROUND (A. Wilder)
   12/31/53*   BC horns/strings/p/b/d

I'LL BE HERE WITH YOU   (BC--words & music)
  • 1968   Billy Eckstine (v)   arr: Jimmy Jones   Motown MS677

I'LL BE YOUR BRIDE AGAIN   (G. Steinman)
  ca. 1958   Lois Peters (v) with the Ravenscroft Singers & Orch.   5brass/4woodwinds/rhythm section/strings/v/vocal group   45:   Decca 9-30269

I'LL CLOSE MY EYES   (B. Reid/B. Kaye)
  6/60   Dakota Staton (v)   large orch/v   Capitol T1490

I'LL NEVER BE THE SAME   (Kahn/Malneck/Signorelli)
  1/63   Sarah Vaughan (v)   4tp/4tb/2as/2ts/1bs/p/g/b/d/v   Roulette R(S)52104

I'LL NEVER FAIL YOU   (V. Mizzy/I. Taylor)
  11/9/38*   Teddy Wilson & His Orch.   (Billie Holiday-v)   1tp/1tb/2as/2ts/p/g/b/d/v

I'LL NEVER GIVE IN   (Freddy Johnson)
  3/24/37*   BC & the Ramblers   2tp/1tb/2as/2ts/p/b/d

I'LL NEVER LEAVE YOU
  1968   Don Wyatt (v)   large orch with strings/v   (unissued)

I'LL NEVER PASS THIS WAY AGAIN   (Bob Friedman)
  11/71-3/72   Carmen McRae (v)   large orch/v   Temponic TB29562

I'LL PLANT MY OWN TREE   (D. and A. Previn)
  1967   film soundtrack: Valley of the Dolls   (unidentified female-v)   large orch with strings/v   Twentieth Century Fox   S4196

I'LL REMEMBER APRIL   (DePaul/Johnson/Raye)
  late 1958 or early   BC   4tp/3tb/5reeds/p/g/b/d
  1959*

I'LL SEE YOU IN MY DREAMS   (I. Jones/G. Kahn)
  1965   Lou Rawls (v)   large orch with strings/vocal group/v   Capitol T2401

ILL WIND   (Koehler/Arlen)
  10/16/41*   BC   3tp/3tb/3as/2ts/p/g/b/d
  probably late 1942*   (AFRS Basic Library of Popular Music P-8)   BC   (Savannah Churchill-v)
                        NOTE: Probably same arrangement as the three others.
  4/10/43*   BC
  May or later 1943*   (AFRS Basic Library P-33)   BC

I'M A LUCKY GUY   (Bob Friedman)
  11/71-3/72   Joe Williams (v)   large orch/v   Temponic TB29561

I'M A THREE TIME LOSER   (BC/lyrics: I. Gordon)
  • 9/22/47*   Joe Alexander (v)

Discography: Arranger/Composer

I'M A WOMAN   (J. Lieber/M. Stoller)
7/62   Peggy Lee (v)   1tp/1ts/p/g/b/d/v   45: Capitol
                4888, LP: Capitol SM386, Capitol STC L576

I'M ALONE WITH YOU   see   LONESOME NIGHTS

I'M ALWAYS DRUNK IN SAN FRANCISCO   (T. Wolf)
1968   Carmen McRae (v)   large orch with strings/v
                Atlantic SD8165

I'M BEGINNING TO SEE THE LIGHT   (Ellington/Hodges/James)
July 1981*   BC   2tp/1tb/3reeds/1violin/p/b/d

I'M COMING VIRGINIA   (D. Heywood)
3/7/38*   BC   2as/2ts/p/g/b/d

4/17/39*   BC   3tp/3tb/2as/2ts/p/g/b/d   NOTE: Saxophone
                arrangement similar to 3/7/38* above.
5/6/39*   BC   (Mercedes Carter-v)

7/22/57*   BC   1tp/1tb/1ts/p/g/b/d

I'M FOREVER BLOWING BUBBLES   (J. Kenbrovin/J. Kellette)
2/14/40*   Freddie Rich & His Orch.   3tp/1tb/3as/3ts/p/g/
                b/d

I'M GETTING SENTIMENTAL OVER YOU   (G. Bassman/N. Washington)
9/11/34   The Modernists [Benny Goodman & Orch.] (Tony
                Sacco-v)   3tp/2tb/1cl/2as/1ts/p/g/b/d   Sunbeam
                SB135, Columbia Special Products P2A 12020

2/15-16/79   Ella Fitzgerald (v) with Count Basie's Orch.
                4tp/4tb/5reeds/p/g/b/d/v   Pablo Today 2312-132

I'M GONNA LIVE TIL I DIE   (A. Hoffman/W. Kent/M. Curtis)
1962   Sarah Vaughan (v)   4tp/4tb/5reeds/p/g/b/d/vib/v
                Roulette R(S)52092, Roulette (E) 2682-043

I'M IN THE MOOD FOR SWING   (BC)
1/11-16/37*   BC   3tp/2tb/2as/2ts/p/g/b/d
4/22/39*   BC
7/24/39*   BC

7/21/38*   Lionel Hampton & His Orch.   1tp/2as/2ts/p/b/d/
                vib
5/30-31/79   Bob Wilber & the American All Stars featuring
                Lars Erstrand   Phontastic 7526

I'M LEFT WITH THE BLUES IN MY HEART   see   BLUES IN MY HEART

I'M LOST   (Otis René)
5/21/44*   BC   (Dick Gray-v)   4tp/3tb/2as/2ts/1bs/p/g/b/d/v

1964   Harry Edison with Benny Carter's Orch.   1tp/4tb/
                14strings/1harp/p/g/b/d   Vee-Jay VJS3065

I'M OUT OF STYLE   (BC/lyrics: Mack David)
 • 12/17/40   Ginny Simms (v) with Eddie South & His Orch.
                1tp/1cl/1as/1violin/p/g/b/d/v   78: OK 5990

I'M PUTTING ALL MY EGGS IN ONE BASKET (Berlin)
    4/4/36   Henry Hall & the B.B.C. Dance Orch. (Dan Donovan-v)   3tp/3tb/5reeds/p/g/b/d/6strings/v   World Records (E) SH172

I'M SORRY   (BC) [appears on LP as SORRY]
    1/4/54*   BC   horns/strings/p/b/d

I'M SUCH A FOOL TO BE IN LOVE WITH YOU   (BC/lyrics: P. Vandervoort)
    • 1950   Virgie Austin (v)   78:   London 17009

I'M THE CARING KIND   (BC/lyrics: I. Gordon)
    1/8/46*   BC (Maxine Sullivan-v)   4tp/4tb/3as/3ts/1bs/p/g/b/d/v
    4/30/46*   BC (Lucy Elliott-v)
    May-June 1946*   (AFRS Jubilee #191)   BC (Lucy Elliott-v)

    • ca. 1950   The Drifters (vocal group)   78:   Coral 65037

I'M TICKLED TO DEATH I'M ME
    ca. 5/36   Henry Hall & the B.B.C. Dance Orch.   large orch   (B.B.C. broadcast, no known aircheck s)

IMMINENT   (BC)
    5/63*   KPM Music Library   4tp/4tb/2fr. horns/5reeds/p/g/b/d   NOTE: See notes for this session in chronological section of discography.

IN A MELLOTONE   (D. Ellington)
    8/14/79   Zoot Sims   4tp/4tb/2as/2ts/1bs/p/g/b/d   Pablo Today 2312-120   NOTE: This arrangement was written for Sarah Vaughan, but at session Sims substituted as featured soloist.

IN A SENTIMENTAL MOOD   (D. Ellington/I. Mills/M. Kurtz)
    4/29/77*   BC   2tp/1tb/3reeds/p/g/b/d

    8/13/79   Sarah Vaughan (v)   1flute/2cl/1bass cl/3fr. horns/1oboe/1ts/9violins/3viola/2celli/1harp/p/g/b/d/v   NOTE: Recorded for Pablo--unissued.

IN THE DARK   (L. Greene/W. Broonzy)
    1957   Ernie Andrews (v) with Benny Carter's Orch.   large orch/v   GNP 28, GNP-Crescendo 10008

IN THE EVENING (WHEN THE SUN GOES DOWN)   (L. Carr)
    7/13/63   Ray Charles (v), The Raelets (v)   4tp/4tb/2as/2ts/1bs/p/g/b/d/v/vocal group   ABC 465

IN THE MIDNIGHT HOUR   (W. Pickett/S. Cropper)
    1/3-4/68   Jackie Wilson (v) with Count Basie's Orch.   4tp/4tb/2as/2ts/1bs/p/g/b/d/v   Brunswick BL54134

INDIANA   (Hanley/MacDonald)
    3/27/36   Henry Hall & the B.B.C. Dance Orch.   large orch   (B.B.C. broadcast, no known airchecks)

6/60   Dakota Staton (v) 1tp/1reed/p/g/b/d/v   Capitol
                        T1597

INTO EACH LIFE SOME RAIN MUST FALL   (A. Roberts/D. Fiseer)
    1965   Lou Rawls (v) 2tp/4tb/2reeds/p/g/b/d/v   Capitol
                        T2273

IT AIN'T THE MEAT, IT'S THE MOTION   (H. Glover/L. Mann)
    12/22/74*   Maria Muldaur (v) 2tp/1tb/1as/1ts/1bs/p/g/b/d/v
    1974   Maria Muldaur (v) Reprise MS2194

IT DON'T MEAN A THING IF IT AIN'T GOT THAT SWING   (D. Ellington/
I. Mills)
    8/2/54*   Mel Torme (v) 4tp/4tb/5reeds/p/g/b/d/v

    12/22/74*   Maria Muldaur (v) 2tp/1tb/1as/1ts/1bs/p/g/b/d/v

    4/29/77*   BC   2tp/1tb/3reeds/p/g/b/d
    4/15/78*   BC
    4/19?/78*   BC

    8/14/79   Zoot Sims 4tp/4tb/2as/2ts/1bs/p/g/b/d   Pablo
                        Today 2312-120 NOTE: This arrangement was
                        written for Sarah Vaughan, but at session Sims
                        was substituted as featured soloist.

IT HAPPENS TO THE BEST OF FRIENDS   (R. Bloom/M. Parish)
    8/16/34   Benny Goodman & His Music Hall Orch. (Ann
                        Graham-v) 3tp/2tb/2as/2ts/p/g/b/d/v   Sunbeam
                        SB139

IT PAYS TO ADVERTISE   (BC/lyrics: P. Vandervoort)
  • 7/8/49*   Kitty White (v) accompanied by Dave Cavanaugh's
                        Orch. arr: Dave Cavanaugh 3tp/1tb/2as/2ts/1bs/
                        p/b/d/v

IT'S ALL RIGHT WITH ME   (C. Porter)
    1966   Pat Dahl (v) large orch with strings/v   Audio
                        Fidelity AFLP2157

IT'S DE-LOVELY   (C. Porter)
    11/56   Billy Daniels (v) accompanied by Benny Carter's
                        Orch. 4tp/4tb/2as/2ts/1bs/p/g/b/d/v   Verve
                        MGV2072

IT'S IMPOSSIBLE   (A. and D. Previn)
    1971   Pearl Bailey (v) 4tp/4tb/5reeds/p/g/b/d/strings/v
                        RCA LSP4529

IT'S MONDAY EVERY DAY   (S. Robin)
    1965   Lou Rawls (v) 2tp/4tb/2reeds/p/g/b/d/v   Capitol
                        T2273

IT'S SO FRIGHTNIN'   (BC/lyrics: D. Overstreet Gray)
    1958   Don Evans (v) with orch. under the direction of
                        Benny Carter p/g/b/d/v   45: Dome 100-1

IT'S UP TO ME AND YOU (Ella Fitzgerald)
5/10/68   Ella Fitzgerald (v) 1fr. horn/20strings/1harp/p/
                  g/b/d/v 45: Capitol P2212

I'VE BEEN IN LOVE BEFORE (F. Hollander/F. Loesser)
10/23/40*   BC (Roy Felton-v) 3tp/2tb/5reeds/p/g/b/d/v

I'VE GOT A FEELING YOU'RE FOOLING (N. Brown/A. Freed)
1/17/36*   Willie Lewis (v) & His Orch. 3tp/2as/2ts/p/g/b/
                  d/v

I'VE GOT TWO LIPS (L. Feather)
late 4/36*   BC 2tp/1cl/1as/1ts/p/g/b/d

JJJJUMP (BC/C. Basie/C. Terry)
• 5/6/76*   Basie Jam #2

JACKSON COUNTY JUBILEE (BC) [One of ten pieces comprising Carter's Kansas City Suite.]
9/6-11/60   Count Basie & His Orch. 4tp/3tb/2as/2ts/1bs/p/
                  g/b/d Roulette (S)R52056, Roulette (E) 2683-013,
                  Roulette RE124 NOTE: See note on recording
                  date under Kansas City Suite.

JAM BLUES (BC/C. Shavers/J. Hodges/C. Parker/F. Phillips/B. Webster/
O. Peterson/B. Kessel/R. Brown/J. C. Heard)
• June or July 1952* Jam Session (Norman Granz)

JAZZ COCKTAIL (BC)
9/21/32   Duke Ellington & His Orch. 3tp/3tb/4reeds/p/g/
                  b/d Gaps 040, CBS (F) 88035
9/23/32   Mills Blue Rhythm Band 78: Banner 32608, LP:
                  Swingfan (G) 1019
10/5/32*   BC

A JAZZ PORTRAIT OF BRIGITTE BARDOT (BC/C. Hawkins/R. Eldridge/
D. Byas)
• 11/22/60*   Jazz at the Philharmonic

JAZZ WALTZ (BC)
5/63*   KPM Music Library 4tp/4tb/2fr. horns/5reeds/p/
                  g/b/d NOTE: Two different brief thematic transi-
                  tion passages for this piece were recorded at the
                  same session. Both were arranged and composed
                  by Carter. Also see notes for this session in
                  chronological section of discography.

JITTERBUG WALTZ (Waller)
4/29/77*   BC 2tp/1tb/3reeds/p/g/b/d

JOHNNY (BC)
• 11/30/76*   BC

JOHNNY KLINGARINGDING (L. Chase)
1953-1954   Lincoln Chase (v) with Spencer-Hagen Orch.
                  small group/v Liberty LRP3076

(THE) JUKE BOX (BC)
3/59*   The Music From M Squad large orch

Discography: Arranger/Composer

7/2/72*　　　　　　BC　5tp/4tb/3as/2ts/1bs/p/g/b/d
12/3/73*　　　　　　BC

　　　　　　　　　　NOTE: Composed for TV series M Squad.

JUMP CALL (BC) [also appears as MELODRAMA IN A V-DISC RECORD ROOM]
1/5/46*　　　　　　BC　4tp/3tb/3as/2ts/1bs/p/g/b/d
April-May 1946*　　(AFRS Jubilee #184) BC NOTE: appears on V-Disc 701 as Melodrama In A V-Disc Record Room.
probably early 1947*　(AFRS Jubilee #246) BC

JUNE COMES AROUND (H. Arlen)
4/9/45*　　　　　　BC　5tp/4tb/3as/2ts/1bs/p/g/b/d

JUNE IN JANUARY (Robin/Rainger)
late 1958 or early　　BC　4tp/3tb/5reeds/p/g/b/d
1959*

JUNE IS BUSTIN' OUT ALL OVER (Rodgers/Hammerstein)
late 1958 or early　　BC　4tp/3tb/5reeds/p/g/b/d
1959*

JUST A MOOD (BC)
1/17/36*　　　　　　Willie Lewis & His Orch.　2tp/1tb/2as/2ts/p/g/b/d
late 4/36*　　　　　　BC NOTE: Arrangement similar to Lewis recording above.

• 9/7/36　　　　　　Garland Wilson 78: Brunswick 03115

JUST A RIDE see SWINGIN' AT THE MAIDA VALE

JUST A-SITTIN' AND A-ROCKIN' (Ellington/Strayhorn/Gaines)
2/15-16/79　　　　　Ella Fitzgerald (v) with Count Basie's Orch.
　　　　　　　　　　4tp/4tb/5reeds/p/g/b/d/v Pablo Today 2312-132

JUST IN TIME (J. Styne/B. Comden)
11/56　　　　　　　Billy Daniels (v) accompanied by Benny Carter's Orch. 1tp/4reeds/p/g/b/d/strings/v Verve MGV2072

JUST SQUEEZE ME (Ellington/Gaines)
1957　　　　　　　Ernie Andrews with Benny Carter's Orch. large orch/v GNP 28, GNP-Crescendo 10008

JUST THE BLUES (L. Stevens/S. Fine)
Sept.-Oct. 1958*　　film soundtrack: The Five Pennies 2tp/2tb/4reeds/p/b/d NOTE: Features Louis Armstrong, tp.

JUST YOU, JUST ME (J. Greer/R. Klages)
3/19/45*　　　　　　(AFRS Jubilee #125) BC 4tp/4tb/2as/2ts/1bs/p/g/b/d
12/12/45*　　　　　BC
Apr.-May 1946*　　(AFRS Jubilee #186) BC
ca. 7/47*　　　　　(AFRS Jubilee #248) BC

KANSAS CITY LINE (BC/C. Basie/C. Terry/Eddie "Lockjaw" Davis)
- 5/6/76*   Basie Jam #2

KANSAS CITY MOODS (BC/A. De Haas)
- 1/24/40   Jan Savitt & His Orch.   arr: Jack Pleis?
    Sounds of Swing LP104
10/25/45   Jan Savitt & His Orch.   (AFRS broadcast One Night Stand ONS #817)

- 9/26/41   Nat Gonella & His New Georgians   78: Columbia FB-2754

NOTE: Although he is listed as co-composer in the copyright records, Carter ascribes primary authorship of "Kansas City Moods" to De Haas, who felt that Carter's name would increase the chances of having the composition recorded.

KANSAS CITY SUITE
This is a collective title for a set of Carter compositions and arrangements recorded by Count Basie and His Orchestra in 1960. For further details see the individual titles:

VINE STREET RUMBLE, KATY DO, MISS MISSOURI, JACKSON COUNTY JUBILEE, SUNSET GLOW, THE WIGGLE WALK, MEETIN' TIME, PASEO PROMENADE, BLUE FIVE JIVE, ROMPIN' AT THE RENO

Jepsen gives recording date as 11/17/60 and location as New York. Carter was present and recalls that session was in Los Angeles. Roulette master tapes list dates as 9/6, 9/7, 9/10 and 9/11 (four sessions). This is probably accurate, because Carter was touring with Jazz at the Philharmonic from early November to December 7, 1960.

KATY DO (BC) [One of ten pieces comprising Carter's Kansas City Suite]
9/6-11/60   Count Basie & His Orch.   4tp/3tb/2as/2ts/1bs/p/g/b/d   Roulette (S)R52056, Roulette RE124
NOTE: See note on recording date under Kansas City Suite.

KEEP A SONG IN YOUR SOUL (T. Waller/A. Hill)
12/2/30*   Fletcher Henderson & His Orch.   3tp/2tb/2as/1ts/p/g/b/d

KEY LARGO (BC, K. Suessdorf/lyrics: L. Worth)
- 1947   Ellington Gang   Queen Disc Q041

1947*   Anita O'Day (v)   12 piece orch/v

- 1947   Jimmy Zito & His Orch.   (Nick Delane-v)   78: Coast 8034

9/52*   BC with the Oscar Peterson Trio & Buddy Rich horns/strings/p/g/b/d

Discography: Arranger/Composer

- 3/4/55   Arne Domnerus Quintet   HMV (Sw) 7EGS17
- 2/56   Jane Fielding (v) with the Kenny Drew Quintet arr: Kenny Drew   Jazz West JWLP5
- 1960   Cal Tjader arr: Eddie Cano   Fantasy 3309 (mono), Fantasy 8053 (stereo)
- ca. 1963   Sarah Vaughan (v)   Roulette (E) 2682-032, New World Records NW295
- date unknown   Tony Lovelle & Orch.   45: Acama X-121

KING SIZE PAPA   (BC under pseudonym "Johnny Gomez"/lyrics: P. Vandervoort)
- 11/11/47*   Julia Lee (v) & Her Boy Friends   arr: Dave Cavanaugh

- 1956-1957   Julia Lee (v)   Foremost 104

KING'S RIFF   (BC)
- 12/27/51*   Ben Webster Sextet

A KISS FROM YOU   (BC/lyrics: J. Mercer) [also recorded as LYDIA]
- ca. 1963   Stanley Wilson & His Orch.   arr: Stanley Wilson   Decca 74481 (as Lydia)

12/3/73*   BC   4tp/4tb/3as/3ts/1bs/p/g/b/d
10/28/78*   BC with the University of Buffalo Jazz Ensemble directed by Sam Falzone   (as Lydia)

                      NOTE: This composition was originally written for TV's Chrysler Theatre and called "Lydia." When Johnny Mercer added the lyrics, the title was changed.

KNOCK ME A KISS   (A. Razaf)
6/60   Dakota Staton (v)   1tp/1reed/p/g/b/d/v   Capitol T1597

KRAZY KAPERS   (BC)
10/10/33*   The Chocolate Dandies   1tp/1tb/1as/1ts/p/g/b/d

LADY BE GOOD   (Gershwin)
5/20/39*   BC   3tp/3tb/3as/2ts/p/g/b/d
7/24/39*   BC

9/9/39   Roy Eldridge & His Orch.   2tp/1tb/1as/2ts/p/g/b/d   Jazz Archives JA14

LADY OH LADY   (B. Blalock)
early 1950's   Bruce Blalock (v)   small group   45: Coral 9-61884

A LADY SINGS THE BLUES   (Stanley Wilson)
3/59*   The Music From M Squad   large orch

THE LADY'S IN LOVE WITH YOU   (B. Lane/F. Loesser)
  1962   Sarah Vaughan (v)   4tp/4tb/5reeds/p/g/b/d/vib/v
                      Roulette R(S)52092, Roulette (E) 2682-043   Roulette
                      RE103

LASSE LASSE LITTEN   (BC/I. Stevens)
  1968   Inger Stevens (v)   large orch with strings/v   45:
                      Dome D506

THE LAST KISS YOU GAVE ME   (H. Ruby)
  10/23/40*   BC   (Roy Felton-v)   3tp/2tb/2as/2ts/1bs/p/g/b/d/v

LAURA   (D. Raksin/J. Mercer)
  1961*   Alfred Newman   large orch with horns/strings/
                      rhythm section

LAZY AFTERNOON   (BC)
  8/17/37*   BC   3tp/2tb/2as/2ts/p/g/b/d

  • 9/20/56   Bertie King Jazz Group   Nixa (E) NJT506

THE LEGEND   (BC)
  10/30-31/61*   Count Basie & His Orch.   4tp/3tb/2as/2ts/1bs/p/
                      g/b/d

LET IT BE ME
  ca. 6/36   Henry Hall & the B.B.C. Dance Orch.   large
                      orch   (B.B.C. broadcast, no known airchecks)

LET THEM TALK
  6/60   Dakota Staton (v)   large orch with strings/v
                      Capitol T1597

LET US DRINK A TOAST TOGETHER   (H. Atwood)
  1/48*   BC (Bob Decker and/or The Enchanters-v)   1tp/
                      1tb/1as/1ts/p/g/b/d/v

LET'S FALL IN LOVE   (Arlen/Koehler)
  9/10/53*   Buddy Rich & His All Stars   1tp/1tb/1as/1ts/1bs/
                      p/b/d

LET'S HAVE A JUBILEE   (A. Hill/I. Mills)
  10/4/34   Mills Blue Rhythm Band   3tp/2tb/3reeds/p/g/b/d
                      Jazz Archives JA10
  10/19/34*   Alex Hill (v) & His Hollywood Sepians

LILACS IN THE RAIN   (P. DeRose/M. Parish)
  1/28/39*   BC (Dell St. John-v)   3tp/3tb/2as/2ts/p/g/b/d/v

LIMEHOUSE BLUES   (P. Braham/D. Furber)
  9/11/34   Fletcher Henderson & His Orch.   3tp/2tb/1cl/2as/
                      1ts/p/g/b/d   Decca DL9228, MCA 1318, Time-
                      Life STL-J21

  1/5/35   Benny Goodman & His Orch.   (aircheck)   Sunbeam
                      SB100

LITTLE BO BOP HAS LOST HER BEEP   see BOP BOUNCE

Discography: Arranger/Composer 307

LIVIN' IN THE SUNLIGHT (LOVIN' IN THE MOONLIGHT) (A. Sherman/A. Lewis)
1/1975   Geoff Muldaur (v) 3tp/2tb/1ss/2as/1ts/1bass sax/p/celeste/banjo/tuba/d/vocal chorus/v Reprise MS2220 NOTE: Vocal arrangement by Amos Garrett.

LIZA (I. and G. Gershwin/G. Kahn)
5/3/38   Chick Webb & His Orch. 3tp/3tb/2as/2ts/p/g/b/d Decca DL79223, MCA 2-4107
8/13/38   Chick Webb, Roy Eldridge accompanied by the Saturday Night Swing Club Houseband (aircheck) Jazz Archives JA33
11/30/70   Time-Life series The Swing Era (Billy May-leader) Time-Life STL342 NOTE: In this series, significant swing era performances are "recreated" including imitations of the solos present on the original recordings.

THE LONE ARRANGER
5/18/40   Cab Calloway & His Orch. 3tp/3tb/3as/2ts/p/g/b/d Jazz Archives JA8, Merritt 12

LONELY AFFAIR (BC)
5/63*   KPM Music Library 4tp/4tb/2fr. horns/5reeds/p/g/b/d

5/63*   KPM Music Library 4tp/4tb/2fr. horns/5reeds/p/g/b/d

NOTE: Two brief thematic transition passages for this piece were recorded at the same session. Both were arranged and composed by Carter. Also see notes for this session in chronological section of discography.

LONELY HOURS (Glaser/Solomon)
1/63   Sarah Vaughan (v) 4tp/4tb/2as/2ts/1bs/p/g/b/d/v Roulette R(S)52104

LONELY WOMAN (BC/lyrics: R. Sonin)
● ca. 7/47   Peggy Lee (v) T: AFRS Jubilee #248

● 12/6/47   Stan Kenton & His Orch. (June Christy-v) arr: Pete Rugolo Creative World ST1037
Nov. 25-Dec. 21 1947   Stan Kenton & His Orch. T: AFRS "One Night Stand"

● 10/48   Charlie Ventura (Jackie Cain-v) arr: Roy Kral? Savoy SJL2243

● 1952   Sylvia Syms (v) with Barbara Carroll Trio Atlantic 1243

● 5/9/55   June Cristy (v) and Stan Kenton Capitol T656

● 4/8/56   Sarah Vaughan (v) arr: Hal Mooney Trip TLP5517

- 9/21/59   Stan Kenton & His Orch.   arr: Bill Matthews
                      Capitol (S)T1394

- 4/9/62   Chris Connor (v) arr: Al Cohn? Atlantic
                      SD8061

1966   Path Dahl (v) large orch with strings/v Audio
                      Fidelity AFLP2157

- 1976   Sylvia Syms (v) arr: Dick Hyman Atlantic
                      SD18177

A LONESOME CUP OF COFFEE   (B. Russell)
    1956   Abbey Lincoln (v) large orch/v 45: Liberty
                      F55035

LONESOME NIGHTS (BC) also entitled TAKE MY WORD
    10/16/33*   BC 3tp/3tb/3as/1ts/p/g/b/d
    8/16/34   Benny Goodman & His Music Hall Orch. Sunbeam
                      SB139, Columbia Special Products P2A 12020 (as
                      Take My Word)
    ca. 7/20/36   Bunny Berigan & His Studio Orch. Thesaurus
                      transcription 273 (as Take My Word)
    5/6/37   California Ramblers (Charlie Barnet Orch.)
                      Ajax 106 (as Take My Word)
    2/15/38   Artie Shaw & His Orch. Thesaurus transcription
                      549, Alamac QSR2434 (as Take My Word)
    8/28/40   Cab Calloway & His Orch. CBS (F) 62950, Epic
                      EE22008, Merritt 12
    1945?   Sam Donahue & His Navy Orch. Big Band Land-
                      marks vol. 23-24 NOTE: May be same ar-
                      rangement as those above.

- ca. 1960   Lionel Hampton & His Orch. arr: Bobby Plater
                      Glad Hamp LP1001
    12/61   Lionel Hampton & His Orch. Glad Hamp LP1005

                      NOTE: There are two recordings by Andy Kirk
                      and His Twelve Clouds of Joy of a Clyde Hart
                      composition and arrangement entitled "Puddin'
                      Head Serenade" which bears a marked resemblance
                      to "Lonesome Nights." The 3/31/36 version is
                      on Mainstream MRL399; the 4/10/36 on 78:
                      Decca 1208. Another recording inspired by
                      "Lonesome Nights" is the Jimmie Lunceford
                      Orchestra's "I'm Alone with You," which even
                      contains a saxophone chorus based on Carter's.
                      This composition is credited to Buff Estes, who
                      was also the arranger. The date is 12/14/39 and
                      it is on Columbia CL2715, and Columbia CS9515.

LOOK AT THAT FACE (Newley/Bricusse)
    Mar. 30-Apr. 1   Pearl Bailey (v) 4tp/4tb/5reeds/p/g/b/d/v
    1965*

LOOK FOR ME, I'LL BE AROUND (Wood/Dee)
    1/63   Sarah Vaughan (v) 4tb/20strings/p/g/b/d/v
                      Roulette R(S)52104

Discography: Arranger/Composer

LOOK OUT FOR TOMORROW (BC/lyrics: P. Vandervoort)
- ca. 1949 Calvin Boze (v) & His All Stars 78: Aladdin 3072

LOOKING FOR A BOY (G. and I. Gershwin)
1/8/46* BC (Maxine Sullivan-v) 4tp/4tb/3as/2ts/1bs/p/g/b/d/v

LOUIS ARMSTRONG MEDLEY
See individual titles:
WHEN IT'S SLEEPY TIME DOWN SOUTH, CONFESSIN', WHEN YOU'RE SMILING

LOU'S BLUES (BC)
1/22-24/62 Louis Bellson Orch. 5tp/3tb/1fr. horn/1tuba/2as/2ts/1bs/p/g/b/d/vib Roulette R52087, Roulette (E) 2934-020

LOVE FOR SALE (Cole Porter)
10/25/43* BC 4tp/3tb/2as/2ts/1bs/p/g/b/d
ca. 7/47* (AFRS Jubilee #203) BC

LOVE IS A FEELING (Bob Friedman)
11/71-3/72 Joe Williams (v) large orch/v Temponic TB29561

LOVE IS CYNTHIA see BLUE MOUNTAIN

LOVE, YOU DIDN'T DO RIGHT BY ME (I. Berlin)
1954* Peggy Lee (v) large orch with strings/v

LOVE, YOU'RE NOT THE ONE FOR ME (BC--words & music)
3/14/33* BC (v) 3tp/2tb/2as/1ts/p/g/b/d/v
11/6/33* Mezz Mezzrow & His Orch. (BC-v)

LOVELESS LOVE (W. C. Handy)
10/15/40* Billie Holiday (v) accompanied by Benny Carter Orch. 1tp/1tb/2reeds/p/g/b/d/v

LOVER COME BACK TO ME (S. Romberg/O. Hammerstein)
4/27/55 Ella Fitzgerald (v) with Benny Carter Orch. 3tp/1tb/2as/2ts/p/g/b/d/v Decca DL4129, MCA Coral (G) 0082.050-2

1957 Ernie Andrews (v) with Benny Carter's Orch. large orch/v GNP 28, GNP-Crescendo 10008

LOVER MAN (J. Davis/R. Ramirez/J. Sherman)
12/22/74* Maria Muldaur (v) 2tp/1tb/1as/1ts/1bs/p/g/b/d/v

LOVE'S GOT ME DOWN AGAIN (Cahn/Chaplin)
11/1/39* BC (Roy Felton-v) 3tp/3tb/3as/2ts/p/g/b/d/v

THE LOVING ROOM (BC/lyrics: Al Stillman)
1968 Inger Stevens (v) large orch with strings/v 45: Dome D506

LULA (BC/lyrics: P. Vandervoort)
- 4/10/62* BBB & Co. 1tp/1cl/1as/1ts/p/g/b/d

LULLABY IN BLUE   (BC)
  7/26/52*   BC   1tp/1tb/3reeds/p/g/b/d

LULLABY TO A DREAM   (BC)
  4/1/41*   BC   3tp/3tb/2as/2ts/p/g/b/d

LUSH LIFE   (B. Strayhorn)
  8/13/79   Sarah Vaughan (v)   1flute/2cl/1bass cl/3fr. horns/
                          1oboe/1ts/9violins/3viola/2celli/1harp/p/g/b/d/v
                          NOTE: Recorded for Pablo--unissued.

LYDIA   see   A KISS FROM YOU

M SQUAD
                          For Carter's contributions to the album The Music From M Squad (RCA LPM2062) which was based on the TV series, see 3/59* in chronological section of discography.

MA (SHE'S MAKING EYES AT ME)   (S. Clare/C. Conrad)
  1964   Ray Charles (v)   5tp/3tb/2as/2ts/1bs/p/g/b/d/v
                          ABC Paramount ABC495

  9/29/70   Mrs. Miller (v)   2tp/2tb/2as/1ts/1bs/p/g/b/d/v
                          45: Mrs. Miller Records (no issue number)

MAKE ME A PRESENT OF YOU   (J. Greene)
  1953   Ernie Andrews (v) with Benny Carter's Orch.
                          large orch/v   78: Trend 68, LP: GNP 28
                          NOTE: Although the discographies list two versions of this title by Andrews, one from 1953 (Trend 68) and one from 1957 (GNP 28), both discs contain the same performance, probably recorded in 1953.

  6/60   Dakota Staton (v)   large orch/v   Capitol T1490

MALIBU   (BC)
  4/9/45*   BC   5tp/4tb/3as/2ts/1bs/p/g/b/d
  11/16-22/45*   BC
  ca. 7/46*   (AFRS Jubilee #205)   BC
  8/14/59   Glen Gray & His Casa Loma Orch.   Capitol (S)T1289, Time-Life STL348   NOTE: This is a recreation of Carter's 4/9/45 version including solos. Carter's alto solo is played by Skeets Herfurt.

  • 2/11/76*   BC

  • 12/5/81*   BC

MAMA, A RAINBOW
  1971   Pearl Bailey (v)   4tp/4tb/5reeds/p/g/b/d/strings/v
                          RCA LSP4529

MAMA DON'T WEAR NO DRAWERS   (BC/C. Basie/C. Terry)
  • 5/6/76*   Basie Jam #2

Discography: Arranger/Composer

MAMA LOU (BC)
  7/26/52*   BC 1tp/1tb/3reeds/p/g/b/d

A MAN CALLED ADAM [film soundtrack]
                              Carter's compositions and arrangements for this 1966 film were released on a soundtrack album of the same name and are listed under the following individual titles, recorded in November, 1965: ALL THAT JAZZ, GO NOW, AIN'T I, SOFT TOUCH, CLAUDIA, CRACK UP, NIGHT WALK, WHISPER TO ONE. The film was about a trumpeter, Adam Johnson (played by Sammy Davis, Jr.), and the soundtrack featured Nat Adderley as trumpet soloist along with contributions by Kai Winding, Jimmy Cleveland (tb), Jerome Richardson, Lucky Thompson (ts), Junior Mance (p), Everett Barksdale (g), Aaron Bell (b), and Herb Lovelle (d) on the titles listed above. In addition, two performances by Louis Armstrong and his All Stars were included, "Someday Sweetheart" and "Back of Town Blues." The personnel for these titles was Armstrong (tp,v), Tyree Glenn (tb), Buster Bailey (cl), Billy Kyle (p), Buddy Catlett (b), and Danny Barcelona (d), although John Brown (b) and Jo Jones (d) appear on the screen.

THE MAN I LOVE (G. and I. Gershwin)
  1/63   Sarah Vaughan (v) 4tb/20strings/p/g/b/d/v Roulette R(S)52104, Roulette RE103 NOTE: Melody Maker (May 30, 1936) reports that Carter was commissioned by Henry Hall to arrange this tune. It may later have been broadcast by Hall and the B.B.C. Dance Orchestra. There are no known airchecks.

A MAN IS A NECESSARY EVIL (W. Shelley)
  Mar. 30-Apr. 1   Pearl Bailey (v) 4tp/4tb/5reeds/p/g/b/d/v
  1965*

MARCH WIND (BC)
  late 1958 or early   BC 4tp/3tb/5reeds/p/g/b/d
  1959*
  11/9/68*   BC with Henri Chaix & His Orch. NOTE: Similar arrangement but performed by 1tp/1tb/2as/1ts/1bs/p/b/d

MARGIE (Conrad/Robinson/Davis)
  1965   Lou Rawls (v) large orch with strings/vocal group/v Capitol T2401

THE MASQUERADE IS OVER (H. Magidson/A. Wrubel)
  11/5-6/56   Abbey Lincoln (v) 1tp/1tb/1fr. horn/3woodwinds/p/g/b/d/v Liberty LRP3025

  6/60   Dakota Staton (v) large orch/v Capitol T1490

ME AND MY JAGUAR (BC)
9/10/53*   Buddy Rich & His All Stars 1tp/1tb/1as/1ts/1bs/
                            p/b/d

ME AND MY SHADOW (Jolson/Dreyer/Rose)
1965   Lou Rawls (v) large orch with strings/vocal
                            group/v Capitol T2401

MEET ME AT NO SPECIAL PLACE (J. R. Robinson)
6/60   Dakota Staton (v) large orch/v Capitol T1490

MEETIN' TIME (BC) [One of ten pieces comprising Carter's Kansas City
Suite.]
   9/6-11/60   Count Basie & His Orch. 4tp/3tb/2as/2ts/1bs/p/
                            g/b/d Roulette S(R)52056, Roulette RE124
                            NOTE: See note on recording date under Kansas
                            City Suite.

 • 12/20-21/63   Lambert, Hendricks & Bavan (v) arr: Jon Hen-
                            dricks RCA LPM2861 NOTE: Lyrics added by
                            Jon Hendricks for this recording.

MELANCHOLY LULLABY (BC/lyrics: E. Heyman)
   4/17/39*   BC 3tp/3tb/3as/2ts/p/g/b/d
   4/22/39*   BC (two versions)
   5/6/39*   BC
   5/20/39*   BC
   6/29/39*   BC
   7/24/39*   BC (two versions)
   10/9/39*   BC
   10/14/39*   BC (two versions)
   4/10/43*   BC
   8/3/70   Time-Life series The Swing Era (Billy May-lead-
                            er) Time-Life STL343 NOTE: This is a recrea-
                            tion of Carter's 6/29/39 Vocalion recording in-
                            cluding note-for-note imitations of the solos.
                            Carter's solo is played by Skeets Herfurt.

 • ca. 8/39   Gene Krupa & His Orch. (broadcast from Steel
                            Pier, Atlantic City)
   2/2/40   Gene Krupa & His Orch. (broadcast from Meadow-
                            brook, Cedar Grove, N.J.)

 • 9/5/39   Jimmy Dorsey & His Orch. (Helen O'Connell-v)
                            Ajax 164

 • 9/11/39   Glenn Miller & His Orch. (Ray Eberle-v) RCA
                            Camden CAL829, RCA (F) 900.028, RCA (E)
                            LFM1-7503

 • 1939   Reggie Childs & His Orch. (Marion Kaye-v) 78:
                            Varsity 8079

 • 1939   Ginny Simms (v) 78: Vocalion 5140

 • 1939   Artie Shaw Helen Forrest (v) Hindsight
                            149 (aircheck)

 • early 1950's?   Peggy Lee (v) Capitol transcription

Discography: Arranger/Composer   313

• 11/60   Arne Domnerus & His Orch.   Metronome
                       MLP15062

MELODRAMA IN A V-DISC RECORD ROOM   see JUMP CALL

A MELODY FROM THE SKY   (L. Alter/S. Mitchell)
  11/56   Billy Daniels (v) accompanied by Benny Carter's
                       Orch. 1tp/4reeds/p/g/b/d/strings/v   Verve
                       MGV2072

MEMORIES OF YOU   (E. Blake/A. Razaf)
  8/64*   BC 2ss/4as/3ts/2bs/p/g/b/d

METROPOLE   (BC)
  5/63*   KPM Music Library 4tp/4tb/2fr. horns/5reeds/p/
                       g/b/d NOTE: See notes for this session in
                       chronological section of discography.

MIDNIGHT   (Gomez/Parker)
  4/1/41*   BC (Maxine Sullivan-v) 3tp/3tb/3as/2ts/p/g/b/d/v
  1943*   (AFRS Basic Library P-34) BC (Savannah
                       Churchill-v)

THE MIDNIGHT SUN WILL NEVER SET   (D. Cockran/H. Salvador/Q. Jones)
  11/13/61*   BC 2as/2ts/p/g/b/d

MIGHTY LIKE THE BLUES   (L. Feather)
  8/18/37*   BC 1tp/1tb/1cl/1ts/p/g/b/d

MILLIONS OF PEOPLE   (BC/lyrics: P. Herrick)
  1955   Larry Barbro (v) with Benny Carter Orch.
                       5brass/4reeds/p/b/d/v 45: Benida No 5033, 45:
                       Imperial X3003

MISS MISSOURI   (BC) [One of ten pieces comprising Carter's Kansas City
Suite.]
  9/6-11/60   Count Basie & His Orch. 4tp/3tb/2as/2ts/1bs/p/
                       g/b/d Roulette (S)R52056, Roulette 2683-013,
                       Roulette RE124 NOTE: See note on recording
                       date under Kansas City Suite.

MR. LOVE   (Bob Friedman)
  11/71-3/72   Carmen McRae (v) large orch/v   Temponic
                       TB29562

MOMENTS TO REMEMBER   (R. Allen/A. Stillman)
  9/8/55   Louis Armstrong (v) with Benny Carter's Orch.
                       3tp/2tb/1cl/2as/2ts/p/b/d/v Vocalion VL73851,
                       MCA Coral 42026, MCA Coral 82051/2

MONA LISA   (R. Evans/J. Livingston)
  8/30/74   Yujiro Ishihara (v) 2tp/1tb/1as/2ts/1bs/p/g/b/d/v
                       Continental (J) C01 NOTE: Instrumental tracks
                       recorded 8/30/74, Los Angeles; vocal added later
                       in Japan.

MOOD INDIGO   (Ellington/Bigard)
  July 1981*   BC 2tp/1tb/3reeds/1violin/p/b/d

THE MOON IS LOW   (N. Brown/A. Freed)
1/22-24/62   Louis Bellson Orch.   5tp/3tb/1fr. horn/1tuba/2as/
                          2ts/1bs/p/g/b/d/vib   Roulette R52087, Roulette
                          (E) 2934-020

MOONLIGHT ON THE GANGES   (S. Myers/C. Wallace)
1962   Sarah Vaughan (v)   4tp/4tb/5reeds/p/g/b/d/vib/v
                          Roulette R(S)52092, Roulette (E) 2682-043

MOPPIN' AND BOPPIN'   (BC/T. Waller/E. Kirkeby)
• 1/23/43*   Fats Waller & His Rhythm

MORE THAN YOU KNOW   (V. Youmans/B. Rose/E. Eliscu)
4/17/39*   BC   3tp/3tb/2as/2ts/p/g/b/d
11/1/39*   BC   (Roy Felton-v)

THE MUGGER   (BC)
3/59*   The Music from M Squad   large orch   NOTE:
                          Composed for TV series M Squad.

THE MUSIC GOES 'ROUND AND 'ROUND   (E. Farley/M. Riley/R. Hodgson)
2/9/42*   Mark Warnow & His Orch.   (The Hit Paraders-v)
                          3tp/2tb/6reeds/8violins/1harp/p/g/b/d/vocal group

MUSKRAT RAMBLE   (Kid Ory)
7/21/38*   Lionel Hampton & His Orch.   1tp/2as/2ts/p/b/d/
                          vib

MY BUDDY   (Donaldson/Kahn)
8/18/37*   BC   1tp/1tb/1as/2ts/p/g/b/d
date unknown   Electrecord Orch. (Roumania)   Electrecord 0971
                          NOTE: This recording is a recreation, including
                          solos, of the 8/18/37* recording above.

1965   Lou Rawls (v)   large orch with strings/vocal
                          group/v   Capitol T2401

MY FAVORITE BLUES   (BC)
4/1/41*   BC   3tp/3tb/3as/2ts/p/g/b/d

MY FUNNY VALENTINE   (R. Rodgers)
early 1970's   The Airmen of Note (U.S. Air Force Jazz En-
                          semble) (Sarah Vaughan-v)   4tp/4tb/5reeds/p/g/b/
                          d/v   NOTE: Promotional album: The Airmen of
                          Note and Sarah Vaughan (no label and issue)

MY GIRL   (W. Robinson/R. White)
1/3-4/68   Jackie Wilson (v) with Count Basie's Orch.   4tp/
                          4tb/2as/2ts/1bs/p/g/b/d/v   Brunswick BL54134

MY GUIDING LIGHT   see   GUIDING LIGHT

MY HEART HAS WINGS
5/20/39*   BC (Mercedes Carter-v)   3tp/3tb/3as/2ts/p/g/b/d/v

MY KIND OF TROUBLE IS YOU   (BC/lyrics: P. Vandervoort)
• 11/11/55   Helen Carr (v)   Bethlehem BCP1027

Discography: Arranger/Composer

- 1959   Felicia Sanders (v)   Time S/2110
- 2/11/76*   BC
- 4/76   Milt Jackson & Strings   arr: Jimmy Jones
                      Pablo 2310-774

2/15-16/79   Ella Fitzgerald (v) with Count Basie's Orch.
                     4tp/4tb/5reeds/p/g/b/d/v   Pablo Today 2312-132

MY MELANCHOLY BABY   (Burnett/Norton/Watson)
date unknown   Meg Myles (v)   large orch/v   45: Capitol F3437

MY PRETTY GIRL   (Fulcher)
2/5/31*   Fletcher Henderson & His Orch. (Lois Deppe-v)
                     3tp/2tb/2as/cl/1ts/p/g/b/d/v   NOTE: Carter is
                     possibly the arranger.

MY TWILIGHT REVERIE   (BC/lyrics: Kay Parker)
- 8/23/45   Fred Waring & the Pennsylvanians (unknown v)
                     arr: Hawley Ades, Roy Ringwald   (aircheck)

MY WISH   (B. Young/Una Mae Carlisle)
2/60   Dakota Staton (v) large orch with strings/v
                     Capitol T1427

NAGASAKI   (H. Warren)
1/21/35   Charlie Barnet & His Orch.   3tp/1tb/2as/2ts/p/g/
                     b/d   Bluebird AXM2-5526

1/11-16/37*   BC (v)   2tp/2tb/3as/2ts/p/g/b/d/v   NOTE: This
                     arrangement is similar to the one recorded by
                     Barnet.

NEVER AGAIN   (J. Moody)
ca. 1970   Benard Ito (v)   large orch   45: Mercury 72686

NEVER SWAT A FLY   (Desylva/Brown/Henderson)
11/4/30*   McKinney's Cotton Pickers (Bill Coty-v)   3tp/1tb/
                     3reeds/p/g/tuba/d/v
9/20/75   New McKinney's Cotton Pickers (Orrin Foslien-v)
                     Bountiful B38003
6/26/80*   New McKinney's Cotton Pickers (Orrin Foslien-v)

THE NEW CONTINENT   (L. Schifrin)
                     This extended work was written and arranged by
                     Lalo Schifrin to feature Dizzy Gillespie. Carter
                     conducted the orchestra at the 1962 Monterey
                     Jazz Festival performance of the piece and during
                     a studio recording of it made in two sessions in
                     September 1962, one before and one after the
                     festival. The recording was originally released
                     on Limelight LS86022 (Dizzy Gillespie, The New
                     Continent) and reissued on Emarcy EMS2410
                     (Dizzy Gillespie, Composer's Concepts).

NIGHT AND DAY   (C. Porter)
5/5/46*   BC (Lucy Elliott-v)   large orch/v

NIGHT HOP   (BC)
   5/20/40*
   1981
                      BC   3tp/2tb/3as/2ts/p/g/b/d
                      Widespread Depression Orch.   Stash ST212
                      NOTE: Carter's 1940 arr. transcribed by John Ellis.

NIGHT WALK   (BC)
   11/65
                      film soundtrack: A Man Called Adam   4tp/4tb/4reeds/p/g/b/d   Reprise 6180

NIGHTFALL   (BC)
   4/15/36*
                      BC   3tp/2tb/3as/cl/2ts/p/g/b/d

   5/7/36
                      Henry Hall & the B. B. C. Dance Orch. (B. B. C. broadcast, no known airchecks) NOTE: May be same as 4/15/36* arrangement above.

   • 8/2/36*
                      BC with the AVRO Orch.   (aircheck)

   • 1963
                      George Shearing   arr: Julian Lee   Capitol (S)T2143

NO LOVE, NO NOTHIN'   (H. Warren/M. Gordon)
   Mar.-Apr. 1943*
                      Alice Faye (v) with Benny Goodman & His Orch. 3tp/2tb/6reeds/strings/p/g/b/d/v   NOTE: This performance is from the film soundtrack: The Gang's All Here.

NOBODY BUT ME   (B. Myles)
   1965
                      Lou Rawls (v)   2tp/4tb/2reeds/p/g/b/d/v   Capitol T2273

NOBODY ELSE BUT ME   (Hammerstein/Kern)
   1962
                      Sarah Vaughan (v)   4tp/4tb/5reeds/p/g/b/d/vib/v   Roulette R(S)52092, Roulette (E) 2682-043

NOBODY KNOWS HOW MUCH I LOVE YOU   (BC, Fats Waller/lyrics: Bud Allen)
   • 1/17/28
                      Andy Razaf (v) 78: Columbia 14285-D   NOTE: Issued under the pseudonym "Johnny Thompson"; Fats Waller plays piano.

NOTHING REALLY FEELS THE SAME   (Rachaels/Hart/Magid)
   1965
                      Lou Rawls (v)   large orch with strings/vocal group/v   Capitol T2401

NOW AND THEN THERE'S A FOOL SUCH AS I   (B. Trader)
   1965
                      Lou Rawls (v)   large orch with strings/vocal group/v   Capitol T2401

NUAGES   (D. Reinhardt)
   4/29/77*
                      BC   2tp/1tb/3reeds/p/g/b/d

O. K. FOR BABY   (BC)   also appears as OKAY FOR BABY
   5/20/40*
                      BC   3tp/2tb/3as/2ts/p/g/b/d

   • 12/23/40
                      Jimmie Lunceford & His Orch.   arr: Lonnie Wilfong   Tax m-8003, Swingfan (G) 1009

Discography: Arranger/Composer 317

Nov.-Dec. 1940   Jimmie Lunceford & His Orch.   Lang-Worth transcription, Circle CLP11

● 8/10/43   Les Brown & His Orch.   Fanfare 30-130 (aircheck) NOTE: Although the notes to the Fanfare LP state that O.K. for Baby is from the Lunceford book, the arrangement is not the same as that on the Lunceford recordings.

● 8/45   Jack McVea & His All Stars   78: Apollo 761

● 6/19/46   Harry Parry   78: Parlophone (E) R3013

● 6/24/58   The Big Eighteen   arr: Charlie Shirley   RCA LPM1983, RCA DPS2058

ODE TO BILLY JO   (B. Gentry)
1/3-4/68   Jackie Wilson with Count Basie's Orch.   4tp/4tb/2as/2ts/1bs/p/g/b/d/v   Brunswick BL54134

OH LADY BE GOOD   see   LADY BE GOOD

OH! LOOK AT ME NOW   (J. Bushkin/J. DeVries)
1963   Jo Stafford (v)   large orch/vocal group/v   Reprise RS6090, Stanyan 10073

OKAY FOR BABY   see   O.K. FOR BABY

OL' MAN RIVER   (Kern/Hammerstein)
10/3/33   Horace Henderson & His Orch. (Red Allen-v) 3tp/2tb/4reeds/p/g/b/d/v   Prestige 7645
3/31/73   New McKinney's Cotton Pickers (Dave Wilborn-v) Bountiful B38001 NOTE: The New McKinney's recording is based on Carter's 1933 arrangement, but differs in places.

12/18/42*   (AFRS Jubilee #4) BC large orch
6/12/44*   (AFRS Jubilee #83?) BC
4/16/45*   (AFRS Jubilee #129) BC NOTE: This arrangement is probably the same as the one above.

OL' MAN TIME   (C. Friend/J. Reynolds)
7/13/63   Ray Charles (v), The Raelets (v. group)   4tp/4tb/2as/2ts/1bs/p/g/b/d/v/vocal group   ABC 465

OLD DEVIL MOON   (B. Lane/E. Y. Harburg)
4/27/55   Ella Fitzgerald (v) with Benny Carter Orch.   3tp/1tb/2as/2ts/p/g/b/d/v   Decca DL4129, MCA Coral CB20024, MCA Coral (G) 0082.050-2

OLD FASHIONED LOVE   (James P. Johnson/C. Mack)
6/11/57*   BC   1as/1tb/1ts/p/g/b/d

OLD FOLKS   (W. Robison/D. L. Hill)
2/60   Dakota Staton (v)   large orch with strings/v   Capitol T1427

AN OLD LOVE STORY   (H. Atwood/L. Herscher)
1/48*   BC (Emma Lou Welch, The Enchanters-v)   1tp/
                   1tb/1as/1ts/p/g/b/d/v

THE OLD MAN AND THE SEA   (Tiomkin/Webster)
ca. 1958*   Kitty White (v) with Benny Carter & the Orch.
                   1tb/1as/1fr. horn/p/g/b/d/v

ON A HOLIDAY see DEVIL'S HOLIDAY

ON CENSORSHIP   (background music: BC/narrative text: V. Lundberg)
1968   Victor Lundberg (v)   2fr. horns/1woodwind/1harp/
                   10strings/p/g/b/d/narrative v   Liberty LST7547

ON GREEN DOLPHIN STREET   (B. Kaper/N. Washington)
6/60   Dakota Staton (v)   large orch/v   Capitol T1490

8/64*   BC   2ss/4as/3ts/2bs/p/g/b/d

ONCE IN A WHILE   (M. Edwards/B. Green)
11/5/57   Stringin' Along   2reeds/p/vib/g/b/d/string quartet
                   Andex LP3001   NOTE: Personnel includes Bob
                   Keene (cl) and session appears in Jepsen under
                   his name.

ONCE UPON A HAPPY TIME (THE BIG BAND DAYS)   (Bob Friedman)
11/71-3/72   Joe Williams (v)   large orch/v   Temponic
                   TB29561

ONCE UPON A TIME   (BC)
10/10/33*   The Chocolate Dandies   2tp/1tb/1ts/p/g/b/d

• 4/6/55   The Bertie King Jazz Group   Jazz Today (E)
                   JTL5

ONCE UPON A TIME (IT HAPPENED)   (BC/lyrics: J. Moen)
• 6/20/58   Dean Martin (v)   arr: Gus Levine   45: Capitol
                   4065

THE ONE I LOVE BELONGS TO SOMEONE ELSE   (I. Jones/G. Kahn)
1963   Jo Stafford (v)   large orch/vocal group/v   Reprise
                   RS6090, Stanyan 10073

ONE SWEET LETTER FROM YOU   (Clare/Brown/Warren)
9/11/39*   Lionel Hampton (v) & His Orch.   1tp/1as/3ts/p/g/
                   b/d/vib/v

ONE, TWO, BUTTON YOUR SHOE   (Burke/Johnston)
1/23/37   Henry Hall & the B. B. C. Dance Orch. (George
                   Elrick-v)   3tp/3tb/5reeds/p/g/b/d/6strings/v   78:
                   Columbia (E) FB1627, LP: World Records (E)
                   SH172

ONE WAY OUT   (BC)
5/63*   KPM Music Library   4tp/4tb/2fr. horns/5reeds/p/
                   g/b/d/perc   NOTE: See notes for this session in
                   chronological section of discography.

ONLY TRUST YOUR HEART (BC/S. Cahn)
- 8/19/64   The New Stan Getz Quartet (Astrud Gilberto-v) Verve V8600, Verve 2352095 NOTE: This performance of Only Trust Your Heart was included in the soundtrack of the film The Hanged Man (1966) in which Getz and Gilberto appeared.

- 1/3/76*   BC

ONLY YOU (B. Ram/A. Rand)
9/8/55   Louis Armstrong (v) with Benny Carter's Orch. 3tp/2tb/1cl/2as/2ts/p/b/d/v   Vocalion VL73851, MCA Coral 52026, MCA Coral 82051/2

OOFDAH! (BC)
ca. 7/46*   (AFRS Jubilee #203)   BC   large orch

ORGAN GRINDER'S SWING (Hudson/Mills/Parish)
2/15-16/79   Ella Fitzgerald (v) with Count Basie's Orch.   4tp/4tb/5reeds/p/g/b/d/v   Pablo Today 2312-132

OUT OF MY WAY (Sid Catlett)
8/23/46*   BC   (Sid Catlett-v)   1tp/1tb/1as/1ts/p/b/d/v

OUT OF NOWHERE (Green/Heyman)
4/28/37*   Coleman Hawkins & His All Star Jam Band   1tp/1as/1cl/1ts/p/g/b/d

PDQ BLUES (Henry/Simpson)
4/28/27   Fletcher Henderson & His Orch.   3tp/2tb/3reeds/p/banjo/tuba/d   78: Columbia 1002-D, LP: Only For Collectors OFC23 NOTE: In an interview in the May 1936 issue of the British periodical Musical News, Carter recalls his first attempts at arranging. He mentions three pieces which he did for Charlie Johnson's Orchestra--"Do, Do, Do" (from the musical Oh! Kay), "Moonlight on the Ganges," and "Rhapsody in Blue." He then states that he was approached by Fletcher Henderson to do an arrangement of "PDQ Blues." The arranger for Henderson's recording of this title (made on April 28, 1927) is not identified by Walter C. Allen, who suggests in Hendersonia (p. 202) that it may be a stock. Although Carter does not recognize the recording today, it is quite possible that this is his arrangement. If so, it is his first on record, preceding by several months the Charlie Johnson session of January 1928, at which two Carter arrangements were recorded.

PAPA TREE TOP BLUES
1951   Little Miss Cornshucks [pseudonym for Mildred Cummings] (v)   small group/v   Coral 65045

PARADISE (N. H. Brown/G. Clifford)
1945   Sam Donahue & the Navy Band   4tp/4tb/6reeds/p/g/b/d   Big Band Landmarks vol. 24, Hep (E) 5

NOTE: This arrangement was originally done for Fletcher Henderson, probably in the early 1930's. Although the Henderson band never recorded it, Walter Allen notes in his chronology that the band in 1943 "was still using some of Fletcher's old charts from the Benny Goodman days, even a couple of tattered Benny Carter pieces like "Paradise," which Fletcher thought was a masterpiece, and which Chet Kruley and Leon Comegys recalled with respect." (Hendersonia, p. 424)

Note on Hep LP sleeve: "Paradise saxophone chorus, originally written for 4 saxes in the Fletcher Henderson band, was raised in key to accomodate [sic] 6 saxes by Sam Donahue."

PARDON ME, PRETTY BABY (V. Rose/R. Klages/J. Meskill)
   8/18/37*   BC 1tp/1tb/1as/1cl/1ts/p/g/b/d

PASEO PROMENADE (BC) [One of ten pieces comprising Carter's Kansas City Suite.]
   9/6-11/60   Count Basie & His Orch. 4tp/3tb/2as/2ts/1bs/p/g/b/d Roulette (S)R52056, Roulette RE124
                     NOTE: See note on recording date under Kansas City Suite.

PATTY CAKE, PATTY CAKE, BAKER MAN (Waller)
   5/13/39*   BC (Mercedes Carter-v) 3tp/3tb/2as/2ts/p/g/b/d/v

THE PAWNBROKER (Q. Jones/J. Lawrence)
   1965   Sarah Vaughan (v) large orch with strings/v 45: Mercury 72417

PEACE (Rogers/Fields)
   1957   Ernie Andrews (v) with Benny Carter's Orch. large orch/v GNP 28 NOTE: This recording also has a vocal accompaniment by an unknown female singer.

PEOPLE (J. Styne/B. Merrill)
   2/19/64   Billy Eckstine (v) 1tp/1tb/2reeds/p/g/b/d/v/vocal group Mercury SR60916, Mercury MG20916

PHANTOM RAIDERS (BC)
   3/59*   The Music from M Squad large orch NOTE: Composed for TV series M Squad.

PHEASANT FEATHERS see FEASANT PHEATHERS

PICK YOURSELF UP (J. Kern/D. Fields)
   6/60   Dakota Staton (v) large orch Capitol T1490

PINKY (A. Newman)
   1961   Alfred Newman large orch with horns/strings/rhythm section Capitol S(T)1652, Capitol SP8639, Angel S36066

Discography: Arranger/Composer 321

PLAY BALL (BC/lyrics: P. Vandervoort)
1954 Jimmy Maddin (v) & His Orch. small orch/v
 78: Skyway 103

PLAYBOY THEME see CRACK UP

PLAYIN' THE BLUES see BLUE LIGHT BLUES

PLEASE DON'T TALK ABOUT ME WHEN I'M GONE (S. Stept/S. Clare)
2/15-16/79 Ella Fitzgerald (v) with Count Basie's Orch.
 4tp/4tb/5reeds/p/g/b/d/v NOTE: Recorded for Pablo--unissued.

PLEASE PLEASE ME (Lennon/McCartney)
ca. 1966 Keely Smith (v) large orch with strings/v Reprise RS6142

PLEASURES AND PALACES (F. Loesser)
Mar. 30-Apr. 1 Pearl Bailey (v) 4tp/4tb/5reeds/p/g/b/d/v
1965*

POINT OF NO RETURN (BC/lyrics: J. Moen)
1968 Don Wyatt (v) large orch with strings/v NOTE: Recorded for Capitol--unissued.

POLKA DOTS AND MOONBEAMS (J. Van Heusen/J. Burke)
11/5/57 Stringin' Along 2reeds/p/vib/g/b/d/string quartet
 Andex LP3001 NOTE: Personnel includes Bob Keene (cl) and appears in Jepsen under his name.

POM POM (BC)
 • 1/15/40* Varsity Seven

 • 4/29/40 Joe Sullivan & His Cafe Society Orch. Blu-Disc T1005

 5/20/40* BC 3tp/2tb/3as/2ts/p/g/b/d

 • 2/29/46 Eddie Heywood & His Orch. Decca DL8202

POOR FOOL (BC/lyrics: P. Vandervoort)
2/19/64 Billy Eckstine (v) 1tp/1tb/2reeds/p/g/b/d/v/vocal group Mercury SR60919, Mercury MG20916

 • date unknown Ernie Freeman Orch. (Lawrence Stone-v) arr: Ernie Freeman 45: Mambo 107

POOR LITTLE RICH GIRL (N. Coward)
5/63* Stanley Wilson Orch. 4tp/4tb/5reeds/p/g/b/d

THE POWER OF LOVE (A. Schroeder/C. Demetrius)
1965 Lou Rawls (v) 2tp/4tb/2reeds/p/g/b/d/v Capitol T2273

PRISONER OF MY EYES (I CAN NEVER LET YOU GO) (L. Pockriss/H. Hackady)
1968* Nancy Wilson (v) 4tp/4tb/5reeds/p/g/b/d/v

PROHIBIDO   (BC)
<u>3/2/66</u>*   BC   2as/2ts/1bs/p/g/b/d
<u>11/10/73</u>*   BC

PROTECT ME   (H. Dietz/A. Schwartz)
<u>1968</u>   Pearl Bailey (v) with Louis Bellson Orch. 4tp/
                              4tb/5reeds/p/g/b/d/v   Project 3 PR5022SD, Project 3 PR4003SD

PUDDIN' HEAD SERENADE   see   LONESOME NIGHTS

QUEEN FOR A DAY   (B. Blalock)
<u>early 1950's</u>   Bruce Blalock (Ketty Lester?-v) small group/v
                              45: Coral 9-61884

RAIN, RAIN, GO AWAY   (J. Green/E. Heyman/M. David)
<u>4/25/39</u>*   Jerry Kruger (v) & Her Orch.   1tp/2reeds/p/b/d/v

RAINBOW RHAPSODY   (BC)
• <u>7/16/42</u>   Glenn Miller & His Orch.   arr: George Williams
                              4tp/4tb/5reeds/p/g/b/d   Bluebird AXM2-5574
<u>1959</u>   New Glenn Miller Orch. directed by Ray McKinley
                              RCA LSP1948   NOTE: This recording is a recreation, including solos, of the 1942 performance.
<u>late 1950's?</u>   Don Raleigh & His Orch.   Palace PST621   NOTE:
                              This recording also appears on Parade SPS385,
                              A Tribute to Glenn Miller which does not identify
                              the orchestra. It may also be the version of
                              Rainbow Rhapsody included on Spinorama M83,
                              also entitled A Tribute to Glenn Miller.

                              NOTE: The Bluebird LP credits Carter with the
                              arrangement, but Carter recalls it was by George
                              Williams.

RAISIN' THE ROOF   (McHugh/Fields)
<u>ca. 4/29</u>   Fletcher Henderson 2tp/2tb/2cl/as/1ts/p/banjo/
                              tuba   Columbia CL1684

RAMBLING IN C   (BC)
• <u>1/11-16/37</u>*   BC

RANDALL'S ISLAND   (BC)
• <u>12/27/51</u>*   Ben Webster Sextet

RE-BOP BOOGIE   (BC) [also entitled BE-BOP BOOGIE]
<u>8/46</u>*   BC   3tp/2tb/3reeds/p/g/b/d

<u>12/16/47</u>   Freddie Slack & His Orch.   1tp/1tb/1as/p/g/b/d
                              Capitol LC6529   (as Be-Bop Boogie)

RED RED RIBBON
<u>1957</u>   Martha Davis (v) 4tp/4tb/2as/2ts/1bs/p/g/b/d/v
                              NOTE: Recorded for ABC Paramount--unissued.

RED ROSE WALTZ
<u>date unknown</u>   Johnny Ridge [pseudonym for Art Kassel] ?/v
                              45: Kady (no issue number)

Discography: Arranger/Composer 323

REINA (H. Atwood)
1/48*   BC (Bob Decker, The Enchanters-v) 1tp/1tb/1as/
                     1ts/p/g/b/d/v/vocal group

RESPECT (O. Redding)
1/3-4/68   Jackie Wilson (v) with Count Basie Orch. 4tp/
                     4tb/2as/2ts/1bs/p/g/b/d/v Brunswick BL54134

RHUMBOOGIE (D. Raye/H. Prince)
1955   Freddie Slack (v) 1tp/1tb/1ts/1bs/p/g/b/d/v
                     Emarcy MG36094, Wing MGW60003

RHYTHM IS OUR BUSINESS (Lunceford/Cahn/Kaplan)
1/17/36*   Willie Lewis & His Orch. (Bobby Martin-v) 2tp/
                     1tb/2as/2ts/p/g/b/d/v

RHYTHM OF THE TAMBOURINE (D. Franklin)
3/2/37   Fletcher Henderson & His Orch. 3tp/3tb/2cl/as/
                     2ts/p/g/b/d Columbia CL1685

RIDING TO GLORY ON A TRUMPET (McCoy)
1955   Horace Heidt & His Musical Knights (unknown v)
                     3tp/3tb/4reeds/p/g/b/d/v 45: Magnolia MS1070

RIFF ROMP (BC)
8/31/39*   BC 3tp/3tb/3as/2ts/p/g/b/d
10/14/39*   BC

RIFFAMAROLE (BC)
• 3/30/45*   Capitol International Jazzmen

RIGHT HERE IN MY HEART (Bob Friedman)
11/71-3/72   Joe Williams (v) large orch/v Temponic
                     TB29561

RIGHT HERE WITH YOU
8/64*   BC 2ss/4as/3ts/2bs/p/g/b/d

RISE AND SHINE see RISE 'N SHINE

RISE 'N SHINE (Youmans/DeSylva)
ca. 5/36   Henry Hall & the B. B. C. Dance Orch. large
                     orch (B. B. C. broadcast, no known airchecks)

THE RIVER OF NO RETURN (K. Darby/L. Newman)
8/30/74   Yujiro Ishihara (v) 2tp/1tb/1as/2ts/1bs/p/g/b/d/
                     14violins/4violas/4celli/v/vocal group Continental
                     (J) C01 NOTE: Instrumental tracks recorded
                     8/30/74, Los Angeles; vocal added later in Japan.

ROCK ALONE see ROCKIN' ALONG

ROCK BOTTOM (BC)
3/4/66*   BC 2as/2ts/1bs/p/g/b/d
11/10/73*   BC

ROCK ME TO SLEEP (BC/lyrics: P. Vandervoort)
• 5/9/50   Helen Humes (v) accompanied by Marshall Royal
                     & His Orch. Discovery 519, Savoy SJL2242

• 11/14/50	Les Brown & His Orch. (Lucy Ann Polk-v) Columbia CL539
• 1950	Peggy Lee (v) 78: Capitol 1428 45: F1428
1951	Little Miss Cornshucks [pseudonym for Mildred Cummings] (v) small group/v Coral 65045
• ca. 1951	Rudy Render (v) with Maxwell Davis & His Orch. arr: Maxwell Davis 78: London 17014
• 6/58	June Christy (v) accompanied by Bob Cooper's Orch. arr: Bob Cooper Capitol T1076
6/60	Dakota Staton (v) large orch/v Capitol T1490
• 1963	Irene Kral (v) accompanied by Junior Mance Trio Ava 33
• 1963	Maynard Ferguson Roulette (S)R52107? NOTE: Although a "Rock Me to Sleep" is listed on the jacket of this Maynard Ferguson LP, the disc does not actually contain a track with this title. Whether the tune was recorded but not issued, and whether it is Carter's composition or a different song with the same title is not known.

ROCKIN' ALONG   (BC)   also appears as ROCK ALONE
7/26/52*   BC 1tp/1tb/3reeds/p/g/b/d

ROCKIN' CHAIR   (H. Carmichael)

3/22/41*	Gene Krupa & His Orch. featuring BC.
6/7/41	Gene Krupa & His Orch. 4tp/3tb/2as/2ts/p/g/b/d (NBC broadcast from Meadowbrook, Cedar Grove, N. J.)
7/2/41	Gene Krupa & His Orch. Columbia C2L29
10/3/41	Gene Krupa & His Orch. (broadcast from Hollywood Palladium)
4/15/49	Gene Krupa & His Orch. (AFRS One Night Stand #1961) (possibly same arrangement)
4/22/49	Gene Krupa & His Orch. (AFRS One Night Stand #1936) (possibly same arrangement)
8/2/71	Time-Life series The Swing Era (Billy May-leader) Time-Life STL347 NOTE: This recording is a recreation of the 7/2/41 Krupa performance.
9/75	Maria Muldaur, Hoagy Carmichael (v) 2tp/1tb/ 1as/1ts/1bs/p/g/b/d/v Warner Brothers MS2235

ROLL WITH THE BOOGIE   (BC under pseudonym "Johnny Gomez"/lyrics:
F. Cadrez)
9/22/49*   Joe Robinson (v) with Benny Carter's Orch. 1tp/
                          1as/1ts/1bs/p/g/b/d/v

ROMPIN' AT THE RENO   (BC) [One of ten pieces comprising Carter's
Kansas City Suite.]
9/6-11/60   Count Basie & His Orch. 4tp/3tb/2as/2ts/1bs/p/
                          g/b/d Roulette (S)R52056, Roulette (E) 2683-013,

Discography: Arranger/Composer 325

                        Roulette RE124 NOTE: See note on recording
                        date under Kansas City Suite.

ROSES IN DECEMBER (Oakland/Jessel/Magidson)
late 1958 or early   BC 4tp/3tb/5reeds/p/g/b/d
1959*

ROSES OF PICARDY (H. Wood/F. Weatherly)
5/63*   Stanley Wilson Orch. 4tp/4tb/5reeds/20strings/
                      p/g/b/d

'ROUND MIDNIGHT (Hanighen/Williams/Monk)
9/52*   BC with the Oscar Peterson Trio & Buddy Rich
                      horns/strings/p/g/b/d

1957   Ernie Andrews (v) with Benny Carter's Orch.
                      large orch/v GNP 28, GNP-Crescendo 10008

6/60   Dakota Staton (v) large orch with strings/v
                      Capitol T1597

ROW ROW ROW ROW
1961*   Pearl Bailey (v) large orch/v

RUBY (M. Parish/H. Roemheld)
8/30/74   Yujiro Ishihara (v) 2tp/1tb/1as/2ts/1bs/p/g/b/d/
                      14violins/4violas/4celli/v Continental (J) C01
                      NOTE: Instrumental tracks recorded 8/30/74,
                      Los Angeles; vocal added later in Japan.

RUMBLE, RUMBLE, RUMBLE (F. Loesser)
1947   Betty Hutton (v) with Joe Lilley & His Orch.
                      large orch/v 78: Capitol 380

ST. LOUIS BLUES (W. C. Handy)
10/15/40*   Billie Holiday (v) accompanied by Benny Carter
                      Orch. 1tp/1tb/2reeds/p/g/b/d/v

11/25/47*   Freddie Slack & His Orch. 4tp/2tb/2as/2ts/1bs/
                      p/g/b/d

SAN FRANCISCO BLUES
4/15-16/61*   Peggy Lee (v) accompanied by Quincy Jones' Orch.
                      6tp/4tb/2as/2ts/1bs/p/g/b/d/v

SATIN LATIN (Bob Friedman)
11/71-3/72   Joe Williams (v) large orch/v Temponic
                      TB29561

SAVOY STAMPEDE see GIN AND JIVE

SAY IT WITH A KISS (J. Mercer/H. Warren)
11/9/38*   Teddy Wilson & His Orch. (Billie Holiday-v)
                      1tp/1tb/2as/2ts/p/g/b/d/v

SCANDAL IN A FLAT (BC)
mid 6/36*   BC 3tp/2tb/3as/1ts/p/g/b/d

4/22/39*   BC 3tp/3tb/2as/2ts/p/g/b/d

| 7/24/39* | BC |
| 10/9/39* | BC |

6/29/39*   BC   3tp/3tb/2as/2ts/p/g/b/d   NOTE: Differs slightly from 4/22/39* arrangement.

THE SEARCH (BC)
3/59*   The Music from M Squad   large orch   NOTE: Composed for TV series M Squad.

SECOND HAND LOVE   (BC/lyrics: P. Vandervoort under pseudonym "Paul Vance")
11/26/47   Kay Starr (v)   1cornet/3tb/1ts/p/g/b/d/v   78: Capitol 15380

SEPTEMBER SONG   (Anderson/Weill/DeSylva/Brown/Henderson)
late 1958 or early   BC   4tp/3tb/5reeds/p/g/b/d
1959*

8/30/74   Yujiro Ishihara (v)   2tp/1tb/1as/2ts/1bs/p/g/b/d/14violins/4violas/4celli/v   Continental (J) C01   NOTE: Instrumental tracks recorded 8/30/74, Los Angeles; vocal added later in Japan.

SERENADE TO A SARONG (BC)
5/20/40*   BC   3tp/2tb/3as/2ts/p/g/b/d

SHANGRI-LA   (Maxwell)
8/64*   BC   2ss/4as/3ts/2bs/p/g/b/d

SHE DOESN'T LAUGH LIKE YOU   (BC/lyrics: K. Suessdorf, L. Worth)
• ca. 1953   Jack Powers (v) & the Cheer Leaders   78: Click JP-503

SHE HAD TO GO AND LOSE IT AT THE ASTOR
9/29/70   Mrs. Miller (v)   2tp/2tb/2as/1ts/1bs/p/g/b/d/v   45: Mrs. Miller Records (no issue number)

THE SHIP THAT NEVER SAILED   (A. Kassel)
date unknown   Johnny Ridge [pseudonym for Art Kassel] (v)   ?/v   45: Kady (no issue number)

SHOE SHINER'S DRAG   (Jelly Roll Morton)
7/21/38*   Lionel Hampton & His Orch.   1tp/2as/2ts/p/b/d/vib

SHOOT THE WORKS (BC)
12/13/34*   BC   3tp/2tb/3as/1ts/p/g/b/d

SHOW BREAK #1 (BC)
5/63*   KPM Music Library   4tp/4tb/2fr. horns/5reeds/p/g/b/d   NOTE: See notes for this session in chronological section of discography.

SHOW BREAK #2 (BC)
5/63*   KPM Music Library   4tp/4tb/2fr. horns/5reeds/p/g/b/d   NOTE: See notes for this session in chronological section of discography.

Discography: Arranger/Composer

SHOW ME THE WAY TO GO HOME   (I. King)
5/63*   Stanley Wilson Orch.   4tp/4tb/5reeds/20strings/
                            p/g/b/d

SHUFFLEBUG SHUFFLE   (BC)
11/1/39*   BC   3tp/3tb/3as/2ts/p/g/b/d

SIGHS AND TEARS   (BC/lyrics: Mack David)
● 12/17/40   Ginny Simms (v) with Eddie South & His Orch.
                            78: OK 5990

SKIP IT   (BC)
8/17/37*   BC   3tp/2tb/2as/2ts/p/g/b/d

● 9/20/56   Bertie King Jazz Group   Nixa (E) NJT506

THE SKY IS CRYING   (BC/lyrics: P. Herrick)
● 2/1/50   Mary Ann McCall (v)   arr: Al Cohn   78: Roost
                            511

SLEEP   (E. Lebieg)
1/30/40*   BC   3tp/3tb/3as/2ts/p/g/b/d
May or later 1943*   (AFRS Basic Library P-33)   BC
4/30/45*   (AFRS Jubilee #131)   BC
7/2/72*   BC
12/3/73*   BC

SLEIGH RIDE IN JULY   (Burke/Van Heusen)
late 1958 or early   BC   4tp/3tb/5reeds/p/g/b/d
1959*

SLIDES AND HIDES   (BC/L. Bellson)
1/18/65   Buddy Rich - Louis Bellson with the George Kawa-
                            guchi Orch.   4tp/6tb/5reeds/p/g/b/2d   Roost
                            SLP2263, Roulette (E) 2432-003   NOTE: Recorded
                            in Tokyo.

SLOW BUT SURE   (BC/lyrics: A. Hansen)
● early 1950's   Kay Brown (v)   arr: Van Alexander   45: Crown
                            45x132

● ca. 1957   Ruth Olay (v)   Emarcy MG36125

SLOW FREIGHT   (Buck Ram)
1/30/40*   BC   3tp/3tb/2as/2ts/p/g/b/d

SMACK DAB IN THE MIDDLE   (C. E. Calhoun)
1964   Ray Charles (v) & the Raelets   5tp/3tb/2as/2ts/
                            1bs/p/g/b/d/v   ABC Paramount 495

SO IN LOVE   (C. Porter)
6/60   Dakota Staton (v)   large orch with strings/v
                            Capitol T1597

SO LONG, MY LOVE   (Cahn/Spence)
1/63   Sarah Vaughan (v)   4tp/4tb/2as/2ts/1bs/p/g/b/d/v
                            Roulette R(S)52104

SOFT AND SWEET   (E. Sampson)
3/30/31*   Chick Webb & His Orch.   3tp/1tb/2as/c1/1ts/p/g/
                         b/d

SOFT TOUCH   (BC)
11/65   film soundtrack: A Man Called Adam   1tb/1ts/p/
                         b/d Reprise 6180

SOLITUDE   (D. Ellington/E. DeLange/I. Mills)
2/60   Dakota Staton (v)   large orch with strings/v
                         Capitol T1427

1/63   Sarah Vaughan (v)   4tp/4tb/2as/2ts/1bs/p/g/b/d/v
                         Roulette R(S)52104, Roulette RE103

8/13/79   Sarah Vaughan (v)   1flute/1ts/9violins/3violas/
                         2celli/p/g/b/d/v   NOTE: Recorded for Pablo--
                         unissued.

SOME OF THESE DAYS   (S. Brooks)
9/12/36*   BC med Sonora Swing Band   2tp/1tb/1cl/1ts/p/g/
                         b/d

SOME OTHER SPRING   (Kitchings/Herzog)
2/15-16/79   Ella Fitzgerald (v) with Count Basie's Orch.
                         4tp/4tb/5reeds/p/g/b/d/v   NOTE: Recorded for
                         Pablo--unissued.

SOMEBODY LOVES ME   (B. Macdonald/B. DeSylva/G. Gershwin)
10/3/30*   Fletcher Henderson & His Orch.   3tp/2tb/2as/
                         1ts/p/g/b/d/v(trio)

8/18/37*   BC   1tp/1tb/1cl/1ts/p/g/b/d

early 1945*   (AFRS Jubilee?)   BC
4/30/45*   (AFRS Jubilee #131)   BC

SOMEONE TO WATCH OVER ME   (G. and I. Gershwin)
12/20/65   Johnny Hodges with Lawrence Welk Orch.   4tb/
                         3fr. horns/1as/p/g/b/d/vib/strings   Dot DLP25682

SOMETHING FOR OCTOBER   (BC)
late 1958 or early   BC   4tp/3tb/5reeds/p/g/b/d
1959*

SONG OF THE WANDERER   (N. Moret)
1957   Ernie Andrews (v) with Benny Carter's Orch.
                         large orch/v   GNP 28, GNP-Crescendo 10008

SOPHISTICATED LADY   (D. Ellington)
8/13/79   Sarah Vaughan (v)   1flute/2cl/1bass cl/3fr. horns/
                         1oboe/1ts/9violins/3violas/2celli/1harp/p/g/b/d/v
                         NOTE: Recorded for Pablo--unissued.

SORRY   see   I'M SORRY

SOUTH SIDE SAMBA   (BC)
  • 3/18/77*   BC

Discography: Arranger/Composer   329

```
4/29/77*              BC  2tp/1tb/3reeds/p/g/b/d
6/2/79*               BC
July 1981*            BC

• 4/18/81*            BC

• 9/26/81*            BC

• 11/28/81*           BC

• 12/5/81*            BC
```

SOUVENIR (BC)   originally entitled THAT'S HOW IT GOES
  12/3/73*   BC 4tp/4tb/3as/2ts/1bs/p/g/b/d (as That's How It Goes)
  4/8/77*   BC with the Princeton University Jazz Ensemble

  4/29/77*   BC 2tp/1tb/3reeds/p/g/b/d NOTE: This arrangement is similar to the one above.

• 1978   Mundell Lowe Dobre DR1018

• 1978   The Capp/Pierce Juggernaut arr: Nat Pierce Concord CJ72

• 4/18/81*   BC

SPRING FEVER BLUES (L. Whenham)
  1954   The Dream Dusters (v) with Jimmie Maddin (v) & His Orch. small orch/v/vocal group 78: Skyway 103

SQUATTY ROO (J. Hodges)
  4/29/77*   BC 2tp/1tb/3reeds/p/g/b/d

SQUEEZE ME (T. Waller/C. Williams)
  12/22/74*   Maria Muldaur (v) 2tp/1tb/1as/1ts/1bs/p/g/b/d/v
  1974   Maria Muldaur (v) Reprise MS2194

STAR DUST (H. Carmichael/M. Parish)
  1/17/36*   Willie Lewis & His Orch. 2tp/1tb/2as/2ts/p/g/b/d

  4/22/39*   BC 3tp/3tb/2as/2ts/p/g/b/d NOTE: This is a slightly altered version of the 1/17/36 arrangement. The saxophone chorus has been retained.

  7/11/44*   (AFRS Jubilee #87) BC large orch
  early 1945?*   (AFRS Jubilee?) BC

STARS AND YOU (BC)
• 1/11-16/37*   BC 1tp/1as/p

STATE FAIR
                    For Carter's work on this movie musical see the individual title THAT'S FOR ME.

STAY OUT OF LOVE (Gerlach/Freniere)
  1/17/36*   Willie Lewis (v) & His Orch. 2tp/1tb/2as/2ts/p/g/b/d/v

STICK OR TWIST   (BC)
  early 1960's   Laurie Johnson Orch.   8brass/5reeds/p/g/b/d
                        NOTE: Test pressing--may have been issued.

STINKIN' FROM DRINKIN'   (BC/lyrics: P. Vandervoort)
  • ca. 1949   Calvin Boze (v) & His All Stars   78: Aladdin
                        3072

STORMY WEATHER   (H. Arlen/T. Koehler)
  Jan.-Feb. 1943*   film soundtrack: Stormy Weather (Lena Horne-v)
                        large orch with strings/v

  Jan.-Feb. 1943*   film soundtrack: Stormy Weather   large orch
                        with strings/vocal group   NOTE: Carter arranged
                        last 29 measures.

STROLL   (BC)
  • 11/30/76*   BC   1as/p/b/d

SUGAR BLUES   (C. McCoy)
  9/61   Jonah Jones with Glen Gray & the Casa Loma
                        Orch.   6tp/4tb/2as/2ts/1bs/p/g/b/d   Capitol T1713

SUMMER NIGHT   (BC/lyrics: Jimmy Kennedy)   also known as WONDERLAND
  • ca. 1961   Harry Williams (v)   45: Pye (issue number unknown)

  • 1962   Mantovani & His Orch.   45: Decca 11500

  • 11/30/76*   BC   1tp/1as/1ts/p/b/d

SUMMERTIME   (G. Gershwin/D. Heyward)
  4/25/39*   Jerry Kruger (v) & Her Orch.   1tp/2reeds/p/b/d/v

SUMMERTIME IN VENICE   (Pinchi/Sigman/Cicognini)
  8/30/74   Yujiro Ishihara (v)   2tp/1tb/1as/2ts/1bs/p/g/b/d/
                        14violins/4violas/4celli/v   Continental (J) C01
                        NOTE: Instrumental tracks recorded 8/30/74,
                        Los Angeles; vocal added later in Japan.

A SUNBONNET BLUE
  ca. 5/36   Henry Hall & the B.B.C. Dance Orch.   large
                        orch   (B.B.C. broadcast, no known airchecks)

SUNDAY   (Miller/Cohn/Stein/Kruger)
  10/16/41*   BC   3tp/3tb/3as/2ts/p/g/b/d
  6/4/45*   (AFRS Jubilee #136)   BC

SUNDAY AFTERNOON   (BC)
  10/2/52*   BC   3tp/3tb/2as/2ts/1bs/p/g/b/d

SUNSET EYES   (T. Edwards/D. Wayne)
  1957   Ernie Andrews (v) with Benny Carter's Orch.
                        large orch/v   GNP 28, GNP-Crescendo 10008

SUNSET GLOW   (BC) [One of ten pieces comprising Carter's Kansas City
Suite.]

Discography: Arranger/Composer

9/6-11/60   Count Basie & His Orch.   4tp/3tb/2as/2ts/1bs/p/ g/b/d   Roulette (S)R52056, Roulette RE124   NOTE: See note on recording date under Kansas City Suite.
8/9/62   Count Basie & His Orch.   NOTE: Recorded live in Stockholm--unissued.

SUPPER TIME   (I. Berlin)
1971   Pearl Bailey (v)   4tp/4tb/5reeds/p/g/b/d/strings/v   RCA LSP4529

SURF BOARD   (BC)
• 5/49*   BC   1tp/1tb/1as/1ts/p/b/d

SUSPICIOUS OF MY WOMAN   (BC under pseudonym "Johnny Gomez"/B. Austin)
9/22/49*   Joe Robinson (v) with Benny Carter's Orch.   1tp/ 1as/1ts/1bs/p/g/b/d/v

SWEDISH JAM   (BC/D. Gillespie/J. J. Johnson/J. Adderley)
• 11/22/60*   Jazz At The Philharmonic

SWEET AND HOT   (J. Yellen/H. Arlen)
2/5/31*   Fletcher Henderson & His Orch.   (Jimmy Harrison-v)   3tp/2tb/2as/1ts/p/g/b/d/v

SWEET GEORGIA BROWN   (B. Bernie/M. Pinkard/K. Casey)
7/11/44*   (AFRS Jubilee #87)   BC   large orch
3/19/45*   (AFRS Jubilee #125)   BC

SWEET LORRAINE   (Burwell/Parish)
2/15-16/79   Ella Fitzgerald (v) with Count Basie's Orch.   4tp/4tb/5reeds/p/g/b/d/v   Pablo Today 2312-132

SWEET RHYTHM   (Maxey/Bechet)
11/15/32   Cab Calloway & His Orch.   3tp/2tb/4reeds/p/g/b/ d/v   Collector's Classics 20

SWEETHEART   (K. Burgan)
12/22/74*   Maria Muldaur (v)   2tp/1tb/1as/1ts/1bs/p/g/b/d/v
1974   Maria Muldaur (v)   Reprise MS2194

SWING IT   (Bretz/Weitz)
3/14/33*   BC (v)   3tp/2tb/2as/1ts/p/g/b/d/v

SWINGIN' AT MAIDA VALE   (BC)   originally entitled JUST A RIDE
3/27/36   Henry Hall & the B. B. C. Dance Orch.   large orch   (B. B. C. broadcast, no known airchecks)

4/15/36*   BC   3tp/2tb/3as/2ts/p/g/b/d   NOTE: This arrangement may be the same as or similar to the 3/27/36 version above.

SWINGIN' IN NOVEMBER   (BC)
late 1958 or early   BC   4tp/3tb/5reeds/p/g/b/d
1959*
11/9/68*   BC with Henri Chaix & His Orch.   NOTE:

                              Similar arrangement but performed by 1tp/1tb/
                              2as/1ts/1bs/p/b/d

SWINGIN' THE BLUES   (BC)
   late 4/36*   BC 2tp/1cl/1as/1ts/p/g/b/d

SWINGIN' WITH RHYTHM AND BLUES (J. Barnett/J. Durante)
   ca. 1957   Jimmy Durante, Peter Lawford (v) 4tp/4tb/2as/
                              2ts/1bs/p/g/b/d/v 45: Decca 9-29581

THE SWIZZLE   (BC)
   11/1-2/61*   Count Basie & His Orch.   4tp/3tb/2as/2ts/1bs/p/
                              g/b/d

SYMPHONY (Alstone/Lawrence)
   1/4/54*   BC horns/strings/p/b/d

SYMPHONY IN RIFFS   (BC)
   10/16/33*   BC 3tp/3tb/3as/1ts/p/g/b/d
   4/28/37   Artie Shaw & His Orch.   Thesaurus Transcription
                              402, Alamac QSR2434
   7/8/38   Artie Shaw & His Orch.   (broadcast, aircheck?)
   7/25/38   Tommy Dorsey & His Orch. RCA (F) FXM1-
                              7171, Historia (G) H628
   ca. 8/39   Gene Krupa & His Orch. (broadcast from Steel
                              Pier, Atlantic City)
   9/20/39   Gene Krupa & His Orch. Bandstand 7117, Colum-
                              bia Special Products JCL641, Ajax 121
   11/5/39   Gene Krupa & His Orch. (broadcast, Sherman
                              Hotel, Chicago)
   2/5/40   Glenn Miller & His Orch. (aircheck, NBC broad-
                              cast, Hotel Pennsylvania, New York)
   3/4/40   Glenn Miller & His Orch. (aircheck, NBC broad-
                              cast, Hotel Pennsylvania, New York)
   6/22/40   Tommy Dorsey & His Orch. featuring Bunny
                              Berigan Fanfare 4-104 (aircheck)
   3/8/58   Glen Gray & His Casa Loma Orch. Capitol
                              SM1022, Capitol (G) IC054-81 710 NOTE: This
                              recording is a recreation, including note-for-note
                              solos of the 9/20/39 Gene Krupa version and is
                              included in the Time-Life series The Swing Era
                              Time-Life STL344.
   date unknown   Electrecord Orch. (Roumania) Electrecord 0971
                              NOTE: This is a recreation, including solos, of
                              Carter's 10/16/33* recording.

 • 4/20/55   The Jazz Today Unit (Kenny Baker-leader, fea-
                              turing Bertie King) Jazz Today (E) JTL5 NOTE:
                              This arrangement is based on Carter's.

SYNTHETIC LOVE   (BC/lyrics: N. Washington)
   3/14/33*   BC (v) 3tp/2tb/2as/1ts/p/g/b/d/v
   12/13/34*   BC (Charles Holland-v)

TAKE BACK YOUR MINK   (F. Loesser)
   Mar. 30-Apr. 1   Pearl Bailey (v) 4tp/4tb/5reeds/p/g/b/d/v
   1965*

Discography: Arranger/Composer

TAKE IT OR LEAVE IT   (BC/lyrics: M. Hammond)
● 11/11/47*   Julia Lee (v) & Her Boy Friends

TAKE MY WORD   see   LONESOME NIGHTS

TAKIN' MY TIME   (BC)
11/19/40*   BC   3tp/3tb/2as/2ts/1bs/p/g/b/d

TEA FOR TWO   (V. Youmans/I. Caesar)
4/22/39*   BC   3tp/3tb/2as/2ts/p/g/b/d
5/27/39*   BC (Mercedes Carter-v)

TEACH ME TONIGHT   (Cahn/DePaul)
2/15-16/79   Ella Fitzgerald (v) with Count Basie's Orch.   4tp/
                       4tb/5reeds/p/g/b/d/v   Pablo Today 2312-132

TENDER LOVING WORDS   (Bob Friedman)
11/71-3/72   Carmen McRae (v)   large orch/v   Temponic
                       TB29562

TENDERLY   (W. Gross/J. Lawrence)
9/61   Jonah Jones with Glen Gray & the Casa Loma
                       Orch.   6tp/4tb/2as/2ts/1bs/p/g/b/d   Capitol
                       T1713

THAT AIN'T IT   (BC/lyrics: P. Vandervoort)
1950   Virgie Austin (v)   small orch/v   78: London
                       17009

THAT OLD BLACK MAGIC   (H. Arlen/J. Mercer)
4/27/55   Ella Fitzgerald with Benny Carter Orch.   3tp/1tb/
                       2as/2ts/p/g/b/d/v   Decca DL8155, MCA Coral
                       (G) 0082.050-2

THAT'S FOR ME   (Rodgers/Hammerstein)
1962   film soundtrack: State Fair (Pat Boone-v)   large
                       orch with strings/v   Dot DLP9011

THAT'S HOW IT GOES   see   SOUVENIR

THEM THERE EYES   (M. Pinkard/W. Tracey/D. Tauber)
4/29/77*   BC   2tp/1tb/3reeds/p/g/b/d
4/15/78*   BC
4/19?/78*   BC

THERE I'VE SAID IT AGAIN   (R. Evans/D. Mann)
1/21/41*   BC (Roy Felton-v)   3tp/3tb/3as/2ts/p/g/b/d/v

THERE'LL NEVER BE ANOTHER YOU   (H. Warren)
early 1970's   The Airmen of Note (U.S. Air Force Jazz En-
                       semble) (Sarah Vaughan-v) 4tp/4tb/5reeds/p/g/b/
                       d/v   NOTE: Promotional album: The Airmen of
                       Note and Sarah Vaughan (no label and issue)

THERE'S A SMALL HOTEL   (Rodgers/Hart)
1/11-16/37*   BC (v)   2tp/2tb/3as/2ts/p/g/b/d/v
1/11-16/37*   BC

THESE FOOLISH THINGS (J. Strachey/H. Link)
 4/15/36*   BC 3tp/2tb/3as/2ts/p/g/b/d

 2/9/42*   Mark Warnow & His Orch. (Barry Wood-v) 3tp/
                    2tb/6reeds/7violins/1harp/p/g/b/d/v

 1/63   Sarah Vaughan (v) 4tb/20strings/p/g/b/d/v
                    Roulette R(S)52104, Roulette RE103

THEY SAY (E. Heyman/P. Mann/S. Weiss)
 11/9/38*   Teddy Wilson & His Orch. (Billie Holiday-v) 1tp/
                    1tb/2as/2ts/p/g/b/d/v

THINGS AIN'T WHAT THEY USED TO BE (D. Ellington)
 4/29/77*   BC 2tp/1tb/3reeds/p/g/b/d
 4/15/78*   BC
 4/19?/78*   BC
 July 1981*   BC

THIS CAN'T BE LOVE (Rodgers/Hart)
 11/5-6/56   Abbey Lincoln (v) 1tp/1tb/1fr. horn/3woodwinds/p/
                    g/b/d/v Liberty LRP3025

THREE O'CLOCK IN THE MORNING (J. Robledo/D. Terriss)
 1965   Lou Rawls (v) large orch with strings/vocal
                    group/v Capitol T2401, Capitol SM2948

THREE TIME LOSER (WITH A TWO TIME GIRL) see I'M A THREE
TIME LOSER

TICKLE TOE (Lester Young)
 8/64*   BC 2ss/4as/3ts/2bs/p/g/b/d

TIGER RAG
                    NOTE: Melody Maker (May 30, 1936) reports that
                    Carter was commissioned by Henry Hall to arrange
                    this tune. It may have been broadcast by Hall and
                    the B.B.C. Dance Orchestra. There are no known
                    airchecks.

TILL WE MEET AGAIN (R. Whiting/R. Egan)
 2/14/40*   Freddie Rich & His Orch. 3tp/1tb/3as/3ts/p/g/b/d

TIME AFTER TIME (J. Styne/S. Cahn)
 11/56   Billy Daniels (v) accompanied by Benny Carter's
                    Orch. 1tp/4reeds/p/g/b/d/strings/v Verve
                    MGV2072

TIRED (B. Lown/T. Kurrus)
 1961*   Pearl Bailey (v) large orch/v

TITMOUSE (BC)
 3/4/66*   BC 2as/2ts/1bs/p/g/b/d
 11/9/68*   BC with Henri Chaix & His Orch.

TO AVA see BLUE MOUNTAIN

Discography: Arranger/Composer

TO THE DESTROYERS (background music: BC/narrative text: V. Lundberg)
1968   Victor Lundberg (v) 2fr. horns/1woodwind/1harp/
                10strings/p/g/b/d/narrative v Liberty LST7547

TONIGHT I SHALL SLEEP WITH A SMILE ON MY FACE (D. Ellington)
8/13/79   Sarah Vaughan (v) 1flute/2cl/1bass cl/3fr. horns/
                1oboe/1ts/9violins/3violas/2celli/1harp/p/g/b/d/v
                NOTE: Recorded for Pablo--unissued.

TOOT TOOT TOOTSIE (T. Fiorito/R. A. King/G. Kahn/E. Erdman)
1961*   Pearl Bailey (v) large orch/v

TRANSATLANTIC (BC)
                NOTE: Melody Maker (May 30, 1936) reports that
                Carter was commissioned by Henry Hall to arrange this tune. It may have been broadcast by
                Hall and the B. B. C. Dance Orchestra. There are
                no known airchecks.

TRAPPED IN THE WEB OF LOVE (Jeanne Burns)
6/60   Dakota Staton (v) large orch/v Capitol T1490

TREE OF HOPE (BC)
10/16/41*   BC 3tp/3tb/3as/2ts/p/g/b/d

THE TROLLEY SONG (H. Martin/R. Blane)
1962   Sarah Vaughan (v) 4tp/4tb/5reeds/p/g/b/d/vib/v
                Roulette R(S)52092, Roulette (E) 2682-043

THE TROT (BC)
10/30-31/61*   Count Basie & His Orch. 4tp/3tb/2as/2ts/1bs/p/
                g/b/d

TRUMPETS HAVE TRIPLETS (DeVol)
1955   Horace Heidt & His Musical Knights 3tp/3tb/
                4reeds/p/g/b/d 45: Magnolia MS1070

TURNABOUT (BC)
11/1-2/61*   Count Basie & His Orch. 4tp/3tb/2as/2ts/1bs/p/
                g/b/d

TUTTI FRUTTI (D. Fisher/S. Gaillard)
8/2/54*   Mel Torme (v) 4tp/4tb/5reeds/p/g/b/d/v

TWELVE O'CLOCK JUMP (BC/S. Shepherd)
8/46*   BC 3tp/2tb/1as/1ts/1bs/p/g/b/d

TWO AGAIN (T. Grouya)
1944*   (AFRS Basic Library P-238) BC (Savannah
                Churchill-v) large orch/v

TWO CIGARETTES IN THE DARK (P. Webster/L. Pollack)
11/5-6/56   Abbey Lincoln (v) 1tp/1tb/1fr. horn/3woodwinds/p/
                g/b/d/v Liberty LRP3025

TWO LEFT HANDS (BC/lyrics: I. Gordon) [registered with ASCAP as
HE'S GOT TWO LEFT HANDS]

• 1947   Freddie Slack   (Charlotte Blackburn-v)   78: Capitol 15035

TWO O'CLOCK JUMP   (H. James)
9/61   Jonah Jones with Glen Gray & the Casa Loma Orch.   6tp/4tb/2as/2ts/1bs/p/g/b/d   Capitol T1713, Capitol (G) IC054-81 710

TWO TICKETS WEST   (R. Stevens/J. Zackery)
1965   Lou Rawls (v)   2tp/4tb/2reeds/p/g/b/d/v   Capitol T2273

UNDER PARIS SKIES   (Gannon/Drejac/Giraud)
5/63*   Stanley Wilson Orch.   horns/strings/vocal group/rhythm section

UPTIGHT (EVERYTHING'S ALL RIGHT)   (S. Moy/S. Wonder/H. Cosby)
1/3-4/68   Jackie Wilson (v) with Count Basie Orch.   4tp/4tb/2as/2ts/1bs/p/g/b/d/v   45: Brunswick 55365, LP: Brunswick BL54134

VAGABOND DREAMS   (H. Carmichael/J. Lawrence)
10/28/39*   BC (Roy Felton-v)   3tp/3tb/2as/2ts/p/g/b/d/v
11/1/39*   BC (Roy Felton-v)

VALLEY OF THE DOLLS
                         For Carter's work on this film soundtrack see the individual title I'LL PLANT MY OWN TREE.

THE VERY THOUGHT OF YOU   (R. Noble)
11/19/40*   BC (Roy Felton-v)   3tp/3tb/2as/2ts/1bs/p/g/b/d/v

2/60   Dakota Staton (v)   large orch with strings/v   Capitol T1427

VINE STREET RUMBLE   (BC) [one of ten pieces comprising Carter's Kansas City Suite.]
9/6-11/60   Count Basie & His Orch.   4tp/3tb/2as/2ts/1bs/p/g/b/d   Roulette (S)R52056, Roulette RE124   NOTE: See note on recording date under Kansas City Suite.

VINHO VERDE   (BC)
5/63*   KPM Music Library   4tp/4tb/2fr. horns/5reeds/p/g/b/d   NOTE: Carter rewrote the melody to this piece and called it "Green Wine" (with lyrics by Leonard Feather) under which title he later recorded it.   See also notes for this session in chronological section of discography.

VOUS QUI PASSEZ SANS ME VOIR   (C. Trenet/J. Hess)
5/63*   BC   1as/p/b/d/vocal group

WALKIN' ONE AND ONLY   (D. Hicks)
12/22/74*   Maria Muldaur (v)   2tp/1tb/1as/1ts/1bs/p/g/b/d/v

A WALKIN' THING   (BC)
7/22/57*   BC   1tp/1as/1ts/p/g/b/d

Discography: Arranger/Composer 337

* 4/1/64   Phineas Newborn   Contemporary S7615

* 5/68   Milt Jackson & the Hip String Quartet   arr: Tom McIntosh   Verve V6-8761

12/3/73*   BC   4tp/4tb/3as/2ts/1bs/p/g/b/d/conga
10/28/78*   BC with the University of Buffalo Jazz Ensemble directed by Phil Sims

* 2/11/76*   BC

WALTZ GAY   (BC)
* 5/63*   BC

WALTZING THE BLUES   (BC)
* 6/20/36*   BC

THE WANG WANG BLUES   (Mueller/Johnson/Busse/Wood)
5/16/29   Fletcher Henderson & His Orch.   3tp/2tb/2cl/as/1ts/p/banjo/tuba/d   Columbia CL1684

WANNA GO HOME   (J. Thomas/H. Biggs)
8/18/52*   BC   3tp/2tb/5reeds/p/g/b/d/10strings/vocal group

WAY DOWN YONDER IN NEW ORLEANS   (Layton/Creamer)
3/27/36   Henry Hall & the B.B.C. Dance Orch.   large orch   (B.B.C. broadcast, no known airchecks)

WE JUST COULDN'T SAY GOODBYE   (H. Woods)
9/75   Maria Muldaur (v)   2tp/1tb/1as/1ts/1bs/p/2g/b/d/v/vocal group   Warner Brothers MS2235

WE SAW THE SEA   (I. Berlin)
4/4/36   Henry Hall & the B.B.C. Dance Orch.   (Dan Donovan-v)   large orch   78: Columbia (E) FB1364

WE WERE IN LOVE   (BC--words & music)
3/4/66*   BC   2as/2ts/1bs/p/g/b/d

* ca. 1966   Irma Curry (v)   arr: Ernie Freeman   45: Vee-Jay 669

WEAK FOR THE MAN   (Jeanne Burns)
6/60   Dakota Staton (v)   large orch/v   Capitol T1490

THE WEEKEND OF A PRIVATE SECRETARY   (B. Hanighen/J. Mercer)
9/29/70   Mrs. Miller (v)   2tp/2tb/2as/1ts/1bs/p/g/b/d/v   45: Mrs. Miller Records (no issue number)

WEST END BLUES   (King Oliver)
9/61   Jonah Jones with Glen Gray & the Casa Loma Orch.   6tp/4tb/2as/2ts/1bs/p/g/b/d   Capitol T1713

WHAT A DIFFERENCE A DAY MADE   (S. Adams/M. Grever)
4/1/41*   BC (Maxine Sullivan-v)   3tp/3tb/3as/2ts/p/g/b/d/v

WHAT ARE YOU DOING THE REST OF YOUR LIFE? (Bergman/Legrand)
   early 1970's   The Airmen of Note (U. S. Air Force Jazz Ensemble) (Sarah Vaughan-v) 4tp/4tb/5reeds/p/g/b/d/v NOTE: Promotional album: Airmen of Note Come Out Swinging (no label and issue)

WHAT IS A MAN? (Rodgers/Hart)
   Mar. 30-Apr. 1   Pearl Bailey (v) 4tp/4tb/5reeds/p/g/b/d/v
   1965*

WHAT KIND OF FOOL AM I? (A. Newley)
   5/63*   Stanley Wilson Orch. 4tp/4tb/5reeds/20strings/p/g/b/d

WHATCHA KNOW JOE? (Young)
   1963   Jo Stafford (v) large orch/vocal group/v Reprise RS6090, Stanyan 10073

WHAT'LL I DO? (I. Berlin)
   1/63   Sarah Vaughan (v) 4fr. horns/p/g/b/d/tuba/v 45: Roulette 4516, LP: Roulette R(S)52104

WHAT'LL IT BE? (BC)
   ● 8/23/46*   BC 1tp/1tb/1as/1ts/p/b/d

WHAT'S NEW? (B. Haggart/J. Burke)
   10/14/39*   BC (Dell St. John-v) 3tp/3tb/2as/2ts/p/g/b/d/v
   10/23/39*   BC (Dell St. John-v)

WHAT'S THE NAME OF THAT SONG? (V. Lawnhurst/T. Seymour)
   5/2/36   Henry Hall & the B. B. C. Dance Orch. (Dan Donovan-v) 3tp/3tb/5reeds/p/g/b/d/6strings/v 78: Columbia (E) FB1400
   1936   Henry Hall & the B. B. C. Dance Orch. (probably Dan Donovan-v) (B. B. C. broadcast, no known airchecks)

WHEN DAY IS DONE (DeSylva/Katscher)
   late 4/36*   BC 2tp/1cl/1as/1ts/p/g/b/d

WHEN IT'S SLEEPY TIME DOWN SOUTH (L. and O. Rene/C. Muse)
   4/29/77*   BC 2tp/1tb/3reeds/p/g/b/d
   4/15/78*   BC
   4/19?/78*   BC
   July 1981*   BC

WHEN IT'S TIME TO TELL (Bob Friedman)
   11/71-3/72   Carmen McRae (v) large orch/v Temponic TB29562

WHEN LIGHTS ARE LOW (BC/lyrics: Spencer Williams)
   ● 6/20/36*   BC (Elisabeth Welch-v) (with bridge)

   8/29/36*   BC (v) with Kai Ewans' Orch. 3tp/2tb/3as/2ts/p/g/b/d (with bridge)

   ● 1937   Teddy Joyce & His Orch. (unknown v) 78: Decca (E) F6063 (with bridge)

Discography: Arranger/Composer

8/31/39*	BC (Dell St. John-v) 3tp/3tb/3as/2ts/p/g/b/d/v (with bridge)
9/11/39*	Lionel Hampton & His Orch. 1tp/1as/3ts/p/g/b/d/vib (with bridge)
5/30-31/79	Bob Wilber & the American All Stars featuring Lars Erstrand Phontastic 7526
• 1940	Svenska Hotvintetten 78: Columbia DS1227
• 5/4/49	Putte Wickmans Orch. 78: Cupol 4225 (with bridge)
• 7/17/52	George Shearing Quintet 45: MGM x4072, LP: Verve 2683-069 (with bridge)
• 5/19/53	Miles Davis Quartet Prestige 7822 (without bridge)
• 9/5/55	Georg Riedel Sextet Metronome MEP152
• 1/19/56	Bud Shank - Bob Cooper Quartet Pacific Jazz PJ1219 (without bridge) NOTE: On this live recording, "When Lights Are Low" is announced as a Miles Davis composition.
• 10/26/56	Kenny Clarke arr: Andre Hodeir Epic LN3376 (without bridge)
• 10/26/56	Miles Davis New Quintet Prestige 7094 (without bridge)
• 1956	Pete Jolly Trio RCA LPM1367, RCA (J) RGP1085
• 4/29/57	Herbie Mann arr: A. K. Salim Epic LN3395 (without bridge)
• 4/57	Cal Tjader Quartet Fantasy S8084
• 6/58	June Christy (v) arr: Bob Cooper Capitol T1076, Capitol W1162 (with bridge)
• 7/58	Oscar Peterson Trio Verve MGV8287 (without bridge)
• 9/58	Chet Baker Riverside RLP12-281, Riverside RS1119, Riverside (J) SMJ6095, Jazzland 998 (without bridge)
• 1958	Nils Bertil Dahlander [Bert Dale] Verve MGV8253
• 1958	Oscar Peterson Trio Verve MGV8268 (without bridge)
• 3/10/59	Arne Domnerus & His Orch. arr: Georg Riedel Telefunken BLE14120
• 6/24/59	Billy Taylor Trio Atlantic SD1329

- 1959   Curtis Fuller Sextet   arr: Curtis Fuller?   United
                 Artists UAS5041

- 1959   Bill Shepherd Orch. with the Beryl Scott Chorus
                 arr: Bill Shepherd   Roulette R25086 (with
                 bridge)

- 1959   Dakota Staton (v) arr: Sid Feller Capitol T1241
                 (with bridge)

- late 1950's   Alice Babs & Ulrick Neuman (v) Dot DLP3128
                 (with bridge)

- 10/31/60   Dick Morgan   Riverside RLP12-347 (without
                 bridge)

- 1/2-4/61   Frans van Bergen   CNR (Holland) LPT35006

- 8/21/61   Webster Young   VGM 0005 (without bridge)

- 8/30/61   Eric Dolphy Inner City 3017 (without bridge)

- 9/6/61   Eric Dolphy Prestige 24027 (without bridge)

- 10/15-17/61   Buddy DeFranco Mercury MG20685, Mercury
                 SR60685

- 1961   Vic Damone (v) arr: Jack Marshall Capitol
                 T1646 (with bridge)

- 3/62   Art Blakey & the Jazz Messengers arr: Cedar
                 Walton   United Artists UAS5633 (without bridge)

- 4/10/62*   BBB & Co. (with bridge)

- 2/12-13/63   Howard Roberts   Capitol ST1887 (with bridge)

- 1963   Tony Bennett (v) with Ralph Sharon Trio Columbia CL2175 (with bridge)

- ca. 1963   Sarah Vaughan (v) Roulette (E) 2682-032 (with
                 bridge)

- 11/28/66   Richard "Groove" Holmes Prestige 7493

- ca. 1966   Harry Edison arr: Julian Lee Liberty LST7484
                 (with bridge)

- ca. 1968   Eric Delaney Saga (Eros) 8050 (with bridge)

- 7/29/71   Jaki Byard Swing (F) 05, Musica (F) 2008 (with
                 bridge)

- 10/7/72   Joe Albany Revelation 16, Spotlight (E) JA3
                 (without bridge)

- 10/22/73*   BC (with bridge)

Discography: Arranger/Composer   341

12/3/73*	BC 4tp/4tb/3as/2ts/1bs/p/g/b/d (with bridge)
4/8/77*	BC with the Princeton University Jazz Ensemble
10/28/78*	BC with the University of Buffalo Jazz Ensemble directed by Sam Falzone
10/28/78*	BC with the University of Buffalo Jazz Ensemble directed by Phil Sims
• 1973	Bobby Hackett, Vic Dickenson Hyannisport HR1002 (with bridge) NOTE: Rhythm section featured on this track--Hank Jones (p), Remo Palmieri (g), George Mraz (b), Jackie Williams (d)
• 2/12/74	Chuck Folds RCA LFL1-5064 (with bridge)
• 5/10/75	Conte Condoli - Frank Rosolino MPS (G) 68.167
• 1/3/76*	BC (Millicent Browne-v) (with bridge)
• 12/27/76	Chuck Wayne Quartet arr: Chuck Wayne? Progressive Records 7008 (with bridge)
• 1976	Elisabeth Welch (v) World Records SH233 (with bridge)
• 9/77	Cal Tjader Galaxy GXY5107 (with bridge)
• 1979	Kenny Burrell Concord CJ83 (without bridge)
• 1980	Joe Kennedy Black and Blue (F) 33.171 (with bridge)
• 1981	Pharoah Sanders Theresa TR112/113 (with bridge)
• 7/18/81*	BC (with bridge)
• 9/26/81*	BC (with bridge)
	NOTE: Many recordings after 1953 follow the Miles Davis version, which does not include Carter's original bridge, but rather repeats the "A" section up a fourth. The presence or absence of the original bridge is noted for those recordings which have been verified by the authors.

WHEN TWILIGHT COMES	(Bob Friedman)
11/71-3/72	Carmen McRae (v) large orch/v Temponic TB29562

WHEN YOU'RE SMILING	(L. Shay/J. Goodwin/M. Fisher)
ca. 5/36	Henry Hall & the B.B.C. Dance Orch. large orch (B.B.C. broadcast, no known aircheks)
4/29/77*	BC (Joe Newman-v) 2tp/1tb/3reeds/p/g/b/d/v
4/15/78*	BC (Joe Newman-v)

4/19?/78*   BC (Joe Newman-v)
July 1981*   BC (Pete Candoli-v)

WHEN YOU'RE YOUNG   (Bob Friedman/lyrics: S. Cahn)
11/71-3/72   Joe Williams (v)   large orch/v   Temponic
                       TB29561

WHERE OR WHEN   (Rodgers/Hart)
5/5/46*   BC large orch

WHISPER TO ONE   (BC/lyrics: A. Stillman)
• 11/65   film soundtrack: A Man Called Adam (Sammy
                       Davis, Jr.-v) Reprise 6180

WHISPERING GRASS   (D. Fisher/F. Fisher)
2/60   Dakota Staton (v)   large orch with strings/v
                       Capitol T1427

1965   Lou Rawls (v)   2tp/4tb/2reeds/p/g/b/d/v
                       Capitol T2273

WHO'S BLUE?   (BC)
11/1-2/61*   Count Basie & His Orch.   4tp/3tb/2as/2ts/1bs/p/
                       g/b/d

WHO'S TIRED?   (L. Bellson)
Mar. 30-Apr. 1   Pearl Bailey (v)   4tp/4tb/5reeds/p/g/b/d/v
1965*

WHO'S WHO   (BC)
1/22-24/62   Louis Bellson Orch.   5tp/3tb/1fr. horn/1tuba/2as/
                       2ts/1bs/p/g/b/d/vib   Roulette R52087, Roulette
                       (E) 2934-020

WHO'S YEHOODI?   (M. Dennis)
5/18/40   Cab Calloway (v) & His Orch.   3tp/3tb/3as/2ts/
                       p/g/b/d/v   Jazz Archives JA8

THE WIGGLE WALK   (BC) [One of ten pieces comprising Carter's Kansas
City Suite.]
9/6-11/60   Count Basie & His Orch.   4tp/3tb/2as/2ts/1bs/p/
                       g/b/d   Roulette (S)R52056, Roulette RE124
                       NOTE: See note on recording under Kansas City
                       Suite.

WILL YOU STILL BE MINE?   (M. Dennis/T. Adair)
6/60   Dakota Staton (v)   1tp/1reed/p/g/b/d/v   Capitol
                       T1597

THE WINE OF SWEET REMEMBRANCE   (BC/lyrics: J. Flint)
• 1967   Martha Mason (v)   ?/v   45: Take V (no issue
                       number)

WISH YOU WERE HERE   (H. Rome)
8/18/52*   BC   3tp/2tb/5reeds/p/g/b/d/10strings/vocal group

WITH A SONG IN MY HEART   (Rodgers/Hart)
1/4/54*   BC horns/strings/p/b/d

Discography: Arranger/Composer 343

WITHOUT A WORD OF GOODBYE (BC/lyrics: P. Vandervoort)
- 1950's   Lawrence Stone (v) with Ernie Freeman's Orch.
                  arr: Ernie Freeman 45: Vita 45-V-115

WONDERLAND see SUMMER NIGHT

WOULDN'T IT BE LOVERLY (A. J. Lerner/F. Lowe)
2/19/64   Billy Eckstine (v) 1tp/1tb/2reeds/p/g/b/d/v/vocal
                  group Mercury SR60916, Mercury MG20916

YASSU (D. Tiomkin)
1961   film soundtrack: The Guns of Navarone large
                  orch with strings Columbia CL1655, Columbia
                  CS8455

YES INDEED (S. Oliver)
1963   Jo Stafford (v) large orch/vocal group/v Reprise
                  RS6090, Stanyan 10073

YOU AIN'T THE ONE (C. Johnson/A. Porter)
1/24/28*   Charlie Johnson's Paradise Orch. (Monette
                  Moore-v) 2tp/1tb/3as/cl/1ts/p/banjo/tuba/d/v

YOU ARE (BC/lyrics: F. Herbert)
7/2/72*   BC 5tp/4tb/3as/2ts/1bs/p/g/b/d

12/3/73*   BC 4tp/4tb/3as/2ts/1bs/p/g/b/d

YOU ARE NOT MY FIRST LOVE
1957   Martha Davis (v) 4tp/4tb/2as/2ts/1bs/p/g/b/d/v
                  NOTE: Recorded for ABC Paramount--unissued.

YOU BELONG TO ME (P. W. King/R. Stewart/C. Price)
8/18/52*   BC 3tp/2tb/5reeds/p/g/b/d/10strings

YOU CALL IT MADNESS (R. Colombo/C. Conrad/G. DuBois/P. Gregory)
6/60   Dakota Staton (v) large orch with strings/v
                  Capitol T1597

YOU GO TO MY HEAD (J. F. Coots/H. Gillespie)
11/56   Billy Daniels (v) accompanied by Benny Carter's
                  Orch. 1tp/4reeds/p/g/b/d/strings/v Verve
                  MGV2072

YOU TURNED THE TABLES ON ME (L. Alter/S. Mitchell)
11/56   Billy Daniels (v) accompanied by Benny Carter's
                  Orch. 4tp/4tb/2as/2ts/1bs/p/g/b/d/v Verve
                  MGV2072

YOU UNDERSTAND (BC/R. Sonin)
mid 6/36*   BC 3tp/2tb/2as/1ts/p/g/b/d

YOU'D BETTER THINK IT OVER (BC/lyrics: P. Vandervoort)
1957   Martha Davis (v) 4tp/4tb/2as/2ts/1bs/p/g/b/d/v
                  NOTE: Recorded for ABC Paramount--unissued.

Mar. 30-Apr. 1   Pearl Bailey (v) 4tp/4tb/5reeds/p/g/b/d/v
1965*

YOU'LL NEVER BREAK MY HEART AGAIN (H. Atwood/L. Herscher)
    1/48*   BC (Emma Lou Welch, The Enchanters-v)   1tp/1tb/1as/1ts/p/g/b/d/v

YOU'LL NEVER GET THE CHANCE AGAIN (BC/lyrics: P. Vandervoort)
    • 1954   Helen Troy (v), Charles Schrouder (bass v) with Van Alexander's Orch.   arr: Van Alexander   45: Vito VO-109X

YOUNG AND IN LOVE
    ca. 1959   Dean Jones (v)   ?/v   MGM K12462

YOUR CONSCIENCE TELLS YOU SO (BC/lyrics: D. Raye)
    • 4/24/46   Ella Mae Morse (v) with Freddie Slack   78: Capitol 278

    8/46*   BC (Lucy Elliott-v)   3tp/2tb/1as/1ts/1bs/p/g/b/d/v

YOU'RE DRIVING ME CRAZY (W. Donaldson)
    1953-1954   Lincoln Chase (v) with Spencer-Hagen Orch.   small group/v   Liberty LRP3076

    1/63   Sarah Vaughan (v)   4fr. horns/p/g/b/d/tuba/v   Roulette S(R)52104

YOU'RE GONE FOR A LONG LONG TIME
    1953   Ernie Andrews (v) with Benny Carter's Orch.   large orch/v   78: Trend 2502

YOU'RE GONNA MISS IT (BC under pseudonym "Johnny Gomez"/lyrics: P. Vandervoort)
    • 7/21/50   Julia Lee (v) & Her Boy Friends   (unissued)

YOU'RE MINE YOU (J. Green/E. Heyman)
    2/60   Dakota Staton (v)   large orch with strings/v   Capitol T1427

YOU'RE MY EVERYTHING (H. Warren/M. Dixon/J. Young)
    11/56   Billy Daniels (v) accompanied by Benny Carter's Orch.   1tp/4reeds/p/g/b/d/strings/v   Verve MGV2072

YOU'RE ON THE RIGHT TRACK BABY (BUT YOU'RE GOIN' THE WRONG WAY) (BC/lyrics: I. Gordon)
    • 12/8/47   Louis Jordan & His Tympany Five (Louis Jordan, Martha Davis-v)   78: Decca 24502

INDEX OF ARTISTS WHO HAVE RECORDED
CARTER ARRANGEMENTS AND/OR COMPOSITIONS

a = Carter arrangement   c = Carter composition

THE AIRMEN OF NOTE   (U. S. AIR FORCE JAZZ ENSEMBLE)
early 1970's
My Funny Valentine (Sarah Vaughan-v) a
There'll Never Be Another You (Sarah Vaughan-v) a
What Are You Doing the Rest of Your Life? (Sarah Vaughan-v) a

ALBANY, JOE
10/7/72   When Lights Are Low c

ALEXANDER, JOE
9/22/47   I'm a Three Time Loser c

ALEXANDER, VAN see Helen Troy

ANDERSON, ERNESTINE see Bob Friedman

ANDREWS, DEBBIE
1949   I Ain't Got Nobody a
                I Lost You a

ANDREWS, ERNIE
1953   All Alone and Lonesome a, c
                Don't Lead Me On a
                Make Me a Present of You a
                You're Gone for a Long Long Time a
1957   But Now I Know a
                In the Dark a
                Just Squeeze Me a
                Lover Come Back to Me a
                Peace a
                'Round Midnight a
                Song of the Wanderer a
                Sunset Eyes a

ARMSTRONG, LOUIS
9/8/55   Christmas in New Orleans a
                Christmas Night in Harlem a
                Moments to Remember a
                Only You a
                See also Soundtrack: The Five Pennies NOTE: The liner notes to MCA 1334 suggest that two 1942 recordings by Armstrong, "Among My Souvenirs" and "Cash for Your Trash," are Carter arrangements. Carter denies this.

THE ARMY AIR FORCE BAND   see   Glenn Miller

AUSTIN, VIRGIE
   1950   I'm Such a Fool to Be in Love with You c
                          That Ain't It a, c

AVRO ORCHESTRA   see   BC 8/2/36

AZAMA, ETHEL
   1959   Friendly Islands c

B. B. C. DANCE ORCHESTRA   see   Henry Hall

BABS, ALICE
   late 1950's   When Lights Are Low (with Ulrick Neuman) c

BACON, LOUIS   see   Chick Webb

BAILEY, MILDRED
   9/15/31   Blues in My Heart (with the Casa Loma Orch.) c

BAILEY, PEARL
   1961   Row Row Row Row a
                          Tired a
                          Toot Toot Tootsie a
   Mar. 30-Apr. 1   Big Nobody a
   1965   Hey There a
                          I Shoulda Quit When I Was Ahead a
                          Look at That Face a
                          A Man Is a Necessary Evil a
                          Pleasures and Palaces a
                          Take Back Your Mink a
                          What Is a Man a
                          Who's Tired a
                          You'd Better Think It Over a, c
   1968   Baby, Don't You Quit Now (with Louis Bellson Orch.) a
                          Protect Me (with Louis Bellson Orch.) a
   1971   Here's That Rainy Day a
                          A House Is Not a Home a
                          I Never Met a Stranger a
                          It's Impossible a
                          Mama, a Rainbow a
                          Supper Time a

BAKER, CHET
   9/58   When Lights Are Low c

BAKER, KENNY   see   Jazz Today Unit

BARBRO, LARRY
   1955   Millions of People a, c

BARNES, MAE
   1958   Blues in My Heart c

BARNET, CHARLIE
   1/21/35   Devil's Holiday (as On a Holiday) a, c
   6/2/38

Arranger/Composer: Artist Index

Nagasaki a
See also California Ramblers

BASIE, COUNT
9/6-11/60
Blue Five Jive a, c
Jackson County Jubilee a, c
Katy Do a, c
Meetin' Time a, c
Miss Missouri a, c
Paseo Promenade a, c
Rompin' at the Reno a, c
Sunset Glow a, c
8/9/62
Vine Street Rumble a, c
The Wiggle Walk a, c
10/30-31/61
The Basie Twist a, c
Goin' On a, c
The Legend a, c
The Trot a, c
11/1-2/61
Amoroso a, c
Easy Money a, c
8/10/62
The Swizzle a, c
Turnabout a, c
Who's Blue? a, c
10/20/69
Blues in My Heart c
5/6/76
JJJJump c
Kansas City Line c
Mama Don't Wear No Drawers c
See also Ella Fitzgerald, Jackie Wilson

BAXTER, LES see Gordon MacRae

BECHET, SIDNEY
10/6-9/50
Blues in My Heart (with Claude Luter) c

BELLSON, LOUIS
1/22-24/62
Amoroso a, c
Blitzen a
Doozy a, c
A Foggy Day a
Gumshoe a, c
Lou's Blues a, c
The Moon Is Low a
Who's Who a, c
See also Pearl Bailey, Buddy Rich

BENNETT, TONY
1963
When Lights Are Low (with Ralph Sharon Trio) c

BERIGAN, BUNNY
7/20/36
Lonesome Nights (as Take My Word) a, c
4/8/38
Devil's Holiday a, c
6/27/38
See also Tommy Dorsey

THE BIG EIGHTEEN
6/24/58
O.K. For Baby c

BIG MAYBELLE [MABEL SMITH] see Christine Chatham

BLACKBURN, CHARLOTTE see Freddie Slack

BLAKE, EUBIE
 ca. 9/31   Blues in My Heart (Dick Robertson-v) c

BLAKEY, ART
 3/62   When Lights Are Low c

BLALOCK, BRUCE
 early 1950's   Bodyguard (Ketty Lester?-v) a
                    Lady Oh Lady c
                    Queen for a Day (Ketty Lester?-v) c

BOONE, PAT see Soundtrack: State Fair

BOWLLY, AL see Ray Noble

BOWMAN, DAVE
 3/46   Cow Cow Boogie c

BOZE, CALVIN
 ca. 1949   Look Out for Tomorrow c
                    Stinkin' from Drinkin' c

BRADLEY, BETTY see Bob Chester

BRONSON, BETTY see Ray Herbeck

BROOKS, KIRBY see Ray Herbeck

BROWN, KAY
 early 1950's   Slow But Sure c

BROWN, LES
 8/10/43   O.K. for Baby c
 11/14/50   Rock Me to Sleep (Lucy Ann Polk-v) c

BROWNE, MILLICENT see BC 1/3/76

BUCKNER, MILT
 5/30/76   Blues in My Heart (with Arnett Cobb/Panama
                    Francis) c

BULLOCK, CHICK see Mills Blue Rhythm Band

BURNS, RALPH see Anita O'Day

BURRELL, KENNY
 1979   When Lights Are Low c

BUZON, JOHN
 ca. 1959   Blues in My Heart c

BYARD, JAKI
 7/29/71   When Lights Are Low c

BYRD, CHARLIE
 1976   Cow Cow Boogie (with Barney Kessel, Herb
                    Ellis) c

Arranger/Composer: Artist Index

CAIN, JACKIE   see   Charlie Ventura

CALIFORNIA RAMBLERS (CHARLIE BARNET ORCHESTRA)
5/6/37   Lonesome Nights   (as Take My Word)   a, c

CALLOWAY, CAB
5/6/31   Blues in My Heart   c
6/9/32   Hot Toddy   a, c
                 9/21/32
                 1932 (Soundtrack: The Big Broadcast of 1932)
11/15/32   Sweet Rhythm   a
10/27/38   Blue Interlude   c
5/18/40   Calling All Bars   a
                 The Lone Arranger   a
                 Who's Yehoodi   a
8/28/40   Lonesome Nights   a, c

CALVIN, ROSEMARY   see   Freddie Rich

CANDOLI, CONTE
5/10/75   When Lights Are Low   (with Frank Rosolino)   c

CAPITOL INTERNATIONAL JAZZMEN
3/30/45   Riffamarole   c

CAPP, FRANKIE
1978   Souvenir   (with Nat Pierce)   c

CARMICHAEL, HOAGY   see   Maria Muldaur

CARR, HELEN
11/11/55   My Kind of Trouble Is You   c

CARROLL, BARBARA   see   Sylvia Syms

CARROLL, DIHANN
1960   Guiding Light   c

CARTER, BENNY, CHORALE   see   Bob Friedman

CARTER, KING
3/23/31   Blues in My Heart   (Dick Robertson-v)   a?, c
                 NOTE: Although his name appears as leader,
                 Carter was not present. King Carter and His
                 Royal Orchestra was an Irving Mills - sponsored
                 unit.

CARTER, MERCEDES
                 See chronological section of discography for vari-
                 ous arrangements and compositions recorded by
                 this vocalist with the Carter Orchestra in 1939.

CASA LOMA ORCHESTRA   see   Mildred Bailey, Glen Gray

CATLETT, SID   see   BC 8/23/46

CAVANAUGH, DAVE   see   Kitty White

CHAIX, HENRI   see   BC 11/9/68

CHARLES, RAY
  7/13/63   Busted (with the Raelets-v) a
  7/13/63   In the Evening (When the Sun Goes Down) (with the Raelets-v) a
                          Ol' Man Time (with the Raelets-v) a
  1964   Feudin' and Fightin' (with the Raelets-v) a
                          Ma (She's Making Eyes at Me) a
                          Smack Dab in the Middle (with the Raelets-v) a

CHASE, LINCOLN
  1953-1954   Johnny Klingaringding (with Spencer-Hagen Orch.) a
                          You're Driving Me Crazy (with Spencer-Hagen Orch.) a

CHATHAM, CHRISTINE
  4/6/44   Hurry Hurry (Mabel Smith [Big Maybelle]-v) c

CHEATHAM, DOC
  5/2/75   Blues in My Heart c

THE CHEER LEADERS   see Jack Powers

CHESTER, BOB
  1941-1942   Blues in My Heart (Betty Bradley-v) c

CHILDS, REGGIE
  1939   Melancholy Lullaby (Marion Kaye-v) c

CHITTISON, HERMAN see Ethel Waters

THE CHOCOLATE DANDIES
  9/18/29   That's How I Feel Today a
  12/4/30   Goodbye Blues a, c
  12/31/30   Bugle Call Rag a
                          Dee Blues a, c
                          Got Another Sweetie Now (Jimmy Harrison-v) a
  10/10/33   Blue Interlude a, c
                          I Never Knew a
                          Krazy Kapers a, c
                          Once Upon a Time a, c
                          See also BC 8/23/46

CHRISTY, JUNE
  5/9/55   Lonely Woman (with Stan Kenton) c
  6/58   Rock Me to Sleep (accompanied by Bob Cooper) c
                          When Lights Are Low c
                          See also Stan Kenton

CHURCHILL, SAVANNAH
                          See chronological section of discography for various arrangements and compositions recorded by this vocalist with the Carter Orchestra during 1943-1946.

CLARKE, KENNY
  10/26/56   When Lights Are Low c

CLUMP, CLARENCE [pseudonym for Benny Carter]   see   BC 12/14/48

COBB, ARNETT
   2/27/59   Blues in My Heart   c
                       See also Milt Buckner

COLEMAN, BILL
   5/24/56   Blues in My Heart   c

COLIN, SID   see   R. A. F. Dance Orchestra

CONNOR, CHRIS
   4/9/62   Lonely Woman   c

COOK, J. LAWRENCE
   date unknown   Cow Cow Boogie   (piano roll)   c

COOPER, BOB   see   June Christy, Bud Shank

COTY, BILL   see   McKinney's Cotton Pickers

CRAYTON, PEE WEE
   ca. 1950   Blues in My Heart   c
   1953-1955   Hurry Hurry   c

CRISS, SONNY
   2/24/75   Blues in My Heart   c

CRISTOBAL, CHICO
   11/15/46   Cow Cow Boogie   c

CROTHERS, SCAT MAN
   ca. 1949   I'd Rather Be a Rooster   c

CUMMINGS, MILDRED   see   Little Miss Cornshucks

CURRY, IRMA
   ca. 1966   A Heart Must Learn to Cry   a
                       We Were in Love   c

DAHL, PAT
   1966   It's Alright with Me   a
                       Lonely Woman   a, c

DAHLANDER, NILS BERTIL [BERT DALE]
   1958   When Lights Are Low   c

DALE, BERT   see   Nils Bertil Dahlander

DAMONE, VIC
   1961   When Lights Are Low   c

DANIELS, BILLY
   11/56   Blue Prelude   a
                       Blue Skies   a
                       Comes Love   a
                       Hallelujah   a

                        How Am I to Know   a
                        It's De-Lovely   a
                        Just in Time   a
                        A Melody from the Sky   a
                        Time After Time   a
                        You Go to My Head   a
                        You Turned the Tables on Me   a
                        You're My Everything   a

DAVIS, BLIND JOHN
    ca. 1976   Cow Cow Boogie   c

DAVIS, EDDIE "LOCKJAW"
    ca. 1951   Blues in My Heart   c

DAVIS, LEM
    10/20/45   Blues in My Heart   c

DAVIS, MARTHA
    1949   I Ain't Gettin' Any Younger   c
    1957   A Hundred Years from Today   a
                        Red Red Robin   a
                        You Are Not My First Love   a
                        You'd Better Think it Over   a, c
                        See also Louis Jordan

DAVIS, MAXWELL   see   Rudy Render

DAVIS, MILES
    5/19/53   When Lights Are Low   c
    10/26/56

DAVIS, SAMMY, JR.   see   Soundtrack: A Man Called Adam

DECKER, BOB   see   BC 1/48

DeFRANCO, BUDDY
    10/15-17/61   When Lights Are Low   c

DELANE, NICK   see   Jimmy Zito

DELANEY, ERIC
    ca. 1968   When Lights Are Low   c

DEPPE, LOIS   see   Fletcher Henderson

DERWIN, HAL   see   Shep Fields

DOLPHY, ERIC
    8/30/61   When Lights Are Low   c
    9/6/61

DOMNERUS, ARNE
    3/4/55   Key Largo   c
    3/10/59   When Lights Are Low   c
    11/60   Melancholy Lullaby   c

Arranger/Composer: Artist Index

DONAHUE, SAM
1945   Paradise (see note in title listings) a
1945?   Lonesome Nights c

DONOVAN, DAN see Henry Hall

DORN, PAT
1965   Blue Train a, c
Brazilian Twist a, c
Gonna Build a Mountain a
High Society Limbo a, c

DORSEY, JIMMY
5/26/39   A Home in the Clouds (Helen O'Connell-v) c
9/5/39   Melancholy Lullaby (Helen O'Connell-v) c

DORSEY, TOMMY
7/25/38   Symphony in Riffs a, c
6/22/40 (featuring Bunny Berigan)

THE DREAM DUSTERS
1954   Spring Fever Blues (with Jimmie Maddin (v) and Orch.) a

DREW, KENNY see Jane Fielding

THE DRIFTERS
ca. 1950   I'm the Caring Kind c

DURANTE, JIMMY
ca. 1957   Swingin' with Rhythm and Blues (with Peter Lawford-v) a

EBERLE, RAY see Glenn Miller

ECKSTINE, BILLY
2/19/64   A Beautiful Friendship a
People a
Poor Fool a, c
Wouldn't It Be Loverly a
1968   I'll Be Here with You c

EDISON, HARRY "SWEETS"
1964   Blues in My Heart c
The Girl from Ipanema a
I Don't Know What Kind of Blues I've Got a
I'm Lost a
ca. 1966   When Lights Are Low c

ELDRIDGE, ROY
9/9/39   Lady Be Good a
3/28/51   I Still Love Him So (as I'd Love Him So) c
1/16/76
See also BC 1/9/55

THE ELECTRECORD ORCHESTRA (ROUMANIAN)
date unknown   Symphony in Riffs a, c

ELLINGTON, DUKE
9/21/32   Jazz Cocktail   a, c
1947   Key Largo (Ellington Gang) c

ELLIOTT, LUCY
                   See chronological section of discography for various arrangements and compositions recorded by this vocalist with the Carter Orchestra during 1945-1946.

ELLIS, HERB   see   Charlie Byrd

ELRICK, GEORGE   see   Henry Hall

THE ENCHANTERS   see   BC 1/48

ERSTRAND, LARS   see   Bob Wilber

EVANS, DON
1958   How Long Is a Moment   a, c
                   It's So Frightnin'   a, c

EWANS, KAI   see   BC 8/26/36, 8/29/36

FAYE, ALICE   see   Soundtrack: The Gang's All Here

FEATHERSTONHAUGH, BUDDY
2/14/45   Blues in My Heart (with the Radio Rhythm Club Sextet) c

FELDKAMP, ELMER   see   Bert Lown

FELTON, ROY
                   See chronological section of discography for various arrangements and compositions recorded by this vocalist with the Carter Orchestra during 1939-1941.

FERGUSON, MAYNARD
1963   Rock Me to Sleep   c

FIELDING, JANE
2/56   Key Largo (with the Kenny Drew Quintet) c

FIELDS, SHEP
5/22/39   A Home in the Clouds (Hal Derwin-v) c

FITZGERALD, ELLA
11/3/43   Cow Cow Boogie (with the Ink Spots-v) c
4/27/55   Between the Devil and the Deep Blue Sea   a
                   Lover Come Back to Me   a
                   Old Devil Moon   a
                   That Old Black Magic   a
5/10/68   It's Up to You and Me   a
2/15-16/79   Ain't Misbehavin' (with Count Basie's Orch.)   a
                   Don't Worry 'Bout Me (with Count Basie's Orch.)   a
                   Honeysuckle Rose (with Count Basie's Orch.)   a
                   I'm Getting Sentimental Over You (with Count Basie's Orch.)   a

Just A-Sittin' and A-Rockin' (with Count Basie's Orch.) a
My Kind of Trouble Is You (with Count Basie's Orch.) a, c
Organ Grinder's Swing (with Count Basie's Orch.) a
Please Don't Talk About Me When I'm Gone (with Count Basie's Orch.) a
Some Other Spring (with Count Basie's Orch.) a
Sweet Lorraine (with Count Basie's Orch.) a
Teach Me Tonight (with Count Basie's Orch.) a
NOTE: In addition, Carter arranged and played on a series of medleys for Ella Fitzgerald's Capitol LP 30 By Ella. See 5/28, 5/29, and 6/3/68 in chronological section of discography.

FOLDS, CHUCK
2/12/74   When Lights Are Low c

FORREST, HELEN see Artie Shaw

FOSLIEN, ORRIN see New McKinney's Cotton Pickers

FRANCIS, PANAMA see Milt Buckner

FREEMAN, ERNIE
date unknown   Poor Fool (Lawrence Stone-v) c
                See also Lawrence Stone

FRIEDMAN, BOB
11/71-3/72   All I Need Is You (Ernestine Anderson-v) a
               Betty (Benny Carter Chorale-v) a
               Bobby (Benny Carter Chorale-v) a
               Bossa Nova Sonata (A Serenade to Genie) (Gene Merlino-v) a
               The Day Your Love Comes True (Ernestine Anderson-v) a
               How Do I Love Thee (Bob Grabeau-v) a
               I Love You (Sue Raney-v, vocal group) a
               Jane (Benny Carter Chorale-v) a
               Jenny (Benny Carter Chorale-v) a
               Little Bit O'Heaven (Bob Grabeau-v) a
               Mary (Benny Carter Chorale-v) a
               Pretty Girl (Bob Grabeau-v) a
               Serenade to Genie (Bob Grabeau-v) a
               Sleepy Baby (Benny Carter Chorale-v) a
               Tender Loving Words (Benny Carter Chorale-v) a
               Thank You, Mr. Moon (Ernestine Anderson-v) a
               That's Love (Benny Carter Chorale-v) a
               NOTE: Amateur songwriter Bob Friedman commissioned Carter to arrange and conduct a number of his compositions for recording. The recordings, made between November 1971 and March 1972 featured vocalists Carmen McRae and Joe Williams among others. Many top jazz players also took part, such as Sweets Edison, Jimmy Rowles, Flip Phillips, Barney Kessel and Jimmy Jones. The Williams and McRae tunes were released on LPs on Friedman's own label, Temponic,

and were widely available commercially. These performances are listed here under Carmen McRae and Joe Williams. The remainder of Carter's arrangements for Friedman appeared on a two-record Temponic limited issue, Twenty-Five Years, which Friedman dedicated to his wife on their anniversary. These items are listed above.

FULLER, CURTIS
1959   When Lights Are Low c

GELLER, HARRY   see   Frankie Laine, Patti Page

GETZ, STAN
8/19/64   Only Trust Your Heart (Astrud Gilberto-v) c

GILBERTO, ASTRUD   see   Stan Getz

GILLESPIE, DIZZY   see   BC 4/27/76

GONELLA, NAT
9/26/41   Kansas City Moods c

GOODMAN, BENNY
8/16/34   It Happens to the Best of Friends (Ann Graham-v) a
                         Lonesome Nights (as Take My Word) a, c
9/11/34   I'm Getting Sentimental Over You (Tony Sacco-v) a
1/15/35   Blue Moon (Helen Ward-v) a
                         Limehouse Blues a
8/8/38   Blue Interlude (Martha Tilton-v) a, c
2/9/39   A Home in the Clouds (Martha Tilton-v) c
10/19/42   Cow Cow Boogie (Peggy Lee-v) c
                         See also Soundtrack: The Gang's All Here
                         NOTE: In addition to the recorded arrangements cited, Benny Goodman's files indicate the following scores were supplied by Carter: "Earful of Music" (signed score, dated 1934) and "Don't Let That Moon Get Away" (1938). Also, a 1934 arrangement of Carter's "Blues in My Heart" may have been by Carter. There are no known airchecks of these arrangements.

GRABEAU, BOB   see   Bob Friedman

GRACEN, THELMA   see   Freddie Slack

GRAHAM, ANN   see   Benny Goodman

GRAY, DICK   see   BC 5/21/44

GRAY, GLEN
3/8/58   Symphony in Riffs (with Casa Loma Orch.)
                         (Time-Life series The Swing Era) a, c
8/14/59   Malibu (with Casa Loma Orch.) (Time-Life series The Swing Era) a, c
                         NOTE: These two recordings are recreations--

Arranger/Composer: Artist Index

                          see notes in title listings.
                          See also Jonah Jones, Time-Life series

HACKETT, BOBBY
   ca. 1958   Blues in My Heart   c
   1973   When Lights Are Low   (with Vic Dickenson)   c

HALL, AL
   1/24/46   Blues in My Heart   c

HALL, HENRY
   4/4/36   I'm Putting All My Eggs in One Basket   (Dan Donovan-v, and the B.B.C. Dance Orch.)   a
                          We Saw the Sea   (Dan Donovan-v, and the B.B.C. Dance Orch.)   a
   5/2/36   What's the Name of That Song   (Dan Donovan-v, and the B.B.C. Dance Orch.)   a
                          1936   (Dan Donovan-v, and the B.B.C. Dance Orch.)   a
   10/24/36   Bye Bye Baby   (George Elrick-v, and the B.B.C. Dance Orch.)   a
   1/23/37   One, Two, Button Your Shoe   (George Elrick-v, and the B.B.C. Dance Orch.)   a
                          NOTE: According to 1936 issues of the Melody Maker, the following Carter arrangements were broadcast over the B.B.C. by Henry Hall and the B.B.C. Dance Orchestra. There are no known airchecks.
   3/27/36   Blues in My Heart   a, c
                          I Got Rhythm   a
                          Indiana   a
                          Swingin' at the Maida Vale   a, c
                          Way Down Yonder in New Orleans   a
   5/7/36   Chickfeed   a, c
                          I Never Knew   a
                          Nightfall   a, c
                          The Melody Maker also lists the following Carter arrangements as being aired around the same time--ca. May 1936 (no known airchecks):
                          Hold Me Tight, I'm Falling   a
                          I'm Tickled to Death I'm Me   a
                          Let It Be Me   a
                          Rise and Shine   a
                          A Sunbonnet Blue   a
                          When You're Smiling   a
                          Finally, the Melody Maker reports that Carter was commissioned to arrange the following tunes for Henry Hall and the B.B.C. Dance Orchestra. They may have been included in a broadcast:
                          Blue Interlude   a, c
                          Dirty Hands, Dirty Face   a
                          I Ain't Got Nobody   a
                          The Man I Love   a
                          Tiger Rag   a
                          Transatlantic   a, c

HALL, RENE   see David Swift

HAMPTON, LIONEL
   7/21/38   Any Time at All a
                              I'm in the Mood for Swing a, c
                              Muskrat Ramble a
                              Shoe Shiner's Drag a
   9/11/39   Early Session Hop a
                              One Sweet Letter from You a
                              When Lights Are Low a, c
                              9/11/39 (take #2)
   ca. 1960   Lonesome Nights c
   12/61

HARRIS, BIXIE see BC 1/5/46

HARRIS, WYNONIE see Lucky Millinder

HARRISON, JIMMY see The Chocolate Dandies, Fletcher Henderson

HAWKINS, COLEMAN
   4/28/37   Crazy Rhythm a
                              Honeysuckle Rose a
                              Out of Nowhere a

HEIDT, HORACE
   1955   Bugle Call Rag a
                              Riding to Glory on a Trumpet a
                              Trumpets Have Triplets a

HENDERSON, BOBBY
   3/69   A Home in the Clouds (two versions) c

HENDERSON, FLETCHER
   4/28/27   P. D. Q. Blues (see note in title listings) a
   12/12/28   Come on Baby a
                              Easy Money a
   ca. 4/29   Raisin' the Roof a
   5/16/29   Blazin' a
                              The Wang Wang Blues a
   10/3/30   Somebody Loves Me a
   12/2/30   Keep a Song in Your Soul a
   2/5/31   My Pretty Girl (Lois Deppe-v) a
                              Sweet and Hot (Jimmy Harrison-v) a
   10/16/31   Blues in My Heart (Les Reis-v) c
   9/11/34   Happy as the Day Is Long a
                              Limehouse Blues a
   3/2/37   Rhythm of the Tambourine a

HERBECK, RAY
   5/17/39   A Home in the Clouds (Betty Bronson, Kirby Brooks-v) c

HERMAN, WOODY
   12/30/48   I Ain't Gettin' Any Younger (as I Ain't Gonna Wait Too Long) c

HEYWOOD, EDDIE
   2/29/46   Pom Pom c

Arranger/Composer: Artist Index 359

HILL, ALEX
   10/19/34   Let's Have a Jubilee a

THE HIP STRING QUARTET see Milt Jackson

THE HIT PARADERS see Mark Warnow

HODGES, JOHNNY
   12/20/65   Someone to Watch Over Me (with the Lawrence Welk Orch.) a

HOLIDAY, BILLIE
   10/15/40   Loveless Love a
                       St. Louis Blues a
                       See also Teddy Wilson

HOLLAND, CHARLES see BC 12/13/34

HOLMES, RICHARD "GROOVE"
   11/28/66   When Lights Are Low c

HORNE, LENA see Soundtracks: Stormy Weather, Thousands Cheer

HUGHES, SPIKE
   2/10/32   Blues in My Heart (Joey Shields-v) c

HUMES, HELEN
   5/9/50   Rock Me to Sleep (accompanied by Marshall Royal and His Orch.) c

HUTTON, BETTY
   1947   Rumble, Rumble, Rumble (with the Joe Lilley Orch.) a

HUTTON, MARION see Glenn Miller

HYMAN, DICK
   ca. 1956   Cow Cow Boogie c

THE INK SPOTS see Ella Fitzgerald

ISHIHARA, YUJIRO
   8/30/74   Again a
                       As Time Goes By a
                       The Call of the Far Away Hills a
                       Mona Lisa a
                       The River of No Return a
                       Ruby a
                       September Song a
                       Summertime in Venice a
                       NOTE: 8/30/74 is the date of recording for the instrumental backing for these tunes (done in Los Angeles); the vocal tracks were added later by Ishihara in Japan.

ITO, BENARD
   ca. 1970   Con Alma a
                       Never Again a

JACKSON, MILT
    5/68   A Walkin' Thing (with the Hip String Quartet) c
    4/76   My Kind of Trouble Is You c

JACKSON, QUENTIN see McKinney's Cotton Pickers

JAZZ AT THE PHILHARMONIC
    11/22/60   A Jazz Portrait of Brigitte Bardot c
                          Swedish Jam c

JAZZ GALA '79, CANNES, FRANCE
    1/22/79   Blues in My Heart (Joe Williams-v) c

THE JAZZ TODAY UNIT
    4/20/55   Symphony in Riffs (Kenny Baker-leader, featuring Bertie King) c

JOHNSON, CHARLIE
    1/24/28   Charleston Is the Best Dance After All a
                          1/24/28 (take #2)
                          You Ain't the One (Monette Moore-v) a
                          1/24/28 (take #2)

JOHNSON, EDDIE
    June-July 1981   Blue Star c

JOHNSON, LAURIE
    early 1960's   Stick or Twist a, c

JOHNSON, PLAS
    1960   Blues in My Heart c

JOLLY, PETE
    1956   When Lights Are Low c

JONES, CLAUDE see Fletcher Henderson

JONES, DEAN
    ca. 1959   The Gypsy in My Soul a
                          Young and in Love a

JONES, JONAH
    9/61   After You've Gone a
                          Apollo Jumps a, c
                          Baubles, Bangles and Beads a
                          Boy Meets Horn a
                          Ciribiribin a
                          Echoes of Harlem a
                          Hot Lips a
                          I Can't Get Started a
                          Sugar Blues a
                          Tenderly a
                          Two O'Clock Jump a
                          West End Blues a
    1962   Blues in My Heart c

JONES, QUINCY see Peggy Lee

Arranger/Composer: Artist Index

JORDAN, LOUIS
    12/8/47   Don't Burn the Candle at Both Ends (Martha Davis-v) c
                                  You're on the Right Track Baby (But You're Goin' the Wrong Way) (Martha Davis-v) c

JOYCE, TEDDY
    1937   When Lights Are Low c

JUGGERNAUT BAND see Frankie Capp

KPM MUSIC LIBRARY
    5/63   Be Cool - A a, c
                                  5/63 - B
                                  5/63 - C
                                  Blue Yonder - A a, c
                                  5/63 - B
                                  Catfish Row a, c
                                  5/63 (link) #1
                                  5/63 (link) #2
                                  Discovery a, c
                                  Gotta Go Home a, c
                                  Heels Up a, c
                                  Imminent a, c
                                  Jazz Waltz - A a, c
                                  5/63 - B (thematic link)
                                  5/63 - C (thematic transition)
                                  Lonely Affair - A a, c
                                  5/63 - B
                                  5/63 - C (thematic transition)
                                  5/63 - D (thematic bridge)
                                  Metropole a, c
                                  One Way Out a, c
                                  Show Break (ending) #1 a, c
                                  5/63 (ending) #2
                                  Vinho Verde a, c
                                  See also notes for this session (5/63) in chronological section of discography.

KASSEL, ART (recorded under pseudonym JOHNNY RIDGE)
    date unknown   Red Rose Waltz a
                                  The Ship That Never Sailed a

KAWAGUCHI, GEORGE see Buddy Rich

KAYE, DANNY see Soundtrack: The Five Pennies

KAYE, MARION see Reggie Childs

KEENE, BOB see "Stringin' Along"

KEITH PROWSE MUSIC see KPM Music Library

KELLER, GRETA
    10/5/31   Blues in My Heart c

KENNEDY, JOE
    1980   When Lights Are Low c

KENTON, STAN
   12/6/47   Lonely Woman (June Christy-v) c
   Nov. 25-Dec. 21 1947
   9/21/59
                       See also June Christy

KESSEL, BARNEY   see Charlie Byrd

KING, BERTIE
   4/6/55   Blues in My Heart c
                       Once Upon a Time c
   9/20/56   Blue Interlude c
                       Lazy Afternoon c
                       Skip It c
                       See also Jazz Today Unit

KIRK, ANDY   see note under "Lonesome Nights"

KRAL, IRENE
   1963   Rock Me to Sleep (accompanied by Junior Mance Trio) c

KRUEGER, JERRY
   4/25/39   Rain, Rain, Go Away a
                       Summertime a

KRUPA, GENE
   ca. 8/39   Melancholy Lullaby c
   2/2/40
                       Symphony in Riffs a, c
   9/20/39
   11/5/39
   3/22/41   Rockin' Chair a
   6/7/41
   7/2/41
   10/3/41
                       4/15/49 (possibly same arrangement)
                       4/22/49 (possibly same arrangement)
   1/23/42   Harlem on Parade (Anita O'Day-v) c
   11/13/42   Cow Cow Boogie (Anita O'Day-v) c

LAINE, FRANKIE
   ca. 1951   I Love You for That (with Patti Page-v, and Harry Geller Orch.) a

LAMBERT, HENDRICKS, BAVAN
   12/20-21/63   Meetin' Time c

LANE, RUBY
   early 1950's   Baby, Won't You Please Come Home a
                       For Sale--One Broken Heart a

LARKINS, ELLIS
   11/74   Blues in My Heart c
   7/21/77

LAWFORD, PETER   see Jimmy Durante

LEE, JULIA
   11/11/47   King Size Papa c

Arranger/Composer: Artist Index

	1956-1957
	Take It or Leave It c
11/13/47	I Didn't Like It the First Time c
4/49	Don't Come Too Soon c
7/21/50	You're Gonna Miss It c

LEE, PEGGY
   ca. 7/47   Lonely Woman c
   1950   Rock Me to Sleep c
   early 1950's?   Melancholy Lullaby c
   1954   Love, You Didn't Do Right By Me a
   4/15-16/61   San Francisco Blues (with Quincy Jones Orch.) a
   8/61   I Believe in You a
   7/62   I'm a Woman a
                    See also Benny Goodman

LESTER, KETTY see Bruce Blalock

LEWIS, WILLIE
   1/17/36   All of Me a
                   I've Got a Feeling You're Fooling a
                   Just a Mood a, c
                   Rhythm Is Our Business (Bobby Martin-v) a
                   Star Dust a
                   Stay Out of Love a

LILLEY, JOE see Betty Hutton

LINCOLN, ABBEY
   1956   I Didn't Say Yes (I Didn't Say No) a
                   A Lonesome Cup of Coffee a
   11/5-6/56   The Masquerade Is Over a
                   This Can't Be Love a
                   Two Cigarettes in the Dark a

LITTLE MISS CORNSHUCKS (pseudonym for MILDRED CUMMINGS)
   1951   Papa Tree Top Blues a
                   Rock Me to Sleep a, c

LOMBARDO, CARMEN see Guy Lombardo

LOMBARDO, GUY
   2/23/32   Blues in My Heart (Carmen Lombardo-v) c

LOVELLE, TONY
   date unknown   Key Largo c

LOWE, MUNDELL
   1978   Souvenir c

LOWN, BERT
   9/16/31   Blues in My Heart (Elmer Feldkamp-v) c

LUNCEFORD, JIMMIE
   12/23/40   O.K. For Baby c
                   Nov.-Dec. 1940
                   1945?
                   See also note under Lonesome Nights (in title listings).

LUNDBERG, VICTOR
1968   On Censorship   a, c
                          To the Destroyers   a, c
                          NOTE: Carter composed and arranged background music for Lundberg's narrative vocal.

LUTER, CLAUDE   see   Sidney Bechet

M SQUAD (TV SHOW)
3/59   (The) Juke Box   a, c
                          A Lady Sings the Blues   a
                          The Mugger   a, c
                          Phantom Raiders   a, c
                          The Search   a, c

McCALL, MARY ANN
2/1/50   The Sky Is Crying   c

McGHEE, STICKS
1/14/53   Blues in My Heart   c

McKINLEY, RAY
1955   Cow Cow Boogie   c

McKINNEY'S COTTON PICKERS
9/8/31   Do You Believe in Love at Sight   (Quentin Jackson?-v)   a
11/4/30   Never Swat a Fly   (Bill Coty-v)   a

McRAE, CARMEN
1968   I Haven't Got Anything Better to Do   a
                          I'm Always Drunk in San Francisco   a
11/71-3/72   All That I Can Do Is Think of You   a
                          All the Time   a
                          Bobby   a
                          The Happy Ones   a
                          I'll Never Pass This Way Again   a
                          Mr. Love   a
                          Tender Loving Words   a
                          When It's Time to Tell   a
                          When Twilight Comes   a

MacRAE, GORDON
1950   Hongi Tongi Hoki Poki   (with the Les Baxter Chorus and Paul Weston and His Orch.)   c

McVEA, JACK
8/45   O. K. For Baby   c

MADDIN, JIMMIE
1954   I Like a Shuffle Beat   a
                          I Stole De Wedding Bell   a, c
                          Play Ball   a, c
                          See also The Dream Dusters

MALONE, ANNIE
date unknown   Debbie's Debut   a
                          Hell's Bells   a

Arranger/Composer: Artist Index

MANCE, JUNIOR see Irene Kral

MANN, HERBIE
    4/29/57   When Lights Are Low c

MANTOVANI
    1962   Summer Night c

MARTIN, BOBBY see Willie Lewis

MARTIN, DEAN
    6/20/58   Once Upon a Time (It Happened) c

MASON, MARTHA
    1967   The Wine of Sweet Remembrance c

MAY, BILLY see Time-Life series <u>The Swing Era</u>

MERLINO, GENE see Bob Friedman

MERRILL, HELEN
    1959   Blues in My Heart c

MEZZROW, MEZZ
    11/6/33   Free Love a, c
                            Love, You're Not the One for Me a, c

MILES, EDDIE see Washboard Rhythm Kings

MILLER, GLENN
    9/11/39   Melancholy Lullaby (Ray Eberle-v) c
    10/9/39   Bluebirds in the Moonlight (Marion Hutton-v) a
    11/17/39
    11/25/39
    2/5/40   Symphony in Riffs a, c
    3/4/40
    7/3/40   Blues in My Heart c
    9/10/40
                              1943-1944 (with the Army Air Force Band)
    7/16/42   Rainbow Rhapsody c
                              1959 (New Glenn Miller Orch.)

MILLER, MRS.
    9/29/70   I Said No a
                            Ma (She's Making Eyes at Me) a
                            She Had to Go and Lose It at the Astor a
                            The Weekend of a Private Secretary a

MILLINDER, LUCKY
    5/26/44   Hurry Hurry (Wynonie Harris-v) c

MILLS BLUE RHYTHM BAND
    6/26/31   Heebie Jeebies (Chick Bullock-v) a
    9/23/32   Jazz Cocktail a, c
    10/4/34   Let's Have a Jubilee a

THE MILLS BROTHERS see BC 10/23/40

MILTON, ROY
    1946   Blues in My Heart   c

MISS RHAPSODY (pseudonym for Viola Wells)
    4/22/72   Blues in My Heart   c

MOORE, JOHNNY
    1951   Blues in My Heart   (Billy Valentine-v)   c

MOORE, MONETTE   see   Charlie Johnson

MORGAN, DICK
    10/31/60   When Lights Are Low   c

MORSE, ELLA MAE
    4/24/46   Your Conscience Tells You So   (with Freddie Slack)   c
    ca. 1948   Cow Cow Boogie   c
                            See also Freddie Slack

"MUCHO CALOR"
    10/57   Autumn Leaves   (features Art Pepper)   a

MULDAUR, GEOFF
    1/75   Livin' in the Sunlight (Lovin' in the Moonlight)   a

MULDAUR, MARIA
    1974   It Ain't the Meat, It's the Motion   a
                            12/22/74
                            Squeeze Me   a
                            12/22/74
                            Sweetheart   a
                            12/22/74
    12/22/74   Any Old Time   a
                            Don't You Make Me High   a
                            Gee, Baby, Ain't I Good to You   a
                            It Don't Mean a Thing If It Ain't Got That Swing   a
                            Lover Man   a
                            Walkin' One and Only   a
    9/75   Rockin' Chair   (with Hoagy Carmichael-v)   a
                            We Just Couldn't Say Goodbye   a

MURPHY, MARK
    1962   Blues in My Heart   c

MUSIC FROM M SQUAD   see   M SQUAD

MYLES, MEG
    date unknown   My Melancholy Baby   a

NEUMAN, ULRICH   see   Alice Babs

NEW McKINNEY'S COTTON PICKERS
    3/31/71   Ol' Man River   (arrangement dates from early 1930's)   a
    9/20/75   Never Swat a Fly   (Orrin Foslien, Jr.-v)   (arrangement originally recorded in 1930 by McKinney's Cotton Pickers)   a
    6/26/80

Arranger/Composer: Artist Index 367

NOTE: New McKinney's LP Bountiful B38003 lists Carter as the arranger of "China Boy" (recorded 9/20/75) but Carter, upon hearing it, finds no reason to believe it is his.

NEWBORN, PHINEAS
4/1/64   A Walkin' Thing   c

NEWMAN, ALFRED
1955   The Girl Upstairs   a
       Blue Mountain (as To Ava)   a
1961   The Bad and the Beautiful   a
       Laura   a
       Pinky   a

NOBLE, RAY
2/12/32   Blues in My Heart   (Al Bowlly-v)   c

NORVO, RED
10/14/47   Hollyridge Drive   a, c

O'CONNELL, HELEN   see Jimmy Dorsey

O'DAY, ANITA
1947   I Ain't Gettin' Any Younger   (with Ralph Burns Orch.)   a, c
       Key Largo   a, c
       See also Gene Krupa

OLAY, RUTH
ca. 1957   Slow But Sure   c
1958   Hurry Hurry   c

OMER, JEAN
ca. 12/40   The Blue Room   a

PAGE, PATTI
ca. 1951   Back in Your Own Backyard   a
           See also Frankie Laine

PARRY, HARRY
6/19/46   O.K. For Baby   c

PAYNE, JACK
ca. 1932   Blues in My Heart   c

PEPPER, ART
10/24-25/60   How Can You Lose?   c
              See also "Mucho Calor"

PETERS, LOIS
ca. 1958   Ask   (with the Ravenscroft Singers and Orch.)   a, c
           How Deep Is the Ocean   a
           I'll Be Your Bride Again   (with the Ravenscroft Singers and Orch.)   a

PETERSON, OSCAR
7/58   When Lights Are Low   c
1958

See also BC 9/52

PIERCE, NAT   see   Frankie Capp

POLK, LUCY ANN   see   Les Brown

POWELL, CHRIS
   4/6/50   Blues in My Heart   c

POWERS, JACK
   ca. 1953   She Doesn't Laugh Like You   (with the Cheer Leaders)   c

PRICE, SAMMY
   4/9/56   Blues in My Heart   c

PRINCETON UNIVERSITY JAZZ ENSEMBLE   see   BC 4/8/77, 11/10/79

PROWSE, KEITH   see   KPM Music Library

R. A. F. DANCE ORCHESTRA (THE SQUADRONAIRES)
   7/27/43   Cow Cow Boogie   (Sid Colin-v)   c

THE RADIO RHYTHM CLUB SEXTET   see   Buddy Featherstonhaugh

THE RAELETS   see   Ray Charles

RALEIGH, DON
   late 1950's   Rainbow Rhapsody   c

THE RAMBLERS (DUTCH)   see   BC 3/24/37

RANEY, SUE   see   Bob Friedman

RAVENSCROFT SINGERS AND ORCHESTRA   see   Lois Peters

RAWLS, LOU
   1965   Blues for the Weepers   a
                     Charmaine   a
                     Cold Cold Heart   a
                     Du Bist Die Liebe   a
                     Gee, Baby, Ain't I Good to You   a
                     If I Had My Life to Live Over   a
                     If It's the Last Thing I Do   a
                     I'll See You in My Dreams   a
                     Into Each Life Some Rain Must Fall   a
                     It's Monday Every Day   a
                     Margie   a
                     Me and My Shadow   a
                     My Buddy   a
                     Nobody But Me   a
                     Nothing Really Feels the Same   a
                     Now and Then There's a Fool Such as I   a
                     The Power of Love   a
                     Three O'Clock in the Morning   a
                     Two Tickets West   a
                     What'll I Do   a
                     Whispering Grass   a

Arranger/Composer: Artist Index

RAZAF, ANDY (recorded under pseudonym JOHNNY THOMPSON)
1/17/28   Nobody Knows How Much I Love You c

REIS, LES see Fletcher Henderson

RENDER, RUDY
ca. 1951   Rock Me to Sleep (with Maxwell Davis and His Orch.) c

RICH, BUDDY
9/10/53   Let's Fall in Love a
       Me and My Jaguar a, c
1/18/65   Slides and Hides (with Louis Bellson and the George Kawaguchi Orch.) a, c
       See also BC 9/52

RICH, FREDDIE
2/14/40   A House with a Little Red Barn (Rosemary Calvin-v) a
       How High the Moon (Rosemary Calvin-v) a
       I'm Forever Blowing Bubbles a
       Till We Meet Again a

RICHARDS, ANN
1958   Blues in My Heart c

RICHARDS, CHUCK
12/19/34   Blue Interlude c

RIDGE, JOHNNY (pseudonym) see Art Kassel

RIEDEL, GEORG
9/5/55   When Lights Are Low c

ROBERTS, HOWARD
2/12-13/63   When Lights Are Low c

ROBERTSON, DICK see Eubie Blake, King Carter

ROBINSON, BILL see Soundtrack: Stormy Weather

ROBINSON, JOE
9/22/49   Don't Scream, Don't Shout a
       If I Can't Have You a, c
       Roll with the Boogie a, c
       Suspicious of My Woman a, c

ROGERS, DICK (pseudonym) see Dick Robertson

ROSOLINO, FRANK see Conte Candoli

ROSS, CANDY
       See chronological section of discography for various arrangements and compositions recorded featuring vocals by this musician with the Carter Orchestra in 1946.

ROYAL, MARSHALL see Helen Humes

SACCO, TONY see Benny Goodman

ST. JOHN, DELL
See chronological section of discography for various arrangements and compositions recorded by this vocalist with the Carter Orchestra in 1939.

SANDERS, FELICIA
1959   My Kind of Trouble Is You c

SANDERS, PHAROAH
1981   When Lights Are Low c

SAVITT, JAN
1/24/40   Kansas City Moods c
10/25/45

SCHROUDER, CHARLES see Helen Troy

SCOTT, BERYL see Bill Shepherd

SHANK, BUD
1/19/56   When Lights Are Low (with Bob Cooper) c

SHARON, RALPH see Tony Bennett

SHAW, ARTIE
4/28/37   Symphony in Riffs a, c
7/8/38
2/15/38   Lonesome Nights (as Take My Word) a, c
12/2/38   Blue Interlude c
1949   Melancholy Lullaby c
NOTE: The liner notes to RCA (F) FXM1-7336 (Artie Shaw and His Orch. v. 1, 1941-1945) state that Carter was responsible for the arrangements from Shaw's 6/24/61 session--"Confessin'," "Love Me a Little Little," "Don't Take Your Love from Me," and "Beyond the Blue Horizon." Shaw, however, has identified these arrangements as his own (letter dated 5/31/77).

SHEARING, GEORGE
7/17/52   When Lights Are Low c
8/57   Blues in My Heart (Dakota Staton-v) c
1963   Nightfall c
See also Joe Williams

SHEPHERD, BILL
1959   When Lights Are Low (with Beryl Scott Chorus) c

SHIELDS, JOEY see Spike Hughes

SIMMONS, ART
4/15/58   Cow Cow Boogie c

SIMMS, GINNY
1939   Melancholy Lullaby c
12/17/40   I'm Out of Style (with Eddie South and His Orch.) c

Arranger/Composer: Artist Index

                          Sighs and Tears (with Eddie South and His Orch.) c

SIMPKINS, ARTHUR LEE
    date unknown   I Long for You a
                         I Resolve a

SIMS, LEE
    ca. 1931   Blues in My Heart c

SIMS, ZOOT
    8/14/79   Black Butterfly a
                         I Got It Bad a
                         I Let a Song Go Out of My Heart a
                         In a Mellotone a
                         It Don't Mean a Thing If It Ain't Got That Swing a

SLACK, FREDDIE
    5/21/42   Cow Cow Boogie (Ella Mae Morse-v) c
                         1955 (Thelma Gracen-v)
    11/25/47   Boogie Minor a, c
                         Chopstick Boogie a
                         St. Louis Blues a
    12/16/47   Re-Bop Boogie (as Be-Bop Boogie) a, c
    1947   Two Left Hands (Charlotte Blackburn-v) c
    1955   Between 18th and 19th on Chestnut Street a
                         Rhumboogie a
                         See also Ella Mae Morse

SMITH, HALE see BC 12/3/73

SMITH, KEELY
    1964   Can't Buy Me Love a
                         A Hard Day's Night a
                         I Want to Hold Your Hand a
                         Please Please Me a

SMITH, MABEL (BIG MAYBELLE) see Christine Chatham

SONORA SWING BAND see BC 9/12/36

SOUTH, EDDIE see Ginny Simms

SPENCER-HAGEN ORCHESTRA see Lincoln Chase

SPIVAK, CHARLIE
    1/7/47   Devil's Holiday a, c
    1/12/47
    2/12/47

THE SQUADRONAIRES see R.A.F. Dance Orchestra

STAFFORD, JO
    1963   Oh! Look at Me Now a
                         The One I Love Belongs to Someone Else a
                         Whatcha Know Joe? a
                         Yes Indeed a

STARR, KAY
 11/26/47   Second Hand Love   a, c

STATON, DAKOTA
 1959   When Lights Are Low   c
 2/60   Be Anything   a
                        Body and Soul   a
                        Close Your Eyes   a
                        Congratulations to Someone   a
                        Dedicated to You   a
                        I Can't Get Started   a
                        My Wish   a
                        Old Folks   a
                        Solitude   a
                        The Very Thought of You   a
                        Whispering Grass   a
                        You're Mine Now   a
 6/60   Don't Explain   a
                        Don't Leave Me Now   a
                        Everybody's Somebody's Fool   a
                        First Things First   a
                        The Folks Who Live on the Hill   a
                        Hey Lawdy Mama   a
                        I Won't Worry   a
                        If I Love Again   a
                        I'll Close My Eyes   a
                        Indiana   a
                        Knock Me a Kiss   a
                        Let Them Talk   a
                        Make Me a Present of You   a
                        The Masquerade Is Over   a
                        Meet Me at No Special Place   a
                        On Green Dolphin Street   a
                        Pick Yourself Up   a
                        Rock Me to Sleep   a, c
                        'Round Midnight   a
                        So in Love   a
                        Trapped in the Web of Love   a
                        Weak for the Man   a
                        Will You Still Be Mine   a
                        You Call It Madness   a
                        See also George Shearing

STEVENS, INGER
 1968   Lasse Lasse Litten   a, c
                        The Loving Room   a, c

STEVENS, RAY
 1975   Cow Cow Boogie   c

STONE, LAWRENCE
 1950's   Without a Word of Goodbye (with Ernie Free-
                        man's Orch.)   c
                        See also Ernie Freeman

"STRINGIN' ALONG"
 11/5/57   Once in a While   a
                        Polka Dots and Moonbeams   a

Arranger/Composer: Artist Index

NOTE: Personnel includes Bob Keene (cl) and session appears in Jepsen under his name.

SULLIVAN, JOE
   4/29/40   Pom Pom c
   1944-1946   Blues in My Heart c

SULLIVAN, MAXINE see BC 4/1/44, 1/8/46

SVENSKA HOTVINTETTEN
   1940   When Lights Are Low c

SWIFT, DAVID
   1962   Cow Cow Boogie (with Rene Hall's Orch.) c

SYMS, SYLVIA
   1952   Lonely Woman (with Barbara Carroll Trio) c
   1976

TATUM, ART
   12/28/53   Blues in My Heart c
                      See also BC 6/25/54

TAYLOR, BILLY
   6/24/59   When Lights Are Low c

TAYLOR, SAM
   1956-1957   Blues in My Heart c

THOMPSON, JOHNNY (pseudonym) see Andy Razaf

THOMPSON, LUCKY
   4/22/47   Boulevard Bounce a, c

THOMPSON, SIR CHARLES
   1/8/61   Cow Cow Boogie c

THE THREE REASONS see Dick Todd

TILTON, MARTHA see Benny Goodman

TIME LIFE SERIES: THE SWING ERA
   8/3/70   Melancholy Lullaby (Billy May-leader) a, c
   11/30/70   Liza (Billy May-leader) a
   7/29/71   Happy as the Day Is Long (Billy May-leader) a
   8/2/71   Rockin' Chair (Billy May-leader) a
   2/17/72   I Surrender Dear a
                      NOTE: These five recordings are recreations--
                      see notes in title listings.
                      See also Glen Gray

TJADER, CAL
   4/57   When Lights Are Low c
                      9/77
   1960   Key Largo c

TODD, DICK
   5/1/39   A Home in the Clouds (with the Three Reasons-
                      v) c

TORME, MEL
8/2/54   It Don't Mean a Thing If It Ain't Got That Swing a
                    Tutti Frutti a
                    See also Soundtrack: A Man Called Adam

TROY, HELEN
1954   You'll Never Get the Chance Again (with
                    Charles Schrouder-v, and Van Alexander's Orch.)
                    c

TURNER, JOE (pianist)
5/29/76   Blues in My Heart c

UNIVERSITY OF BUFFALO JAZZ ENSEMBLE   see BC 10/28/78

U. S. AIR FORCE JAZZ ENSEMBLE   see   The Airmen of Note

VALENTINE, BILLY   see   Johnny Moore

VAN BERGEN, FRANS
1/2-4/61   When Lights Are Low c

VARSITY SEVEN
1/15/40   Pom Pom c

VAUGHAN, SARAH
4/8/56   Lonely Woman c
1962   After You've Gone a
                    Falling in Love with Love a
                    A Garden in the Rain a
                    Great Day a
                    Honeysuckle Rose a
                    I Believe in You a
                    I Can't Give You Anything But Love a
                    I'm Gonna Live Til I Die a
                    The Lady's in Love with You a
                    Moonlight on the Ganges a
                    Nobody Else But Me a
                    The Trolley Song a
1/63   Always on My Mind a
                    Friendless a, c
                    If I Had You a
                    I'll Never Be the Same a
                    Lonely Hours a
                    Look for Me, I'll Be Around a
                    The Man I Love a
                    So Long, My Love a
                    Solitude a
                    These Foolish Things a
                    What'll I Do a
                    You're Driving Me Crazy a
ca. 1963   Key Largo c
                    When Lights Are Low c
1965   The Pawnbroker a
8/13/79   Day Dream a
                    In a Sentimental Mood a
                    Lush Life a
                    Solitude a

Arranger/Composer: Artist Index 375

                        Sophisticated Lady a
                        Tonight I Shall Sleep with a Smile on My Face a
                        See also The Airmen of Note

VENTURA, CHARLIE
  10/48   Lonely Woman (Jackie Cain-v) c

VENUTI, JOE
  10/13/33   Everybody Shuffle a, c

WALLER, FATS
  1/23/43   Moppin' and Boppin' c

WARD, HELEN see Benny Goodman

WARING, FRED
  8/23/45   My Twilight Reverie c

WARNOW, MARK
  2/2/42   Cocktails for Two (Barry Wood-v) a
  2/9/42   The Music Goes 'Round and 'Round (The Hit Paraders-v) a
                        These Foolish Things (Barry Wood-v) a

WARREN, EARLE
  2/9/74   Blues in My Heart c

WASHBOARD RHYTHM KINGS
  9/23/31   Blues in My Heart (Eddie Miles-v) c

WATERS, ETHEL
  1931-1934   Blues in My Heart (with Herman Chittison Trio) c

WAYNE, CHUCK
  12/27/76   When Lights Are Low c

WEBB, CHICK
  3/30/31   Blues in My Heart (Louis Bacon-v) a, c
                        Heebie Jeebies a
                        Soft and Sweet a
  5/3/38   Liza a
  8/13/38

WEBSTER, BEN
  12/27/51   King's Riff c
                        Randall's Island c

WELCH, ELISABETH
  1976   When Lights Are Low c
                        See also BC mid 6/36, 6/20/36

WELCH, EMMA LOU see BC 1/48

WELK, LAWRENCE see Johnny Hodges

WELLS, VIOLA see Miss Rhapsody

WESTON, PAUL   see   Gordon MacRae

WHITE, KITTY
  7/8/49   It Pays to Advertise (accompanied by Dave Cavanaugh's Orch.)   c
  ca. 1958   I Am Your Dream   a
                        The Old Man and the Sea   a

WHITEMAN, PAUL
                        The Whiteman Archive at Williams College has scores of three Carter compositions from the Whiteman book. None were arranged by Carter and there are no known recordings. The titles are: "Blue Interlude," "Blues in My Heart," and "Devil's Holiday."

WICKMAN, PUTTE
  5/4/49   When Lights Are Low   c

WIDESPREAD DEPRESSION ORCHESTRA
  1981   Night Hop   a, c

WILBER, BOB
  5/30-31/79   I'm in the Mood for Swing (with the American All Stars featuring Lars Erstrand)   c
                        When Lights Are Low (with the American All Stars featuring Lars Erstrand)   c

WILEY, LEE
  7/25/57   Blues in My Heart   c

WILLIAMS, HARRY
  ca. 1961   Summer Night   c

WILLIAMS, JOE
  3/1-2/71   Blues in My Heart (with George Shearing)   c
  11/71-3/72   Always on Sunday   a
                        Care   a
                        God Bless You   a
                        Got That Feeling   a
                        I'm a Lucky Guy   a
                        Love Is a Feeling   a
                        Once Upon a Happy Time (The Big Band Days)   a
                        Right Here in My Heart   a
                        Satin Latin   a
                        When You're Young   a
                        See also Bob Friedman (note); Jazz Gala '79, Cannes, France

WILSON, GARLAND
  9/7/36   Just a Mood   c

WILSON, JACKIE
  1/3-4/68   Chain Gang (with Count Basie's Orch.)   a
                        Even When You Cry (with Count Basie's Orch.)   a
                        For Your Precious Love (with Count Basie's Orch.)   a
                        Funky Broadway (with Count Basie's Orch.)   a

Arranger/Composer: Artist Index 377

	I Never Loved a Woman (with Count Basie's Orch.) a
	I Was Made to Love Her (with Count Basie's Orch.) a
	In the Midnight Hour (with Count Basie's Orch.) a
	My Girl (with Count Basie's Orch.) a
	Ode to Billy Joe (with Count Basie's Orch.) a
	Respect (with Count Basie's Orch.) a
	Uptight (Everything's All Right) (with Count Basie's Orch.) a

WILSON, NANCY
1968   Prisoner of My Eyes (I Can Never Let You Go) a

WILSON, STANLEY
1960-1961   Champagne Waltz a
5/63   Cherchez La Femme a, c
    Dance with Me a, c
    Domino (vocal group) a
    If You Go a
    Poor Little Rich Girl a
    Roses of Picardy a
    Show Me the Way to Go Home a
    Under Paris Skies (vocal group) a
    What Kind of Fool Am I a
ca. 1963   A Kiss from You (as Lydia) c

WILSON, TEDDY
10/31/38   Here It Is Tomorrow Again (Billie Holiday-v) a
11/9/38   April in My Heart (Billie Holiday-v) a
    I'll Never Fail You (Billie Holiday-v) a
    Say It with a Kiss (Billie Holiday-v) a
    They Say (Billie Holiday-v) a
    11/9/38 (take #2)

WOOD, BARRY see Mark Warnow

WYATT, DON
1968   All Tore Down a
    Do I Need You a
    I'll Never Leave You a
    Point of No Return a, c

YOUNG, WEBSTER
8/21/61   When Lights Are Low c

ZITO, JIMMY
1947   Key Largo (Nick Delane-v) c

SOUNDTRACKS

NOTE: Listed here are Carter arrangements and compositions which have been released on Soundtrack LPs. For a complete listing of his film work see Filmography.

THE BIG BROADCAST OF 1932   see   Cab Calloway

THE FIVE PENNIES
   Sept.-Oct. 1958
                   Bill Bailey, Won't You Please Come Home (Louis Armstrong, Danny Kaye-v) a
                   Just the Blues a   NOTE: Features Louis Armstrong, tp.

FLOWER DRUM SONG
                   Carter played in the orchestra and assisted in the orchestration of parts of this 1961 production. The soundtrack is on Decca DL79098 (later labelled MCA 2069).

THE GANG'S ALL HERE
   Mar. or Apr. 1943
                   No Love, No Nothing (Alice Faye-v, and the Benny Goodman Orch.) a

GUNS OF NAVARONE
   1961
                   Yassu a

THE HANGED MAN   see   Stan Getz

A MAN CALLED ADAM
   11/65
                   Ain't I   a, c
                   All That Jazz (3 versions) (Mel Torme-v) a, c
                   Claudia (2 versions) a, c
                   Crack Up (Playboy Theme) a
                   Go Now a, c
                   Night Walk a, c
                   Soft Touch a, c
                   Whisper to One (Sammy Davis Jr.-v) c

STATE FAIR
   1962
                   That's for Me (Pat Boone-v) a

STORMY WEATHER
   Jan.-Feb. 1943
                   Ain't That Something (Bill Robinson-v) a
                   Good for Nothin' Joe (Lena Horne-v) a
                   I Can't Give You Anything But Love (Lena Horne, Bill Robinson-v) a

Stormy Weather (Lena Horne-v) a
Jan.-Feb. 1943 (vocal group) (Carter arranged last 29 measures)

THOUSANDS CHEER
  1943   Honeysuckle Rose (Lena Horne-v) a

VALLEY OF THE DOLLS
  1967   I'll Plant My Own Tree a

CHRONOLOGICAL INDEX
OF COMPOSITIONS AND ARRANGEMENTS

a = Carter arrangement   c = Carter composition

1927
PDQ Blues   a

1928
Charleston Is The Best Dance After All   a
Come On Baby   a
Easy Money   a
Nobody Knows How Much I Love You   c
You Ain't The One   a

1929
Blazin'   a
Raisin' The Roof   a
The Wang Wang Blues   a

1930
Bugle Call Rag   a
Dee Blues   c
Goodbye Blues   ac
Got Another Sweetie Now   a
Keep A Song In Your Soul   a
Never Swat A Fly   a
Somebody Loves Me   a

1931
Blues In My Heart   ac
Do You Believe In Love At Sight   a
Heebie Jeebies   a
My Pretty Girl   a
Soft And Sweet   a
Sweet And Hot   a

1932
Hot Toddy   ac
Jazz Cocktail   ac
Sweet Rhythm   a

1933
Blue Interlude   ac
Blue Lou   a
Devil's Holiday   ac
Everybody Shuffle   ac
Free Love   ac
I Never Knew   a

Krazy Kapers   ac
Lonesome Nights   ac
Love, You're Not The One For Me   ac
Ol' Man River   a
Once Upon A Time   ac
Swing It   a
Symphony In Riffs   ac
Synthetic Love   ac

1934
Dream Lullaby   ac
Happy As The Day Is Long   a
I'm Getting Sentimental Over You   a
It Happens To The Best of Friends   a
Let's Have A Jubilee   a
Limehouse Blues   a
Shoot The Works   ac

1935
Blue Moon   a
Nagasaki   a

1936
Accent On Swing   ac
All Of Me   a
Big Ben Blues   ac
Blue Interlude   a [c: 1933]
Blues In My Heart   a [c: 1931]
Bye Bye Baby   a
Chickfeed   ac
Gin And Jive   ac
Gloaming   a
Hold Me Tight, I'm Falling   a
I Got Rhythm   a
I Gotta Go   ac
I Never Knew   a
If Only I Could Read Your Mind   ac
I'm Putting All My Eggs In One Basket   a
I'm Tickled To Death I'm Me   a
Indiana   a
I've Got A Feeling You're Fooling   a
I've Got Two Lips   a
Just A Mood   ac
Let It Be Me   a

Nightfall   ac
Rhythm Is Our Business   a
Rise 'N Shine   a
Scandal In A Flat   ac
Some Of These Days   a
Star Dust   a
Stay Out Of Love   a
A Sunbonnet Blue   a
Swingin' At Maida Vale   ac
Swingin' The Blues   ac
These Foolish Things   a
Waltzing The Blues   c
Way Down Yonder In New Orleans   a
We Saw The Sea   a
What's The Name Of That Song   a
When Day Is Done   a
When Lights Are Low   ac
When You're Smiling   a
You Understand   ac

1937
Blues In My Heart   a [c: 1931]
Crazy Rhythm   a
Honeysuckle Rose   a
I Ain't Got Nobody   a
I'll Never Give In   a
I'm In The Mood For Swing   ac
Lazy Afternoon   ac
Mighty Like The Blues   a
My Buddy   a
One, Two, Button Your Shoe   a
Out Of Nowhere   a
Pardon Me, Pretty Baby   a
Rambling In C   c
Rhythm Of The Tambourine   a
Skip It   ac
Somebody Loves Me   a
Stars And You   c
There's A Small Hotel   a

1938
April in My Heart   a
Blue Light Blues   c
Farewell Blues   a
Here It Is Tomorrow Again   a
I'll Never Fail You   a
I'm Coming Virginia   a
I'm In The Mood For Swing   a [c: 1937]
Liza   a
Muskrat Ramble   a
Say It With A Kiss   a
Shoe Shiner's Drag   a
They Say   a

1939
Blue Evening   a
Blue Orchids   a
Bluebirds In The Moonlight   a
Early Session Hop   a
The Fable Of A Fool   ac
A Home In The Clouds   ac
Honeysuckle Rose   a
How Strange   a
I Cried For You   a
I'm Coming Virginia   a
I'm Forever Blowing Bubbles   a
Lady Be Good   a
Lilacs In The Rain   a
Love's Got Me Down Again   a
Melancholy Lullaby   ac
More Than You Know   a
My Heart Has Wings   a
One Sweet Letter From You   a
Patty Cake, Patty Cake, Baker Man   a
Rain, Rain, Go Away   a
Riff Romp   ac
Scandal In A Flat   a [c: 1936]
Shufflebug Shuffle   ac
Star Dust   a
Summertime   a
Tea For Two   a
Vagabond Dreams   a
What's New   a
When Lights Are Low   a [c: 1936]

1940
All Of Me   a
Among My Souvenirs   a
Blue Room   a
Boogie Woogie Sugar Blues   a
By The Watermelon Vine, Lindy Lou   a
Calling All Bars   a
Cocktails For Two   a
Fish Fry   ac
A House With A Little Red Barn   a
How High The Moon   a
I'm Out Of Style   c
I've Been In Love Before   a
Kansas City Moods   ac
The Last Kiss You Gave Me   a
The Lone Arranger   a
Loveless Love   a
Night Hop   ac
O.K. For Baby   ac
Pom Pom   ac
St. Louis Blues   a
Serenade To A Sarong   ac
Sighs And Tears   c
Sleep   a
Slow Freight   a
Takin' My Time   ac
Till We Meet Again   a
The Very Thought Of You   a

Compositions/Arrangements: Chronological Index   383

Who's Yehoodi a

1941
Babalu a
Back Bay Boogie ac
Cuddle Up, Huddle Up ac
Ev'ry Goodbye Ain't Gone ac
Ill Wind a
Lullaby To A Dream ac
Midnight a
My Favorite Blues ac
Rockin' Chair a
Sunday a
There I've Said It Again a
Tree Of Hope ac
What A Difference A Day Made a

1942
Cocktails For Two a
Cow Cow Boogie c
Harlem On Parade c
I Can't Get Started a
The Music Goes 'Round And 'Round a
Ol' Man River a
Rainbow Rhapsody c
These Foolish Things a

1943
Ain't That Something? a
Good For Nothin' Joe a
Honeysuckle Rose a
Hurry Hurry c
I Can't Get Started a
I Can't Give You Anything But Love a
Love For Sale a
Moppin' And Boppin' c
No Love, No Nothin' a
Stormy Weather a

1944
I Can't Escape From You a
I Never Mention Your Name a
I Surrender Dear a
I'm Lost a
Star Dust a
Sweet Georgia Brown a
Two Again a

1945
All Alone a
Bunbelina ac
Cuttin' Time ac
Daddy Daddy a
June Comes Around a
Just You, Just Me a
Malibu ac
My Twilight Reverie a
Paradise a (arrangement probably dates back to early 30s but first recorded 1945)
Riffamarole c
Somebody Loves Me a

1946
Dream Castle ac
I Cover The Waterfront a
If I Can't Have You ac
I'm The Caring Kind ac
Jump Call ac
Looking For A Boy a
Night And Day a
Oofdah! ac
Out Of My Way a
Re-bop Boogie ac
Twelve O'Clock Jump ac
What'll It Be c
Where Or When a
Your Conscience Tells You So ac

1947
Boogie Minor ac
Boulevard Bounce ac
Chopstick Boogie a
Congoroo ac
Don't Burn The Candle At Both Ends c
Hollyridge Drive ac
I Ain't Gettin' Any Younger ac
I Didn't Like It The First Time c
I'm A Three Time Loser c
Key Largo ac
King Size Papa c
Lonely Woman c (composed 1937 but first recorded 1947)
Re-bop Boogie a [c: 1946]
Rumble, Rumble, Rumble a
St. Louis Blues a
Second Hand Love ac
Take It Or Leave It c
Two Left Hands c
You're On The Right Track (But You're Goin' The Wrong Way) c

1948
Baby, You're Mine For Keeps a
Bop Bounce ac
I Don't Want It No More c
Let Us Drink A Toast Together a
An Old Love Story a
Reina a
You'll Never Break My Heart Again a

1949
Don't Come Too Soon c
Don't Scream, Don't Shout a
I Ain't Got Nobody a
I Lost You a
I'd Rather Be A Rooster c
If I Can't Have You a [c: 1946]
It Pays To Advertise c
Look Out For Tomorrow c
Roll With The Boogie ac
Stinkin' From Drinkin' c
Surf Board c
Suspicious Of My Woman ac

1950
Hongi Tongi Hoki Poki c
I'm Such A Fool To Be In Love
  With You c
Rock Me To Sleep c
The Sky Is Crying c
That Ain't It ac
You're Gonna Miss It c

1951
Back In Your Own Backyard a
I Love You For That a
I Still Love Him So c
King's Riff c
Papa Tree Top Blues a
Randall's Island c
Rock Me To Sleep a [c: 1950]

1952
Bewitched, Bothered And Be-
  wildered a
Blue Mountain a
Cocktails For Two a
Cruisin' ac
Georgia On My Mind a
Jam Blues c
Key Largo a [c: 1947]
Lullaby In Blue ac
Mama Lou ac
Rockin' Along ac
'Round Midnight a
Sunday Afternoon ac
Wanna Go Home a
Wish You Were Here a
You Belong To Me a

1953
All Alone And Lonesome ac
Beautiful Love a
Blue Star ac
Don't Lead Me On a
Flamingo a
I'll Be Around a
Johnny Klingaringding a

Let's Fall In Love a
Make Me A Present Of You a
Me And My Jaguar ac
She Doesn't Laugh Like You c
You're Driving Me Crazy a
You're Gone For A Long Long
  Time a

1954
Can't We Be Friends a
I Like A Shuffle Beat a
I Stole De Wedding Bell ac
I'm Sorry ac
It Don't Mean A Thing If It Ain't
  Got That Swing a
Love, You Didn't Do Right By Me
  a
Play Ball ac
Spring Fever Blues a
Symphony a
Tutti Frutti a
With A Song In My Heart a
You'll Never Get The Chance Again
  c

1955
Between 18th and 19th On Chestnut
  Street a
Between The Devil And The Deep
  Blue Sea a
Blue Mountain a
Bugle Call Rag a
Christmas In New Orleans a
Christmas Night In Harlem a
The Girl Upstairs a
Lover Come Back To Me a
Millions Of People ac
Moments To Remember a
My Kind Of Trouble Is You c
Old Devil Moon a
Only You a
Rhumboogie a
Riding To Glory On A Trumpet a
That Old Black Magic a
Trumpets Have Triplets a

1956
Blue Prelude a
Blue Skies a
Comes Love a
Hallelujah a
How Am I To Know a
I Didn't Say Yes (I Didn't Say No) a
It's De-Lovely a
Just In Time a
A Lonesome Cup Of Coffee a
The Masquerade Is Over a
A Melody From The Sky a

Compositions/Arrangements: Chronological Index

This Can't Be Love a
Time After Time a
Two Cigarettes In The Dark a
You Go To My Head a
You Turned The Tables On Me a
You're My Everything a

1957
Autumn Leaves a
Blue Lou a
But Now I Know a
How Can You Lose? ac
A Hundred Years From Today a
I'm Coming Virginia a
In The Dark a
Just Squeeze Me a
Lover Come Back To Me a
Old Fashioned Love a
Once In A While a
Peace a
Polka Dots And Moonbeams a
Red Red Ribbon a
'Round Midnight a
Song Of The Wanderer a
Sunset Eyes a
Swingin' With Rhythm And Blues a
A Walkin' Thing ac
You Are Not My First Love a
You'd Better Think It Over ac

1958
Ask ac
August Moon c
Bill Bailey, Won't You Please Come Home a
February Fiesta a
How Deep Is The Ocean a
How Long Is A Moment ac
I Am Your Dream a
I'll Be Your Bride Again a
I'll Remember April a
It's So Frightnin' ac
June In January a
June Is Bustin' Out All Over a
Just The Blues a
March Wind ac
The Old Man And The Sea a
Once Upon A Time (It Happened) c
Roses In December a
September Song a
Sleigh Ride In July a
Something For October ac
Swingin' In November ac

1959
Friendly Islands c
The Gypsy In My Soul a

The Juke Box ac
A Lady Sings The Blues a
The Mugger ac
Phantom Raiders ac
The Search ac
Young And In Love a

1960
Be Anything a
Blue Five Jive ac
Body And Soul a
Champagne Waltz a
Close Your Eyes a
Congratulations To Someone a
Dedicated To You a
Don't Explain a
Don't Leave Me Now a
Everybody's Somebody's Fool a
First Things First a
The Folks Who Live On The Hill a
Guiding Light c
Hey Lawdy Mama a
I Can't Get Started a
I Won't Worry a
If I Love Again a
I'll Close My Eyes a
Indiana a
Jackson County Jubilee ac
A Jazz Portrait Of Brigitte Bardot c
Katy Do ac
Knock Me A Kiss a
Let Them Talk a
Make Me A Present Of You a
The Masquerade Is Over a
Meet Me At No Special Place a
Meetin' Time ac
Miss Missouri ac
My Wish a
Old Folks a
On Green Dolphin Street a
Paseo Promenade ac
Pick Yourself Up a
Rock Me To Sleep a [c: 1950]
Rompin' At The Reno ac
'Round Midnight a
So In Love a
Solitude a
Sunset Glow ac
Swedish Jam c
Trapped In The Web Of Love a
The Very Thought Of You a
Vine Street Rumble ac
Weak For The Man a
Whispering Grass a
The Wiggle Walk ac
Will You Still Be Mine a
You Call It Madness a
You're Mine You a

1961

After You've Gone a
Amoroso ac
Apollo Jumps ac
The Bad And The Beautiful a
The Basie Twist ac
Baubles, Bangles And Beads a
Blue Star a [c: 1953]
Body And Soul a
Boy Meets Horn a
Cherry a
Ciribiribin a
Cottontail a
Crazy Rhythm a
Doozy ac
Easy Money ac
Echoes Of Harlem a
The Flower Drum Song (soundtrack) a
Goin' On ac
Honeysuckle Rose a
Hot Lips a
I Believe In You a
I Can't Get Started a
Laura a
The Legend ac
The Midnight Sun Will Never Set a
Pinky a
Row Row Row Row a
San Francisco Blues a
Sugar Blues a
Summer Night c
The Swizzle ac
Tenderly a
Tired a
Toot Toot Tootsie a
The Trot ac
Turnabout ac
Two O'Clock Jump a
West End Blues a
Who's Blue ac
Yassu a

1962

After You've Gone a
Amoroso a [c: 1961]
Blitzen a
Doozy a [c: 1961]
Falling In Love With Love a
A Foggy Day a
A Garden In The Rain a
Great Day a
Gumshoe ac
Honeysuckle Rose a
I Believe In You a
I Can't Give You Anything But Love a
I'm A Woman a
I'm Gonna Live Til I Die a
The Lady's In Love With You a
Lou's Blues ac
Lula c
The Moon Is Low a
Moonlight On The Ganges a
Nobody Else But Me a
That's For Me a
The Trolley Song a
Who's Who ac

1963

Always On My Mind a
Around The World In Eighty Days a
Bagatelle c
Be Cool ac
Black Knight a
Blue Yonder ac
Busted a
Catfish Row ac
Cherchez La Femme c
Cherokee a
Cuando Caliente El Sol a
Dance With Me a
Discovery ac
Domino a
Friendless ac
Gotta Go Home ac
The Gypsy a
Heels Up ac
If I Had You a
If You Go a
I'll Never Be The Same a
Imminent ac
In The Evening (When The Sun Goes Down) a
Jazz Waltz ac
A Kiss From You c
Lonely Affair ac
Lonely Hours a
Look For Me, I'll Be Around a
The Man I Love a
Metropole ac
Oh! Look At Me Now a
Ol' Man Time a
The One I Love Belongs To Someone Else a
One Way Out ac
Poor Little Rich Girl a
Roses Of Picardy a
Show Break #1 ac
Show Break #2 ac
Show Me The Way To Go Home a
So Long, My Love a
Solitude a
These Foolish Things a

Compositions/Arrangements: Chronological Index   387

Under Paris Skies   a
Vinho Verde   ac
Vous Qui Passez Sans Me Voir   a
Waltz Gay   a
What Kind Of Fool Am I   a
Whatcha Know Joe   a
What'll I Do   a
Yes Indeed   a
You're Driving Me Crazy   a

1964
Alto Ego   ac
A Beautiful Friendship   a
Don't Get Around Much Anymore   a
Fairy Tales   a
Feudin' And Fightin'   a
The Girl From Ipanema   a
The Great Lie   a
I Don't Know What Kind Of Blues I've Got   a
I Wanna Be Around   a
I'm Lost   a
Ma (She's Making Eyes At Me)   a
Memories Of You   a
On Green Dolphin Street   a
Only Trust Your Heart   c
People   a
Poor Fool   ac
Right Here With You   a
Shangri-La   a
Smack Dab In The Middle   a
Tickle Toe   a
Wouldn't It Be Loverly   a

1965
Ain't I   ac
All That Jazz   ac
Big Nobody   a
Blue Train   ac
Blues For The Weepers   a
Brazilian Twist   ac
Charmaine   a
Claudia   ac
Cold Cold Heart   a
Crack Up   a
Du Bist Die Liebe   a
Gee, Ain't I Good To You   a
Go Now   ac
Gonna Build A Mountain   a
Hey There   a
High Society Limbo   ac
I Shoulda Quit When I Was Ahead   a
If I Had My Life To Live Over   a
If It's The Last Thing I Do   a
I'll See You In My Dreams   a
Into Each Life Some Rain Must Fall   a
It's Monday Every Day   a
Look At That Face   a
Margie   a
Me And My Shadow   a
My Buddy   a
Night Walk   ac
Nobody But Me   a
Nothing Really Feels The Same   a
Now And Then There's A Fool Such As I   a
The Pawnbroker   a
Pleasures And Palaces   a
The Power Of Love   a
Slides And Hides   ac
Soft Touch   ac
Someone To Watch Over Me   a
Take Back Your Mink   a
Three O'Clock In The Morning   a
Two Tickets West   a
What Is A Man   a
Whisper To One   c
Whispering Grass   a
Who's Tired   a
You'd Better Think It Over   a
  [c: 1957]

1966
Can't Buy Me Love   a
Come On Back   ac
Doozy   a   [c: 1961]
Fantastic, That's You   a
A Hard Day's Night   a
A Heart Must Learn To Cry   a
I Want To Hold Your Hand   a
If Dreams Come True   a
It's All Right With Me   a
Lonely Woman   a   [c: 1937]
Please Please Me   a
Prohibido   ac
Rock Bottom   ac
Titmouse   ac
We Were In Love   ac

1967
I'll Plant My Own Tree   a
The Wine Of Sweet Remembrance   c

1968
All Tore Down   a
Baby, Don't You Quit Now   a
Chain Gang   a
Do I Need You   a
Even When You Cry   a
For Your Precious Love   a
Funky Broadway   a
I Haven't Got Anything Better To Do   a

I Never Loved A Woman   a
I Was Made To Love Her   a
I'll Be Here With You   c
I'll Never Leave You   a
I'm Always Drunk In San Fran-
  cisco   a
In The Midnight Hour   a
It's Up To You And Me   a
Lasse Lasse Litten   ac
The Loving Room   ac
My Girl   a
Ode To Billy Joe   a
On Censorship   ac
Point Of No Return   ac
Prisoner Of My Eyes (I Can
  Never Let You Go)   a
Protect Me   a
Respect   a
To The Destroyers   ac
Uptight (Everything Is All Right)
  a

Right Here In My Heart   a
Satin Latin   a
Supper Time   a
Tender Loving Words   a
When It's Time To Tell   a
When Twilight Comes   a
When You're Young   a

1972
Blues For Beginners   ac
Doozy   a [c: 1961]
Honeysuckle Rose   a
I Can't Get Started   a
The Juke Box   a [c: 1959]
You Are   ac

1973
Coalition   ac
Cottontail   a
Doozy   a [c: 1961]
A Kiss From You   a [c: 1963]
Souvenir   ac
A Walkin' Thing   a [c: 1957]
When Lights Are Low   a [c: 1936]
You Are   a [c: 1972]

1969
(none)

1970
Con Alma   a
I Said No   a
Ma (She's Making Eyes At Me)
  a
Never Again   a
She Had To Go And Lose It At
  The Astor   a
The Weekend Of A Private Secre-
  tary   a

1974
Again   a
Any Old Time   a
As Time Goes By   a
The Call Of The Far Away Hills   a
Don't You Make Me High   a
Doozy   a [c: 1961]
Gee, Ain't I Good To You   a
It Ain't The Meat, It's The Motion
  a
It Don't Mean A Thing If It Ain't
  Got That Swing   a
Lover Man   a
Mona Lisa   a
The River of No Return   a
Ruby   a
September Song   a
Squeeze Me   a
Summertime In Venice   a
Sweetheart   a
Walkin' One And Only   a

1971
All That I Can Do Is Think Of
  You   a
All The Time   a
Always On Sunday   a
Bobby   a
Care   a
God Bless You   a
Got That Feeling   a
The Happy Ones   a
Here's That Rainy Day   a
A House Is Not A Home   a
I Never Met A Stranger   a
I'll Never Pass This Way Again
  a
I'm A Lucky Guy   a
It's Impossible   a
Love Is A Feeling   a
Mama, A Rainbow   a
Mister Love   a
Once Upon A Happy Time (The
  Big Band Days)   a

1975
Livin' In The Sunlight (Lovin' In
  The Moonlight)   a
Rockin' Chair   a
We Just Couldn't Say Goodbye   a

1976
A Tea Vista   c
Blues in D Flat   c
The Courtship   c

Compositions/Arrangements: Chronological Index

Green Wine c
JJJJump c
Johnny c
Kansas City Line c
Mama Don't Wear No Drawers c
Stroll c

1977
All My Love a
Chinatown a
Confessin' a
Cottontail a
God Bless The Child a
Hobnobbin' ac
In A Sentimental Mood a
It Don't Mean A Thing If It Ain't
  Got That Swing a
Jitterbug Waltz a
Nuages a
South Side Samba ac
Souvenir a [c: 1973]
Squatty Roo a
Them There Eyes a
Things Ain't What They Used To
  Be a
When It's Sleepy Time Down
  South a
When You're Smiling a

1978
(none)

1979
Ain't Misbehavin' a
Black Butterfly a

Day Dream a
Don't Worry 'Bout Me a
Feasant Pheathers c
Honeysuckle Rose a
I Got It Bad a
I Let A Song Go Out Of My Heart
  a
I'm Getting Sentimental Over You
  a
In A Mellotone a
In A Sentimental Mood a
It Don't Mean A Thing If It Ain't
  Got That Swing a
Just A-Sittin' And A-Rockin' a
Lush Life a
My Kind Of Trouble Is You a
  [c: 1955]
Organ Grinder's Swing a
Please Don't Talk About Me When
  I'm Gone a
Solitude a
Some Other Spring a
Sophisticated Lady a
Sweet Lorraine a
Teach Me Tonight a
Tonight I Shall Sleep With A Smile
  On My Face a

1980
(none)

1981
The Courtship a [c: 1976]
I'm Beginning To See The Light a
Mood Indigo a

A BASIC SELECTION OF BENNY CARTER'S LPs

This list will help readers who want to obtain a basic selection of Carter's recordings. Most of these LPs are domestic labels or widely-distributed imports that are either still in print or only recently cut out. Essential items are marked with an asterisk.

In addition, at any given time there are usually available several bootleg LPs of Carter's recordings for the Armed Forces Radio Service by his mid-1940s orchestra. Most of them are imports carried by large record stores or by mail-order dealers.

*The Giants of Jazz: Benny Carter (Time-Life Records STL-J10, 3 records). Highlights of Carter's recording career from 1929 to 1977. Includes samples of Carter as multi-instrumentalist, arranger and composer with the Chocolate Dandies, Fletcher Henderson, McKinney's Cotton Pickers and his own orchestras among others. Available by mail from Time-Life.

*Benny Carter 1933 (Prestige 7643). First important recordings of the Carter orchestra and the 1933 Chocolate Dandies. Includes such seminal arrangements as "Symphony In Riffs" and "Lonesome Nights."

*Benny Carter (French RCA Black & White PM42406, Jazz Tribune series, no. 4, 2 records). A cross-section of recordings for Victor, 1928-1952. Includes Carter's first recording (with Charlie Johnson), Lionel Hampton all-star dates 1938-39, and a good representation of Carter's 1940-41 orchestra.

The Early Benny Carter (Everest Archive of Folk and Jazz FS225). British recordings, 1936-37.

Benny and the Hawk on the Loose in Europe (On the Loose, vols. 1-5). Recordings of Carter and Coleman Hawkins in Europe, together and separately. Includes many items never before on LP as well as previously unissued alternate takes. Limited edition import, not easily obtainable.

Benny Carter 1933/1939 (Tax m-8031). Includes 1933 Mezz Mezzrow date, 1934 Carter orchestra, 1936 British recordings with Elisabeth Welch, 1937 Dutch recordings with Hawkins and 1939 Carter orchestra. Swedish import.

Melancholy Benny (Tax m-8004). 1939-40 orchestra: studio recordings and Savoy Ballroom airchecks. Swedish import.

*Big Band Bounce (Capitol M11057, Capitol Jazz Classics series, vol. 11). 1943-45 West Coast recordings of Carter orchestra with Max Roach, J. J. Johnson and other younger musicians. (One side is Carter, the other Cootie Williams.)

*Jazz Giant (Contemporary S7028). 1957 small group and quartet including Ben Webster.

*Swingin' the Twenties (Contemporary S7561). Carter's only recordings with Earl Hines, 1958.

*Further Definitions (Impulse A12). Carter leads and arranges for sax quartet including Coleman Hawkins, Phil Woods and Charlie Rouse, 1961.

Additions to Further Definitions (Impulse A9116). 1966 date featuring Carter's arrangements and compositions played by five-man reed section.

The King (Pablo 2310-768). "Comeback" date in 1976 featuring Carter with Milt Jackson, Tommy Flanagan and Joe Pass playing Carter originals.

Carter, Gillespie, Inc. (Pablo 2310-781). 1976 reunion with his former trumpeter.

*Benny Carter 4 - Montreux '77 (Pablo Live 2308-204). Live at 1977 Montreux Jazz Festival, with Ray Bryant; finest example of Carter's alto in the 1970s as well as his first recordings on trumpet in fifteen years.

'Live and Well in Japan (Pablo Live 2308-216). Ten-piece band recorded live in Tokyo, 1977; new Carter arrangements include tributes to Louis Armstrong, Billie Holiday and Duke Ellington.

The Best of Benny Carter (Pablo 2310-853). One side of material from 'Live and Well in Japan album and one side from Benny Carter 4 - Montreux '77 album.

Benny Carter Jazz All Star Orchestra, Live in Japan '79 (Paddle Wheel GP3199). Ten-piece band, loose jam-style arrangements leaving much solo space, as well as a ballad medley. Japanese import, hard to obtain.

Street of Dreams (LOB LDC1030). Carter plays standards backed by Japanese trio; recorded 1981. Japanese import, hard to obtain.

FILMOGRAPHY

1. Theatrical Films by Major Studios

Carter's work on theatrical films made by the major Hollywood studios has been of two kinds. (a) On about a hundred films he plays on the soundtrack but has not written music. This category is omitted from this filmography. (b) We have traced thirty-three films, included in this filmography, in which he arranges, orchestrates, or composes music; in some of them he also plays or conducts on the soundtrack and appears on screen. The films are listed in chronological order by date of release, showing title, studio, music director, and Carter's specific contributions as indicated by the following abbreviations:

cmp:	composes
at:	arranges or orchestrates tunes or songs
ab:	arranges or orchestrates backgrounds
ps:	plays on soundtrack
cs:	conducts on soundtrack
scr:	appears on screen

Studio abbreviations: TCF--Twentieth Century-Fox; MGM--Metro-Goldwyn-Mayer.

1943	June 11	Jitterbugs. TCF. Alfred Newman (probably). at
	July 16	Stormy Weather. TCF. Alfred Newman. at ps
	August 2	Young Ideas. MGM. George Bassman. ab
	August 14	This Is the Army. Warner Brothers. Ray Heindorf. at ps
	September 17	Wintertime. TCF. Alfred Newman. at ps
	December 24	The Gang's All Here. TCF. Alfred Newman. at ps
1944	January	Thousands Cheer. MGM. Herbert Stothart. at ps cs scr
	July 29	The Canterville Ghost. MGM. George Bassman. ab
	December	Here Comes the Waves. Paramount. Robert E. Dolan. at
1949	April 22	Portrait of Jennie. Selznick. Dmitri Tiomkin. at ab
1950	March 3	Love Happy. United Artists. Ann Ronell. at cs
	September	My Blue Heaven. TCF. Alfred Newman. at ps cs
	September	Panic In the Streets. TCF. Alfred Newman. at ab cmp ps cs
	September 30	Edge of Doom. RKO Radio. Hugo Friedhofer. ab ps

393

	September 30.	I'll Get By. TCF. Lionel Newman. at
	October.	No Way Out. TCF. Alfred Newman. at
1951	November 9	An American in Paris. MGM. Johnny Green. at ps cs scr
1952	June	Clash by Night. RKO Radio. Roy Webb. at ps cs scr
	November	Night Without Sleep. TCF. Cyril Mockridge. at ps
1953	April	The Glass Wall. Columbia. Leith Stevens. at ps cs
	July	The Snows of Kilimanjaro. TCF. Bernard Herrmann. at ps scr Note: release date is July 1953 but this film was reviewed in the New York Times, September 19, 1952, p. 19.
1954	March	Red Garters. Paramount. Joseph L. Lilley. at
1955	November	The View from Pompey's Head. TCF. Elmer Bernstein. at ps cs scr
1957	September	The Sun Also Rises. TCF. Hugo Friedhofer. at ps
1959	August	The Five Pennies. Paramount. Leith Stevens. at ps
	December (probably)	The Gene Krupa Story. Columbia. Leith Stevens. at ps
1961	July	The Guns of Navarone. Columbia. Dmitri Tiomkin. ab
	October	Town Without Pity. United Artists. Dmitri Tiomkin. ab
1962	January	Flower Drum Song. Universal. Alfred Newman. at ps Note: release date is January 1962 but this film was reviewed in the New York Times, November 10, 1961, p. 40.
1966	July	A Man Called Adam. Embassy. Benny Carter is music director: composer, arranger-orchestrator, conductor on all music (does not play).
1967	December 14	Valley of the Dolls. TCF. John Williams. at
1971	no release date given	Red Sky at Morning. Universal. Billy Goldenberg. at Reviewed in New York Times, May 13, 1971, p. 53.
1972	April	Buck and the Preacher. Columbia. Benny Carter is music director: composer, arranger-orchestrator, conductor on virtually all music (does not play).

2. Short Animated Films

Carter has written music for five short (four to ten minutes) animated films by John and Faith Hubley, as shown in The Hubley Studio list, "John Hubley: Faith Hubley," N.Y., n.d., ca. 1977.

Year of Release	Title
1957	Adventures of an Asterisk
1957	Harlem Wednesday
1966	Urbanissimo
1967	The Cruise
1975	People People People

In 1980 Carter composed for a short animated film, Opens Wednesday, by Barry Nelson Productions.

3. Television

Carter has written at least ninety-five episodes ("segments") of twenty television serials or shows with an overall title for unrelated segments. There is no documentation to show all his television work, nor does he remember it all, but the following table certainly includes almost all. The list comes mainly from his statement of October 10, 1976 in connection with the composers' (CLGA) law suit against the major studios. The table shows the year, the overall name of the series, and the approximate number of segments Carter composed. All these shows were productions of the Universal studio, except for the last series, Banyon, which was by Warner Brothers.

Year of Contract or Airing	Overall Name of Series	Approximate No. of Segments
1958-1960	M Squad	35
1960	17 Battery Place	Pilot + 1
1961	The Investigators	Pilot
1963	Kraft Suspense Theater	1
1963-1966	Bob Hope Chrysler Theater	20
1964	Expose	Pilot
1964	Alfred Hitchcock	1
1964	General Electric Theater	4
1964	Project 120	1
1965	Jean Arthur	1
1965	Run for Your Life	1
1968	World Première	2
1968-1969	Ironside	8
1968-1970	Name of the Game	8
1969	It Takes a Thief	Pilot + 1
1969	The Outsider	1
1970	The Doctors	1
1970	Night Gallery	2
1970	The Bold Ones	2
1971	Banyon	1

Carter has also written for two feature telefilms: Man Hunter, 1968 (Universal), and Louis Armstrong, Chicago Style, 1976 (independent).

BIBLIOGRAPHY OF WORKS CITED

Adderley, Julian "Cannonball." "Paying Dues: The Education of a Combo Leader," In Williams, ed., q.v., pp. 258-263.

Albertson, Chris. Bessie. New York, Stein and Day, 1972.

Allen, Leonard. "The Battle of Tin Pan Alley." Harper's Magazine, October 1940, pp. 514-523.

Allen, Walter C. Hendersonia: The Music of Fletcher Henderson and His Musicians, A Bio-Discography. Highland Park, N.J., The Author, 1973.

Armstead-Johnson, Helen. "Blacks in Vaudeville: Broadway and Beyond." In Myron Matlaw, ed. American Popular Entertainment. Westport, Conn. and London, Greenwood, 1979, pp. 77-86.

Arvey, Verna. "Memo for Musicologists." In Robert B. Haas, ed., q.v., pp. 88-93.

The ASCAP Biographical Dictionary of Composers, Authors and Publishers. 3d ed. New York, ASCAP, 1966.

Atterbury, Grosvenor. "The Phipps Model Tenement Houses." Charities and the Commons (later, The Survey), October 1906, pp. 49-65.

Balliett, Whitney. "Profiles." New Yorker, February 14, 1977, pp. 43-52.

_____. Such Sweet Thunder. Indianapolis and New York, Bobbs-Merrill, 1966.

Barker, Danny. "Jelly Roll Morton in New York." Jazz Review, May 1959, pp. 12-14.

Barnouw, Erik. Tube of Plenty: The Evolution of American Television. New York, Oxford, 1975.

Bazelon, David. Knowing the Score: Notes on Film Music. New York, Van Nostrand Reinhold, 1975.

Bechet, Sidney. Treat It Gentle. New York, Hill and Wang, 1960.

Bérard, Madeleine. "Un Dîner avec Benny Carter." Hot-Revue (Lausanne). 1946 (month not indicated), vol. 1, no. 12, pp. 12-15.

Berg, Charles Merrell. An Investigation of the Motives for and Realization of Music to Accompany the American Silent Film, 1896-1927. New York, Arno, 1976.

Berger, Edward. "Benny Carter: A Discographical Approach." Journal of Jazz Studies 4, no. 1 (1976): 47-74, and 5, no. 1 (1978): 28-80.

Berger, Morroe. "Jazz Caravan." Aramco World Magazine, July-August 1977, pp. 1-2.

──────. "Jazz: Resistance to the Diffusion of a Culture-Pattern." Journal of Negro History 32 (October 1947): 461-494. Reprint, Charles Nanry, ed., q. v., pp. 11-43.

Berlin, Edward A. Ragtime: A Musical and Cultural History. Berkeley and Los Angeles, University of California Press, 1980.

Bernstein, Elmer. "What Ever Happened to Great Movie Music?" High Fidelity and Musical America, July 1972, pp. 55-58.

──────. "The Man with the Golden Arm." In Limbacher, ed., q. v., pp. 94-96.

The Billboard. Band Year Book. Suppl. September 26, 1942.

──────. Music Year Book. 5th annual ed. 1943.

──────. Music Year Book. 6th annual ed. 1944.

Blesh, Rudi. Shining Trumpets: A History of Jazz. New York, Knopf, 1946.

──────, and Harriet Janis. They All Played Ragtime. 4th ed. New York, Oak, 1971.

Bontemps, Arna, and Langston Hughes. Arna Bontemps-Langston Hughes Letters 1925-1967. Charles H. Nichols, ed. New York, Dodd, Mead, 1980.

Borneman, Ernest. A Critic Looks at Jazz. London, Jazz Music Books, 1946.

Bourne, Michael. "His Royal Majesty of Reeds: Benny Carter." Down Beat, February 24, 1977, pp. 20-21, 50.

Bowen, Louise De Koven. "Dance Halls." The Survey, June 3, 1911, pp. 383-387.

Boyer, Richard O. "Profiles: The Hot Bach--III." New Yorker, July 8, 1944, pp. 26-31.

Bradford, Perry. Born With the Blues: Perry Bradford's Own Story. New York, Oak, 1965.

Braithwaite, R. B. Theory of Games As a Tool for the Moral Philosopher. Cambridge, England, Cambridge University, 1955.

Brooks, Aubrey. "About Musicians." The Inter-State Tattler, September 13, 1929, p. 13.

Burley, Dan. "So He Laid His Bible Down." New York Amsterdam News, October 21, 1939, p. 20.

Bibliography

Burns, Jim. "Jazz and the Beats." Jazz Monthly (London), January 1971, pp. 17-22.

Burton, Jack. The Blue Book of Hollywood Musicals. Watkins Glen, New York, Century House, 1953.

_____. The Blue Book of Tin Pan Alley. New York, Century House, 1951.

Butler, Jack, and Jean Poinsot. "Harlem en 1928." Bulletin du Hot Club de France, September 1960, pp. 5-7.

California Advisory Committee to the United States Commission on Civil Rights. Behind the Scenes: Equal Opportunity in the Motion Picture Industry. U. S. Commission on Civil Rights, Washington, D. C., 1978.

Calloway, Cab, and Bryant Rollins. Of Minnie the Moocher and Me. New York, Crowell, 1976.

Carpenter, Paul S. Music: An Art and a Business. Norman, Oklahoma, University of Oklahoma Press, 1950.

Carter, Benny. "Benny Carter Hits Out." Melody Maker, April 10, 1937, p. 2.

_____. "Benny Carter Sifts LA Union Issues." Down Beat, August 27, 1952, p. 14.

_____. Interview, 1976. Jazz Oral History Project, Institute of Jazz Studies, Rutgers University, Newark, N. J.

_____. "My Nine Lives." Swing Music (London), May-June 1936, pp. 55, 71.

_____. See Feather, The Pleasures of Jazz.

_____. See The Giants of Jazz.

Castle, Irene (as told to Bob and Wanda Duncan). Castles in the Air. New York, Doubleday, 1958.

_____. Irene and Vernon. Modern Dancing. New York, Harper, 1914.

Ceplair, Larry, and Steven Englund. The Inquisition in Hollywood: Politics in the Film Community 1930-1960. New York, Anchor/Doubleday, 1980.

Cesana, Otto. "Have Dance Orchestras Reached Their Peak?" Down Beat, March 1, 1942, p. 9.

Charters, Samuel B., and Leonard Kunstadt. Jazz: A History of the New York Scene. New York, Doubleday, 1962.

Cheatham, Adolphus "Doc." Autobiographical statement accompanying record album, Jezebel JZ-102-ST. New York, 1973.

Coleman, Bill. Interview, 1978. Jazz Oral History Project, Institute of Jazz Studies, Rutgers University, Newark, N. J.

Chilton, John. McKinney's Music: A Bio-Discography of McKinney's Cotton Pickers. London, Bloomsbury Book Shop, 1978.

──────. Billie's Blues: Billie Holiday's Story 1933-1959. New York, Stein and Day, 1975.

──────. Who's Who of Jazz. Rev. ed. Alexandria, Virginia, Time-Life Records, 1978.

Cogley, John. Report on Blacklisting. 2 vols. New York, Fund for the Republic, 1956. Vol. 1: Movies.

Cole, Bill. Miles Davis: A Musical Biography. New York, Morrow, 1974.

Collier, James Lincoln. The Making of Jazz: A Comprehensive History. Boston, Houghton Mifflin, 1978.

Collins, John. Interview, 1975. Jazz Oral History Project, Institute of Jazz Studies, Rutgers University, Newark, N.J.

Connor, D. Russell, and Warren W. Hicks. BG on the Record: A Bio-Discography of Benny Goodman. New Rochelle, New York, Arlington House, 1969.

Cook, Bruce. Dalton Trumbo. New York, Scribner, 1977.

Cook, Mercer. "Benny Carter Plays for Italian Students." New York Amsterdam News, March 19, 1938, p. 19.

──────. "From 'Clorindy' to 'The Red Moon' and Beyond." Typescript of lecture at CUNY Graduate Center, New York, October 1978.

Cook, Will Marion. "Clorindy, the Origin of the Cakewalk." Theater Arts, September 1947, pp. 61-65. Reprint, Eileen Southern, ed., q.v., pp. 217-223.

──────. Letter dated December 19, 1926, New York Times, December 26, 1926, sec. 7, p. 8. Reprint, Cuney-Hare, q.v., pp. 135-136.

Cressey, Paul G. The Taxi-Dance Hall. Chicago, University of Chicago Press, 1932.

Cripps, Thomas. Slow Fade to Black: The Negro in American Film, 1900-1942. New York, Oxford, 1977.

Crosland, Margaret. Jean Cocteau. London, Peter Nevill, 1955.

Cuney-Hare, Maud. Negro Musicians and Their Music. Washington, D.C., Associated Publishers, 1936.

Dance, Stanley. "Benny Carter Interviewed by Stanley Dance." Jazz, July 1966, pp. 12-14.

──────. "Jazz at the White House." Saturday Review, November 15, 1969, pp. 73, 75, 101.

──────. The World of Count Basie. New York, Scribner, 1980.

Bibliography

_____. The World of Duke Ellington. New York, Scribner, 1970.

_____. The World of Earl Hines. New York, Scribner, 1977.

_____. The World of Swing. New York, Scribner, 1974.

Davis, Clive, with James Willnerth. Clive: Inside the Record Business. New York, William Morrow, 1975.

Davis, Fred. Yearning for Yesterday: A Sociology of Nostalgia. New York, Free Press, 1979.

Delaunay, Charles. "Biographie de Benny Carter." Jazz Hot, September-October 1935, p. 5.

_____. Django Reinhardt. Translated by Michael James. London, Cassell, 1961.

_____. Hot Discography. (1st ed. 1936.) Rev. ed. New York, Commodore Record Co., Inc., 1943.

de Lerma, Dominique-René, ed. Black Music in Our Culture. Kent, Ohio, Kent State University Press, 1970.

_____. "Will Marion Cook, Antonín Dvořák, and the Earlier Afro-American Musical Theater." Morgan State University Music Department, Baltimore, Maryland, 1979.

de Toledano, Ralph, ed. Frontiers of Jazz. New York, 1947. 2d ed. New York, Ungar, 1962.

Dexter, Dave, Jr. Jazz Cavalcade. New York, Criterion, 1946.

_____. Playback. New York, Billboard, 1976.

Dimmitt, Richard Bertrand. A Title Guide to the Talkies. 2 vols. New York, Scarecrow, 1965.

Dorr, Rheta Childe. What Eight Million Women Want. Boston, Small and Maynard, 1910. Reprint ed., New York, Kraus, 1971.

Driggs, Frank. "Don Redman, Jazz Composer-Arranger." In Williams, ed., q.v., pp. 91-104.

_____, Franklin S. [Frank] "Kansas City and the Southwest." In Hentoff and McCarthy, eds., q.v., pp. 189-230.

DuBois, W. E. Burghardt. "The Future of Wilberforce University." Journal of Negro Education 9(October 1940):553-570.

Durante, Jimmy, and Jack Kofoed. Night Clubs. New York, Knopf, 1931.

Dvořák, Antonin. "Music In America." Harper's, February 1895, pp. 429-434.

Edey, Maitland. "Dizzy Gillespie. An Interview." Paris Review, Fall 1965, pp. 137-146.

Eisen, Jonathan, ed. The Age of Rock. New York, Vintage Books, 1969.

Eldridge, Roy. "Little Jazz." Interview with Nat Hentoff, q. v.

Ellington, Edward Kennedy (Duke). Music Is My Mistress. New York, Doubleday, 1973.

Ellington, Mercer, with Stanley Dance. Duke Ellington in Person: An Intimate Memoir. Boston, Houghton Mifflin, 1978.

Emge, Charles. "Jazz' Most Underrated Musician? Benny Carter." Down Beat, May 18, 1951, pp. 2, 16, 18.

Ertegun, Nesuhi. "Benny Carter." The Record Changer, May 1948, pp. 5-6.

Esquire's Jazz Book. See Miller, Paul Eduard, ed.

Evans, Mark. Soundtrack: The Music of the Movies. New York, Hopkinson and Blake, 1975.

Ewen, David. A Journey to Greatness: The Life and Music of George Gershwin. New York, Holt, 1956.

―――. Panorama of Popular Music. Englewood Cliffs, N. J., Prentice-Hall, 1957.

Falter, John, and Richard Gehman. "Greatest Jazz Band." Saturday Evening Post, Spring 1972, pp. 60-63, 153.

Fass, Paula S. The Damned and the Beautiful: American Youth in the 1920s. New York, Oxford, 1977.

Faulkner, Robert R. Hollywood Studio Musicians: Their Work and Careers in the Recording Industry. Chicago and New York, Aldine-Atherton, 1971.

Feather, Leonard. "Bennett L. Carter, Esquire." Melody Maker, October 31, 1936, p. 2.

―――. The Encyclopedia of Jazz in the Sixties. New York, Bonanza, 1966.

―――. "The Enduring Benny Carter." Down Beat, May 25, 1961, pp. 15-16.

―――. Inside Jazz. New York, Da Capo, 1977. (1st pub. as Inside Be-bop, New York, J. J. Robbins, 1949.)

―――. The New Edition of the Encyclopedia of Jazz. New York, Bonanza, 1962. (1st ed., New York, 1955.)

―――. The Pleasures of Jazz. Introduction by Benny Carter. New York, Horizon, 1976.

Feather, Leonard, and Ira Gitler. The Encyclopedia of Jazz in the Seventies. New York, Horizon, 1976.

Federation of Social Agencies of Pittsburgh and Alleghany County, Bureau of Social Research. "Social Facts Concerning McDonald Borough." Pittsburgh, Pa., 1940.

Fitzgerald, F. Scott. "Echoes of the Jazz Age" (1931). The Crack-Up. New York, New Directions, 1945.

Fletcher, Tom. 100 Years of the Negro in Show Business: The Tom Fletcher Story. New York, London and Toronto, Burdge, 1954.

Flower, John. Moonlight Serenade: A Bio-Discography of the Glenn Miller Civilian Band. New Rochelle, N.Y., Arlington House, 1972.

Foote, Timothy. "Benny Carter." The Swing Era: One More Time. Philip W. Payne and Joan S. Reiter, eds. Time-Life Records, New York, 1972, pp. 28-38.

Foreman, Ronald Clifford, Jr. Jazz and Race Records, 1920-1932: Their Origins and Their Significance for the Record Industry and Society. Ph.D. Thesis, U. of Illinois, Urbana, 1968.

The Giants of Jazz: Benny Carter. Philip W. Payne, ed. Recordings by Carter, biography by Morroe Berger, music notes by Edward Berger. Time-Life Records, Alexandria, Va., 1980.

Gifford, Denis. The British Film Catalogue, 1895-1970. New York, McGraw-Hill, 1973.

Gillespie, John Birks. "Conversation with John Birks 'Dizzy' Gillespie." By Josephine R. B. Wright. The Black Perspective in Music 4(Spring 1976):82-89.

_____. to BE, or not ... to BOP: Memoirs. New York, Doubleday, 1979.

Gitler, Ira. Jazz Masters of the Forties. New York, Macmillan, 1966.

Goddard, Chis. Jazz Away from Home. New York and London, Paddington, 1979.

Goffin, Robert. Aux Frontières du Jazz. 2d ed. Paris, Editions du Sagittaire, 1932.

_____. Horn of Plenty: The Story of Louis Armstrong. Translated by James F. Bezou. New York, Towne and Heath, 1947.

_____. Jazz: From the Congo to the Metropolitan. Translated by Walter Schaap and Leonard G. Feather. New York, Doubleday Doran, 1944.

Goldberg, Isaac. Tin Pan Alley: A Chronicle of the American Popular Music Racket. New York, John Day, 1930.

Goldblatt, Burt. Newport Jazz Festival: The Illustrated History. New York, Dial, 1977.

Goldman, Albert. Freakshow. New York, Atheneum, 1971.

Goldstein, Richard, ed. The Poetry of Rock. New York, Bantam, 1969.

Goodman, Benny, and Irving Kolodin. The Kingdom of Swing. New York, Stackpole Sons, 1939.

Granz, Norman. Just Jazz 2. Sinclair Traill and Gerald Lascelles, eds. London, Peter Davies, 1958, pp. 15-21.

Green, Johnny. "Johnny Green Tells Duties, Functions, and Details of Motion Picture Musical Director." Down Beat, August 22, 1956, pp. 13, 41.

Guback, Thomas H. The International Film Industry: Western Europe and America Since 1945. Bloomington and London, Indiana University Press, 1969.

Gutman, Herbert G. The Black Family in Slavery and Freedom, 1750-1925. New York, Pantheon, 1976.

Haas, Robert Bartlett, ed. William Grant Still and the Fusion of Cultures in American Music. Los Angeles, Black Sparrow, 1972.

Hall, Ben M. The Best Remaining Seats: The Story of the Golden Age of the Movie Palace. New York, Clarkson N. Potter, 1961.

Hammond, John, with Irving Townsend. John Hammond on Record. New York, Summit, 1977.

Handy, W. C., ed. Blues: An Anthology. New York, Boni, 1926. Introduction by Abbe Niles.

Harris, Rex. Jazz. Harmondsworth, England, Penguin, 1952.

Haskins, Jim. The Cotton Club. New York, Random House, 1977.

Henderson, Horace. Interview, 1975. Jazz Oral History Project, Institute of Jazz Studies, Rutgers University, Newark, N. J.

Henderson, Mae Gwendolyn. "Portrait of Wallace Thurman." In Arna Bontemps, ed. The Harlem Renaissance Remembered, chap. 8. New York, Dodd, Mead, 1972.

Hennessey, Thomas Joseph. From Jazz to Swing: Black Jazz Musicians and Their Music, 1917-1935. Ph. D. Thesis, Northwestern University, 1973.

Hentoff, Nat. "Dr. Jazz, and His Son, the Professor." New York Times Magazine, April 14, 1974, pp. 12-13, 28, 30, 32-35.

_____. "Little Jazz." Down Beat, September 19, 1956, pp. 13-14, 48.

Hentoff, Nat, and Albert J. McCarthy, eds. Jazz: New Perspectives on the History of Jazz. New York, Rinehart, 1959.

Heyward, Sammy. "Résumé of the New Amsterdam Musical Association." New York, 1974.

Hippenmeyer, Jean-Roland. Jazz sur Films (1917-1972). Yverdon, Editions de la Thièle, Switzerland, 1973.

Bibliography

Hobson, Wilder. "Fifty-second Street." In Ramsey and Smith, eds., q.v., chap. 11.

──────. "Introducing Duke Ellington." Fortune, August 1933, pp. 47 ff. Reprint, Ralph de Toledano, ed., q.v., pp. 137-147.

Hodeir, André. Toward Jazz. Translated by Noel Burch. New York, Grove, 1962.

──────. The Worlds of Jazz. Translated by Noel Burch. New York, Grove, 1972.

Hoefer, George. Liner notes to The Sound of Harlem, record album, C3L33, Columbia Jazz Archive Series, "Jazz Odyssey," Frank Driggs, producer. New York, 1964.

Holiday, Billie, with William Dufty. Lady Sings the Blues. New York, Lancer, 1965. (1st ed., New York, Doubleday, 1956.)

Horricks, Raymond, et al. These Jazzmen of Our Time. London, Gollancz, 1959.

Huggins, Nathan Irvin. Harlem Renaissance. New York, Oxford, 1971.

Hughes, Langston. The Big Sea: An Autobiography. New York, Knopf, 1940.

──────. Letters. See Arna Bontemps and Hughes.

──────. Something in Common and Other Stories. New York, Hill and Wang, 1963.

Hughes, Langston, and Milton Meltzer. Black Magic: A Pictorial History of the Negro in American Entertainment. Englewood Cliffs, N.J., Prentice-Hall, 1967.

Hughes, Patrick Cairns (Spike). Second Movement. London, Museum Press, 1951.

──────. "Sweet Sorrow." Swing Music (London), November-December 1935, pp. 250-252, 268, 270.

Hughes, Rupert. "A Eulogy of Rag-Time." Musical Record, April 1, 1899, pp. 157-159.

Hunt, David C. "Benny Carter: Controversial Jazz Giant." Jazz and Pop, May 1970, pp. 42-44.

International Cyclopedia of Music and Musicians. 9th ed. New York, Dodd, Mead, 1964.

International Motion Picture Almanac. Annual. New York, 1933--present.

Jablonski, Edward. Harold Arlen: Happy with the Blues. New York, Doubleday, 1961.

Jackson, Edgar. "Maestros of Jazz--No. 4. Benny Carter." "His Master's Voice" Record Review (London), December 1942, pp. 17-20.

"The Jazz Composers in Hollywood: A Symposium with Benny Carter, Quincy Jones, Henry Mancini, Lalo Schifrin, Pat Williams." Conducted by Harvey Siders. Down Beat, March 2, 1972, pp. 12-15, 34.

Jepsen, Jörgen Grunnet. Jazz Records 1942--. 11 vols. Copenhagen, Knudsen, 1963-1970.

Johnson, J. Rosamond. "Why They Call American Music Ragtime." The Colored American Magazine 15(January 1909):636-639.

Johnson, James Weldon. Along This Way. New York, Viking, 1933.

_____. Black Manhattan. New York, Knopf, 1930.

Johnson, James Weldon, ed., and J. Rosamond Johnson and Lawrence Brown, arrangers. The Book of American Negro Spirituals. New York, Viking, 1925.

Johnson, James Weldon, ed., and J. Rosamond Johnson, arranger. The Second Book of Negro Spirituals. New York, Viking, 1926.

Jones, Isham. "American Dance Music Is Not Jazz." The Etude 42 (August 1924):526.

Jones, LeRoi. Blues People: Negro Music In White America. New York, William Morrow, 1963.

Jones, Max, and John Chilton. Louis: The Louis Armstrong Story 1900-1971. Boston, Little, Brown, 1971.

Joplin, Scott. The Collected Works of Scott Joplin. Vera Brodsky Lawrence, ed. New York, New York Public Library, 1971.

Karshner, Roger. The Music Machine. Los Angeles, Nash, 1971.

Katkov, Norman. The Fabulous Fanny: The Story of Fannie Brice. New York, Knopf, 1953.

Kellner, Bruce. Carl Van Vechten and the Irreverent Decades. Norman, Oklahoma, University of Oklahoma Press, 1968.

Kennington, Donald. The Literature of Jazz: A Critical Guide. Chicago, American Library Association, 1971.

Kimball, Robert, and William Bolcom. Reminiscing with Sissle and Blake. New York, Viking, 1973.

Kinkle, Roger D. The Complete Encyclopedia of Popular Music and Jazz 1900-1950. 4 vols. New Rochelle, New York, Arlington House, 1974.

Kirkeby, Ed, with Duncan P. Schiedt and Sinclair Traill. Ain't Misbehavin': The Story of Fats Waller. New York, Dodd, Mead, 1966.

Klamkin, Marian. Old Sheet Music: A Pictorial History. New York, Hawthorn, 1975.

Kolodin, Irving. "The Dance Band Business Today: A Study in Black and White." Harper's Magazine, June 1941, pp. 72-83.

Bibliography

Kunstadt, Leonard. "The Story of Louis Metcalf." Record Research, October 1962, pp. 3-12.

Langeweg, Hans. "Benny Carter." Doctor Jazz (Utrecht, Holland), No. 93, September 1980, pp. 33-41.

Larkin, Dick. "Sir Bennett Arrives." Orchestra World, December 1943, p. 27.

Larkin, R. L. "Are Colored Bands Doomed as Big Money Makers?" Down Beat, December 1, 1940, pp. 2, 23.

Lees, Gene. Letter, Down Beat, December 29, 1966, pp. 8-9.

Leitch, Alexander. A Princeton Companion. Princeton, N.J., Princeton University Press, 1978.

Leiter, Robert D. The Musicians and Petrillo. New York, Octagon, 1974. (1st ed., New York, Bookman, 1953.)

Leonard, Neil. Jazz and the White Americans. Chicago, University of Chicago Press, 1962.

Levin, Floyd. "New Orleans--July 4, 1976." Fanfare (Southern California Hot Jazz Society), August 1976, pp. 3-6.

Lewis, Willie. "I Was Driven Out of Europe by Fascist Armies." Music and Rhythm, January 1942, pp. 18, 45.

Limbacher, James L., comp. and ed. Film Music: From Violins to Video. Metuchen, N.J., Scarecrow, 1974.

_____. Keeping Score: Film Music, 1972-1979. Metuchen, N.J., Scarecrow, 1981.

Locke, Alain. The Negro and His Music. Port Washington, N.Y., Kennikat, 1968. (1st ed., Washington, D.C., Associates in Negro Folk Education, 1936.)

_____, ed. The New Negro: An Interpretation. New York, Johnson Reprint Corp., 1968. (1st ed., New York, Boni, 1925.)

Lyons, Jimmy, with Ira Kamin. Dizzy, Duke, the Count and Me: The Story of the Monterey Jazz Festival. San Francisco, San Francisco Examiner, 1978.

Mannes, David. Music Is My Faith. New York, Norton, 1938.

Marbury, Elisabeth. My Crystal Ball: Reminiscences. New York, Boni and Liveright, 1923.

Marks, Edward B. They All Sang. New York, Viking, 1934.

McCarthy, Albert. Big Band Jazz. New York, G.P. Putnam's Sons, 1974.

_____. The Dance Band Era: The Dancing Decades From Ragtime to Swing 1910-1950. London, Spring Books, 1971.

McCarthy, Albert J., and Nat Hentoff. See Hentoff and McCarthy.

McCarty, Clifford. Film Composers in America: A Checklist of Their Work. New York, Da Capo, 1972. (1st ed., Glendale, California, distributed by J. Valentine, 1953.)

McDonald Diamond Jubilee, Inc. Souvenir Booklet: 75th Anniversary of the Founding of the Borough of McDonald, Pennsylvania, 1889-1964. McDonald, 1964.

McGinnis, Frederick A. A History and an Interpretation of Wilberforce University. Wilberforce, Ohio, 1941.

McKay, Claude. Home to Harlem. New York, Harper, 1928.

McLaughlin, Robert. Broadway and Hollywood: A History of Economic Interaction. New York, Arno, 1974.

McRae, Barry. "June Clark." Jazz Journal (London), May 1963, pp. 17-18.

Meeker, David. Jazz in the Movies: A Guide to Jazz Musicians 1917-1977. New Rochelle, N.Y., Arlington House, 1977. (1st ed., London, 1972.)

Mezzrow, Milton "Mezz." Really the Blues. New York, Random House, 1946.

Mialy, Louis Victor. "Benny Carter." Jazz Hot (Paris), February 1970, pp. 14-16.

Milhaud, Darius. Ma Vie Heureuse. Paris, Belfond, 1973.

Miller, Paul Eduard, ed. Esquire's Jazz Book. New York, Smith and Durrell, 1944.

_____. Esquire's 1945 Jazz Book. New York, Barnes, 1945.

_____. Esquire's 1946 Jazz Book. New York, Barnes, 1946.

Millinder, Lucky, as told to Dan Burley. "Negro Bands Are Not Doomed, Says Millinder." New York Amsterdam News, December 21, 1940, pp. 20-21.

Mills, Irving, with Charles Emge. "I Split With Duke When Music Began Sidetracking." Down Beat, November 5, 1952, p. 6.

Mooney, Hughson F. "Rock as an Historical Phenomenon." Popular Music and Culture 1(Spring 1972):129-143.

Morgenstern, Dan. Liner notes to record Bean and the Boys: Coleman Hawkins, Prestige 7824, New York, 1970.

_____. "Jazz on Film." Down Beat, 12th Yearbook, Music 67, suppl. to vol. 33, 1966, pp. 64-67, 69, 88-91.

Morgenstern, Dan, with Ole Brask. Jazz People. New York, Abrams, 1976.

Bibliography

Moss, Harry. "The Future of the Ballroom." 3 articles. Orchestra World, April 1933, p. 19; May 1933, p. 19; July 1933, p. 19.

Murray, B. J. "Dance Hall Versus Ballroom." Orchestra World, April 1931, p. 20.

M. W. "Benny 'King' Carter Confides." Musical News and Dance Band (London), May 1936, pp. 25-26.

Nanry, Charles. "Jazz and All That Sociology." In Nanry, ed., q. v., pp. 168-186.

Nanry, Charles. ed. American Music: From Storyville to Woodstock. New Brunswick, N. J., Transaction, 1972.

_____, with Edward Berger. The Jazz Text. New York, Van Nostrand, 1979.

Niles, Abbe. Introduction to Handy, q. v.

Noble, Peter. The Negro in Films. New York, Arno, 1970. (1st ed., London, Skelton, 1948.)

Osofsky, Gilbert. Harlem: The Making of a Ghetto, Negro New York, 1890-1930. 2d ed. New York, Harper 1971. (1st ed., New York, 1966.)

Ovington, Mary White. Half a Man: The Status of the Negro in New York. New York, Negro Universities Press, 1969. (1st ed., London, Longmans, Green, 1911.)

_____. The Walls Came Tumbling Down. New York, Schocken, 1970. (1st ed., New York, Harcourt, Brace, 1947.)

Owens, Thomas. Charlie Parker: Techniques of Improvisation. Ph. D. Thesis, University of California at Los Angeles, 1974.

Panassié, Hugues. Hot Jazz. The Guide to Swing Music. Translated by Lyle and Eleanor Dowling. New York, Witmark, 1936.

_____. Le Jazz Hot. Paris, R.-A. Corrêa, 1934.

Panassié, Hugues, and Madeleine Gautier. Guide to Jazz. Translated by Desmond Flower. Boston, Houghton Mifflin, 1956.

Paque, Glyn. "Bennet [sic] Carter." Jazz News (Basel), December 1940, pp. 7-8.

Pepper, Art and Laurie. Straight Life: The Story of Art Pepper. New York, Schirmer, 1979.

Perelman, S. J. Crazy Like a Fox. New York, Random House, 1944.

Pleasants, Henry. Serious Music--and All That Jazz! New York, Simon and Schuster, 1969.

Prendergast, Roy M. A Neglected Art: A Critical Study of Music in Films. New York, N. Y. U. Press, 1977.

Raksin, David. "What Ever Became of Movie Music?" Filmmusic Notebook, Autumn 1944, p. 22.

Ramsey, Frederic, Jr., and Charles Edward Smith, eds. Jazzmen. New York, Harcourt, Brace, 1939.

Randle, William, Jr. "Black Entertainers on Radio, 1920-1930." The Black Perspective in Music 5(Spring 1977):67-74.

Rapee, Erno. Encyclopedia of Music for Pictures. New York, Arno, 1970. (1st ed., New York, Belwin, 1925.)

Reis, Claire R. Composers, Conductors and Critics. New York, Oxford, 1955.

Reisner, Robert George. Bird: The Legend of Charlie Parker. New York, Citadel, 1962.

Riley, Clayton. "We Thought It Was Magic." New York Times Magazine, November 7, 1976, pp. 38 ff.

Roberts, John Storm. Black Music of Two Worlds. New York, William Morrow, 1974.

Rogers, J. A. "Jazz at Home." In Locke, ed., q.v., pp. 216-224.

Rolontz, Bob. "Whatever Became of Jazz and Poetry?" Jazz Review, February 1959, pp. 26-27.

Rosenkrantz, Timme. Dus Med Jazzen: Mine Jazzmemoirer. Copenhagen, Erichsen, 1964.

Rosenthal, Harold, and John Warrack. Concise Oxford Dictionary of Opera. London, Oxford, 1964.

Rowland, Mabel, ed. Bert Williams: Son of Laughter. New York, The English Crafters, 1923.

Russell, Ross. Bird Lives! New York, Charterhouse, 1973.

Rust, Brian. The American Dance Band Discography 1917-1942. 2 vols. New Rochelle, N.Y., Arlington House, 1975.

_____. The Dance Bands. New Rochelle, N.Y., Arlington House, 1974. (1st ed., London, 1972.)

_____. Jazz Records 1897-1942. 2 vols. 4th ed. New Rochelle, Arlington House, N.Y., 1978.

Rust, Brian, with Allen G. Debus. The Complete Entertainment Discography from the Mid-1890s to 1942. New Rochelle, N.Y., Arlington House, 1973.

Rust, Frances. Dance in Society. London, Routledge and Kegan Paul, 1969.

Rye, Howard. "Visiting Firemen. 4: Benny Carter." Storyville, No. 93, February-March 1981, pp. 84-87.

Bibliography

Sampson, Henry T. Blacks in Black and White: A Source Book on Black Films. Metuchen, N. J., 1977.

Sanford, Herb. Tommy and Jimmy: The Dorsey Years. New Rochelle, N. Y., Arlington House, 1972.

Sargeant, Winthrop. Jazz: Hot and Hybrid. New ed. New York, Dutton, 1946. (1st ed., New York, 1938.)

Schary, Dore. Heyday: An Autobiography. Boston, Little, Brown, 1979.

Schiffman, Jack. Uptown: The Story of Harlem's Apollo Theater. New York, Cowles, 1971.

Schuller, Gunther. Early Jazz: Its Roots and Musical Development. New York, Oxford, 1968.

Schwartz, Charles. Gershwin: His Life and Times. Indianapolis, Bobbs-Merrill, 1973.

Shand, Gwendolyn Vaughan. "The Sociological Aspects of an Industrial Community." M. A. Thesis, Carnegie Institute of Technology, Division of Social Work. Pittsburgh, 1923.

Shaw, Arnold. Honkers and Shouters: The Golden Years of Rhythm and Blues. New York, Macmillan, 1978.

_____. The Street That Never Slept: New York's Fabled 52d St. New York, Coward, McCann and Geoghegan, 1971.

Sheean, Vincent. Oscar Hammerstein I. New York, Simon and Schuster, 1956.

Shih, Hsio Wen. "Count Basie." In Stewart, q. v., pp. 195-206.

_____. "The Spread of Jazz and the Big Bands." In Hentoff and McCarthy, eds., q. v., pp. 171-187.

Simon, George T. The Big Bands. Rev. ed. New York, Macmillan, 1971.

_____. "Carter Clan Clean." Metronome, November 1940, p. 16.

_____. Glenn Miller and His Orchestra. New York, Crowell, 1974.

_____. Simon Says: The Sights and Sounds of the Swing Era, 1935-1955. New Rochelle, N. Y., Arlington House, 1971.

Skvorecky, Josef. The Bass Saxophone. Translated by Kaca Polackova-Henley. New York, Knopf, 1979.

_____. The Cowards. Translated by Jeanne Nemcova. New York, Grove, 1970.

Smith, Charles Edward. "Jazz: Some Little Known Aspects." The Symposium 1(October 1930):502-517.

_____. Liner notes to Swing Street, record album, Epic SN 6042, Frank Driggs, producer. New York, 1962.

Smith, Willie the Lion, with George Hoefer. Music on My Mind: The Memoirs of an American Pianist. New York, Doubleday, 1964.

The Sound of Harlem. See Hoefer.

Southern, Eileen, ed. "Black-Music Concerts in Carnegie Hall, 1912-1915." The Black Perspective in Music 6(Spring 1978):71-88.

_____. The Music of Black Americans. New York, Norton, 1971.

_____, ed. Readings in Black American Music. New York, Norton, 1971.

Spaeth, Sigmund. A History of Popular Music in America. New York, Random House, 1948.

_____. They Still Sing of Love. New York, Horace Liveright, 1929.

Stearns, Marshall W. "Is Jazz Good Propaganda? The Dizzy Gillespie Tour." The Saturday Review, July 14, 1956, pp. 28-31.

_____. The Story of Jazz. New York, Oxford, 1956.

Stearns, Marshall W., and Jean Stearns. Jazz Dance: The Story of American Vernacular Dance. New York, Macmillan, 1968.

Stefan, Paul. Anton Dvořák. Translated by Y. W. Vance. New York, Greystone, 1941.

Steiner, Max. "Scoring the Film." In We Make the Movies, ed. Nancy Naumburg, chap. 14. New York, Norton, 1937.

Stevens, Leith. "The Wild One." In Limbacher, ed., q.v., pp. 120-122.

Stewart, Rex, "The Benny Carter I Knew." Jazz Masters of the Thirties, pp. 168-180. New York, Macmillan, 1972. (Original publication: Down Beat, October 7, 1965, pp. 20-23.)

_____. "Rex Stewart Remembers Cuban Bennett." Down Beat, March 10, 1966, p. 13.

Still, William Grant. "A Composer's Viewpoint." In de Lerma, ed., q.v., chap. 8. Reprint, Haas, q.v., pp. 124-139.

_____. "How Do We Stand in Hollywood?" Opportunity: Journal of Negro Life, Spring 1945, pp. 74-77.

Stuart, Fredric. The Effects of Television on the Motion Picture and Radio Industries. New York, Arno, 1976.

Suber, Charles. "Jazz Education." In Feather and Gitler, q.v., pp. 366-381.

Sudhalter, Richard M., and Philip R. Evans. Bix: Man and Legend. New Rochelle, N.Y., Arlington, 1974.

Sutak, Ken. The Great Motion Picture Sound-Track Robbery: An Analysis of Copyright Protection. Hamden, Conn., Archon, 1976.

Bibliography

The Swing Era: One More Time. Philip W. Payne and Joan S. Reiter, eds. Time-Life Records. New York, 1972.

Sylvester, Robert. No Cover Charge: A Backward Look at the Night Clubs. New York, Dial, 1956.

Tendes, Antonio. "Figuras del Jazz." Ritmo y Melodia (Barcelona), no. 2, p. 3. (Date or volume not indicated. This was 2d issue of 1st year; in retrospect, November 1943.)

──────. "Galeria de Figuras del Jazz: Benny Carter, el Versatil." Jazz Magazine (Barcelona), June 1936, pp. 1-2.

Terrace, Vincent. The Complete Encyclopedia of Television Programs 1947-1976. 2 vols. South Brunswick, N.J. and New York, A. S. Barnes, 1976.

Terry, William E. "The Negro Music Journal: An Appraisal." The Black Perspective in Music 5(Fall 1977):146-160.

Thomas, Tony. Music for the Movies. South Brunswick, N.J. and New York, A. S. Barnes, 1973.

Thurman, Wallace. The Blacker the Berry ... A Novel of Negro Life. New York, Collier, 1970. (1st ed., New York, Macaulay, 1929.)

Tiomkin, Dmitri. "Composing for Films." In Limbacher, ed., q.v., pp. 55-61.

Tirro, Frank. Jazz: A History. New York, Norton, 1977.

Tynan, John. "Jazz in Hollywood Studios." Down Beat, March 1, 1962, pp. 14-15.

Ulanov, Barry. Duke Ellington. New York, Creative Age, 1946.

──────. "Thanks, Mr. Redman, for Modern Style." Metronome, June 1941, pp. 20-21, 25.

United States Copyright Office. Library of Congress. Catalogue of Copyright Entries. Part 3: Musical Compositions. Washington, D.C., annual.

United States Department of Labor. Children's Bureau. Publication No. 189. Public Dance Halls: Their Regulation and Place in the Recreation of Adolescents. By Ella Gardner. Washington, D.C., 1929.

United States Senate. Use of Mechanical Reproduction of Music. Hearings before a Subcommittee of the Committee on Interstate Commerce Pursuant to S. Res. 286, September 17, 18, and 21, 1942. Washington, D.C., 1943.

Valburn, Jerry. "Armed Forces Transcriptions as Source Materials." Studies in Jazz Discography I. Institute of Jazz Studies, Rutgers University. New Brunswick, N.J., 1971, pp. 47-52.

Walker, Leo. The Wonderful Era of the Great Dance Bands. New York, Doubleday, 1972.

Walker, Stanley. The Night Club Era. New York, Frederick A. Stokes, 1933.

Wall, Joseph Frazier. Andrew Carnegie. New York, Oxford, 1970.

Waters, Ethel, with Charles Samuels. His Eye Is On the Sparrow. New York, Doubleday, 1951.

Wells, Dicky, as told to Stanley Dance. The Night People: Reminiscences of a Jazzman. Boston, Crescendo, 1971.

Whiteman, Paul. "The All-America Swing Band." Collier's, September 10, 1938, pp. 9-12, 63-64.

──────. "So You Want to Lead a Band." Collier's, September 9, 1939, pp. 14, 51-52.

Williams, Martin. "Jazz at the Movies." Saturday Review, July 15, 1967, p. 49. Reprinted in Limbacher, ed., q.v., pp. 42-44.

──────, ed. Jazz Panorama. New York, Crowell-Collier, 1962.

Wilson, John S. "Cabaret and Jazz Are Active, But...." New York Times, August 29, 1976, sec. 2, p. 15.

Wilson, John S. The Collector's Jazz: Traditional and Swing. Philadelphia, Lippincott, 1958.

──────. "Jazz Makes a 'Comeback' With Broadest Range Yet." New York Times, January 24, 1974, p. 46.

──────. "Jazz: Serenading the Rock Fans." New York Times, August 28, 1977, sec. 2, p. 17.

──────. Jazz: The Transition Years. New York, Appleton-Century-Crofts, 1966.

──────. "Meet Professor Carter." Down Beat, April 2, 1970, pp. 19, 32.

Winkler, Max. A Penny from Heaven. New York, Appleton-Century-Crofts, 1951.

Witmark, Isidore, and Isaac Goldberg. From Ragtime to Swingtime: The Story of the House of Witmark. New York, Lee Furman, 1939.

Woll, Allen L. Songs from Hollywood Musical Comedies, 1927 to the Present: A Dictionary. New York and London, Garland, 1976.

Woodson, C. G. The Education of the Negro Prior to 1861. Washington, D. C., Associated Publishers, 1919.

Worthington, George E. "The Night Clubs of New York." The Survey 61(January 1, 1929):413-417.

Wright, Josephine R. B. See Dizzy Gillespie, "Conversations...."

Zissu, Leonard. "The Copyright Dilemma of the Screen Composer." Hollywood Quarterly 1(April 1946):317-320.

Bibliography

Zolotow, Maurice. "Harlem's Great White Father." Saturday Evening Post, September 27, 1941, pp. 37 ff.

Zwerin, Mike. "You're Not Going to Like This, But...." Down Beat, November 3, 1966, pp. 18-19.

DISCOGRAPHICAL ADDENDA

Changes to sessions already listed:

[94] Updated matrix and take information:

SLEEP: 1126-1 (complete); -2 (complete); -3 (breakdown); -4 (issued)

AMONG MY SOUVENIRS: 1127-1 (complete); -2 (complete); -3 (breakdown); -4 (issued)

FISH FRY: 1128-1 (breakdown); -2 (complete); -3 (breakdown); -4 (issued); -5 through -8 (breakdowns); -9 (complete); -10 (breakdown)

[371] Following titles issued in June 1982 on Storyville SLP4047, SUMMER SERENADE: INDIANA/LIKE SOMEONE IN LOVE (listed on LP as ALMOST LIKE BEING IN LOVE)/SUMMER SERENADE/ALL THAT JAZZ (vocal Richard Boone)/BLUE STAR/WHEN LIGHTS ARE LOW/TAKING A CHANCE ON LOVE

Additional Sessions:

Probably May 22, 1973   Holbaek Jazz Club, Denmark

Carter (as), Harry Edison, Arnvid Meyer (tp): John Darville (tb), Ben Webster, Jesper Thilo (ts), Niels Jorgen Steen (p), Hugo Rasmussen (b), Hans Nymand (d)

I CAN'T GET STARTED/SUNDAY/WHEN LIGHTS ARE LOW/KEESTER PARADE

July 19, 1973   Tokyo, Toranomon Hall

Carter (as), Gildo Mahones (p), Larry Gales (b), Duffy Jackson (d)

LULLABY OF BIRDLAND/ROBBINS NEST/I CAN'T GET STARTED/ UNDECIDED

July 22, 1975   Nice Festival

Carter (as), Joe Venuti (violin), George Barnes (g) Michael Moore (b)

SOMEBODY LOVES ME/DEEP PURPLE/UNDECIDED/SOMETIMES I'M HAPPY

July 25, 1975   Nice Festival

Carter (as), Illinois Jacquet (ts), Kenny Drew (p), Arvell Shaw (b), Bobby Rosengarden (d)

LADY BE GOOD

same date

Carter (as), Doc Cheatham (tp), Vic Dickenson (tb), Budd Johnson (ts), Kenny Drew (p), Arvell Shaw (b), Bobby Rosengarden (d)

JUST YOU, JUST ME/'DEED I DO

July 17-25, 1975   Nice Festival

Carter (as), Ruby Braff (tp), George Barnes (g) unknown b, d

WRAP YOUR TROUBLES IN DREAMS/I CAN'T GET STARTED/LOVER COME BACK TO ME

July 17-25, 1975   Nice Festival

Carter (as), Earl Hines (p) with several horns

CONFESSIN'

April 25, 1977   Fukuoka, Japan

same personnel as session no. 351

EASY MONEY/THEM THERE EYES/IN A SENTIMENTAL MOOD/NUAGES/ ARMSTRONG MEDLEY/CHINATOWN/THINGS AIN'T WHAT THEY USED TO BE/ ALL MY LOVE/GIRL TALK/THE COURTSHIP/JITTERBUG WALTZ/ SOUVENIR/COTTONTAIL

early July 1977   probably London, Pizza Express

Carter (as), Ralph Sutton (p), Jim Richardson (b), Tony Mann (d)

UNDECIDED/PERDIDO/IN A MELLOTONE

September 6, 1980   Osaka, Japan (Aurex Festival)

same personnel and similar titles to sessions no. 372 and 372A

May 21, 1982   Princeton University (Morroe Berger Memorial Concert)

Carter (as), Harry Edison (tp), Derek Smith (p), George Duvivier (b) Ronnie Bedford (d), Stanley Jordan (g--on last four titles)

Discographical Addenda

EASY MONEY/AUTUMN LEAVES/THE COURTSHIP/LOVE FOR SALE (feat. D. Smith)/IN A MELLOTONE/AIN'T MISBEHAVIN' (feat. H. Edison)/ BASICALLY THE BLUES (feat. G. Duvivier)/SOUTH SIDE SAMBA/UNDECIDED/ SOUVENIR/MISTY (S. Jordan solo)/PERDIDO/COTTONTAIL/BLUES

Arrangements: Julian Claes notes three Carter arrangements for the Ink Spots on Verve MGV2124, Favorites (released 1960).

Spelling correction: Phil Schaap has verified correct spelling of saxophonist Ben Whittett's last name to be Whitted.

Session no. 57 (8/18/37)

Newly released alternate takes (-2) of "Somebody Loves Me," "Pardon Me, Pretty Baby," and "My Buddy" on Panachord (Dutch) H2005.

Ella Fitzgerald/Count Basie Arrangements

Pablo Today D2312110 (A Perfect Match) recorded in Montreux, Switzerland 7/12/79 contains three Carter arrangements: "Please Don't Talk About Me When I'm Gone," "Some Other Spring," and "Honeysuckle Rose." These are the same arrangements recorded in L.A. 2/15-16/79; "Honeysuckle Rose" from that session was issued on Pablo Today 2312-132 with other Carter arrangements from that date.

Sessions 277 and 278 (Impulse album Further Definitions) reissued on Jasmine JAS14.